CONTENTS

PENGUIN BOOKS

THE HUNDRED YEARS' WAR

A. H. Burne was born in 1886 and educated at Winchester and RMA Woolwich, and was commissioned in the army in 1906. He served in the First World War and was awarded the DSO. During the Second World War he was Commandant of the 121st OCTU, 1939–42. He was editor of the *Gunner* from 1938 to 1957 and Military Editor of *Chambers Encyclopedia*. Described by Sir Arthur Bryant as 'one of the most distinguished living authorities on the history of land warfare and one of its finest teachers', he was the author of many works of military history, including *Lee, Grant and Sherman* (1938), *The Art of War on Land* (1944), *The Noble Duke of York* (1949), *The Battlefields of England* (1949; Classic Penguin, 2001) and *More Battlefields of England* (1953). *The Crecy War* (1954) and *The Agincourt War* (1956) are published here for the first time in one volume. He died in 1959.

EDWARD III (*left*) AND ST. GEORGE

A reconstruction by Professor E. W. Tristram of a contemporary painting in the old
St. Stephen's Chapel, Westminster.

Reproduced by permission of the Lord Great Chamberlain.

THE CRECY WAR

TO GLADWYN TURBUTT

who took me to Crecy

CONTENTS

PLATES

SKETCH-MAPS

PREFACE

THE Hundred Years War was, in all but name, four wars. The first was the invasion of France by Edward III; the second saw the almost total expulsion of the English; the third was the war of Henry V; the fourth resulted in the loss of all our territories in France except Calais.

This book chronicles, in its military aspect, the first of these wars, from 1337 to 1360, terminating in the Peace of Bretigny. This war possesses no name, so I have been obliged to coin one, and have fixed upon *The Crecy War*, which at least is self-explanatory, as every historical title should be: the word CRECY conjures up in the public mind the great war of Edward III in France better than any other.

Yet, though it enjoys no name, this war is in all essentials self-contained. It is only because historians when writing of it have presumed the future, that it has been merged in the war that followed it. The peace that ensued was, it is true, of short duration, but this was solely because of the premature and unexpected death of the French king. It lasted for nine years – not a long period, but longer than the interval between the War of the Austrian Succession and the Seven Years War.

The fact remains that the Crecy War has an individuality, a coherence, a continuity, and a central theme that gives it ample claim to be considered and treated as a single whole. That central theme is the struggle carried on for twenty-one years by one dominant personality for one over-riding purpose – to extirpate, once and for all, the root cause of the abiding enmity between England and France – namely the homage due by the English king for his French dominions. That was the aim which Edward III kept ever before him, in good times and in bad, and that aim was secured and sealed by the Treaty of Bretigny, as the direct result of the most continuously successful war that England had ever fought.

9

England was a young nation, only recently moulded into one, and the cement was still damp. Mainly as a result of this war the cement hardened rapidly, and such a spirit of pride and national consciousness was engendered in its people that, long afterward, Jean Froissart noticed and recorded the proud mien of Englishmen everywhere. This may or may not be a good thing—I am not arguing the point—but it was at least an important result of the war, and for this if for no other reason the Crecy War deserves to be rescued from anonymity.

There are other reasons too. For the soldier and the military student the war will repay study, as it marks a step in the progress of the military art, in the age-long contest between mounted and dismounted troops, between "missile" and "personal" weapons, and in the emergence of a third arm—the artillery. It is thus all the more surprising that no soldier, French or English, has hitherto written a history of this war. A few, a very few, battles have been dealt with by military writers, but the grand strategy has been left, for the most part, to civilian historians. These men seem to compete with one another in deriding the strategic ability of Edward III and their verdict may be summed up thus: "He was a good tactician, but he did not understand strategy." I was brought up on Victorian accounts of his campaigns (for practically nothing has been written on the subject during the past half century) and I was therefore prepared to endorse this adverse verdict on Edward III. But the deeper I studied the subject the more firmly I became convinced that the English king, so far from not understanding, was a master of strategy, and that he never showed it more strikingly than in his last and much criticized campaign of 1359.

Thus I came to the conclusion that a military study of the war of Edward III was overdue. That king has been hardly treated by historians. Not only have they failed to eradicate from their minds the ultimate sequel to Bretigny, but they cannot forget that Edward died in his dotage. What of that? Other great men have done the same, Marlborough for example, but what possible bearing has that on events that had taken place 30 years earlier? There has also been a tendency to judge him from the standpoint of Victorian morality, by which criterion there is of course much to reproach in his character and conduct. He was not so judged by his contemporaries: he was everywhere regarded as in all respects a great and gifted man. He was indeed described by an opponent as *le plus sage guerrier du monde*. It is one of the objects of this book to justify and establish this contemporary assessment of one of our greatest kings.

No one can study this war for long without becoming conscious of the fact that England in those days bred a race of masterful men: both leaders and led were men mighty in spirit. Well did Henley sing of them:

> *Such a breed of mighty men*
> *As came forward, one to ten* . . .

Yet their reputations and their very names have been forgotten (for Shakespeare never wrote *The Life of King Edward III*). Let these resounding names therefore be set down at once: Henry of Lancaster, Northampton, Warwick, Oxford, Salisbury, Stafford, Lord Bartholomew Burghersh, Sir Thomas Dagworth, Sir William Bentley, Sir James Audley, Sir Robert Knollys, Sir John Chandos, and the Black Prince. Only the last two of these names are now widely known, yet never did such an illustrious band of English soldiers take the field. When the paragon of them all, Henry of Lancaster, was buried in the Collegiate Church at Leicester (his grave has now vanished) the greatest in the land came to do him honour, for his passing was looked upon as a national disaster.

The Hundred Years War as a whole is a sealed book to most Englishmen, apart from Crecy, Poitiers, and Agincourt, and this may in part be due to the strange fact that no English professional historian—let alone professional soldier—has ever written a history of the War or of any of its phases, although it looms so large in our history. Nor has the task been attempted by a French soldier. Recently there has appeared a single-volume history of the war (*The Hundred Years War*, by Edouard Perroy) brilliant in its own way, and particularly under the circumstances in which it was written, but the author is a French civilian and the book is confined mainly to the political aspect of the war. It was indeed the appearance of this book in Paris in 1946[1] that inspired me to tackle the task from the military point of view.

*   *   *

The reconstruction of all history is largely conjectural, and this applies more to military than to any other branch of history. It should therefore be clearly understood that there is this element of the conjectural in all the events described in this book, but it would become wearisome to the reader were I to qualify almost every sentence with such expressions as "It would seem that", "In all probability", or "The evidence points to the fact that. . .". When in particular doubt or difficulty, I have applied the test of what I call Inherent Military Probability to the problem, and what I.M.P. tells me I usually accept. All military historians to some extent do this—they are bound to—but they do not all admit it.

*   *   *

This book is designed primarily for the general reading public and I have not cumbered it with voluminous notes and references,[2] nor have I interrupted the narrative appreciably in order to discuss controversial points. But for those who wish to delve into such matters there is an appendix to each chapter in which the principal sources are also listed, and controversial points are discussed in greater detail. This appendix can of course be skipped by those who wish for narrative, pure and simple.

The space devoted to political considerations is confined to

[1] English edition published by Eyre & Spottiswoode.
[2] In footnote references I have only included the specific page reference in cases that I consider particularly important.

a minimum in order to allow greater space to the military operations, but the political side cannot of course be completely omitted: for instance the effect of shortage of money upon the operations must be mentioned, but not the cause of that shortage, or the means taken to remedy it; the strength of armies must be gone into, but not the method of providing the men. (The latter subject is dealt with in the Appendix to Chapter I.)

On the political side I am much indebted to Professor Lionel Butler, of All Souls, Oxford, and to Mr. Robin Jeffs, of Trinity College, Oxford, for reading my MS with such eagle-eyed care, and for pointing out slips and errors of which I had been guilty and pitfalls into which I should have fallen but for their help. On the military side, for the reason given above, I have no acknowledgements to make.

ALFRED H. BURNE.

THE CRECY WAR

"Such a breed of mighty men"

CHAPTER I

PRELIMINARIES

THE seeds of the Hundred Years War were sown as far back as A.D. 1152 when Henry Plantagenet, count of Anjou, married Eleanor, the divorced wife of Louis VII of France and heiress to the duchy of Aquitaine. Two years later Henry succeeded to the throne of England and Normandy and thus found himself in possession of the whole of western France from the English Channel to the Pyrenees. For all this vast area—a good half of France—he was the nominal vassal of the king of France and thus the unnatural position was established of a king in his own right being also the vassal of another king. What made it worse was that the vassal was often more powerful than his suzerain. It is therefore not surprising that for the next 300 years every king of England was at some time or another at war with the king of France.

The situation was aggravated in 1259 by the complicated Treaty of Paris which made various adjustments and new enactments and reaffirmed the vassal status of the English dominions in France. No king of France enjoyed the sight of a rival monarch in occupation of a large portion of the land of France, and no king of England could stomach the thought of having to do homage to another monarch whom he regarded as his equal. It made matters worse when the two were blood relations. The Treaty of Paris produced so much confusion and conflict that some historians have dubbed the ensuing 80 years "The First Hundred Years War".

Edward III was only 14 years of age when, in 1327, he succeeded to the throne of his luckless father, Edward II. Although he had a French mother, the notorious Isabella, he was born and brought up in an atmosphere and tradition of enmity with France; his ears were filled with stories of

17

French insolence and bad faith and he smarted with humiliation at having to travel to France and do homage to his rival.
The seeds of war had been so well sown that it would have
been little less than a miracle if the peace had been maintained
throughout his reign. In fact we need look no further than the
duchy of Aquitaine to explain the outbreak of a conflict that
was to last off and on for over 100 years.

But wars are seldom the effect of a single cause. Like most
events in life they are the result of several causes or factors.
In this case there were at least three minor and predisposing
causes: the wool trade with Flanders, the relations between
France and Scotland, and the succession to the throne of
France.

The county of Flanders, occupying roughly the areas
between the sea and the Lower Scheldt, was a fief of the French
crown. The count of Flanders had to do homage for his
domains in just the same way as the English king had to do
homage for his French possessions, but, unlike Edward, he was
on friendly terms with his suzerain. But the Flemish merchants
and the lower classes were favourably disposed to England for
there were close trade links between the two countries. English
sheep provided the wool for the cloth mills of Flanders. Without
this wool the artisans of Flanders would starve—just as the
cotton operatives in Lancashire starved when American cotton
was denied them during the American Civil War. The great
cloth towns realized that their true interests resided in an
English alliance, and they appealed to Edward for help against
the exactions and harsh treatment of their count and their
suzerain. Thus began the long era of community of interests
and friendship between England and the Low Countries.

The relations between England and Scotland had been
unhappy for half a century and they were destined to remain
unhappy for a further 100 years.

Young Edward, at the outset of his reign, had one over-
ruling ambition—to restore the ascendancy established by his
grandfather, Edward I, over Scotland, and to give the island

of Great Britain a single government. Yet when he invaded
Scotland, and seemed on the verge of complete success, the
French king, Philip VI, twice intervened diplomatically, and
secretly helped the northern country by all possible means.
Thus was induced in the minds of both the English king and
his parliament a deep feeling of suspicion and distrust of the
French king and the belief steadily grew that war between
the two countries was inevitable. This suspicion of Philip was
not fully justified, but it became ingrained nevertheless. The
damage was done.

The third predisposing cause of the war was the disputed
succession to the French throne on the death of Charles IV,
the last of the Capetians, in 1328. When in 1314 Philip IV
("the Fair") died, he left a younger brother, Charles of Valois,
three sons and one daughter. Each son wore the crown in
succession, none of them having surviving male issue. When the
last of them died the French barons selected his first cousin
Philip, son of Charles of Valois, thus passing over Isabella, the
sister of the late Capetian kings. It was understandable that
Isabella should be passed over; there were two precedents for
it, and a woman had never been sovereign of France. But
Isabella had a son, who was thus nephew of the late kings,
and a nephew is nearer in kinship than a cousin.[1] Isabella's
son was in English and in some French eyes the lawful claimant
to the throne. Why then was he also passed over? The answer
is because he was born and bred in a foreign country, and was
moreover the king of that country, for the name of this son
was, of course, Edward III of England. Philip was thus a
natural choice on the part of the French barons. England was
at the time a hated rival, and it will be easy for us to appreciate
their motives when we think of Philip II of Spain as king of
England when he married Mary Tudor.

The selection of Philip VI did not create much stir at the time,

---

[1] "*Neveu des derniers rois et leur parent au troisième degré, Edouard III leur était plus
proche que le Comte de Valois, qui n'était que leur cousin germain et par conséquent parent
au quatrième degré.*" PERROY, ÉDOUARD. *La Guerre de Cent Ans*, p. 54 (1945).

and indeed within a year Edward III crossed to France to do homage for his French possessions, thereby recognizing his rival as sovereign. It is true that he added some qualifying words which became afterward the subject of argument, but there is no evidence that he at the time wished for the French throne. Scotland was much nearer his heart.

Even when he eventually broke with France, he did not officially put forward the claim. The war had been in operation nearly two years before he officially advanced it, and then only at the request of the Flemings whom he was trying to bring into active alliance against France.

The assertion made in so many history books that Edward III went to war for the crown of France is thus incorrect. Confusion has been induced by the intrusion of the "Salic Law" into the controversy. It is alleged that the so-called Salic Law prevented Isabella or her son from sitting on the throne of France. But the truth is that this law was not mentioned or thought of by the French jurists till over 30 years later. The truth of the matter can be summed up in a sentence: the legitimate heir was passed over because he was a foreigner.

In any case, it was a wise decision. The law of female inheritance has been responsible for much misery in European history. We have seen how disastrous in its effects was the marriage of Eleanor of Aquitaine with Henry Plantagenet; almost equally unfortunate was the marriage of another French princess, Isabella, to Edward II.

*   *   *

Though the dynastic seeds of discord were powerful, the overriding cause of the war was, as we have seen, the fact that Aquitaine was a fief of the French crown and this fact alone would have been sufficient cause for war to break out, or rather for the "First Hundred Years War" to be resumed. When we add the further predisposing causes which we have listed, it becomes clear that the war was not only natural, but practically inevitable.

*   *   *

We pass now from the fundamental causes of the conflict to the events that brought matters to the breaking point. The first move that led to the final breach came from the French side. In the spring of 1336, when Edward was on the point, as it seemed, of clinching his Scottish war, Philip sent his fleet round from the Mediterranean and settled it threateningly in the ports of Normandy. Both Edward and his parliament interpreted this as a threat to invade England, and it is difficult to see what other interpretation they could have placed on it. They seem to have decided from that hour that war was unavoidable and they started to make methodical preparations for it. Subsidies were voted, funds and military stores were sent to Gascony, and troops both naval and military were moved to the south coast.

War now looked imminent, in spite of the efforts of the pope, Benedict XII, to avert it. The fact that Benedict was a Frenchman told against him in English eyes, though he seems to have been sincere in his efforts.

Both sides now looked round for allies in the coming struggle. On the English side one soon came to hand unbidden. Robert of Artois, the dispossessed lord of that county, a thoroughly disgruntled man, took refuge at the English court late in 1336, pressed the king to lay formal claim to the throne of France, and promised his personal support in a war with his hated suzerain.

Before we follow Edward in his search for allies we must glance at the composition of the Low Countries at that epoch. For it was to the Low Countries that Edward's eyes naturally turned. What is now modern Belgium was then occupied by the three provinces of Flanders, Brabant, and Hainault. Flanders, as we have seen, was a fief of France, and occupied the seaboard from the estuary of the Scheldt to Dunkirk, its southern boundary running along the river Scheldt almost as far as Cambrai. Brabant stretched in a rather narrow belt from Antwerp to Mons and Namur, while Hainault formed a sort of buffer State between Brabant and France. Both Brabant and Hainault were provinces of the German Emperor. The boun-

dary of France proper ran much as it does today as far as Tournai
and along the upper Scheldt (spelt Escaut in modern French).
The county of Artois lay, as it still does, round Arras, which was
its capital.

It was, as we have said, natural for the English king to look
to the Low Countries for allies. They were the nearest communities to our shores; there was a tradition of friendship and
commerce between them and us, and through his wife, Philippa
of Hainault, Edward had many connections by marriage with
these parts. Above all, the Low Countries formed the best
jumping-off point for an attack on France. Gascony, an English
possession, was threatened, but Gascony was a long way off. In
the days of sailing ships it might take weeks before troops or
military stores could be landed there, whereas the prevailing
westerly wind ensured that the Low Countries could be reached
in a few days at the most. Moreover the Low Countries were
nearer Paris, the French capital, than was Gascony. Edward
saw, as clearly as did the duke of Marlborough four centuries
later, that a threat to the capital from the Low Countries was
the most effective way of conducting a war with France.
Edward would save Gascony on the plains of Flanders, just as
Pitt four centuries later "conquered Canada on the plains of
Germany".

Of the three communities comprising the Low Countries,
Flanders was the most eligible as an ally. She was the nearest,
direct access could be obtained to her by sea; she was a traditional friend and she had commercial and trade interests in
common with England. If it had been left to her burgesses, she
would gladly have joined in a war against France. But unfortunately her count was a Frenchman, Louis of Nevers, and
although he probably had little love for Philip VI he retained
considerable fear of him and he dared not risk open revolt
against his suzerain. Flanders therefore was not responsive to
Edward's wooing, and in retaliation for this cold attitude,
Edward took the drastic step of cutting off all imports of wool
to the Flemish towns. Where Flanders lost, her neighbours

stood to gain–in particular, Brabant and the Dutch principalities. Where Ypres and Ghent lost, Brussels and Amsterdam
gained. Partly by this means, and partly by lavish expenditure,
Edward built up an imposing alliance comprising Brabant,
Hainault, and a number of towns and counties. Against this, the
king of France–apart from his Scottish alliance–had few
allies outside his own vassals, some of whom displayed little
zeal in the cause of their suzerain.

Furthermore, the duchy of Brittany inclined to the English
cause, and best of all, the Emperor, Louis of Bavaria, who was
married to the king's sister-in-law, signed an offensive and
defensive alliance with Edward in the summer of 1337.

On May 24, 1337, Philip took the decisive step; he solemnly
confiscated all the territories of his English vassal. This, in the
view of a modern French historian,[1] was tantamount to a
declaration of war, and we may conveniently accept this date
as the official beginning of the war. As if to clinch matters,
French troops, who were already stationed on the border,
invaded Gascony and the French fleet raided Jersey, following
up with a raid on Portsmouth and the south coast. The war
was on!

Edward III responded in October by repudiating his
homage and addressing his rival as "Philip", describing himself
as "king of France". He declared that he was the rightful
occupant of the French throne, though he did not proclaim himself king. That claim was not put forward for nearly two years.

The English king followed up words with deeds: in November
he sent a small expedition under Sir Walter Manny (a compatriot of his queen) to raid the Flemish island of Cadzand.
This was accomplished successfully, largely because of the
striking action of the archers, who put down what would now
be described as a barrage of arrows to cover the landing of
the infantry. The English troops then drew up in a formation
that was afterward to become familiar–the men-at-arms in line
and the archers massed like two bastions at the ends of the line.

[1] Edouard Perroy, in *The Hundred Years War*.

During all this time the pope was striving to avert the conflict, but was trusted by neither side. All he succeeded in doing was to delay the outbreak of serious operations for six months. But in the summer of 1338 naval operations began again in the English Channel and the French fleet made itself again uncomfortably familiar off the south coast of Hampshire, burning Portsmouth and other towns.

Meanwhile Edward carried on his preparations steadily for an invasion of the Continent, and on July 12, 1338, he set sail from Orwell, with a considerable fleet and army, his flagship being the *Christopher*, of which we shall hear later.

THE YEAR 1338

When Edward III of England landed at Antwerp amid scenes of pomp and pageantry on July 22, 1338, his first object was to complete and cement his grand alliance against France. Hitherto he had had no practical experience of working with allies. The task was to tax all the power, patience, and talents of the 26-year-old king. He found his new allies slippery, tepid and timid. They were hesitant and dilatory and the months passed without anything being effected.

The immediate task was to meet the Emperor in person. Louis of Bavaria, Emperor of the Holy Roman Empire, sometimes loosely called the German Empire, or even Germany, came to Coblenz, 160 miles from Antwerp, on the Middle Rhine. After careful preparations the king of England set out with an immense retinue and arrived at Cologne on August 23. Here he was received with enthusiasm, which was intensified when he made a handsome contribution to the building fund for the great new cathedral that was then slowly rising. From Cologne he went to Bonn, where the scenes of welcome and rejoicing were repeated: thence by water to Coblenz, cheering crowds greeting him at every halting place. It was a royal progress, the like of which had not been seen within memory.

When the king reached Coblenz on August 31 all the world seemed gathered to meet him. The emperor's train was even larger and more magnificent than that of the king, and included all the imperial electors save one. A few days were spent in preparation; then the king and emperor took their seats on two thrones that had been erected in the market place, the emperor with crown, orb and sceptre. The market place was packed with a huge throng, upward of 17,000 in number, of the nobility of western Europe and their trains. None could recall such a scene of pomp and magnificence. The emperor opened the proceedings by proclaiming that Philip of Valois had forfeited the protection of the empire because of his perfidy. Next, he bestowed on the English king the gold wand, symbolizing his appointment as the emperor's vicar, or vice-regent in western Europe. Edward then spoke, declaring that Philip had usurped the crown of France, which was his own by right. The impressive ceremony passed off without a hitch, and on the morrow the nobles of the empire did homage to Edward III as their vicar for the next seven years. In fact "all went merry as a marriage bell".

The season was too far advanced for a campaign that year, so Edward summoned the princes to attend him in the following July in a campaign for the recovery of Cambrai, which belonged by rights to the empire. This was a shrewd move, for it did not necessarily involve an invasion of France, a course to which some of the principalities were averse. This accomplished, Edward returned to Antwerp where, surprisingly, he spent the winter, instead of returning home. As the result of over a year's labours he had built up a grand alliance, as it might well be called, against France, almost as wide in its scope as the more famous Grand Alliance of the duke of Marlborough. Though the month of July was distinctly late for the opening of the campaign, the prospects appeared bright. But before describing Edward's first campaign in the Low Countries we must glance briefly at the respective strengths and natures of the rival countries.

Though conditions and numbers on the two sides necessarily varied from time to time, the following general statement for the whole period of the war, omitting allies, will never be very far from the mark.

The population of England was between three and four million, while that of France was well over ten million. It may thus be supposed that the French armed forces normally outnumbered those of England by three or four to one. This was not the case, for two particular reasons. England's methods of recruitment were better developed than those of France, and she had at command from time to time both Welsh and Irish troops. These were only slightly offset by the Scottish contingents that from time to time fought under the French colours.

Fairly exact estimates can generally be made about the English strength in the great battles, but that of the French must always remain in doubt because of a marked absence of official records. This book, being primarily a military history, is not directly concerned with the method by which armies were raised and maintained, but rather with the way they operated and fought. The subject is however dealt with in some detail in the appendix to this chapter. Here it will suffice to epitomize the system that obtained in the army of Edward III.

The old English army, inherited by Edward, consisted of two categories: the feudal array or levy, and the national militia. Under the feudal system the barons were obliged to provide retinues of mounted men-at-arms for the service of the crown.[1] But feudalism was decaying and Edward III, shortly before the outbreak of the war with France, had started substituting for it a system of indenture which produced a body of paid professional soldiers and gradually replaced the old feudal levy.

[1] The French had a similar feudal array, called "Hosting", but though every knight in theory was liable for service, in practice vassals were no longer obliged to provide more than one-tenth of their number. PERROY, E. *The Hundred Years War* (Eng. trans.), Eyre & Spottiswoode (London, 1951), p. 44.

The national militia (the old fyrd) was raised from the able-bodied male population between the ages of 16 and 60, selected by Commissioners of Array in each shire. It consisted of hobilars, or mounted lance-men (corresponding to the dragoons and mounted infantry of later ages) and foot soldiers who were subdivided into bowmen and spearmen (later billmen).

To complete the army, there were some foreign mercenaries and Welsh spearmen (for the longbow was by now used exclusively by Englishmen).

The French system of raising and organizing armies was much the same as the English, that is to say the core of the army was made up of the feudal levy of mounted men-at-arms and this was supplemented by the national levies, whose organization and composition was very loose and vague. Broadly speaking the French knights reckoned to win their battles without much assistance from the "communes" or common, base-born men.

But the feudal retinues were only obliged to fight for 40 days outside their own provinces. To induce them to extend their service they had to be paid, but as the royal treasury was generally almost empty the number who could be so paid was very small. Even so the armies that were raised invariably exceeded in number the English armies against which they were pitted.

The French also engaged mercenaries, who in their case were almost exclusively Genoese crossbowmen.

ARMS AND EQUIPMENT

Arms and equipment in the two armies were very similar. Knights and men-at-arms were armed with lance, sword, dagger, and occasionally battle mace. They wore mail armour for the most part, but it gradually gave place to plate armour in the course of the Hundred Years War. A helm, shield, and spurs completed the full outfit. It became customary for each knight to have with him some armed attendants, the usual number being three, two mounted archers and one *coutillier* (swordsman), the whole constituting a "lance". Thus when a certain number of lances is mentioned we must multiply by about four to arrive at the total of effectives.

The English archer, whether mounted or dismounted, carried a longbow and sword, and usually a dagger. The long-bow could be discharged six times a minute: it had an effective range of 250 yards and an extreme range of about 350 yards. The French archers, on the other hand, carried a crossbow. This weapon, though more powerful than the longbow, could only discharge one bolt to four of the longbow. Moreover it was more inaccurate and had a shorter range.[1]

But though both armies were armed and equipped in sub-stantially the same way there was a considerable difference in their efficiency. For over a generation the military exper-iences of the French army had been limited to occasional operations against their vassals, notably in Gascony, whereas the English army was fresh from its successes in the Scottish campaigns. These successes had gone far to expunge the memory of Bannockburn and to link up with the victories of Edward I, who was remembered as the Hammer of the Scots. Edward III had also, by the introduction of the indenture system of service, in effect transformed his army into a body of long-service professional soldiers, highly trained and disciplined. Nothing like it existed on the Continent at the time and it may be compared to the British Expeditionary Force which landed in France in 1914.

As for the third arm, the artillery, at the opening of the war, there is no reliable evidence for the presence of cannon in the English fleet in the battle of Sluys in 1340, nor is it likely that Edward III took any with him to Flanders; and though the French did undoubtedly use cannon in the defence of Tournai in 1340 the first occasion that artillery was used in the field was at Crecy, six years later. Until that date, then, we may ignore its existence.

---

[1] For further details of arms and armour see the article under that heading by Sir James Mann in the new edition (1950) of *Chambers' Encyclopaedia*.

Of the rival fleets there is not much that need be said. Each country had a small nucleus of royal ships of war, the exact number of which is unknown. The bulk of the fleet was collected in an emergency by the simple means of requisitioning ships, so many from each port. In his efforts to raise a large fleet against the increasing activity and threatening moves of the French fleet, Edward went as far afield as Bayonne, demanding and begging in turn for a contingent of vessels from that distant port. The French had in addition a number of war-galleys which had been rowed round from the Mediterranean.

But naval warfare was at a primitive stage, and the only big engagement at sea approximated to a land battle.

APPENDIX

The Army of Edward III

RAISING THE ARMY

From the time of the Norman Conquest to the accession of Edward I a medieval army was raised from two sources: the national militia (fyrd), and the feudal levy. Regarding the first, every able-bodied man between the ages of 16 and 60 was liable to serve if called upon, and to provide himself with suitable arms. Service was, in the first instance, for 40 days (unpaid) and the summons was for the repelling of invasion. The feudal levy or array came in with William I, who allotted lands to his barons on the stipulation that they provided military service for the crown with their own tenants and retinues. The lands so allotted were called fiefs of the crown. The tenants-in-chief could, and did, enfeoff their lands on sub-tenants who thus owed fealty to their immediate lords in the first instance and then to the crown. The size of the contingent that each lord was required to produce varied. Later, tenants were allowed under certain conditions to pay "scutage" to the crown in lieu of military service.

Such, in broad outline, was the military system in vogue at the time of the accession of Edward I. Sixty-five years later, when his grandson embarked on the first campaign of the Hundred Years War, the situation had been transformed. The army, for all practical purposes, consisted of long-service professional volunteers and was based on the indenture system introduced by Edward III himself. The explanation of this almost startling change was that the feudal system was in decay and had ceased to function satisfactorily as a troop-raising medium. The causes of this decay of feudalism form an interesting constitutional study, but one outside the province of this military history. Suffice it to say that the system was no longer providing the crown with the number of men-at-arms required. To give an example: In 1277 only 375 knights answered the summons, out of a possible total (as calculated by Dr. J. E. Morris)[1] of about 7,000. Thus the number had been whittled down to less than one-eighteenth of the available figure.

Edward I set about alleviating this weakness by issuing pay (confined to the mounted troops). "The key was the systematic use of pay. The paid squadron under the professional captain could be combined, and was more efficient than the incoherent units of a feudal host."[2] The earliest example of such pay contracts was in 1277. Other such payments followed, but the contracts remained merely verbal, so far as is known, throughout the reign, and indeed until 1338. The first crack in the old feudal system had appeared, and Edward III extended it. But only gradually. In his first campaign against the Scots he seems to have relied mainly on the impressed national militia. He summoned the whole force of the country; but the results were so disappointing that he resorted to the tentative methods of contract applied by his grandfather. But he went further; he instituted a system of written indenture and gradually extended it throughout his army till the biggest and most important part of it consisted of indentured soldiers. Of this innovation A. E. Prince writes: "In the history of the English army in the

---

[1] *The Welsh Wars of Edward I*, pp. 41 and 45.   [2] Op. cit., p. 68.

middle ages there is no more significant development than that
of the indenture system of recruitment."[1]

By this system a commander contracted with the king to
provide a specified force for military service. The indenture
laid down precisely the size and composition of the force, rates
of pay, place of assembly, length of service, and obligations
and privileges such as "regards" (bonuses) to which the men
would be entitled. Such a force was generally one of all arms;
i.e., men-at-arms, mounted and foot archers, hobilars, foot
spearmen, and even miners, artificers, surgeons, chaplains, and
interpreters. (This system was, no doubt unconsciously,
followed in the British army of the eighteenth century when a
colonel contracted with the king to raise a regiment for his
service.) The terms of service varied, the shortest being the
traditional 40 days, and the longest normally one full year,[2]
though in exceptional cases this term was exceeded. For
instance, in the army that the Black Prince took to Gascony
in 1355 the engagement was "during the king's pleasure" –
which was just as well, for the men had little chance of returning
home by any specified date. The indenture system had other
advantages. It was found to be a convenient method of providing regular garrisons for certain of the royal castles; and
foreign mercenaries could also be obtained by this means.

It also became quite common for captains to resort to sub-
contract on the same principle as sub-tenancy. The effect of
this system was that a long-service professional army was
produced. The transformation that had taken place is vividly
expressed by Carl Stephenson: "The English army . . . had
definitely ceased to be feudal. Rather it was a mercenary force,
in which the mounted noble, as well as the yeoman archer,
humbly served at the King's wage."[3]

[1] MORRIS, (*Edited*) W. A., and WILLARD, J. F., 'The Army and Navy' in *The
English Government at Work, 1327-1336* (Medieval Academy of America, 1940),
p. 352.
[2] PRINCE, A. E., 'The Indenture System under Edward III' in *Historical Essays
in Honour of James Tait* (1937), p. 291.
[3] *Medieval Feudalism*, p. 100.

THE MILITIA

The National militia was raised in the following manner. When the force was to be mobilized, writs were issued to the sheriffs of counties giving the quotas to be provided by them. The county quotas were then subdivided between the hundreds and large towns. The selection of the men to fill these quotas was made by Commissioners of Array, normally one per county, appointed by letters patent by the crown. These commissioners were sent round with instructions to pick out "the strongest and most vigorous men". The men selected received pay from the central government from the date they marched out to the rendezvous appointed.[1] As the numbers raised by indenture increased, so the number of impressed men diminished. This leads Professor Prince to declare: "It was the retinue, based on an indenture contract, rather than the man impressed by commission of array, who superseded the feudal levies and formed the backbone of the Hundred Years War armies."

ORGANIZATION AND EQUIPMENT

Each member of the nobility[2] from the king downward possessed a retinue. These retinues consisted of two categories: the men-at-arms (sometimes loosely called cavalry, though in the reign of Edward III they almost invariably fought on foot), and the mounted archers. There were three degrees in the hierarchy: first came the earls (with whom we must include the Prince of Wales and the duke of Lancaster); second came the bannerets; and third the knights bachelor (so called to distinguish them from the knights banneret). Banneret was not a degree of nobility but a purely military term[3] denoting an officer who was entitled to carry a banner (rectangular); knights bachelor could be promoted to this rank. The knight

---

[1] Before the reign of Edward III the first 40 days had been done without pay.

[2] And some knights. For example, Sir John Chandos in the 1359 campaign had a retinue of seven knights, 54 esquires and 34 archers. PRINCE, 'The strength of the English armies of Edward III' in *E.H.R.* (1931), p. 362 n.

[3] PRINCE, *The Army and Navy*, p. 337.

bachelor carried a pennon (triangular). What we might term the rank and file of the men-at-arms were the esquires. These were usually the younger sons of the nobility or others who were aspirants to knighthood.

But the term men-at-arms comprises the whole body, including the officers. Thus a knight was a man-at-arms, but a man-at-arms was not necessarily a knight. The retinue, as mentioned above, also included the mounted archers. To king Edward must be given the credit for the creation of this corps. Before his reign the only mounted troops outside the men-at-arms had been the hobilars, or light-armoured mounted infantry. The technical difference between the hobilars and the men-at-arms was that their horses were unprotected whereas those of the men-at-arms were "covered", *i.e.*, they wore a coverlet of mail or stuffed material. Usually the hobilars carried lances. They had been found very useful in the mountains of Scotland in pursuit of the agile inhabitants whom the heavy cavalry could not reach. J. E. Morris states that the mounted archers were first formed in 1337.[1] But Prince has shown that it can be antedated by three years.[2] As the numbers of the mounted archers rose, those of the hobilars fell, till by the end of the War they had reached negligible proportions. Similarly the numbers of foot archers fell.

The proportion of mounted archers to men-at-arms was consequently variable. Nominally a banneret was expected to find one archer for every man-at-arms, but naturally this provision was not strictly complied with. Even in the king's last campaign, that of 1359, when conditions might be expected to have become standardized after 21 years of war, it is impossible to descry any fixed proportion between the two. Some of the retinue figures for this campaign will repay examination. Thus, the Prince of Wales's retinue consisted of seven bannerets at 4s. a day, 136 knights at 2s., 143 esquires at 1s., and 900 mounted archers at 6d. On the other hand the duke of

[1] 'Mounted Infantry in Medieval Warfare', in *Transactions of the Royal Historical Society*, 3rd Series, vol. VII, p. 94.
[2] *The Army and Navy*, p. 341.

Lancaster's retinue consisted of six bannerets, 90 knights, 486 men-at-arms, and 423 archers.[1] These figures show the rates of pay at a time when they had become reasonably standardized, but they also show that the proportion of archers to men-at-arms was still far from standardized. From the above figures we see that in the Prince's retinue a banneret commanded on an average 210 men, whilst in that of Lancaster he commanded only 130. (These figures omit some Welsh levies in the retinues whose numbers are unknown.) A banneret, it would seem, can be equated with a battalion commander of the present day. It should be noted that the headquarters staff of the army was provided by the bannerets of the king's own retinue of the Household.

Each knight possessed three or four horses, including two destriers (heavy chargers). He also had one or two pages whose duty it was to clean and polish his armour and help him into and out of it, and to assist him to mount his charger.[2] A page also acted as horseholder and groom to his master.

THE INFANTRY

Thus far we have dealt with the cavalry. The infantry in medieval days consisted of archers and foot spearmen, but since the introduction of mounted archers, who may be designated mounted infantry (as well as the hobilars) we should confine the term infantry, pure and simple, to the foot archers and spearmen. These consisted principally of "the men impressed by the Commissions of Array" as thus described above by Professor Prince. The remainder of the infantry was made up by foreign mercenaries, Irish, Gascons, etc. (though it is likely that many of the Gascons were genuine volunteers and would not have appreciated the term mercenaries).

The foot archers, except that they drew less pay (2d. a day was the basic wage), were almost indistinguishable from their

---

[1] Tout, T. F., *Chapters in Administrative History*, vol. iv, p. 144, n. 3, as amended by Prince's *Indenture System*, p. 308, n. 2.
[2] The scene in the film *Henry V* depicting knights being hoisted by winches into the saddle may be disregarded.

mounted comrades once the battle had commenced, being similarly armed, though devoid of armour except for a steel cap.

The foot spearmen were drawn mostly from Wales. Although the longbow originated in the Principality, it had soon crossed the border, and first the Cheshire men and then the archers of the other counties were armed with it. In fact, all the archers in Edward's armies were Englishmen.

Though the pay of the army varied from time to time there was one basic rate that was invariable—the pay of the foot archer. That, as we have seen, was fixed at 2d. a day. It remained stationary—just as the basic wage of foot soldiers of later days remained fixed at one shilling a day for over a century. As long as feudalism remained strong the earls scorned to accept any pay, but by the beginning of the Hundred Years War not only the earls, but even the Prince of Wales, accepted pay.[1] A soldier drawing regular pay for his services is naturally more amenable to discipline than one who is not dependent upon it. This was an important factor in building up the cohesion of the English army.[2]

TACTICAL ORGANIZATION

Chronicles and records alike are reticent on the details of organization in the field. What was the tactical unit? How did it deploy? What was the formation on the march? Did the troops march in step? What non-commissioned officers (as we should now call them) were there? What was the system of picquets and outposts? These and suchlike questions we cannot answer with any degree of certainty. Chroniclers were generally monkish clerks, sequestered in distant monasteries, devoid of practical knowledge of war and dependent upon the tales of old soldiers.[3] Hence they failed to record or explain details of routine which we nowadays are so avid to learn about. It is however known that men-at-arms were grouped in "con-

[1] The Prince's pay was one pound per day.
[2] "Pay produces discipline", writes Morris tersely (op. cit., p. 68.)
[3] Froissart, and still more le Bel, who served under Edward in the Scottish campaigns, were of course exceptions.

stabularies" and that impressed men were formed into units of 1,000, 100, and 20, which may be termed battalions, companies, and troops.[1] Further than this we cannot safely go. No doubt both organization and drill were tentative and fluid, varying according to the character, will and whim of the local commander. A strong man, in command of a small force, such as Sir Thomas Dagworth in Brittany, could weld his force into a remarkable and well-disciplined body of men, as we know by the results.

EQUIPMENT

The best guide to arms and armour carried at any period is provided by the effigies and brasses of knights to be seen in churches all over the country. Perhaps the best example of a knight in armour during the reign of Edward III is that of the Black Prince in Canterbury Cathedral.[2] It was a transition period: the days of mail armour were ending, and it was being replaced by plate armour. The Prince is shown wearing plate except for his gorget, which is of mail; but the ordinary knight may be presumed to have worn a bigger proportion of mail–still more the esquires. Over the breastplate or hauberk was worn a loose-fitting surcoat, emblazoned with the arms of the knight. This, besides being spectacular, had practical advantages. For example, in an emergency, such as an ambuscade, or night attack, the knight would hastily don his surcoat, which became the rallying point for his men, who would automatically gather round his person.[3]

It is interesting to note that as the strength of armour increased the need for the additional protection of a shield diminished. Consequently its size decreased, till eventually it was discarded altogether–just as portions of the body that have ceased to have a function gradually wither and eventually

[1] PRINCE, *The Army and Navy*, p. 340. Morris speaks vaguely of "brigades", but without citing his authority.

[2] See article 'Arms and Armour', by Sir James Mann in *Chambers' Encyclopaedia* (1950 edition), p. 608, for a photograph of this, and also for general information.

[3] A good example of this occurred in the battle of Auberoche. See chapter V *infra*.

disappear.[1] The spur, on the other hand, so far from diminishing, tended to increase in size with the introduction of the rowell.[2] Archers, both mounted and foot, wore a steel cap, and breastplate or padded hauberk, and spearmen were similarly attired except that they seldom wore a breastplate.

Rudimentary forms of uniform can be traced at this time. Thus, some Welsh levies raised for the war in Brittany were ordered to be clothed in uniform clothes.[3] And other local authorities were frequently enjoined to dress the impressed men alike.[4]

WEAPONS AND THEIR EMPLOYMENT

Men-at-arms carried swords, lances, and daggers. The lance was an inheritance of the days of mounted charges. It was the *arme blanche par excellence*. Although it could also be used dismounted we do not hear much of its use in the bigger battles of the war. The sword was the main stand-by of the knight in Edward's army. The lance was unwieldy and out of place in a mêlée, and even the sword often gave place to the dagger in such engagements. Effigies of knights are invariably shown armed with daggers. For a set battle the knights would dismount and hand over their horses to their pages, who would lead them to the rear[5] and establish themselves in the baggage leaguer, for which they formed the guard or garrison during the ensuing battle. Meanwhile the men-at-arms were deployed in line by the two marshals, after which, if the enemy was still motionless, they would be allowed to fall out and refresh themselves. Normally each division[6] of the army (of which there were three) would form up in a single line, flanked by the archers. On the rare occasions when a pursuit was undertaken

[1] It would not be surprising if many of the knights in this war discarded their shields just as our troops discarded their gas-masks in the 1940 campaign.
[2] Sir J. Mann, op. cit., p. 608.
[3] EVANS, D. L., 'Some Notes on the Principality of Wales . . .' in *The Transactions of the Honourable Society of Cymmrodorion* (1925), p. 48.
[4] WROTTESLEY, THE HON. G., *Crecy and Calais*, p. 1.
[5] Just as did the artillery horseholders in pre-mechanized days in England.
[6] Many are the Latin and early French words all denoting the same formation, which I translate division.

the pages brought up the chargers, assisted their knights to mount, and probably followed them in the ensuing charge (for there would be no one to restrain them). The archers also dismounted, as stated above. We hear little about the disposal of their horses, but clearly a proportion of the men, perhaps one in ten, led them away to the wagon leaguer. The bowmen then formed into "herces", or hollow wedges, in conjunction with the archers of the next division. These were easily and simply constructed: each body inclined diagonally forward, pivoting on the flank of its own men-at-arms; where the two contiguous lines of archers joined up an apex was formed. The effect was that a bastion-like formation was created in the intervals between the divisions, and the flanks of the army were similarly enfiladed. Thus:—

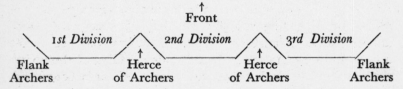

The obvious advantage of this formation was that the front of the men-at-arms could be enfiladed by the archers. Each archer carried two quivers; each quiver contained 24 arrows. With this very limited supply the ammunition problem became acute. When the last arrows had been discharged, three possible courses were open to the archer. He could await the arrival of a fresh supply of arrows; he could pick up the arrows discharged by the enemy; or he could join in the mêlée with his sword. Poitiers is a good example of the second case, Agincourt of the third. Being less encumbered with armour than the men-at-arms, the archers were more nimble and therefore more effective in the hand-to-hand fighting. Moreover they were probably more muscular; only a strong man could wield the longbow.

The few hobilars that Edward still retained with his army were employed as messengers, scouts and orderlies, and as a support to the reserve.[1] The bulk of the reserve was composed of spearmen, and they were utilized after a battle in the rather inglorious task of "clearing up" the battlefield, a task in which the Welsh found that their long knives came in handy. At Crecy some of them broke ranks in their enthusiasm and joined in the mêlée.

SUPPLY AND TRANSPORT

Regrettably little information has come down to us on these all-important subjects. In his otherwise admirable chapter on the Army and Navy in *The English Government at War*, Professor Albert Prince, under the heading "Commissariat arrangements", confines himself to the bald remark that armies mainly lived on the country except at the beginning of a campaign, and he then describes the administrative arrangements at home for procuring supplies for the army abroad.[2] These administrative arrangements concern us here but little; they do not add one iota to the better understanding of the operations in the field, with which this work is primarily concerned. We may therefore confine ourselves to recording that the official responsible for the collection and dispatch of supplies was known as The Receiver and Keeper of the King's Victuals.

As for arms and ammunition, they were stored at the Tower of London, which was the main arsenal of the country and contained, so far as we know, all the cannon in existence in the country at that time. They were under the charge of the Clerk of the Privy Wardrobe. It is from this official's journal and accounts that we get practically all the extant information about the early history of artillery in this country.[3]

On the subject of transport in the field Prince has nothing to say. Very few people have. Some of the things we should like to know are the type of carts and wagons employed;[4] the proportion of stores carried on pack, and on wheels; the number

---

[1] MORRIS, J. E., *Mounted Infantry.*   [2] Op. cit., p. 364.
[3] TOUT, T. F., 'Firearms in England in the 14th Century', in *E.H.R.*, vol. 12, and in *Collected Essays*, II, p. 233.
[4] For the 1359 campaign the king had special wagons constructed.

and nature of roads traversed; the speed at which the transport could travel; and the extent to which it was "road-bound".

Some light is thrown on the last-named point by an incident in the Poitiers campaign. At one place in the English retreat the combatant troops left the road and pushed on across country, in order to shorten their route, leaving the wagons to continue by the road. This is a clear indication that in Poitou at any rate vehicles were road-bound. And I think there can be little doubt that this was the case in most other campaigns.

Not only were they road-bound, but road-bogged in winter operations, for roads were unmetalled, and the wagon train was often a long one. Especially was this the case in the 1359 campaign, which opened in November and continued without a break till the following April. This campaign does furnish some interesting particulars about the composition of the train. Here are some of the stores carried:—

Field-forges, horseshoes, hand-mills for "man-corn" and "horse-corn", fishing boats, a pack of hounds (60 couple), and so on, the whole carried in an enormous train of wagons, variously given as 1,000 to 6,000 in number.

But this campaign was exceptional. In his previous campaigns the king had never cut himself deliberately adrift from the home country, and the campaigns had been of limited duration. In this one the army plunged into the heart of France, and its length was foreseen and planned to be of unspecifiable duration. Nevertheless the general trend of the evidence is that the armies of Edward III lived on the country less than did many of more recent times, for example the French armies in the Peninsular War. There were some surprisingly modern features about Edward's campaigns, such as his carrying on operations in the winter season; but perhaps the most marked of them were his supply and transport arrangements. We only once hear of his army running short of food–that was in the Calais campaign. Indeed, in his first campaign in Flanders he offered to share with his allies the bread that he was carrying for his own troops in wagons. Bread was always the staple food of military life.

Marlborough's bread wagons are famous[1] and Edward's bread wagons have the right to be equally celebrated.

It should go without saying that the fullest possible recourse was had to local supplies, but they were necessarily an uncertain quantity and the king took steps not to be entirely dependent upon them. To sum up: the result of the various measures and efforts designed by Edward, and indicated above, was that during his war in France the English army became the most powerful and highly trained army of its time, and it is not surprising that successive kings of France evinced a strong disinclination to cross swords with it in the field.

[1] They still exist and are in use in Austria under the name of marlbrooks.

Scale of Miles
0   5   10   20   30

ANTWERP

•Sluys

•Bruges

Ghent

FLANDERS

Dunkirk

Vilvoorde

Ypres•

R. Lys

R. Scheldt

Audenarde•

Brussels•

St. Omer•

LILLE

R. Marque

Tournai•

BRABANT

FRANCE

ARTOIS

•Arras

Valenciennes•

HAINAULT

Cambrai•

Marcoing•

Peronne•

Flamengerie•

La Capelle•

St. Quentin•

Guise•

Origny•

THIERACHE

I. THE CAMPAIGNS OF 1339–40

42

CHAPTER II

THE 1339 AND 1340 CAMPAIGNS

KING EDWARD had fixed on Vilvoorde, six miles north of Brussels, as the rendezvous for the army, but July came round without any sign of the allied contingents. Week after week passed while the English army fumed, but the king exercised what patience he could, sending out constant letters of exhortation or reproof. It was not till well on in September that the Elector of Brandenburg, the Emperor's son, arrived at Vilvoorde and the army at length set forth.

It is impossible to make a close estimate of numbers, though it is fairly certain that the English contingent was about 4,000 strong. The allies varied from time to time, and though greatly outnumbering the English, the army total probably at no time reached 20,000. Still, that was a formidable number for those days. The king of England had, in accordance with the chivalrous etiquette of the time, sent a formal challenge of "defiance" to Philip VI in Paris, by the hand of the bishop of Lincoln. The French king thereupon collected an army, also formidable in numbers, and ordered a concentration at St. Quentin, 25 miles south of Cambrai. Three potentates joined its ranks—the blind king of Bohemia, the king of Navarre, and the king of Scotland.

The route for the allies was the shortest possible, namely that *via* Mons and Valenciennes. Sir Walter Manny led the van and his first brush with the enemy occurred at Montaigne, about ten miles north of Cambrai. Though successful in rushing the town he failed to capture the castle. Passing on, he attacked Thun, a few miles further south, and here managed to take both town and castle. A young squire of the name of John Chandos was prominent in these operations. Many engagements were these two destined to share in. Sir Walter Manny seems to have been the "maid of all work" for the king, just as Lord Cadogan was for the duke of Marlborough (though we must discount some of the claims made by Froissart for this remarkable man, both being Hainaulters). The army swept on, the English portion paying its way in the countryside, but the Germans showing themselves "bad payers".

Cambrai was reached on September 20 and its surrender was demanded. Its gallant bishop, who was in control, refused; so siege was laid. Without waiting to "soften up" the city, Edward tried to storm it. A simultaneous attack was made upon its three gates, but in spite of heavy fighting which lasted all day no impression could be made. Froissart asserted in his earliest edition (the only one translated into English) that the defenders had some artillery, but he gave no details and omitted the assertion in both the Amiens and Rome editions. I do not credit the presence of artillery in Cambrai.

Edward now changed his plans; deciding not to waste time on a lengthy siege but to push on into France proper and ravage the dominions of his opponent. At this point a curious incident occurred, illustrating the sort of difficulties with which the English king had to contend. Count William of Hainault, brother of Queen Philippa, and therefore brother-in-law of Edward, solemnly marched off, declaring that he could not enter France as that would mean fighting against his uncle, the king of France. It is surprising that he was allowed to depart without any sharp words being uttered by the king. Still more surprising, three days later he offered his services to the other king. This was more than Philip could stomach and he dismissed the traitor in a rage. As the super-cautious duke of Brabant had now put in a tardy appearance the desertion of the count of Hainault did not amount to much.

Pursuant to the new plan, the army broke up the siege of Cambrai on September 26 and the same day entered France proper seven miles to the south-west, at Marcoing (a town that figured prominently in the 1917 battle of Cambrai). Advancing another ten miles to the south, the king set up his headquarters in the abbey of Mont St. Martin, near Le Catelet. Here he remained for a fortnight whilst his army ravaged and burnt the surrounding country systematically in the hopes that the king of France would be forced to come forward in defence of his subjects and property.

Meanwhile where was Philip VI? When the allies advanced to Cambrai, he was seated in his château at Compiègne. When he heard of the hostile advance he returned to Peronne, *via* Noyon and Nesle. At the latter place he saw on the eastern skyline the smoke of burning villages. This was the work of an expedition under the earls of Salisbury and Derby. They penetrated down the Oise valley, almost to the gates of Laon, burning, among other places, Moy–the scene of a brilliant cavalry action in the 1914 retreat from Mons. Other contingents laid fire to villages further west up to St. Quentin and within sight of Peronne.[1]

It is difficult for us to understand the military object to be achieved by this systematic burning, but two things may be said. In the first place, it was a very usual custom in those days for an invading army not only to pillage but to burn a hostile country. In the second place, Edward by this time thought he knew his man; his own object was to cross swords with his rival while the great army that he had spent so much time, trouble and money to build up was under arms and in the field. Philip, he knew, was loth to fight, but surely the sight of the misery that his subjects were suffering would force him to action. But Edward did not really know his man. Philip, on arriving at Peronne, where his main army was concentrated, instead of advancing boldly against the evil invader sat still, waiting stolidly for laggard contingents to arrive or for the English to advance. So we have the curious spectacle of two rival kings and armies, 12 miles apart, each waiting for the other to advance.

After halting at Mont St. Martin for a fortnight without inducing any offensive move on the part of his opponent,

[1] In 1794 the Austrian invaders, in spite of the expostulations of the Duke of York, burnt the same villages. The famous Hindenburg Line of 1917 ran through the middle of this devastated area.

Edward decided to change his strategy. He would move east
into the province of Thierache (the modern Aisne). This move
would have the appearance of running away from his opponent,
who might thereby pluck up his courage and follow him. A
sudden stand might then produce the desired battle. Such a
manoeuvre would have the additional advantage that the
allies would be moving parallel to and near the frontier
between France and Hainault, and so could easily slip across
the border if need be.

On October 16, therefore, the army struck east. Leaving
St. Quentin some miles on its right, it crossed the Oise near
Mont Origny. But a cruel shock was in store for the English
king. His lukewarm allies suddenly came to him and announced
that they must go home! The army, they averred, had done
enough; their supplies were well-nigh exhausted, the season
was far advanced, and it was high time to seek winter quarters.

Edward must have experienced the same feelings as did
Christopher Columbus when his crew demanded to turn back
before they had sighted America. It was the moment for the
young English king to show his true metal. He expostulated, he
argued, he pleaded and finally he bargained. If they were short
of supplies he would supply them from his own resources; he
would scrap the huge wagon train (rivalling in size that of an
eighteenth-century monarch) and mount the whole army on
horseback. His allies withdrew to consult among themselves
in private. Coming back, they stuck to their decision and then
they went off to bed.

Edward no doubt spent a restless night, but next morning
the situation was unexpectedly saved. A messenger arrived
in the camp from the French lines. He carried a proposal from
the French king. According to the testimony of two French
chroniclers, Philip had at last been stung into action by the
"scandal and murmurs" both of the army and of the unfortunate inhabitants. He thereupon advanced to St. Quentin
directly his enemy had cleared off to the east. The events of the
next few days are difficult to unravel from the confused mass

of evidence. Dates especially are in dispute, but the general trend is clear.

From St. Quentin Philip sent his message. The exact wording of it would help us to appreciate the course of events could we be sure of it. Unfortunately we cannot. Edward himself, in a letter to his son, the Guardian, gave the import of it and Knighton in his chronicle practically repeated it. The English king was to "seek out a field, favourable for a pitched battle, where there is neither wood, nor marsh, nor river". These words are accepted by most historians, but Hemingburgh gives in Latin what purports to be the exact terms of the letter. Unfortunately, the grammar is bad and the meaning rather obscure, but it seems that no onus was placed on the English king of selecting the battlefield. Probably Philip made the message intentionally obscure, and Edward was left to interpret it as he liked.

The message, whatever its exact terms, had an unexpected effect upon the allies. Instantly their martial spirit revived and they declared that they were willing to stand and fight. But it was decided to continue the march another 24 miles to the east, drawing the French army after them. The march was accordingly resumed and on the evening of October 21 a suitable place for battle was found.

The position selected by Edward was near La Flamengerie, three miles north of La Capelle, and 30 miles east of Cambrai. A little stream runs in an east-west direction just to the north of the village and the English position was probably on the ridge beyond, facing south. The French army followed up, and halted the same night, October 21, at Buironfosse, four miles west of La Capelle. The road to La Flamengerie ran through La Capelle, and thus approached the English position from the south. Edward, on learning of the proximity of the enemy on October 22, sent a herald with a challenge to battle on the morrow, a challenge which was accepted by the French king.

In the early morning the following day, the English army drew up in its position in the following order: there were three "battles" or divisions in line, with a fourth in reserve, the foremost division being English and the rearmost the Brabanters. The order of battle from right to left seems to have been:—Derby, Suffolk, Northampton, Salisbury, Pembroke. Robert of Artois and Sir Walter Manny were present and probably held minor commands. The English archers were, it seems, on the wings, flanking the line of men-at-arms, and the whole army was dismounted. This was a repetition of the formation that Edward had found so successful at Halidon Hill six years before and the formation adopted by Walter Manny at Cadzand.

The king himself set his army in order of battle and extorted the admiration of his allies by the skill with which he did it. Then he rode along the ranks in a last review. Finally he posted himself in front of the line and awaited, with what patience he could command, the approach of the French host.

In the official report to parliament the strength of the army was given as "15,000 men and more, and people without number". Make what you can of this! Eugene Deprez, who has made the most detailed study of this campaign, does not even attempt to appraise the strength of either army.

The French army was also drawn up in three divisions in line. It probably outnumbered the English, and was extraordinarily comprehensive. All the great vassals were present, the six dukes of Normandy, Brittany, Burgundy, Bourbon, Lorraine and Athens. Besides the three kings (of Scotland, Navarre, and Bohemia) there were 36 counts, Douglas of Scotland included.

It must have taken some hours to marshal the rival arrays. When both armies were drawn up a prolonged pause ensued. Evidently, though so much had been prepared by mutual arrangement, the question of who should attack had been omitted. Clearly Edward expected from the terms of the challenge to be attacked. But Philip made no move.

Suddenly there was a long, rolling shout in the English ranks. This was followed by clamour and excitement in the opposing army: the English were attacking! A French vassal hastily knighted several of his officers—a usual procedure on the eve of a battle. But the English did not move, the shouting died down, and the two hares which had sprung up in the English lines, thus producing the "view halloas", had met their end. The unhappy new knights were afterwards dubbed the Knights of the Order of the Hare.

Meanwhile Philip was engaged in hot dispute with his captains. They were equally divided between attacking and standing; arguments in support of both views were advanced, but apparently none that the English were holding an unfairly strong position. Finally the king was informed that the astrologer of king Robert of Sicily had seen in a horoscope that he would be defeated if he attacked. This decided the vacillating king, and the absurd day came to an end with the German princes suggesting at vespers that it was time to go home. The allies thereupon mounted their horses and moved a stage toward home. This brought them to Avesnes, ten miles further north. There the army halted for the night and Edward sent to inform the enemy that he would offer battle at that place. Next day he halted, but the French army did not appear; in fact it was already on its way back home. "Our allies would stay no longer" explained the English king to his son, and the whole army returned to Brussels and afterward to Antwerp.

Thus ended in fiasco a campaign on which so many preparations and so much good English money had been lavished. Condensed accounts in most histories make this campaign appear not only ridiculous but puzzling. But there is nothing to be puzzled about. Edward's allies had no heart in the venture; on the one hand they feared the power of France, on the other they coveted English gold. The two forces nearly balanced; when they had received all the gold they could expect the latter motive disappeared, but fear of the French remained. Hence they seized every excuse to be done with it. Edward was as powerless to control his allies as was Marlborough 400 years later, and Edward probably lacked some of the patience and tact of John Churchill.

At the end of the campaign the king wrote a long letter to his son, which is particularly helpful because it provides a type of information that is almost always lacking in accounts of military operations of the period, that is, it tells us what information about the enemy the king had from time to time. Here are some extracts from this unique letter, which may be described as the first military dispatch in English history. On reaching Marcoing,

"we heard that Philip was coming towards us at Peronne, on his way to Noyon (i.e. moving south). . . . On Monday there came a messenger from the king of France saying that he would . . . give battle to the king of England on the next day. . . . In the evening (after arriving at La Flamengerie) three spies were taken who said that Philip was a league and a half from us and would fight on Saturday. On Saturday we went in a field a full quarter of an hour before dawn, and took up our position in a fitting place to fight. In the early morning some of the enemies' scouts were taken and they told us that his vanguard was in battle array and coming out towards us. The news having come to our host our allies, though they had hitherto borne themselves somewhat sluggishly, were in truth of such loyal intent that never were folk of such good will to fight. In the meantime one of our scouts, a knight of Germany, was taken, and he showed all our array to the enemy. Whereupon the foe withdrew his van and gave orders to encamp, made trenches around him and cut down large trees in order to prevent us approaching him. We tarried all day on foot in order of battle until towards evening it seemed to our allies that we had waited long enough. And at vespers we mounted our horses and went near to Avesnes and made him to know that we would await him there all the Sunday. On the Monday morning we had news that the Lord Philip had withdrawn. And so would our allies no longer abide."

The first campaign of the Hundred Years War had ended in disappointment and almost in farce. Moreover, in spasmodic fighting in Gascony the French were gaining ground. But Edward III, though naturally disappointed, was not discouraged. He displayed a tenacity of purpose and a serenity of spirit unusual in one so young. The first thing he did on arrival at Antwerp, and before the army had dispersed, was to hold a Diet, or conference of nobles, to decide on the following year's campaign. For the next two months he was busied in important political and diplomatic negotiations, which can be more conveniently dealt with in connection with the next year's campaign.

THE 1340 CAMPAIGN

Flanders had observed an uneasy neutrality during the previous campaign. But though the count of Flanders kept her faithful to her overlord, the King of France, the heart of the country was against him. The opposition was led by Jacques van Artevelde, a merchant prince of Ghent. By advancing money to Edward he had procured the removal of the restrictions on the import of wool and thus became popular with all classes. By the winter of 1339 he had become the virtual ruler of the country and the count fled to France.

The way was now open for an Anglo-Flemish alliance. The stumbling-block lay in the fact that if Flanders took up arms against the king of France, her lawful suzerain, she would incur heavy ecclesiastical penalties. But Artevelde pointed out to Edward, with cunning casuistry, that if Edward laid official claim to be king of France, then the Flemings would acknowledge this claim and recognize him as their overlord and fight for him. All that was necessary was for Edward to undertake to help them recover their lost cities of Lille, Douai, Tournai, and Bethune.

All this suited Edward's purpose admirably and in January, 1340, he made a state entry into Ghent, where, on January 24, he was proclaimed king of France with much pomp, the ceremony taking place in the market place, and the three towns of Ghent, Bruges, and Ypres swearing allegiance to him as their overlord. In order to clinch the matter Edward had a new Great Seal made, quartering the lilies of France with the leopards of England.

When all this was settled, the king took boat for England where he spent the next five months bargaining with his parliament—with some success—for fresh subsidies for the war, and strengthening the new alliance by various treaties.

Meanwhile fighting of a rather sporadic nature flared up in the Low Countries. Philip sent an army to wreak vengeance on the towns of Hainault in revenge for the ravages committed by the Hainaulters—the chief offenders—in the preceding campaign. He sent his son John, duke of Normandy, to ravage Hainault to such a degree that it should never recover. John attempted to carry out his father's behests, and certainly did a vast amount of damage, but his progress came to an end at Quesnoy, where the garrison startled his men and horses by discharges from a number of small cannon.

Flanders was also involved in these raids and Jacques van Artevelde set off from Ghent with an army to which the earls of Suffolk and Salisbury attached themselves with a small contingent. On the way to Valenciennes, near Lille, the two earls were captured in an ambush and taken in triumph to Paris. King Philip had now joined his army, and it looked as if there would be a clash between the two armies just to the north of Cambrai. But, as in the previous year, it came to nothing. This time the cause was the arrival of the news of a great naval victory by the king of England and of his landing in Flanders with a large army. On receipt of this news Philip took the course that we are beginning to expect of him. He fell back to Arras, where he disbanded part of his army, and dispersed the remainder into the neighbouring garrisons.

THE BATTLE OF SLUYS

We must now hark back a few weeks, in order to see how this naval battle came about. It will be remembered that in the early stages of the war the French navy held the upper hand in the Channel, and there was a real danger of invasion. Right through 1339 the danger persisted, and one of the king's pre-occupations on his return to England was to strengthen his own shores. While he was gradually amassing a large fleet the French were doing the same. It was a polyglot affair, consisting

mainly of Normans and Genoese. By this means Philip was able
to concentrate, according to king Edward, 190 ships of war in
Sluys harbour in the month of June, in readiness for Edward's
expected return to Flanders. It was a shrewd selection of
position, for whether the English made for Antwerp or for the
ports of Flanders, the French fleet could intercept them or cut
their communications.

Meanwhile Edward was collecting his new army in Suffolk,
and arranging for the concentration of his fleet at Orwell, near
Ipswich. At the last moment, when he was about to embark,
the archbishop of Canterbury came hot-foot from London
beseeching him to defer his journey as the French fleet was in
waiting and the risk was too great to take. The admirals
backed up the archbishop; but the king would not be deterred.
"Ye and the archbishop", he exploded, "have agreed to tell
the same story to prevent my crossing. I will cross in spite of
you, and ye who are afraid where no fear is may stay at home."

He did, however, stay a few days longer, awaiting the arrival
of a northern squadron, and at length, on June 22, the great
fleet weighed anchor and set sail for Flanders.

It is impossible to compute exactly the strength of either
fleet or army, but it would seem that the English fleet was
inferior in numbers to that of France, while Froissart may not
this time be greatly exaggerating when he estimates an army
of 4,000 men-at-arms and 12,000 archers. The king commanded
in person, having as navigator the veteran John Crab, who had
deserted the Scottish service because of bad treatment. His
chief admirals were Sir Robert Morley, the earls of Huntingdon
and Northampton, and the ubiquitous Walter Manny. (It must
be remembered that admiral and general were almost synonymous terms in those days, and for long after.)

The king wrote another admirable letter to his son a few
days after the battle that ensued, the first naval dispatch that
we possess, just as the letter on the Cambrai campaign was the
first full military dispatch. Other and later accounts of the
battle of Sluys are so confusing and conflicting that they can

almost be ignored and the story built up round the royal dispatch, from which we are quoting. After setting out:

"we sailed all day and the night following and on Friday about the hour of noon we arrived upon the coast of Flanders, before Blankenberg, where we had a sight of the enemies' fleet who were all crowded together in the port of Sluys. And seeing that the tide did not serve us to close with them we lay to all that night. On Saturday, St. John's Day [June 24] soon after the hour of noon at high tide [the actual hour has been computed at 11.23 a.m.] in the name of God, and confident in our just quarrel, we entered the said port upon our said enemies, who had assembled their ships in very strong array, and who made a most noble defence all that day and the night following. . . ."

It was indeed a "very strong array"; the ships were drawn up in four lines, all except the rear line being bound and clamped together with ropes and chains. They thus formed four gigantic floating platforms. Since land armies were to contest the battle, it was natural that the arena should be made as near as possible like the dry land. The first requisite of a battle is a battlefield. It is perhaps appropriate that the place where the battle took place is now land. Long ago the port silted up and there is now nothing but a flat sandy plain.

In the English fleet each vessel containing men-at-arms had on each side of it a vessel containing archers—the Crecy formation on the high sea. Fleets in those days were regarded merely as vehicles to convey armies, much as horses convey mounted infantry: neither was expected to take a part of its own in the battle. That was reserved for the soldiers. The only missiles the French fleet seem to have possessed were stones, thrown on to the English decks by soldiers perched in the rigging.

After what has been said, the reader will not be surprised to learn that the battle took the form of a land battle. The English attacked, each vessel clamping itself to its opposite number, and the chivalry of England clambered (without their horses) on board the French vessels and engaged in a hand-to-hand fight on the decks.

Early in the engagement a striking success was gained. The royal flagship, the great *Christopher*, the pride of the navy, had been captured in a Flemish harbour the previous year and the French had the effrontery to station her in the very forefront of their line. The English naturally made a dead set at her and speedily effected her recapture. They also recaptured a second great ship,. the *Edward*. Hastily manning these warships with English crews they sent them back into the fight with the English flag aloft.

The English army was a picked one; the cream of the chivalry and nobility of the country was on board. The long-bowmen had "sitting targets", each arrow found its billet in the massed ranks on the French decks, and the lusty and expert men-at-arms carried on the slaughter, pushing back their opponents step by step across the decks and into the sea. It must have been an extraordinary sight. Even in France the story got about. King Philip's clown was heard to ask his master: "Do you know, Sire, why the English are cowards? Because, unlike the French, they dare not jump into the sea."

The rear squadron of the French fleet, 24 ships in number, made its escape under cover of darkness. Every other ship was captured. It must have been easy to count them and Edward's statement about numbers (190 vessels in the fleet) can be accepted as accurate. But when it comes to computing the number killed or drowned, the case is different—unless the king captured the French strength return, which is most unlikely. Therefore his estimate of 30,000 French lost is probably a wild exaggeration. More than that we cannot say.

After spending a few days on the spot and at Bruges, Edward III entered Ghent on July 10 where he was greeted by the burgesses like a conquering hero. This was gratifying, but he received another greeting which he appreciated even more. It was from his wife, Philippa, who presented him with his new-born son, John, born while the king was in England. John was, in accordance with the custom of the time, called by the name of his birthplace, John of Ghent; but as our forefathers pronounced the word Gaunt, he has come down to us as John of Gaunt.

Edward's great victory added immensely to his prestige and his vassals came flocking to congratulate him. He lost no time in taking advantage of his good fortune. He summoned a Diet to meet at Vilvoorde on July 18, and there the alliance between England and her three allies, Brabant, Hainault, and Flanders, was sealed. The Diet was then turned into a war council and plans were made for the season's campaign. This war council was numerously attended—too numerously for secrecy. A simple plan was formed. While Robert of Artois took an army of Flemings against St. Omer, the main blow was to be struck against Tournai by the remainder of the forces, under the personal command of Edward III. The king assured the Home government that there were 100,000 Flemings— probably a deliberate exaggeration, for he had contracted to pay them, and he depended upon friends in England to do so. He was, in fact, the first of a long line of English commanders who had under them a mixed army of varying tongues and nationalities, most of whom were in the pay of the English government.

Situated in the middle of the cockpit of Europe, Tournai has repeatedly figured in our military annals, and the surrounding ground has been plentifully watered by English blood. The duke of Marlborough captured it in a brilliant siege, and his armies marched and counter-marched around it for two years. Forty years later the duke of Cumberland, with another allied army, marched to its relief and fought the marvellous battle of Fontenoy under its walls. In 1793 the duke of York made it his headquarters on several occasions, besides fighting three battles in the vicinity in the area between it and Lille. In the war of 1914–18 it was taken by our 55th Division only two days before the end of the war, and finally in the Second World War it was liberated by the Guards Armoured Division on September 3, 1944. At the time of the Hundred Years War, and for long after, Tournai was the chief town on the French north-eastern border, greater even than Lille, and its fortifications were immensely strong. In the days of Henry VIII its population was, according to Cardinal Wolsey, 80,000, and it probably was nearly that size in the time of Edward III, though Wolsey's figure must be over-high.

The all too public plan of Vilvoorde had reached the ears of the king of France and Philip VI promptly sent the garrison a large reinforcement of his best troops, under count Raoul, the Constable of France. He also supplied it with "l'artillerie, engiens, espingalls, et kanons" to use Froissart's terms. Here we encounter a difficulty. When a new invention appeared in the Middle Ages it took some time to coin a word for it, and usually an old word was made to do duty. Thus "engine" may mean "cannon" or merely "mediaeval siege weapon", such as balista, trebuchet, mangonel, etc. In the same way, "artillery" may mean merely archery. "Kanon", however, can have but one meaning, as also ribaudequin, which Froissart explains as three or four guns bound together. Now from other sources we know that ribaudequins were employed by the English and Flemings, so it is clearly established that artillery was used by *both* sides in this famous siege. We will return to the subject presently.

CHALLENGE TO COMBAT

After the Vilvoorde council Edward III had sent his allied commanders to their various capitals to collect their armies for the coming campaign. It was arranged that they should concentrate for the siege on July 22. The king, with the English army, marched along the course of the Scheldt through Audenarde–later to become famous in our history (see sketch map). After a skirmish at Espierres, ten miles north of Tournai, he reached Chin, three miles north-west, on July 22, according to plan. From here he sent a remarkable letter to the king of France, in which he offered him three alternatives, first that the two of them should decide the issue by single combat; second, that they should engage each other at the head of

100 picked men a side; third, that the complete armies should engage. As he addressed the letter to "Philip of Valois" and not "King of France" the latter pretended at first not to have received it as it was incorrectly addressed. Eventually he rather astutely agreed to single combat on condition that if he won he would have the kingdom of England as well as that of France. This of course was tantamount to a refusal, and probably did not come as a surprise to the English king. We are not however warranted in ridiculing the whole affair. King Edward was the embodiment of chivalry, and he conceived himself merely to be acting in accordance with its tenets.

Meanwhile the other allies were drawing near, and the defenders of the city were putting the finishing touches to their defence measures. A vast amount of food had been collected in the town, the walls had been strengthened, as also had the gates (some which had been blocked up entirely). Booms had been placed across the river where it entered and left the town. The guns, or–to be on the safe side–the engines, had been stationed mainly at the various gates. Of the old defences, a bridge in the town and the twin towers of the Marvis still stand. The four national contingents of which the allied army was composed took up their position as follows:

English, opposite the St. Martin gate, on the south-west.
Flemings, opposite the St. Fontaine gate, on the north-west.
Brabançons, opposite the Marvis gate on the north-east.
Hainaulters, opposite the Valenciennes gate, on the south-east.

Thus the city was completely surrounded and pontoon bridges were thrown across the river in order to link up the different contingents in closer union. The siege commenced in earnest on July 31–remarkably punctually.

While the English king was thus engaged in methodically encompassing the threatened city his French counterpart appeared to be dawdling supinely at Arras, nearly 40 miles to the south-west. In reality he was concentrating an army for

the relief of Tournai. But there seemed no need for particular
haste; the numbers of the allied armies, reasoned Philip, were
so great that it would not do to venture forward with a weak
host and Tournai was well defended and well supplied.

The allies were indeed taking advantage of their preponder-
ant force. Leaving only a fraction of their numbers engaged
in the actual siege they carried out raids and forays throughout
the surrounding countryside. Seclin, to the south of Lille, was
captured, pillaged and fired; so was Orchies still further south;
St. Amand nearly suffered the same fate. The French were
powerless to prevent all this. As their enemies closed in on
Tournai the garrison ejected all Flemings, English, and
Brabançons within the city. Otherwise they would only become
"bouches inutiles" (an expression that had been coined at the
famous siege of Chateau Gaillard). With great magnanimity,
Edward allowed three days for this evacuation, a sign that
humanity was not entirely absent from medieval warfare.

Edward's plan for conducting the siege had a distinctly
modern flavour. Instead of attempting to carry it at once by
storm, he decided to do the job as cheaply as possible, sparing
his infantry until the "artillery" (by which term I include both
mechanical and gunpowder weapons) had effected breaches
in the walls and gates, and the inhabitants had been "softened"
by bombardment and hunger. It thus became largely an
artillery siege. From the difficulty already mentioned of
distinguishing between ancient and modern "artillery" and
"engines" we will not attempt to discriminate in the following
account, except in the case of the ribaudequins, which were
incontestably cannon.

The besieging artillery was concentrated against the various
gates, each national contingent bombarding its own sector
of the defence. A number of incidents have been recorded in
the local archives, and nowhere else.[1] Three "engines" were
placed in action opposite the Porte Marvis, but they do not

[1] Fortunately for us they have been collected by the Baron Kervyn de Lettenhove and inserted as notes in his edition of Froissart's *Chronicles* (vol. III, 1867).

seem to have effected a breach. The walls of the two still existing towers are very massive and strong, and the probability is that the projectiles did little material damage. The same applies to the other gates. The English used two against the Porte Cocquerel in their sector, while the Flemings, somewhat injudiciously, placed their artillery in the camp of their commander, the famous Jacques van Artevelde. Thereat ensued the first "artillery duel" of which we have record: the French had placed an "engine" just inside the Porte St. Fontaine, which engaged the Flemish "engine" and knocked it out. The Flemings repaired and brought it into action again, only to be knocked out a second time. The French had evidently got the range to a nicety. Not to be outdone the English now took up the contest and knocked out a French gun in the Marché-aux-Vaches.

And so the contest went on. The ribaudequins were otherwise employed, being wholly anti-personnel weapons. Now in order to hit the defenders upon the battlements, plunging or at least horizontal fire was required. The ribaudequins had therefore to be raised by some means to an equal height with the tops of the walls. Wooden towers were constructed for this purpose and the ribaudequins mounted upon them. What damage they did we are not told, but it is related that at the end of the siege the towers were dismantled and the wood of which they were constructed sold to the inhabitants. The ribaudequins were then floated down the Scheldt to Ghent.

After the siege had been in progress for nearly a month a series of assaults was made upon the walls where they had been weakened by artillery fire. On August 26 the Flemings made a vigorous assault; they also endeavoured to smash the boom which had been placed across the river in their sector, with some of their own boats. But the current was against them and the attempt failed. It is even said that the French sallied forth in their own boats and that a miniature naval engagement then took place. Two days later the French took the initiative, making an attack against the English lines. This was not only repulsed, but the English followed the French so closely that they almost succeeded in getting into the town.

By this time food was running short inside the city and the garrison smuggled out a message crying for relief. It did not fall on heedless ears. Philip VI had by this time collected his army at Arras and he advanced to the relief of the beleaguered town.

Midway between Tournai and Lille flows the River Marque. It is about 15 feet wide, but boggy and deep, and in most places unfordable.[1] There were (and are) bridges at Bouvines and Pont-à-Tressin. King Edward occupied the line of river between these two bridges in what would afterwards be called "lines of contravallation". (Marlborough's army marched and fought over this ground nearly 400 years later, and again it was the scene of a victory by the duke of York in 1794.) The French king, finding both bridges occupied by the enemy, formed his camp midway between the two. This was on September 7, and the garrison of Tournai, being now in their sixth week of siege, were getting to the end of their tether, and were clamorous for relief. Philip, however, made no sign of attempting to storm the river crossings and to relieve the city.

But the king of England also had his difficulties. When a number of allies are collected together it is seldom that trouble and friction does not arise between some of them, and Edward's heterogeneous army was no exception to this rule. The Brabançons, who had no common frontier with the French, were not so zealous in the cause as the other allies, and some of them began to clamour to go home.

One day king Edward was sitting in his tent, discussing matters with Artevelde and the duke of Brabant, when the former acidly remarked that it was about time the Brabançons made an assault on the city, as had all the other allies. A Brabançon knight who was also present told Artevelde sharply to hold his tongue and get back to Ghent and get on with his

[1] The duke of York in the 1794 campaign once saved his life by fording it.

brewing—an allusion to his plebeian origin. The Flemish leader drew his sword in fury and ran him through on the spot. The duke of Brabant then rushed from the tent and sprang to his horse, with the evident intention of leading his army away. But Edward was equal to the occasion. Following the duke out of the tent he seized the charger by the bridle before the duke could gallop off, and used all the eloquence at his command to mollify the outraged Brabançon leader. So successful were his entreaties that the duke ultimately consented to patch up the quarrel. To clinch the matter king Edward gave a great banquet to which he invited all the leaders and he so arranged the seating that the duke of Brabant and Jacques van Artevelde found themselves seated next each other. The English king must have possessed that gift of harmonizing warring elements which both the duke of Marlborough and the duke of York afterwards exhibited with the same sort of allies in the same sort of country.

Peace reigned once more in the allied lines, and the end of the siege seemed near. The garrison was famished and the French king was at his wits' end. Like Masséna before the lines of Torres Vedras, the longer he looked at the lines of the Marque the less he liked them. But help came to him from an unexpected quarter—a woman, and an abbess. Philip had a sister, the Lady Jeanne de Valois, who was also the mother of the count of Hainault and Philippa, and therefore Edward's mother-in-law. This good woman, leaving her abbey of Fontenelle, came to the French camp and prevailed upon Philip to consider negotiations for a truce. Then she crossed over the river to the rival camp, and put the same suggestion to the English king. The Brabançons were now seething with discontent and Edward had no money with which to quieten them. He called a council to consider the Lady Jeanne's appeal. All the allies were in favour of a truce, while the king and Artevelde alone held out against it. This was too serious a matter to ignore and eventually Edward, though much against his will, agreed to negotiate. His money troubles, which

were likely to grow worse, partly reconciled him to this course.
A meeting was therefore held on September 25 and a truce for
one year was signed – the truce of Esplechin.

By this truce, Edward's allies all acquired some slight
advantages, but he gained nothing. Things were left as they
were at the outset between France and England; everything
remained in suspense. Thus the second campaign had ended as
inconclusively as the first, and the disappointment was cumulative. The main blame for this dismal conclusion Edward
placed, not on his miserable allies, but on his Home government, who had sent him no subsidies or reinforcements in spite
of his urgent appeals. If he had been able to keep his allies in
gold he could have kept them in the field. Such was his belief,
and it was probably justified. Rage boiled up within his
breast, and he took the first opportunity he could (it did not
come for two months) to slip away home. He landed at the
Tower unexpectedly and in savage mood. Within 24 hours he
had dismissed his ministers and appointed others. But the
damage was done, and it was irremediable. Early in 1341 the
emperor rescinded Edward's appointment as his Vicar of the
Holy Roman Empire and the grand alliance collapsed in ruins.
The first round of the great war on sea was to our advantage,
but on land a pointless draw. The king of England would have
to start all over again.

APPENDIX

PRINCIPAL SOURCES

The sources for the first two chapters of this book can be
grouped together. They are few and straightforward, and most
can be found in any standard reference library.

On the English side the usual chroniclers of the period cover
most of the ground, the most useful being Henry Knighton,
Adam Murimuth, Walter de Hemingburgh and Robert of
Avesbury. The last two, with Rymer's collection of *Foedera*,
contain all the letters referred to here. The French chroniclers

are, as throughout the Hundred Years War, disappointingly meagre. The *Grandes Chroniques* belies its name. More reliable are the *Continuation* of *Guillaume de Nangis* and *Chronographia Regum Francorum* (not cited in Ramsay's *Genesis of Lancaster* for some reason).

On the neutral side, as we must call it, there are the Chronicles of Jean le Bel, the Liégeois, and Jean Froissart of Valenciennes. Le Bel had served in the army of Edward III in Scotland and he had an unbounded admiration for the English king. His Chronicle attains a high standard of accuracy when judged by the historical standards of the period. Not so Jean Froissart, who in his first edition copied unblushingly the chronicle of the Liégeois, and added to it–embellished it would be a more exact expression–according to his information and his fancy. His reckless irresponsibility is the despair of all who search for the truth in his pages. Broadly speaking, any statement by him, except such as are inherently probable, should not be accepted unless corroborated by another source. There are two standard editions of his *Chronicle*, one by a Belgian, the Baron Kervyn de Lettenhove (1866–onward) and the other by a Frenchman, Simeon Luce (1869–onward). Though the Belgian started publishing his colossal edition first, the two ran simultaneously. It is essential to work on one or other of these, since English translations give only the first edition; to read the *Amiens* or *Rome* or the *Abrégées*[1] editions one must go to the original French. Lettenhove's edition is set out the more conveniently, but it contains some grave errors of transcription (as his French rival did not fail to point out). For general notes Luce is best, but Lettenhove prints many hitherto unpublished or unknown MSS, such as the *Récit d'un Bourgeois de Valenciennes*, which is useful here and elsewhere.

These remarks on the neutral chroniclers should be borne in mind throughout this book.

The best bibliography is contained in *Les Préliminaires de la Guerre de Cent Ans* (1902) by Eugène Deprez (who died in

---

[1] So named in Lettenhove. Luce describes it as MSS B6.

1953). Professor Deprez was fully acquainted with English writings on the period (which is more than can be said for some French writers). The most detailed account in English is that of the American, H. S. Lucas, *The Low Countries and the Hundred Years War* (1929), but the period as a whole has been sadly neglected.

CHAPTER III

BRITTANY TO THE BATTLE OF
MORLAIX, 1341–42

AFTER his return to England, Edward III was for a year occupied with Home and Scottish affairs. He undertook a short campaign north of the Tweed where the Scots were slowly recovering the territories lost in the earlier campaigns. Meanwhile an event occurred in Brittany which was to have a lasting effect upon the fortunes of the Hundred Years War. In April, 1341, duke John III of Brittany died, leaving no son to succeed him. His father, duke Arthur II, had a second son, Guy, who had died young but had left a daughter, Joan. Duke Arthur's second wife was Yolande, the widow of Alexander II of Scotland. By her he had a third son, John. Both Joan de Penthièvre and John de Montfort claimed the succession. Thereby arose the war of succession in Brittany, which was to last for 24 years. In this war England and France became increasingly involved. It brought to the front a succession of notable English soldiers and proconsuls (as we should now call them), and produced some notable battles. (Both soldiers and battles have alike passed almost into oblivion.)

The dispute arose in this way. Joan had married Charles, count of Blois, who was a nephew of the French king. Joan therefore claimed the throne for her husband, and appealed to Philip VI for approval. This approval the French king was anxious to give, for obvious reasons. With his own nephew duke of Brittany, the province was more likely to remain faithful to its suzerain than it would under John, who inclined to the English cause. For the same, or rather for the opposite reason, England favoured John. Charles de Blois based his wife's claim on the fact that she was the nearest blood relation of the dead duke, whereas John de Montfort based his on the fact that he was the nearest *male* relation, invoking the Salic law. Thus we find the king of France supporting a claim that ignored the Salic law, whereby he himself wore the crown, and the king of England supporting a claim the principle of which he had rejected in the case of the French crown. The irony of this situation has not been lost upon historians.

But for the moment neither England nor France was drawn into the contest. John was first in the field. He entered Nantes, was well received by the citizens, and in a short campaign of two months rapidly overran most of the country. He then crossed to England where he obtained promise of support from the king, in return for acknowledging Edward as his lord, and king of France.

Meanwhile Charles de Blois was collecting an army at Angers. With it he advanced on Nantes in November, 1341. This count de Blois was a pious man with saintly habits. He put pebbles into his shoes and wore a hair shirt swarming with vermin. This may have made him irritable in mind as well as in body, for after capturing some of John's men in a sortie from Nantes, this holy man beheaded 31 of them and threw their heads into the town with his catapults. The inhabitants, fearing for the fate of their relatives outside, quickly came to terms. De Blois entered the city, and count John was captured and sent to Paris, where he lay imprisoned in the Louvre for four years.

Charles in his turn now overran most of the country, helped by a French army under the king's son John, duke of Normandy.

All seemed lost for the Montfort party, but men had forgotten the countess. This heroic woman, Joan of Flanders, took energetic measures to restore the situation, and for a time she was successful. But the Blois party advanced in overwhelming numbers, and eventually the countess of Flanders was besieged in Hennebout. This town lies at the head of an estuary on the south coast midway between Vannes and Quimper.[1]

---

[1] Lorient, the famous German submarine base in the Second World War, is lower down the estuary.

The countess naturally appealed to Edward to redeem his promise of help. This the English king was quite willing to do, and a small expedition under Sir Walter Manny was fitted out. In March, 1342, it sailed for Hennebout, but the voyage took 60 days, incredible as this may sound. Consequently it did not

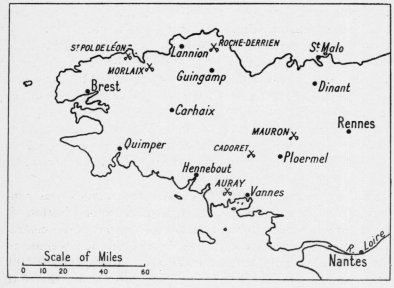

2. BRITTANY

arrive till May, by which time the countess was hard pressed and almost in despair. Froissart, in a well-known passage, describes the dramatic moment when the countess, standing on the roof of a tower and scanning the horizon anxiously, caught sight of the gleaming white sails of the English fleet, slowly making its way up the estuary.

The relieving force ran the blockade without much difficulty, and was received with unrestrained joy by the famished garrison. A great banquet in honour of the English was given that same night, while a "great engine" (doubtless a catapult) kept hurling projectiles into the town. This led Sir Walter

Manny, in the course of the banquet, to remark that he would like to capture that engine. Leave was given, and next morning he led out a sortie of English troops, drove off the defenders, seized the catapult and broke it to pieces.

This was only the beginning of a series of exploits by Sir Walter Manny and his gallant band, which we will not recount in detail. It is Froissart who relates them, and as we have said his statements about his fellow Hainaulter, when uncorroborated, must be accepted with caution. Be this as it may, the net result of Manny's activities was that the siege was raised, as was also that of Auray, 20 miles east, and Louis de la Cerda, the skilful Spanish general in the service of de Blois, was defeated at Quimperlé (12 miles to the west).

We must leave Sir Walter Manny and Charles marching and countermarching in southern Brittany, in order to follow a more serious attempt on the part of England to intervene in the war.

The strategical pattern of the war that ensued was conditioned by geographical and ethnological factors. Brittany is a peninsula; Upper Brittany (Haute Bretagne) is the central zone stretching from the eastern border through Rennes to Pontivy. It was French in tongue and sympathies, and the bulk of the nobility of French blood resided there. It was therefore natural that Upper Brittany should espouse the cause of the French king's nephew. The northern district of Penthièvre also came under French influence, since Joan countess of Blois was the daughter of Guy de Penthièvre. Thus the essentially Montfort regions were confined to the south and west. (This, with many fluctuations, was the line of demarcation throughout the war.) Hence, if an English army was to fight a French army on Breton soil it would have a long and precarious sea passage round Cape Finisterre, and it would be the aim of the French to cut this line of communications by naval operations. *Per contra*, the French had a short and easy approach by land from the east. Two main gateways guarded this approach, Nantes and Rennes. It was therefore the English object to seize these gateways (just as the duke of Wellington seized the two main gateways from Portugal to Spain, Badajoz and Ciudad Rodrigo).

These factors gave France a big advantage. It was like the war between England and Germany in Italy in 1944; the Germans could reinforce their armies speedily by land, whereas we had to reinforce by a long and dangerous sea route.

This strategical handicap, much greater in the days of sail than of steam, dogged the English efforts throughout the war, especially in Gascony, and should be kept in mind throughout, for attention will not be incessantly drawn to it.

In July, 1342, Edward III appointed the earl of Northampton, whom we last met in Flanders, as his lieutenant in Brittany, assisted by the earls of Derby and Oxford, with Robert of Artois as his "chief of staff",[1] all four of whom had shown their military talents in the Flanders campaigns.

On August 14, 1342, a fleet of 260 sail transported Northampton's army, about 3,000 strong, to Brest, where it arrived four days later. Charles de Blois, who had now overrun nearly all the provinces, was besieging the port, so the English army had to land on the open shore near by. But only light resistance was offered and Northampton entered the town amid scenes of rejoicing. Charles immediately raised the siege and fell right back to Guingamp, 40 miles to the east, leaving the country open to the invaders. Western Brittany was strongly pro-Montfort, and some Bretons may be presumed to have joined the English army. Advancing without impediment, Northampton arrived within sight of Morlaix on September 3, and at once attempted to take it by storm. The attempt lasted all day, but failed, and Northampton sat down to besiege it methodically. This did not seem likely to be successful as the town was strongly fortified and amply supplied.

Meanwhile de Blois, at Guingamp, was vigorously strength-

---

[1] Robert of Artois had impressed the king with his military ability, and Edward had brought him back to England and kept him at Court. As to the relative share in the operations of the forthcoming campaign, historians are at variance. But Northampton was with the army, and as the king's representative had to bear the responsibility and must therefore be regarded as the commander in chief.

ening his army and enlisting local levies, until it attained
prodigious numbers for those days. The careful French historian of Brittany, A. de la Borderie, estimates these numbers at
30,000, which seems quite impossible. If they did not pass
15,000, however, they still outnumbered the little English
army by more than four to one, a proportion that seems well
substantiated. With this large and probably rather unwieldy
army, Charles de Blois began an approach march for the relief
of Morlaix. His route lay *via* Lanmeur, a large village seven
miles north-east of Morlaix. On Michaelmas Day the earl
of Northampton received news of this advance. Its purpose was
obvious; it would never do to allow his own army to be caught
between the two forces, the town on one side and the relieving
army on the other. Northampton immediately broke up the
siege and that night marched out towards Lanmeur.[1]

By dawn a suitable position was reached. This position
strides the road, and is just on the beginning of a gentle slope
into a dip about 300 yards in front. The road then ascends an
equally gentle slope and disappears some 500 yards from the
position. Immediately in rear is a wood. The spire of (the new)
Lanmeur church can be seen over the horizon. If this is in
truth the position occupied by the English army, the wood
that I have mentioned is the veritable wood that figures so
prominently in the battle that took place that day.

THE BATTLE OF MORLAIX (SEPTEMBER 30, 1342)

The English army took up position just in front of this wood,
in a line astride the road, and perhaps 600 yards in length. The
selection of a position with a wood in rear was popular with
English troops in those days, because it could not be effectively

---

[1] No attempt has ever been made, so far as I can ascertain, to establish the
site of the battle that ensued. It is usually called vaguely Morlaix, or the battle
near Morlaix. The battle itself, in spite of its great military significance, has passed
almost unnoticed by English historians, with the sole exception of Professor Tout,
who touched on it in an article in the *English Historical Review* for 1906. The
obscurity in which the battle has been allowed to remain is no doubt in large
measure due to this fact that the site is unknown. The one given here is of course
conjectural, but I give my reasons for this site in the appendix to this chapter.

attacked in flank by cavalry, and formed a useful baggage
park.[1] Some hundred yards in front of it, on a line now marked
approximately by a hedge and a cottage, they dug a trench,
and covered it with grass and other herbage as a "booby-
trap" for the horsemen of the enemy. It was only 30 years
since the battle of Bannockburn and the English troops had
not forgotten the lesson taught by the "pots" of the Scots.

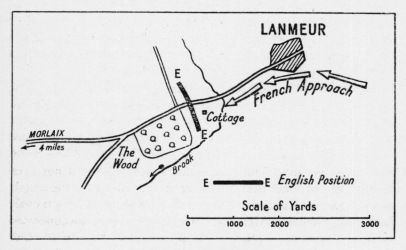

3. BATTLE OF MORLAIX

The dismounted men-at-arms occupied the centre of the line,
the archers were stationed on the flanks. During that morning
the French army was apparently stationary a league away,
which would seem to indicate billets in the village of Lanmeur
—at least for the mounted troops—and we may suppose that
the footmen arrived on the scene next morning. This would
account for the fact that the French did not attack till three
o'clock in the afternoon. In the battle that ensued there were
at least four points of resemblance with the battle that was to
take place at Poitiers 13 years later. It is not too fanciful to

[1] It should be noted that Northampton had a responsible command at Crecy
four years later, and some features common to both battles may be due to his
influence.

suppose that the Black Prince was mindful of this battle when making his dispositions at Poitiers.

The count of Blois drew up his army in three huge columns, one behind the other, with an appreciable space between each. The leading column consisted of irregulars, presumably local levies. These were all dismounted troops. On the order being given they advanced straight to their front, descending the hill into the slight dip and up the other side. When they got within effective range the English archers drew bow, and a hail of arrows dispersed the column before it had got into close contact with the men-at-arms. The contest was short; the Bretons went reeling down the hill.

Charles was disconcerted by this sudden disaster and took counsel with his chief captains regarding the next step. Eventually it was decided to launch the second column, the men-at-arms, in a mounted attack. This was, of course, exactly what Northampton wished and had prepared for. His stratagem worked admirably. The French horsemen, who had not been warned of the concealed trench by the irregulars for the simple reason that they had not reached it, rode forward impetuously and unsuspectingly. Men and horses plunged into the concealed trench; the archers plied them with arrows to add to their confusion, and the attack practically came to a standstill. A few horsemen, 200 in all, did manage to negotiate the trench and, indeed, to penetrate the line. But local reserves came up and they were cut off and captured, including their commander, Geoffrey de Charni.

The second attack had ended as disastrously as the first, and again there was a considerable pause while the attackers licked their wounds and consulted on what to do next.

Northampton waited to see if there were any signs of a general retreat. But there was none. Though two columns, each greater in number than his own tiny army, had been worsted, the third column, also bigger than his own, remained drawn up on the opposite ridge. His archers were by this time short of ammunition, each man carrying 36 arrows at most. Had time allowed, the archers would doubtless have run forward to recover their arrows (as did their successors at Poitiers). But the hostile column was now on the move, and at the sight of the huge mass of fresh troops approaching, the English showed signs of discouragement. The trench was by this time battered in or filled with corpses; it was no longer a defence. Moreover there are indications that the third French column extended beyond the flanks of the position and thus threatened the flanks. Seeing and weighing all this, the earl (with or without the advice of Robert d'Artois, of whom we hear nothing in the battle) decided on a novel manoeuvre. If he did not retreat he could not prevent the enemy surrounding him if they had the will. He decided to adopt a course of action in battle that is almost unprecedented in that era: he would fall back into the wood less than a hundred yards in rear, and form what we now call a "hedgehog", a defensive line along the edge of the wood and facing in all directions. No doubt he had this eventuality in mind when he selected a position immediately in front of a wood. So into the wood his victorious troops fell back in good order, taking with them their prisoners, and a new position, facing all ways, was taken up.

The details of what followed are scanty and rather puzzling. What seems clear is that the English reserved their "fire", preserving their scanty ammunition, and that the French came on and engaged, but everywhere failed to penetrate the wood. Some of them swung round the flanks, till the occupants were practically, if not quite, surrounded.

A fresh pause now ensued. We are reminded of the *Ballad of the Revenge*:

> "The Spanish fleet, with broken sides, lay round us all in a ring,
> But they dared not touch us again, for they feared that we still could sting."

Charles was at his wits' end. Many of his troops had fled the field, including his Genoese crossbowmen; the English position was still intact and unbroken, and there seemed to be no means of getting at it. Night was coming on, and Charles decided to abandon the contest, to give up his intention of relieving Morlaix, and to beat a retreat. Orders were issued accordingly and gradually the troops still left on the battlefield drew back and retreated to Lanmeur.

Northampton had been doing some thinking too. Food had run out, and his troops were, according to one chronicler, famished. The French had been fought to a standstill, and their advance on Morlaix had been frustrated. Darkness was falling; his immediate task was accomplished; he would return to the siege of Morlaix. So, collecting his little band, he charged out of the wood in a body, cutting his way through the still encircling enemy, and returned with his prisoners to the siege lines of Morlaix. This decision was reached approximately simultaneously with that of his opponent. The curious spectacle was thus witnessed of both armies falling away from one another, as if by mutual consent.

The two armies disengaged, but whereas the English army had achieved its purpose, although outnumbered by four or five to one, its opponent had failed in his purpose, and had retreated the way he had come. He is next heard of in the south, resuming the siege of Hennebout.

*　　　　*　　　　*

The battle of Morlaix was the first pitched battle on land of the Hundred Years War, and it made a deep impression at the time. Le Baker, writing some 18 years later, declared that such desperate fighting was not seen at Halidon Hill, Crecy or "Petters".[1] Regarded from the point of view of the art of war, the battle has great interest. The tactics pursued by the English were evidently founded on the lessons of Bannockburn and Halidon Hill. The men-at-arms were used dismounted; the trench took the place of the marsh as an obstacle in front; a defensive position on a ridge was selected;

---

[1] Phonetic spelling of course: the Black Prince spelt it Peyters. These two examples are an indication to the pronunciation of the day—far removed from the modern French pronunciation, Poitiers.

the fire power of the archers was a feature in both battles, and lastly the two arms cooperated skilfully in defeating the mounted attack. It is not surprising that Edward's first great victory should form the prototype for Morlaix and for all the other great battles of the Hundred Years War—except the last.

APPENDIX

SITE OF THE BATTLE OF MORLAIX

At first sight the paucity of information concerning the site of the battle might well deter us from further investigation. Yet I think something can be made of it. The only positive and unimpeachable information is provided in a letter written only two days after the battle by Carlo de Grimaldi, a captain of the Genoese crossbowmen (who, he clearly implies, ran away at the end of the day). He states definitely that the battle took place between Lanmeur and Morlaix. This is only what we should expect. Lanmeur is on the road from Guingamp to Morlaix. It is seven miles from Morlaix. Northampton would hardly wish to march further from Morlaix than the seven miles to Lanmeur if he wished, as he did, to resume the siege after repulsing the approaching army—even if Charles de Blois allowed him the requisite time to advance beyond Lanmeur. On the other hand, he would hardly select a position close to Morlaix, the garrison of which might sally out and attack him when his back was turned. One would expect a position at least three miles away. Now the Genoese captain also states that in the evening the French army retreated to Lanmeur, so the battlefield must be appreciably short of that village, say over a mile. Thus we should expect to find the field somewhere between the third and fifth milestone from Morlaix.

Next, we must consider the type of position favoured by English armies of the period. Almost invariably they would seek for a ridge or hill or commanding ground which would allow of a position on the forward slope with a long view to the front, so as to get as much warning as possible of the hostile approach and of any attempt to turn the flanks. This position, being defensive, should stride the road by which the enemy was expected to approach. Examining the map, we find that the ground slopes upward gradually from Morlaix more than half-way to Lanmeur, thus offering commanding positions facing Morlaix, but not in the opposite direction. At about four miles from Morlaix the ground becomes flat, the top of the table-land, and so continues for about one mile. It then—nearly two miles short of Lanmeur—begins very gradually to fall, to rise again one mile short of Lanmeur, thus forming the dip we have mentioned. *A priori* one would expect the battle to be fought near here.

There is a further consideration. There was a largish wood in rear. Now ancient records show that the table-land was wooded—as it still is—in medieval times. It was only after I had hit upon this site that I noticed the passage in Knighton's *Chronicon*, which states that the English army occupied the whole night (*tota obscura nocte*) in advancing to the position. This must imply a march of several miles, indicating that it could not be far short of Lanmeur. Everything therefore points to the position being near where I have indicated. There is today a bus service from Morlaix to Lanmeur, with a bus-stop at a small café, three kilometres short of Lanmeur. By alighting here, one finds oneself almost surrounded by woods, and on walking forward 1,000 yards, the position I have described, just in front of the wood, is reached. If my elucidation is sound we have here the identical wood that played so large a part in the battle. The English position would be, say, 50 yards in front of it, the trench 100 yards further forward, along a tall hedge.

SOURCES

There is no need to list sources, since they are practically the same as for the preceding chapter. But the following comparatively modern works are essential for a close study of the campaign: *Mémoires pour servir de preuves à l'histoire . . . de*

Bretagne, edited by Dom. P. H. Morice, in 1749; this work, as its title implies, contains many additional sources for the battles of the campaign; *Histoire de Bretagne*, by G. A. Lobineau (1707); and *Histoire de Bretagne*, Vol. III, by A. de la Borderie (1898). I can trace practically no modern work written from the English side (apart from the standard histories) except two papers by Professor T. F. Tout: an account of Mauron in *E.H.R.* for 1905, and an account of Morlaix in his *Collected Papers* (1932).

CHAPTER IV

BRITTANY, 1342-47

LONG before sending out the Northampton expedition, Edward had decided to undertake a campaign in Brittany in person; the earl's army was merely an advanced guard, which should establish a foothold, as it were, and fight the first battles.[1] He accordingly instructed Northampton, as soon as he was established on shore, to send back the ships for the second "lift", *i.e.*, for the main army under the king. They were to return to Sandwich, and there the king collected his army. As the day approached when he calculated the fleet should appear, Edward went down to Sandwich, after appointing his son Edward, then aged 12, as Governor of the kingdom in his absence.

He arrived at Sandwich on October 4, but there was neither sign nor news of the expected fleet. After waiting by the sea for a fortnight with as much patience as he could muster, the king changed his plans and marched his army along the coast to Portsmouth. Here he chartered the bare minimum of ships, placed his troops on board, and on October 23 set sail for Brest. According to Adam Murimuth, who was alive at the time, the king collected no less than 400 ships, into which he embarked 6,000 men-at-arms and 12,000 archers. These figures are evidently "round numbers", and almost certainly exaggerated, but by how much it is impossible to say. Certainly 400 vessels should suffice to transport that number of troops, but it is doubtful if the king could have collected at Portsmouth at short notice anything like that number of ships.

The army landed safely at Brest on October 27, to find that much fighting had gone on since the battle of Morlaix three

[1] In just the same way in 1799 General Abercrombie was sent with an advanced guard army to capture the Helder, where he fought the opening battle, being joined later by the main army under the duke of York.

79

weeks before. The second siege of Hennebout by Charles de
Blois proved as unsuccessful as the first, although de Blois
brought up 18 large "engines" against it; the walls had been
strengthened since the first siege and his "artillery" was not
powerful enough to breach them. After only ten days Charles
had had enough of it and departed for Nantes, where he
proposed settling into winter quarters.

Such was the medieval custom, but the English leaders had
unorthodox ideas. They had come over to Brittany to fight, not
to languish in winter quarters. The siege of Morlaix was therefore resumed, and with assistance from inside, it fell shortly
afterward. Robert of Artois then conceived the bold plan of
laying siege to Nantes, the largest city of Brittany, and the count
de Blois's capital. Embarking a little army, less than 5,000
strong, he sailed round the coast, intending to land opposite
Nantes. But he was forestalled by the French fleet, attacked,
and obliged to sheer off. Not disconcerted by this, he landed
opposite Vannes–then the second city of Brittany–and besieged that place. In the course of the Hundred Years War
there were literally hundreds of cases of fortified places being
besieged, but the siege of Vannes by Robert d'Artois and his
little band of English men-at-arms and archers is different
from them all.

The city of Vannes was small, confined to a peninsula of
elevated land jutting out to the south like a sort of appendix.
It had three main gates. They all remain to the present day,
as also does much of the wall. It is thus easy to picture the
course of events. After spending the first few days in making
preparations for the assault, d'Artois delivered it early one
morning. The opening move had a modern flavour. The
archers–the artillery of the period–put down what we should
now call a standing barrage on to the battlements. So fierce
and accurate was it that, according to Froissart, the battlements
were soon cleared and not an enemy dared show his head.
Covered by this fire the men-at-arms advanced to the assault.
The attack met with a strenuous resistance and was everywhere

repulsed. Not discouraged by the first failure, d'Artois put in attack after attack throughout the day, but when dusk fell the defences were still intact. Silence descended with night and the inhabitants went to bed; hoping for a respite at least till dawn. But they had reckoned without d'Artois's resource.

Suddenly in the middle of the night there arose a great din: trumpets sounded, drums beat, a heavy fire was poured upon two of the gates, where the attackers could be seen to be massing. Amid the cries and hubbub two fires burst alight opposite the gates, lighting the sky. All available troops were rushed to the threatened points, where they then awaited the attack. But no attack came—from without. Instead the watchers suddenly found themselves assailed from within—by English soldiers. What had happened was that when the walls had been denuded of defenders except near the threatened gates, a party if English men-at-arms had crept up to the walls at a spot as far removed as possible from the two gates, armed with scaling ladders. Silently putting these against the walls they as silently mounted them and attained the battlements without a blow being struck. Then, penetrating into the town, they rushed forward to the two gates, attacked the defenders from behind and dispersed them, and then opened the gates to their waiting comrades without. Robert's brilliant stratagem had won the powerful city of Vannes at practically no cost. The French garrison, including Olivier de Clisson, the city's governor, fled toward Nantes. The triumph of Robert d'Artois was complete and the countess de Montfort came over from Hennebout to congratulate the victors.

But Robert d'Artois and his English band had not long to enjoy their triumph. Olivier de Clisson gradually rallied his troops, de Blois sent reinforcements, and in less than a fortnight after the fall of Vannes he reappeared with an army that vastly exceeded that of d'Artois. De Clisson was intent on revenge, but his opponent again did the unexpected. Instead of shutting himself up in the city and sending for help to Hennebout, d'Artois left a small garrison in the town and

boldly advanced with the remainder to face his enemy in
the open. The clash took place some distance outside the city,
but the odds were too great for Robert and his little band.
He was obliged to fall back upon Vannes, closely followed by
de Clisson. But to his consternation he found the gates shut
in his face, and no sign of his garrison within. In his absence
the inhabitants of the town, strongly pro-Blois, taking advantage
of the absence of the main body, had risen against the depleted
garrison and driven them out of the city. Thus caught between
two enemies and vastly outnumbered, the plight of the English
force was desperate. D'Artois did the only thing possible: he
fought a rearguard action all the way back to Hennebout,
25 miles away. He got them there fairly intact, but he was faint
from the loss of blood, caused by wounds. A few days later in
the last days of October, this gallant Frenchman in the service
of England breathed his last—one of the most remarkable of
the many remarkable soldiers produced by the Hundred Years
War. Thus, when on October 30, 1342, Edward III set foot on
land at Brest, it was to learn that though a great part of
Brittany had been won back for the Montforts, one of the chief
instruments in that achievement, and one of his right-hand
men, had fallen.

The beginning of November is a curious time of year in any
age to undertake a campaign, and it was especially so in
medieval days. Charles had done the conventional thing in
going into winter quarters, but the English king was not a
conventional soldier. Like Northampton and d'Artois before
him, he had not risked the passage to Brittany to find a pleasant
spot in which to winter. He made a plan of campaign, a plan
that has been described by a French historian as "simple and
sound". Only a limited number of troops can play an effective
part in the siege of a town. When, as frequently happened, a
large army concentrated to besiege a fortified place (as did
Edward at Tournai or Cambrai), the principle of "economy
of force" is broken. The English king did not repeat this
mistake. The three most important towns in Brittany were still

in the hands of the enemy. Edward decided to attack all three
simultaneously. But before he could do so he must make good
the intervening territory. Most of the south of Brittany except
Hennebout held Bloisian garrisons. These must first be dealt
with and the speediest way of doing it would be by advancing
on a broad front. This is what Edward did. Setting out from
Brest about November 8 he marched with concentrated forces
as far as Carhaix, 50 miles to the east, which he quickly captured and made his base of operations. Here he split his army
into two; the northern column, under Northampton, was to
advance in an easterly direction towards Rennes, which it was
to capture, while the southern column, commanded by the
king, would strike south to the coast and then work east to
Vannes which it would attack, at the same time sending a
detachment forward to besiege Nantes. It was certainly an
ambitious plan, but its very audacity favoured its prospects.

On November 11 the two columns set off. The northern one
marched by Pontivy, Ploermel, and Redon, capturing all
places en route with ease, whilst the southern column marched
by Hennebout to Vannes, which it promptly besieged. In
accordance with his plan the king now sent a small force under
the earls of Norfolk and Warwick to besiege Nantes, which
they did, Charles de Blois fleeing the city before their arrival.
It is noteworthy that Edward found time en route to write
home formal instructions that the body of his good friend and
servant, Robert d'Artois, which he was sending to England,
should have a ceremonious burial in the Black Friars in London.

As the English troops swept through the country, only
feebly opposed, the king imposed on them a strict discipline,
forbidding all pillage and burning; it was a friendly country—
indeed in his eyes his own—and the inhabitants were to be
treated as friends. This sensible policy probably conduced to
the ease and rapidity of the operations.

Vannes was besieged about November 25 and Nantes at
the end of the month; Rennes not till a week later, for Northampton had been taken out of his direct route by going by

Redon. The reason for this apparent detour was doubtless to keep the two columns within mutual reach of one another as long as possible. Thus they were never more than 30 miles apart – a nice example of the principle of advancing in parallel columns.

After setting siege to Rennes, Northampton sent flying columns in various directions, including one under the earl of Warwick to Dinant. This town was strongly held, so Warwick contented himself with burning its suburbs and he then returned to Rennes.

Charles de Blois was naturally surprised and perturbed by the rapid advance of the English army at such an unusual season of the year, yet he dared not oppose it, although his available troops were probably numerically superior. Instead he fell back from Nantes and appealed for help to his suzerain and uncle. Philip VI responded, and not only assembled a large army at Angers, 50 miles north-east of Nantes, but came there to command it in person. Thus, after a lapse of two years, the kings of France and England seemed likely to confront each other face to face once more.

The French army, when augmented by Bloisian contingents, was big, though we can dismiss the figure of 50,000 given by the chroniclers (and accepted by la Borderie). It was however greatly superior to the English army. Edward did the only possible thing; he called off the sieges of Nantes and Rennes, and concentrated his army in strong lines of circumvallation and contravallation before Vannes. He had no intention of abandoning the siege of this town – if only out of respect for the memory of Robert d'Artois, who had received his lethal wound outside its walls. The siege was therefore carried on with energy and with all the means and processes available at that period – catapults, battering rams, snaps and mines.

Meanwhile the great Franco-Breton array was on the move. But instead of advancing straight toward Vannes – that is, due west – the duke of Normandy marched north-west on Rennes, where he arrived on or about Christmas Day. Thence he turned

south-west towards Vannes, but halted midway at Ploermel,
where his army was joined by the French king. This curious
halt can only be explained by the assumption that it was done
under the orders of the king. The situation had suddenly
become exciting. The English were between the garrison of
Vannes on the one side and the combined Franco-Breton army
on the other. It was the Morlaix situation again. But Edward's
solution differed from Northampton's. He did not throw up
the siege, but prepared to fight it out in his own lines if
attacked, as he had every reason to suppose he would be. It
was an anxious time, and the king sent repeated and urgent
messages to England for reinforcements.

But the unexpected happened, as it so often did in this
extraordinary war. The French army at Ploermel was 25 miles
away, but apart from sending out patrols which bickered with
the English patrols, Philip sat still for over a fortnight. At the
end of that time, just as the English army was about to assault
the town, two cardinals, sent by Pope Clement VI, descended
on the scene of operations and in a remarkably short time had
arranged a truce, the Truce of Malestroit, between the two
parties. By this truce, which was to last for three years (unless
peace was declared in the meanwhile), both sides were to hold
what they had, with the exception that the Franco-Bretons
were to depart from Vannes, which was to be "neutral" for
the duration. Accordingly the French king departed with his
army, and shortly afterward the bulk of the English army sailed
for home. Edward remained on the spot in camp opposite
Vannes for some weeks, suspecting that Philip might suddenly
reopen hostilities. Thus abruptly and unexpectedly the first
English campaign in Brittany came to an end.

On the surface it appears something of a fiasco, like the two
Flanders campaigns, but in reality the English intervention
had saved the Montfort party at a time when their position
seemed desperate. Half the country was now in their hands,
the south and west, and though the north and east remained
under Bloisian control, many of the nobility who had thrown

in their lot with de Blois began to waver and some came over to the Montfort party, notably the influential Olivier de Clisson.

It is possible that the truce saved the English army, though de la Borderie believes that if the French had attacked, it would have been *"une première édition de la journée de Crecy"*. As for Philip VI, any remnants of military reputation left over from his two abortive Flanders campaigns had now vanished. Thrice had he come face to face with an inferior English army when by a single stroke he might have ended the struggle for the French throne, and thrice had he shirked the challenge. The conclusion is inescapable; whatever bellicose intention he may have had when he collected an army and marched to war, his resolution failed him when he found himself confronted by the redoubtable English king and his formidable troops.

On February 22, 1343, king Edward set sail for home, accompanied by the indomitable countess Joan of Flanders, and after a terrible storm which blew his ship almost to the coast of Spain, he landed at Weymouth ten days later and went straight to London, while the countess went to Exeter. To Edward the storm was the work of Philip's necromancers, and it was frustrated by the direct intervention of the Almighty, and to show his thankfulness he went on pilgrimage to Waltham Abbey, Canterbury, and Gloucester.

*   *   *

SIR THOMAS DAGWORTH

The following two years were distinguished by great tournaments at home, in most of which the king took a prominent part. It was the zenith of the age of chivalry, signalized by the revival of the Knights of the Round Table and the building of the Round Tower at Windsor to accommodate them. But while junketings were the order of the day in England, war again threatened in Brittany because of repeated breaches of the truce by Philip VI. He unlawfully seized and put to death some of the Breton nobility, and the English retaliated by occupying Vannes. In May, 1345, the unfortunate John de

Montfort escaped from France to England, where he did homage to Edward, recognizing him as the lawful king of France. Next month de Montfort and the indispensable earl of Northampton took ship for Brittany. This time Northampton's right-hand man was another notable soldier, Sir Thomas Dagworth. They landed with a powerful army at Brest about June 10.

Sir Thomas Dagworth immediately set out with a flying column through the centre of Upper Brittany. In seven days he covered over 100 miles. Just short of Ploermel he met and put to flight a French army at the village of Cadoret. Following up his success he almost reached Rennes, capturing many places in its vicinity. The strategical object of this operation in Upper Brittany had been to relieve the pressure on the Montfort region of the south, where the count de Blois had made incursions and had captured Quimper. John de Montfort attempted its recapture, but the siege lasted so long that Blois had time to come to its relief. This he effected, and John count de Montfort and earl of Richmond, to give him his full title, died shortly afterward. The countess Joan had gone mad and their son, the young John, was in England and only six years of age. The affairs of Brittany appeared to have reached their nadir. But the king of England was not easily discouraged, as we have seen, and he now took the war completely into his own hands. It thus became more than ever a contest between France and England, fought out on Breton soil. Operations were to continue, though winter was at hand.

The next move was made by Northampton himself. Setting out from Carhaix on November 29 in the dead of night, he marched with such rapidity that by dawn of November 30 he had covered the 25 miles to Guingamp, which he summoned to surrender. It closed its gates against him, and Northampton, having no siege engines with him, and having a further target in view, pushed on another 20 miles to the north and before nightfall arrived opposite Roche-Derrien. Thus he made the remarkable march of 45 miles or more in under 24 hours, and in winter too. It is evident that the whole of his force must have been mounted. Roche-Derrien surrendered after a three-day siege, and Treguier, five miles further north, fell without resistance. Thus the English had obtained a footing in a region that had been Bloisian throughout the war. Moreover Treguier possessed a harbour, which might prove of the greatest value to the English. Lannion, 12 miles further west and also connected with the sea, fell early next year (1346). This considerable success de Blois seemed incapable of averting or avenging, and the English offensive was continued. Dagworth was sent out with a flying column which mopped up a number of towns in the north and centre, including Ploermel. De Blois at last brought up his army to deal with this enterprising and elusive Englishman and on June 9, 1346, managed to come up with him, at St. Pol de Léon, N.W. of Morlaix.

The French army was, as usual, greatly superior in numbers. Its first attack was repulsed, but, as at Morlaix, the second line came on, and overlapping the diminutive English force on each flank, put in a simultaneous attack from three sides. An astonishing thing then happened. The English army, standing its ground and taking steady aim, poured in such a stream of arrows that "a veritable massacre" ensued. The French were crushingly defeated and put to flight. Thus again was exhibited the power of the English longbow: Dagworth's victory was just in time to add to the morale and prestige of the English archers at Crecy. It is unfortunate that we have not full details of this remarkable action. At Morlaix the archers are not specifically referred to in the accounts, and Dagworth's great victory of St. Pol de Léon was thus the first field battle in Brittany where the work of our archers was specifically mentioned. Dagworth's surprising victory made a big impression at the time and a chivalrous Frenchman, writing of him a hundred years ago, described him as: "The English Achilles who covered himself with glory in resisting with a handful of men the whole army of Charles de Blois."

It was only one of many victories in this *Annus Mirabilis*, or

Year of Victories (strictly speaking two years) in four different and distant but simultaneous campaigns, extending from the south of France to the north of England.

King Edward had finished with tournaments, for the time being at least. By 1345 the defeat of France had become the predominant object of his life, and Northampton's expedition to Brittany was only a part of the king's wider plan for the conquest of France. Simultaneously with sending one expedition to Brittany he had sent another, under the earl of Derby, to Gascony, while he himself crossed to Flanders, to cement the alliance and concoct plans with the faithful Artevelde.

The king had conceived the tremendous scheme of an attack on France on exterior lines–from Flanders in the north-east, from Brittany in the north-west, and from Gascony in the south-west. The first of these was still-born, for on the very day of his interview with Artevelde the latter was murdered. With the Gascony attack we will deal in the next chapter. In Brittany Dagworth's operations had already played their part in attracting French troops away from the vital spot–Normandy.

*   *   *

The count of Blois took several months to recover from his severe defeat at the hands of Sir Thomas Dagworth. Meanwhile the English victors looked upon the Penthièvre territory as a foreign country, and "made the war pay for itself" by stern exactions from the inhabitants. They did not resort to the senseless burnings that had disfigured the campaigns in Flanders (albeit the chief offenders there were not English troops but Hainaulters). But the inhabitants were antagonized still more, and may be presumed to have appealed to Charles to drive out their unwelcome guests. Charles was burning to avenge his humiliating defeat, but it was not till the following spring (1347) that he could get together an army sufficiently strong, in his opinion, to meet the English in the open field. Hence he had not dared to attempt the recapture of Roche-Derrien in the meantime. Crecy had saved it.

By May, 1347, his preparations were complete and on May 20 he appeared before the walls of the doomed Roche-Derrien, plentifully equipped with all that was requisite for a full-scale siege.

THE BATTLE OF ROCHE-DERRIEN (JUNE 20, 1347)

The little town of Roche-Derrien stands picturesquely on a rocky foundation (as its name implies). The west side falls almost precipitously to the river Jaudi, here about 30 feet wide. To north and east the ground slopes down gently, but to the south it slopes up towards a wooded plateau. In other words it forms a sort of appendix from the high ground, jutting out to the north.

Though small in area it was a walled town, complete with a castle that commanded the bridge over the river below. The Bloisian army had been recruited from Bretons, French, Normans, and other nationalities. Charles set about the siege systematically. He first constructed an extensive camp, entrenched it, and cleared the ground around it of trees in order to provide a good "field of fire". The camp was laid out like a town complete with streets and houses, and even markets were held. This camp—it is quite clear from the terrain—was on the south side of the town. In addition, de Blois stationed a detached force in an old earthwork, called the Black Castle (see appendix), 500 yards to the west of the bridge over the river. Its special mission was to guard against the inevitable attack by Dagworth, which it was reckoned was likely to come from that side. The garrison of the Black Castle had strict instructions that they were on no account to quit their post without express orders from the count.

The siege now commenced. It took the usual form: siege "engines" were brought up and the walls were bombarded in order to make a breach. Charles had nine of them, all of considerable size, but one so huge that it discharged stones of up to 300 lb. in weight. One of these landed on a house where the governor, Richard Totsham, and his wife were sitting, and half the house was destroyed. The good lady then pleaded for the town to be surrendered, as did others whose nerves were shaken. But Totsham held on resolutely, though

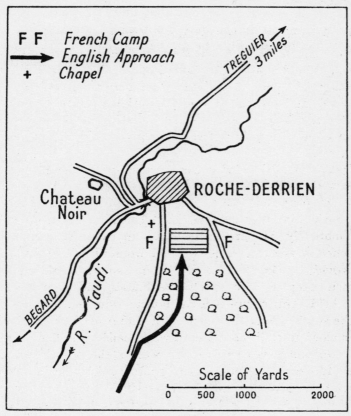

F F *French Camp*
→   *English Approach*
+   *Chapel*

TREGUIER 3 miles

ROCHE-DERRIEN

Chateau Noir

BEGARD

R. Jaudi

Scale of Yards

0   500   1000   2000

4. ROCHE-DERRIEN

three weeks elapsed without a sign of any approach by the relieving army.

Why Sir Thomas Dagworth delayed so long in going to the relief of the sorely stricken town is a mystery. The reason cannot have been that he required time in which to assemble a large army, for the one with which he eventually set out was astonishingly small. It consisted of but 700 combatants, 300 men-at-arms and 400 archers. Even if we add a few armed attendants on the knights, the total number cannot have exceeded 1,000, while the army with which it was about to cross swords was several times that number. And Dagworth knew it. He had ample time to obtain the information, and one is lost in astonishment at the audacity of the attempt that was about to be made, even while allowing something for the reputation and moral supremacy that the English army had attained.

Sir Thomas Dagworth collected his little army at Carhaix, his headquarters, and set out. Roche-Derrien is 45 miles north-east of Carhaix. Nine miles short of it was the village of Begard. The force (all presumably mounted) arrived there that night and halted in the large monastery that evening. The inmates, we are informed from French sources, were well treated, and after supper Dagworth attended divine service in their chapel.

He then gave out his orders on the information he had doubtless received from the staff of the monastery (most of the monks had fled). There was only one obvious line of approach to the beleaguered town, that by a road along the western bank of the river Jaudi. It was by this route that Charles assumed the English army would come. But Dagworth took the hazardous course of approaching by the east bank, which involved a cross-country march through woods and enclosed country, without a map and in the dark, hoping to arrive opposite the Bloisian camp just before dawn. What a hope! The camp was to be rushed by surprise; after which a mêlée was bound to take place in the darkness. The far-seeing Dagworth allowed for the inevitable confusion that would characterize it and resolved to profit by it. The mêlée usually sorted itself out into duels. In the dark neither side would be quite sure who was friend and who was foe. Sir Thomas Dagworth therefore gave out a secret signal, or password. When two men met in the mêlée and were not sure of each other's nationality, one was to ask for the signal, and the man challenged was to give it in a low voice; if he gave it in a loud voice he was to be despatched by his comrade.[1] The reason for this is obvious: if it were given out loud the French would soon learn it and use it themselves to deceive their opponents.

The army then moved off. It was about midnight. By some extraordinary means (Froissart says there were three guides, which is quite likely), the column found its way without mistake or mishap and arrived "at the right place at the right time", that is, opposite the Bloisian camp "a quarter before dawn". The French had no sentries out, and no password had been circulated. The English emerged from the woods, charged across the open space and entered the camp. The surprise was complete. Most of the defenders were asleep, and the knights were of course not clad in their armour. To struggle into it in the dark, with the enemy running amok and hacking down the tents and pavilions, was a difficult task, as may be imagined. The scene would baffle description even if we knew all the details, which no one at the time did, and no one ever will. Suffice it to say that the attackers carried all before them in their first impetuous rush. But then the temptation to indulge in destruction proved too strong for most of the elated troops. According to Froissart's Amiens version, they began cutting down the tents, as mentioned above. The delay thus caused gave a breathing space to those defenders who occupied the outlying parts of the camp, and presently a counter-attack was thrown in. It was repelled. A second met with the same fate. It was still dark, but some Frenchmen had made and lit some torches with which they were enabled to take stock of the situation and to concert plans. Eventually, while it was still dark, a third attack, stronger and better organized than the preceding ones, was made. The band of Englishmen was in a sea of enemies, still outnumbered in spite of its initial success. The tide began to turn against them.

---

[1] Somewhat similar orders were given by the duke of Monmouth for the march to Sedgmoor fight.

In one mêlée Dagworth was wounded and captured. A prompt counter-attack was then launched by the English and their beloved leader was rescued. But ever fresh enemies were coming up, and as daylight gradually appeared, the slender numbers of the attackers became evident and their plight began to look serious. But with daylight came help. The struggle was taking place on the plateau some 500 yards from the town. During the night the garrison heard a great clamour, but the men did not dare leave their posts till the situation clarified with the dawn. Then they took in the situation; the relievers were evidently in a bad way; help must be sent them at once. Leaving a skeleton force to hold the walls in case of a sudden attack from across the river, Totsham made a spirited sortie with the remainder into the backs of the French. Only a few hundred men were available for this attack, but it proved enough. Dagworth's men cooperated and everywhere the French gave way, till eventually there was a general flight from the field.

Meanwhile the besiegers on the far bank of the river remained inactive. Some historians, anxious to find a scapegoat, have blamed them for this inactivity. But they were not only obeying orders, but doing the only sensible thing during the hours of darkness. Their camp was about a mile from the scene of action and separated from it by the river. Though they could hear the clamour they could not know or even guess that the defenders were being put to rout. For all they knew it was a feint attack designed to draw them over the river, after which the real attack, led by Dagworth in person, might come on their own front. By the time it got light enough to establish the situation, it was too late to help. The bridge over the river led into the town. They would have to go some way up stream, ford the river, and then climb a steep bluff. It was too late.

An army had defeated another army several times its own strength, largely because of the inherent advantage the attacker possesses of being able to concentrate his strength against a single point, whereas the defender has to try to defend everywhere and fritter his strength accordingly all along the line.

Large numbers of the French were killed and many captured. The rest fled. And what of the French commander? Charles de Blois had fought the fight of his life. Surprised in his tent (according to Froissart) he managed to get out, but evidently not to don his armour. For, fighting heroically, he received wound after wound, yet continued to fight. Eventually, covered with blood, he was overpowered late in the fight and captured. He was taken to various castles in Brittany while he made a slow recovery, after which he was taken to England. On the voyage he was serenaded by eight guitar players, presumably in order to ward off sea-sickness. On arrival in London he was placed in the Tower, alongside the king of Scotland, who had recently been captured in the battle of Neville's Cross.

The results of this shattering victory were considerable. The tables were now turned: a short time before, the Montfort party had lost its leader; now a like fate had met the de Blois party, while their rivals had found a fresh leader in their new suzerain, king Edward III of England. One thrust of the English king's triple attack on France was going well.

EPILOGUE

This victory had a grim sequel. After his signal triumph Dagworth crossed to England and the defeated side took advantage of his absence to appeal for help to the French king. Philip complied and sent an army to retake the town. Its attack came as a surprise, and after three days' siege and some good sapping by Genoese soldiers, a breach was made, an entry forced, and all the inhabitants, men, women and children, slaughtered. The English garrison, 250 strong, had withdrawn to the castle, but they surrendered on condition that they were given a safe conduct to friendly territory. They were therefore escorted unarmed out of the town by two French knights, but on reaching Chateauneuf they were set upon by the butchers and carpenters of the town, in spite of the efforts of their French escort, and massacred to a man. The story sounds almost incredible, but we have a French source for it.

APPENDIX

BATTLEFIELD OF ROCHE-DERRIEN

There can be little doubt about the site of Charles's camp. The one obvious place is on the wide, gently-sloping plain, on the high ground overlooking the town from the south. This area seems made for a camp, and we get partial corroboration from a statement by the *Grandes Chroniques* that it was the opposite side of the town from the Black Castle, which it approximately is. I estimate the northern edge of the camp at 300 yards from the town. A wayside shrine or chapel to Notre Dame de Pitié runs through this line. The upper or southern edge would be a few hundred yards south. Beyond that the country was wooded and it is easy to picture the English troops charging down the slope to that astonishing battle.

The Black Castle is popularly supposed to have been constructed by the earl of Northampton when besieging the town in the previous year. That is impossible. That siege only lasted a few days; it would have taken Northampton's troops over six months to construct the great earthwork which still exists. Compare it, for example, with the earthwork that Jean Bureau made opposite Castillon in four days before besieging that town. It is still visible, but a mere scratch in the ground. The Black Castle on the other hand has a circumference of about 500 yards, and a height of vallum up to 18 feet. It is no doubt much older than the fourteenth century, though de la Borderie cannot be right in thinking it Roman.

NUMBERS

There seems no reason to doubt Dagworth's statement about his numbers, astonishingly small though they be, "about 300 men-at-arms and 400 archers". He gave this figure in an official dispatch soon after the battle. It would be published in England and Brest, and if it was badly wrong his veracity would soon be impugned. De la Borderie gives no reason for his estimate that the English numbers were 2,000 to 2,500.

It is a quite different matter with the French. Dagworth would have no exact knowledge of the French strength when he wrote, or at any other time. Indeed, even de Blois was probably ignorant of the exact number of his army. Throughout the war we find this vagueness about French numbers. For what it may be worth, here are Dagworth's figures: 1,800 men-at-arms, 600 archers, 2,000 crossbowmen, and an unknown number of "commune" (probably Breton infantry). Knighton gives the French 25,000; Froissart makes the number 1,600 men-at-arms and 12,000 footmen, a figure accepted by Laconteau in his *Histoire de Bretagne*. No doubt this is exaggerated, but it seems clear that the army was exceptionally large. Charles had spent a long time in amassing it, and the *Grandes Chroniques* assert that it consisted of "a great quantity of people, both French and Bretons and other nationalities". However much we scale down these figures we are left with an army many times the strength of its opponents.

SIR THOMAS DAGWORTH AND COUNT CHARLES DE BLOIS

De la Borderie retails a story to the effect that "Dagworth, after his victory, coming to regale himself with the sight of the generous, defeated Charles de Blois, and finding him drenched in blood dripping from his seventeen wounds, lying on a feather bed, supported by charitable hands, had the infamy to snatch this bed from him and cast him brutally on to the straw."

He asserts that this tale is "perfectly true" and speaks of "the dastardly and odious blackguardism of this Dagworth" (*le goujaterie odieuse et lâche de ce Dagworth*).

Considering how much at variance with Dagworth's chivalrous character this story is, I had the curiosity to examine de la Borderie's evidence. It is printed in *Mémoires pour servir de preuves à l'histoire . . . de Bretagne*. It is contained in the deposition made at the inquiry regarding the canonization of

Charles de Blois by Georges de Lesnen. It is in Latin, and I
translate the salient passage thus: "On his bed there was a
feather mattress. Dagworth . . . had this mattress drawn from
under him (*ipsam calcitram* [sic] *sustrati de subtas ipsum*) in order
to insult him, as it appeared, and thus remained the lord
Charles on the straw, only one linen cloth remaining on the
straw."

Notice first how de la Borderie has embellished the story,
more in the manner of Froissart than of a serious historian
whose history is accepted as standard.

Now let us examine the credentials of this witness. Lesnen
had been Charles's doctor for 20 years. He does not claim to
have been captured with him in battle, which he would
scarcely have omitted when giving evidence if it were true.
Thus his evidence, at best, must be hearsay. His deposition is
one long unadulterated paean of praise for his hero. Such
testimony by a friend should be treated with the same caution
that one treats the evidence of witnesses at the Rehabilitation
of Joan of Arc. Moreover, this witness had been guilty of
prevarication in another case. In short, his testimony must be
regarded as suspect unless corroborated by another witness or
unless it is inherently probable in itself.

In this case it is inherently improbable. Dagworth had been
brought up in the Edwardian school of chivalry. Knights
might treat lower orders with harshness and cruelty, but once
the battle was over, they observed a strict rule of chivalry and
courtesy among themselves. Dagworth's comrade-in-arms,
the earl of Derby, had recently set the fashion in Gascony by
inviting to sup with him his defeated opponent, a fashion that
the Black Prince followed on the night of Poitiers. Dagworth's
later conduct also gives the lie to this story, for he allowed the
defeated count to have with him his own friends during his
convalescence, and to allow his wife to visit him.

The serious historian must regard this story as, at the
most, "non proven". If there is any basis for it the culprit was
probably some subordinate, whose name Lesnen would not

be likely to know, and in order to add verisimilitude to the
story he inserted the only English name he did know.

In most respects de la Borderie is careful in his facts (if rather
credulous regarding numbers), but in this case national bias
seems to have got the better of his cool judgment.

CHAPTER V

THE WAR IN GASCONY,
1345–47

THOUGH the first act of aggression that precipitated the outbreak of the war occurred in Gascony[1]–it was the seizure of Penne on the Lot, 30 miles north-east of Aiguillon–little of moment happened in that province for the first seven years. The French commander, the count de l'Isle, contented himself with a leisurely advance against inappreciable resistance (from Penne), down the rivers Lot and Garonne as far as St. Macaire (ten miles below La Réole) and thence down the Dordogne as far as Libourne, where he halted. Libourne is 25 miles from Bordeaux, the capital of Gascony, and St. Macaire is about twice that distance. Practically all that was left of the old English dominion in the south of France was a strip of territory bordering on the sea between Bordeaux and Bayonne, 100 miles further south. But the exact boundary between the contending forces at any time during the war was vague and ill-defined, and very indented. It amounted to this: the country was studded with castles and *bastides* (roughly corresponding to the peel castles on the Scottish border). These castles changed hands frequently, and the domain of the castle-owner at any time could be considered the territory of whichever king the castle-owner acknowledged. Thus the war assumed the pattern of a struggle for castles, and as these castles were chiefly grouped along the two great rivers, the Garonne and the Dordogne, the war became in practice a struggle for the possession of these two rivers. Although the French carried all before them in the early

---

[1] Most of the fighting took place in Guyenne, which is to the north of Gascony, but the two words are almost synonymous in the Chronicles and, as the inhabitants are indiscriminately described as Gascons, it seems more convenient to keep to the word Gascony. It is also taken to include the whole of Aquitaine.

THE WAR IN GASCONY, 1345–47   101

stages of the war, a large number of the Gascon barons remained faithful to the English connexion. They instinctively
looked to England for help, and when an appeal of this nature
reached Edward III in 1344, he took heed of it, and all the more
readily because it fitted in with his grand triple design of
attack on France which we have noticed in the previous
chapter. An army was therefore fitted out and a commander
appointed–the earl of Derby, who had been so prominent in
the Flanders campaigns. It is time to say something about
this remarkable man, who may be described as one of England's
"forgotten worthies". Henry of Lancaster, or of Grosmont, as
he was sometimes called after the place of his birth, was the
son of the first earl of Lancaster. From the days of his early
manhood until his death 40 years later, Henry was almost
continually engaged in war or diplomacy, and for the latter
third of that time he was the right-hand man of his sovereign
in both those callings. His name became almost legendary
during his lifetime all over Europe, for he had fought on the
Continent and in the Mediterranean, in crusades as well as in
"home wars" in Scotland, Flanders, Brittany, Gascony, and
on the sea. That his name is not now better known is partly
due to Froissart, who was inclined to ascribe the credit for his
achievements to his subordinate, Sir Walter Manny, as a fellow
Hainaulter who was Froissart's especial *protégé*. As an example
of Derby's fame in his own time, when in 1352 he led a deputation to visit the Pope in Avignon, the road leading into the
town was so thronged with the populace that he found it
almost impossible to get over the bridge into the city.

This was the man to whom the king of England entrusted
the command of the southern arm of his grand offensive against
France. He was now 46 years of age–that of Wellington and
Napoleon at Waterloo–and at the height of his powers. The
army he took with him consisted of only about 500 men-at-arms
and 2,000 archers. But it required ships and sailors as well, and
the fact that Edward could send from these shores two expeditions simultaneously–one to Brittany and one to Gascony–

illustrates the expansion in warlike resources that the war had
brought about at home. The principal officers in the army were
the earls of Oxford and Pembroke, Lord Stafford, and the
indispensable Sir Walter Manny.

The expedition was ready in the spring, but adverse winds
prevented it setting sail from Southampton till late May. It
landed at Bayonne on June 6 and Derby very sensibly remained
there seven days in order to refresh the men, and particularly
the horses, after their long sea voyage. Then he marched
straight to Bordeaux where great crowds came out of the city
to give him a rapturous welcome. The earl of Derby (as we will
continue to call him during this campaign, for though his
father died in the course of it he continued to be known generally as Derby for some time) had been given a free hand; he
was to act as he saw fit in the military sphere, while in the
civil sphere he became "the king's representative", and
shortly after his arrival he was nominated "the king's
lieutenant". Thus his hands were full, and the 14 days that
he spent at Bordeaux must have been among the busiest of
his life.

Meanwhile the count de l'Isle, still in command of the
French forces, heard of the earl's arrival and summoned a
council of war to decide on a plan of campaign. The conclusion arrived at was to make a stand at Bergerac on the
Dordogne, 70 miles east of Bordeaux, and thither reinforcements were hastened from all sides. The earl of Derby learned
of this concentration and decided to attack the town before
the enemy had time to make it impregnable. For this purpose
he assembled his army at Libourne, which the French had not
managed to capture. Accompanied by a fleet of small boats,
he pushed on up the river, through the little town of Castillon–
later to become famous–thence along the south bank to
Bergerac. This town lies on the north bank of the river, connected by a bridge with a suburb on the south bank. This
suburb the enemy were holding, so that it became necessary
first to eject them from the suburb and then to capture the

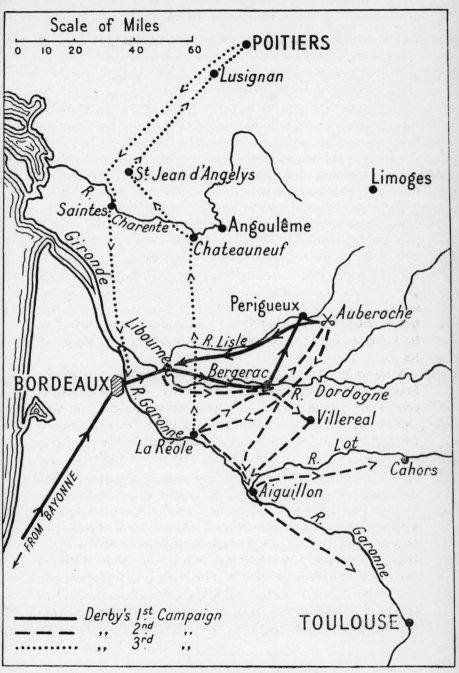

Scale of Miles

0 10 20 40 60

POITIERS

Lusignan

St Jean d'Angelys

Saintes

R. Charente

Angoulême

Chateauneuf

Limoges

Gironde

Perigueux

Auberoche

R. Lisle

Libourne

Bergerac

R. Dordogne

BORDEAUX

R. Garonne

Villereal

R. Lot

La Réole

Cahors

FROM BAYONNE

Aiguillon

R. Garonne

Derby's 1st Campaign

,,   2nd   ,,

,,   3rd   ,,

TOULOUSE

5. DERBY'S CAMPAIGNS IN GASCONY

bridge. When he saw the approach of the English, the count de l'Isle sent out a force of local levies, supported by some men-at-arms, to engage the attackers before they should reach the suburb. Derby's rejoinder to this was simple and sound: he ordered his archers forward to engage the defenders with "fire". This had an immediate and devastating effect upon the raw foot-soldiers, who fell back toward the suburb. There was a watercourse surrounding the suburb, and the fugitives crowded upon the bridge that spanned it, making it impossible for the supporting men-at-arms to take action. To make matters worse for them, Derby now loosed his men-at-arms in a mounted charge. (It goes without saying that Froissart makes Walter Manny lead this charge, and makes him get so far ahead in the midst of the enemy that he was in danger of being cut off.) The rout was complete, and the French men-at-arms scurried back across the river and dropped the port-cullis in time to stop all but a handful of English pursuers from getting into the town. The elated English spent that night in the suburb, where they found enough wine and victuals to last the army for a month or more.

Next morning the attack was resumed, but without success. The earl now realized that the front of attack must be extended; to do this necessitated crossing the river, but he had no bridging material. He therefore waited for the fleet, and on its arrival he transported a portion of his men-at-arms and archers to the north bank. In order that the fleet could co-operate, the point selected for attack was at a portion of the wall quite close to the river. Vessels were filled with archers who, as soon as a breach had been made, kept up so heavy a "fire" that the garrison did not venture into the open to repair it. They also engaged in a long duel with Genoese cross-bowmen in the town. It now seemed to the count de l'Isle that nothing could save the town, but that there was still time to save his own life. In the dead of night he took horse with most of his men-at-arms and rode out on the side that was not besieged and did not draw rein till he had reached La Réole,

40 miles to the south. Next morning the inhabitants awoke to
find their French leaders fled, and they at once entered into
negotiations for the surrender of the town. These were carried
out by the earls of Oxford and Pembroke and, as a result, on
August 26 the gates were opened and the English army
entered the town.

This was an encouraging start, for Bergerac was a considerable town, in a strong position, and a great road centre—even
in those days. Thus it effectually blocked progress along the
river valley by whichever side did not hold it.

After halting for a few days at Bergerac the earl of Derby
resumed his advance, first upstream 12 miles to Lalinde in a
northerly direction, capturing a number of small places, till
he arrived before Périgueux, the capital of Périgord. But when
he saw how strongly fortified this old Roman city was, he left
it alone and marched nine miles eastwards to the castle and
hamlet of Auberoche. Here he made serious preparations for
assault, but when they saw this the garrison surrendered at
discretion. It was now autumn and, the presence of the king's
lieutenant in Bordeaux being desirable, a garrison was left in
Auberoche and the remainder of the army returned with its
prisoners and booty to Bordeaux. The earl of Derby's first
campaign had gone almost without a hitch, and much of
Agenais and Périgord had been recovered.

DERBY'S SECOND CAMPAIGN

While the victorious English army returned to Bordeaux, the
defeated French army was being reconstituted at La Réole
by the count de l'Isle. As soon as his preparations were complete
and siege engines constructed, this enterprising commander
sallied forth from La Réole, marched rapidly to Auberoche,
and laid siege to it. Froissart retails a fantastic story (repeated
gravely by the historians) that a messenger sent out by Sir
Frank Halle, the governor of the castle, with an appeal for
help, was captured by the besiegers, placed alive in a great
"engine" and catapulted back into the castle where he landed

more dead than alive. The fact is, Halle did manage to get word to Bordeaux and Derby responded at once. Hastily he collected a small army at Libourne, consisting of 400 men-at-arms and 800 archers, and ordered the earl of Pembroke, who had a force at some unspecified spot, to join him at once. Pembroke failed to keep the appointment so, after waiting for 24 hours, the earl of Derby marched off toward Auberoche, hoping that the other earl would join him en route. At Bergerac there was still no sign of the missing Pembroke, so Derby went a stage further, marching swiftly and under cover of the woods. He was thus able to reach a concealed position in the woods only two miles from Auberoche without the enemy having any suspicion of his presence.

The castle of Auberoche is picturesquely situated on a rocky prominence overlooking the little river Auvezere, some nine miles east of Périgueux in one of the most secluded and little-known valleys of Gascony. Its situation in many respects resembles that of Chateau Gaillard. Each is a "promontory fort", one side precipitous, the other nearly so; each overlooks a river which it completely commands and each is on slightly lower ground than the *massif* to which it is joined. The valley is narrow at this point and the castle dominates and blocks it as effectually as a cork blocks a bottle. Its strategic importance is thus obvious.

The surroundings have, in all probability, changed but little during the 600 years that have elapsed since the battle. The little valley was, and is, meadow-lined; the slopes on each side were, and are, heavily wooded; as sketch-map 2 shows, the meadow to the west of the river is about 220 yards wide. In this valley de l'Isle placed his main camp, with a smaller one in the still narrower valley on the north side of the castle. The little hamlet of Auberoche lies at the foot of the castle at the junction of the two valleys. As sketch-map 2 shows, the river Auvezere hereabouts makes a series of hairpin bends and the English line of approach from the south-west involved crossing at least two of them.

THE BATTLE OF AUBEROCHE (OCTOBER 21, 1345)

On the evening of October 20, 1345, the tiny English army settled down silently into its bivouacs, hoping to be joined at any time by Pembroke, to whom a message had been sent indicating the position of the new rendezvous. Dawn broke on October 21, but still there was no sign of Pembroke. Strict

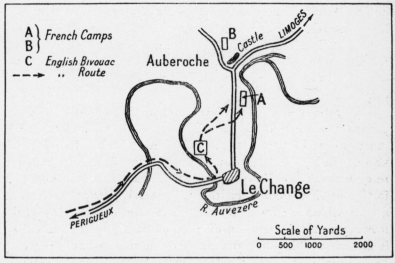

6. BATTLE OF AUBEROCHE: I

orders had been issued for the preservation of secrecy and so far the presence of the English army had not been discovered. Foraging was forbidden, though the horses were grazed near the bivouac. All food for the men had purposely been brought on pack-horses, and from this supply a morning meal was served.

As the morning wore on and still there was no sign of the reinforcements, anxiety began to reign in the camp. The English knew they were hopelessly outnumbered; they could only muster 1,200 whereas the French were reported to be 9,000 to 10,000 strong. Though the real figure was only 7,000 the proportions were six to one, formidable odds indeed. It was impracticable to remain indefinitely awaiting the reinforcements that might never arrive; the food brought with them was practically exhausted, and to forage for more would probably involve detection and the loss of surprise. To give up the venture and retreat, apart from playing false with Frank Halle and his English garrison, would damage the high morale of the troops, who had known no reverse since their landing in the country. In this dilemma Derby summoned a council of war. The problem was thoroughly examined and conflicting advice was given. After all had had their say the earl announced his decision: he would await Pembroke's contingent no longer, but would throw all his forces into an immediate attack. (Froissart, in his first edition, as may be supposed, attributed the credit for this decision to Sir Walter Manny, who was acting as Derby's chief of staff, but he omitted it in the later editions. Unfortunately it is only the first edition that has been translated into English).

Having decided to attack, the earl of Derby, it would seem, made a personal reconnaissance on foot through the wood, groping his way stealthily through the undergrowth. Thus he was able to reach undetected a point on the edge of the wood only a few hundred yards from the French camp. What a sight met his gaze! In the open space between wood and river he could see the French tents and pavilions in serried lines. All was quiet, the afternoon was well advanced and coils of smoke were rising above the tent tops: the enemy was cooking his evening meal.

The question was, how to take advantage of this unexpectedly favourable situation. A mounted charge from the wood seemed indicated, but the ground sloped down so steeply through the wood opposite the camp that this was out of the question. About 300 yards south of the camp, however, there was a fairly level approach, practicable for horsemen. Moreover there is, and probably was then, a track through the woods leading out into the meadow at that point. If this point could be

attained without detection, the camp could be charged from
the rear. At the same time, the archers, dismounted, could
creep through the undergrowth to the edge of the wood dead
opposite the camp and from there give supporting "fire" to
the charging cavalry–a good example of "fire and movement". For, thus situated, the archers could keep up their
"fire" till the cavalry had reached the camp, and by
switching it continuously to the left they could continue to
provide covering "fire" even after the arrival of the horsemen
in the camp.

Derby went back and gave his orders. A ticklish operation
with very nice timing was involved, so orders must be precise
and detailed and discipline perfect. Froissart specifically states
that they were thorough. When all understood their orders and
the final preparations had been made, the attackers cautiously
advanced and silently took up their respective positions. The
signal for the attack was to be given by the earl himself; on
receipt of it the archers were to utter their battle cry: "Derby!
Guyenne!" at the same time unfurling their banners. At the
sound of the battle-cry the cavalry were to emerge from the
wood and charge. It must have been an exciting moment when
all were in position awaiting the signal from their leader,
while the smoke continued to rise lazily above the French tents,
so close that the smell of the repast may even have been wafted
into the wood; and still there was no movement in the hostile
lines.

"Derby! Guyenne!" The signal is given, the archers wave
their banners and discharge their arrows; the cavalry utter
their war-cry, gallop out of the wood, form some sort of ragged
line and charge straight forward over the 200 or 300 yards
of intervening meadow into the outer line of French tents.
The surprise was as complete as that of their comrades at
Roche-Derrien was to be (indeed, the one may have inspired
the other). A scene of utter confusion ensued in the French
camp, that may be likened to that which arises when a stone
is raised from on top of an ants' nest. The French chief officers,

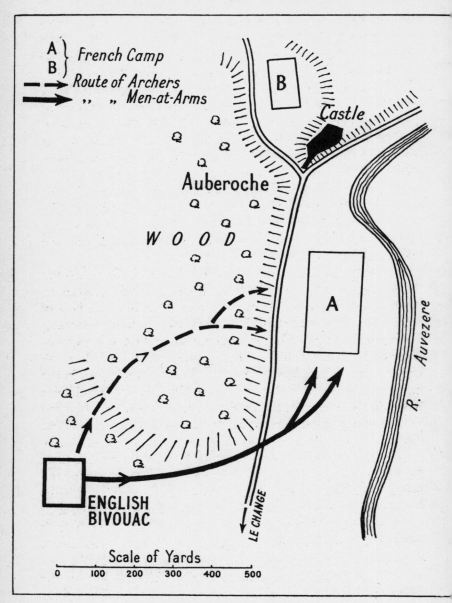

A } French Camp
B }

- - - ▶ Route of Archers
━━━▶ ,,   ,, Men-at-Arms

B

Castle

Auberoche

WOOD

A

R. Auvezere

ENGLISH
BIVOUAC

LE CHANGE

Scale of Yards

0   100   200   300   400   500

7. BATTLE OF AUBEROCHE: 2

110

out of their armour and mostly supping in their tents, rushed out and tried frantically to don their armour, while all the time a hail of arrows was striking them from one direction and the mounted charge was coming from another. The casualties caused by the first flights of arrows into those crowded lines were immense: Murimuth estimates them as over a thousand, though this is of course a pure guess and no doubt exaggerated. As the horsemen penetrated further into the centre of the camp and became invisible to the archers, the latter were obliged for the time to cease their "fire". A few French officers managed to struggle into their armour and to unfurl their banners on the outskirts of the camp, as a rallying point for their own men. But as they thus began to form clumps, a fresh target was provided for the English archers, who opened on them once more.

How long this extraordinary contest lasted no man knows. Contestants lose all sense of time under such circumstances. But before it was over a fresh assailant came into the field of action. Not only were the French men-at-arms hastily donning their armour. High up in the castle the same thing was happening. For Sir Frank Halle, from his eyrie, had the whole scene laid out before him. His course was clear; he would join in the battle with every available horseman. The French detachment blocking the exit from the gateway had its attention attracted to the exciting events directly in its rear, whither their gaze was riveted, so the garrison's mounted troops found no difficulty in bursting out and charging into the French camp from their side. Even before this the archers in the castle joined in the attack with their "fire",[1] though it must have been at extreme range and could only have reached the near edge of the French camp. Be that as it may, the sudden irruption of Halle's little band of horsemen proved "the last straw". The last semblance of resistance crumpled, every man who could fled the field, and the English were left in possession of it. The French to the north of the castle took no effective part in the battle, and by

---

[1] According to a local tradition, told me on the spot.

their hasty flight only added to the immense booty. (This inaction is discussed in the appendix.)

The victory was complete and staggering. Though no two accounts agree about the casualties, there is no doubt that the flower of the chivalry of the south of France was accounted for that day in killed, wounded, and captured. Many of the French leaders were prisoners, including the count de l'Isle himself.

That evening the great-hearted Lord Derby, anticipating the Black Prince 11 years later,[1] entertained at dinner in the castle his captive generals. During the meal, whc should appear but the dilatory earl of Pembroke. While approaching the rendezvous, he explained, he was met by fugitives from the field who told him that a battle was proceeding. He had hurried forward at his best pace, but had arrived to find all was over. Derby was in a jovial mood and welcomed his brother earl with mock delight. "You have arrived just in time – to help us finish off the venison!" he exclaimed.

The results of the battle of Auberoche were considerable, indeed astonishing, considering the small number which took part. The French immediately abandoned the sieges of three towns that they had hoped to take, a campaign that was being prepared by the duke of Normandy was delayed by six months, while his communications with the duke of Bourbon in the south were abandoned. For the capture of Auberoche by count de l'Isle had been intended as the prelude to a general campaign for the recovery of the territory recently lost to the earl of Derby. The latter's sudden attack against vastly superior forces was almost breath-taking in its audacity and dazzling in its brilliance. A French historian of our time has described it as *un choc terrible*.[2]

In the psychological domain the results were equally important; though judged by the numbers engaged Auberoche was one of the lesser battles of the war, it established in Gascony

[1] I suspect that the Black Prince followed the example of his second cousin the earl of Derby in this and in other ways.
[2] BERTRANDY, HENRI, in *Études sur les Chroniques de Froissart*.

the moral supremacy that Morlaix had established in Brittany, and that Crecy was nine months later to establish in Picardy. Henceforth till almost the end of the war 100 years later no French army engaged an English army in the field if it could honourably avoid doing so.

The earl of Derby only allowed two days' rest at Auberoche — a short breathing space — for there was much to be done. His troops required a rest, the wounded required tending, arrangements had to be made for the prisoners to be escorted to Bordeaux, the army had to be reorganized with Pembroke's contingent incorporated in it, and plans had to be made for the future after this surprisingly complete victory. Should Derby return to Bordeaux with his captives? As Governor-General — as we should now call him — he would find plenty of work awaiting him. Moreover he had left the capital at short notice with much business half completed. Froissart guessed that the earl did return to Bordeaux and he couched his guess in a positive statement. But the chronicler guessed wrong. Far from returning, Derby resolved to "strike while the iron was hot", and while the enemy was still reeling under his blow. In which direction should he strike? The dukes of Bourbon and Normandy were keeping prudently out of his reach. The duke of Normandy had been on his way south from Limoges when he heard of the disaster at Auberoche. Though only a few leagues from that place, this ineffective commander, instead of hurrying forward to avenge the defeat, fell back to Limoges — fell back before a tiny band of Englishmen.

So Derby resorted to the recovery of more territory and castles. But in which direction? Of the two main approaches to Bordeaux — the valleys of the Garonne and the Dordogne — the latter was now effectually blocked. There remained the Garonne valley. Here there were two strong and important fortified towns still in French possession, La Réole, recently the French headquarters, 65 miles to the south-west of Auberoche, and Aiguillon, the same distance almost due south. Derby seems to have divided his forces, sending one body under Pembroke and

Lord Stafford against Aiguillon, while he led the other against La Réole.[1]

Pembroke and Stafford attacked and captured Monségur, a few miles north of Aiguillon, and then besieged Aiguillon itself. Meanwhile Derby had marched direct to La Réole, to which he laid siege about October 26. This town had a more remarkable history during the period of English dominance in Gascony than any other town except the capital. It has a striking situation, perched on an outcrop of rock overlooking the river Garonne. The walls were strong, and the castle, situated at the south-west angle, was considered almost impregnable because of the thickness of its fortifications and the fact that it was founded on rock and so could not be mined.

The earl of Derby was doubtless aware of its strength, for it had been a favourite abode of English kings and princes, and though it had changed hands with almost bewildering frequency this had been due to starvation or treachery rather than to direct assault. The English commander therefore went about his task methodically. This was no Bergerac, where he could break in at the first attempt without the assistance of siege engines. These had first to be constructed. Catapults were of comparatively simple construction, but they were not by themselves sufficient for the work; Derby also had built two enormous *beffrois*–to use the technical French term–*i.e.* movable towers, so high that they overtopped the town walls. Such towers were manhandled right up to the wall to be breached and archers stationed on the summit discharged their arrows on to the garrison manning the parapet walk below them. By this means the battlements were soon cleared of defenders. The next stage was for pioneers to advance into the ditch and up to the foot of the wall to be breached, which they would then hack away or mine beneath with their picks.

While these two *beffrois* were being made, the ditch at the points selected for their attack was filled in till it was level

[1] Here I accept the suggestion first made by Simeon Luce in his edition of Froissart, vol. III, xx Note.

with the surrounding ground, and beaten down firm. Then the *beffrois* were hauled right up to the walls, at points some hundred yards apart, and, the garrison having been driven from the walls by the archers, the pioneers began their breach in the section between the *beffrois* comparatively unmolested. When the inhabitants saw this they surrendered at discretion—indeed with relief and gladness for the most part. It should be noted that the French had only been in occupation for 21 years, and the sympathies of the Gascons were more favourably inclined toward the English than the French.

The commander of the garrison, Agout des Baux, was not however a Gascon. He and his troops hailed from distant Provence, and he refused to surrender. Instead he withdrew into the castle when the town was seen to be lost. Here he sustained a siege of anything up to ten weeks. All we know for certain is that it fell very early in the New Year (1346). According to Froissart, its fall came about in the following way. The English opened proceedings by bombarding the walls and two towers with their catapults, but the stones they threw made little or no impression on the massive walls. (One of the towers was so strongly built that it is still occupied as a private domicile.) They then had recourse to mining, but this also proved almost insuperably difficult, for the castle, as we have said, was founded on the solid rock and before the era of gunpowder the work of hacking out the naked rock was extremely slow. Nevertheless it was persisted in for so long that the garrison became alarmed, and a deputation to the commander suggested that honour was now satisfied and that the place should be yielded up before it was destroyed and taken by storm, in which case all their lives would be forfeit. Agout yielded to their representations and descended from the top of the tower to the lowest floor, where (following Froissart) he put his head out of the window and asked the besiegers if he might parley with Lord Derby. The earl appeared, in company with Sir Walter Manny, opposite the foot of the tower on horseback, and the following remarkable conversation ensued:

AGOUT: "Gentlemen, you know the King of France has sent me
to this town and castle to defend them to the best of my ability.
You know in what manner I have acquitted myself, and also
that I should wish to continue it: but one cannot always remain in
the place that pleases one best. I should therefore like to depart
from hence with my companions, if it be agreeable to you."
EARL OF DERBY: "Sir Agout, Sir Agout, you will not get off so.
We know that you are very much distressed, and that we can
take your place whenever we please, for your castle now only
stands upon props" (referring to the mining). "You must surrender yourselves unconditionally, and so shall you be received."

Sir Agout went on pleading in a wheedling tone till Derby
withdrew for a short distance and discussed the matter with
Manny. Then he came forward again and addressed the
French commander as follows:—

"Sir Agout, we shall be happy always to treat every stranger knight
as a brother at arms and if, fair sir, you and yours wish to leave the
castle you must carry nothing with you but your arms and horses."

Sir Agout joyfully agreed, and the last view we get is that
of the French marching out with their six remaining horses,
and bartering with the English soldiers for fresh ones. The
English, we are told, charged heavy prices for them. Thus,
by a magnificent piece of bluff, Derby secured the strongest
castle on the Garonne without having to assault it.

*　　　*　　　*

The siege of Aiguillon was shorter. Though the exact date
of its surrender is not known it must have taken place before
December 10 and there are indications that it may have been
the work of what we should now call "fifth columnists" inside
the place. However that may be, Lord Derby had now secured
the two bastions, as it were, that barred the approach to
Bordeaux of a hostile army, or, conversely, the two gateways
that opened the way to further advances into Agenais and
Quercy.[1]

[1] In these respects his action may be compared with that of Wellington in
capturing the twin bastions of Badajos and Ciudad Rodrigo before embarking
on his invasion of Spain.

The earl of Derby was quick to take advantage of the opening. It would seem that he retained his army in two columns,
one of which advanced up the Lot and the other up the
Garonne, capturing or receiving the submission of all the towns
in succession right up to the frontier of Quercy.

*   *   *

Derby's first two campaigns had been brilliant in the
extreme. He had regained a large area of territory, he had
routed the best army that the French could put into the field
against him, and he had established the moral superiority of
the English army. And all this had been accomplished with a
tiny force and at inconsiderable cost in lives.

Neither Froissart nor any of the other chroniclers report
details of the latter campaign, but the evidence for it rests upon
incontestable local documents which have been collected by
Bertrandy, while the broad results are attested to by three
English chroniclers who state that about 50 towns and castles
fell into English hands. (Curiously enough, however, Agen, the
next town up the Garonne and only 15 miles from Aiguillon,
seems to have remained in French hands.)

The actions and intentions of John duke of Normandy
during these first campaigns of Derby are extremely obscure.[1]
The *Grandes Chroniques* alleges that in the course of them he
returned to Paris in despair, where he was roundly taken to
task by his father the king and sent south again. This French
source would hardly have invented such a story (though it is
often discredited by historians), but it is a fact that Philip, in
spite of his dissatisfaction with his son, left him in command
of the huge army that he now set about amassing for the
reconquest of the lost province.

This army was drawn from all over France and it took
several months to collect. The duke of Burgundy brought a
contingent and the duke of Bourbon, who was the king's

---

[1] Bertrandy has with great ingenuity traced the main movements of the duke
of Normandy during this period, but they throw little light on his intentions nd
plans.

lieutenant at Agen, accompanied it. Jean le Bel gave its
strength at the round figure of 100,000. Froissart blindly
repeated this preposterous figure in his first *rédaction*, but later
reduced it to 60,000. (Here again this correction has been overlooked by historians, who continue to repeat the figure 100,000).
The sober and careful Robert of Avesbury gives 12,000 men-
at-arms and a grand total of, say, 40,000 and this figure is corroborated by a French source, which includes large numbers
of Genoese crossbowmen and many siege engines. Everything
points to the fact that this army was exceptionally large for
the period and it must have approached 20,000 in numbers.
There is also good evidence that 24 cannon were constructed
at Cahors for the siege of Aiguillon, at least five of which were
taken to that siege by the army.[1]

The chroniclers are at variance about the rendezvous of the
French army. By one account it was at Orleans, whence it
advanced south toward Aiguillon, capturing en route various
places including Angoulême, said to have been taken by
Derby. It seems, however, that the rendezvous was Toulouse,
80 miles south-east of Aiguillon, and that the army advanced
thence without opposition to Agen, which it reached on
April 5, 1346. Here the duke tried to enlist some local levies,
but was outwitted by the governor. A few days later the army
moved forward to Aiguillon, apparently approaching it from
the south.

Aiguillon is a small town with a dwindling population,
prettily situated in the angle formed by the confluence of the
Garonne and the Lot, both considerable rivers at this point.
The castle is on an eminence commanding the Lot, and not far
from the Garonne. The duke of Normandy rightly recognized
its strategic importance, and accordingly selected it for his
main objective. It was held by an English garrison under Lord
Stafford, assisted by Walter Manny, and, according to some
accounts, by the earl of Pembroke. Stafford had the foresight,
on the approach of the enemy, to lay in a good store of pro-

[1] See LACABANE, LEON, *De la Poudre à Canon* (1845).

visions and warlike stores. He was thus well prepared for the siege that ensued. The French on the other hand experienced great difficulty in providing enough food for their immense host, the very size of which proved an embarrassment. The country round was soon swept bare of food and the lack of food may partly explain the large number of deserters from the invading army.

The siege was one of the most famous of that age and Froissart gives a spirited description of it. The French army took up its station in the first instance along the south bank of the Garonne, that is, on the far side to the town and castle. Here I follow Froissart, though it is hard to understand why the French did not approach along the north bank. No bridge was available, so the first task was to construct one, and this the French proceeded to do. Twice the English made a sortie and destroyed it, but eventually it was completed and the French crossed to the north side and the siege proper began. The duke of Normandy had such enormous forces that he was able to divide them into four parties or "shifts", one of which was always at work bombarding, attacking, and threatening the beleaguered town. The English, however, repelled every attack, and made constant sorties, in some of which it would seem they managed to replenish their supplies. In one audacious sortie they destroyed two barges full of supplies from Toulouse. John's next step was to get eight large catapults from Toulouse, together with four vessels specially constructed or adapted to convey them as close as possible to the walls. In a subsequent age they would be called bomb vessels, and in a still later age, monitors. The garrison received them with such a heavy "fire" from four large catapults of their own, that when one of the attacking machines had been damaged the attempt was abandoned. This was only one of many examples of what we should now call "counter-battery work" between the two "artilleries". Nothing could quench the spirit and resolution of the garrison, and John decided to sit down and reduce the castle by starvation, a course in which Philip VI at first concurred. To effect this he placed a blockading force down-stream, cutting off completely communication with La Réole.

All this time Edward III was preparing a great expedition for the relief of Aiguillon—as it was supposed. On July 11 the expedition set sail from the Isle of Wight, but instead of steering for Bordeaux it touched land in Normandy and soon overran that province. The situation was thus suddenly altered; Philip's best and biggest array was far away in the south, conducting a never-ending siege; it must be recalled at once. Messengers conveying orders to this effect were sent off hot-foot. As soon as he heard of the landing in France of Edward III, John sued for a truce. But Derby had also received the news and he contemptuously rejected it. There was nothing left but to raise the siege and depart for the north. On August 20, just six days before the battle of Crecy was fought, the great army of the duke of Normandy hastily broke up the siege and marched away to the north, leaving tents standing and an enormous quantity of supplies. The English army was left in undisputed possession of all its conquests.

During the siege the earl of Derby had taken up his head-quarters at La Réole. Here he collected supplies of troops and food, and on one occasion at least, June 16, he succeeded in running the blockade and throwing reinforcements of men and food into the beleaguered place. When, later in the siege, the blockade was tightened, this became impossible.

A week before the end of the siege Derby moved north to Bergerac, where he received and rejected the truce overtures to which we have already referred. Immediately following this he received the news that the French had abandoned the siege of Aiguillon.

The successful outcome of the siege of Aiguillon had an effect only slightly less striking than that of the victory of Auberoche. It was known throughout France that the king was making a supreme effort and concentrating overwhelming forces to drive the English into the sea. But the gallant defenders of Aiguillon, Gascon inhabitants and English soldiers, took on themselves the full brunt of the blow, and parried it. The duke of Normandy, who conducted more abortive operations against the English than any other general of his time, showed a pitiful lack of enterprise in this campaign. With his vast army it should have been possible both to ensure a more effective blockade of Aiguillon and at the same time to take the offensive elsewhere with a portion of his troops. As it was, "a handful of troops"—in the generous words of a French historian—"braved the united efforts of a complete *grande armée*, while another French historian declared that "the defence of Aiguillon covered with glory Sir Walter Manny and the earl of Pembroke".

When news of the abandonment of the siege of Aiguillon reached the earl of Derby he was at Bergerac with a small force. Immediately he set off for Aiguillon, which was 40 miles due south. He did not, however, take the direct road, but marched south-east to Villereal, 25 miles distant, which he captured. It is likely that his intention was to cut off any stragglers from the French army in its march to the north; but of this we have no particulars. He reached Villereal on August 27, seven days after the departure of the duke of Normandy, and next day pushed on to Aiguillon, where it is easy to imagine the scenes of rejoicing and congratulations when he met the victorious garrison. Here Derby remained for five days. There was much to be done: the place had to be "re-established", revictualled, sick and wounded removed, defences repaired and detachments sent out to keep touch with the retreating French and to restore English rule in the towns that had temporarily fallen to duke John.

DERBY'S THIRD CAMPAIGN

But Henry of Lancaster, as he was beginning to be called, had no intention of letting the grass grow under his feet: the campaign of the English army in the north of France was in full swing, and diversions must be made in the south to detain as many enemy troops there as possible. Offensive operations must therefore be carried out in all possible directions, even though his numbers were pitiably small. The earl envisaged three campaigns; two based on Aiguillon were to recover and extend the English conquests in Agenais and Bazardois, while the third, under his own command, should operate in Saintonge and Poitou. To this end he reorganized his forces in three armies, and it is highly significant that he gave the command of the two southern armies not to English but to Gascon captains, for they were operating in the old English dominion of Aquitaine, and were themselves liege subjects of the king of England. Their task was to recover and hold, by friendly action rather than by force, those parts that had been lost. The army left available for the expedition into Poitou was a very small one, only 1,000 men-at-arms, according to Derby's own statement. It seems incredible that there should be no archers included, and he may have meant "lances" rather than "men-at-arms", and that one or possibly two mounted archers were attached to each man-at-arms. Froissart gives the numbers as 1,200 men-at-arms and 2,000 archers, and here the chronicler may for once not be so very far from the mark. He also mentions 3,000 infantry, and as Derby himself mentions posting some infantry in St. Jean d'Angelys later in his campaign, it may be that some infantry followed up the expedition on foot, catching up at towns where halts were made. Froissart's Rome edition also mentions the use of archers at the capture of Poitiers.

Derby spent eight days at La Réole, September 4 to 12, making these preparations, and on the 12th he set out on his third and last campaign. At the same time the other two armies set off in opposite directions. It has been suggested that by this dispersion of force the earl transgressed the principle of concentration of force. It would be truer to say that he fitted the means to the end. His French opponent had indeed kept his whole force concentrated in front of Aiguillon and to what end? The principle of economy of force implies a nice appreciation of the minimum number of troops required for a given task, and such a distribution of forces that the maximum effect can be produced. Judging by results, this right distribution was attained by Derby. Though the chroniclers are disappointingly silent as to the operations in the south and east, it is established that all went well and that English troops penetrated far into Quercy, and almost to the walls of Toulouse. The consternation aroused extended to the shores of the Mediterranean.

Henry's own campaign can be followed in more detail and without having recourse to the unreliable and imaginative Froissart, for fortunately we possess the dispatch that Derby wrote toward the end of his campaign, the accuracy of which cannot be impugned.[1]

Poitou, whose capital was Poitiers, had not been in English hands since Henry III lost it, but parts of Saintonge, which lies immediately to the north of the Gironde, had had a more chequered history and might be expected to return willingly to the English allegiance. Derby's little army therefore set out full of hope on September 12, and spent that night at Sauve-terre, nine miles to the north. For the next eight days they marched on the most direct route to Chateauneuf on the Charente, a distance of 75 miles, and arrived on September 20. The inhabitants closed their gates and as the town was on the north side of the river, which was unfordable, and the only bridge was broken down, they might well feel secure. But Derby set about repairing the bridge, and with such vigour did his men work that next day it was passable and the army marched over it to the attack of the town. Then some totally unexpected news arrived, to explain which we must hark back a little way.

On the relief of Aiguillon, Sir Walter Manny had pleaded to be allowed to join his old master the king in his Normandy campaign. The ways of medieval chivalry never cease to surprise us, and incredible as it may seem, this redoubtable

---

[1] This remarkable document is in medieval French, and is given with an English translation in the Rolls Series edition of Robert of Avesbury's chronicle.

knight, who had so often been a thorn in the side of the French, was by them granted a safe-conduct, not only for himself but for his own retinue, across France. They promptly set off, and no more was heard of them. But now, just as Derby was about to assault the town of Chateauneuf, the startling news arrived that Sir Walter Manny and his companions had been seized, in spite of their safe-conduct, and imprisoned in the castle at St. Jean d'Angelys. Manny and two others had "with great trouble" escaped, but the remainder were still incarcerated. Had Froissart heard of this adventure of his hero, what a story he would have made of his "great trouble"! St. Jean is 40 miles north-west of Chateauneuf, and the army was about to assault that town; but the good faith of an English knight had been violated, and Henry of Lancaster blazed with anger. His mind was made up at once; everything else must give place to the rescue of Sir Walter Manny's comrades in distress. The attack was called off, and the whole army marched that very day post haste to St. Jean. They arrived by the following day at the latest and promptly assailed and stormed the town. "We marched on towards the said town and assailed it and it was won by force, thank God, and the men brought forth from prison", wrote the earl in simple soldierly language.

It might be supposed that Derby would wreak his vengeance on the town for this shocking breach of faith, but he evidently realized that it was the fault of an individual, not of the whole town, and his treatment of it was lenient and statesmanlike. To quote his own words again: "And we stayed there eight days and established the town, and they of the town took oath and became English, and were bound at their own cost during the war to find 200 men-at-arms and 600 foot soldiers as garrison of the said town. . . ."

The comment of the French historian Henri Bertrandy is worth recording:—

"This conduct seems to me most honourable to the memory of Derby and also of Walter Manny. I do not descry anything more beautiful in the Guyenne war. The efficacy of the protection of

England could not show itself in a fashion more striking, more just or more happy. The act of Derby was at once the act of an honourable man, a courageous soldier and a skilful diplomat."

Henry of Lancaster spent nine days at St. Jean d'Angelys, occupying himself less as a soldier than as a diplomat, a role in which he had already had ample experience. The fruits of his activities will be seen presently. On the last day of September he departed, setting his face for Poitiers. The capital of Poitou lay 70 miles to the north-east, and, with little to impede the army, good progress was made. Three days later they came to Lusignan, described by Derby as "a strong town", but they took it by assault in the minimum of time. Continuing their advance early next morning, October 4, they reached Poitiers, after a march of 15 miles, early enough in the morning to deliver an attack that day, after summoning it to surrender in vain. The first assault failed, so the earl made more elaborate preparations for the next attempt.

The historic city of Poitiers, which gave its name to three famous battles, occupies a striking position on a crescent-shaped knoll, with a great bend of the river Clan sweeping round its eastern face. Thus the easiest approach is from the opposite side – the west – and the English probably approached from that side. (If they approached from the south-east, they must have crossed the swelling upland on which almost exactly ten years later another English army was to repeat the glories of Crecy.)

Derby seems to have acted with amazing speed. His troops had already marched 15 miles that day and had failed in an attack on a strong walled city. One might have supposed that the commander would spend the remaining hours of daylight in reconnaissance and preparations for another attack on the morrow. But that was not the way of Henry of Lancaster. Reconnaissance, plan, preparations and execution were all squeezed into what remained of that same day. Reconnaissance showed what appeared to be three weak spots in the defences. Derby decided to assault these three simultaneously. Dividing his slender army into three (it is unlikely that his dismounted troops had yet come up) he posted them opposite the three indicated points. Then at a signal the concentric assault was delivered under the usual covering fire from the archers, and was crowned with success. The French leaders managed to escape (probably swimming the river), but most of the garrison were rounded up inside. By the custom of the time, a town which, after being summoned, refused to surrender, could expect no quarter, and Derby in his dispatch writes: "All those in the city were taken or slain." Froissart avers that "the earl's people put everyone to the sword, men, women and little children". French historians have accepted and repeated Froissart's statement. But it is not true. Such conduct was foreign to Derby's nature and previous conduct. He had won golden opinions from the inhabitants of those parts since his arrival in the country; nor had the city offended in the way that St. Jean d'Angelys had in his eyes. Moreover, Froissart himself states that the earl prohibited any burning of churches or houses "under pain of death". Wholesale looting there was, and no doubt indiscriminate killing in hot blood by the excited assailants in the moment of victory, as there usually was in such circumstances until quite recent times. (For further examination of Froissart's statement see the appendix to this chapter.) But there is documentary proof that Derby undoubtedly showed greater sternness with the capital of Poitou, which he regarded as practically a foreign country as it had been outside the English dominion for so long, whereas St. Jean d'Angelys was situated in Saintonge, which had more recently accepted the king of England as its lord. More than that we cannot say.

On October 13 the army marched out of Poitiers on its return journey. The main body returned to St. Jean d'Angelys and detachments were dispatched throughout Saintonge during the next fortnight seizing or accepting the submission of most of its towns. It is almost certain that the towns which Froissart reports Derby as taking in the course of his advance to Poitiers were in reality taken during this fortnight. Meanwhile Henry established his headquarters at St. Jean, for which town he had acquired a liking. His diplomacy and moderation had procured a rich dividend. In Saintonge he came to be regarded as a popular hero. He was in excellent spirits and he entertained royally, by no means forgetting the ladies of the neighbourhood, who came flocking to his banquets. He was naturally pleased with what he called a *belle chevauchée*–inadequately translated "raid" by historians: it was more than a mere raid–it was an expedition.

On October 30 the earl re-entered Bordeaux amid the plaudits of an enthusiastic populace. After a short stay he handed over the duties of King's Lieutenant and sailed for England. On New Year's Day, 1347, he landed in the home country. On January 14 he arrived in London and the very same day he visited David king of Scotland, who had been captured at the battle of Neville's Cross and incarcerated in the Tower. Henry of Lancaster was not the man to let the grass grow under his feet.

*   *   *

In just 14 months the diminutive English army which had landed in Bayonne in June, 1345, had fought three campaigns and, under the inspiring leadership of Henry of Lancaster, had not only driven the French out of most of the old dominions of our Angevin kings, but had spread the dread of the English arms far and wide, even to the shores of the Mediterranean. The first campaign, on the Dordogne, had removed the threat to Bordeaux from the direction of Paris, and recovered a large part of Périgord; the second, on the Garonne, had safeguarded the capital from the direction of Toulouse, had regained most of Agenais and Quercy and had penetrated into Languedoc almost as far as Toulouse itself; the third campaign, with a minimum of fighting, had recovered Saintonge and subdued most of Poitou. For the moment there was no fight left in the French. The land had peace: for the moment.

Before leaving the war in Gascony, a final word must be said about the illustrious Englishman who, with a mere handful of troops, had so signally reversed the fortunes of his country in south-western France. For though Comte d'Erbi, as the French called him, lived to do important work, both military and diplomatic, and indeed became the king's right-hand man, his "maid of all work" . . . his most notable campaign was that in Gascony. In spite of the regrettable paucity of records, such as do exist point unerringly in one direction: Henry of Grosmont, Derby and Lancaster, was a *chevalier sans peur et sans reproche*. There were giants in the land in those days and Derby was one of the greatest of them. But an assessment made by a compatriot may be biased and suspect. Let us hear then what a dispassionate French historian, one who has made a deeper study of Derby's campaigns than anyone, has to say. I refer, of course, to Henri Bertrandy. He has sensed the grandeur of this redoubtable opponent of his country, so that he is able to write on the last page and in the last paragraph of his *Études:*

"These campaigns have imprinted upon the memory of Derby an indestructible glory. This illustrious Englishman displayed all the qualities which in their entirety form the appanage of the truly great."

A soldier is not without honour – save in his own country.

APPENDIX

THE BATTLEFIELD OF AUBEROCHE

This battle, though the most important of the whole war in Gascony until the final contest at Castillon, is so little known that a rather extended note on the subject seems justified. Its very site had been forgotten, and even Sir James Ramsay, whose reputation for accuracy is great, located it wrongly. The correct site was suggested by a French monk in 1742 and was established definitely in 1865 by the French historian, M. Bertrandy, Director of the Archives at Bordeaux, but his researches in this field have never been translated into the English language. They are tucked away in a series of *Études* on Froissart's *Chroniques*, and thus have been too easily overlooked. Further reference to Bertrandy and his *Études* will be found later.

THE SOURCES FOR AUBEROCHE

There are, so far as I can discover, eight sources for the battle. Four of these give only bald facts, such as numbers and names of participants. From the remaining four sources, the story of the actual battle must be reconstructed. The first of these is Adam Murimuth's *Chronicle*, written within two years of the battle. The second is the *Continuatio chronicarum*, written a few years later. The third is *Istoria Fiorentini* by Giovanni Villani. (It has never been translated into English.) The fourth is Froissart's *Chronicles*. His original edition dates from 1369-72; the Amiens edition about 1376, the Rome edition about 1400, and the *Abrégées* (or abridged version) a few years later. The first two sources are naturally the most reliable, but they differ on the important question of the relative damage inflicted by the archers and men-at-arms. Villani's account, though useful for numbers, gives few details. We thus have to rely almost entirely on Froissart for details of the actual fighting. A further cautionary word must therefore be said about the reliability of the famous chronicler. Where he could, he followed Jean le Bel, whose bald story he shamelessly embellished with figments of his own imagination. But among these fanciful passages he frequently inserted stories that he had heard from the lips of participants or at second or third hand from them. This is particularly the case where Gascony is concerned, for he twice visited the country and picked up many of his details on or near the spot. We must therefore look for circumstantial details which seem to ring true. Where they seem to do this there is no *a priori* reason to reject them entirely, though embellishment had become so ingrained in Froissart's work that even here it may be present. M. Henri Bertrandy, probably the most profound Froissart scholar for the period, sums up the Chronicler as "une autorité des plus suspectes".[1]

In judging the reliability of any of his stories where they are not corroborated by other sources, one is therefore reduced to the test of inherent military probability. If his account of a battle can be shown to fit in with the terrain about which he can have had no personal knowledge, it follows that he probably received it from an eye-witness. In the case of Auberoche, that is precisely what it does. To prove this I must record my own experiences when visiting the battlefield. From his description I formed in my mind a picture of the terrain and scene, indeed a clear-cut one. When I approached the field and, turning a corner in the road, came into full view of it, I felt almost as if I had seen it before, so exactly did it agree with the picture in my mind's eye. This, I felt, justified me in accepting all the essentials of Froissart's account of the battle.

LOCATION OF THE BATTLEFIELD

It is no easy matter to ascertain the approximate location of the field, and then to get to it. In 1865, M. Bertrandy visited Auberoche and described it. Probably very few Englishmen have visited the place since then, or indeed since the end of the Hundred Years War. As to the location, there are several places with the name Auberoche in Gascony. In 1863 the French historian of Gascony, Henri Ribadieu, identified it with Caudrot on the river Garonne.[2] Five years later he was refuted by M. Bertrandy who established the location as Auberoche-en-Périgord, and his location holds the field. If anyone doubted it he would obtain instant corroboration by visiting this place and noting how exactly it tallies with Froissart's description.

This Auberoche must be one of the hardest to find and most inaccessible places in southern France. The region lies in a backwater; it is sparsely inhabited, and there are few roads and

<hr/>

[1] *Études sur les Chroniques de Froissart* (1865), p. 84.
[2] In *Les Campagnes du Comte de Derby* (1863).

railways though a good road traverses the battlefield. It is practically impossible to obtain a large-scale map of it, and I found the only practicable method of reaching it was by taxi from Périgueux. This involved a nine-mile journey, and even the taxi driver was doubtful of its location.

The castle occupies a striking situation, dominating two straight stretches of the valley. A few houses cluster round the foot of the rock on which the castle is perched. Of the castle itself nothing remains above ground except the chapel and owing to thick undergrowth it is difficult to trace out the lines in places. But the natural strength of the place is obvious at a glance, and the anxiety of the Comte de l'Isle to recapture it is understandable.

LA RÉOLE

No town in Gascony was more closely connected with the English occupation than La Réole. Six English kings, one after another, made their mark on it. Henry II on succeeding to it demolished the main tower known as *Des Soeirs:* Richard Coeur de Lion often resided there; he restored the walls—some of his handiwork remains to this day—as also does the house in which tradition declares he stayed; he is also reputed to have made it the rendezvous for the contingents that accompanied him on his famous crusade, though this is disputed. John granted it commercial rights; Simon de Montfort was once its governor, so was Richard of Cornwall, king of the Romans; Henry III besieged it twice and took it once. Prince Edward (afterward Edward I) came here to receive the fealty of his barons; his son, the earl of Kent, occupied it, but eventually lost it to Charles le Bel, king of France. In the course of 300 years I calculate that it changed hands between English and French, sometimes peacefully but more often by violence, no fewer than 16 times. All the above is eloquent testimony to the value placed upon it by succeeding generations of kings and soldiers, this being mainly because of its strong strategic situation, blocking or protecting the line of approach to Bordeaux from the south-east. The river does not now lap the foot of the castle but no doubt it did so originally. The walls, still immensely strong, remain for a large part of the perimeter.

FROISSART'S ACCOUNT OF THE SIEGE OF LA RÉOLE

I have so frequently had occasion to warn readers against statements by the old chronicler, that readers may be surprised at the amount of credence I have placed upon his accounts of La Réole, but it is almost certain that he visited the scene during either or both of his sojourns in Gascony. No doubt he over-dramatized the story, but if we allow for such embroideries there still remains a solid core of fact. Froissart, in his account of the war in Gascony, is weakest in his chronology. This was first thoroughly probed by Henri Bertrandy, who in 1870 exposed the errors that had been accepted by Henri Ribadieu in his *Les Campagnes du Comte de Derby*–the only attempt at a detailed account of these campaigns that has been written. Unfortunately it is very difficult to obtain a copy of this book. It is printed in a rare French publication entitled *Actes de l'Académie des beaux arts . . . de Bordeaux*, Vol. XXV for 1863. The author subsequently admitted that he had been mistaken in his chronology, which he had accepted unquestioningly from Froissart, and it is significant that he skated very lightly over all Derby's campaigns in his subsequent *La Conquète de la Guyenne*. But for the student, a study of his "Campagnes" is indispensable.

FROISSART AND POITIERS

In the text we have discussed the inherent improbability of Froissart's assertion that all the women and children were put to the sword. The following note examines in greater detail the passage in question.

(1) There is documentary proof that Froissart exaggerated, to say the least, for the names of certain Frenchmen who were ransomed are known.

(2) The words "every man, woman and child" tripped too easily off the irresponsible tongue of the chronicler. He made the same accusation (though with more imaginative detail) against the Black Prince at the sack of Limoges, and its falsity has since been proved up to the hilt[1] Froissart was more an artist than an historian, and he required ample light and shade for his picture.

(3) The only local and contemporary French account that I can trace does not mention killings at all; its indignation is centred on the pillaging of ecclesiastical property. It is contained in the little-known *Cronique de Maillezais* and the Latin may be translated as follows:

"In the year 1346 on October 4 was captured the city of Poitiers and the castle of Lusignan on the previous day, by Henry count of Lancaster, lieutenant of the king of England. For nine days with all his army he devastated much and seized the goods of the said city and took away with him ornaments from the churches."

But the most revealing proof that Froissart was in error comes from Froissart himself. In both the *Rome* and *Abrégées* editions he quietly omitted the offending passage that all women and children were put to the sword; in the *Rome* edition he substituted the statement that there was much killing ("grand ocision") and in the *Abrégées* he borrowed from le Bel the statement that many women were violated. Le Bel adds that the earl of Derby was much distressed thereby, but could do nothing about it. That is likely enough. But the trouble is that both our English translations were made before the discovery of the *Amiens*, *Rome* or *Abrégées* editions, none of which has been translated into English. It is as if, for example, only the original edition of Oman's *Art of War in the Middle Ages* had been published, the second edition being left in manuscript.

BIBLIOGRAPHICAL NOTE ON DERBY'S CAMPAIGNS

The earl of Derby's campaigns in Gascony have been studied by English historians less than almost any other

---

[1] By A. Leroux, *Le Sac de la Cité de Limoges* (1906). See also *The Sack of Limoges*, by A. H. Burne (*The Fighting Forces*, Feb. 1949.)

campaign in the Hundred Years War: indeed it would not be far from the truth to say that they have not been really studied at all. It may therefore be of help to the student of the war if I devote some space to the literature on the subject.

The sources, as will have been apparent from the preceding pages, are scanty. That erudite scholar Henri Bertrandy, after burrowing into the deepest recesses in his efforts to arrive at the truth, wrote despairingly of the "dense and distant darknesses" (épaisses et lointaines ténèbres) that cloud the path of the researcher. The French chronicles of the period pass it by almost in silence. The *Grandes Chroniques* for example allot but a single page, and the *Chronique de Richard Lescot, Chronique Normande* and *Chronographia* are equally brief. The English chronicles provide a good deal more, particularly *Robert of Avesbury* (Bertrandy alludes aptly to "the bald but accurate laconicisms of Robert of Avesbury"). Also useful, but in a lesser degree, are *Knighton, Murimuth* and *Walsingham*. The above must be supplemented by contemporary documents – mostly local – which have been collected by two Benedictine monks, Vaisseté and Duvic,[1] in their *Histoire de Languedoc* and published in 1742. On the above sources a framework of the war in Gascony can be built up. But detail is almost completely absent. For this we have to depend upon Jean Froissart (who in turn based his Chronicles on another Jean, the Liégois Jean le Bel).

Fortunately, in the case of the war in Gascony, we have an admirable guide in Henri Bertrandy, to whom we have frequently referred in the foregoing chapter. The closer one examines his work the deeper becomes one's admiration for this erudite and fair-minded scholar. His book is a curious one. It was published in 1870 under the misleading title *"Etudes sur les chroniques de Froissart"*. It takes the form of six letters addressed to Leon Lacabane "Mon cher Oncle et très excellent Maître". These letters are primarily directed to an examination of Henri Ribadieu's *Les Campagnes du Comte de Derby*, and by deft and penetrating criticism he demolished the claims of

[1] Cited as Vic in Ramsay's *Genesis of Lancaster*.

the book to be genuine history. This, though we must accept it, is regrettable, for Ribadieu's book is the only single work on the war in Gascony that exists. M. Ribadieu sets out to prove that Froissart did not deserve the criticism and suspicion heaped upon him, but that his chronicle of the War in Gascony was accurate in chronology, indeed more so than even Derby's dispatch. The book, however, contains some useful notes and identifications of places.

Yet another invaluable book hides its nature in an unexpected title: *La Désolation des Églises . . . en France pendant la Guerre de Cent Ans* by Father Henri Deniflé, published in 1899. It is factual, accurate and precise, and can be used conveniently to establish the chronological and topographical framework for the war and is admirably documented. (This applies to the whole war, not only to the campaigns in Gascony.)

The above exhausts the list of essential books. It will be noted that it is not only short, but contains not a single work written by an Englishman, or even translated into English. The best edition of Froissart is that of Simeon Luce, and it is invaluable for its notes. Incidentally, it makes full use and acknowledgment of Bertrandy's work, so that it to some extent replaces that work if it cannot be procured (though there is a copy in the British Museum Library).

CHAPTER VI
THE CRECY CAMPAIGN, 1346

ALL through the winter of 1345 and spring of 1346 Edward was preparing for the invasion of northern France. His plan of campaign was what we should now describe as a strategical combination on exterior lines: in other words three armies, operating from three widely distant points, were to face inward toward the centre, from the north, the north-west, and the south-west respectively. This must not be understood too literally: there was no question of the three armies advancing on three radii, as it were, all directed on Paris, the centre; but there was *the threat* of such an operation, and it was calculated to upset the mental equilibrium of the French king. The fact that, in reality, one army might not get very far in the direction of Paris mattered little if it drew away hostile forces from the other two, thus making their progress the easier.

But Edward's plan went further than this: a fourth army was involved, that of the Anglo-Flemings. This army, small in numbers, was to advance south-westward through Artois simultaneously with that of the king, whose landing was to be somewhere on the north coast of France. These two armies while approaching the enemy's capital would be approaching each other, and before the main French army was engaged they looked forward to uniting their forces.

It was an ambitious plan in any period of warfare, but particularly so for a medieval army whose communications were slow and, when dependent on the sea, very precarious. Even as late as Napoleonic times this form of strategy was looked upon askance until it succeeded signally against the Corsican himself in the Leipzig campaign of 1813. How far Edward planned ahead and what measure of success he expected to reap from it is a fascinating question, but one that will never be answered, for the English king was secretive in his words and writings where military operations were concerned. Just before his Flanders campaign of 1340 he had ordered all foreigners trying to leave the country to be detained till after he had sailed. In the present case he gave out that his objective was Gascony: he was going to the help of the earl of Derby in general and to the relief of Aiguillon in particular. He may indeed at one time have had the intention to act in the South, and if so it is again a fascinating but insoluble speculation about when and why he changed his mind. On April 6, 1346, he had ordered certain troops to collect at Portsmouth "for service wherever he might lead them", but on May 6 he informed the church authorities in London that he was going to Gascony. This was evidently dust in their eyes, being intended to reach the enemy, for prayers were to be said for the success of the expedition. We have related the part played in this plan by Brittany and Gascony. Let us now follow the king's army.

For months preceding the actual invasion, desultory negotiations were going on with France through the Pope, for a renewal of the truce. Edward can hardly have been serious in these negotiations, and at times his conduct appears to us as uncomfortably reminiscent of that of Adolf Hitler. But it would seem that if the king of England was not serious and was utilizing the time gained to increase his armed forces, the king of France was doing the same. Apart from the large army that Philip had sent to Gascony under his eldest son, he was taking various measures to strengthen his forces in the north, and in particular to collect a formidable fleet in the English Channel. Whether this was for offensive or defensive purposes was never made really clear. Probably the French king had both eventualities in mind. As for the morality of preparing for a possible war under the cloak of pacific utterances, this has been an almost normal procedure throughout recorded history. An aggressor will obviously do all he can to prevent his potential opponent strengthening his forces *pari passu* with his own. This may sound like casuistry, but it at least shows that Edward was not any worse than the normal commander of an army about to invade another country.

By early April Edward had concentrated at Portsmouth and Southampton an army of about 15,000 combatants, over twice as large as had ever previously crossed the Channel. Only 2,000 were men-at-arms. They were, as far as possible, picked troops. Froissart's *Abrégées* is careful to point out that the king called for "the best" archers. (For details see the appendix.) To transport this army a fleet of upward of 700 vessels had been brought round the coast to Spithead and Portsmouth harbour. The flat expanse of Southsea Common was a mass of tents and pavilions: but it could be hidden from prying French eyes more effectually than if the base had been Dover or Margate.

All through May and June foul winds blowing up from the south-west prevented the fleet from setting sail. At length, on July 5, all seemed favourable and the leading vessels of the great armada set off. But again adverse gales forced them to turn back. The whole fleet then anchored off St. Helen's and prayed for a favouring wind. For nearly a week they were obliged to wait and it would be surprising if the morale of the wretched troops, cooped up for long days in their cockleshells, did not suffer; for "hope deferred maketh the heart sick".

On July 11 Edward again gave orders for the whole fleet to weigh anchor and follow him out to sea, under sealed orders. When out of sight of land these orders were announced, and to nearly everyone's surprise the destination was found to be, not Gascony, but Normandy. The landing was to be made on the Cotentin peninsula, at St. Vaast la Hogue, 18 miles east of Cherbourg. It is natural to inquire the reasons why Edward selected this point. The answer usually given is that the king was merely following the advice of Godfrey de Harcourt, a French baron who had been banished from his ancestral estate of St. Sauveur le Vicomte. Harcourt was thirsting for revenge and did not hesitate to go over to his king's enemies and offer to serve under the English banner in Normandy. This may appear treasonable conduct to us, but we must remember that the instinct of nationalism was not fully developed in those days, that Edward was by many regarded as the lawful king of France, and that Normandy had been throughout the twelfth century an English possession. Harcourt knew the country all over the Cotentin and should thus prove a valuable guide, if nothing more. Moreover, quite a number of the Cotentin nobility favoured the English cause. Furthermore, the Cotentin was the nearest land to the Isle of Wight, and a short sea crossing provided obvious attractions in those days of sail, and especially in that summer of storms.[1] But Edward may have had other and deeper strategical reasons for selecting the Cotentin. Cherbourg and Ghent are equidistant from Paris. Now Ghent was the base from which the "Three Towns"–Ghent, Bruges and Ypres–were to operate in the combined operation. The two lines–Cherbourg-Paris and Ghent-Paris–enclose a right angle. Thus, if Paris was the common objective Philip VI would be confronted with two widely separated but equidistant opponents. In approaching each other they would be approaching his capital, and he would find it difficult to know how to distribute his forces in order to oppose each enemy successfully.

As for the French, Philip had just achieved a notable diplomatic success: he had drawn the shifty duke of Brabant partially, and John of Hainault wholly, to his side; indeed John fought under his banner at Crecy. Hence Philip was not very concerned about the upshot of the fighting in Flanders; he decided to concentrate the bulk of his army against the English attack. As his land troops were slow in gathering he depended for immediate protection on his fleet. This he collected in the English Channel; but he made the mistake of scattering it all along the coast in such a manner that it was weak every-

----

[1] Probably as bad as the summer of 1944.

where, for, as has been pointed out by Frederick the Great,
Napoleon, and Sir Winston Churchill, "if you try to defend
everywhere you will be weak everywhere". The French fleet
was weak everywhere and was quite ineffective in preventing
the English from landing.[1] Meanwhile the French army was
concentrating in the neighbourhood of Paris, but the records
are distressingly scanty on the subject.

THE OPENING MOVES

The voyage of the English expeditionary force across the
Channel was a speedy and uneventful one, the French ships
keeping at a prudent distance, and on the morrow, July 12, the
expedition made land at St. Vaast. The first thing the king
did on setting foot on land was to knight his son, the Prince of
Wales, and several of his companions. There was a practical
reason for this, as the Prince was to be the titular commander
of the advanced guard. He was now 16 years old, quite a usual
age for a prince in medieval times to be given a military
command. Besides the royal prince, the other leaders of the
army were the earls of Warwick (the Marshal) and Northampton (the Constable) and Sir Richard Talbot; but most of
the baronage of England who were of military age and not
employed in other theatres of the war were also with the army.

Edward decided to direct his march slightly to the south of
Rouen in the first stage. This was the shortest route to Flanders,
as Rouen was the lowest point on the river Seine that was
bridged. Moreover, this route would not be far distant from
the sea in its early stages, and the fleet would thus provide a
sort of movable base. Finally, it was almost the direct route to
Paris.

The headquarters of the army moved inland three and a half
miles to Morselines on July 13, while the troops and stores
were being disembarked. Allowing five days more for organization—a short enough period—the army set off on its great

[1] Almost exactly 600 years later Rommell made the same mistake on the same
coast.

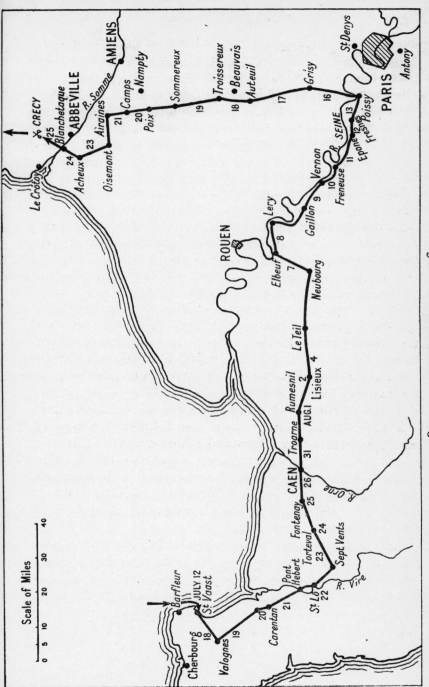

8. THE CRECY CAMPAIGN, 1346

venture on July 18, 1346, while the fleet kept abreast of it, sailing along the coast. Valognes, nine miles to the south-west, was reached that night and occupied without resistance. Next day a long march of 16 miles was made to St. Come-du-Mont, three miles short of Carentan, which town was occupied next day. The inhabitants had broken down the bridge over the Douve just short of the town, but it was promptly repaired by Edward's very efficient pioneers. On July 21 the army pushed on for St. Lô, which entailed a long march of 16 miles over marshy low-lying ground, with the river Vire to cross. The programme was too ambitious, especially as the bridge over the river was broken down at Pont Hebert, four miles short of the town. The king therefore was obliged to halt here, but he immediately ordered his pioneers to repair the bridge. Working continuously throughout the night, they had made the bridge passable by dawn. It seems likely that special stores for the repair of bridges had been brought out with the expedition. St. Lô was reached next day, July 22.

The Cotentin was now behind them and the road lay open for Caen, 26 miles further east. Up to date resistance had been negligible and the army had marched well, but the same cannot be said for its conduct. The English were marching through the old patrimony of the Norman kings. Throughout the advance across Lower Normandy there was widespread pillaging and burning by the army. It may be asked, what military advantage did Edward expect to gain thereby? The answer is that it was done against his orders. A certain amount of pillaging was condoned by him: it came under the category of "living on the country" and was usual procedure for an invading army at that time, and indeed for centuries later. But the king disapproved of deliberate damage and burnings and Michael Northburgh, writing home a few days later, stated that "much of the town (Carentan) was burnt, for all the King could do." The lawless acts and excesses can be partly attributed in the opinion of James Mackinnon to "the wild Welsh and Irish mercenaries, an element which would not be kept in control by the canons of chivalry". But there was probably a further explanation of the widespread and apparently senseless burnings. A considerable number of the English army came from the south coast, where there had been many recent burnings by French sailors; Portsmouth and Southampton were sufferers in this respect. To such people it was a mere act of revenge. Also the fact that the army advanced on a wide front made effective control by the senior officers impossible. There were however times when the king did resort to burnings for a military object. For example, he wrote complacently to the archbishop of York that his fleet had ravaged and burnt the whole coast-line including every ship they could find. This seems to have been both an act of revenge and one of security. If the French had no ships they could not repeat their raids on the Hampshire coast.

We need not therefore be too exercised by the incessant accusations by the old chroniclers of burning and pillaging— *ardant et gastant*—the words come tripping off their pens with almost mechanical reiteration. At the same time it must be admitted that a vast amount of damage was done, and that the peasants fled in terror before the advancing army—an act that made the pillaging all the worse, for soldiers will pillage an abandoned domicile when they will respect one still lived in.

After passing St. Lô the army opened out, marching on a front of several kilometres. The king marched in the centre with the main body, the right wing had with it Godfrey de Harcourt, while the left wing was under the earl of Warwick. On July 23 the main body reached Sept Vents, one mile south-west of Caumont, 14 miles east by south of St. Lô, the left wing taking the more direct Caen road—that is, due east—to Comolain. The next day only five and a half miles were covered, to Torteval. On July 25, still making straight for Caen, the army reached Fontenay, an eight and a half miles march. The reason for the shortness of these two last marches is not apparent. Possibly the fleet was lagging behind, or possibly Edward suspected the near approach of the French king and army. If so, he was mistaken: Philip was far away. At Fontenay the army was only ten miles from Caen, and Edward that evening sent a cleric as envoy to the city with a message to the burgesses that their lives and property would be respected if they would submit peaceably. The message was contemptuously rejected by the bishop of Bayeux, who was the leading spirit in the threatened city. Indeed, so spirited was he that he ostentatiously tore up the message and threw the unfortunate cleric into prison. The glove of defiance having been thrown, the militant bishop withdrew into the castle with 100 men-at-arms and 200 Genoese archers, leaving the constable, count Eu, and the chamberlain, count Tancarville, to defend the town as best they could.

Receiving no reply to his peace overtures, next morning, July 26, Edward resumed his advance, his army now narrowed into a single column—advanced guard, main body (with the baggage), and rearguard.

CAPTURE OF CAEN

The historic old town of Caen, the stone of which enriches so many great English buildings and the story of which is so intimately connected with William the Conqueror, was—and is—curiously situated. At the point where the river Odon runs into the Orne, the latter river divides into two branches, thus forming an island. The northern branch of the river divided the town into two parts; the old town to the north, and the new town, on the island to the south, known from its church as the Île de St. Jean. The castle is on a slight eminence on the northern edge of the old town. Neither old nor new town was fortified, but the latter, being on an island, possessed a natural line of water defences; moreover its three bridges—those of St. Pierre and the Boucherie on the north, and the Millet on the south—were protected by fortified gateways. The castle, largely the work of William I and Henry I, with its forbidding moat on two sides, constituted a formidable obstacle to an army that did not possess engines for siege warfare. Situated a

few hundred yards west and east of that old town lie respectively the famous Abbayes aux Hommes and aux Dames. The
weakest sector was the old town which, apart from what protection the castle could give it on the north and the river on the

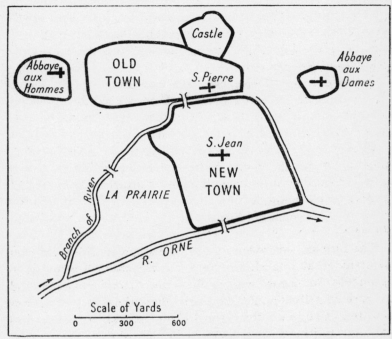

9. CAEN IN 1346

south, was quite defenceless. Edward rightly resolved to
concentrate his first attack against the old town, leaving the
castle for the time being unmolested. The advanced guard was
therefore ordered to march round the north side of the castle
and take possession of the Abbaye aux Dames as a first step to
a general assault. The remainder of the army followed in three
columns, and formed up facing the northern and western sides
of the old town. When the whole army was thus deployed for
action the king ordered the troops to be rested after their ten

mile march and for food to be served out. The advantage of
having the baggage in the middle of the long column was now
apparent, for no long delay was required before it should
appear. By the time all had fed it was about nine o'clock.
Meanwhile the inhabitants of the old town had evacuated it,
some taking refuge in the new town and some from both towns
fleeing into the open country. It was thus possible to proceed
straight to the assault on the new town, and the king gave
orders accordingly.

The main assault centred on the two bridges of St. Pierre
and the Boucherie, 200 yards apart. Warwick led the attack on
the former, and was backed up by the contingents of Northampton and Richard Talbot. But here the defence was stout
and little impression could be made. At the other bridge,
however, the assailants were more successful and an entry was
at length forced. At the same time other attackers found a ford
over the river by means of which they crossed and entered the
town. The Normans holding the bridge of St. Pierre thus found
their position turned from the left and fell back hurriedly. This
in turn allowed Warwick's party to enter, capturing both Eu
and Tancarville in the gateway. (By a similar manoeuvre the
bridge of St. Pierre was again captured 74 years later by
Henry V.) Other bodies captured French vessels in the river
and effected a crossing thereby. Soon the whole garrison was
in flight and the English were swarming over the town.

While this attack was going on under the very eyes of the
garrison of the castle, scarcely 300 yards away, not a single
attempt was made to assist the hard-pressed townsmen, or
even to make a demonstration on their behalf. The castle
defenders were ideally situated for this purpose, and we can
only suppose that Edward, anticipating some such action, had
taken counter-measures of which no record has survived.

The navy also played its part in the capture of Caen. Whilst
the army had, as related above, been marching eastward
towards the town, the fleet had kept abreast of it, sailing along
the coast of Normandy and ravaging and burning various ports

on the way. Reaching the estuary of the Orne at Ouistrehan it
had sailed up the river and arrived opposite the town at
approximately the same time as the army. It is possible that
the simultaneous arrival was deliberately planned, but such
synchronization of land and sea forces was extremely difficult
to effect, as King John had discovered to his cost when attempting to relieve Chateau Gaillard 150 years before. Whether
fortuitous or not, the arrival of the fleet was a happy one, for
30 French vessels were afloat in the port or in the river, and
the army and fleet between them speedily accounted for every
one of them. The arrival of the fleet was happy in another
respect: prisoners had been taken, also spoil; there were sick
soldiers to be sent home, including the earl of Huntingdon.
All these returned to England, accompanied by part of the fleet.
The prisoners were, of course, those who were fortunate enough
to be able to offer a ransom; the remainder met with no
quarter, for by the custom of the time the defenders of a town
which had been duly summoned and had refused to surrender
had no right to quarter once the town had been stormed.
Looting also was widespread, again a custom of the time,
especially in the case of a town from which the bulk of the
inhabitants had fled. The number of Frenchmen who perished
that day is put by our best authority at 2,500.

The army halted for five days at Caen. This halt is not as
easy to explain or justify as the halt at St. Vaast. There was,
of course, much to do; reorganization, dispatch of the sick,
wounded, prisoners and spoil, the latter including an in-
criminating letter written by Philip VI to the burgesses of the
city in 1338, enjoining them to prepare for an invasion of
England. The troops also required some rest, having marched
82 miles in nine days, shortly after being cooped up for days on
board ship. During the halt Bayeux, which had been by-passed,
surrendered to the English army.[1]

[1] A portion of the fleet sailed for home without orders and this has led to the
untenable suggestion that Edward had intended to abandon the expedition and
sail home by it, but that its departure obliged him to carry on with the campaign.

THE ADVANCE TO PARIS

By July 31 all was in order and the advance was resumed. Marching at a steady pace due east, the army made eight miles that day to Troarne, ten miles on August 1 to Rumesnil, and nine on August 2 to Lisieux. If the army continued on the same line it would strike the river Seine midway between Rouen and Paris. Its future movements were likely to depend on the counter-moves of the French king and on the supporting moves of the Flemish allies. It is time therefore to glance at both these armies.

Though Philip had, of course, been aware that an invasion was to be expected he had no inkling of where it would take place. Prudently therefore he retained his main army centrally situated at Paris. News of the invasion reached him at his chateau at Becoiseau. He repaired instantly to the capital, arriving at Vincennes on July 19, the second day of the English advance. Three days later he went to St. Denys to obtain the sacred Oriflamme, with which to lead his army against the invader. The next move was obvious – to Rouen, the capital of Normandy – and thither he marched at a rapid pace. He and his army, of which we have no indications as to the strength, arrived at Rouen on August 2, the day on which the rival army reached Lisieux. The two opponents were now 40 miles apart, and the French held a commanding strategic position in a straight line between their two opponents, and in possession of the main crossing of the river Seine, here about 300 yards wide. Up to date it is difficult to criticize Philip's strategy. He had correctly gauged the route taken by Edward, and had acted accordingly.

And now, what of the Flemish army? To answer this it will be necessary to go back to June 24. On that date a meeting at Ghent of the Three Towns – Ghent, Bruges and Ypres – had agreed to cooperate with the king of England in the forthcoming campaign, and to go wherever he should desire them. Taking advantage of this satisfactory development, Edward had fitted out a small expedition, consisting of some men-at-arms and 600 archers, under the command of Sir Hugh Hastings, John Molyneux and John Maltravers. On July 16 this force sailed for Flanders in 20 vessels and joined the Flemish army at Ghent. The whole allied army was put under the command of count Henry of Flanders. On August 2, as Edward was marching into Lisieux, the Anglo-Flemish army set out, probably from Ypres, to cooperate with the English army that was advancing to meet it. Edward's plan of campaign was, it will be remembered, to unite these two armies before committing his own forces to a close engagement with the probably superior French army. But Ypres was distant 190 miles from Lisieux, and there were at least two formidable rivers in the way, the Seine and the Somme. The shortest line of approach for the Flemish army would take them via Arras and Amiens, where, if both armies advanced at the same pace, they should join forces. The combined allied grand army could then turn with some assurance of success against the main French army. Such was the plan, and despite its ambitious nature, it was one to be commended. Communication between the two armies was, of course, the main difficulty and, though we are told that each army was informed of the other's progress, it must have been only at wide and uncertain intervals, as communications had to go by sea.

The English army, as we have said, reached Lisieux on August 2. It halted for one day at Lisieux, while two cardinals, sent by the Pope, put out fruitless pleas for peace, and news or rumours of the French king's movements probably reached it at the same time. But Edward pursued his march next day, August 4, on the old line, reaching Le Teil Nollent that night, a long march of 16 miles. Next day, still continuing eastward, the march was even longer and 19 miles were covered. The route was via Brienne, and Neubourg was reached that night.

On Sunday August 6, the main body halted while a reconnaissance under Godfrey de Harcourt was thrown out toward Rouen, which now lay 23 miles to the north-east. The French king had put in charge of the defences of Rouen the count de

Harcourt, elder brother of the traitor Godfrey. The count dug
trenches on the southern outskirts of the city and sent forward
a small body which had a skirmish with Godfrey's party. The
latter, having obtained the required information, fell back to
the main body and reported. If Edward had ever hoped to
cross the Seine at Rouen (which is unlikely) he now realized
that it was impossible. Only one course remained open–to
attempt a crossing higher upstream between Rouen and Paris.
His previous advance had had this possibility in view. Instead,
however, of continuing on the same line and meeting the river
at about Gaillon, Edward turned sharp to his left on August 7
and after marching 11 miles touched the river at Elbeuf.
This rather surprising move brought him within a dozen miles
of the main French army, but Edward no doubt banked on
securing the river crossing by this sudden unexpected move.
In this, however, he was disappointed; the bridge was destroyed
and on August 8 he was obliged to push on upstream, looking
for a further crossing. Pont de l'Arche was the first place
bridged, but he hardly expected to obtain this crossing for the
town lies to the south of the bridge and was walled and strongly
fortified (as Henry V discovered 70 years later). The river Eure
joins the Seine just east of Pont de l'Arche and the army pushed
up it to Lery, a march of nine miles. While passing Pont de
l'Arche, according to the *Grandes Chroniques*, Edward received
from Philip a challenge to single combat. To this he sent answer
that he would fight his rival in front of Paris. What did either
king mean by these exchanges? It is hard to say, but probably
Philip's reason was a psychological one: he had declined
Edward's challenge to single encounter seven years before, and
his conscience was no doubt a trifle uneasy on the subject. He
may have overheard some caustic comments in his Court and
may have decided to "wipe out the stain". If this be so,
Edward no doubt saw through it. He possessed a continental
reputation in the lists, and Philip would have received short
shrift had it come to a duel. It would not come to that: both
kings were convinced on that point. Edward's reply–that he

would fight at Paris—may have been a case of deceptive bluff: he had no intention of going as far as Paris if he could manage to cross the Seine short of that place. If his answer induced Philip to hurry back to Paris so much the better.

On August 9, the English army made a long 18-mile march to the suburbs of Vernon, skirting Louviers (which they sacked), and past Gaillon (the castle of which they took), and along the river, looking vainly for a crossing-place. All bridges had been either broken down or were adequately defended; moreover the French army, which had had ample warning of the movement of its opponents, who were clearly visible from the line of lime cliffs on the north bank of the river, was marching abreast of them. For several miles the English army followed the road by which King John's troops had gone to the relief of Chateau Gaillard 150 years before; but no attempt seems to have been made to cross at Les Andelys. Vernon was too strongly held to justify an attempt to storm it: both time and English lives were too valuable. The army accordingly bivouacked outside the town, a short distance to the south. August 10 was a repetition of the day before, except that the march was only half as long. That night was spent at Freneuse, well inside the Moisson bend of the river. It looks as if they were heading for that town, but next day, August 11, they quitted the bend, marching the 13 miles *via* Mantes to Epone. The army was now inside another bend of the Seine and Warwick and Northampton took a strongish force to attempt the crossing at Meulan, in the middle of the bend. Unsuccessful here also, the army continued on its way to Equevilly, a march of only five and a half miles. The shortness of this march was probably due to the delay caused by the Meulan operation: till the issue was decided there the rest of the army could hardly push on beyond that possible crossing-place.

On August 13 a six and a half miles march brought the army to Poissy, where the bridge, though broken down, was only weakly guarded. Philip, with his main army, had gone right past to Paris. Had Edward's bluff succeeded? The English king was quick to take advantage of this situation. Strong parties crossed the river on boats and drove off the guard on the bridge. Then the carpenters and pioneers started repair work on the bridge, working desperately day and night, for they realized their lives depended upon it. Not content with this bridge alone, Edward is said to have started the construction of other bridges in the vicinity (though the *Acta Bellicosa*, which is very detailed at this point, is silent as to this). The inactivity of the French is hard to understand. It is true that on August 14 a considerable force did come up to the bridge and for a time there was a fierce contest, but they were driven back by Northampton, who crossed by a single beam 60 ft. long and 1 ft. wide spanning two piers, and killed 500 of the enemy.

It took nearly three days to repair the bridge, and meanwhile two things happened. The English king sent Prince Edward to demonstrate opposite the south-western suburbs of Paris, burning nearby villages including St. Cloud in full view of Paris, in order to complete the deception. This had the desired effect of keeping the French king in a painful state of indecision. He kept shifting about from one side of his capital to the other, St. Germain des Prés to the west, St. Denys to the north, and Antony to the south, being all in turn occupied —anywhere except the right place, which was Poissy. The second event was that during this period Philip sent a further letter to the English king, this time suggesting a set battle between the two armies, on some mutually agreeable ground. But was Philip serious? Edward, remembering what had happened after a similar challenge in Flanders, might well doubt it. He seems to have taken the measure of his opponent, and to have treated the suggestion with contempt. For the moment, however, he gave no formal answer but went on bridge-building. The Parisians became incensed by the lack of activity and enterprise exhibited by the French army which, grossly superior in numbers, made no attempt to come to grips with the invaders, but which rested supinely in its quarters while the suburbs of the city were aflame. It was probably the inflamed state of public opinion that induced Philip to send that second letter to Edward; it was in fact a "face-saver".

Meanwhile what progress was being made by the Flemish allied army? It had set out, as mentioned earlier, on August 2, under the command of Henry count of Flanders, probably from Ypres (though Li Muisis, the chronicler, does not say so specifically). From there it advanced through the Bailleul area—so familiar to our troops in the 1914–1918 war—to the river Lys. After engagements along the course of this river at Estaires, Merville and St. Venant (where the French hanged an Englishman by the heels and the town was stormed and burnt as reprisal by the allies), they reached Bethune on August 14, and laid siege to it, while the English army was halted at Poissy. It is doubtful if Edward had up-to-date information of the movements of the Flemish army, but he must have been aware of its general line of advance. Bethune is 125 map miles from Poissy. If both armies approached one another continuously at a speed of ten map miles a day, they should meet within a week. Amiens is in a direct line and midway between these two places, and the junction, if all went well, might be expected to take place near that town. But it was far more likely that the English army would move the faster and have to cross the Somme before meeting the Flemings. To make straight for Amiens would entail delay, for it might be presumed to be strongly held by the French. The same applied to Abbeville, 28 map miles to its north-west. Edward therefore decided to direct his march midway between these two towns towards an area where there were at least three bridges over the unfordable river Somme.

THE ADVANCE TO THE SOMME

August 15 was the Feast of the Assumption of the Virgin Mary and Edward ordered no burnings or military activity to take place that day, but next day the English army crossed the now completed bridge, Prince Edward's division having presumably been called in on the previous evening. The army marched due north, fast and straight–uncannily straight. For no less than 68 miles its halting-places did not diverge as much as one and a half miles from a dead straight line, a straightness of march unparalleled in military history, so far as my knowledge goes. How Edward managed to steer so straight a course in the absence of maps–if he had none–must always remain a mystery, for Harcourt can have been of no assistance as a guide once the army was north of the Seine. Edward had not only marched fast, he had given his enemy the slip, for he had not answered Philip's challenge to battle till the end of the first day's march, at Grisy, 16 miles north of Poissy and the same distance from St. Denys. Edward's letter was couched in sarcastic, almost jocular terms. It was, in fact, barely polite. The *Grandes Chroniques* stigmatizes the English king's conduct in all this as deceitful; and deceitful it was. One of the maxims of war is to deceive your opponent, but the good cleric of the abbey of St. Denys would not be conversant with such maxims. Edward had deceived Philip and gained at least one day's march on him in the race to the Somme. But his success was even greater than he had a right to expect, for Philip did not immediately pursue. When he received Edward's letter, presumably early on August 17, he was at Antony to the south of Paris with his main army, daily expecting an attack in that quarter. He moved from there through Paris to St. Denys that night and only set out on his pursuit to the Somme on August 18.

Thus Edward had completely outwitted Philip. He had two days' start, and marched rapidly into the bargain, averaging 14½ miles for the first five days. We hear little of pillage and burning on this march: no doubt its speed did not allow much time for such things and the troops were getting sated with their excesses. His route took him two miles to the west of Beauvais, which the prince of Wales wished to assault, but his father forbade it. Thence the only town traversed was Poix, on August 20, where his exuberant troops stormed the town

with scaling ladders against his orders, for speed—not fighting—
was for the moment his aim. Later two advanced-guard actions
were successfully fought against the king of Bohemia's contingent. This king, whose crest was a plume of feathers, was
a fine soldier and was frequently instrumental in opposing the
English advance. Edward slowed the rate of march on
August 21 to six miles, for he was by all calculations well ahead
of his enemy, and no doubt he heaved a sigh of relief on
arriving safely at Airaines on August 21. Here he was ideally
placed for his purpose, which was to find and utilize a crossing-
place over the Somme, for Airaines is midway between Amiens
and Abbeville, five miles north of the river, while roads branch
off to Picquigny, Longpré, Long and Pont Remy, all of which
had bridges over the river. The precision of his march direct
to this point from Poissy, 67 miles distant, is quite remarkable.
King Edward must have been well pleased with the situation
in which he found himself.

But King Philip with his army was that night on the Somme
at Amiens! How had he managed it? Historians, both French
and English, have slurred over this truly remarkable performance on the part of the French king, the finest military feat of
this somewhat unmilitary monarch. The bald facts speak for
themselves. He left St. Denys on August 18 and was reported
in Amiens on August 20. The distance is 73 miles, *i.e.*, 24 miles
a day. Amiens was undoubtedly the right place to make for,
and the king had sent orders in advance for the levies north of
the Somme to meet him in that town. His route also was nearly
as direct as that of his rival; it took him through Clermont,
which he is reported as reaching on August 18, a 35-mile
march. How are we to account for this phenomenal speed? In
three possible ways. First, though he himself did not set out till
August 18 he may have dispatched the dismounted portion of
his army on the previous day. Second, though he himself
arrived at Amiens on August 20, the bulk of his army may not
have arrived till later. Third, he did not in fact reach Amiens
on August 20, but Nampty, which is described as "near" the

city. In point of fact it is a good nine miles to the south-west. If we plot out on the map the respective itineraries of the two armies in this exciting race, we shall find that, when the French were at Clermont, the English were four miles north of Beauvais, 18 miles to the north-west; when the French reached Nampty the English were at Camps, only ten miles west-northwest; the two armies were now each distant eight miles from the Somme. But next day the French entered Amiens, across the river, while the English army stopped five miles short of it at Airaines. Clearly the moral victory went to the French. Could they exploit it?

The strategical situation was becoming exciting. The gap between the English and Flemish armies had narrowed to 55 map miles; in only two days they might join hands, but the formidable obstacle of the river Somme, with its broad marshy valley and numerous channels strongly defended by French troops, blocked the way. Edward's immediate object was to force this line. With that object in view he sent out on the morning of August 22 a strong reconnaissance force under the earl of Warwick, to discover the most favourable place for the attempt. Warwick's party made straight for the river at Longpré. The bridge there was strongly guarded. He turned left and found the same thing at the neighbouring bridge of Long. He pushed on another four miles to Pont Remy where a considerable engagement took place between his party and the detachment of the king of Bohemia. Warwick was obliged to return and report that no impression could be made on any of the crossing-places. A similar report came from the crossing at Picquigny, midway between Longpré and Amiens. The situation of the English army had suddenly become critical. Boots were worn out, bread was scarce, the army was reduced to eating the fruit—ripe and unripe—on the wayside (just as did its descendants over ground not far distant in the same month of August, 1914, during the retreat from Mons). They had lost heavily in horses, and many of the knights were reduced to riding rough country horses captured during the advance. The army was out of touch with the fleet and out of up-to-date information regarding the Flemings. Reinforcements had flocked to the French army at Amiens and it was now of overwhelming numerical superiority. The half-despised Philip had, to all appearances, out-manoeuvred his rival. Froissart describes Edward III as almost distracted with anxiety. Doubtless this was only a guess on his part, and Northburgh gives the impression that the English king was not in the least put out – at the same time he dared not risk a battle here except in the last extremity. Like Admiral Jellicoe in 1916, he was in a position to lose the war in an afternoon, for in the event of defeat there was little chance of his army ever seeing England again.

Edward that night, after careful thought, came to the conclusion that to force a crossing between Amiens and Abbeville was now out of the question. This was reasonable enough. But the action he decided on taking was surprising. Next morning, August 23, he marched his whole army eight miles due west – away from the river – and carried by storm the town of Oisemont. The rearguard was about to move off from the old billets at Airaines at 10 a.m. when news came of the approach of the French army from the Amiens direction – Philip had recrossed the river! Quartermasters bustled about their business, but there was not time to pack up and remove everything, and when the French arrived in the town two hours later they saw evident signs of a hasty departure.

But why had Edward marched in such a curious direction and why did he waste time in attacking Oisemont? It reminds one of a hunted fox stopping in the course of its flight to rob a hen roost. The clue to his motive is found in his next movement: making almost a right-angled turn to the right he marched straight to Acheux, eight miles north-north-west, where he halted for the night. His object must have been twofold: to mislead the French king – in his "deceitful" way – by appearing to abandon the attempt to cross the river, and to reduce the danger of being seen by the Abbeville garrison as he would have been if he took the direct road to Acheux.

Whether he succeeded in his stratagem or not, his position still remained anxious and precarious. His new intention was to cross the river between Abbeville and the sea if it proved practicable, but he was utterly ignorant of the condition of the lower reaches of the river, which in any case widened out a few miles below Abbeville into an estuary nearly two miles broad. The faithful Harcourt was now of no service, being out of his home country. The king therefore did the only possible thing. That night he summoned to his headquarters all prisoners who had been captured that day and offered handsome rewards to any who could give him reliable information about the possible crossing-places below Abbeville. Tempted by this bribe, one Gobin Agache (whose name still stinks in French nostrils) averred that he knew of a practicable ford at Blanche-taque—The White Spot—where at low tide a man could cross with the water only knee-high. It ran from Saigneville on the south bank to a point nearly one mile north-west of Port on the north bank, its length being exactly 2,000 yards. Edward decided to trust the man, and gave orders for departure before dawn next day. Meanwhile, Philip had halted his main body for the night at Airaines, sending a division to Abbeville.

BLANCHETAQUE

Before dawn on August 24, the English army set out on its desperate venture. It marched in a single column. Warwick led the advanced guard with a force of archers, followed by his men-at-arms. Then came the baggage, while the rear was brought up by the king's own division. When the French king heard of the move he set off in pursuit, but had much leeway to make up. Acheux was 14 miles distant and Blanchetaque nearly 18 by the shortest road. Philip had however posted a force of 500 men-at-arms and at least 3,000 infantry, including Genoese crossbowmen under Godemar du Fay, on the north bank guarding the ford, and they could, if necessary, be reinforced from Abbeville, five miles away. Thus he had little fear that the bottle was not firmly corked.

The English army had a six-mile march in the half-light of a summer dawn. They made good progress and their leading units are reported to have reached the ford at dawn, which seems scarcely credible. In any case, there was no great cause for haste as the tide was only just starting to ebb at dawn and at least four hours' wait was involved before the ford would be practicable. During this long and anxious wait the rear of the column closed up till the whole army was concentrated on the south bank, immediately opposite the ford. It was about 10 a.m. before the first man stepped into the water of the ebbing tide. Hugh Despenser seems to have led the vanguard of archers. Progress along the causeway–one and a half miles in length–was uneventful and unopposed till the leading files came within a few hundred yards of the shore. Here they were greeted with a discharge from the Genoese, to which they could not for the moment effectively reply, and considerable casualties resulted. But the English archers marched on doggedly and silently till they came within effective range, when they opened on the Genoese and a duel took place between the two "artilleries". The causeway was sufficiently broad for about 11 men to stand abreast; the remainder must have shot over the heads of the front file. But the English "fire" was effective: the Genoese fire began to slacken. This was the signal to launch the men-at-arms of Warwick's advanced guard to the attack. The archers edged to the sides of the causeway to make room for the passage of the horsemen and the latter splashed and plunged past them slowly towards the bank. Some French cavalry pushed forward into the water to dispute the passage and a strange contest took place, with much confused splashing and shouting–a type of mounted mêlée for which neither men nor horses had been trained.

This contest was of short duration (and has entirely missed the attention of most chroniclers). The French fell back to dry ground and Hugh Despenser led his fellow knights up the bank and out of the water, while the archers covered their advance with a steady "barrage" of arrows.

Godemar du Fay's troops had had enough; they took to flight, making for the safety of Abbeville. Northampton and Reginald Cobham, bringing forward the main body of the leading division, took up the pursuit, following closely and giving the fugitives a rough handling, till the latter gained the refuge of Abbeville.

It was a brilliant and inspiriting piece of work and according to one account—probably exaggerated—no less than 2,000 Frenchmen fell. So precipitate was their flight that Godemar du Fay was later accused of treachery, though without any real foundation.

While Northampton swung to the right towards Abbeville, Hugh Despenser swung to the left, charging through Noyelle two and a half miles down the estuary, and on as far as Crotoy, another five miles. Here he quickly seized the town and with it a large number of ships which he burnt, and returned in triumph to the main army.

To return to Blanchetaque; just as the last vehicles were entering the water, which was now becoming uncomfortably deep, the vanguard of the French army, under the king of Bohemia, came in sight. There was a short sharp engagement and a few wagons and men fell into French hands, but the bulk of the wagons with their precious load of arrows, under which lay some strange-looking iron tubes, escaped. While this was happening the remainder of the rearguard, already in the water, pushed on as rapidly as possible, so that when the engagement was over the tide was too far up to allow of any pursuit. At any rate, Philip, perhaps mindful of the fate of Pharaoh's army in the crossing of the Red Sea, did not make the attempt. In any case, a mere vanguard of French troops were not in a position to do more than capture a few stragglers; an attempted pursuit over the ford would have been hazardous in the extreme. Philip therefore called off his forward troops and turned his army into Abbeville for the night. His prey had escaped him.

*   *   *

The English had gained an improbable–indeed a near-impossible–success. All the factors conspired against them. Let us for a moment consider them. The English were devoid of surprise, cover or protection; they were hampered by the still-flowing waist-deep tide, they were massed into a narrow target for the powerful crossbows of the Genoese; they wielded their own bows awkwardly, some with wet bow-strings; the cavalry stumbled in the churned-up water, frequently slipping off the causeway into deep water, and eventually emerging in no sort of order, to face the strong infantry force lining the bank. Three Anglo-Saxons had sufficed to hold up a whole Danish army at Maldon; three thousand Frenchmen did not suffice at Blanchetaque. Richard Wynkeley, who made the crossing, wrote home "It was marvellous in the eyes of all who knew the place". Taken all in all, there have been few feats of arms so astonishingly successful against odds in the whole of our proud military history.

*   *   *

It was August 24: the English army was safe across the Somme, no big natural obstacle now separated them from the Flemish army. But where was that army? By a sour coincidence, at the very moment when Edward's troops were ploughing their way successfully through the waters of the Somme the troops of Henry of Flanders were in the act of breaking up the siege of Bethune and falling back on Merville.

How had this come about? Details are scarce, but the outline of events is as follows. On August 14, as related above, Henry of Flanders had laid siege to Bethune. The town was energetically defended by Godfrey d'Annequin. On August 22 he learnt that the Flemings who were also besieging Lillers, ten miles to the north-west, had suffered heavily, and hearing also that there was considerable dissension in Bruges between the war and peace parties, he decided to make a sortie. This he effected with striking success, burning a number of tents of the besiegers and getting back into the town practically unscathed.

This achievement so disheartened the Flemings, who cannot have been aware of the rapid advance of the English army toward them, that on August 24 they incontinently broke up their camp and retreated to the line of the Lys.

Edward, of course, did not know of this untoward turn of events, but three new factors decided him to offer battle to his old opponent. In the first place, he now had a fair chance of escape should he be worsted in the battle; for friendly Flanders now lay behind him and so long as he did not allow Philip to outmarch him, his line of retreat was secure. Secondly, he was now in Ponthieu, his grandmother's patrimony, on soil that he considered his own; he would not give up this possession without a struggle. Thirdly, the success of his army in crossing the Somme in the very face of the foe appeared, in that age of faith, to be a miracle; the God of battles was evidently on his side, his cause was a just one in the eyes of the Almighty, who would not allow them to be defeated. The morale of the troops rose with a bound, their trust in their leader was now absolute; he could "go anywhere and do anything" with such troops; if Philip wanted a fight, he should have one.

*   *   *

The English army encamped that night at some undefined spot in the forest of Crecy, which covered a wide strip of land north of the Somme. The French army had had a long march that day, and it bivouacked near the ford, chagrined and disheartened. Next day, August 25, it doubled back to Abbeville where it spent that night. The same day the English marched to the edge of the forest, nine miles north-east of Blanchetaque, looking for a suitable battlefield, and halted, still in the forest, on the banks of the little river Maye. Beyond the river lay a village called Crecy-en-Ponthieu.[1]

[1] There are several towns named Crecy in France, just as there are several places named Mons. Gobin Agache came from Mons-en-Vimeu.

APPENDIX

THE SOURCES

So deep is the interest in the Crecy campaign and so wide the literature on the subject that I will devote more space to the subject than I have done in the preceding chapters. It can conveniently be divided into three sections:

I. The evidence of eye witnesses;
II. The contemporary or near-contemporary chroniclers;
III. Modern writings.

I. We have accounts by at least four eye-witnesses: King Edward, Bartholomew Burghersh, Michael Northburgh, and Richard Wynkeley. The king wrote four or five letters during the campaign, the longest and most important being that to Sir Thomas Lucy, written from before Calais on September 3 and covering the whole campaign. He also wrote to "his subjects in England", to the archbishop of Canterbury and the archbishop of York.

Burghersh's letter is contained in Adam Murimuth's chronicle, as are those of Michael Northburgh and Richard Wynkeley. The last two were priests in the army, Northburgh being Clerk of the Privy Council and Wynkeley being the king's confessor. Theirs are the most valuable of the letters. (The letters are also given in Robert of Avesbury's chronicle.)

II. Of the original chronicles the best is, curiously, the least well-known, not having been used by Sir James Ramsay, General Köhler, nor any of the biographers of Edward III except the first, Joshua Barnes, who wrote in 1688. It is contained in MS No. 370 of Corpus Christi College, Cambridge. It is variously cited as *Chronique Anonyme*, Corpus Christi Fragment, *Acta Bellicosa* (from its opening words) or *Moisant*, the name of the transcriber. I favour the title *Acta Bellicosa*. It appears in Moisant's *Le Prince Noir en Aquitaine* – an unlikely place in which to find such a transcription. The document has never been edited, but it must have been written by someone present, for on one (and only one) occasion he qualifies a statement by the words "as I later heard". Delbrück describes it as of the highest value, and I agree with him. It starts with the landing in France, evidently intending to cover the whole campaign, but unfortunately it ends abruptly on August 18, in the middle of a sentence.

The chief English chroniclers are the above-mentioned Murimuth and Avesbury, Geoffrey le Baker and Henry Knighton. There are also two documents useful, indeed essential, for the itinerary of the army. They are the *Journal of the King's Kitchen* and the *B.M. Additional MS 25461, f.11*.

The French chroniclers of this campaign are very weak, and only the *Grandes Chroniques de St. Denys*, the Continuation to Guillaume de Nangis' Chronicle, the *Chronographia* (called *Berne Chronicle* by Lettenhove) and the *Chronique Normande du XIVe Siècle* need be mentioned here.

Of what may be called neutral sources, we have two from the Low Countries, those of Jean le Bel of Liége, and of Gilles li Muisis the Fleming, whose chronicle–a weighty one–is contained in the *Chronique de Flandres*. The third is Giovanni Villani, an Italian who based his account largely on the stories of Genoese crossbowmen returning from the war. His account is absolutely contemporary for he died two years after the battle of Crecy.

III. Lastly come modern books. There are three substantial biographies of Edward III, those of Barnes cited above, Longman (1864) and Mackinnon (1900). They all tend to slur over the campaign prior to the actual battle of Crecy. The same applies to Sir James Ramsay's *Genesis of Lancaster* (1913) and T. F. Tout's volume in the Political History of England (1906). Finally, E. Maunde Thompson has some useful notes in his edition of le Baker (1889). It is not an impressive list of English contributions to this world-famous campaign.

The French, on the other hand, have produced some very helpful works dealing with the campaign. The massive edition of Froissart's *Chronicles* edited by Simeon Luce contains valuable notes. *La Désolation des Églises,* by P. H. Deniflé (1899), contains a short but extremely useful account, because it is so thoroughly documented. The same applies to *La Prise de Caen* by Henri Prentout (1903), which is the standard work on the subject. But far and away the best work on the campaign in any language is *La Campagne de Juillet et Août 1346* by Jules Viard (1926), whose notes in his edition of le Bel are also useful.

Of neutral writers only two need be mentioned. The first is Belgian, Baron Kervyn de Lettenhove, whose massive edition of Froissart contains some useful documents and references and gives in full the little-read *Chroniques Abrégées*, or shortened edition of Froissart. The second is the German, General Gustav Köhler, whose *Die Entwickelung des Kriegswesens* appeared in 1886–1890. This distinguished author was not, however, fully acquainted with the English sources, nor with modern researches by Ramsay and Tout.

I have omitted Jean Froissart because this list is confined to sources and writers who I consider have something of original value to offer, and I do not think that Froissart can be said to provide that to any material degree. So far as he copies le Bel he may be considered fairly reliable, but not original; where he is original he is not reliable–no, not for a single statement–without corroboration from another source. When, however, we come to Crecy we shall be able to use him.

ITINERARY OF THE ENGLISH ARMY

Some readers may feel surprise at the precision with which Edward's itinerary has been established. But the material has always been available. It was Maunde Thompson who first "married" the different accounts into one whole. Geoffrey le Baker's chronicle, written only a few years after the event, formed the basis, but the most detailed and precise evidence was obtained by him from two other sources. The first is the

King's Kitchen Journal. This was evidently compiled by some unlearned member of his household who jotted down *as he heard them* the names of the places where the royal kitchen spent the night. His spelling was arbitrary and sometimes rather humorous in our eyes, but by comparing it with the second source, the Cotton MS *Cleopatra* D. vii. f. 170 and the Corpus Christi MS (which Maunde Thompson did not use), certainty and exactitude as to the king's own movements is attained.

Subsequent historians seem to have accepted the distances given for these marches by Maunde Thompson on trust. As a matter of fact they do not quite tally with my own measurements: in nearly all cases they appear to be too long if map miles are indicated, and too short if march miles are indicated. I fancy the latter was intended. It is, of course, impossible to assess with any degree of exactitude such mensuration, but marches always tend to be longer than would appear from a study of the map. Be this as it may, I have in the preceding pages made the marches on an average nearly two miles longer than Maunde Thompson.

The only modern historian, so far as I know, who does not accept Maunde Thompson's itinerary completely is Hilaire Belloc, who cuts out the two-day halt at Airaines, and makes the army halt from August 21 to 23 at Acheux. This is quite contrary to inherent military probability, for the king wished to cross the Somme between Amiens and Abbeville, so he would not be likely to march right past this sector of the river before making his attempt at a crossing. Moreover, both the Cotinian MS and le Baker agree in making the two-day halt at Airaines and it is confirmed by the *Chronographia* on the French side.

NUMBERS OF THE ENGLISH ARMY

It would be pointless to record the varying figures given by the chroniclers: the modern method is to discount them and to trust only to written contemporary rolls and lists such as the exchequer pay rolls. Wynkeley, writing only a few days after the battle of Crecy, gave the number present at that battle as 17,000, which, allowing for wastage, would mean slightly under 19,000 at the landing.

General Wrottesley, writing in 1898, after careful research computed a total of 19,428, which agrees remarkably with Wynkeley's, but this figure was subjected to damaging criticism by, among others, J. E. Morris, Sir James Ramsay and General Köhler. They show that Wrottesley's figure for the Welsh troops must be cut by 3,500 which, without allowing for other slight deductions made by them, brings the figure down to 16,000. Ramsay bases his computation of 10,100 on two sets of figures: the number of those for whom there is written record of having been called up for the campaign, and the total number on the pay roll during the siege of Calais. The first figure reached by him is 10,123, and the latter 31,294. He maintains that this figure refers to all who had been on the pay roll *at any time since the landing*, from which he reasons that only about one-third of these were actually at Crecy. But A. E. Prince[1] has shown that Ramsay has no grounds for this assumption. Nor is the evidence of the pay rolls sufficient. J. E. Morris has shown that some soldiers did not appear on the exchequer rolls, and instances an error on the part of Wrottesley caused thereby, where a category given by him as 600 should be 1800. This seems to put the whole computation into the melting pot, but Morris himself seems to favour 4,000 cavalry and 10,000 infantry, total 14,000.

Retaining in mind these figures and Wrottesley's (corrected) figure of 16,500, let us make a cross check from the number of ships required to transport the army. The number varies considerably, and it will be safest to take the lowest figure given, which is about 700 ships. Allowing for non-combatants, horses and war stores, we can hardly allow an average of more than 20 to 25 combatants per ship. If 20 per ship, the total would come to 14,000, and if 25 per ship, it would come to 17,000 – the two figures arrived at by the two above-named

[1] In the *English Historical Review*.

authorities. I am content to leave it at that, suggesting the round figure of 15,000, which is not far short of the figure given by Wynkeley (for Crecy), our most reliable contemporary source.

CONDUCT OF THE ENGLISH ARMY

The following passage from the *Acta Bellicosa* (Corpus Christi MS No. 270), as translated for me by a friend, seems to have been overlooked by recent biographers who are severely critical of Edward III. The order in question was issued while the king was at Valognes. It reads:

"The most mild king of the English, having mercy in many ways on the miserable population of that country issued an order throughout the army, that nobody should set on fire towns or manors, nor rob churches or holy places, do harm to the aged, the children or women, of his realm of France, nor do harm to any other person if they did not follow, by punishment to life and limb. Further he commanded that anyone who brought to the King anyone caught guilty of the same should obtain 40 solidos reward."

CHAPTER VII

THE BATTLE OF CRECY

WHEN the English king decided on August 26, 1346, to take up a defensive position on the Crecy ridge, he can have had no assurance that the French king would accept the challenge and attack him. Indeed he might well have had grave doubts in the matter. Philip VI had so often in the past exhibited hesitation – to put it no stronger – when confronted by his old opponent that he might well be expected to show it again. Edward III in his "haughty and ironical letter" of July 16 had made pointed, indeed scornful, reference to the fact that Philip had had ample opportunity to attack him during the three days he halted at Poissy, but so far from doing so, had broken the bridge and taken up a defensive position behind the Seine. This suspicion might have been strengthened in Edward's mind by the passivity of his opponent on August 25th. Instead of pursuing the English army, the French king had, ostensibly in order to observe the feast of St. Denys, remained halted at Abbeville. Whether this was the true reason or whether it was an excuse to allow time for laggard contingents to join him, as suggested by one chronicler, is not evident. He did, however, make use of the day to strengthen the bridges across the river. Why then should Edward appear so confidently to expect attack next day! The explanation probably is that by some unknown channel of communication he had received certain information, of which we know nothing, pointing to the probability of an immediate pursuit. This may be so, for his intelligence service, considering the fact that it was acting in a foreign country, was good. But it remains an interesting speculation as to how long he would have remained at Crecy had he not been attacked on August 26.

August 25 was evidently spent by Edward in reconnaissance,

while his army remained hidden in the forest of Crecy, enjoying a well-earned rest, for they had covered 335 miles in 32 marching days: that is, just over ten miles per day. A nice position was found on the ridge immediately to the north-east of Crecy. This ridge is formed by a little valley (known as La Vallée aux Clercs) which is scooped out of the prevailing high ground on the east side of the valley of the little river Maye. This river runs through the lower end of Crecy, from the south-east, and the Vallée aux Clercs joins it one mile from the centre of that village. The Vallée aux Clercs is only 2,000 yards long, its left or upper end merging into the plateau just in front of the village of Wadicourt. The ridge thus formed between Crecy and Wadicourt was about 2,000 yards long, exclusive of both villages. The depth of the Vallée ranges from nothing on the left to nearly 100 ft. on the right.

Edward decided to make this ridge his position. On the highest point of the ridge, only 700 yards from the centre of Crecy, stood a windmill. A few hundred yards behind the centre of the ridge was a small wood, the Bois de Crecy-Grange. The slope in front of the right flank of the position was about one in twelve, and on the left of the position it was almost imperceptible. The right flank was protected against cavalry attack by the village and river (which was wider than it now is) whereas the left had merely the small village of Wadicourt as protection, with open country beyond: it was thus much the weaker flank of the two.

THE ENGLISH POSITION

The strength of the English army, allowing ten per cent. for wastage since the landing, was between 12,000 and 13,000. A front of 2,000 yards was distinctly extensive for an army of such a size, but it is probable that there were slight gaps between the two flanks and the two villages, thus reducing the frontage to about 1,700 yards. Even this may appear rather wide for a medieval army, but there is a feature of the terrain that tends to remove this objection. There are, on the forward slope, three terraces or *raidillons* as the inhabitants call them, 350 yards in length and forming in all probability ancient cultivation strips. No reference is made to these terraces in the chronicles, which may seem surprising because they must have been in existence at the time of the battle, but it must be remembered that we have no eye-witness account of the actual fighting. These terraces would prove an effective obstacle to the French horsemen and thus could be very weakly held; by this means a longer frontage could be held than would otherwise be the case. The terraces no doubt formed a convenient boundary between the two divisions that held the front line.

The division on the right was, in accordance with normal custom, the vanguard of the army–the division of the Black Prince.[1] His chief executive officers were the earls of Warwick and Oxford, and the king put his trusted Godfrey Harcourt to act as his escort and "tutor", as we might say, his chief duty being to see that the boy came to no harm. He placed his troops well down the slope, almost, if not quite, within 300 yards of the valley bottom, the right half standing on a smaller terrace than that mentioned above. (It is not marked in the sketch map, p. 179, which should be consulted here.) The rear-guard held the left of the position under the experienced leadership of the earl of Northampton, who selected a line slightly higher up the slope than the first division. The third division, that of the king, was kept in reserve a short way behind the centre of the line. The baggage was parked in a "leaguer" abutting on the Bois de Crecy-Grange. The sides were made of the wagons and carts, one entrance only being made, for greater security. The interior was occupied by the horses, for the king intended to fight the battle dismounted, no doubt advised thereto by Northampton who had so successfully adopted that course at Morlaix a few years before. It had also been adopted at Falkirk, Halidon Hill and Dupplin

---

[1] It is convenient to use this title, although its first appearance in writing did not take place until 1569 (Grafton).

Moor. The king selected as his post of command the windmill which, though not centrally situated, allowed an uninterrupted view of the whole position and of the French advance.

The reconnaissance being completed, the divisions took up their appointed positions–carefully and methodically. Of the exact nature of the dispositions there has been much controversy. It centres round the meaning to be attached to the word "herce", the formation in which Froissart states that the archers were drawn up. Herce means a harrow, and there have been two interpretations given to the word in this connection. One school maintains that it means that each archer represented the prong of a harrow, the prongs being placed chequerwise, an interval of perhaps four to eight feet separating the archers. Each archer could thus shoot unimpeded and over the head of the archer immediately in his front. The other school maintains that the word means "wedge" and that the archers were drawn up in a series of hollow or solid wedges along the line, each wedge projecting slightly in front of the line of men-at-arms like a bastion flanking the curtain-wall of a castle. This would provide a double advantage: attacking horsemen tend to shoulder away from hostile fire as they advance, and the fire from these wedges would thus tend to "herd" the enemy cavalry charge towards those portions of the line held by the men-at-arms; when the cavalry got close up to the line they would be enfiladed by fire from both flanks whilst at the same time engaged by the men-at-arms in their front.

I unhesitatingly favour this latter school on grounds of inherent military probability. A wedge formation for infantry against cavalry was adopted by the Saxons against King Arthur's Britons at Mount Badon: we get a semblance of the same idea in Wellington's measure to frustrate the French cavalry charges at Waterloo, namely by forming squares between which the French horsemen surged, being raked from both flanks as they did so.

The only point that remains in doubt is how many of these

herces were formed, and were they solid or hollow? I think it is fairly clear that each division had a wedge on each flank, *i.e.* that there were four *herces* altogether;[1] and that they were solid, each *herce* being in the harrow formation favoured by the first school. The gap between the two divisions filled by the terraces would be covered by the fire from the inner flank wedges. Some Welsh spearmen may have lined the terraces.

Each man in the army was allotted his exact position and he took it up as for a review. The archers dug small holes in front of themselves and planted a plentiful supply of arrows in the ground, recourse being had to the ammunition wagons for this purpose; for a longbowman could shoot off his own supply of 24 or 48 arrows in a very few minutes.

When all was in order the "review" took place. It was one of the most momentous inspections in our history, for on it might depend whether the reviewing officer would continue to wear a crown on his head next day. The king rode on a white palfrey slowly along the line, unarmed but carrying a short white staff in his hand. With his experienced eye he peered intently at every man, occasionally halting to utter a few words of encouragement and good cheer to each unit in turn. (Battle orders would have been issued previously by the marshals.)

It was perhaps midday before the review was over and still there was no sign of the enemy. Meanwhile the cooks had been busy in the wagon leaguer; a meal was prepared and the king now gave orders that each man should fall out, relax and feed. At the sound of the trumpet everyone was instantly to resume his place. Each archer laid his bow alongside his arrows to mark his position, while each man-at-arms removed his helm.

The meal was served, nature satisfied, and the men stood about in little groups discussing whether that Philip would dare show his face, and many a bet was made.[2]

Still the hours passed; vespers (4 p.m.) approached but no

---

[1] This seems to be in accordance with file Baker, a good authority on military points.

[2] At Agincourt the archers had a sort of sweepstake on the number of Frenchmen each would account for: much the same may have happened here.

French army. The heavens became black with clouds, and at the threat of rain there was a sudden rush by the archers to protect their precious bowstrings; each man unstrung his bow, coiled up the bowstring and placed it inside his cap. The storm, when it came, was of short duration and it passed off before any appearance of the French.[1]

THE FRENCH ARMY

Meanwhile, what was the French army doing? Philip, whose intelligence service was strangely bad, assumed that the English had retired to Crotoy, the smoke of which could be seen from the walls of Abbeville. If this were so he might yet coop up the English between the Somme and the sea, as he had hoped to do on August 24, only this time on the right bank of the river. Soon after dawn therefore he gave the order to his unwieldy army to advance along the right bank of the river heading for Crotoy. But when his leading troops reached Noyelle they discovered the mistake and informed the king accordingly. The leading units were therefore switched sharp to their right, while those in rear who had not advanced far, if at all, were put on to the Hesdin road that runs north-east from the city.[2]

The old road to Hesdin was even straighter then than it is today, passing through Canchy and Marcheville and leaving Fontaine and Estrées a short distance on its right. Even the longest and slowest march comes at length to an end, and just when the English were beginning to assume there would be no battle that day the van of the French army hove in sight, descending the gentle slope into the valley of the Maye. It is usually assumed that the army marched in a single column. If

[1] Jules Viard in his book queries the historical accuracy of the storm, but I feel that there are too many witnesses to it for it to be doubted, though I agree in doubting the French statement that the Genoese let their bowstrings get wet and thus could not shoot; this was a palpable excuse for their defeat.

[2] The only evidence for this faulty opening move is local tradition at Noyelle and the existence of a road from there towards Crecy, with the name "Le Chemin de l'Armée", but such will explain, as nothing else will, the tardy appearance of the French army on the battlefield. Noyelle is six miles from Abbeville and the detour added a good seven miles to the leading troops, giving them a 17 miles march, whereas those who went from Abbeville direct had ten miles.

that were so the leading troops would, by a rough reckoning, be on the battlefield ere the tail had left Abbeville, but it is unlikely that all units kept to the Hesdin road. Philip had strengthened "bridges", not "a bridge", over the Somme and no doubt this was with the object of marching on as broad a front as possible, thus shortening the length of the column. Allowing for the detour by the leading troops, it is likely that every village in the whole triangle Abbeville–Noyelle–Fontaine saw some French troops passing through it that day.

NUMERICAL STRENGTH OF THE FRENCH ARMY

It is time to say a word about the strength and composition of the French army. As to its strength, the investigation is hedged about with difficulties owing to the almost complete silence of the extant French sources in the matter. We are in the domain of inferences and conjecture. Subject to the above qualifying remarks, the following assessment is probably not far from the facts.

The French army that fought at Crecy was composed of three broad groups or categories of troops. First there come what may be called the regular contingents, consisting in the main of the king's personal retinue of household troops and the Genoese mercenaries–a composite well-trained body under their own commander, Ottone Dorian. They are usually assessed at 6,000 in number.[1] They had played a prominent part in what fighting there had been during the previous ten days, and had suffered heavily at the hands of the English archers. Next come the foreign notabilities, each with his own contingent. The principal of these were the grand old blind king of Bohemia, who had lived for years at the French Court, with his son Charles king of the Romans, and with his contingent of Luxemburgers; John count of Hainault, the turncoat brother-in-law of the English king; James I king of Majorca; the duke of Savoy, and various German mercenaries.

---

[1] Villani gives and Luce accepts this figure, but it is probably too high, though the French figure 2,000 is too low.

Their total contribution must have gone into the thousands. Lastly come the provincial levies, who answered the call of what amounted to a *levée en masse*. Even if we knew their total number we should still not know what proportion of them had actually joined the army in time for the battle; stragglers and distant contingents from the south were continually swelling the ranks, and the number present at any given time would be as difficult to assess as the numbers of Harold's shire levies that straggled on to the field of Hastings. The English chroniclers give figures, the favourite being the suspiciously round number of 100,000, but they are no real guide. The only point on which there can be hardly a doubt is that the French vastly outnumbered the English. Giving what amounts to no more than a guess, I would suggest that the French army approached 40,000 in number and was about thrice as numerous as the English army.

THE FRENCH APPROACH

At about 4 p.m. the French army started to descend the slope from Marcheville into the valley of the Maye. Its leading elements were spotted by the look-out posted, no doubt, in the top story of the windmill. From there the news could be signalled direct to the king's tent, which would be between the ridge and the Crecy Wood. Edward, having rushed forward to verify that his enemy was indeed approaching, gave the signal: the trumpets sounded, the groups broke up, the knights donned such armour as they had temporarily cast off; and all returned to their allotted posts. The French army was coming at last.

But there was a wait of nearly an hour before the enemy came within striking distance. Throughout this period every movement of the French could be seen from the English position, and what the troops saw was calculated to inspire them with confidence. To explain, we must return once more to the French column—if it can be called a column.

It follows from what has been said above that good order

and march discipline was not to be looked for in the French
ranks. The inevitable disorder was accentuated by the sudden
change in direction of the march, and contingents jostled
against contingents, units bumped into one another and
crossed each other, while the king looked on helplessly. His
army was out of hand before a shot had been discharged.
Eloquent testimony to this initial disorder can be gleaned from
the astonishing discordance in the statements of the chroniclers about the formation of the French army. The number
of "battles" or divisions varies from three to over twelve; which
implies that they were never properly sorted out at the start,
still less toward the end, of a long march. When the English
position burst into view, just three miles away, Philip was
taken by surprise. His intelligence, which failed him right up
to the end of this campaign, had given him no warning and
any idea of fighting a battle that day was far from him. His
first action was to take hasty counsel with his leading officers.[1]
Should he accept the challenge that day, or should he halt
for the night? The predominance of opinion was strongly in
favour of postponement till the next morning; the troops were
wearied by the march, hungry, disordered and probably
dispirited after their wanderings; furthermore fresh contingents were known to be on the way: a few hours' delay might
enable them to join up. This advice was to the king's liking;
always when it came to the pinch he shrank from taking
decisive and irrevocable action. So much was at stake—his
crown, perhaps his liberty! Orders were therefore dispatched
along the line for all units to halt. But the order was only in
part obeyed; impulsive French knights, knowing the vast size
of the French army and supremely confident in their ability
to win a great victory, ignored the order and pushed forward
on top of those in front. Thus the Genoese who led were pro-
pelled forward whether they liked it or not and, if only in self
defence, attempted to deploy and march against that portion

[1] Accounts of the actions and conduct of the French king in the battle are more
discordant than almost any other feature of the battle, but the account that follows
seems the one most in accordance with inherent military probability.

of the English position that appeared opposite them. A glance at the map will show that the line of approach of the French army was oblique to the line of the English position. In order to form front to the position and march straight on the windmill which towered above it they had to turn through some 40 degrees. For a large body, nearly 6,000 strong, to change direction to this extent and simultaneously deploy, while being hustled by rude French knights in their rear, required a higher tactics dexterity than even the experienced Genoese were capable of. In spite of their efforts the line became hopelessly ragged and out of dressing and in the course of the mile or so to be covered before the Vallée aux Clercs was reached their commander was obliged to halt his men no less than three times.

THE BATTLE

Meanwhile the English, now drawn up in position, looked on in grim and confident silence. Everything was ready, nothing had been overlooked and, although at extreme range the archers could reach the bottom of the valley with their shafts, orders were, it seems, issued that their fire was to be withheld till the Genoese were within decisive range. The Genoese slowly crossed the valley and started to ascend the gentle slope to the hostile position. As they advanced occasional shafts were discharged, as was the custom with these crossbowmen, but they all fell short. Not till they were within 150 yards of the motionless line in front of them did their enemy respond. Then a sharp word of command rang out and instantly the heavens were, as it appeared, black with the swarm of arrows discharged from the trusty English longbows. The result of this discharge, striking the closely-knit lines of the Genoese, was devastating. The ranks of crossbowmen staggered and reeled while, to add to their discomfiture, a series of thunderclaps and belches of flame, followed by the swift hurtling through the air of great balls of iron and stone, shook the men and stampeded the horses. It was Edward's "secret weapon"–those

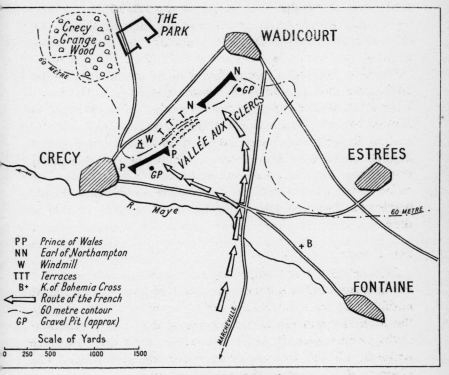

Within the map:

Crecy Grange Wood

THE PARK

60 METRE

WADICOURT

CRECY

N

GP

W T T T N

P

P

VALLÉE AUX CLERCS

GP

ESTRÉES

R. Maye

60 METRE

+ B

FONTAINE

MARCHEVILLE

PP   Prince of Wales
NN   Earl of Northampton
W   Windmill
TTT   Terraces
B+   K. of Bohemia Cross
⟵   Route of the French
— ·   60 metre contour
GP   Gravel Pit (approx)

Scale of Yards

0   250   500   1000   1500

10. BATTLE OF CRECY

mysterious tubes that had for so long laid hidden on the bottom of the ammunition wagons—the first cannon to be fired in open warfare.[1] It was too much: the Genoese broke and fled.

But their troubles were not over. Some of the élite of the knights of France under the count d'Alençon, the king's brother, spoiling for a fight and crowding forward hard on top of the unfortunate Genoese, suspected treachery on the part of these foreign mercenaries. The hot-headed Alençon shouted orders to the men-at-arms behind him to ride down the traitors and, clapping spurs into his horse's flanks, he suited action to the word and drove his horse into their midst, fiercely reviling them the while for their treachery. Some of the Genoese, finding themselves thus between two fires, opened at close range against their new enemies, and an internecine battle began. Alençon's men-at-arms, relentlessly treading underfoot the "traitorous" Genoese, at length reached and engaged the Prince of Wales's division in a hand-to-hand mêlée.

Meanwhile the divisions in rear, brushing past the Genoese, deployed and formed line in succession on their right, wheeling to the left into line as they did so. Eventually a continuous line was formed roughly equal and parallel to the English line. They then closed with Northampton's division in irregular and spasmodic efforts. All along the battle line the French mounted men-at-arms, forcing their reluctant steeds up the hill in the teeth of a hail of arrows from the *herces* of archers, closed with their terrible opponents.

Multitudes fell by the way, but the remainder struggled on with typical French *élan* and fierce hand-to-hand conflicts took place between the mounted Frenchmen and the dismounted Englishmen. The scene must have closely resembled that of the third stage of the battle of Hastings, when the mounted French knights vainly attempted to penetrate the stolid and solid

[1] For evidence on the presence of cannon at Crecy see the appendix to this chapter.

"shield-wall" of the Saxon housecarls. It could not be done; the French horses, in spite of the monstrous medieval spurs worn by their riders, declined to face the human wall in their front, while a crossfire of arrows at close range assailed them from the flanks. Casualties rapidly rose, but whenever a man fell another was found to take his place from the apparently inexhaustible supply of the French host. The pressure on the English line increased, and was especially strong on the right. Godfrey Harcourt, feeling a natural anxiety for the safety of his precious *protégé*, took two measures: he ran across to the nearest unit of Northampton's division on his left–that commanded by the earl of Arundel–and begged him to put in a counter-attack across the slight re-entrant that divided the two divisions, and strike the Prince's opponents in their flank. This Arundel agreed to do. Harcourt's second step was to send to the king for reinforcements. By the time the messenger had reached the king, in his command post high up on the windmill, Arundel's counter-attack was beginning to take shape. It was not lost upon the king; this was not the moment to launch his precious reserve into the fight. "Let the boy win his spurs," he remarked briefly to the messenger. The latter returned with this ungracious message. But in the meantime the counter-attack had relieved the pressure on the Prince's division and the messenger arrived to find the Prince and his troops seated on the ground amid the heaps of dead Frenchmen, quietly awaiting the next attack. But the brief words of the king remained engraved on the memory of the messenger and, years later, he recounted them to a foreign cleric, inquisitive for information about the great battle, and his story is now immortalized in the pages of Froissart's *Chronicles*. In point of fact, the king did send his son a token force of 20 knights, probably under the command of the warlike bishop of Durham. The carnage opposite the Prince's division was particularly great. According to the testimony of the king, in a small space in front of the Prince's troops there lay no less than 1,500 French knights.

"The sun went down and the stars came out" far over the battlefield, but the fight went on into the night under the light of a rising moon. Everywhere it was the same story; the French chivalry boldly and gaily spurred up to the motionless English lines in wave after wave, till all men lost count of the number, but nowhere could a penetration be effected. Line after line "reeled back with their dead and their slain".

> "God of battles. Was ever a battle
> Like this in the world before?"

It is said that there were as many as 15 separate attacks on the English position. But they were not continuous. In all battles there are pauses, of varying duration. During these pauses we can picture the English archers running forward down the slope to retrieve their precious arrows from the bodies of the slain—just as they did at Poitiers ten years later. A little before midnight the battle-flame flickered and died out; silence, except for the groans of the wounded, descended upon the battlefield.

The English army, wearied with slaughter and gorged with victory, lay down on the spot and went supperless to sleep. The king had issued strict and sensible orders against any attempt at pursuit under those unusual circumstances, and his orders were obeyed. Indeed there can have been little temptation to disobey them.

The French army melted away silently into the night, each man selecting his own line of retreat, for there was no one left in command to give him orders, the slaughter among their leaders having been particularly heavy. Their king had shown signs of wishing to fling himself into the midst of the battle—no one could suspect a Valois of physical cowardice—but John count of Hainault, taking a firm hold of his horse's bridle, led him off the field (much as 300 years later the earl of Carnworth led the reluctant Charles of England off the doleful field of his greatest defeat). Both monarchs probably lived to regret that they had survived the battle. For the battle was in each case irretrievably lost. *La dolente bataille* (as the *Grandes Chroniques* calls it) was over.

The king of France rode, or was led, off the field, accompanied by a small band of faithful servants. At about midnight he reached the château of Labroye, three miles away in a north-easterly direction.[1] Here, with some difficulty, he obtained admission and refreshment. His subsequent movements have been slurred over by chroniclers and commentators alike, but they are full of significance. At dawn next day he set out again, not for Abbeville where he might expect to regain touch with a portion at least of his army, but to Amiens, a 43-mile ride to the rear, halting en route at Doullens for a meal. At Amiens he was eventually met by four of his allied chiefs: Charles of Bohemia, John of Hainault, the count of Namur, and the new count, Louis of Flanders. They all reported that their troops had dispersed. They then politely "took their leave" and returned to their respective homes. They had finished with the war; the great alliance had come to an end; the most powerful monarch in western Europe, the head, only a few hours previously, of a mighty army, was abandoned. He had lost in the battle his own brother the count d'Alençon, his brother-in-law John of Bohemia, and his nephew the count de Blois (elder brother of Charles de Blois). Moreover there had been a "clean sweep" of generals. The army was leaderless. The flower of the chivalry of France, as the *Grandes Chroniques* sorrowfully relates, lay dead on the field of battle.

The king was utterly dumbfounded: he dallied in Amiens for a few days, his only recorded activities being to request a three days' truce to bury the dead, and to execute some of the unfortunate Genoese for suspected treachery. He then set off for the château of Pont St. Maxence, situated in a secluded spot on the edge of the great forest of Hallate, 35 miles north of Paris. He arrived there on September 8 and remained in solitary retreat till well on in October, leaving his army and

---

[1] An extraordinary direction to take—square to the right flank instead of to the rear with the bulk of his army—was it intentional?

his country to fend for themselves as best they could. Philip of Valois was, to use a modern term, deflated.

*   *   *

Meanwhile John duke of Normandy was hastening north with the mounted portion of his army. Arrived in Paris (also on October 8) he made inquiries about his father's whereabouts, and then pushed on into the forest, and eventually tracked down the king. The meeting of father and son must have been piquant: Philip *père* had lost his army; just ten years later John *fils* was to lose both his army and his liberty. The duke persuaded the king to return with him to Paris.

*   *   *

We must return to Crecy. Sunday August 27 dawned with a thick fog spread over the battlefield, as if Nature was trying to throw a veil over the scars of war. It was useless for the moment to send out reconnaissance parties in search of the enemy, but two other measures could be taken. The valley was black with the bodies of dead and dying. The English king arranged for the monks of the nearby abbey of Crecy-Grange to tend the wounded and he sent Sir Reginald Cobham with his clerks to make a careful tally of the dead knights and men-at-arms (the "communes" were seldom included in a tally). The clerks carried out their task methodically, and the scene of their work is to this day known as the valley of the clerks. The tally of knights and men-at-arms amounted to 1,542. That is the only reliable data on which to calculate the total French casualties. As a pure guess the figure for the "communes" would be 10,000. It may be exaggerated, although it only amounts to about three notches to each archer.[1]

The exact figure matters not; whatever the total, the great French army had ceased to exist. The Genoese, receiving no pay—for the administration of the army had come to a standstill—for the most part wandered off to their homes in far-off

---

[1] At Agincourt the English archers made a notch in their bows for each Frenchman killed.

Italy (whence the news of the defeat spread through Europe). The remainder of the army dispersed to their own homes, just as did the defeated armies in our Wars of the Roses. The English losses were astonishingly light, though it is not necessary to accept the grotesque assertion of one chronicler that only two knights were killed.

The king of Bohemia was buried with special honours, Edward himself being present decked in funeral trappings, as no doubt was the Prince of Wales, who from then onward adopted his badge of the three plumes.[1]

Before the clerks had completed their gruesome task the fog lifted and Northampton and Warwick were sent out with a strong force, in search of the enemy—if there still was one. There was. At some undisclosed spot not very far from the battlefield a large hostile force was seen advancing toward them. They prepared to receive it. Here we get a rare example of that *friction de guerre* that must have been even more prevalent in those days than at the present time. The corps in question consisted of the levies of Rouen and Beauvais, hurrying forward to take part in the battle. It is hard to credit the assertion that they were unaware that the battle had already taken place for they must have passed some fugitives from the field. However that may be they spotted the English force and, in the foggy atmosphere, mistook it for French. Approaching without adequate precautions they were speedily made aware of their mistake; the English archers took a heavy toll of them and then the men-at-arms charged and drove them back several miles, accounting, it is said, for "several thousands" of them.

CAUSE OF THE VICTORY

How are we to account for what appears at first sight to be an astonishing result to the battle of Crecy? Many explanations have been put forward and indeed the issue of all battles is

---

[1] The traditional spot where the king fell is on the road midway between Crecy and Fontaine and is marked by a cross. On the 600th anniversary of the battle the only gathering on the battlefield was a small party of Czecho-Slovaks, who held a service round the cross in honour of their revered monarch.

decided by many and complex factors. The combination of all these factors on the two sides, weighed against one another, decides the issue. Nevertheless in this case there was, as it seems to me, one supremely important factor which almost outweighed the total resultant of the remainder. It was the quality of the two armies. On the one side was a trained, disciplined, well-armed and confident army, fighting for all it knew with its back to the sea, with no hope of escape if it were defeated. On the other was a largely untrained army, hastily collected from differing lands, races and tongues, each unit unknown to and distrusted by its neighbours, lacking cohesion, order and respect for authority. Such an army was calculated to disintegrate when buffeted, and disintegrate is precisely what it did. There is no need to look further for some reasons or excuses for the French disaster in the "*dolente bataille de Crecy*".[1]

APPENDIX

FRENCH NUMBERS AT CRECY

The last word, but not, it is to be hoped, the final word, comes from the historian Ferdinand Lot, writing in 1946 in his *L'Art Militaire et les Armées au Moyen Age*.[2] After computing the English army at fewer than 9,000 effectives, he writes:

"Everything leads us to believe that the French army was inferior in numbers to the English."

By what channels does he reach this rather startling conclusion—so utterly at variance with all the written evidence and the consensus of opinion from the day of the battle until the present time? The Professor produces two reasons. He prepares the ground by arguing that when Edward wrote that the French army numbered "more than 12,000 men-at-arms, of whom 8,000 were gentlemen, knights and squires" he meant that 12,000 was the whole French total. This would leave only

---

[1] Ferdinand Lot calls it, from the French point of view, "*le chef d'oeuvre de l'incoherence*".

[2] Professor Ferdinand Lot died in 1953.

4,000 for the Genoese and infantry, country levies and allies, making the gentlemen-at-arms more than half the army. Edward was an experienced soldier, and he can never have believed that: when he said "men-at-arms" he *meant* "men-at-arms". It is to be noted that his confessor, Wynkeley, gives the same figure, 12,000 men-at-arms, as his master.

But let that pass, it matters not, for even were we to concede the point it would still leave the French superior in numbers according to Lot (12,000 French to "less than 9,000 English"). How does Professor Lot pare down the French numbers to fewer than "less than 9,000"? Philip had sent the bulk of his troops under the duke of Normandy to Gascony, "Philip could therefore only bring against Edward III improvised levies. The slowness of mobilization of the feudal contingents was such in those times that it is impossible that the king of France could assemble serious forces in the short time that elapsed between the landing of his enemy at St. Vaast, July 12, and the battle."

Let us see. The great English expeditionary force must have been signalled by French ships, who were on the look-out all along the coast. It might take them two or three days to put into Harfleur with the news, which should reach Paris within a week of the landing. As a matter of fact we know that Philip must have heard by July 19, for he returned from his country residence to his capital on that day, and presumably ordered what Ferdinand Lot calls "mobilization". This mobilization proceeded so rapidly that only ten days later he was in possession of an army so numerous that he dared confront his opponent with it. As we know, the battle did not take place for another four weeks, by which time considerable accessions had been made to the French army, notably in Amiens, whereas the English army had diminished in size owing to casualties and sickness. The probability is therefore *a priori* that the French army by August 26 was markedly superior in numbers to the English, quite apart from the written evidence pointing to that, both explicitly and by the *argumentum a silentio*; for is it to be supposed that, if the French army were indeed inferior in numbers, not a single French chronicler would have seized on that excuse to lessen the bitterness of defeat! "Only improvised levies" fails to take into account the 1,542 knights and men-at-arms dead on the field, and the numerous allied and mercenary contingents. Nor were the Genoese "improvised levies". Professor Lot asserts that "everything" points to the French inferiority. I assert that "nothing" points that way.

DEFEAT OF THE GENOESE

Three excuses for the defeat of the Genoese have been variously given by French sources:

1. That the rain wetted their bowstrings;[1]
2. That they were outranged by the English and their arrows all fell short;
3. That part of their ammunition and personal armour had been left in the wagons in rear.

These excuses do not ring true. The rain "falleth on the just and the unjust" and it is not to be supposed that trained troops, such as the Genoese were, would be caught out by it any more than were the English archers. The same applies to their arrows falling short; they would not all have made this elementary misjudgment of the range; and even though the longbow had a greater extreme range than the crossbow, the fact is irrelevant since the English archers shot at effective, not at extreme, range. They may have been only lightly armoured, but so were the English archers; and no doubt their reserves of ammunition were not immediately available, but they were routed in the very early stages of the battle, before reserves of ammunition would be likely to be required; in any case excuse 3 invalidates excuse 2, for if all their arrows fell short it did not matter how many or how few they possessed.

No; the main reason for the defeat was inferiority of morale, induced by their recent experiences of the longbow, especially

[1] Given by one French chronicler and repeated by Froissart in his *Abrégées*.

at Blanchetaque, and accentuated by the surprise of the "new weapon"–the cannon–employed by the English.

SOURCES FOR THE BATTLE

As may be supposed, the sources for the battle are much the same as those noted in the last chapter. We should however add Froissart, who took great trouble over his account of the battle, and undoubtedly did produce some fresh evidence, notably about the presence of English cannon. Jean le Bel still, however, remains our chief source for battle incidents. He was a friend of John of Hainault, from whom mainly he received his information on the French side. Le Baker is our next best source. One might expect that the three eye-witnesses who wrote almost from the field of battle–king Edward, Northburgh and Wynkeley–would produce a fund of details of the battle, but they do not. Edward, in his letter to Sir Thomas Lucy, had to cover the whole campaign, and had not much space left for the actual battle. He does however record the interesting fact that the army went to bed that night supperless and drinkless. Still, they had had a good meal in the middle of the day and one good meal a day should suffice a soldier. But drinkless on that summer night!

Neither Northburgh nor Wynkeley give details of the fighting, the reason no doubt being that they were herded into the park, out of sight and almost out of sound of the fighting. But le Baker can be depended upon for he wrote only a few years after the battle. The French chroniclers can hardly be expected to give long or reliable accounts, but their side of the story is well told by the Fleming, Gilles li Muisis. He was obviously at pains to give an accurate account, but complains pathetically that he finds it hard to know what to believe. Nevertheless his material came almost entirely from the French side, so his version reflects their side of the story only. Another valuable neutral account is that of "A Bourgeois of Valenciennes", printed by Lettenhove in his edition of Froissart as *Valenciennes Chronique*.

There are of course a large number of modern accounts. In
1844 F. C. Louandre wrote *L'Histoire d'Abbeville*, containing
a fund of useful information, topographical and local, of which
subsequent writers have made ample use. Two years later–the
500th centenary of the battle–the Baron Seymour de Constant
established the exact site of the battle, and the road by which
the French army approached. Lettenhove and Luce in their
editions of Froissart added useful notes; in 1887 General
Gustav Köhler in his great work *Die Entwickelung des Kriegswesen*
produced an interesting account, but it would have been more
weighty if he had shown himself better versed in the English
chronicles and commentators. Of all the modern accounts
I prefer that of the Rev. H. B. George, written in 1896. It is
rather short but he was the first to suggest the formation of the
English archers which is basically accepted nowadays. J. E.
Morris supported this view next year in the *English Historical
Review* as also did Colonel E. M. Lloyd, the only soldier to
make a deep study of the battle. Little of note has been written
since then in England.

THE BATTLEFIELD

Within the past few years the local authorities have allowed
a great sprawling beet factory to be placed right on the
battlefield. It is at the lower end of the Vallée aux Clercs,
precisely where the Genoese first came into action, and the
scene of their discomfiture. In the last century vestiges of one
of the grave-pits were visible here. The factory forms an ugly
gash on the panorama of the field that can be seen from
the windmill mound. The mill itself was deliberately pulled
down by a "patriotic Frenchman" in 1898 in revenge, it is
said, for the episode of Fashoda in that year. The foundations
on the mound remain, but recently it has been selected as the
site of a water tank. Whether this selection of site was another
patriotic act is not known.

Apart from these "encroachments" the ground is quite
unspoilt and, standing on the windmill mound, it is easy in

imagination to follow every incident of the fight. Of the grave-
pits dug after the battle two were still visible in 1844, one on
the spot now occupied by the beet factory, and the other high
up the Vallée aux Clercs where a slight ravine strikes north to
Wadicourt. This indicates that the left of the English line was
heavily engaged.

Of the old road from Marcheville by which the French army
advanced few traces remain. It still is known locally as *le Chemin
de l'Armée*.

French accounts emphasize the strong defensive line constructed by the English, consisting of trenches, hedges and
barricades of carts and wagons. The only partial corroboration
from the English side comes from le Baker who speaks obscurely
of "openings", or holes, being dug. I think these must have been
pot holes dug by the archers, reminiscent of Bannockburn and
more recently of Morlaix. If there had been any strong obstacle
in front of the men-at-arms we should have heard something
about it in the course of the fight. On the other hand, it would
be a natural story for the French to circulate in explanation
of their defeat. The wagons were parked in the rear.

The ground has never been accurately contoured, but a
roughly contoured 1 over 20,000 map was produced in
England during the 1939-45 war. Of modern maps, that of
Ramsay in his *Genesis of Lancaster* is the best, though I do not
entirely agree with the dispositions shown on it. Belloc's map
would be more helpful than it is if the scale had been drawn
correctly: it is only half the correct size.

CONDUCT OF PHILIP VI

Few things are more difficult to ascertain regarding the
battle than the actions and conduct of the French king. The
most contradictory stories are told of him; he was too impulsive
and from hatred of the English ordered his army to attack; he
was surprised by the presence of the English and tried to
prevent his army attacking at all; during the fighting he kept so
far in the rear that he was obliged to enquire of John of

Hainault how the battle was faring; he was so forward in the fight that he had two horses killed under him, on one occasion being unhorsed by king Edward; at the end of the battle he tried to ride forward but was forcibly prevented. These stories contradict each other and most of them smack of propaganda, just as does the French story that the Prince of Wales was at one moment captured by a French knight but afterwards rescued. It is easy to see how such stories gain currency.

The conduct of the French king after the battle certainly seems to call for comment. The *Grandes Chroniques* confines itself to stating that he returned to Paris, but I do not think we can reject the circumstantial story told by the Bourgeois de Valenciennes (or the *Valenciennes Chronicle*), printed by Lettenhove. The chronicler was a neutral and his account does not seem to show conscious bias against the French. Philip, in fact, seems to have been so utterly shattered morally that for several weeks he just allowed affairs of state to take their own course.

CANNONS AT CRECY

The long dormant controversy whether the English used cannons has reappeared. In 1942 M. Paul Schaepelynck read a paper before the *Société d'Emulation d'Abbeville*, which disputed the presence of cannons on the battlefield, and his views appear to have received favour with that Society.[1] The same point of view has also been voiced in the correspondence columns of the *Sunday Times*. It seems therefore desirable to review the evidence for and against the presence of the cannons in order to see if some final conclusion can be reached in the matter. I will first enumerate the arguments in favour of their presence and then examine those opposed to it.

[1] I sohuld perhaps add that I have recently had a very pleasant meeting with the leading members of that Society at which they expressed no definite opinion on the subject.

ESTREES

FRENCH ARMY APPROACHING

VALLÉE AUX CLERCS

CRECY

NORTH RIDGE.

ROAD TO POITIERS

LA CARDINERIE (MAUPERTUIS)

THE HEDGE

GUE DE L'HOMME.

POITIERS.

ARGUMENTS IN FAVOUR OF THE USE OF CANNON

These can be grouped under three headings: A–documentary, B–inherent probability, and C–the evidence of the spade.

A. Documentary

There are five apparently independent contemporary sources, the first two of which can be bracketed for the purpose of examination.

1. Giovanni Villani

"The English guns cast iron balls by means of fire. . . . They made a noise like thunder and caused much loss in men and horses. . . . The Genoese were continually hit by the archers and the gunners . . . (At the end of the battle) the whole plain was covered by men struck down by arrows and cannon balls."

2. Istorie Pistolesi

"The English knights, taking with them the Prince of Wales and many bombards, advanced to attack the French."

Villani certainly, and the author of the *Istorie* probably, died of the Black Death in 1348, two years after the battle. So both are absolutely contemporary sources. Both writers enjoyed a high reputation. Whence did they get their accounts? There can be little doubt that they emanated from the Genoese fugitives from the battlefield who, making their way back to Italy as no pay was forthcoming in a chaotic France, spread the first stories of the battle. The stories of nearly all fugitives are exaggerated and self-exculpatory, and the Genoese crossbowmen would naturally be tempted to make the most of the "new weapon" that had been used against them. On the other hand they would not be likely to invent the presence of a new arm of which few, if any, of them had ever heard. There is nothing in common between the above two passages. The *Istorie* is in error in asserting that the English knights advanced with the Prince of Wales. This certainly shows that the author had received some erroneous information, but the very dissimilarity between his account and that of Villani shows also that they were working on different sources, both of which however agreed in asserting the presence of English cannons. The conclusion is inescapable that within two years of the battle stories were current in Italy, brought there by eyewitnesses, that the English had indeed used the New Weapon at the battle of Crecy.

3A. *Les Grandes Chroniques de France* (or of St. Denys)

"Thus the King, with all his people assembled, went to meet the English, which English fired three cannons, by which it happened that the Genoese crossbowmen who were in the front line turned their backs."

Les Grandes Chroniques was about the best contemporary French record, the monk of St. Denys being in close touch with the French Court when he wrote it.

3B. *Continuator of William de Nangis*

"Then the English began to shoot on our people and they fired three cannons so that the said crossbowmen were dismayed."

At one time I regarded this passage as but a slavish copy of the *Grandes Chroniques* and rejected it entirely; but a close examination of the original shows that only three words in the two passages correspond, namely "getterent trois canons". Admittedly these are the key words and they point to the strong probability that both passages are derived from the same source, but they can be independent passages and yet coincide in using those three words, for if the common source stated that the English fired three cannons, "getterent trois canons" would be the natural words for them both to use. I do not claim two sources, and for that reason have bracketed them 3A and 3B, but it does seem that two independent chroniclers at the same time heard and believed the report that the English used cannons. Or it can be put in another way: The *Grandes Chroniques* are corroborated or supported by another contemporary writer. Who was this writer? Auguste Molinier, the unrivalled French expert for the period, is correct in identifying him as Jean de Venette, whose work is "a chronicle of the first rank".

4. Froissart's *Chronicles* (Amiens MS)

> "And the English kept quite still and discharged some cannons which they had with them in order to disturb the Genoese."

This version of the *Chronicles* only came to light in Amiens in 1839, previous to which date it was believed that Froissart had not heard of the presence of the cannons as he did not mention them in his first version. Various explanations of this silence have been put forward and the matter has been needlessly complicated by the fact that Lettenhove (followed, I regret to say, by Sir Charles Oman) wrongly placed the Amiens version earlier than the first version. This was rectified by Simeon Luce in his definitive edition of Froissart. The usual explanation of Froissart's silence in his original version is that as he was attached to the English Court he did not care to mention a new weapon whose intervention in the battle might take away some of the credit for the victory from the knights and archers. This may be so; but there is another and even simpler possibility—that Froissart had not heard of the cannons when he first wrote, but received the news before his second edition.

5. Froissart's *Chroniques Abrégées*

Late in life Froissart set to work to compile a condensed or abbreviated version of his Chronicles. This is known as the *Abrégées*. Strangely little notice has been taken of it, though Luce considers, in view of the new matter that it contained, that it deserves to be considered as a completely new edition. This applies to the passage about the Crecy guns which now reads in this version:

> "The English had with them two of the bombards[1] and they made two or three discharges on the Genoese who fell into a state of disorder when they heard them roar (ruer)."

This account is more explicit than the Amiens version, to which it clearly owes nothing. It must represent a further item of information that had reached Froissart in the interval

---

[1] English writers without exception translate this "two or three bombards". The French original is *deul des bonbardieaulx*.

between the two editions. It is in close accord with the *Grandes Chroniques*.

To sum up the documentary evidence, we have six passages emanating from at least five different sources, but all testifying to the (then surprising) fact that the English were in possession of cannons at the battle of Crecy.

N.B. If it be asked why in the Rome edition of the *Chronicles* no mention is made of the guns, the simplest explanation is that Froissart was working on the first edition (there were probably only two copies of the Amiens version, neither of which was to hand) and he forgot to incorporate the rather vague passages in the Amiens edition. The new information that appears in the *Abrégées* probably reached him after he had compiled the Rome version.

B. *Inherent probability*

This argument can be stated concisely. Edward III had suffered from the attentions of hostile artillery at the siege of Tournai, and had since exhibited great activity in amassing a force of cannons himself. I am informed by Brigadier O. F. G. Hogg that he has discovered documentary evidence that Edward III ordered some "gunnes" for use in France as early as 1339. Professor Tout has shown that he expressly ordered some cannons[1] to be constructed to take with him on his expeditions to France in 1346, and though there is no documentary evidence that they were actually embarked there is no reason to suppose that he left them behind. Unless we happened to possess an inventory of the stores actually placed on board we could hardly expect the contemporary chroniclers to relate the fact.

If the cannons were embarked but did not reach Crecy, what happened to them? It has been suggested that they were captured while crossing the ford at Blanchetaque, along with some of the baggage wagons. But this cannot be the case for the Prince's own division crossed the ford *behind* the baggage wagons.

---

[1] Some lead or iron balls were also made for them.

After his victory at Crecy, one of the first things that Edward III did was to write to England asking for all available cannons in the Tower of London to be sent to him before Calais. Evidently he had cannons in his mind, and if he had used some in the recent battle and had been pleased with their performance this action of his would have been eminently natural and inherently probable.

C. The evidence of the spade

Two journals, Le Courrier de la Somme and L'Abbevillois, reported in September, 1850, within a week of the occurrence, the discovery of a cannon-ball weighing 560 grammes (about $1\frac{1}{4}$ lb.) and measuring 24 centimetres in circumference (about 79 mm. or 3 in. calibre), and that it was made of iron, and was badly rusted. The name of the farmer who found it on the battlefield was M. Douvergne, and the cannon-ball was placed on view in the café of M. Lejeune of the Rue de l'Hotel de Ville at Abbeville. M. Lejeune's house was destroyed by a bomb in May, 1940, and there is no trace of the cannon-ball.

The above details are circumstantial, and there can be no doubt that a cannon-ball as described was in fact found on the battlefield in 1850. One would expect such a ball to be of from 2 in. to 4 in. calibre. Also it agrees with Villani's statement that iron balls were fired. Thus the ball found accords with expectation, and it is scarcely conceivable that such a ball, found on the battlefield, had no connexion with the battle. L'Abbevillois stated that the ball came without doubt from the battle of 1346. Moreover it was found, according to the Town Clerk of Crecy, in the precise area that one would expect—namely, the area where the Genoese attacked the Black Prince's division. The only fact that could cause any lingering doubt would be if fighting had taken place on the same field at a later date. I have searched the history of Crecy for that purpose. This can be found in L'Histoire d'Abbeville by F. L. Louandre (1844). From this it appears that the only fighting in the neighbourhood occurred in 1625, during the Thirty Years' War. It was of a minor nature and there is no mention of cannons being present. Moreover the fighting seems to have been confined to the village itself, which is well to the flank of the Crecy battle-field. M. Ridoux, late Mayor of Crecy (and the local historian), corroborates that there has been no subsequent fighting on the battlefield of 1346.

But this does not complete the contribution made by the spade to the elucidation of the problem. At various dates in the period 1800 to 1850, at least four other cannon-balls were unearthed by farm labourers and collected by Madame Desjardins, the great-grandmother of the present M. Desjardins, who resides in Froyelles Chateau, three miles south of the battlefield. They are described as being found in the area between the Vallée aux Clercs and the monument to the king of Bohemia, which is about a mile further south. This is rather vague, and evidently no exact record was made of the dates and spots where they were all found. The natural presumption is that they were found in the Vallée aux Clercs alongside the 1850 ball, and perhaps subsequently removed to the king of Bohemia's monument as being the only spot identified with the battle.

I inspected these balls in July, 1950, and took a photograph of them. Two are of stone and two of iron. One of each has a calibre of 92 mm. (3·6 in.) and the other two of 82 mm. (3·23 in.) as compared with the 1850 ball of 79 mm. calibre. In those primitive days there can be no doubt that the 79 and 82 mm. balls would be fired from the same piece. It seems likely that the 92 mm. balls were fired from a slightly larger cannon, though there may have been only the one calibre: even as late as Peninsular War days cannon-balls of widely varying calibre were fired from the same piece.

We thus have strong evidence that at least five cannon-balls, three of iron and two of stone, were found in or near the Vallée aux Clercs during the last 150 years.

ARGUMENTS AGAINST

The chief argument, and the only one that requires detailed examination, is the argument from the silence of the English chroniclers. This argument was, till the discovery of the Amiens MS, strengthened by the supposed silence of Froissart. Michael Northburgh and Richard Wynkeley might have been expected to mention the cannons, but both were civilians and both, in the opinion of Maunde Thompson (whose name carries un-rivalled weight in this matter), "probably watched the battle from the rear". Now, the battle took place just over the crest on the forward slope and consequently it was quite invisible from the rear. Our two clerks would be with the baggage which was half a mile or more in rear and they would from there see precisely nothing of the battle. It is therefore probable that these two clerks were dependent for their account on what the soldiers told them after the battle. But, it may be advanced, surely they would hear the discharge of the cannons? Not necessarily. It is a notable fact that nearly all chroniclers stress the noise of a medieval battle; the shouts of the soldiers, the clash of weapons, etc. What does Isaiah say? "Every battle of the warrior is with confused noise." Amid this confused noise of the warriors, a few – only a few – discharges of the cannons took place. The tiny charge for the crazily-constructed tubes would not make a loud report. Such report as there was, would be more audible in front of than in rear of the gun muzzles. Now, the clerks were in rear, and perhaps half a mile or more away with a ridge intervening between them and the guns. Thus they may not have heard the discharges, and even if they did, not knowing of the presence of the cannons, they would not connect any noise they heard with these new weapons.

But how could they be ignorant of the presence of the cannons with the army? Perfectly easily. These cannons must have been very small, they were simply tubes, perhaps as much as six feet long, each lying in a wooden crate. They would be carried in carts, lying on the floor of each and doubtless covered with a tarpaulin or spare weapons. Until occasion arose for action they would remain unseen and unsuspected by the great mass of the troops and Edward no doubt reserved his "secret weapon" till it could be employed in the decisive battle.

If, however, the clerks did know of the presence of the cannons, that silence can be explained in one of two ways. The letters that they wrote home were not very long, and when they come to the details of the actual battle they become exceedingly brief. Wynkeley has only 43 words on the actual course of the battle, which may be slightly condensed as follows:—

"The enemy, wishing to take the person of the king, thrust himself forward. The struggle was hard and long, twice the enemy was repulsed, and a third time. There was a great mass of men who fought strenuously."

He then goes on to recount the casualties.

Northburgh's account is even shorter, extending to exactly 30 words:—

"The battle was hard and long, for the enemy fought well, but they were defeated and their king fled."

Neither of these accounts, it will be noted, gives a single detail worth relating. There is not even mention of the vital work performed by the archers. By the *argumentum a silentio* we might assert that Edward III had no archers on the field, since neither of the eye-witnesses mentions them. But if the part played by the archers was not deemed suitable for mention in these letters *a fortiori* the action of the cannons was not.

There is another possible explanation for the silence of these eye-witnesses—that of motive. If the English victory had been due in the smallest degree to the use of the new weapon, and one not possessed by the enemy, there would be a natural reluctance to proclaim the fact; for artillery fire seemed to run counter to the tenets of chivalry, of which there was no more ardent supporter than Edward III. He above all would be anxious to keep the matter quiet, and it is at least conceivable that he positively enjoined his clerks not to mention it in their letters. The Germans have never boasted about their victory

in the second Battle of Ypres when they used a "new weapon" –
gas – and we had none. If it had been possible to keep its
employment quiet they would undoubtedly have done so.

The same motive for silence would apply to the contemporary
chroniclers also, assuming that they were cognizant of the
presence of cannons. But were they? Let us now consider them.
For practical purposes they were four in number, and I will
deal with each briefly in turn.

First comes Geoffrey le Baker, whose account of the battle
is the longest (excluding Froissart the Fleming of course). The
actual battle is described in 50 lines of Latin. Geoffrey was a
clericus living in Oxfordshire. He took Murimuth's chronicle
as the basis of his account, adding a few details that probably
reached him at second or third hand from eye-witnesses. Now,
if our two eye-witnesses, Northburgh and Wynkeley, did not
care to mention the new weapon in writing, other eye-witnesses
may have been chary about mentioning it to writers in England.
This would account for Geoffrey's silence without looking for
any other reasons. Next we have Robert of Avesbury, a canon
lawyer, who transcribed Northburgh's letter and only added
a half-dozen lines of his own. The third, Adam Murimuth, was
a canon of St. Paul's. He also contented himself in the main
with transcribing Wynkeley's letter and translating Northburgh's from French into Latin (a significant sign of the rapid
decay of the French language in England). Lastly comes
Henry Knighton, a canon of Leicester. His account of the
battle is almost equally short. He mentions three charges by the
French and the wounding of the French king in the face by an
arrow. This is the only reference to the archers in his account.

We can conveniently bracket these four chroniclers together,
observing that all of them got their information at second or
third hand, and that they omitted any detailed description of
the work of the archers, the main feature of the battle, so that
a fortiori they could not be expected to refer to the three small
cannons which cannot have played anything like so important
a part in the fighting.

Finally it may be observed that the motive for silence on the part of the eye-witnesses would apply in only slightly less degree to the English chroniclers. We can sum up by saying that our chroniclers were probably unaware of the presence of cannons at Crecy, but that if they were aware of it they preferred not to chronicle the fact.

SUMMING UP AND VERDICT

We have seen that the documentary evidence for the presence of cannons at Crecy is strong and precise; that their presence is inherently probable from what went before and what followed, and that the evidence of the spade is what the French would call *frappant*. Weighing all these considerations together, and bearing in mind the weakness of the objections to their presence, I subscribe to the conclusion of that profound historian, the late Colonel Henry Hime, "The presence of our guns at Crecy is one of the best established facts of the Hundred Years' War".

SOME TACTICAL POINTS

The dominant tactical point on the English side was the fact that every man in the army fought dismounted, and that the two arms–archers and men-at-arms–mutually supported one another all along the line. The French, on the other hand, concentrated their missile-throwers, *i.e.*, the Genoese crossbowmen, in one mass, directed against one portion only of the line. This was probably because the Genoese refused to fight except in a single body under their own leaders. The result was a complete lack of cooperation between the arms, with the disastrous results that we have seen.

The battle was a rare example of decisive results being obtained from a wholly passive defence. How is this to be explained? Undoubtedly the decisiveness of the French defeat was self-inflicted. It was largely due to the desperate and unthinking bravery of the French knights, who, undeterred by the awful fate that overtook each body in turn, still continued the unequal conflict till practically all the flower of the chivalry of France had fallen. It is, however, probable that the English king did not contemplate fighting such a purely defensive battle. He kept a large portion of his army in reserve under his own firm hand. He was chary about reinforcing his own son. It seems therefore likely that, like Harold at Hastings, he intended to launch his reserve in a great counter-attack as soon as the enemy should have completely shot his bolt, but as this did not happen until far into the night, Edward wisely retained his troops in hand.

Criticism has sometimes been directed against the French king for not undertaking a flank attack against the obviously strong position of the English. But his attacking troops were all mounted and a mounted charge through either of the villages on the flanks was impracticable. No doubt a wide enveloping movement right round Wadicourt followed by an attack on the English left rear might have produced good results; but such things were not done in the pitched battles of the time, and the French chivalry would have considered it rather derogatory to shirk a direct frontal attack against a numerically inferior enemy. (It required a woman to set the fashion—at St. Albans— of a flank attack delivered by the whole army.[1])

[1] This, of course, was Margaret of Anjou, the wife of Henry VI when she routed Warwick the Kingmaker.

CHAPTER VIII

THE SIEGE OF CALAIS

EDWARD III must have been a trifle dazed at the extent of his success on August 26, 1346. The great French army had ceased to exist: it had crumbled, as it were, into dust and the winds had swept it away. Clearly a review of his plan of campaign was now necessary.

Three courses seemed open to him. He could maintain his original plan of joining forces with the Flemings; he could attack Calais; or he could advance on the French capital. There was obviously no longer any urgency about joining forces with the Flemish army, for the danger threatening each had, for the time at least, disappeared. Moreover he had by this time probably heard of the abandonment of the siege of Bethune and the withdrawal of his allies toward their own base. Calais, on the other hand, presented a very tempting target. The English army was sadly in need of warlike stores of all kinds: boots and horse-shoes were worn out or worn thin; transport vehicles were in need of repair; above all, the stock of precious bows and arrows needed replenishment. But a wide stretch of water separated the army from a renewal of all those things, and a powerful French fleet roamed these waters; St. Vaast and Caen were now far distant—while Harfleur and the mouth of the Seine were in enemy hands. The same applied to Boulogne and the mouth of the Somme, and the little port of Crotoy was the sole link with England that the army possessed. The capture of Calais would secure not only a firm base for future operations, supported on its eastern flank by the friendly Flemings, but would provide the shortest possible sea route between the army and the home country—a big consideration in the days of sail. If France was to be conquered, Calais would have to be captured sooner or later, and the sooner this difficult task was tackled the easier it should be. But the third course–an advance on Paris–also had its attractions. The possibility of this course has been ignored by most commentators on the campaign, doubtless because there is a paucity of precise information about the strength and dispositions of the French military forces at this time. This is not surprising, because the internal condition of the country verged on chaos, and French sources skim lightly over this disastrous period. It is thus difficult for us, and must have been quite impossible for the English king, to "appreciate the military situation" with any degree of assurance. We are reduced largely to guess-work; but two fairly safe guesses may at least be made: the first is that Edward was not at first fully aware of the extent of the success he had achieved and the second that he was equally unaware of the strength and position of the army that the duke of Normandy was bringing north, though he must have guessed that it was approaching. There would seem to the king to be weighty reasons against making the attempt on Paris. His army, as we have seen, was badly in need of further supplies, and by marching on Paris it would be marching away from those supplies, even if the march was practically unopposed; it would be necessary to capture the French capital, which was strongly fortified and would almost certainly involve a long siege, for Edward had no siege engines capable of breaching the walls, with the army. It is significant that, on September 1, only five days after Crecy, he sent orders for all available cannons in the Tower of London to be sent out to him, but it would be weeks before they could be counted upon. The time that would elapse before the city fell would allow Philip to collect a new army. We know that he did manage to collect a large army before the siege of Calais was over, and he would have been able to do the same in the case of Paris. The situation of the English army, cut off from its base and surrounded by enemies, would have been desperate– or so it would seem at first sight. But that is not quite the whole story. There were some favourable factors beneath the surface. Let us take first the size of the army with which the duke of

Normandy was approaching. At first sight there is little inkling
to be obtained of its strength or composition, and it is generally
assumed that the great army of Gascony was brought north in
its entirety. But that is probably not the case. In the first place,
the duke left in Gascony certain garrisons. We know two facts
about his northward march: he heard the result of Crecy at
Limoges, and he arrived at Paris on September 8. The news
of Crecy could have reached Limoges about September 1 at
earliest. He cannot therefore have left till September 2, and
he reached Paris seven days later. The distance is 220 miles,
i.e., he must have covered over 30 miles a day. This pace
would be impossible for foot soldiers, so it points to the fact
that the duke had only mounted troops with him. We get
apparent corroboration for this from the Bourgeois de Valenciennes, who states that John pushed on from Paris "with a
strong force of cavaliers". On meeting the king in his forest
retreat, he did not persuade him to march north with this fresh
army and either relieve or reinforce the threatened city of
Calais; on the contrary the two quietly returned to Paris, and
no attempt at relief of Calais was made for over six months. All
this is good evidence that the duke of Normandy brought only
a portion of his army from Gascony, and that he did not
consider it strong enough to confront the invaders.

The English army should thus have had little difficulty in
approaching and laying siege to Paris. Its shortage of ordnance
stores would not become evident unless and until the French
opposed it in the field: to the enemy it would appear to be
simply a victorious and all-powerful army.

This brings us to the final objection, namely that the siege
of Paris was bound to be a long one and before it was over
Philip would have raised a large army and would have cut
off the English from their base. The length of the siege of
Calais, and later of Rouen and Orleans, may affect our military
judgment here. Is it right to assume that Paris would have resisted the summons to surrender? The inhabitants had the awful
example of Caen before their eyes: the English king had been

uncannily successful in everything he had undertaken: he had overrun Normandy and twice when he appeared trapped he had eluded his opponent and had then administered an unheard-of defeat on an immensely larger army. The Parisians had murmured against their king when the English army had appeared outside their walls a few weeks before; Philip, though possessed of superior numbers, had shrunk from engaging his opponents until practically obliged to do it and, having been utterly defeated, had secreted himself in the forest, not choosing to face the wrath of the burghers of his capital. It was about the last straw. National sentiment was not fully developed in western Europe in the fourteenth century, the precise amount of French blood that a claimant to the throne of France possessed did not greatly interest Frenchmen; in any case Edward was half a Frenchman and many thought his claim to the throne was stronger on legal grounds than that of his rival. In short, it seems conceivable, if not probable, that the gates of Paris would have been thrown open to Edward, and that he would have been accepted as king.

If Edward, marching on Paris, had put down with a stern hand the senseless burnings that had marked and marred his march through Normandy, I believe it possible that the Hundred Years War might have been concluded in a single campaign. No doubt a second war would eventually have taken place, but militarily speaking I hold that Edward had it in his power, on the morrow after Crecy, to win for himself the crown that he sought.

ARRIVAL BEFORE CALAIS

By August 28 Edward III had made up his mind: Calais should be his next objective. The same day his army set out and, marching by easy stages via Montreuil, Etaples, the outskirts of Boulogne and Wissant, they arrived on the western side of Calais probably on October 4.[1] The commander of the

---

[1] Three sources give the date as the 4th, one gives the 3rd and one gives the 2nd.

garrison, a stout-hearted Frenchman named John de Vienne, closed the gates, and the siege commenced.

The outskirts of Calais have changed greatly since those days. An early map printed toward the end of the English occupation shows a broad belt of waterlogged country surrounding the town. Through it meandered the little river Hem, passing 1,800 yards to the west of the walls, and then bending to the right and entering the sea immediately to the north of the town.[1] This last stretch of the river formed the town haven, which provided a secure anchorage for a large number of ships. To the east of the town a line of low sand dunes stretched away toward Gravelines, while on the west another and higher line of dunes commenced about 3,000 yards from the walls and ran out to the sea in the headland of Cape Gris Nez.

A double wall and double ditch surrounded the town and there was a citadelle and several angle towers. King Edward cannot have possessed accurate information as to the defences of the town, but a glance of his experienced eye would show him that they were immensely strong, and that to take them by storm was, for the moment at least, out of the question. Nor did he wish to subdue the town by prolonged bombardment and extensive breachings of the wall, for he intended that it should henceforth be, not merely an English possession, but a part of England. It is true that he directed all the cannons in the Tower of London to be sent out, but these were not breaching guns; catapults were still the breaching weapon, and the marshy ground rendered the provision of steady platforms for these heavy engines impracticable. Edward therefore was driven to the lengthy procedure of a blockade. For this purpose he encamped his army on the west side of the town; his left flank stayed by the sea, his Flemish allies held the dunes on the east side and detached posts guarded the approaches across the marshes on the south side. It was thus comparatively easy to blockade the landward side, owing to the marshes that surrounded the town, but to prevent entry of supply ships was

[1] But see the note on terrain in the Appendix.

a more difficult undertaking. Though we cannot give the
relative strengths of the French and English fleets in the
Channel, it would seem that the English fleet could not
maintain absolute command of the sea in the vicinity of the
port. Enterprising Norman ships could, and did, run the
gauntlet and enter the haven with supplies till late in the siege,
thus prolonging its length. Another cause for its prolongation
was that in the early days de Vienne expelled from the town
1,700 (according to Froissart) old men, women and children
who were of no assistance to the defence but whose mouths
had to be filled. Thus they became *bouches inutiles*—useless
mouths to feed. In so doing de Vienne was following a very
common custom, and indeed he may have had in mind the
famous siege of Chateau Gaillard 150 years previously, when
the English commander adopted the same procedure and
Philip Augustus of France refused to allow the ejected civilians
to pass, thus condemning them to a pitiful existence in the no-
man's-land outside the walls of the castle. Edward, however,
did not follow the example of Philip Augustus: he not only
allowed them to pass through his lines but provided them
with a hearty meal. It may be that policy rather than natural
kindness of heart prompted this action, for if Calais was to
become an English town it would be highly desirable that the
French inhabitants of it should be well disposed to the English
connexion. The inevitable result however was that, with
fewer mouths to feed, the food lasted the longer, and the siege
was thereby prolonged. Edward realized this, and when late
in the siege de Vienne repeated the action, expelling another
party of 500, the English king sternly refused to allow them to
pass, and another tragic instance of *les bouches inutiles* was
witnessed.

The siege was bound to be a long one—unless the French king
attempted to relieve the town, and of this there was at first no
sign. Edward therefore sat down to blockade it methodically.
This provided a striking example of his thoroughness and
foresight: he realized that it would be a lengthy operation;

autumn was come and winter was not far ahead. If his troops were to maintain their health during the winter months in that swampy neighbourhood, something better than canvas tents became imperative. A wooden town was therefore laid out in the space between the river Hem, the town walls and the sea. It was planned symmetrically, all roads radiating to the centre, where a large market square was formed–a nice example of town planning.[1] The town was even given a name–Nouville, or New Town. The king appointed two regular market days a week to which the inhabitants of the countryside were invited to bring their wares–an astute move from every point of view.

FLEMISH FORCES

It is time to speak of the Flemish armed forces. We left them relinquishing the siege of Bethune two days before the battle of Crecy and falling back to Aire. After that, precise information about their movements becomes scarce, and–what is still more important–the nature of communications that were established with the English army is unknown. It is, however, clear that close liaison was established before long, for we find Flemish troops serving under the English king at Calais, and combined Anglo-Flemish bands operating inland in raids and operations. Thus Edward's primary object–a junction with the Flemish army–was eventually realized, and such delay as there was mattered little because of the upshot of the battle of Crecy.

But the future of the Flemish alliance appeared uncertain, and all through the winter and early spring of 1347 a pretty contest of wits between the kings of England and France took place, each paying court to the new and youthful count of Flanders. It will be remembered that the old count had been killed at Crecy, and his son Louis was only 15 years of age. Having a French mother, his sympathies were naturally French, but his subjects inclined to the English connexion.

---

[1] Cardinal Wolsey seems to have copied Edward's example at the famous siege of Tournai nearly 200 years later.

Both England and France aimed at inducing him to marry a wife who would favour their own cause, Edward's selection being his own daughter Isabella, and Philip's the daughter of the duke of Brabant, who was now openly on the French side. The youth must have felt flattered at the efforts of two powerful kings to provide him with a wife. At the outset he declared boldly for the Brabant marriage, but the Flemish government practically forced him to agree to the English marriage. At a meeting at Bergues with the king and queen of England in March, 1347, Louis signed an agreement to marry Isabella. Great was the joy at the English Court; but it was short-lived. Though practically a prisoner of his own subjects the boy count managed to give his gaolers the slip while out riding, in a manner reminiscent of Prince Edward's escape on the eve of the battle of Evesham. Louis fled to France and no more was heard of the English marriage.

Philip of Valois then addressed himself to the Flemish government and tried to bribe them into alliance by offering the restitution of Lille, St. Venant, Lillers and other towns. But the Flemings remained faithful to their English allies.

Apart from these diplomatic activities, Philip VI appeared to take little interest in the war with England and he took no steps to relieve the town of Calais.

INVASION AT HOME

Meanwhile the siege dragged on in an uneventful way. There were numerous skirmishes and feats of arms, but details are lacking and even Froissart could not work up his imagination sufficiently to retail them. There were also forays into the neighbouring country, some as far as St. Omer and Boulogne, but they were devoid of military significance. Much more significant operations were taking place in England and Scotland during the early months of the siege, in the shape of a formidable invasion of England by David II. This will be referred to in due course; here we are only concerned with the impact of the news on Edward III. One might suppose that, having set under way the siege of Calais, which was bound to be a long one, the English king would hurry home on hearing of the invasion, or impending invasion, of his own country, leaving the trusty earl of Northampton to carry on the siege. Not so: Edward had had an elaborate headquarters constructed in Nouville and there he remained. One may feel surprise at this decision. The English king had been absent from his capital for over three months, Philip was showing no signs of attempting operations of any sort, while mortal danger loomed at home. Why then did Edward persist in remaining in France? The conclusion is inescapable: he had assessed the military chances and outcome of the operations in the north of England correctly, and he attached such importance to the capture of Calais, and to the bad moral effect that would be caused if he left his army before his objective had been gained, that he decided to accept the risk: he would continue, in principle at any rate, to share the privations of his soldiers outside the walls of Calais. Edward had, to use a modern expression, appreciated the situation correctly.

FRENCH MOBILIZATION

On March 25, 1347, Philip of Valois at last bestirred himself. He summoned a meeting in Paris of the leading persons, political and ecclesiastical, and he asked them for support in raising an army for the relief of Calais. Support was promised him, and the summons went out for a fresh levy of troops. The king appointed May 20 as the date and Arras as the rendezvous for the new army.[1]

The king's vassals played up unexpectedly well, and contingents came forward from all parts of the country, while Hainault and Brabant also sent contingents. But the concentration was deplorably slow and it was not till mid-July that all was ready. The army, when it did collect, was however greater in numbers than ever; one chronicler goes so far as to give the phenomenal figure of 200,000. We have no real clue about the

[1] Amiens is usually but wrongly given as the rendezvous.

correct figure, but it must have exceeded that of the Crecy
army. If we put it at over 50,000 strong that is by no means an
impossible figure for a country whose population was several
times that of England. It was however a badly balanced
army, most of the Genoese having gone home. War-wearied,
short of cash, and with the accusation of treachery hanging
over them, it is not surprising if they "had no stomach for the
fight". The army was also said to be lacking in infantry, for
Philip had a contempt for foot soldiers–in spite of his experience
at Crecy.

While the new French army slowly collected, events of some
consequence took place around Calais. In the month of April
a huge convoy, estimated at 300 ships, succeeded in running
the blockade, and not only entering the haven without loss
but in getting away also without loss, under the eyes of the
English army who were helpless to prevent or even to harm it.
Presumably the French ships kept to the centre of the fairway
where they were out of range of the puny English cannons.
What the English fleet was doing to allow this successful
blockade-running is not recorded.

King Edward was naturally upset by this humiliating
incident; he realized that if it were repeated the garrison of
Calais might never be reduced by starvation, and he took
energetic steps to prevent its recurrence. He constructed a fort,
which he named Rysbank, on the spit of land between the sea
and the haven, overlooking the Gollet (as the entrance to the
haven was called) and on it he mounted the most powerful
weapons he had. (Rysbank remained a permanent part of the
defences throughout the English occupation). He constructed
groynes or piers running out into deep water all along the shore
towards Wissant, in order to prevent single vessels creeping
inshore at high tide, thus eluding his deep-water fleet; and most
important of all, he increased the size of the fleet, which enabled
it to keep a closer blockade. At times he placed aboard the fleet
some of his most trusty army officers, such as Northampton,
Pembroke and Talbot, in order to keep his admiral–John de

Monte Gomery as the *Foedera* writes the name–up to his work.
He also called for reinforcements from England, prominent
amongst whom was Henry of Lancaster, who soon made his
presence felt in successful raids.

On June 25 a curious naval action took place. A portion of
the fleet with Northampton and Pembroke on board[1] was
cruising off the mouth of the Somme. A French fleet of 44 sail
tried to slip past them with supplies for Calais. The English
fleet gave chase, and the French ships scattered in all directions.
Not one reached Calais, and many were captured. One ship
in particular ran ashore and the captain was seen to attach
a paper to an axe-head and throw it overboard before surrendering. The spot was marked and at low tide the axe-head
was found, with the paper still attached. It was indeed a find.
It was none other than a letter from John de Vienne to King
Philip describing the desperate state of the garrison and
imploring help before it should be too late.

"Everything is eaten up–dogs, cats, horses–and we have nothing
left to subsist on, unless we eat each other."

This illuminating letter was dispatched to King Edward who,
with grim irony, courteously forwarded it to the addressee.
This action shows how sure of himself and of his army the
English king was.

*   *   *

The army that set out for the relief of Calais in mid-July
had nearly all its old leaders. There were the two sons of the
king, the dukes of Normandy and Orleans; the dukes of
Burgundy and Bourbon, the count de Foix, Louis of Savoy and
the ever-faithful John of Hainault. All being in order, the army
set out, marching *via* Hesdin to Therouanne. Philip had
intended to make for Gravelines and approach Calais from
the east along the dunes. This would have been sound strategy,
but he could not obtain the assent of the Flemings to this

[1] Historians generally show these earls as being in command, but the chronicle
does not state this: the relationship between them and the admiral was probably
a delicate one.

course, so he weakly decided to approach from the west. This submission to the wishes of the Flemings by the leader of an army 50,000 strong seems astonishing, but we are now past experiencing astonishment at any of Philip's actions, or inactions. Be this as it may, the march was resumed, and on July 27 the French army camped on the dunes immediately to the south of the little fishing village of Sangatte, five miles west of the walls of Calais.

A look-out tower on top of the dunes (here over 300 ft. high) was captured by a *coup de main*, but that was the limit of the French success. Philip had got his army into a hopeless position, the sea was on his left flank, thickly lined by the English fleet; there were marshes on his right flank and in his front was the river Hem, with only one bridge, that at Neuillay,[1] which was strongly held by the earl of Lancaster. Philip recognized his position as hopeless, after a couple of days, and decided to get away with the least possible damage to his prestige. For this purpose, after three days of fruitless parleys,[2] he played his old card of challenging his opponent to engage in battle on some selected spot.[3] Edward, knowing his man, promptly accepted the challenge, and then, as usual, nothing happened. While the parleys – aided and abetted by the usual pair of cardinals sent by the Pope – were proceeding, Philip was making secret preparations to retreat, and on the night of August 1-2 – the day before the battle was to take place – the whole French army crept silently away. There is indeed evidence which points to an actual panic having hastened and accompanied the movement, but we are left to conjecture its cause: it may have been some superstitious motive, caused by some phenomenon in the sky. Whatever the cause, the fact

[1] Now the site of Fort de Neuillay.
[2] The English Commissioners at the parleys—Lancaster, Northampton, Burgersh, Cobham and Manny—may be considered the five senior generals in the army.
[3] The appraisal of the eminent French historian Simeon Luce is probably the correct one. "It seems, to tell the truth, that the challenge had been sent scarcely more seriously by Philip than it had been received by Edward, and the king of France no doubt only proposed battle to his opponent in order to cover his retreat or at least to provide himself with a reasonable explanation for it."

remains that the army burnt its tents, left great quantities of food and stores *in situ* and retreated in such disorder that the pursuing English, under the dashing Henry of Lancaster, were able to make large captures of men and stores and to harry the retreating army for many miles. A great French army was for the second time within 12 months in ignominious flight.

THE FALL OF CALAIS

Our commiseration must go out to the gallant defenders of Calais. From the summit of the towers in the town the relieving army could be seen, but all communication was cut off; only a rough-and-ready method of contacting their saviours could be extemporized. This was done in an ingenious way. On the first night of the relieving army's arrival a great beacon was lit on the highest tower, in full view of the relieving army: on the second night a similar but much smaller beacon was lit and on the third night only a mere flicker of a beacon could be seen—a dramatic and sure method of depicting the desperate position of the garrison.

But they had not lost hope; Philip's huge army covered many acres of ground, and its extent could be descried from the town walls; surely the French king would make a fight for it before tamely withdrawing! But the hope of speedy relief was cruelly dashed when on the morning of August 2 the Sangatte dunes were seen to be an empty smouldering heap, with English troops swarming all around. Philip had deserted his noble city of Calais.

There could be no doubt of what their next course must be. That which de Vienne had hinted at in his letter to the king must now be carried out; Calais must surrender at discretion.

The story of the surrender is one of the best-known episodes of the Hundred Years War, thanks mainly to Froissart's graphic account of it. But Froissart and le Bel are not our only evidence for the circumstances of the surrender. There can be no doubt that the English king intended the surrender to be accompanied by every circumstance of humiliation. Six of the

leading burgesses with de Vienne at their head were required
to come into the king's presence bearing the keys of the town
and castle, bare-headed and footed, with halters round their
necks. Le Bel states—and Froissart embroiders the picture—that
the king would have had them executed but for the inter-
cession of Queen Philippa, and the chroniclers assert that he
was influenced by his hatred of the townspeople. It may be so,
and modern historians seem to be satisfied with this explanation; but it is hard to see what good purpose could be served by
thus gratuitously antagonizing the people who were about to
become his subjects. Edward was a purposeful monarch, he
was farseeing, astute, even crafty, and all his actions, so far as
we can see, were directed to a single end—his establishment as
the predominant power in France. He was not cruel by nature,
and he later treated de Vienne graciously,[1] while a prisoner in
England. Ramsay is probably right in describing the scene of
the surrender as "a solemn pageant". Edward wished to impress
not only the inhabitants of Calais but all other towns with a
sense of his own power and of the terrible fate that, but for his
royal clemency, would overtake any town that refused, as
Calais had done, his summons to surrender.

Immediately after the surrender the king had food sent into
the town for the relief of the starving population, after which
he had everyone ejected whose adhesion to their new sovereign
liege was in doubt. Calais, henceforth, was to be an English
town and the king could not afford to allow inside it large
numbers whose loyalty might be suspect; moreover he required
space within its walls for the English settlers whom he designed
to plant therein. Shortly afterwards a truce was made, to last
till June 24 of the following year. The defences having been set
in order and the administration settled to his liking, a task
that occupied him for another two months, King Edward set
sail on October 12 for the home that he had not seen for 15
months.

[1] A French historian goes so far as to assert that the king "overwhelmed him
with gifts". Professor Tout agrees that "the defenders were treated chivalrously
by the victor, who admired their courage and endurance".

NEVILLE'S CROSS

Reference was made above to the invasion of England by the Scottish king. This invasion does not strictly belong to the Hundred Years War, but strategically it affected the war, for Scotland was the ally of France, and King David, in invading England, was acceding to the request of Philip of Valois to make a diversion in his favour. A brief account of it must therefore be given. Early in October, 1346, David II crossed the Cumberland border at the head of a large army, and advanced toward Durham, laying waste many places as he passed, and burning the famous abbey of Lanercost. He expected an easy progress south, as the English army was far away oversea. But Edward, who never quite trusted his northern neighbour, had with careful foresight prepared for this very contingency before leaving the country. In recruiting his army for the invasion of France he had deliberately excluded all the country north of the Humber. Usually the task of defending the border against a Scottish incursion was the responsibility of the Prince Bishop of Durham, but the soldier bishop Hatfield was, as we have seen, fighting lustily with his king in France; his task therefore devolved on the archbishop of York, who speedily collected an army, and with it confronted the Scots at Neville's Cross, just outside the walls of Durham. On October 17, 1346, the Scots attacked and were decisively defeated, and King David was taken prisoner and lodged in the Tower of London, shortly to be the companion in adversity of Charles de Blois. Few tears need be shed over his fate. As Professor Tout observes: "In thus playing the game of the French, King David began a policy which from Neville's Cross to Flodden, brought embarrassment to England and desolation to Scotland. It was the inevitable penalty of two independent and hostile states existing on one little island."

The "desolation" was not long in coming. As punishment, the English king resolved on the subjugation of the northern kingdom, which he felt powerful enough to achieve, in spite of the fact that 30,000 English soldiers were campaigning in northern France, with further armies in Brittany and Gascony. His calculation, however, appeared to be justified; he had Edward Baliol brought forward as king, raised two armies and sent them across the border in the spring of 1347, while he and his own army were still sitting before the walls of Calais. Earl Percy led one army across the eastern border, the other, under Baliol, marching by the western route. They speedily overran Lothian but Percy, for some reason, did not attempt to take Edinburgh. Instead he swung to his left, probably by previous arrangement with Baliol, and joined forces with the other army, which had been ravaging the Galloway country. All southern Scotland now acknowledged Baliol as king. His rule was to prove of short duration, but the important point as regards the war with France was that danger of Scottish aggression had definitely passed away, and Edward could draw freely on the whole of England in his efforts to maintain the strength of the army before Calais. To such good purpose did he do this that his army eventually topped 30,000 in number.

ANNUS MIRABILIS

A truce having been signed with France, a survey of the English achievements up to date will be appropriate. The English king was received with acclamation when he returned after a long absence to his capital, as well he might be. In spite of the heavy taxation and the calls on manpower needed to sustain the war in so many spheres, the country had prospered materially, but—more important—it had been welded and stimulated by the long series of victories achieved wherever King Edward's armies had fought. The year 1346-7 may well be called *Annus Mirabilis*, the year of victories. The Tower of London was bulging with royal and noble prisoners from Gascony, from Brittany, from Ponthieu and from Scotland.

There were almost simultaneous victories in four different and widely separate theatres, for if we regard the earl of Derby's victory of Auberoche in June, 1345, as a "curtain-raiser", we get four victories in four different campaigns in the space of five months in 1346: Aiguillon, Dagworth's victory of St. Pol de Léon, Crecy and Neville's Cross, while 1347 witnessed the victory of Roche-Derrien and the capture of Calais. To all this can be added the conquest of Poitou by Henry of Lancaster. Wherever men looked, there the soldiers of Edward III were victorious. In an astonishingly short space of time English soldiers had established a world-reputation, and had come to be looked upon everywhere as invincible. Little wonder is it that the inhabitants of Calais soon transferred their allegiance from a Valois to a Plantagenet, led by the man whom, only two months previously, Edward was credited with the intention of hanging—Eustache du Pont St. Pierre.[1]

How are we to explain these remarkable and sustained successes? The reasons may be comprised under two headings—strategical and tactical. Taking the latter first, it has come to be recognized that Edward's tactical methods were derived from his grandfather. Edward I had realized the advantage to be gained from the cooperation of archers and men-at-arms, between cavalry and infantry. The younger Edward carried this principle a step further and at Dupplin Moor his *protégé* Baliol, and at Halidon Hill Edward in person, employed dismounted men-at-arms and archers in skilful combination. The lesson was well learned by Edward's lieutenants, and Northampton at Morlaix and Derby at Auberoche employed the two arms in close cooperation. Crecy only put the seal on what had become an established practice. Needless to say, no method of tactics will avail unless the tool to be employed is sound and sharp. This was so. The English men-at-arms were the pick of the country, and the English archers had graduated by long training and practice at their craft.[2] The unanimity with which the French chroniclers emphasize the

---

[1] This action of the French hero of the siege has led some people to doubt the historical accuracy of the story of the halters.

[2] On many a sandstone village church the grooves are still be be seen where the archers sharpened their arrows after mass, preparatory to undertaking their weekly butt-practice.

skill and prowess of the English archers is significant of the deadly impression–literal and figurative–they had made upon their opponents. So, tactically, Edward had forged a sound and sharp weapon and employed it effectively.

Strategically the English king is assessed very low by most historians. It is said that his only idea in the realm of strategy was to embark upon aimless and purposeless raids. But Edward was the most purposeful of monarchs. Of that we have seen ample evidence. The siege of Calais was *par excellence* a strategical project, and the most outstanding feature of that famous siege is the tenacity of purpose exhibited by the English king: like a snake that has its fangs embedded in its victim, he never let go, jeopardizing everything for the attainment of his objective. And what a tremendous objective that was! A permanent base on French soil at the point where the Channel was at its narrowest fulfilled the triple function of facilitating a subsequent invasion of France, an increased control of home waters and a commercial pipeline, as it were, to the Continent. It was as useful as a Channel tunnel would be in modern days.

If anything is open to criticism in Edward's conduct of the siege it is the inadequacy of his measures to close the port until late in the day. As to this, it is a fact that such blockading was not as simple in the days of sail as in these of steam; the failure of the Spaniards, during the three-year siege of Ostend, to block the harbour, is a good example of this. Yet the fact remains that Edward did eventually find means to effect a total blockade, and there seems no reason why he should not have found them several months earlier.

But that is not the end of the matter. In another sphere his strategy was brilliantly successful, namely his conception of a concentric attack on France by means of exterior lines, possible to an island power that has command of the sea. It was largely as a result of this far-flung strategy that neither of the two great French armies was enabled to achieve anything. The army of John duke of Normandy had as its mission the expulsion of the English once and for all from Gascony. The

duke had merely to march straight forward in order to drive
the tiny English army into the sea, but instead he allowed
himself to become involved in the siege of a petty town, and
then he marched north, too soon to win Aiguillon and too late
to prevent Crecy. Such transferences of armies when operating
on interior lines are common, and Edward's operation on
exterior lines thus produced a rich dividend.

The contrast between the strategical prowess of Edward
of England and Philip of France was glaring. The latter,
throughout his campaigns, exhibited no coherent, continuous
military strategy or design; he wavered, fumbled and faltered,
and may well go down to history as Philip the Fumbler.

APPENDIX

THE TERRAIN

No historian, as far as I can discover, has attempted to pin-
point the exact site of the English camp before Calais. It is
described vaguely as "to the west of the town". Now, the
country directly to the west of the town was all marshy,[1] to
such an extent that the English could not find firm platforms
for their siege ballistas. Are we to believe that the English
army sat down for almost a year in this marsh? The nearest
approach to an exact description of the site is contained in an
anonymous work entitled *Le Siége de Calais* published in 1739,
which states that the English camp was between the river
Hem, the sea and the town.

The oldest printed map that I can discover dates from 1555,
and this shows the course of the river Hem as I have described
it above.[2] A still earlier map of 1547 in the MS room of the
British Museum unfortunately does not clearly show the course
of the river. If it then flowed, as indicated above, into the town
haven, the English camp must have been situated on the marsh.
But, in view of the fact that there was a strip of firm ground

[1] It is now built over, and excavations would not be likely to uncover any remains
of "Nouville".
[2] In the map-room at the British Museum.

to the north between the marsh and the sea, it is contrary to
inherent military probability that the English camp was sited
anywhere else. It was the obvious place. It is however possible
that the river Hem did not at the time of the siege flow into the
town haven; there is a dip in the line of dunes immediately
to the north of Neuillay, still covered with water channels,
which may have been the old channel of the river Hem. If
this was so, the statement that the English camp was between
the river, town and sea becomes clear and plausible. Strength
is given to this supposition by a phrase in King Edward's letter
to the archbishop of Canterbury in which he states that the
French king encamped "opposite the marsh". This implies
that the English army was not situated on the marsh, but on
firm ground beyond it. Since we know that the French camp
was on the Sangatte dunes, the only possible place for the
English camp must therefore be on the low spit of dunes
between the town and the sea, though it probably extended
as far south as the bridge of Nieullay on the west side of the
town. This is where I have placed it in my narrative.

THE SOURCES

The sources are naturally much the same as for the preceding
chapter. Edward III's chaplains desert us, and Knighton
becomes our chief authority. Rymer's collection of *Foedera*
assumes increasing importance, showing the steps taken by
the king to sustain the siege.

On the French side there is practically nothing of importance
—if we perhaps except the *Continuation of Guillaume de Nangis*—
but the *Bourgeois de Valenciennes* again comes to our help, as does
Gilles li Muisis for the part played by the Flemings, though
here we could wish for fuller and more precise information
regarding the cooperation between the English and Flemish
armies, which appears to have been closer and more important
than historians have given credit for.

There is no extant account of the siege by a participant or
even by an eye-witness of any nationality.

CHAPTER IX

BETWEEN CRECY AND POITIERS

THE truce of 1347 and the Black Death (bubonic plague) that followed it in 1348 might have been expected to bring the fighting to an end, and it certainly languished during those years, but it is far from the truth to maintain, as has been done, that there was little fighting and that of no particular interest between the battles of Crecy and Poitiers. On the contrary there was much fighting, and there were operations of considerable interest to military historians. Indeed, apart from the fact that the two kings did not lead armies in person against each other, the truce was a truce in name only. Moreover, the Black Death had a direct influence on the war. It was, curiously enough, more severe in England than on the Continent; indeed nearly half the population is said to have perished during those dreadful years (though this is probably an exaggeration.) This enhanced the already enormous preponderance of potential French over English soldiers, and made reinforcement of the many English garrisons in France ever more difficult. Recruits were drawn from all quarters, from Ireland, from Brittany, from Gascony even, from Flanders, from Italy, and from "Germany". But not from Scotland. England and Scotland–both sprung in the main from the same Anglian stock–remained the bitterest of enemies.

Though the Black Death ravaged the common people more than the upper classes, it carried off the king's youngest daughter, and also the queen of the French king. Philip of Valois married a young girl of 18 exactly one month after the death of his first wife, but did not live many months to enjoy his new spouse: he died on August 22, 1350, and was succeeded by his eldest son as John II, or John the Good.[1]

[1] The appellation "The Good" refers not to his moral qualities, but to his fame for being a "good fellow well met".

Almost constant warfare of one kind or another went on in Picardy, in Brittany, and in Gascony. In the latter duchy the English were steadily enlarging their conquests, and in the summer of 1349 the tireless duke of Lancaster (as Henry of Lancaster was now to become) carried a whirlwind "push", as we should call it, to the gates of Toulouse. Failing to induce the French to meet him in the field he fell back, ravaging the country as he went. In this operation he captured more than 40 towns and villages (many of which were subsequently retaken by the French).

In the same summer a notable battle took place in Poitou at a place called Lunalonge.[1] The allies, English and Gascons, were commanded by the Captal de Buch–shortly to become famous–and the French commander was Jean de Lisle. The allies, as usual, dismounted for the battle, parking their horses in rear. Jean de Lisle, thinking to take advantage of this separation of the English from their horses, sent a mounted party round the rear of the line to capture the horses, which they were completely successful in doing. They then attacked the English line mounted, from the front, with the remainder of their force, but met with the same fate as their predecessors at Crecy, their commander being captured. As Professor Tout observes, "the real interest of the battle lies in the effort of the French to seek out the weak points of the new English system". In this they were indirectly successful, for the English, though victorious, feeling lost and insecure without their horses, fell back on their base during the following night.

Meanwhile spasmodic fighting around Calais was incessant; the French were looking for an opportunity and a means to regain what a French historian has aptly called "the Gibraltar of the North", while the English were forever attempting to enlarge their "pale", thereby increasing their security and providing a surer and wider source of supplies. The French efforts culminated in the next year in an elaborate plot or ruse to capture the place. An Italian named Amerigo, who had

---

[1] Identified as Limalonge (Deux Sevres) by Denifle.

been made governor of the Calais garrison, was bribed by
Geoffrey de Chargny, the French governor of St. Omer, to
open the gates to him. However, Amerigo, thinking better of
it, crossed in secret to England and informed the king. Edward
was delighted at the news: it would give him the opportunity
for an exciting adventure, wherein he might teach the Frenchman that it did not pay to work "underground" in an age of
chivalry. He instructed Amerigo to return, continue with the
plot, and on the appointed day admit to the castle the first
contingent of French troops. But the king was determined to
play an active part in the counter-plot himself: he faced the
unpleasant sea crossing[1] and he allowed his eldest boy to come
too, accompanied by the inevitable Walter Manny. They
crossed in disguise, and on arrival at Calais the king made
certain arrangements. . . .

On the last night of the year 1349 the postern gate was
opened, as arranged, and a party entered, the main body
remaining outside the main gate. Everything appeared to be
in order, no English soldiers being in evidence. But on a prearranged signal, a false wall in the courtyard that the king
had had constructed was thrown down and a party of English
soldiers rushed out and overpowered the Frenchmen. At the
same moment a watchman, posted on top of the tower over
the main gate, hurled a great stone down on to the already
weakened drawbridge and broke it. De Chargny and his main
body were thus prevented from entering in support of their
advanced party, and they could only look on helplessly. But
that was not the end. The king had prepared two assault
parties, one of which he himself led, dressed as a simple knight,
while the Prince of Wales led the other. Simultaneously they
sallied forth, the king by the east gate, the Prince by the west
gate, and attacked de Chargny from both sides at the same
moment. It seems to have been a beautifully prepared and
executed operation—none too easy in the dead of night. The
French were routed and Geoffrey de Chargny was captured.

[1] In nearly all his crossings of the Channel, Edward was caught in bad storms.

King Edward, on good evidence (by which I mean not merely on the "picturesque romancing" of Froissart), dashed into the thick of the fray and crossed swords with and captured Eustace de Ribaumont. That night the chivalrous element in the character of the English king was in evidence; de Chargny was now a prisoner, but, far from punishing him for his breach of the truce, Edward invited him and other prisoners to dinner and even loaded honours on his own captive, de Ribaumont, whom he afterward set at liberty.

BATTLE OF WINCHELSEA

The interest of 1350 lies mainly on the sea. It is typical of the uncertain and uncharted relations between countries of the fourteenth century that, while England and France were formally at war, the fleets of Spain and of Genoa should plan an informal but important part therein. The narrow strip of water separating England from France formed a veritable life-line to the English armies engaged overseas. If that lifeline were permanently severed, slow death to those armies would follow. None knew this better than King Edward, and he exerted himself to build up a powerful fleet. But the seas are wide and, as we have seen at Calais, ships cannot be everywhere at the same time. Castilian and Genoese galleys traded on this well-known fact and openly waged war on English shipping in the Channel. They went further and talked of actually invading the country. No doubt it was an idle threat, but their activities jeopardized the English forces in Brittany and even in Calais. Eventually King Edward decided that this nonsense must be stopped. Hearing that a great Castilian fleet was making up Channel for the ports of Flanders he planned to intercept it on the return voyage. For this purpose he assembled a fleet at Sandwich and went there himself with the Black Prince and his second son, John of Gaunt, now a boy of ten years. The *élite* of the country joined him, William Bohun of Northampton, Henry of Lancaster and Walter Manny of course; others included Warwick, Arundel, Salisbury, Huntingdon, Sir

Reginald Cobham and young John Chandos. The Spanish fleet was commanded by Don Carlos de la Cerda, whose valiant brother we met in Brittany in 1342. The English fleet, 50 sail in all including small pinnaces, put to sea on August 28, the Spanish fleet being reported on its return voyage from Sluys. Though it numbered only 44 ships it was more powerful than the English fleet, for its great galleons towered over the smaller English vessels as did those of the Spanish Armada 200 years later. But in this respect only did the battle that ensued resemble that of the Armada. In the latter the two fleets engaged in a running fight, thanks to their guns, but in 1350 if either side possessed guns they were too weak for this purpose and the only method of engaging was to turn it into a land fight by grappling the hostile ships and boarding them. Therefore the men-at-arms donned their armour as soon as the enemy fleet was sighted.

King Edward hoisted his flag in the *Thomas*, and the ten-year-old John of Gaunt presumably accompanied his father. Prince Edward on the other hand sailed in his own ship; after all he was now in his 21st year, and may be considered a grown man. Both father and son were in high spirits, in spite of the fact that they were about to encounter a superior fleet. The young John Chandos, accompanied by a minstrel, sang before his master a war ballad. For there was a long wait in front of them. The wind was in the east, and the Spanish fleet was running before it. At 4 p.m. on August 29 the two fleets came in sight of one another. By this time the English fleet had dropped down-wind about 40 miles and was off Dungeness. Large ships could not beat against the wind in those days and we may picture the English as tacking backward and forward across the Channel at its narrowest point during those 24 hours. When the Spaniards drew near, the English admiral, Lord Morley, so manoeuvred his fleet that his ships were dead in front of the Spaniards, and a collision was inevitable.

If the English ships put their helms down and lay up into the wind the enemy would sail past them at too great a speed to grapple them; the only possible method was to put their helms up and run on a parallel course to their opponents, shortening sail the while in order to be overtaken, albeit only slowly. This required nice judgment and good seamanship. The skipper of the *Thomas* did not possess these qualities to the full, for he closed with the nearest Spanish ship as it passed at too great speed or at too sharp an angle; there was a mighty thud, the *Thomas* shivered and rebounded from the heavier and stronger-built Spaniard, and sprang a bad leak. According to one account the ship was even dismasted. This seems unlikely, for the ship was still navigable and the skipper was successful at his second attempt: a big Spaniard was grappled and after its stone-throwing crew had been silenced by the archers, a detachment of men-at-arms, with scaling ladders, swarmed up the sides of the loftier ship and fought on deck a similar land battle to that they had fought just a decade previously at Sluys. The other ships in the royal navy followed suit and soon the scene of Sluys was being repeated in the English Channel—and with similar results. By sheer force of arms, and superior skill, though the odds were against them, the highly trained English men-at-arms under their renowned captains brought off a rather astonishing victory. Ship after ship of the proud dons succumbed in turn, till no less than 17 had struck their colours and the remainder were in full flight down the Channel, with every stitch of canvas unfurled. After capturing his opposing vessel, King Edward transferred his own flag to her, as the *Thomas* was now in a sinking condition. Meanwhile the Prince of Wales was in a parlous situation. His ship, too, was badly holed and about to sink, but he had not been successful in boarding his opponent. Fortunately Henry of Lancaster was disengaged at the moment and managed to sail his ship up to the Spaniard on the other side and board her. The enemy was overpowered and the prince transferred to her in the nick of time.

While the fight was in progress, both fleets of course continued to sail before the wind and so passed within sight of

Winchelsea. Great was the excitement in that little harbour, and the cliffs were black with the multitudes, cheering wildly as each Spanish ship in turn was captured. Winchelsea had suffered sorely in the past from sea rovers and now its reward had come, and the great battle has rightly gone down to history as the sea battle of Winchelsea.

The Channel was cleared of its Spanish pests and safe communication with the armies in Gascony and Brittany was restored.

BRITTANY

The scene now shifts to Brittany, where a new King's Lieutenant, or viceroy, had been installed. The gallant Sir Thomas Dagworth had been killed in an ambush near Auray by a Breton named Raoul de Cahours, who had been made viceroy of Poitou, but had quarrelled violently with Dagworth and at the same time was bribed by the French king to desert the English cause. Edward was about to relieve him of his command when his murder of Dagworth took place. Dagworth was succeeded by Sir William Bentley, another remarkable English captain, about whom it is time to say a few words.

Sir William Bentley was now 47 years of age. He had previously served in the wars in Flanders. Coming out to Brittany in 1342 he was placed in charge of the garrison of Ploermel, 26 miles north of Vannes. From this place he had made a lightning march and attack on the besiegers of Annesin, which marked him out for high command. This exploit won him, it is said, the admiration of his enemies. A man of forceful character, he had twice earned the displeasure of his sovereign by openly opposing him. But Edward had an unerring eye for character and military talent and Bentley was restored to favour. Thus, when Dagworth was killed, Bentley was his obvious successor.

Though we are not concerned with his civil government of Brittany, it should be explained that the English king was, in the absence of an adult member of the house of Montfort, directing and controlling the affairs of the duchy more and more. Whether he intended to retain his hold over it when the young John Montfort came of age it is impossible to say, but this English control naturally antagonized the Breton nobles, who were, as has been pointed out before, mainly of the Bloisian faction. Moreover, Edward confiscated the lands of these nobles and granted them to his English captains. This may not have troubled the common people, but the king's policy was "to make the war pay for itself" and this policy naturally led to exactions which rendered the English rule still more unpopular. It may well be that the French would have acted in the same manner, but this was not an argument that would carry much weight with those who suffered the exactions necessary to pay for the war.

All this may explain the Battle of the Thirty, which has been rendered famous by a Breton ballad. It has in itself no intrinsic importance, but is interesting as throwing a light on military manners during the age of chivalry, so it is worthy of relation. It took the form of a mounted mêlée between 30 Breton knights of the French faction and 30 nominally English knights. (Actually there were only 20 Englishmen, the balance being Bretons and Germans.) Accounts differ about the cause; French writers assert that it was due to exasperation caused by the exactions of Bentley; English writers give as the cause the anger induced by the murder of Dagworth. The French account is probably the correct one, for the "battle" which occurred on March 27, 1351, was fought over six months after the death of Dagworth. Whatever the real cause, the engagement took place midway between Ploermel and Josselin seven miles to the west. Two of the English knights were afterward to become famous, Hugh Calveley and Robert Knollys, both Cheshire gentlemen. The fight resolved itself into a series of duels, which lasted an astonishingly long time, with a break for refreshments in the middle. Eventually nine on the English side were killed and the victory rested with the Franco-Bretons.

THE BATTLE OF SAINTES

Eleven days after the Battle of the Thirty a battle of a more orthodox character was fought. In the spring of 1351 the new king of France decided to make an effort to recover the province of Poitou and started making preparations. By some means, news of this intention reached the English king and he immediately took what counter-measures he could. Since the departure of Henry of Lancaster from Gascony there was no outstanding English captain of proved ability in Bordeaux. Someone must be sent there at once and Edward's choice fell upon Sir John Beauchamp, brother of the earl of Warwick and governor of Calais. As always, the king made a sound choice. Beauchamp hurried out to Bordeaux, and so slow were the preparations of King John that the English John arrived at Bordeaux in time to take steps to confront the impending invasion. But he was only just in time. From the moment of his arrival, messengers came one after another hot-foot from the north, imploring help against the invading French army. These invaders were under the command of two marshals of France, Guy de Nesle (Sire d'Offremont) and Arnaud d'Endreghem. Advancing slowly, the French drove back the slender English garrisons and laid siege to St. Jean d'Angelys. Sir John Beauchamp advanced north to meet them and in early April reached the province of Saintonge and entered the town of Taillebourg, between St. Jean d'Angelys and Saintes. According to one source a force under Sir William Bentley had joined the English army near the coast, and had advanced to Taillebourg, but this seems unlikely; Robert of Avesbury would scarcely have omitted to mention it had it been the fact.

The French were besieging Saintes at the time, and when the two armies approached one another near St. Georges-la-Valade, the English dismounted, as was their custom, and formed line of battle, leaving their horses in the rear. The French, on seeing this, did likewise, but retained two mounted bodies, one on each wing. Beauchamp had sent for reinforcements from Taillebourg and Fontnay-sur-Charente, and so slow was de Nesle in forming up his army that they arrived in time for the battle. The French then attacked on foot and, though details are lacking, it is clear that they suffered a bloody and decisive defeat, 600 Frenchmen being killed or taken, the remainder fleeing to Saintes. Among the prisoners were the two French marshals and 140 esquires and gentlemen. Guy de Nesle was promptly ransomed for a large sum by King John and was soon in arms again against the English.

The numbers engaged were not large and the results of the battle were not great, but it is of interest as showing the growing custom of the French to counter the English dismounted array on foot.

THE CALAIS PALE

The interest shifts north again. In May, 1351, the ubiquitous and high-spirited Henry of Lancaster, newly created duke (the second of that rank to be created in the English peerage, the first being the Prince of Wales), landed at Calais on his way to join a crusade in Prussia. As Ramsay expresses it, "Having set foot in France he felt bound to do something". This "something" consisted in nothing less than an attempt to take the strongly fortified town of Boulogne. He succeeded in capturing the lower town, alongside the river and haven, but his attempt on the upper town failed because his scaling ladders were too short. He therefore contented himself with a great raid right up to St. Omer, and then passed on eastward to his crusade.[1]

On June 6 following, Sir John Beauchamp, who had with great promptitude returned to Calais, met a French army under the count de Beaujeu at Ardres, midway between St. Omer and Calais, in a pitched battle. Once again the French followed the English procedure of fighting on foot, and on this occasion were successful, and Beauchamp himself was captured. Unfortunately details of the battle are lacking.

Throughout this period the English were gradually extending and strengthening their hold on the Calais pale. A notable

[1] On arrival in Prussia he was arrested, but eventually set free.

example of this was the capture of Guines, eight miles south of Calais, which occurred in the following January or February (1352).

BRITTANY

The same year was marked by important events in Brittany. Shortly after the battle of Saintes, Sir William Bentley returned to Brittany (if indeed he had ever left it), recaptured the enormously strong castle of Fougeres, which had been seized by a young Breton named Bertrand du Guesclin, and installed as its captain Sir Robert Knollys. But signs of an approaching campaign of reconquest on the part of the new king of France were not lacking, and Bentley hurried home to implore reinforcements from the king. Edward would willingly have provided them were that possible, but the country was still suffering from the effects of the Black Death, and the number of possible recruits to the army had been almost halved. Bentley had therefore to return early in 1352 disappointed, bringing with him a mere handful of men-at-arms and archers of doubtful quality.

Meanwhile the threatened French offensive had begun to take shape, and Fougeres had been invested. Knollys was in sore straights, and Bentley dashed to his rescue. In this he was entirely successful: he drove off the besiegers and levelled the "bastides" or towers that they had constructed round the castle. A few months were still available in which to organize and strengthen the scattered defences of Brittany and Sir William Bentley took full advantage of this breathing space.

Meanwhile King John also was busy. He collected recruits from places far and wide. By August all was ready, and Guy de Nesle, in spite of his defeat and capture the previous year, was again placed in command, with the high-sounding but empty title of "Governor-General of Brittany".

Several of the barons and knights of Brittany served under him, and it is probable (though it cannot be proved) that the young Bertrand du Guesclin was also present with the army.

Early in August, then, Marshal de Nesle led his army over the French border, and directed his march on Rennes, his ultimate objective being Brest. Thus his plan of campaign was exactly the opposite of that pursued by King Edward just ten years before. Leaving Fougeres wide on his right hand, de Nesle pushed straight on and apparently had no difficulty in gaining possession of Rennes. Bentley was wisely husbanding his resources, well knowing that if you try to defend everywhere you are weak everywhere and likely to be defeated in detail. He therefore concentrated his whole available field army in the vicinity of Ploermel, the defences of which he had just strengthened. Ploermel is 36 miles west by south of Rennes and the direct road to Brest runs several miles further north. If, therefore, Bentley remained at Ploermel after news of the French capture of Rennes reached him, he might find his position turned by his northern flank, and his army might thus be cut off from Brest. Two possible courses were open to him. He could either fall back towards Brest or he could advance northward toward the Brest road in order to cut off his enemy and offer him battle. He decided on this latter course, though he must have been aware that he would be heavily outnumbered.

On August 14 the little Anglo-Breton army set out. Most of its senior officers were Bretons, but Sir William Bentley had as his right-hand man Robert Knollys. The route took the army through the small town of Mauron, 12 miles north of Ploermel, the Brest road being a further ten miles on. But either Bentley had miscalculated the time required (which seems unlikely) or the French had left Rennes earlier than reported, for they had already passed through Montfort, 12 miles north-east of Mauron, and had only to march straight on in order to by-pass or get behind the English army. But such was not de Nesle's intention; he desired an encounter and on hearing that the English army was on his left hand he turned south, leaving the Brest road, and marched straight on Mauron. Thus it happened that about noon on August 14 both armies were approaching

Mauron from opposite directions. An encounter seemed inevitable.

THE BATTLE OF MAURON—AUGUST 14, 1352

The little town of Mauron is pleasantly situated on a low ridge about 150 ft. above the valley which sweeps round its foot to the east and south. This valley contains a tiny stream, the head waters of the river Ivel. A spur runs forward from the town to meet this rivulet 1,200 yards to the east, the highest point on this spur being 300 yards short of the rivulet. On the far side of the rivulet the ground slopes up very gently except to the north-east where it is for a short distance very steep.

A narrow belt of trees ran across the top of this spur. The country around was open, devoid of hedges, ditches or woods. Two roads now approach this ridge from the Rennes direction. On the right hand one there was till the last century a château named Brembili; it is now replaced by a warehouse on the side of the railway which runs along the foot of the ridge, between it and the rivulet. At the time of the battle the herbage was at its strongest and most luxuriant. From the top of the spur on the outskirts of the town a distant view can be obtained towards the east and north-east.

We may picture Sir William Bentley riding forward to the top of the spur on hearing that dust columns were rising in the distance to the north-east. From here he would verify the fact for himself. It could only mean one thing—the French army was approaching. Though it was greatly superior to his own in number, Bentley had already resolved to accept battle, and to accept it in what had now become the traditional English manner, that is, dismounted and in a defensive position. Such a position was not difficult to find, for the English commander must have been standing upon it at the time. It was not ideal— no position ever is ideal—but it had certain points in its favour. Though the approach was easy for the enemy (for the tiny rivulet offered no appreciable obstacle), it was on commanding ground and the long rank undergrowth immediately in its front would slow up the French advance, that is, if they dismounted for the purpose, as they were becoming accustomed

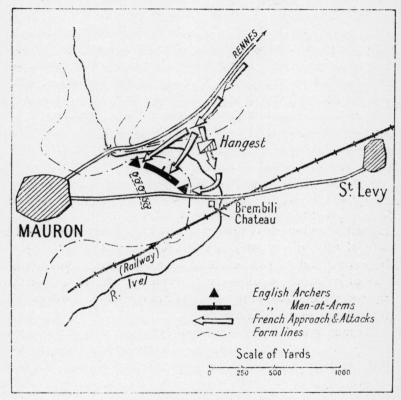

II. BATTLE OF MAURON

to do. Its weak feature was that it was over-extensive for his slender force, about 3,000 all told. For such a force a frontage of over 500 yards was on the large side. But this position required a frontage of over 600 yards, and because of the shape of the ground it must either be very curved, with flanks drawn back, or the centre of the position must be much higher than the flanks. But it was possible to compromise, and this is probably what Bentley did; he placed his centre midway between the belt of trees and the rivulet, while his right rested on the château Brembili and his left on the valley bottom at the main Rennes road, making a total frontage of nearly 700 yards. (See sketch map.)

As the French host drew near it became obvious to both sides that they vastly outnumbered the defenders, though exactly by how much it is impossible to say. Guy de Nesle deployed his army in full view of the English position on the opposite side of the little valley. He then sent forward a herald courteously offering his old antagonist the opportunity to withdraw unmolested if he would undertake to quit the country. This the proud Bentley scornfully declined; and a pitched battle became unavoidable.

The English position was as indicated above. With only about four men per yard it was impossible to form a reserve. As was to be the case at Agincourt, every man had to be placed in the front line. The formation followed that so successfully employed in all the great battles of the war, that is, men-at-arms in the centre and archers on the flanks—probably in the form of bastions or "herces" as at Crecy. In the centre the line would follow the crest nearly 200 yards in front of the belt of trees. Whether or not the flanks were refused (as I think they were), the archers, because of the conformation of the ground, could not cover with their fire the whole front of the position. This was a faulty disposition under the circumstances, as we shall presently see.

THE ATTACK

It was a hot summer day, and during the pause while the parleys were proceeding the English soldiers could hear the hum of innumerable bees sucking honey in the flowering herbage to their front.

As the afternoon wore on, Guy de Nesle formed up his army in battle array. Somewhat surprisingly, considering his recent defeat, he formed his army in the same fashion, that is, all dismounted except a small body of horse. The only difference was that in place of two such bodies, one on each flank, he confined them to a single body of 700 men under the count Hangest, with orders to operate on the left flank. The nature of the ground on the other flank will explain this limitation for, as stated above, the slope here was very steep – in places almost precipitous for a few yards – and would handicap the heavily armoured men and horses.

It was the hour of vespers, about 4 p.m., before all was ready and the French advanced to the attack. The assault was delivered practically simultaneously all along the line. Hangest's cavalry, being on the flank, naturally came into contact with the right wing archers. The slope at this point is about the same as that at Crecy, but the upshot was quite different: the English archers gave way, and several of them – 30 at least – fled to the rear. The consequence was that the men-at-arms on their left could receive little or no covering fire from the archers, even if the ground allowed it; their own right flank became uncovered and they fell back up the slope till they reached the belt of trees on the summit. This double setback boded ill for the English, but two things helped them. The archers on the left, having steeper ground to their front and no mounted attack to face, stood their ground and exacted such a heavy toll of their opponents that the French men-at-arms broke and fled down the hill. This in turn threatened the right flank of their advancing centre column. The second aid to the English was the belt of trees, which constituted a natural "anchor" for the men-at-arms who formed a firm line along its front edge. The same belt of trees handicapped the French horsemen, checking them in their pursuit of the fleeing archers, and brought them to a partial halt. But it was an anxious moment for the little English army and its commander, who was "horribly wounded" according to le Baker.

But he cried "Fight on! Fight on!" and the archers on the left, with that rare initiative and offensive spirit that was the hall-mark of the English archers throughout the Hundred

Years War, charged down the hill after their opponents, thus
still more exposing the right flank of the centre column of the
French army. Encouraged by the sight of this, the English
men-at-arms advanced once more, gradually pushing the
enemy down the slope. Into the valley bottom the French
knights were rolled and as they struggled across the valley they
were caught by the archers, to whom they presented an easy
target. Worse still befell the right wing of the French, for after
re-crossing the valley they encountered the steepest part of
the opposite slope referred to above. Here, loaded down by
their armour, exhausted by their flight in the heat of the
sun, they became practically immobile and were shot down
mercilessly.

Soon the French army had dissolved in flight, Hangest's
men alone preserving any order. The main body was leaderless, and it became a case of *Sauve qui peut*, for their commander,
Guy de Nesle, was dead on the field, and most of his senior
captains were dead or captured. Very few of the leaders can
have escaped, and Bentley, in his official dispatch, rolls off an
impressive list of knights and nobles. The dead included Raoul
de Cahours, the ambusher of Sir Thomas Dagworth.

The victory was complete and crushing. The French army
had ceased to exist as completely as that of Philip VI at Crecy;
2,000 dead, it is said, being left on the battlefield and the
remainder scattered to the four winds. No fewer than 89 of the
knights of King John's newly formed Order of the Star had
fallen, and this Order, intended as a rival to the Order of the
Garter, came to an early and inglorious end. The victory made
a painful impression in France, and its results were important.
For the next 12 years the French abandoned all attempts to
interfere in the English rule of Brittany. Yet the battle has
been allowed to fall into semi-oblivion. The French historian
of Brittany, A. de la Borderie, is candid enough to admit this.
"Our historians have in general ignored the importance of this
day; none of them say much about it although adequate
sources for the battle are not lacking."

COMMENTS ON THE BATTLE

Apart from the important results of the battle of Mauron, it is a significant link in the contest between the English archer and the French man-at-arms – a conspicuous and continuous feature of the Hundred Years War. At first sight the defeat of the English archers on the right flank may puzzle some people and induce them to question whether the predominance of the archer that has been claimed for him is altogether justified. To this there are several replies. The first is of a general nature. Nothing is certain in war: there are no fixed rules by which one might calculate in advance the outcome of any engagement, for even though one has accurate information as to the material forces on each side there are two intangible, invisible and incommensurable factors: there is what the Baron de Jomini has named *friction de guerre*, or more simply the element of luck; and there is the morale factor, which, since it is not outwardly visible, can only be guessed at. Hence a single apparent contradiction of what may appear to be the general rule may prove nothing. In this particular case the morale of the English archers probably was not as high as the archers of Crecy. Bentley had scraped together his army from all quarters, they were far from being picked men, as were the Crecy archers, indeed the Black Death may have physically weakened a number of them. On the other hand, Hangest's horsemen may have been the *élite* of the French army; we have no information on the point. But putting aside these unknown factors, the terrain and the tactics employed by Hangest may alone have been responsible for the result. Why did de Nesle employ only *one* body of mounted men whereas at Saintes he had used two? The formation of the ground is, as I have hinted, one answer. On his right it was no place for mounted action, the slopes on both sides of the valley being much too steep. But his experienced eye may have indicated the possibility of an enveloping, flanking movement against the right flank of the English archers. Such enveloping movements, though the exception, were by no means unknown in medieval warfare:

indeed we shall see a conspicuous example of its employment in only four years' time. The slope of the spur on which the English were posted was at its gentlest in the neighbourhood of Brembili château. If Hangest took the route indicated on my sketch map he would have fairly favourable ground for mounted action once he had crossed the rivulet; further, by approaching the archers from the flank the French would render about half the archers incapable of engaging them with fire, for they would not only be facing the other way but would be screened from view of them by their own comrades (always assuming that the Crecy "herce" formation was adopted). Looking at the problem on the ground such a manoeuvre seems the obvious thing and quite sufficient to explain the setback to the archers without invoking inferior quality in these particular archers. It is true that on the day after the battle the stern Bentley had 30 archers executed for running away. Thirty, however, is not a large proportion of the whole, and as Bentley was himself horribly wounded he was not in a good position to appraise calmly and accurately the behaviour of these men. Be this as it may, when we turn to the opposite flank we see the lesson and experience of Crecy being repeated most emphatically. Here the archers had things all their own way, in spite of the rearward movement of the men-at-arms on their immediate right. I think it may also help to explain the sudden reversal of fortune in the centre of the line if we suppose that a portion of the victorious archers, instead of pursuing their own opponents straight down the hill, swung to their right and attacked the hostile centre in flank – a winning manoeuvre, as Henry's archers showed at Agincourt and Cromwell's troopers showed at Naseby.

Properly viewed, therefore, Mauron is an interesting link between Crecy and Poitiers. It confirmed the predominance of the archers in a frontal fight and passed on to Poitiers the idea of an enveloping mounted attack. So the battle of Mauron can claim importance both historically and technically, and it is strange that it has been ignored by historians and soldiers alike.

EPILOGUE

Sir William Bentley was not the least notable in a notable line of English soldier-statesmen whom the war in Brittany threw up. He was soon to show a third example of his courage in opposing his own sovereign. Charles de Blois had been all this time an inmate of the over-populated Tower of London. For the sake of an enormous ransom King Edward now was prepared to grant him his liberty on very lenient terms. Under certain stipulations he was to be recognized as duke of Brittany and certain strongholds were to be given up to him. On receipt of this intelligence Sir William Bentley reacted so strongly that he returned home in order to expostulate in person with the king. On arrival he was clapped into the Tower and kept there for nearly two years. This was a rather rough-and-ready method of justice on the part of the king, but as Bentley met as Constable of the Tower his old comrade-in-arms and brother-in-law, Sir John Beauchamp, his sojourn was no doubt rendered as little irksome as possible. The proposed treaty with Charles de Blois eventually fell through, and de Blois, who had returned to Brittany on parole, surrendered himself once more; such was the binding power of chivalry in those days. King Edward at length realized his mistake, and Bentley was restored to favour. He returned to Brittany where the king granted him numerous possessions, including the tactful gift of Ploermel Castle. Bentley now took part in affairs of state; but he had never fully recovered from his desperate wounds and in the summer of 1359 he died. Within a few months two other great viceroys of Brittany also passed away – William Bohun earl of Northampton, and Thomas Holland earl of Kent. Brittany "bred a breed of mighty men".

APPENDIX

THE SOURCES FOR MAURON

There is little change in the sources for the foregoing chapter, but a word must be said about those concerned with the battle of Mauron. There are really only three sources for the battle, but they are all good ones and it is a relief not to have to go to Froissart for battle details. These sources were for a long time considered to be confined to the letter from Sir William Bentley to the Chancellor (printed in Avesbury) and le Baker's account. The latter relies on Bentley for the early portion of the battle, but adds some later details. But all the while there was a good account of the battle available in the *Chronique Normande du XIVe Siècle*, edited by Auguste Molinier in 1882. M. Molinier, one of the most eminent bibliographers then living, held it in high esteem where military information is concerned, and there is no reason to doubt the inherent accuracy of the Chronicle's account of the battle. To Professor Tout must go the credit for rescuing and applying this long forgotten account and for drawing the battle out of the oblivion into which it had sunk. This he did in an article in the *English Historical Review* for October, 1897. This was followed next year by A. de la Borderie's *Histoire de Bretagne*. But the fullest examination of the battle appeared in a curious book published anonymously in 1917, of which apparently only 100 copies were produced. It is called *A brief note upon the battles of Saintes and Mauron* and appears from internal evidence to have been intended as a memoir of Sir William Bentley. It is useful for biographical details. The publisher's name is not given.

THE BATTLEFIELD

At first sight the evidence on which to fix the exact battle-field seems scanty. We know that the English were marching from Ploermel toward Mauron and the French from Rennes toward the same town; that the battle took place near Mauron, and (from the *Chronique Française*, quoted by Dom H. Morice in his *Preuves* . . .) that "the year 1352 was the battle of Mauron at the château of Brembili and the English won it". These facts do not appear to provide much to work upon, but if we place ourselves in the shoes of Sir William Bentley when he saw or heard the approach of the enemy, standing on the

Mauron spur, and if we apply the test of inherent military probability, it should be possible to pin-point the position with a reasonable degree of certainty. Indeed, if we accept the position suggested in the text above it seems to fit the description as a glove fits a hand. The position seems the natural, indeed the only, possible one; the whole course of events becomes comprehensible, especially the success of the French horse on the southern flank and of the English archers on the northern flank. Though the château of Brembili has long since disappeared (probably during the construction of the railway) its situation is known, and that seems to confirm the supposition, made on the grounds of inherent military probability, that the English position was on the spur to the east of the town.

The only battlefield monument or memorial is that erected to three American soldiers who were killed there on August 3, 1944.

CHAPTER X

THE BLACK PRINCE'S "GRANDE CHEVAUCHÉE"[1]

FOR three years after the battle of Mauron the war (or rather "truce") languished in all theatres. Prolonged negotiation for permanent peace, conducted under the aegis of the new pope, Innocent VI, at his palace at Avignon, finally broke down early in 1355 and both countries prepared once more for open war.

The plan of campaign evolved by Edward III followed closely that of 1346, which had been attended with such success; that is, it comprised a triple attack on France, directed from the north-east, the north-west and the south-west. That from the south-west—Gascony—was to be under the command of the Prince of Wales, and it will be described presently; that from the north-east was to be under the king and was based on Calais; while that from the north-west was to be under Henry duke of Lancaster, and was to be carried out in Normandy.

The last-mentioned campaign need not detain us long. While Henry of Lancaster had been conducting the negotiations at Avignon he met Charles "The Bad", king of Navarre. This monarch had been one of the claimants to the French crown, but had recently married the infant daughter of King John. He soon quarrelled with his father-in-law and came to Avignon, where he suggested to Lancaster a joint campaign against France in Normandy, where he held wide possessions. When next spring open war was resumed he undertook to join in the

---

[1] *Chevauchée* is translated by most English writers as a raid. The word literally means a procession of mounted men; thence, more loosely, a march or expedition of all arms, as here. An operation wherein the commander wished and tried to bring the French army of the south to battle is emphatically not a raid. A French historian describes this operation as an expedition, which it was.

Normandy campaign, and it was arranged that both armies should cooperate from Cherbourg. But when Lancaster set sail, after vexatious delays, Charles the Bad backed out of the undertaking without informing Edward and patched up his quarrel with the French king. The Normandy campaign was thus still-born.

EDWARD III IN PICARDY

"What you lose on the swings you gain on the roundabouts." The troops earmarked for Normandy now became available for the Picardy campaign. For this campaign Edward amassed a considerable army. After incipient trouble with Scotland all seemed quiet on the Border, and Earl Percy and the bishop of Durham came south with their troops and joined the continental expedition. A third accession to the strength of Edward's army was a large force of mercenaries from Flanders and beyond. Edward took with him as his second in command his favourite general, Henry of Lancaster. His other principal officers were the earls of Northampton, Stafford and March, and Sir Walter Manny.

Because of various delays, inseparable from such an ambitious operation, the English army was not concentrated at Calais till October 26. It was strong in numbers – being possibly as numerous as the Crecy army. But the king of France had not been idle. Among other measures, he had concentrated an army under his own command in the area between Amiens and St. Omer, ready to confront the English invader. There is no means of computing the strength of this army, but it is reasonable to suppose that it was larger than that of the English king. After spending a week organizing his rather heterogeneous army, Edward moved off in search of his old opponent on November 2, very late in the year for the inception of field operations. Groping for the enemy, Edward made first for St. Omer. He reached this town on November 4, but did not attack it. Pushing on south to Blangy, he was met by an envoy from King John, who was then, it appeared, at Amiens.

Edward sent by the envoy a return message to the French king that he was ready to accept battle and would await him for three days with that object. John was not responsive; on the contrary he shut himself up in Amiens, first wasting the country in the path of the English army. At this stage he does not seem to have been much more aggressive-minded than his father had been when in the vicinity of the king of England. Evidently there was to be no fight, and Edward returned with his army via Boulogne to Calais, reaching it on November 11 after the shortest and most baffling campaign of the whole war.

It would be fruitless to spend time in vain speculation as to the reason for this sudden *volte face*, but the presumption is strong that news or rumours of a disturbing nature had reached the king at Blangy, the nature of which will shortly transpire.

The French army seems to have followed up slowly, and John sent an advance challenge to Edward to come out and fight a battle on November 17. A long and confused correspondence then took place, strongly reminiscent of the old verbal manoeuvring between Edward and Philip. The fact is, as Sir James Ramsay suggests, that "neither king had any serious intention of fighting". If actions speak louder than words, this is certainly the case with John. As for Edward, the reason for his declining battle now becomes clear; whether or not rumours or presentiment had reached him at Blangy, he received at Calais definite news that the Scots were besieging the border castle of Berwick.

Edward took prompt and drastic action. He paid off his mercenaries, ordered up his ships and took his army back to England. How came it that his reaction was so different from that of ten years previously when a Scottish king and army penetrated to the walls of Durham? The answer is that the Border was this time defenceless. "Rashly relying on an armistice concluded with the Douglas", Percy had, as we have seen, led away the Border defence force to France and the Scots had, as usual, taken advantage of the cat being away to come out and play the Border game.

The accounts that reached Calais may have been exaggerated; we cannot say; but there can be no doubt that the safety of northern England was in jeopardy, and the course taken by the king was the only possible one in the circumstances.

THE SCOTTISH CAMPAIGN

In order to explain the situation that had arisen we must hark back to the spring of that year (1355). While the king of England was busy with his plans and preparations, his French rival was no less busy. One of his measures took the customary form: Scotland must be induced to make trouble in the north. To this end he sent an envoy offering—and indeed bearing—money and troops, if the regent, William Douglas, would take the offensive.[1] Douglas took the bait, but Percy had not then gone south, and the regent soon signed the armistice mentioned above. But as soon as Percy and the king were safely oversea, egged on again by King John, the Scots made the attack on Berwick recorded above.

Edward was, not unnaturally, furious, but the Scots advanced no further and the king was able to make methodical preparations for the delivery of his retributive blow. While concentrating an army at Durham for the purpose, the king sent forward Sir Walter Manny to relieve the garrison of the castle, which was still holding out. In the dead of winter, about New Year's Day, the English army set out toward the Border. A few days later the Scots evacuated Berwick and the regent sued for peace.

It was too late, for Edward had "taken the bit between his teeth". An unexpected turn of events now seemed likely to ease the task of the English king. Baliol, still in Edward's eyes the nominal and rightful king of Scotland, came to the English king, who had then reached Roxburgh, and surrendered to him his kingdom of Scotland, in respect of which Edward granted him a life pension. Douglas then professed friendship and asked for a truce of ten days, on the pretext that he re-

---

[1] The northern Irish were also inveigled into taking offensive action, but were speedily subdued.

quired time to consult his government. Edward granted this, but on discovering that it was not asked in good faith he resumed his advance. Meeting with practically no opposition he moved north, bearing the twin banners of England and Scotland, and burning the countryside as he passed. He entered Edinburgh without difficulty. Here he expected to be recognized as king, but his savage and senseless burnings and devastation had so incensed the people that he met with no response. Recognizing the futility of obtaining recognition as king by force of arms, he, as suddenly as he had made his *volte face* in Picardy, marched back to England and disbanded most of his army.[1]

Sir James Ramsay sums up this unedifying campaign in the following words:

"The inroad was one of the worst experienced in Southern Scotland. For many a day the horrors of 'Le Burnt Candelmas' marked an epoch in the national memory; and for it Scotland had again to thank the French alliance."

Two of Edward's three campaigns for the year 1355 had crashed. There remained the third–that of the Black Prince in Gascony. And that was of a very different complexion.

THE GRANDE CHEVAUCHÉE

For two years Count Jean d'Armagnac, the French king's lieutenant in Languedoc (the southern province of France), had been nibbling away at the territory won by the earl of Derby. The Gascons applied for help to England, and the expedition of the Black Prince was sent out ostensibly in response to this appeal. But there were other reasons of a strategic nature. Not only was it desirable to restore the waning English prestige in Gascony and to punish d'Armagnac for his harsh treatment of the people and land that he had lately overrun, but a diversion in the south would, it was thought, help the campaign in the north just as it had so signally done in the year of Crecy.

[1] He was also short of supplies, his ships having failed to keep their rendezvous at Dunbar.

On that occasion the army of the duke of Normandy, torn between two objectives, was successful in neither. And there was another way in which a punitive expedition in Languedoc might help the general war effort. It was one of the richest parts of France, and the king was wont to draw plentifully upon it for military resources in supplies, money and men. If the province could be systematically devastated this source of supply would dry up and the French war effort be correspondingly reduced. Great hopes were therefore placed in the new expedition.

After the usual delay, chiefly because of foul winds, the Black Prince set sail from Plymouth on September 9, 1355, with 3,500 troops. By September 20 he had disembarked at Bordeaux, where he was greeted with enthusiasm. He was not only to be commander of the army but the king's viceroy in the duchy, endowed with the widest powers.

After his installation as the king's deputy, he summoned a council of war, and to it he wisely called the Gascon lords. It would seem that they took the lead in preparing the plan of campaign, and the prince showed his good sense in following their advice. The Gascons were insistent on vengeance against Jean d'Armagnac. He was not at the moment in the field, having presumably gone into winter quarters. But this did not deter the eager young prince, now for the first time, at the age of 25, enjoying a command of his own. There were two methods whereby d'Armagnac might be brought to battle: by advancing straight toward him or, if he did not react to that, by devastating his country, until he was forced to take action in its defence. The plan formed envisaged both these possibilities. The army was to march as one complete integrated body, ready to fight, with all forces united, at the shortest notice; at the same time systematic devastation was to be carried out while inside the enemy's territory. It was hoped to march through Languedoc from end to end, from sea to sea.[1] For this purpose elaborate

[1] The original Languedoc had stretched across the whole of southern France from the Atlantic to the Mediterranean.

preparations were made. For instance, the march would take the army close to the foothills of the Pyrenees, where numerous swiftly flowing rivers would have to be crossed, and the enemy might be expected to break down the bridges; so a number of portable bridges were constructed and carried on the line of march.

The prince pushed on with his preparations with all speed and by October 5, 1355, the expedition set out. The army was about 5,000 strong, mainly English, but with a backing of Gascons. Marching south-east at a leisurely pace at first—for the army had to get into its stride—the frontier at Arouille was reached on October 11. It had so far been a peace march, but now battle formation was adopted, the vanguard being under the earl of Warwick with Sir Reginald Cobham of Blanchetaque fame, as Constable; the main body was commanded by the Prince in person, with Oxford and Burghersh the leading English officers, while the Captal de Buch (Jean de Greilly) and the Sire d'Albret were the chief Gascons. The rearguard was under the two earls, Salisbury and Suffolk.[1]

On entering enemy territory the work of devastation began. The orders were that the maximum amount of destruction to crops, stores and buildings (churches and monasteries being spared) was to be carried out. Now the speediest, simplest and surest method of destruction is by fire, and it was by fire that the bulk of the damage was done, a work, we are told, in which the Gascons showed the greatest zeal. The slight feeling of embarrassment that we sense when trying to excuse or explain the burnings in the Normandy campaign have no place here, for the work had a clear military object, which had not been the case in Normandy, which was an old appanage of the English crown, and which it was hoped would become so again. But Languedoc was a foreign country and it met the fate of most invaded countries in the Middle Ages.

In any case, the soldiers were only carrying out their orders, and offences against the persons of the inhabitants seem to have

[1] Le Baker curiously omits the name of Sir John Chandos.

been few. A modern biographer of the Black Prince speaks glibly of the butchery of "men, women and children", a stock phrase of that reckless romancer, the Canon of Chimay. If there had been such outrages it is fairly certain that they would have been recorded in Father Denifle's definitive work *La Désolation des Églises.* . . . But he records none; his complaints concern the burning of religious houses. This was contrary to the Prince's general policy, and in at least one case he tried in vain to save such a building from the flames. Most likely such burnings were accidental; when a fire gets out of control religious buildings are not immune, as we all well know in England, and on one occasion the very house in which the Prince was asleep caught fire by accident.

I have said that these burnings were much to the liking of the Gascons, to whom they were a form of revenge; but the English soldiers no doubt enjoyed them too – there is something exhilarating about a bonfire – in fact the whole army enjoyed the expedition enormously. The weather was fine, the country was beautiful and rich, the inhabitants for the most part abandoned their houses and possessions, which were given up to unlimited looting, and the danger to life and limb was practically nil. Early in the march the count de l'Isle was killed, but that was in a quarrel. There was no enemy to quarrel with, for Jean d'Armagnac and his army took care to keep well out of the way. In short, the army must have enjoyed itself as much as did Sherman's army "marching through Georgia" in 1865.[1]

After marching a hundred miles to the south (see sketch map), the army turned east, and 80 miles further on came opposite Toulouse, the capital of Languedoc. It was a fortified city and it was not the policy of the Black Prince to spend time and blood in capturing places that he had no intention of

[1] Perhaps I may be permitted to quote what I have written elsewhere: "Sherman exhibited his intention to 'make Georgia howl' by destroying the country on a sixty-mile band. This march was in effect a peace march. The average day's march was 15 miles." The Black Prince's average was 14 miles. Otherwise the parallel is startlingly close.

holding. He therefore by-passed Toulouse by the south. To do
this he was obliged to cross two large rivers, the Garonne and
the Ariège, on both of which the bridges had been destroyed.
Much to the astonishment of the inhabitants living on the far
side of the Garonne, a ford was discovered and the army
waded across.[1]

It was not till they were past Toulouse that they learnt from
prisoners that d'Armagnac with his whole army had shut

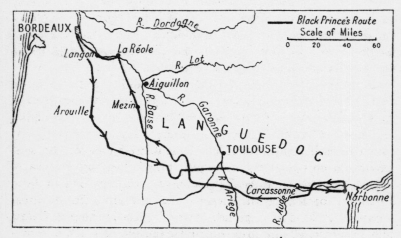

12. THE GREAT CHEVAUCHÉE

himself up in that city (like the other Jean who had shut
himself up in Amiens at the approach of the Black Prince's
father). This inactivity of the king's lieutenant in the south so
incensed the citizens that they threatened his life and eventually
galvanized him into action, as we shall see. Meanwhile opposition remained negligible, and the Anglo-Gascon army
continued merrily on its way, its face ever to the east. Five
marches and one rest day brought them to the wonderful city
of Carcassonne, the sight of which still seems to transport the
visitor into the Middle Ages. The old walled town is situated

---

[1] The season was abnormally dry and the water lower than it had been for
29 years.

on a hill, and the outer town nestled at its foot (as it still does). After some feeble resistance in the lower town the population took refuge in the upper town. The citizens then tried to avoid the destruction of the lower town by offering a large ransom, to which the prince haughtily replied that his father did not require gold, it was justice that he was after. With that, he set fire to the lower town and departed, for the walls were practically unscalable and he possessed no siege engines for breaching them. The army had spent three days at Carcassonne, and on November 2 they departed, crossing to the south bank of the river Aude and reaching Narbonne, 30 miles further east, on November 8. The English were now within ten miles of the Mediterranean, and all southern France was in a whirl of excitement and apprehension. Some English scouts appeared outside the walls of Bezières, 30 miles to the north-east; Montpelier, another 60 miles on, began looking to its defences, and even in Avignon, over 100 miles away, the Pope barricaded himself inside the gates of his fortress-palace, and sent an urgent embassy to the English prince begging for peace. Prince Edward, after keeping the envoys waiting for two days, sent them back with the message that the Holy Father must apply to the king of England, news of whose landing at Calais had just reached the army–a nice example of what is sometimes called "passing the buck".

Meanwhile there was at last some serious fighting to be done, for the outer town was held and resistance was at first fairly strong. It was captured, but the citadel held out. Before he had decided what course of action to adopt the Prince received more news from the outer world. Two armies were reported on the move in his direction. D'Armagnac had at last been stung into action, or an appearance of action; the second army was that of Jacques de Bourbon, who had been collecting an army at Limoges for the assistance of d'Armagnac, and was now drawing near. According to Froissart their intention was to hem the English between the Garonne and the Pyrenees, and the chronicler may here be right. The truth is, we know very

little about the two French armies, their movements and their
plans, nor about a force of militia that was reported approaching Narbonne from Montpelier.

The Prince of Wales summoned a council of war to consider
the new situation, though the course to be adopted must have
required little debating. To remain at Narbonne, where the
storming of the citadel might take several days, whilst possibly
three hostile bodies were drawing near, would be foolish. If
forced to retreat the English would be driven into the sea. On
the other hand a prompt advance against d'Armagnac before
he could unite with Bourbon offered obvious attractions. The
decision was therefore taken to withdraw from Narbonne and
to seek battle with d'Armagnac. On November 10 the return
march began. But instead of taking a westerly direction towards
Toulouse, whence it may be assumed the Limoges army was
approaching, the prince marched due north for eight miles and
halted at Aubian where he crossed to the north of the Aude.
The reason for this move is puzzling. This, no doubt, is because
we know so little as to the French movements; their armies
appear from time to time and disappear like ghosts. This
paucity of information does not appear to worry the historians,
but it worries me. Without more knowledge on the point it is
impossible to descry the strategy, or to assess the ability of the
Black Prince in the field. The northern move may have been
intended, as Ramsay suggests, to mislead the enemy, but as the
prince's aim was to bring them to battle, not to elude them, it
seems more likely that d'Armagnac, having joined forces with
Bourbon to the north of the Aude (and possibly with the
Montpelier contingent also), was preparing to bar the advance
of the English in that direction. What however is clear, is that
on the approach of the invaders the French fell back westward
toward Toulouse, and next day the English followed them in
that direction. But the French were a day's march ahead: the
next night the Prince's headquarters were in the place occupied
by Jean on the previous night. The pursuit through the hilly
country was an arduous one; the drought continued, there was

a shortage of water, and even the horses had to drink wine—in some cases with rather ridiculous results.

But the French showed a clean pair of heels, and after covering 23 miles in two days the English made another sudden turn, this time to the south. The Aude was recrossed and the march continued well to the south of it. Again we must resort to conjecture; the reason may well be that to continue on the northern bank of the Aude would mean retraversing the country already devastated in the advance; the south side was virgin land and the prince had no intention of abandoning his devastation policy. The work of destruction—and the march—therefore went on, leaving Carcassonne well to the right and crossing the Garonne 20 miles south of Toulouse by another opportune ford. In the course of this march the Prince had been greeted by the young Gaston de Foix, later to play a prominent part in the war.

When the English army was safely past Toulouse, d'Armagnac ventured forth from that city of refuge as if to pursue. Prince Edward turned to meet him, sending a reconnoitring party forward under John Chandos, James Audley, and Lord Burghersh. By the time they had obtained contact, any resolution that Jean might have made to confront his opponent now deserted him; he turned and started on the return journey to Toulouse. Chandos and his little party charged boldly into the retreating rearguard and returned with 200 prisoners.

Prince Edward made another sharp turn, this time to the north, in the hope of regaining contact with his elusive opponent. But another incomprehensible turn of events supervened. On the next day, November 21, the French army again came in sight—not on the side of Toulouse but to the west—on the far side of the river Save down which the English were now marching. The French had put the river between the two armies and broken down the bridges. There was nothing for it but to continue on down the valley until a crossing became possible. This was effected at Aurade next day, after which the army pushed on for Gimont. D'Armagnac was now marching on a parallel road, making no effort to close. During the day contact was, however, obtained and the French were roughly handled. But their main body marched on and reached the strongly defended Gimont that night. Edward encamped in the vicinity on the south side, fully expecting a battle next morning. Before daylight he arrayed his army in battle order, but when it got light it was seen that "the bird had flown": the combined armies of d'Armagnac and Bourbon, which must have heavily outnumbered that of the Anglo-Gascons, had brought the farce to an end by slipping away to Toulouse in the night.

*   *   *

Thereafter it became a peace march once more, and on December 2 the weary troops entered the friendly and historic La Réole—a town that witnessed the departure of Richard Coeur de Lion on his famous crusade and the return of the Black Prince from his *grande chevauchée*. After resting a day or two in La Réole the army resumed its homeward march, and entered Bordeaux on December 9, nine weeks and five days after setting out.

There were great rejoicings in the city when the Anglo-Gascon army entered with its huge train of booty and long column of prisoners. The Prince of Wales had every reason to be pleased with himself, according to his own lights. He was only 25, the commander of an army already become famous. He had set out on a bold and ambitious project and had accomplished all that he had set out to do. He had diminished the French war effort by an enormous and incalculable amount; he had restored the prestige of the English name, and had removed all danger to the frontiers of Aquitaine; his main body had marched, as nearly as I can compute it, 675 miles, as far as from London to the north of the Orkneys, averaging 14 miles a marching day on the outward and nearly 17 miles on the return journey. And all this had been accomplished at practically no cost in human lives. Thousands of the unfortunate inhabitants had lost their homes and sustenance, but not their lives; indeed the conduct of the army seems to have been correct throughout and they had humiliated the armies of their opponents in the eyes of the populace. The *chevauchée* was of good augury for the future.

* * *

Christmas was at hand and the army and its leaders must have looked forward to a period of rest and recuperation in the great city of Bordeaux. If so, they were to be cruelly disappointed. So far from resting, the already stern and implacable young prince sent off detachments under his chief officers to strengthen weak places and extend the frontier in all directions. This went on throughout the winter and spring and by May, 1356, over 50 towns and castles of the old English dominion had been recovered.

APPENDIX

SOURCES

There are only three real sources for the Languedoc expedition, but they are good ones. On Christmas Day the Prince wrote a letter, which may be called an official dispatch, to Bishop Edinton of Winchester, the Treasurer (as he believed the king to be still in Picardy). A few days earlier his secretary, John Wingfield, had written a similar but longer letter to the same address. Our third source is le Baker, who managed to obtain possession of a detailed itinerary of the Prince's main body throughout the march—an invaluable document, though the spelling of names is mostly phonetic and some of the places named cannot be identified. One would expect that one of the Prince's many biographers would have annotated this itinerary and produced a detailed analysis of the march, but no; it has been left to the editor of le Baker to do the work and to do it very thoroughly. Maunde Thompson's notes to his edition, written in 1889, are as useful for this campaign as were his notes for the Crecy campaign. Of French writers, again one must go to an unexpected source for the most detailed account; it is contained in Father Deniflé's *La Désolation des Églises* . . . which has already been frequently referred to. It is a valuable guide on sources throughout the war.

In the brief account of the Scottish campaign I have followed Sir James Ramsay closely.

CHAPTER XI

LANCASTER'S "CHEVAUCHÉE" IN NORMANDY

HISTORY does not record the feelings of Edward III on the results of the opening year, 1355, of the renewed war, nor his views and plans for the second year. But disappointment cannot have been entirely absent. The Languedoc expedition, it is true, had been unexpectedly successful, but it was too far distant to produce any immediate effect on the operations in the north. Here everything had gone wrong: both his expeditions had ended in fiasco and the king of Navarre had been reconciled to his French overlord.

But human events are always unpredictable, for luck and chance play a sometimes decisive part. An unlooked-for chance came the way of the English king in the spring of 1356. Charles of Navarre had again fallen out with the king of France, and it came about in the following way. Because of increased taxation, unrest became rampant in the Norman possessions of the king of Navarre, an unrest that Charles the Bad secretly encouraged. Rumours of this reached King John, and he suddenly put in an appearance at a banquet given at Rouen by his eldest son Charles, who had recently succeeded him as duke of Normandy. The guest of honour at the banquet was the king of Navarre. The story goes that John rushed into the hall at the head of 30 armed men while the banquet was in progress, seized Navarre by the collar, and exclaimed "Abominable traitor! You are not worthy to sit at my son's table. By the soul of my father, I will neither eat nor drink as long as you live." John was not quite as good as his word, for whereas he had the count of Harcourt summarily beheaded, he sent the king of Navarre to imprisonment in Paris.

The upshot was what might have been expected. Philip, the younger brother of the arrested monarch, declared war against John and appealed to Edward III for help. Nothing could have fitted the English king's purpose better. The appeal reached him on May 28, when he was in the process of fitting out a small expedition to Brittany under the duke of Lancaster, who was to be the king's new lieutenant in the duchy. The young duke of Montfort, who had now come to man's estate, was to accompany the expedition and presumably assume some share in the government of his father's duchy. Quickly Edward switched the expedition to Normandy. Henry of Lancaster embarked his troops at Southampton on June 4 and on June 18 he landed at La Hogue. Here he was met, by arrangement, by Philip of Navarre with a token force, and soon was joined by "the famous Robert Knollys" as Froissart calls him, or "the terrible Robert" as a French historian dubs him.

Henry was about to undertake one of his breathless *chevauchées*. We fortunately know nearly all the essential facts about this expedition, thanks to an official report drawn up by one of his staff officers only three days after the return of the expedition to its base. We know the exact composition and strength of his army, his orders, his marches and his timetable.

First, the army. The duke brought with him from England 500 men-at-arms and 800 archers; Robert Knollys brought from Brittany 300 men-at-arms and 500 archers; Philip of Navarre brought 100 men-at-arms "of the country"; *i.e.*, Normans. The total was thus 900 men-at-arms and 1,300 archers. To this must be added a small advance guard that had preceded the main body. The total cannot have exceeded 2,500, a small force with which to carry out the orders given him. These were to relieve and revictual the three Navarre towns then being besieged by French troops. They were Evreux, Pont Audemer and Breteuil, and all three were over 130 miles distant from La Hogue. Practically all the fighting men in the English army were mounted, but the victualling train, etc., would be on foot.

Let us now look at the French plans. Unfortunately, because of the dreadfully inadequate French records and chronicles of the period we know little of the French king's movements and still less of his strength. As for his movements, we do know that he immediately answered the challenge thrown down so courageously by Philip by sending forces to besiege the chief towns in the Navarre territories—the three above-named—and that he then set to work to collect an army and lead it in person into the field. It is quite evident that this was a large army. The *Grandes Chroniques* merely says that it was a very great assembly of men-at-arms and foot soldiers. We know, however, that it included his son the duke of Normandy and his brother the duke of Orleans, and most of the leading soldiers of France.[1] In other words it was the main French army.

The English official report, it is true, gives the figures for the French army with some precision, making them 8,000 men-at-arms and 40,000 others. Simeon Luce accepts this figure without demur, but I do not find it acceptable. The English staff officer cannot have been in a position only three days after the return of the expedition to compute the strength of the French army. He probably accepted unquestioningly figures given him by one of the prisoners. It is not of course literally impossible that the French army was 48,000 strong, but utterly unlikely. But even if we reduce it to a quarter of that figure it leaves it many times larger than the English army. Indeed, when fully concentrated, it may quite well have been ten times as large as Lancaster's little army.

When the campaign opened the French king was at Dreux, 25 miles east of Breteuil and the same distance from Evreux. The latter town had already surrendered, so Lancaster's objective was thus confined to Pont Audemer and Breteuil. On conclusion of this task the duke was evidently intended to pass on into Brittany, taking with him young Montfort, who was in the meantime presumably left at the base. This base was

[1] *Les Quatre Premiers Valois* gives an impressive list of these leaders, and frequently emphasizes the great strength of the army.

13. LANCASTER'S CHEVAUCHÉE

Scale of Miles

0 5 10 20 30

$\dfrac{23}{23}$ March of English (& date)
March (conjectural) of French (& date)

the abbey of Montebourg, seven miles south-east of Valognes. Robert Knollys was also left here, somewhat surprisingly.

The expedition set out on June 22, only four days after landing. (The march can be followed on the sketch map.)

The first day's march took the army to Carentan, 16 miles, where a day's halt was allowed in order to sort things out. The next march took the army past St. Lô, which was garrisoned by the French. Henry of Lancaster kept his eye steadily on his objective and had no intention of incurring delays by attacking strongly defended towns. He therefore skirted to the north of St. Lô, marching rapidly in order to avoid becoming involved with its garrison. That evening he reached Torigny, a 30-mile march. On June 25 the army halted, but the next four days saw marches averaging 21 miles per day. The first three marches to Lisieux were in an almost dead straight line, reminding one of Edward's marches through Normandy ten years previously. As on that occasion, we no doubt see the experienced hand of Godfrey Harcourt as guide, for he had again thrown in his lot with the English. He was the chief landowner in the Cotentin, and his château of St. Sauveur-le-Vicomte,[1] situated in the centre of the Cotentin, dominated almost the whole peninsula. The route followed also had the merit of avoiding Caen.

Approaching Lisieux a slight detour to the north had been necessary in order to cross the marshy valley of the river Dives. The bridge at Corbon was held by a French post who fled on the approach of the English and the crossing was secured, much to the satisfaction of the staff officer, who described it as "a very great stronghold, the strongest pass in the realm".

From Lisieux on June 29 the army marched direct to Pont Audemer, 23 miles. They encountered no opposition on the way, and entered the town without sighting any enemy. The explanation is that the post at Corbon had fled to Pont Audemer, where they had given the warning. This so worked upon the besiegers, who guessed what was coming, that they

---

[1] This château afterwards came into the possession of Sir John Chandos and underwent one of the most famous sieges of the war.

fled incontinently during the night, leaving "all their engines, artillery, crossbows, bucklers and other divers harness". The fugitives met strong reinforcements on their way, coming out from Rouen, who were so impressed by the exaggerations of the fugitives that they also turned and returned to the city. Henry revictualled the town from his train, according to instructions, and also left 50 men-at-arms and 50 archers from his scanty force for their additional protection. He remained in the town for the next two days, a curious reason being given for it, namely "to fill up the mines which the enemy had made right well and strong, so close to the castle that they were but four feet from the wall". One would have supposed that the townspeople could do the necessary spade-work themselves, and there must have been some other reason, the nature of which we cannot guess.

Half Henry's task was now accomplished, and still there was no sign of the king of France, or even of a detachment of his army. On July 2, therefore, the march was resumed and in 16 miles they reached the famous abbey of Bec, whence two great archbishops had come to England, Anselm and Lanfranc. Here they were placidly received, though most of the army must have camped outside in the open. It was near midsummer and mattered not. On July 3 a 23-miles march brought them to the French-owned town and castle of Conches. A prompt attack was made on the castle; an entry was effected into the outer ward and the place was then set on fire. This is all the staff officer says, but as the army spent the night there we may presume that all opposition was overcome.

Still no news of King John and his great army, yet he could not be far off. The next day, July 4, was indeed an eventful one. Setting off due south the army reached its second objective, Breteuil, again without opposition, after a ten-mile march, while it was still quite early. Once again the French abandoned the siege on hearing of the English approach and the army entered without losing a man. Extensive victuals, calculated to last the garrison for one year, were here unloaded and stored.

But though his double objective had now been accomplished, Henry of Lancaster evidently felt he must "do something more". His gay spirit cried out for adventure and he decided to try and capture the moated and walled town and castle of Verneuil, then considered by some the capital of Normandy. This venerable city is still outwardly strong, and the gaunt keep of Henry I, called not inaptly *le Tour Gris*, and as grim as its builder, might be expected to offer strenuous resistance.

Revictualling Breteuil must have occupied most of the morning, and eight more miles had to be covered before Verneuil was reached. During the afternoon, however, the English appeared before its walls and summoned it to surrender. But the gates were closed and an assault became necessary. This was successful; that is all we know, but it is reasonable to suppose that the change in procedure from avoiding defended towns before Audemer was reached may have sprung from the fact that siege equipment was captured at that town, which thus simplified, and indeed made possible, the assault of walled towns. Thus we see the speedy fall of two of them, Conches and Verneuil.[1] The assault on the town walls was successful, but a tower in the castle held out obstinately, and it was not till 6 a.m. two days later that it fell into English hands. Many troops were wounded in this assault, but none killed.

By this time the tiny English army had pranced through Lower Normandy, relieving two important towns and taking two others by storm, and still no army had appeared against them in the field. It could not go on much longer; Verneuil is only 20 miles from Dreux where the French army had been on the opening day of the *chevauchée*. Where was it and what was it doing? Henry did not know, and it was tempting fortune to dally another day at Verneuil, badly though men and horses wanted rest. But it was in Henry's nature to take risks.

[1] The army marched across the battlefield-to-be of Verneuil, just outside the town—that of a great victory of the duke of Bedford which the French have called "une seconde Agincourt".

July 7 was, therefore, devoted to rest and refreshment, and the following day the army set off on its long return journey. The direct route would take it through Laigle, 14 miles to the west. Thither the duke set his face. The march was uneventful to start with, and the headquarters had reached the town when word came that the French army was in contact with the rearguard. At Tuboeuf, four miles east-south-east of Laigle, the French army, coming from the direction of Breteuil, had bumped into the English.

King John had at last got within striking distance of his unpredictable and elusive opponent. Now was the chance to crush this disturber of the peace of Normandy. And how did he set about doing it? The answer is that he followed the trail so clearly and so disastrously blazed for him by his own father, Philip VI: he resorted, not to actions, but to words. He halted his army and sent two heralds to the English army with a solemn challenge to battle. Goliath challenged David. Such a gesture from the French king could hardly take the English duke by surprise, knowing his antecedents as he did. Henry was ready for it and he returned an adroit answer. His staff officer was evidently so pleased with the wording that he gives it fully. "Whereupon my lord gave answer that he was come into these parts to do certain business, which he had well accomplished, thank God, and was returning back to the place where he had business, and that if the said King John of France willed to disturb him from his march he would be ready to encounter him."[1] No reply was received.

Darkness fell, the two armies still sitting opposite one another. A report ran through the French lines that evening that the formidable duke of Lancaster was about to attack. A near-panic was caused, and the troops hurriedly stood to arms. No attack followed, but a battle seemed inevitable next day, July 9. Early that day trumpets sounded in the French camp, banners were unfurled and the marshals made busy to set out the troops

---

[1] There is a "Froissartian" twang about this message, but the author of the *Chroniques* had nothing to do with it.

in array. The English could be dimly descried, but they showed no sign of coming out into the open, nor did they send out a herald to inform the French king what they intended to do. Odd! After some time it was observed that the English became less and less visible and eventually there was not a man to be seen. Patrols were sent forward. They came back and reported that Laigle was empty. The English army had vanished.

The English commander had no intention of being so imbecile as to engage the huge French army in battle, but his astute answer to the herald, though containing a *suggestio falsi*, was not a downright lie; it contained a hidden element of truth. For Lancaster calculated that, with a little skilful management, he could get clear away, even though he was now weighed down with prisoners and loot. His plan to this end was simple (as war plans should always be). He deployed a small force of picked men along the front, just in view of the enemy, with orders to keep them amused next morning as long as possible, and then to slip away, mount and follow after the army as fast as possible. Meanwhile in the dead of night the main body was assembled in silence, a witness to the high state of discipline the troops had attained to under Lancaster's firm and experienced tuition. The army moved off shortly after midnight. It "swiftly and silently melted away".

By the time the ruse was discovered by the French their opponents were well on the way to Argentan, and pursuit would have been useless. The author of the *Grandes Chroniques*, in his anxiety to excuse the ineptitude of his king, produced an absurd story that someone unnamed had told the king when the English army was first sighted that there were vast forests in front and that it would be useless to attack. The real truth of the matter is stated bluntly by Simeon Luce: "The king of France, instead of falling on the English, sent heralds to offer battle to the Duke of Lancaster, who profited by this warning to escape."[1] John had not learned from Philip's example: in

---

[1] Delachenal writes that John "showed as much incapacity as chivalrous naivety".

fact one is tempted to liken the early Valois to the Bourbons—they learnt nothing and they forgot nothing.

Argentan[1] was reached that evening, a distance of 35 miles having been covered. Of course this was done in two stages, a night march and a day march. Even so, it was a fine achievement for the dismounted men left in the army. I put it that way because in the course of the *chevauchée* over 2,000 horses were captured, sufficient to mount the whole army, train, prisoners and all. But it is probable that the big haul of horses was made in Argentan, for next day the length of march suddenly shot up to the prodigious figure of 52 miles, which, coming on top of one of 35 miles, must be considered phenomenal. Lancaster must have believed he was still being followed (and he may have been, by light forces). But after Torigny, which was reached on July 10, the pace slackened. Delay was caused at the crossing of the river Vire at St. Frommond. Since their outward journey the bridge had been cut by French troops, who laid an ambush at the spot. But something went wrong; To quote the official report once more: "Sixty men-at-arms and other soldiers lay in ambush, to do what mischief they might to our people, and with them 15 of our English men-at-arms fought and killed them all, which thing was held for a miracle."

But even better was to come! Next day the army reached Carentan in home country, and on the morrow they got back to Montebourg. Robert Knollys, who had been left in charge of the base camp, hearing of the advent of the army, rode out to meet them and lead them into the quarters that he had prepared for them. He had but seven armed men with him and they ran into an ambush of 120 Frenchmen. "And the said Robert and the said seven men-at-arms slew them all except three which were taken at ransom." The "terrible Robert" indeed!

The army had covered, according to my reckoning, about

---

[1] The duke must have lodged in the forbidding-looking castle in which Henry II, 200 years before, had uttered the fateful words: "Who will rid me of this turbulent priest?"

330 miles in 15 marches and 22 days, at an average distance of 22 miles a march–a remarkable record. The summing up of the expedition by Roland Delachenal in his *Histoire de Charles V* reads:

"Complete success crowned the enterprise. The soldiers of Lancaster had captured or secured several fortresses, they brought back numerous prisoners, 2,000 horses taken from the enemy, an enormous booty, and they themselves had had very few casualties."

As a result of this expedition, Philip of Navarre crossed over to England and did homage to Edward III for his Norman possessions. The alliance was sealed and for some years English and Navarre-Normans fought shoulder to shoulder.

The achievement of Henry of Lancaster speaks for itself. Not so the lack of achievement of King John. This is due to the regrettable lack of written evidence. In order to assess his operations we must try to fill in the gap between June 22 when he was at Dreux and July 8 when he appeared before Laigle. I believe it can be done with a fair degree of plausibility.

If we make one big assumption everything seems to fall into place and fit into the picture. That assumption is that Rouen, not Dreux, was the concentration point for his army. Dreux was not a large town, and the record does not state that the main French army was there, or was going to concentrate there, though most writers seem to assume that. The natural place would be Rouen. It had obvious administrative and geographical advantages and it was in keeping with the policy of both John and his father before him to order such concentrations at large towns: Amiens, Arras, Chartres, Rennes, etc. Moreover, Rouen would be the best possible strategical centre, for it faced the heart of the Navarre territories, and was almost equidistant from the two towns then being besieged, Pont Audemer and Breteuil. Let us assume then that John left Dreux for Rouen on June 23 or very soon after, and see how the picture of the campaign can be filled in. He arrives at Rouen on June 25 and for the next four days is busied with the organization of his army as contingents arrive, one after the other. During the night of June 29 fugitives from the besieging force at Pont Audemer arrive. They are full of excuses for the abandonment of their post, and in self-defence wildly exaggerate the numbers of the English army that is approaching. John takes this seriously, not realizing that the stories of fugitives from the battlefield must ALWAYS be heavily discounted. He therefore makes careful and deliberate arrangements to march toward Pont Audemer with his whole army, not realizing the need for haste against such a slippery opponent. Two ponderous marches bring him to the vicinity of Pont Audemer where he arrives on the evening of July 2, only to find that the English army have departed that morning in a southerly direction. The pursuit, of which the *Grandes Chroniques* speak, then begins. Following in the tracks of the enemy, John reaches the vicinity of Breteuil on July 5 – a day and a half behind his enemy – and encamps at Condé, three miles to the east of that town.

The king is now separated by only ten miles from the English and as Henry is going to stay another two full days at Verneuil there is ample time and opportunity to bring him to battle. But John for some reason remains halted at Condé during those two vital days. Our evidence for this is a curious sentence (which seems to have escaped notice) in the message of the heralds: "The said king knew well, by reason that . . . my lord had tarried so close to him at Verneuil. . . ." This remark implies that both sides had tarried. We know why Henry tarried; the only reason we can suggest for John tarrying at this juncture was that as soon as he arrived within striking distance of his famous opponent, of whom he had unhappy recollections in Gascony, his professed desire to measure swords with him evaporated and he waited to bring up all the stragglers in his host before risking a battle. Hence he tarried two days, July 6 and 7, at Condé, and when he was on the point of setting out for Verneuil on the morning of July 8 news reached him that the English were on the march along the road to Laigle. He therefore cut the corner, marching along the river valley towards Laigle, and at Tuboeuf, as we have seen, he obtained contact with the rearguard of the English army at last. The rest we know.

The French king did not pursue with his main army, but turned back to resume the siege of Breteuil which had been so rudely broken off. Here he met with a determined defence, and had to resort to all the known methods of reducing a fortress. An enormous *beffroi*, or moving tower, was constructed that would overtop the walls and enable the attackers to set foot from it on to the parapet. But when it approached, the cannons in the town opened fire and set it alight.[1] This episode, combined with the mention of artillery at Pont Audemer, is interesting evidence as to the progress of artillery in siege warfare, of which we have heard little since the siege of Tournai 16 years previously. Contingents of Scottish troops joined the French army here under the command of Lord William Douglas, whom King John took into his paid service.

In mid-August, disturbing news was received from the south. That young son of the English king was again on the warpath, and this time was reported marching straight for Paris. It was therefore essential to bring the siege of Breteuil to a speedy conclusion and John granted it easy terms and departed in haste with his army to Paris.

APPENDIX

SOURCES

The main sources are the Official Report, printed in Avesbury, the *Grandes Chroniques*, and the *Chronique des Quatre Premiers Valois*, which is steadily becoming more important for the French side. Subsidiary sources: in English, Knighton; in French, the *Continuation* of de Nangis; neutral, Froissart. The campaign has been scarcely even recognized by English writers with the exception of Mackinnon (two pages) and Ramsay

---

[1] During the famous siege of Ostend in 1601, Spinola, the Italian, constructed a similar tower which he named "Pompey". It was the wonder of the day, but the English gunners fired at its wheels, broke one of them, and brought it to a standstill. History repeats itself.

(one page) both of whom, however, ignore the *Quatre Premiers Valois*. The best account, as usual, comes from a Frenchman, Roland Delachenal, in his *Histoire de Charles V*.

LENGTH OF A FRENCH LEAGUE

The staff officer in his report gives the interesting information that the French league was twice as long as the English league. He does not say how long that was, but as he gives the length of most of the day's marches, it is possible to calculate it approximately. Only an approximation is possible because of our ignorance of the exact roads traversed. One can, however, strike an average and my calculations made it equal to about three modern miles. M. Delachenal calculates the league as only 4,200 metres, say two and a half miles, but he evidently measures each stage in a straight line, *viz.* map miles, whereas the staff officer who presumably had no map must have judged the distance actually travelled along the road. The length of a league at any given period or place must be the bugbear of military historians (though they usually evade this difficulty by merely using the word "league" without defining it).

CHAPTER XII

POITIERS

THE king of France had brought the siege of Breteuil to a premature end because he received a report that the Black Prince was heading north for Paris. The report was in its essence true. The Prince of Wales and his army were heading not for but toward the French capital. It was part of another of those wide strategic plans that distinguish the warfare of Edward III.[1]

What then was the plan on which the Black Prince had set out? It was in essence a replica of the Crecy plan of campaign, which had worked so well. There were to be two, if not three, simultaneous and widely separated operations, acting on exterior lines; that is, facing inward as it were, and directed toward the Loire, where it was hoped they might join hands. No attempt was made to concert synchronized plans: experience had taught that the elements–that is the weather on the various sea passages–made any such plans impossible. The greatest latitude was therefore left to each commander and no great hopes of complete success were entertained: the subsidiary aims might at least be carried out–the ravaging of the enemy's territory and the defeat of his forces in the field.

The first part of the plan–an invasion *via* Calais by the king–was, as we have seen, still-born (if it was ever seriously contemplated) and the second–an invasion from Brittany *via* Normandy by Henry of Lancaster–had been delayed by the operations in Normandy. But in mid-July Henry had passed on into Brittany and in a few weeks this indefatigable soldier

[1] Most historians, both English and French, find little trace of strategy in any of the king's campaigns, probably because the documentary evidence for it is slight. But actions may be more convincing than words, and the actions of Edward III, which have been and which will be described in these pages, point to the fact that the English king was in advance of his time as a strategist. Indeed he may be described as the Father of English strategy.

was again in the field, marching toward the Lower Loire. His advance took him through southern Normandy where he captured the strong castle of Domfront and other castles on the border of Maine. Thence he advanced south on Angers, hoping to cross the Loire south of that city and to join forces with his second cousin, the Prince of Wales.

The third army was that of Gascony, still under the Black Prince. During the spring of 1356 he had extended and steadily strengthened his dominion and his task had been rendered the easier thanks to the number of Gascon nobles (who had held aloof from the previous expedition) now coming forward with their retinues. For nothing succeeds like success. It was therefore with an army nearly, if not quite, double the size of the previous one that the Prince marched out of Bordeaux on July 6. Making his first headquarters at La Réole, he took active steps for warding off a possible attack by Jean d'Armagnac, who had been showing unwonted activity of late. For this purpose the Prince detached approximately half his troops, nearly all of them being Gascons, for the defence of his borders during the absence of his main army. As a matter of fact, d'Armagnac's activities were of a purely defensive nature, but it would have been unsound for the Prince to march over 200 miles away from his base without first rendering it secure.

By the beginning of August all was ready and an Anglo-Gascon army about 6,000 strong set out on its second great *chevauchée*. The prince used this word *chevauchée* to describe it; it was a word with a wide connotation (for the French vocabulary was small in those days) and it covered the three aims of the expedition, *viz.*, to carry fire and sword into the heart of the enemy's country, thus showing that he was not master in his own domains; secondly to meet and defeat his armies in the field; and thirdly to join hands, if possible, with the king or with Lancaster, or both, somewhere on the line of the river Loire. Sketch map 14 (p. 282) should here be consulted.

On August 4 the army passed through Bergerac, and advanced by easy stages of about ten miles a day, *via* Périgueux,

Brantôme, Rochechouart (leaving Limoges on the right hand), Lussac (where Sir John Chandos was afterwards to meet his death), Chateauroux and Issudun. Up to this point the army was heading for Bourges, where the count of Poitiers, one of the sons of the French king, was believed to be lying. But Bourges did not hold him, and the English army continued on its way, leaving Bourges on its right hand. At Vierzon the border from Aquitaine into France proper was crossed and destruction of the countryside was systematically carried out. It did not, however, reach the height of the Languedoc devastations, and Father Deniflé (whose reconstruction of the itinerary is accepted by all) records the burning of only a few religious houses.

Next day, August 29, French patrols sent out by King John's approaching army were met for the first time. They were chivvied back to the castle of Romorantin, where they were shut up and besieged. The main castle fell next day, but the keep held out for another three days. Eventually it was set on fire[1] and captured.

Some information was obtained from the prisoners, to the effect that the French king was approaching and that one of the sons of the king was in Tours. The Black Prince went in that direction, marching westward down the right bank of the Cher for 40 miles to the Loire, which he struck near Amboise, 17 miles short of Tours. The Prince seems to have had a hope that his father might be not far off on the northern bank of the river. His aim was therefore to cross and join him, but no crossing could be found; all the bridges were either cut or strongly defended and the river was in spate and unfordable. The prince, who had taken up his quarters at Montlouis Castle, near the river, now turned his attention to the city of Tours. The vanguard of his army, on arrival opposite its walls, found that fresh defences had been

---

[1] No doubt with Greek Fire. I do not credit the report that cannons were used. If it were so the *Eulogium*, which notices the use of arrows in the siege, would hardly have remained silent. There is no record of the presence of cannon at any other time during this campaign.

thrown up and that there was a numerous and vigilant garrison. In default of a siege train, and in view of the approach of the French army, an attempt to capture the town would be fruitless, and the Black Prince was reduced to sitting down, in the hopes that the Valois prince might be induced to come out and fight. For four days, therefore, the English army sat down and rested. They had need of it. They had marched some 320 miles in 32 days, an average of 10 miles a day, including halts. Some of their wide-ranging foraging parties had, of course, covered very much more.

But prospects appeared gloomy. The broad river was uncrossable, the enemy was beginning to swarm everywhere, forage was becoming increasingly difficult to procure, the French main army was now within striking distance, and, worst of all, there was no news of either the king of England or of the duke of Lancaster. Evidently the Prince's army could not hope to push further into France unless one or other of the northern armies could get to him, which now seemed unlikely. Meanwhile his train of booty had become rich and lengthy[1]; parties of the enemy were reported crossing the river both above and below Tours, while the duke of Normandy, if he really were in Tours, had evidently no intention of venturing out. Would it not therefore be wise to set his face toward home?

Such may well be the thoughts that passed through the mind of the young Prince during those critical and anxious days. By September 10 his mind was made up; and orders were issued for the army to proceed to Montbazan, 12 miles south of Tours, on the following day. The reason given by the Prince for this move was that he wished to join the duke of Lancaster, and this may truly have been one reason, as we shall shortly see.

THE FRENCH MOVES

It is time to follow the movements of the rival army. We left King John in mid-August abandoning his Normandy campaign

---

[1] The extent of his booty has probably been exaggerated. There are no exact records.

and repairing to Paris in order to take steps to repel the greater
danger from the south. Unfortunately, the French chronicles
are as scanty and as vague as ever during this period; all we
know for certain is that the king ordered a great army to concentrate at Chartres, whither he went himself, arriving not later
than August 28. His old army must have formed the nucleus
of the new one, for operations in Normandy had practically
ceased with the departure of the English army to Brittany. The
orders convening the new army were as widespread as ever, all
parts of the country except Languedoc being bidden to send
their levies. The size of the army that collected at Chartres
must therefore have been about as large as any the king had
previously commanded, if not larger.

Through the latter half of August, then, detachments of
French troops were hurrying toward the city of Chartres,
whilst the Anglo-Gascon army was wending its leisurely way
through the heart of the country. In the first days of September,
King John set out for the Loire, on receipt of the intelligence
that the Black Prince was approaching. His army was not
fully concentrated, indeed it is doubtful whether it ever was,
for we have the extraordinary fact that whereas he himself
crossed the Loire at Blois on September 6, some of his detachments crossed at Orleans, Meung, Tours, and even Saumur–
the latter obviously being Breton and Norman contingents–
that is, on a front of 110 miles in a direct line. If the king
believed a hostile army to be somewhere in the centre of this
line his dispersion was either an extremely rash act or, if exactly
co-ordinated and synchronized, a skilful strategic operation. But
such synchronization was practically out of the question at that
date. However that may be, on September 10, John crossed the
river at Blois, and next day reached Amboise, a 21-mile march.

The following ten days are easily the most controversial ten
days of the whole Hundred Years of War, and the reader is
advised to consult sketch map 15 closely and to construct for
himself a simple march table, showing the two armies in
parallel columns. The sources are puzzling and conflicting

and in attempting to establish the true course of events I shall
have to make great demands on inherent military probability.
The famous German military historian, Delbrück, when he
examined the sources for the battle, gave up the task of describing it in despair—which was *grand pitié*—as Jean Froissart
would have said.

There are two main problems: the first concerns the preliminaries of the battle and the second the conduct of the
actual battle of Poitiers. The first problem may be simplified
in the following terms: What was John's object in marching
round the flank of the English army, and did the Black Prince
seek to cross swords with his opponent or try to elude him?
For convenience I will give a *précis* of the ascertained facts first
and then go over the problem in detail.

The ascertained facts for the preliminaries are that on
Monday September 12, the French were halted at Amboise,
the English at Montbazan. On Tuesday the English marched
to La Haye (30 miles) and the French to Loches (24 miles). On
Wednesday the English marched to Chatellerault (17 miles),
the French to La Haye (16 miles). On Thursday the English
halted, the French marched to Chauvigny (33 miles). On
Friday the English continued their halt, the French also
halted.[1] On Saturday September 17, the English went to
Chabotrie, four miles south-east of Poitiers (30 miles), the
French to Poitiers (18 miles), the English crossing the path of
the French and colliding with their rearguard near Chabotrie.

What construction are we to put on these curious marches
and halts? The two opposing schools of thought may for
convenience be called the French and the English, though
this is by no means an exact definition. The French school
avers that during these days the Black Prince was continuously retreating from King John who, by a brilliant
flanking manoeuvre, put his army right behind that of his
opponent and had it in his power to cut off the English

[1] That is, the main body. The king seems to have pushed on with his vanguard
towards Poitiers, though the statement that he spent the night of September 16
at Chabotrie is most unlikely.

retreat. These critics stress the fact that when the Prince heard at Chatellerault that the enemy had got past him and were at Chauvigny he made a hurried retreat, being prepared if necessary to sacrifice his booty-train in his desperate effort to get out of the net. The English school, on the other hand, avers that so far from trying to avoid the enemy in that hurried march of September 17, the Black Prince' was hastening to set a trap for his opponent on the road from Chauvigny to Poitiers, and that it nearly came off. Most of the chroniclers support the French school, only three supporting the English; but these three happen to be the three most reliable sources we have. Moreover until Father Deniflé wrote his *Désolation des Églises* . . . in 1899 two out of these three sources were, incredible though it may sound, unknown to the French historians, so their adherence to the French school is understandable. These sources are two letters written by the Prince on October 20 and 22 to the mayor of London and to the bishop of Worcester respectively. There is also the Chronicle of Geoffrey le Baker de Swynbroke. Both these sources state that the Prince throughout was anxious to engage the French king in battle and that his march from the Loire to Poitiers was a manoeuvre for that purpose, not a retreat. Father Deniflé himself accepts this claim, but he has not been followed by subsequent French historians. Professor Tout and Sir James Ramsay are the chief exponents of the English school, though biographers of the Black Prince seem generally to side with the French school.

THE PRELIMINARIES

The ground is now cleared for an examination of these rival contentions. If in the course of it I constantly refer to *L'Histoire de Charles V* by Roland Delachenal it is because it contains what is on the whole the most detailed, thorough and well-documented examination of the problem in print, and because Professor Delachenal's views have been in the main accepted by subsequent French writers since the book was published

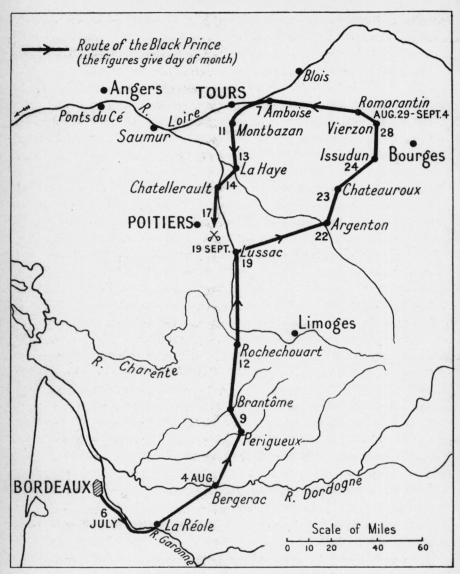

Route of the Black Prince
(the figures give day of month)

Angers
Ponts du Cé
Saumur
R. Loire
TOURS
Blois
7 Amboise
Romorantin
AUG.29 - SEPT.4
11 Montbazan
Vierzon 28
13
La Haye
Issudun
24
Bourges
Chatellerault 14
Chateauroux
23
POITIERS 17
Argenton
22
19 SEPT.
Lussac
19
Limoges
R. Charente
Rochechouart
12
Brantôme
9
Perigueux
BORDEAUX
4 AUG.
6
JULY
Bergerac
R. Dordogne
La Réole
R. Garonne

Scale of Miles
0   10   20   40   60

14. THE POITIERS CAMPAIGN

(1909) till the appearance in 1946 of Professor Ferdinand Lot's *L'Art Militaire et les Armées au Moyen Age*.

Let us open this examination on the morning of Monday September 12, when the English army was halted at Montbazan and the French at Amboise, 20 miles north-east of it. That day the two inevitable cardinals appeared in the English camp, beseeching that an end be put to hostilities. Prince Edward, who had his mind full of other things, treated the cardinals civilly but explained blandly that he was not authorized to negotiate a truce, and that they should refer to his father the king. It was either on this day or on September 11 that he received a message from his "dear cousin" Henry of Lancaster. The faithful Lancaster was doing his best to carry out his instructions. It is a pity that we have few details of them, but it is clear that he had reached the river Loire at Les Ponts du Cé, due south of Angers, where he also was held up.[1] One would give a good deal to know the exact nature of the information that the Prince received: it is reasonable to suppose that it was to the effect that Henry was trying to get across the river but had not yet succeeded. If he did eventually succeed where would be the best junction point? Midway between the two armies lay Saumur, which was in hostile hands. Lancaster would therefore have to give it a wide berth. This would take him through Montreuil (a dozen miles south of Saumur) and, continuing the same line, he would converge on to the Black Prince's road at or near Chatellerault. It may indeed well be that the Prince sent back a message making this suggestion. The latter resumed his march next day, through La Haye to Chatellerault, where he arrived on September 14. Meanwhile he had lost touch with the French army. Had it stopped at La Haye, 17 miles in his rear? He would send to ascertain this; for though he would sooner have the battle after joining forces with Lancaster, he did not wish to lose sight of his opponent. As far back as September 5 he had warned his troops to

[1] Ramsay is candid enough to say that he cannot find the place on his map, which is a pity, for he might have developed the point I am about to make.

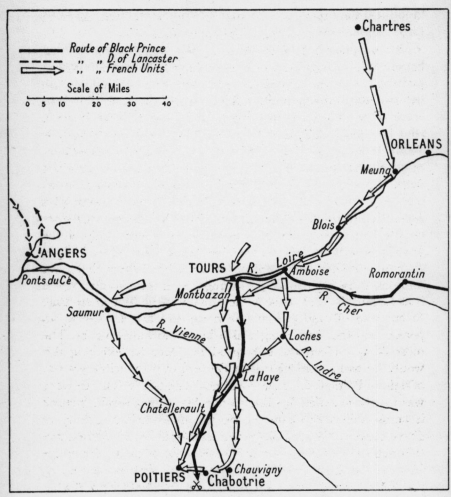

Route of Black Prince
  ,,   ,, D. of Lancaster
  ,,   ,, French Units
Scale of Miles
0 5 10   20   30   40

Chartres

ORLEANS

Meung

Blois

Loire R.

TOURS   R.   Loire

Amboise

Romorantin

Ponts du Cé

ANGERS

Montbazan

R. Cher

Saumur

R. Vienne

Loches

R. Indre

La Haye

Chatellerault

Chauvigny

POITIERS   Chabotrie

15. FROM THE LOIRE TO POITIERS

284

"prepare their harness" for the coming battle. He therefore halted on the next day, September 15, at Chatellerault. But why did he also halt the following day, too? This has puzzled all commentators and worried some of them. He was still without information of his opponent's whereabouts and he gives this as his reason for remaining halted for a second day. But if he was also waiting for more news from Lancaster it was natural that he should dally as long as he dared at Chatellerault. It was thus not surprising that he should halt for two days running. But on the evening of the second day he at last received definite news of the French army: he could not remain halted any longer, unless he was to abandon all hope of meeting his opponent. In that case the latter might in his absence devastate Gascony in revenge for the Black Prince's devastations. King John was reported halted in Chauvigny. The Prince judged that his immediate destination was Poitiers, where there was a strong French garrison; John might even shut himself up in it as he had done at Amiens the previous year. Was there time to cut him off and perhaps even capture him by taking up position on the road along which he would have to pass! The most likely, indeed the only possible, place for effecting this would be as far removed from Chauvigny as possible yet out of sight of Poitiers, in other words near Chabotrie. The distance was nearly 30 miles. By disengaging his baggage-train, getting it across the river Clain during the night and marching at dawn, it should be possible for the mounted portion of the army to reach the Chauvigny road by early afternoon. Orders were issued accordingly, the baggage crossed the river bridge during the night, and at dawn on September 17 the march began. The baggage was left to follow on, and after marching down the Roman road towards Poitiers for about 12 miles[1] the vanguard turned off the road and pushed on across country, leaving the baggage to its own devices, far in rear. It was an exciting race, and everything had to give way to the main consideration.

[1] Following Hilaire Belloc here.

As the vanguard reached the Chauvigny-Poitiers road, the French rearguard was just passing. It was promptly charged and received a rough handling from the English men-at-arms, many prisoners being taken, including two counts. But King John had escaped the trap, and was already safe in Poitiers. The English army was now short of food and water, especially water. The Prince therefore decided to go no further, he would give time for his baggage to catch up. So the night was spent in the forest near the little village of Chabotrie.

That, at least, is how I reconstruct the motives of the Black Prince, based on his known actions and his own statements.[1]

As to whether the Prince really wished an encounter with King John, Ferdinand Lot implies that his actions belie his words. Let us see. The crucial date is the Friday evening, when the Prince learnt that his opponent was at Chauvigny. If he had wished to avoid an encounter with the French king would he have remained halted for two days out of touch with his pursuers? Would he not rather have seized the opportunity to get his booty-wagons further toward Bordeaux and safety? His opponent had vanished. When on the second day his opponents were still unlocated, would not the Prince have grown apprehensive? Two days ago they were at La Haye; where might they not be now? Again, when, that Friday evening, the Prince learnt that King John had reached Chauvigny, 20 miles in his rear, would he not have looked for some way of escape? It was a very obvious guess that the French king would join forces with the Poitiers garrison; therefore the Chauvigny-Poitiers road would probably be in enemy hands ere now. Would not that line of escape offer the least likely chance of success? Would it not be better to march south-east, making for Lussac and then returning home by the same road that he had traversed in his outward march, or, better still, work to the south-west, leaving Poitiers on his left hand, and thus placing it between himself

---

[1] His statement that he wished to cross swords with King John has been questioned in many quarters, but that fair and indefatigable historian, Father Denifié, though bitter against the prince for his devastations, accepts his statement here at its face value.

and the French army? Surely the answer to all these questions is in the affirmative, unless the Black Prince, and his experienced generals, were imbeciles. Yet he did none of these things. So it seems that when the prince told the mayor of London that he had wished to cross swords with King John he was speaking the truth.

KING JOHN'S MOTIVES

Now let us consider the motives and generalship of the French king. At first sight the generally held view of his march to Chauvigny seems the natural one; *viz.*, that he wished to turn the English flank and cut off their retreat to Bordeaux. But there are some awkward questions. On what grounds did he calculate at La Haye that he could outmarch the English and get in their rear? To cut them off near Chabotrie his army would have to march over 45 miles if it went, as it did, *via* Chauvigny; whereas the English army had less than 30 to traverse, as we have just seen. How could he foretell that the English would halt for two whole days running at Chatellerault? Moreover the English troops were in harder condition than his own, having been campaigning for over six weeks. Even with the two halts included, the English, as we have seen, nearly won the race. That is the first awkward question, and I do not know the answer, nor how it showed "brilliant generalship", as a modern English biographer of the Black Prince has claimed.

Next, admittedly the king made a rapid and unexpected march to Chauvigny; but if speed was essential why did he throw away its fruits by halting at Chauvigny next day?[1] There are two possible explanations for this. The king may have found on the morning of the Friday that so many of his troops had straggled that he did not feel strong enough to continue with his plan until they had all caught up the main body. This would certainly apply to all his infantry, who had marched

[1] Most historians slur over this, some of them even asserting that he only reached the town on the Friday, but the evidence on the point is clear.

62 miles in four days, but it should have been an easy stage for his mounted troops.

The other possible explanation is that, as the prospect of crossing swords with the redoubtable and so far ever-victorious English army appeared more likely, he relished it less and less. King John was by no means a physical coward: he fought with magnificent bravery at Poitiers, like a true Valois, but his past record seemed to indicate a certain shrinking from the "final argument" when the time for it drew near. Those are the two explanations that I hazard, and the true explanation may well be a combination of the two.

There is, however, an entirely different view that may be taken of John's famous flank march. It may not have had an aggressive intent; its real intention may have been to get into Poitiers before the English could either get there first or stop him getting there at all. There is a good deal to be said for this theory. Let us go back to September 10, when the French army was crossing the Loire on a 120-mile front. How did the king manage to collect these widely dispersed detachments on the southern side of the river? A glance at the map shows that the English army was sitting down between him and the Tours and Saumur contingents. He could scarcely expect them to get past the vigilant English scouts during the next four days. Hence, if he was to obtain their services in a battle near Poitiers, they must march direct on that city instead of attempting to join him and accompany him to Chauvigny. Thus he would order Poitiers rather than Chartres as his concentration point as far as the Normandy and Brittany contingents were concerned (and we know he had both). If this be the correct explanation it means that the Chauvigny march, instead of being intended to hold up and bring to bay the English army, was on the contrary an attempt to keep well clear of that army until John had completed his concentration, which would be in Poitiers. In favour of this view is the fact that, whatever his intention, that is what in fact happened. The French army during those famous and critical ten days was spread out over a huge area of country, with the minimum of control and communication between the component parts. As an example, a few hours after the English had marched out of Chatellerault on that Saturday morning, a French detachment marched over the same bridge in the same direction, a fact which seems to have puzzled Delachenal.[1] An objection to this view is that, had the king desired to get into Poitiers first, he would not have made the wide circuit *via* Chauvigny, but would have cut the corner from Pleumartin onward, and ridden into the city on the Thursday.

If none of the above speculations is the truth it seems we must fall back on the view, expressed tentatively by one French commentator, that after his arrival at Chauvigny King John hesitated and wobbled for some time before deciding on his next step. If his opponent was in the dark, so also was he. The French chroniclers who might be expected to assist here throw no light on the king's motives. The problem will therefore never be finally solved. My own view, on balance, is that King John, in making his flank march, hoped by some means to shake off and evade the English army until he had fully concentrated his own army at Poitiers. If the facts are as suggested above, note how exactly they are corroborated by the Prince's letter to the mayor of London, which may be translated as follows:

"(King John) came with his army to Chauvigny, in order to pass to Poitiers; on which we decided to hasten towards him, on the road by which he must pass, intending to meet him on the road to Poitiers. . . ."

Here the Black Prince makes a definite statement as to the king's intentions. Did John tell him this when a prisoner!

SUNDAY, SEPTEMBER 18

The second great point of controversy concerning the battle of Poitiers centres round the events immediately preceding the battle and the nature of the battle itself. Was the Black Prince attacked while holding a position or while in the act of retreat-

---

[1] He calls it "fort singulier".

ing? The French school asserts the latter, the English school
the former. As before, we will first give a *précis* of the events
up to the moment in dispute. Early on Sunday, September 18,
the English mounted units filed away to water in the Moisson
stream, at Nouaillé, four miles due south of Chabotrie, while
the marshals presumably reconnoitred the ground for a suitable
position covering the river line and facing Poitiers, Nouaillé
being distant eight miles from that city. Warwick's division led,
followed by the Prince's, while Oxford's brought up the rear.
At Nouaillé there was a narrow stone bridge. In order that the
two leading divisions could water their horses simultaneously,
Warwick's division would cross over the bridge and water on
the southern bank. The rear division probably found sufficient
water in Chabotrie and the neighbouring farms, and would
then proceed direct to the selected position. Here it would be
joined by the leading two divisions when watering was completed, the Prince's division doubling back up the road by
which it had descended to the river, Warwick's division re-
crossing the river by a ford 600 yards further west (see sketch
map), which was the direct line of approach to its portion—
the left—of the selected position.

Meanwhile the two indomitable cardinals had put in
another appearance. It is generally said that they spent the
day "passing backwards and forwards between the two armies".
This is hardly correct. They came from the French camp to
Edward, who listened with courteous patience to their tearful
pleadings for a truce. He ultimately agreed to a conference
between delegates from the two armies, which accordingly
assembled with the cardinals in no man's land. Discussions
went on most of the day, but without result. The terms proposed by King John were too humiliating for the Prince to
accept, and he fell back on the plea that he was not authorized
to arrange a truce and that reference must be made to his
father the king. Darkness fell, and both sides lay on their arms,
the outposts, according to one source, being within bowshot
of each other.

During the night the English held a war council, for the question had to be faced–supposing King John declined to attack the English position indefinitely, what was to be done? There were three possible courses. First, to take the offensive themselves. This was not in the English tradition, and as it had now become clear that the French army had attained great proportions such an attack was not likely to succeed. Second, to remain in position. But if the French remained stationary also there would be an impasse, which would redound to the advantage of the enemy, for the king could continually increase the size of his army whereas the Prince could not. Third, to retreat to Bordeaux. Such a move must sooner or later be carried out, for there was no longer any question of joining up with either of the two English armies to the north of the Loire. Might it not be advantageous to slip away quietly and so obtain a good lead for the slow-moving baggage and booty-wagons? The council decided upon the third course, provided the French king showed no signs of attacking next morning. The Prince, however, took the same preparatory step that he had taken before the withdrawal from Chatellerault: he passed his booty-wagons over the Nouaillé bridge during the night.

MONDAY, SEPTEMBER 19

Early in the morning the cardinal of Périgord again approached the Prince (who probably had pitched his tent on the ridge top in full view of the ridge held by the French outposts 1,500 yards distant). His keen eye detected continual movement from rear to front in the hostile lines: the French were evidently utilizing the unofficial armistice to bring up reinforcements and to collect stragglers after their hasty march. His own army was concentrated and ready for action. Any further delay would be in the interests of the French king. Indeed, the Prince is said to have accused the cardinal of working in the interests of King John. The Black Prince would listen to him no longer; the armistice was at an end. The die was cast. The Prince invited battle, and passed along his line, addressing encouraging

words to all within earshot. It is noteworthy that, so great an
importance did the English commander place on the moral
effect of this harangue, that he instructed his subordinate commanders to pass on the gist of it to all.

The above narrative is, in general, common to both schools
of thought up to the dawn of Monday. After that they diverge.
The English school holds that no retreat took place before the
battle and that the whole English army was drawn up awaiting
battle when the French advanced. The French school asserts
that the retreat had already begun, that Warwick's division had
already crossed to the south of the river and, with the baggage,
was on its way toward Bordeaux when the attack was launched.
Roland Delachenal, who may be said to represent the extreme
French school, asserts that while Warwick was on the south side
of the river the remainder of the army was also on the march,
quitting the position and heading for the Gué de l'Homme.

This divergence of view arises from a famous passage in the
Chandos Herald's poem, which states:

"The French book says, and the account likewise, that the earl of
Salisbury ... discomfited the (French) marshals ... before the
vanguard could be turned and brought across again, for it was over
the river." (The herald had previously stated that Warwick was
in command of the vanguard.)

Written at approximately the same time, *i.e.*, some 30 years
after the battle, the *Anonimalle Chronicle* states that Warwick's
division crossed a narrow causeway, but later, when the French
vanguard approached the English position, "Warwick and his
people, passing the marsh, found a good passage which had
not been found before", and attacked and worsted the French
vanguard, after which Salisbury with the rearguard came to
the aid of Warwick so that the French were defeated.

Thirdly, le Baker. He narrates how the Prince addressed
his whole army and then, turning to the archers, gave them
a special harangue. Thus saying (*talia dicens*), he looks up and
notices a hill; and le Baker proceeds:

"Between us and the hill was a broad deep valley and a marsh, which was fed by a certain stream. At a fairly narrow ford the Prince's division crossed the stream, with its carriages, and occupied the hill. . . ."

Le Baker then describes the position held by the other two divisions, one flank of which rested on a marsh.

The above three accounts agree in one thing, *viz.*, that at some time before the battle a portion of the English army was on the opposite side of a valley from the position to be held. This has led the French school to believe that the herald's story is substantially true, and that the English army was in the act of retreating when the French attacked them. I hold to the traditional, or English, school. I must here support my case by examining the above passages.

Let us first take le Baker, easily the most reliable of the three sources. Though not himself present at the battle he must have obtained his story from eye-witnesses—indeed from several, for a single one could not have given the full coherent and detailed account that le Baker retails. But the author gives no indication of his division of sources: they merge into one in a flowing narrative that reflects the accomplished historian. Let us see whether we can break down into its components the story related by him. I suggest that the above passage originates from at least two informants, one in the Prince's division and one in Warwick's. Number one was present when the Prince made his harangue (probably an archer). The fiery harangue made a vivid impression on him, and in giving his story of the battle he starts off with it. Number two had crossed the river with Warwick, and had halted on the far side to water and feed. From here he well remembered looking across the valley toward the ridge up which he was shortly to toil on the way to the allotted position. This he retailed to his auditor, and then described in detail the position, how one flank rested on a marsh, etc. Le Baker no doubt heard other accounts, but having neither map nor photograph of the field was not able to form a clear and correct picture of the terrain. He did his best to piece the accounts together, but his chronology was the weakest part (as it nearly always is when relating battle or any exciting episode, or when listening to the accounts afterward). Thus in his effort to merge his various stories into one smooth-flowing account, he joined them into one continuous narrative with such conjunctive phrases as *talia dicens*. But is it conceivable, on the ground of inherent military probability, that the Prince should decide to stand his ground and announce the fact formally to his troops with the greatest publicity *before he had decided on the position to be held*, or had even reconnoitred the ground? Thus we are bound to place the speech after, not before, the scene in the valley. The speeches must have been delivered on the actual position occupied by the troops, either on the Sunday evening or, more probably, the Monday morning.

Thus regarded, le Baker does not lend any support to the herald's story. The *Chronicle Anonimalle* must be tackled in another way. The only essential point on which it supports the herald is in the statement that immediately before the battle, Warwick's division was on the far side of the river. In other respects it directly contradicts the herald, for it brings Warwick's division into action before, not after, Salisbury's. According to him, though at one time Warwick was over the river he returned in time to encounter the French vanguard, in other words, at the very beginning of the battle. This agrees with the other chroniclers, and with the English school. Incidentally, the *Anonimalle* account is full of obvious errors[1]; indeed, only one original statement in it "rings true", *viz.*, that some wagons retiring during the night over what is evidently Nouaillé bridge caused a traffic jam—a very likely occurrence before the days of traffic policemen—and even since their appearance for that matter. The episode is, however, of importance as showing that during the night the Prince prepared for an eventual withdrawal, by getting his booty-wagons clear of the river crossing

---

[1] A statement by the Chronicler regarding the siege of Romorantin is characterized by his editor, Professor Galbraith, "a wilful perversion of the truth".

overnight—just as he had so wisely done at Chatellerault a few nights before.

We must now consider the French school, which accepts implicitly the herald's statement quoted above. How can it be "explained away"? First, we must allow some licence to a poet who for the sake of rhyme and scansion must at times use an inexact word. Thus "rivière" was used by him irrespective of the size of the stream in question in order to rhyme with "pière".

But apart from this, whence did the herald obtain his information? In the first place it was already known that there was talk of retirement, and indeed that preparations had been made for it. Such preparations are evidently alluded to by Froissart when he makes the French marshals argue as to whether what they saw indicated a retirement or not. Then we are now all agreed, I hope, that at one time a portion of the English army had indeed crossed to the south side of the river (in order to water). But, allowing for all this, whence did the herald obtain his assertion that Warwick was actually in retreat when the battle opened? The herald himself tells us (though, rather surprisingly, his statement seems to have been overlooked by the commentators). Twice when describing the battle he informs us that he owes his information to "the French book", and the story of Warwick's retreating division is one of the occasions. So it was a French source—now lost—not a very good source for what was going on "the other side of the hill" to the French. We can safely attribute it to a patriotic and imaginative Frenchman anxious to impart a gleam into the gloom of that dolorous day and for this purpose inventing an English "retreat". Such a book would probably not come into the hands of the herald till after the death of his master, Sir John Chandos. It is generally and naturally supposed that the herald obtained his story of the battle from that master, with a view to his poem. But the idea of the poem perhaps occurred to him after the death of his master, when it was too late to question him. How often does one regret not having questioned the actor in a scene while he was still alive!

Let us now examine the theory of the French school, as
portrayed by Roland Delachenal in his *Histoire de Charles V* and
adopted by J. Tourneux-Aumont in *La Grande Goule* for 1935
(in reply to an article from my pen in the same issue).

The theory of M. Delachenal is that the battle took place
in the bend of the Moisson river at Champ d'Alexandre where
the English army was attacked while "en plein marche"
toward the south, the English right being near Bernon and
their left approaching the Gué de l'Homme. In other words,
the English faced west and the French east. His ground for
placing the French army in such a curious position is that the
Champ d'Alexandre is described in a sixteenth-century MS as
the place where certain French soldiers who had fought in the
battle died. But Professor Lot has shown that this passage is
wrongly transcribed from a fourteenth-century MS which
refers to "plusieux des bons et loyaux amis du Roy qu'ils
fussent ou non de sa bataille". Thus "bataille" means battalion
or unit—not battle. But apart from the weakness of the written
evidence, Delachenal's theory is open to attack on six grounds
of inherent military probability.

1. In order to reach this position the French king would
have to make a flank march across and in sight of the English
position and then form line to his left, having altered the
direction of his front by almost a right angle. This would be
a hazardous and difficult manoeuvre for a badly trained
medieval army, especially as the ground was wooded and hilly.

2. The French army would form up in line, facing east, the
bulk of it on a narrow-backed ridge sloping down so steeply to
both front and rear that the horsemen of that day would have
found it practically unnegotiable—hardly an ideal place for an
army that relied to a large degree on its mounted men.

3. The southern half of the army would be confined by the
narrow loop of the river, with that river only 250 yards to its
front and to its rear. In the event of being defeated it would be
driven into the marshy ravine.

4. The position would thus have no depth; it would be

impossible to station any reserve behind the centre of the line, still less could the army approach in three or four columns, as we know it did.

5. If the French army had been seen approaching such a position and it had been the intention of the Black Prince to retreat he would scarcely have selected the Gué de l'Homme for that purpose, but would have taken the natural one–the Nouaillé crossing.

6. The Valois princes who fled at the end of the battle could not have gone in an easterly direction to Chabotrie (as they did) for that would have taken them right through the enemy army.

Even if King John had seriously proposed to occupy such a position he would have been dissuaded by his experienced generals, or if he had persisted in it and the manoeuvre had been attempted it would have foundered in the course of execution.

Whatever possible sites there may be for the battlefield there is one impossible one–Delachenal's.

In short, the conception is one that is refuted by inherent military probability. It is hard to believe that Professor Delachenal can have ever visited the terrain.[1]

THE ENGLISH POSITION

The English position can be easily defined, for it ran along a hedge–the famous hedge mentioned by three of the chroniclers–which faced north-west, and the centre of which was 500 yards due south of La Cardinerie farm. Portions of this hedge are still in existence. The hedge crosses two roads from Poitiers, that to Nouaillé and that to Le Gué de l'Homme, and the two roads, interrupting the line of the hedge, formed two gaps in it. That on the Nouaillé road was left open, but that on the Gué de l'Homme road was barricaded with carts and

[1] Since penning the above pages, I have read Ferdinand Lot's account of the battle in his *L'Art Militaire*. He appears to abandon Delachenal's theory, but though he says that my article in *English Historical Review* (1938) subjects it to "*des critiques les plus vives*" he does not specify how far he agrees with them.

brushwood. The lower, or left-hand, end of the hedge rested upon marshy ground in the slight "Depression" (so marked on the sketch map) that runs down to join the Moisson river. The upper or right-hand flank rested on open ground on top of the plateau, and was strengthened by the construction of a leaguer made of the war-stores wagons, surrounded by a trench.[1] Behind the position lay the wood of Nouaillé, which stretched down the slope for about 50 ft. to the winding narrow valley of the river Moisson. At the highest point of the ridge, on the edge of the wood, are two tall trees, which probably mark the approximate situation of the Black Prince's command-post during the battle. From it there is a good view of the position, and of the parallel ridge 800 yards beyond it (which I call the North Ridge) on which the French troops deployed for action.

The English army was about 6,000 strong, and the French over 20,000. The English army took up its position along or close to the hedge, Salisbury's division being on the right, Warwick's on the left, while the Prince's was in reserve in rear. The archers were for the most part drawn up in the Crecy formation, that is, on the two flanks of their respective divisions, in wedges slightly in advance of the line of men-at-arms. (They were, as usual, dismounted, but the Prince retained a small body of mounted men, as a reserve.)

The French army was formed into four bodies. In the van were two small contingents of mounted men-at-arms, about 250 in each, under the command of the two marshals, Clermont and Audrehem. Next came the division of the duke of Normandy, then that of his uncle, the duke of Orleans, and last of all that of the king. All except the van were dismounted. They had left their horses in the city of Poitiers, and for convenience in marching had cut off the long toes of their riding boots and had removed their spurs, and they had also shortened their lances to about five feet.

[1] Vestiges of this trench were still visible in the seventeenth century, and an air photograph might still disclose them. I made an ineffectual effort to obtain such a photograph in 1946.

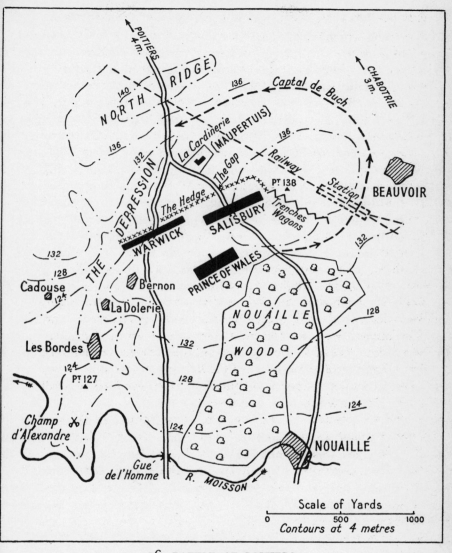

POITIERS
4 m.

NORTH RIDGE

140

136

132

136

Captal de Buch

CHABOTRIE
3 m.

La Cardinerie
(MAUPERTUIS)

The Gap

136

Railway

PT 138

Station

BEAUVOIR

THE DEPRESSION

The Hedge

WARWICK

SALISBURY

Trenches
Wagons

PRINCE OF WALES

132

132

128

124

Cadouse

Bernon

La Dolerie

128

NOUAILLE

Les Bordes

132

WOOD

124

PT 127

128

124

Champ
d'Alexandre

124

NOUAILLÉ

Gué
de l'Homme

R. MOISSON

Scale of Yards

0   500   1000

Contours at 4 metres

16. BATTLE OF POITIERS

THE BATTLE

The truce terminated at about 7.30 a.m. on Monday,
September 19. The French showed no signs of advancing, and
the Prince who had, as we know, during the night discussed the
desirability of slipping away, began seriously to consider doing
so. The first step was obviously to get on the move the wagons
containing the personal baggage and tentage (the booty-
wagons having already cleared the position). Orders were
issued accordingly and the wagons and their escort began to
move off. The move was spotted by the French vanguard, and
received different interpretations.[1] After an altercation whether
the English were really retiring, the two French marshals led
the vanguard to the attack.[2] They advanced by divergent
paths. Why? The terrain seems to afford the answer. Consider
the situation. The French horses were heavy and unwieldy;
their course led through the vineyard, which constituted a big
obstacle and would tend to break up the line formation into a
series of small columns, each column taking a track or pathway
between the vines in "follow-my-leader" style. Now we have
seen that there were two distinct tracks or roads, leading to the
English hedge in divergent directions. Clermont's column on
the French left would tend to "bunch" on the Nouaillé road,
and that of Audrehem on the Gué de l'Homme road. This
would bring both columns up against the two gaps where the
respective roads passed through the hedge. That confronting
Audrehem was barricaded and occupied; consequently he had
no success and was in fact captured (probably by jumping the
hedge and not being followed by the less well-mounted
troops); but that of Clermont met with more immediate
success, for it came up to the open unguarded gap on the

---

[1] Just as at the battle of the Aisne, the sight of German transport moving to
the rear led some to believe that it was the beginning of a general retirement.
I have here accepted the herald's account, but it is possible that Villani's statement that smoke from some burning wagons precipitated the battle is the
correct one.

[2] I cannot accept Froissart's unsupported statement that the battle began at
"prime" and ended at "nones": more likely it began at "nones" (noon) and ended
at vespers (4 p.m.).

Nouaillé road, and the leading files passed through it and swung to their right in support of Audrehem, already held up opposite his gap. It was only the prompt manoeuvre of Salisbury that frustrated this well-devised operation of Clermont's. Quick to sense the danger, he advanced his line right up to the hedge, thus effectually closing the gap and scotching the flank attack on Warwick's division.

Meanwhile on the English left some of our archers were carrying out a noteworthy manoeuvre. As the French cavalry approached, the bulk of them moved still further to their left into the marsh. Here they were comparatively safe from the hostile horsemen, and were able to gall them with a flanking fire. An obscure passage in le Baker[1] describes how the cavalry advanced direct upon the archers hoping to protect themselves by their breast armour and at the same time protect the infantry following behind them. The English arrows ricocheted off the French breastplates and the archers were consequently at a disadvantage till the earl of Oxford, appreciating the situation, ran down from the Prince's head-quarters and directed the archers to fire obliquely, not at the armoured riders, but at the unprotected hindquarters of their horses. It was in order to do this that the archers moved to their left into the marsh. This action was completely successful and the French attack was repulsed. The struggle had, how-ever, been severe and in some places (probably in the centre) some cavalry had managed to break through the hedge.[2] Rigid discipline reigned in the English ranks, and no pursuit was allowed. It was recognized that only the vanguard had as yet been encountered.

The Dauphin's column now advanced, on foot.[3] Their horses had been left in the rear, as already mentioned. The English men-at-arms had also dismounted, with this difference,

---

[1] Omitted by Stow in his translation.

[2] No doubt making use of the "*pluseurs brèches*" mentioned by the *Chronique Normande du XIVe Siècle*.

[3] King John has been blamed for dismounting the bulk of his army, but he was well advised to do so. It was no innovation in the French army, as we have seen.

however, that they had kept their horses at hand, and did not remove their spurs.

The *élan* of the oncoming column cannot have been increased by the spectacle of disaster that had befallen the vanguard. Nor would the impact with the panic-struck horses of the vanguard, galloping to the rear, add to their order and cohesion.[1] But the column came stolidly on, in spite of all that the archers could do, and engaged the men-at-arms in hand-to-hand fighting. At this stage the hedge vanishes almost completely from the story. There are two possible explanations. Either it was by now so battered down that it ceased to be an obstacle for the dismounted French, or the English advanced slightly beyond the hedge for the hand-to-hand contest that ensued. The archers were running short of arrows, and the major credit for the defeat of the Dauphin's column goes to our men-at-arms. During the course of this fight the Prince reinforced Warwick's portion of the line with the bulk of his own column; but he was careful to keep a small mounted force in his own hands, which he later used to good purpose.

It is useless to attempt to compute how long the struggle lasted; but that it was prolonged is evident from the extreme state of exhaustion to which it reduced the English army. The accounts are clear and frank on this point. When at last the Dauphin drew off, defeated but in good order, the English heaved a sigh of relief, believing the battle was over. From this it is clear that the two remaining columns of the French army were still out of sight behind the North Ridge. A lull now descended on the battle, which the English utilized to replenish ammunition, exchange broken for sound lances, recover spent arrows and tend the wounded. Water was no doubt brought up from the river, as they must have been very thirsty by now—especially the men-at-arms. The pause was happily increased by the failure of the duke of Orleans' column to engage. What exactly happened to it is obscure, but it appears to have been seized with panic and to have fled toward

[1] A similar impact at Agincourt had serious results.

Chauvigny.[1] The duke of Orleans has, of course, been unmercifully blamed for this; but it must be remembered in his
defence that, though the uncle of the Dauphin, he was himself
under 21 years of age. Moreover the fugitives from two defeated
columns had passed through his ranks and such people are
not prone to underestimate the strength and hitting power of
their opponents.

THE KING ATTACKS

The column of the king of France alone remained. King
John had to make a momentous decision. Should he attack,
or should he cut his losses and retreat while yet there was time?
Retreat would certainly be the more prudent course to adopt,
but in those days considerations of chivalry were held of
greater account than those of strategy. King John therefore
ordered his column to the attack.

All the indications point to the fact that during the battle
of the Dauphin the king's column was a long distance in rear.[2]
This curious aloofness from the battlefield of King John's
column is one of the enigmas of the battle. Whatever the cause,
it was undoubtedly the gravest fault committed by the French
king in his conduct of the battle, though it has been almost
universally ignored by the commentators.

There was a long distance to traverse and no doubt the
advance was slow as the knights moved forward on foot. But
when the column topped the rise and appeared all along the
North Ridge, it presented a formidable spectacle to the exhausted and depleted English ranks.[3] For it was the largest of
the three columns, and superior in numbers to its opponents,
besides being fresher.

[1] Ramsay's assertion that the column fought and was defeated is directly
refuted by Villani's statement that it "had fled for fear without taking or giving
a blow".
[2] The *Chronique Normande* expressly says so and it is implied in Villani's statement
that "the Dauphin's column was defeated and dispersed before the king had news
of it".
[3] Some of the English were still absent in pursuit of the Dauphin, and perhaps
also of the duke of Orleans. Le Baker and Chandos Herald agree on this point.

The English chroniclers are strikingly frank about the disturbing moral effect the unexpected apparition of this huge and well-appointed column had upon the Anglo-Gascons. Historians, with that wisdom that comes after the event, have a tendency to regard the defeat of King John's column as fore-doomed and inevitable. But there seems no warrant for this. In the first place the extreme exhaustion of the Prince's army has not been sufficiently emphasized. Next comes the moral exhaustion, and reaction after a hard-fought fight.

"The great number of the enemy frightened our men", le Baker says bluntly. The *Eulogium* confirms that "many of our men were frightened; nor is it to be wondered at". Le Baker adds the interesting detail that at this juncture many of our wounded began to leave the field[1] (no doubt "escorted" by unwounded comrades, as the custom is!). Other men were heard to grumble that the Prince had left more than half his army behind to defend Gascony. No wonder Prince Edward offered up a fervent prayer to heaven! The depth of discourage-ment that reigned about him, contrasted by the Prince's own high courage, is well reflected in le Baker's story of how a prominent member of the Prince's staff cried out: "Alas, we are beaten!" and the Prince's stinging retort: "Thou liest, thou knave, if thou sayest that we can be conquered as long as I live!"

It was the critical moment in his career. Let us consider his perplexing position. He could not at the moment be aware of the flight of Orleans' column, which would be hidden by the North Ridge. He would imagine that he had the main body of the French army still in his front. Should he, in view of the weakened state of his own array, rest content with the blow he had struck against the Dauphin and now fall back? His horses were handy and there yet was time if he was prepared to sacrifice some of his foot men and wagons. Or should he accept battle in his defensive position? Or, thirdly, should he take the offensive himself?

Somewhat unexpectedly, when we consider all the circum-

---

[1] Discreetly omitted in Stow's translation.

stances, he chose the third course. Probably two considerations induced this decision.

1. He had already noted that his defensive position was more effective against mounted than dismounted men. The latter had fought upon fairly even terms. No benefit was therefore to be gained by awaiting attack behind what remained of the hedge.

2. At the crisis of a battle, moral superiority may just turn the scale. His men were then experiencing that reaction after a fight, that *lassitudo certaminis* that so frequently supervenes toward the end of a fight when physical and moral powers are at their lowest ebb. If he was content merely to sit still and await attack, the moral of his troops would scarcely be higher–it might indeed be lower–than that of the enemy. But if, with splendid audacity, he ordered an attack–and a mounted attack at that–the old moral superiority of mounted over dismounted men would assert itself and compel victory. The French were in the open, and on the move; they were deficient in archers, and dismounted; and would not be in a good posture to protect themselves against a mounted attack. Some such reasoning as this probably led the son of Edward III to the dazzling decision which stamps him for all time as a great captain.[1]

It is to be noted that the English attack was not to be the wholly frontal operation customary in those days. Combined with the frontal attack, the prince arranged a flank attack by the mounted reserve to which I have already referred. This he placed under the Gascon leader, the Captal de Buch. The force was small in numbers, but the ground was admirably suited to the operation. From point 138 the ground slopes down gently in all directions. Thus, from the northern edge of Nouaillé wood it is possible to skirt round to the east of the (present) railway station and swinging to the left approach the North Ridge unobserved. Such was the manoeuvre that was

[1] Ramsay is fully justified in claiming that "the daring attack on the king's big battalion is one of the finest things in military history".

entrusted to the Captal. No exact synchronization of the two attacks was probably either hoped for or aimed at. The final struggle was bound to be prolonged; a few minutes either way would be immaterial, though it was desirable, but not essential, that the frontal attack should slightly precede the flank attack.

From a study of the ground, and the identification of the place-names, the final clash must have taken place in the dip in the immediate vicinity of La Cardinerie.

The scene must have been a striking one. The English men-at-arms sprang to the stirrup, as they had done 23 years before at Halidon Hill, and charged down the hill upon the slowly oncoming column of dismounted men. A homeric contest then ensued in which the French crossbowmen were prominent. In the midst of the fighting and above the din was heard the familiar English battle-cry "St. George!" and from the right a body of mounted troops was seen galloping into the un-suspecting flank of the French column. It was the Captal de Buch with his gallant band. The result of this sudden onslaught was probably out of all proportion to the numbers of those engaged. Indeed it may have been the deciding factor—"the last straw" which so often settles destiny.

The contest was long, but yard by yard the sturdy English men-at-arms forced their way forward, as they had done across the decks of the French ships at Sluys and the Spanish ships at Winchelsea, while the mounted archers, having exhausted their arrows, put aside their bows and drawing their swords, entered the mêlée. The great French column, attacked on two sides, gradually crumbled, then disintegrated and fled from the field, leaving its king a prisoner in English hands. So much attention has naturally been lavished on this resounding and world-famous capture that the subsequent remarkable English pursuit right up to the walls of Poitiers has been generally overlooked. But it was yet another of the unusual features of the battle. The pursuers no doubt got out of hand, as all pursuers do, and the Prince had no means of reassembling them, save by hoisting

his banner on one of the bushes on the hill-top, as recommended
by Sir John Chandos.

There, amid the dead and dying, the Black Prince pitched
his pavilion, and there, when darkness descended, he sat down
to supper with the king of France as his guest.

The losses in the French nobility were staggering—nearly
2,000 knights and men-at-arms were prisoners and over 2,000
of them lay dead on the field. Of casualties to the infantry
levies, no record was attempted. A great charnel-pit was made
for the corpses, and it would be interesting to know the exact
spot where it was sited. As for the English, their casualties were
slight, but they included the dashing Lord Audley. That evening he was found lying half-dead on the field, and was carried
on his shield to the pavilion of the Prince of Wales, who was at
that moment at supper with King John. The Prince interrupted
his meal to tend the wounds of one of the staunchest of his
captains.

*   *   *

Next day the Anglo-Gascon army resumed its homeward
march, and entered the city of Bordeaux some days later in
triumph—while the Anglo-Breton army sorrowfully retraced
its footsteps to Brittany. Henry of Grosmont, Derby and
Lancaster had failed for the first and only time in his military
career.

CAUSES OF THE VICTORY

It is not surprising that French commentators have pondered
deeply the problem of how the English came to win this
sweeping victory against such odds, adding one more to the
line of consistent English victories during the previous 16 years
of warfare. Simeon Luce, in the notes to his edition of
Froissart, writes: "The incontestable military superiority of
the English in the 14th century resided above all in the
dexterity, the good weapons and the large proportion of their
archers to other arms." Professor Delachenal starts with very

similar words, but comes to different conclusions: "The intrinsic quality of the English army largely made up for its weak
numbers. The military superiority of the English was established in the first encounters of the Hundred Years War, and
it was maintained throughout the 14th century. Du Guesclin
himself recognized this, for he never risked a set battle against
them." But Delachenal finds other causes for this superiority
than those given by Luce. In general he attributes the English
success to superior organization, recruitment and training.
Neither of these authors, in my opinion, gives the most fundamental cause. While recognizing that battles and wars are
won, not by one single factor but by the resultant of several,
it is usually possible to single out one factor as predominant in
any given case. In this case I believe this factor to be *morale*—
that mysterious quality that induces one man to persevere in
the fight longer than another. An army, or a nation, gains a
victory by certain means; its morale is thereby raised, with the
result that a second victory is gained; this in turn still further
strengthens the morale of the troops by the reverse of the
"vicious circle" and until some greater antagonistic factor
supervenes the army goes from strength to strength. The
English army started the Hundred Years War possessed of a
fairly high state of morale, born of their recent success against
the Scots, with the victories of Edward I as a background. They
went "from strength to strength" just as, for example, did
Napoleon's *Grande Armée* 450 years later, or as did the British
Eighth Army after its victory at Alamein. By the time of
Poitiers the English morale was at its zenith.

THE TACTICS

A word regarding the tactics, that is the dispositions and
handling of troops in the battle, on the part of the rival commanders. As for the Prince of Wales, I can find no flaw at any
stage. The only really difficult problem is to decide how far the
young Prince really "took charge" in the battle and how far
he was swayed or indeed governed by the counsel of others. It

is clear that he was wont to hold a war council before making any important decision; but this was in accordance with the normal procedure of medieval times, and indeed of later times; even the duke of Marlborough conformed to this practice. As regards advice given by individuals, the only name mentioned is that of Sir John Chandos. At one time I was disposed to regard this famous knight as what we should call chief of staff to the Prince. But this is doubtful. Sir John Chandos at times roamed far from the main column, once at least as much as 25 miles; at such times he could be of little help to his master. The earl of Warwick was probably the most experienced soldier in the army and his high rank and station indicates him as the nearest in the line of succession to the Black Prince; but we hear nothing specific about this rather shadowy commander. The matter cannot be resolved on the available evidence; but it is reasonable to suppose that the Prince relied wholly upon his advisers in the early stages of his first campaign, but became progressively independent of them, until when the day of Poitiers dawned he was as much the commander-in-chief as his father had been at Crecy.

Though Poitiers was at the outset fought in the Crecy tradition, two important differences should be noted – the ascendancy of the men-at-arms, and the success of mounted versus dismounted troops in the final phase of the battle. In these two respects Poitiers was a hark-back to the previous century.

As for the king of France, we possess no account by an eye-witness from the French side, so must judge as best we can, solely from the evidence of the facts. This evidence shows no indication of control by one supreme commander. Indeed there seem in essence to have been three armies, if not four, for the two marshals with their mounted troops acted on their own initiative in opening the battle. These armies fought entirely separate battles (when they fought at all). This disconnected-ness was the weakest feature in the French tactics, and must be attributed to the king who, during the greater part of the battle, was far in rear of the field. His decision to fight dismounted was taken, we are told, on the advice of a foreigner, Sir William Douglas, and that is the only decision we hear of. As far as one can see, the battle would have been fought no worse had the French army possessed no commander at all.

As the unfortunate French king passed down the Bordeaux road into captivity, he passes out of these pages. What are we to say of him? Jean le Bon, John the Good Fellow, a man of stainless honour, during his military career encountered little but disappointment, defeat and disaster. He was more consistently unsuccessful than any captain of his century—with the possible exception of his own father. Some leaders are born so, some are made. John was neither born so nor made. The French nation was unfortunate, from a military point of view, in its first two Valois kings.

APPENDIX

SOURCES

No battle in the Hundred Years War is better supplied with sources than that of Poitiers.[1] There exist over 20 fourteenth-century sources, some, of course, very brief. Here I will only list the dozen that I consider the most useful in elucidating the many problems of the campaign and battle.[2] I list them in roughly chronological order:

1 and 2. *Letters of the Black Prince to the mayor of London and to the bishop of Worcester*, dated respectively October 22 and 20. The first is the longer, and is particularly valuable for the campaign; the actual battle is passed over in a few words.

3. *Letter from Lord Bartholomew Burghersh*, who was present throughout the campaign. This letter also is more concerned with the campaign than with the battle, of which he gives only the strengths and losses.

[1] For a more complete list see my article in the *English Historical Review* (1938).
[2] The old-fashioned English pronunciation "Poy-teers" is nearer how our ancestors pronounced the word than the modern French pronunciation now taught in schools. English writers of the period spelt proper names phonetically: the Black Prince spelt it Peyters, and another Englishman Petters.

4. *Eulogium Historiarum.* Written by a monk of Malmesbury, but believed to be the record of an eye-witness. In it is what is called the *Itinerary of the Prince of Wales* in the campaign. From it Father Deniflé was able to compile a day-to-day journal of the march. It fortunately gives some space to the battle, and is incomparably the most reliable account of the battle, so far as it goes.

5. *Chronicle of Geoffrey le Baker de Swynbroke.* The author was not present, but most of his facts were probably gathered from eye-witnesses. His is the most detailed account of the battle except that of Froissart. Stow translated it in parts, quietly omitting difficult passages. Maunde Thompson, in his edition (1889), reproduces some of Stow's translation.

6. *Scalacronica,* by Sir Thomas Gray. The author served in the Black Prince's division in the 1359 campaign, whence he obtained most of his information. Unfortunately it is a muddled account, marred by some obvious errors, and written in execrable French—almost as bad as that of the Black Prince himself.

7. *Istorie Florientine,* by Matteo Villani, an Italian banker. Unbiassed, independent and contains some interesting details, but Villani naturally could not discriminate between true and false reports.

8. *Chronicles of Froissart.* Jean Froissart is here in his most tantalizing mood. He intersperses obviously genuine information received from participants with gross embellishments of his own. But it is an intellectual delight trying to sift the chaff from the good grain, of which there is plenty. The *Amiens* edition (never translated into English) should be consulted wherever possible.

9. *Chronicle of Henry Knighton.* Useful for the later stages of the battle.

10. *Le Prince Noir,* by Chandos Herald. A long poem by Sir John Chandos' herald, written some 30 years after the battle (with English translation in the edition of Pope and Lodge, 1910). The necessity for scansion and rhyming tells against it as exact history. All we can safely say is that here and

there it contains accurate statements not found elsewhere. The lines dealing with the battle have caused all historians many sleepless hours.

11. *Chronicle Anonimalle.* Written about the same time as the last-mentioned, and is about as unreliable. But it contains at least one statement not found elsewhere that rings true–the story of the traffic jam in the night at Nouaillé bridge. It has not been used by modern historians, having only been edited by Professor V. H. Galbraith in 1927 (though the MS was used by Stow).

12. *Chronique Normande du XIVe Siècle.* Written by a French soldier, not by a monk, consequently its military information is always of interest and no doubt fairly reliable. His is the best French account of the battle that we possess.

The other French sources help us very little, nor do the remaining English chronicles, or le Bel.

It is a regrettable fact that the only sources of which we possess a full modern rendering in English are the Prince's letter to the mayor of London, the *Scalacronica*, and the poem of the Chandos Herald. The others have to be studied in their original medieval French or Latin.

THE NUMBERS

English Army

It has been established that the army that went to Gascony in 1355 was 2,600 strong. To this figure must be added the number already serving in that country, plus the reinforcements received in 1356. From this total must be deducted wastage by death, sickness, etc., and troops left behind to guard Gascony. Unfortunately, none of these figures is known. Another unknown quantity is the number of Gascons in the army. There are indications that a large number joined up in 1346 as a result of the successful campaign of the previous year. Indeed the total field force that the Black Prince led out of Bordeaux in July, 1356, has been estimated as high as 12,000. But a large portion of this, almost entirely Gascon in composition, was, as we have seen, left behind watching the Armagnac border. Thus our original figure of 2,600 is no guide, except as setting a kind of scale of values on which to work. The total numbers were evidently very small. The estimates given in the chronicles do not vary greatly, 7,000 being an average figure. I see no reason for not accepting the figure given by Burghersh, who was in a position to know the facts. He gives 3,000 men-at-arms, 2,000 archers and 1,000 sergeants, making a total of 6,000. The only estimate well below this is that of Ramsay, who suggests 3,500, on the unwarranted assumption that there were less than 1,000 Gascons in the army.

French Army

This is, as usual, a more difficult problem. Figures vary between 11,000 and 60,000. In default of reliable figures I will approach the problem from four different aspects.

1. There is ample evidence that the appearance of the French king's division on the battlefield dismayed the English because of its vast numbers. It must therefore have outnumbered the victorious English nearly, if not quite, twofold. If the English were 6,000 the king's division would thus be at least 10,000 strong. The other two divisions were much smaller than the king's. Stragglers and late detachments joining the army on the morning of the battle would be hastily drafted into the rear division, which was the king's. In addition, some of the stouter-hearted soldiers in the duke of Orleans' division joined that of the king, which we can thus assess at about twice the strength of each of the other two. Thus the total would amount to about 20,000, excluding the 500 mounted troops of the marshals.

2. King John had a large army in Normandy. Coville in Lavisse's History computes it at 50,000. We can scale this down to perhaps 20,000 but scarcely lower. As no operations were going on when John left for Chartres, he presumably took the great proportion of this army with him. To it he added levies from all over France – the chronicles are emphatic on the point.

At least another 5,000 must have joined his army from this source, making a total of rather more than 20,000.

3. Burghersh states that the French had 8,000 men-at-arms, 3,000 foot soldiers, totalling 11,000. He must have obtained these figures from French prisoners (who would be tempted to scale down the numbers from obvious motives) for neither Burghersh nor any other Englishman saw the whole French army, since Orleans' division never came in view of them. But if Burghersh was given some official French figure the only one available would be that of the permanent force (what we should now call regulars) that accompanied the king on his campaigns. The numbers obtained by the nation-wide levy called for so insistently by the king could not be known, for the simple reason that detachments were still arriving right up to the day of the battle, and after the battle the king was a prisoner and all internal organization of the army had vanished (and with it the records). It is, however, reasonable to suppose that the total of the levies equalled, if it did not exceed, that of the regulars. This would bring the grand total to something over 20,000.

4. Approximately 2,500 French are reported killed, and 2,000 captured. If we allow two men wounded for one killed that would make the total casualties including captured about 8,500. In so heavy a defeat as this one might expect the casualties to amount to nearly 50 per cent. of combatants, which would thus be 17,000. To this we must add the 5,000 or so of Orleans' division which presumably had no casualties. This brings the grand total to approximately 23,000. Thus by four several lines of approach we get a grand total of slightly over 20,000.[1]

Until quite recently all chroniclers and historians have been in agreement that the French army outnumbered the English. But in 1946, Professor Ferdinand Lot in his *L'Art Militaire* attempted to show that the French were inferior numerically

[1] Delachenal computes the French as being twice as numerous as the English. As he puts the latter at about 10,000 he evidently agrees with our figure of 20,000 for the French.

to the English, or rather, he "suspects it". As the professor endeavours in this book to show that the French never had a numerical superiority at Crecy, Agincourt or Verneuil, or at least to throw doubt on the matter, it is desirable to examine his methods of calculation rather closely, for they constitute "the last word" and have never been answered from the traditional point of view.

He starts by arguing that King John cannot have had a large army because he was completely unable to turn the English position because of lack of men. This is a weak argument; especially when referring to a medieval battle where a frontal attack, when two armies were ranged in opposing lines, was almost a foregone conclusion. But he bases his main argument on the figures supplied by Jean le Bel, a foreigner writing hundreds of miles away, and not a particularly reliable authority. However, let us accept his figures for the sake of argument. Le Bel gives very low figures for the French cavalry, but adds: "The King had in his own division all the remnants of the men-at-arms and infantry, of whom there were such a large number that it was a marvellous sight." Lot accepts the first statement which supports his case, but rejects the second, which he explains away by the airy remark that "no doubt John sacrificed all to the desire to cut the Anglo-Gascon retreat to Bordeaux, and did not embarrass himself with a lot of infantry: they would have retarded his march. . . ."

As we have seen above, it is by no means certain that John tried on the Friday or the Saturday to cut the retreat of the English, but even if we allow that argument, King John was halted at Chauvigny for the best part of a day, and two whole days at Poitiers (thus allowing time for the infantry to come up) before the battle began. M. Lot also makes the assertion (copied from the German Lampe and not verified by him) that "there is no question of the presence of any crossbowmen . . . in the accounts of the action". This is not so: le Baker (p. 151, 1.6) refers to "a threatening body of crossbowmen" who made the sky dark with their arrows.

The professor concludes by asserting that the *Grandes Chroniques* says that the two armies were equal. What the *Grandes Chroniques* actually said was: "Although the king of France had as many men as the Prince . . ." which Delachenal describes as a statement made "très habilement, trop habilement" thus indicating that it was a *suggestio falsi*. But Ferdinand Lot seizes on it and twists it to his own purpose.

On such flimsy grounds and by such questionable methods does the learned historian seek to upset a hitherto universally accepted belief.

THE HEDGE

We come now to the consideration of the exact location of the English position. The commentators are agreed that it was somewhere to the north of Nouaillé wood and near Maupertuis (La Cardinerie). Can we define it within narrower limits? Can we even aspire to discover the actual hedge, and the *"fameuse brèche"* in it? Let us see.

On grounds of inherent military probability we would naturally look for the position on a ridge facing toward Poitiers, and covering the road or roads by which the ultimate retirement to Bordeaux would have to be carried out. Now, the road running just west of La Cardinerie to Gué de l'Homme existed at the time of the battle, and would thus form a possible line of retreat. Maupertuis was a village or hamlet, and some sort of road connected it with the near-by abbey of Nouaillé, for a road crossed the river at that spot. Maupertuis lay in the direct line from the abbey to the city of Poitiers, another reason for the existence of this road. It seems natural that this road should take the approximate course of the present road, and that it would constitute a second possible line of retreat. Thus, we have two roads, both still in existence, to be covered by the English position. All accounts agree that this was a strong natural position. Looking at the ground to-day, there appear to be two possible positions and two only. The foremost lies on the ridge 400 yards to the north-west of La Cardinerie, which I call the North Ridge. The rear one is 400 yards south of La Cardinerie. Between the two runs the slight depression (which I call the "Depression") which joins the valley of the Moisson just south of Les Bordes, deepening as it descends.

Let us now see what light the study of place-names and discovery of relics may throw upon the subject. This study has been well summarized by Lettenhove in his edition of Froissart.

Le Champ de la Bataille. "Between Les Bordes and Maupertuis." Babinet puts it just south of the railway bridge west of Maupertuis. Broken swords and battle debris have been found here.

La Masse Aux Anglais. "A mound 500 metres from Maupertuis."

L'Abreuvoir Aux Anglais. "Further on." Probably the same as *Mare Aux Anglais*, a small pool at the head of the depression, at which the English watered some horses.

In addition, a silver coin of Edward III was picked up near Maupertuis; near the same place was found the "escarboucle" or jewel of the French king.

Finally, in Lettenhove's time "one still sees vestiges of field works constructed by the English", in the same locality. The cumulative effect of all these identifications is overwhelming; the inference is inescapable. The battle took place in the immediate vicinity of the present La Cardinerie.

Now the bulk of the fighting seems to have taken place slightly in advance of the English hedge; certainly the fight with King John's column was in front of it. Consequently the battlefield debris would be mainly in front of the hedge. This would point to the hedge being slightly to the south of La Cardinerie; *i.e.*, on the rearmost of the two positions I have suggested.

There are other considerations that point in the same direction. Here le Baker comes to our assistance. He describes an uncultivated hilltop, thick with scrub and undergrowth, bounded by a long hedge and ditch; beyond this hedge lay the cultivated land, partly vines and partly fallow at that season of the year. The first and third columns lay behind the hedge, one end of which fell away into a marsh. Toward the other end of the hedge, a good way from the marsh, was a large gap. The position that I have indicated south of Maupertuis exactly fits this description, if we allow the assumption that "marsh" refers to my "Depression". Doubts have been expressed on this point because of the words "wide and deep valley". That description is true of the Moisson valley, but not of the depression near Maupertuis. I suggest, however, that the "marsh" *does* refer to the depression. Though shallow at this point, it gets deeper as it runs south, till on joining the Moisson valley south of Les Bordes it is just as deep as that valley. It would be easy for an absentee chronicler, relying on verbal accounts, to confound the main valley with its tributary "marsh". Even this assumption is not absolutely essential. Le Baker, in speaking of a "wide deep valley and a marsh", may have intended, as I have hinted above, to discriminate between them, the valley being the Moisson valley, and the marsh being the Depression. But what of the stream running through it? There is now no stream, but it is probable that before the days of drainage surface water trickled down it, especially as there was a "reservoir" at its head. An alternative solution is that both informants spoke of a marsh and le Baker incorrectly assumed that they were referring to the same marsh, whereas there were really two quite separate marshes–one in the Moisson valley, and one in the Depression.

If my assumption is accepted, we can now fix the site of the hedge within very narrow limits. It would face roughly north-west; its left end resting on the "marsh", that is on the Depression, its right on the high ground near point 138 (see Map 37.[1]

H. B. George says, "There is now no long hedge anywhere *east* of the wood of Nouaillé," but it is to the *north-west* that we must look. "Hedges and ditches disappear easily in fertile soil," he continues, and certainly a visitor to the field nearly

[1] Hilaire Belloc favoured such a position, which he claimed extended for 1,000 yards "almost to a foot".

600 years later would scarcely expect the good fortune of
finding and identifying that famous hedge, but there are in
fact considerable portions of an old hedge exactly fitting the
requirements. In places it has disappeared and been replaced
by wire or fresh planting; but the line is marked by a continuous track which runs along in front of it (corresponding
to the ditch which we know lay in front of it). This hedge and
track start on the left at the Gué de l'Homme road, and run
north-east for 500 yards, crossing the Nouaillé road 300 yards
south-east of La Cardinerie. There is now no sign of the hedge
to the left of the Gué de l'Homme road, but if it indeed is the
actual hedge, we must picture it continuing another 200 yards
down to the Depression. Assuming that this is the veritable
hedge, where should we expect to find the equally famous
gap? The obvious spot would be where the road passes through
it. Now, we have seen that in all probability two roads, or
tracks, passed through it. Either of these might be the gap,
were it not that le Baker distinctly states that the gap was
"well removed from the marsh". This rules out the Gué de
l'Homme road, leaving only the Nouaillé road. The lower
gap would be barricaded[1] while the upper gap was left open.
This also we know from le Baker, who records that Warwick
held the lower part of the hedge, but that Salisbury kept back
"a stone's throw" from the gap.

We will now see how this identification of the position fits
in with a reconnaissance report[2] made by Marshal Ribaumont
just before the battle. We can picture him viewing the English
position from where the railway bridge now is. The intervening
ground, he reported, was partly planted with vines and partly
fallow. (This agrees with le Baker.) Since vines generally grow
on a southward-facing slope, the ground on his side of the
depression was probably covered with vines, with fallow ground

[1] An illustration in the copy of Froissart in the *Bibliothèque de l'Arsenal* in Paris
shows a gap barricaded with stakes interlaced with vine branches—a very natural
precaution.
[2] Delachenal describes this reconnaissance as "derisoire"—ridiculous—but I can
find nothing ridiculous in it—although Froissart is our only authority for it.

on the far side, immediately in front of the hedge. In his front was the hedge, pierced by the single obvious gap, through which a road ran.[1] To his right (English left) was a "petite montagne" on which he saw some horses. This would be Bernon, where the ground falls on three sides, and would have the appearance of a hill from the French side ("montagne" need mean no more than "hillock"). On his left was "ung petit plain", which is evidently represented by the flat-topped ridge about point 138. This was fortified, and a sort of laager of wagons was made to protect that flank, which was the most vulnerable of the two. No doubt this flank was "refused" and may have touched the extreme north edge of the Nouaillé wood.[2]

Thus Ribaumont's report is consistent with the site of the hedge suggested above. This site is satisfied by the other chronicles and is consistent with inherent military probability. In short, I believe the vestiges of hedge still visible are those of the famous hedge of Poitiers.

THE BLACK PRINCE'S SPEECHES

I have already in the narrative suggested that the Prince of Wales attached great importance to the maintenance of morale. In this connection le Baker reports in great detail two speeches made by the Prince before the battle, the first to the whole army, the second to his archers. After the manner of his age, the chronicler uses *oratio recta*. Obviously the speeches cannot be literally correct, but I do not feel that they deserve the almost universal disregard that they have received from historians. Le Baker was not writing a panegyric, such as that of the herald, but sober history. So far as one can tell, in no single respect did he deliberately fabricate. Why should there be any difficulty in accepting the fact that le Baker received

[1] There is no foundation for the fable that it was a hollow road—any more than for the fable of the hollow road of Ohain at Waterloo; there is no trace of a hollow road now. Hollow roads tend to get deeper, not shallower, with the passage of time. Nor, of course, was there a double hedge.

[2] Luce, vol. v, p. vi, quotes from *Gallia Christiana* II, col. 1243, under date 1720, "*Saltus Nobiliacensis* (Nouaillé wood), *ubi etiamnum Anglorum castra fossis munita cernere est*". There are no visible signs now, but an air photograph might disclose something.

reports from various sources of what the Prince had said, and of what a powerful impression his words had made on the English host? It may certainly be accepted that he *did* address his army. Villani, Froissart, and the *Eulogium* all testify to the fact, and the account of the last named is in accord with le Baker's as far as it goes. So also is that of Villani, two of whose passages had their almost exact counterpart in le Baker. Froissart adds the interesting point that the Prince caused his words to be passed on by the leaders to their own units. Obviously he could not address the whole army personally, and the fact that he made a point of ensuring that his words should reach all his troops shows that he attached considerable importance to his utterance. Who can doubt but that these speeches contributed to the glorious issue of the battle that followed them? Indeed, they have every right to enjoy as much fame as the speech put by Shakespeare into the mouth of Henry V on the eve of Agincourt.

MODERN WORKS

The chief modern works on the battle have been referred to in this chapter. The two outstanding ones on the French side are those by Roland Delachenal and Ferdinand Lot. Colonel Babinet's researches are also essential. They are printed in the *Bulletin des Antiquaires de l'Ouest* for 1883. The most detailed account in English is Hilaire Belloc's *Poitiers*, but it is difficult in this book to distinguish between what is fact and what is inference.

CHAPTER XIII

EDWARD'S LAST CAMPAIGN

ON March 23, 1357, a two-year truce was signed at Bordeaux. But for unhappy, distracted France there was to be no peace. In fact the following two years were to be among the most miserable in her history. This for several reasons. The war in Brittany carried on as before; the Navarre war also smouldered; bodies of disbanded soldiers, later known as the Free Companies, roamed through France, seizing castles, living on the country and pillaging as they pleased, for there was no strong central authority or army to prevent them,[1] and France, deprived of her king, sank under the feeble government of the boy Dauphin into a state of chaos; peasants fought against nobles, fields were left untilled, and the king's writ practically ceased to run.

The Navarre war was kept alive largely by English soldiers. In June, 1347, the king of Navarre (well called "The Bad", for he was guilty of repeated treasons to the king of France and England in turn) obtained his freedom, and the Navarre war flared up once more; eventually nearly the whole of Lower Normandy—from Cherbourg to the Seine—was controlled by bands of Navarre and English soldiers. But only one event of great military interest occurred during those troublous two years and that was the siege of Rennes, to which we will now turn.

THE SIEGE OF RENNES

When, at the conclusion of his Normandy campaign, the duke of Lancaster marched into Brittany to take up his post

[1] The most celebrated of these commanders was Sir Robert Knollys, whose "Company" was said to number 3,000. After assisting the king of Navarre, Knollys operated in the centre of France to the south of Paris, and no one dared to oppose him. All nationalities were in these free companies, but the English predominated.

as king's lieutenant, he at once appreciated that in order to get the whole duchy completely and firmly under English and Montfort control it would be necessary to take the capital Rennes and the county of Nantes.[1] But soon after his arrival, Charles de Blois, who had been released on payment of the bulk of his ransom, landed at Treguier and took up his residence at Guingamp. This could not be allowed, and Henry of Lancaster marched there himself. Charles, warned of the danger, made his escape to Nantes, and Henry took possession of Guingamp and recaptured Roche-Derrien.

No sooner was this effected than Henry learnt of the approach of the Black Prince from the south. Of his march *au grand galop* to join hands with his cousin we have already spoken. This attempt proving both abortive and unnecessary, Lancaster retraced his steps with his usual speed, covering the 100 miles in a few days, and he laid siege to Rennes on October 3.

The task was likely to prove a difficult one for the small Anglo-Breton army, for the circuit of the walls was large, and Lancaster possessed no siege engines. In several respects it resembled the siege of Calais. In both cases a direct assault was impracticable; blockade and starvation was the only obvious procedure, but was bound to be a lengthy one. Calais had held out for over ten months; could Henry of Lancaster better that? He determined to try, and, according to a French heroic poem the reliability of which, however, is no greater than the poem of the Chandos Herald, he swore that he would not desist till it surrendered.

During the autumn months, the siege, or rather blockade, took the usual dull course of all such blockades in their early stages. Then a youthful Breton leader, named Bertrand du

---

[1] The military historian of Brittany, la Borderie, pays this notable tribute to Henry of Lancaster: "An illustrious prince, renowned for his chivalrous courtesy, he enjoyed by his birth and his great reputation an almost regal authority. Such a general could not confine himself to a series of petty skirmishes and ambushes such as had, since the battle of Mauron, been the nature of the war raged in Brittany." The next sentence cannot be adequately rendered in English, "*Grand homme de guerre, il voulut faire la grande guerre.*"

Guesclin, appeared upon the scene. This young Breton was remarkable alike for his extreme ugliness and his martial virtues. At first he did not attempt to enter the city, but contented himself with harassing the besiegers from without.

This went on till the depth of winter, when Charles the Dauphin, duke of Normandy and now regent of France, sent two columns for the relief of the city. The first made a night attack on the besiegers but was completely cut up and its commander captured with 400 of his men. The other commander decided to proceed more cautiously, and settled down in the town of Dinan, 30 miles to the north. From there he harassed the besiegers to such an extent that Lancaster, without abandoning his grip on Rennes, took upon him the additional task of laying siege to Dinant, a town that had narrowly avoided being captured by Edward III 15 years before. Meanwhile du Guesclin was chafing to take a more active part in the defence of Rennes, and if we are to believe the poem, he effected his entry by the following stratagem. One of the garrison passed through the lines and pretended to give himself up as a deserter. Admitted into Lancaster's presence, he averred that a relieving army was approaching from the east, and was due to arrive that very night. The duke took the bait and marched out with his striking force to meet the relieving army. In his absence that night, Bertrand du Guesclin slipped in, and not only did so, but brought with him a captured train of supplies. Whatever the truth, du Guesclin did effect an entry, and is said to have heartened the garrison considerably.

Spring had now come, and more active methods of capturing the place were put in hand. The first was by mining—a slow process at the best of times, but particularly so in those days of primitive warfare. The essential technique of mine and counter-mine has not, however, altered through the centuries, and the French dug a successful counter-mine, and thus brought that line of attack to an end. The second method (indeed, the only other method possible, since the English possessed no breaching engines) was to employ a *beffroi*, or portable tower. This also was tried but met with the same method of defence as at La Réole: the French made a sortie by night and set it on fire.

The siege then relapsed into its old languid condition. On March 23 a truce was signed at Bordeaux between England and France to which Brittany was a party. Information of this was sent to Lancaster, but he anticipated Nelson by putting "his deaf ear to the trumpet" (if we may coin the phrase) and inflexibly carried on the siege for two months. Then in June, on receipt of a third order to cease operations, he entered into pourparlers with the garrison for surrender, not informing them that he must in any case give up the siege. The city was by this time suffering greatly from hunger, and "consented to be delivered from the siege on payment of 100,000 crowns". The siege thus came to an end on July 5, 1357, after exactly nine months, compared with the siege of Calais which lasted over ten months. Before departing the duke of Lancaster entered the town with ten knights carrying his banner which he placed on one of the city gates. Bertrand du Guesclin came forward and offered him a drink. The duke quaffed it and then departed. At once the banner was of course removed and thrown into the city ditch.

This qualified military success was seized upon by the French and broadcast through the country, no doubt "with advantages", as some solace for the recent disaster of Poitiers. But its real significance is the emergence of Bertrand du Guesclin into fame as the potential "saviour of France".

There seems now to have developed some coolness between the English king and his headstrong subordinate, and Henry asked to be allowed to return to England. To this the king consented when the duke had settled affairs in the following year, 1358. The truce was thenceforth observed in Brittany as elsewhere.

In glaring contrast to France, England was now enjoying

a period of peace and prosperity in spite of the Black Death. The king engaged in jousts and tournaments to his heart's content, and his royal prisoner, who was treated like a king and given almost complete freedom of person, seems to have found the time pass without undue tedium.

But Edward III now sincerely desired peace, and took advantage of a new approach by the persevering Pope, to come to terms with King John. Together they signed a treaty that may be called the First Treaty of London, by which the old duchy of Aquitaine was to revert to the English crown in absolute sovereignty, the king no longer being obliged to do homage to the king of France for it. In return, Edward agreed to abandon his claim to the French crown.

King John was also to return to France on payment of an immense ransom. There is no actual record of these terms, but the above gist of them was established by "the learned Dominican" Father Deniflé, and elaborated by Roland Delachenal.[1]

It is important to keep the terms of this treaty in mind if we are to understand the motives of Edward III in his next campaign.

The First Treaty of London was still-born. Parliament seems to have opposed it, being evidently more bellicose than the king himself, and Charles of Navarre also made objections. The two kings decided to try once more, and in March, 1359, actively encouraged by the Pope, they signed a second Treaty of London, more favourable to the English, for it included the return of the old Angevin possessions to England. But now it was the turn of the French government, despite their internal troubles, to demur. This intransigence, as he considered it, made Edward furious. He now lost all faith in peaceable negotiations and came to the conclusion that the only way to settle the matter for good and all was by force of arms; he must invade France once more.

---

[1] Professor Tout is the only English historian to notice this important treaty. See *E.H.R.* 1910.

But, he recollected, he had already invaded France five times, and each time he had expected it to be the last. This sort of thing could not go on; it had already lasted for 21 years. There must be no mistake about it; he would this time attain his object—"an honourable peace"—or die in the attempt. He made a solemn resolution and announced it in a speech to his army, that he would not return to England till peace had been secured.

He was prudent enough not to specify what sort of a peace, but it appears that he had two alternative objectives—"an optimum", the crown of France, and, failing that, one of the two Treaties of London. If nothing was to be left to chance this time prolonged preparations would be necessary, several months at least. That would involve an autumn, perhaps even a winter campaign. But that prospect did not affright or deter this iron-willed monarch. Preparations were methodically put in hand, and many of the measures may be read in Rymer's *Foedera*—but by no means all. We saw as far back as 1346 how far-seeing and provident the king was when preparing his Crecy campaign. But this time his problem was to be far more difficult and complex, for, instead of marching parallel to the sea-coast—the line that linked him with England—he would have to cut adrift from it, he must "burn his boats" almost literally; for months perhaps, he would be out of touch and communication with England, and consequently he must depend for all manner of war stores and weapons, ammunition, equipment, food, clothing and tentage, largely on what he could carry with him. For France was steadily becoming a desert. A few examples of his foresight are instructive. The stores included field forges and horseshoes, hand-mills for grinding "man-corn and horse-corn", and a large number of portable leather fishing coracles, in case the campaign should last into Lent, when fish would not be procurable from home. It is a remarkable fact that there is no record of cannons being taken on this campaign.

A vast train of wagons was therefore built and transported across the sea to Calais; numbers vary from 1,000 to 6,000, each wagon drawn by four horses. No such baggage-train had ever been seen in European warfare, nor was to be seen again till the armies of Louis XIV lumbered across Europe.

Not only did the king prepare with much thought everything requisite and necessary for a great army on a possibly long campaign; he prepared also the plan of campaign referred to above months ahead, a most unusual proceeding in the fourteenth century when little attention seems to have been paid to such things. We know this because the intelligence service of the French government was good, and it obtained possession of the outlines of this plan. It was a simple one, as all military plans should be in their initial stages: the king of England intended to march to Rheims, in the hopes that he might be crowned and anointed king of France in that holy city of Clovis, or if he failed in that object, that he might at least induce the regent to come to its relief and thus to fight him in the field. A shrewd plan, for the action of the archbishop of Rheims had recently been suspect and he might be won over to Edward's cause.[1]

Edward hoped to be able to open his campaign before August was out, which should give at least two good campaigning months; but because of the usual and inevitable hitches and delays, chiefly due to the shortage of shipping, it was not till the beginning of October that the vanguard of the army landed in Calais. The value of this port as a "pistol pointed at Paris"–as it might truly be described–was now seen. The king must have been thankful that he had persisted to the end in the siege of Calais. Not only did it possess a nucleus of war-stores useful for the campaign, but it was already the home of English merchants and could speedily be turned into an arsenal. It was also accessible to foreign volunteers and would-be mercenaries, of whom a large number flocked to the town during the late summer, for the king had made no attempt to keep his expedition secret, and indeed encouraged volunteers.

[1] This is the view of H. Moranville (Bibliothèque de l'École des Chartes, vol. LVI, p. 91.)

Flemings, Hainaulters, Brabançons, and Germans came to lodge in the town in large numbers–too large; they began to "own the place", and to eat up its victuals and drink up its drinks while waiting week by week for the English army to appear. Something had to be done to cope with this potential menace; a trusted subordinate must be sent ahead to cope with the situation before it got out of hand. Readers will have no difficulty in guessing on whom the king's choice fell. . . .

On October 1 Henry of Lancaster landed at Calais with 2,400 troops, and addressed himself immediately to the task of controlling the unruly band of foreigners. He explained to them that the king, with the main body of the army, could not arrive for a fortnight or more. There was meanwhile a growing shortage of food in the town and no money available for the troops. But, he pointed out, he was about to undertake a little chevauchée into the interior of France, to see what could be picked up. Would not they like to accompany him, instead of kicking up their heels aimlessly in Calais? The bait was taken, a little army formed, and the duke of Lancaster sallied forth on what may correctly be termed a raid.

Leaving St. Omer and Bethune on his left hand, he pushed on to the monastery of St. Eloi on the ridge a few miles north of Arras, where he halted for four days. Proceeding south, he struck the river Somme at Bray, where a strongly held castle barred the crossing. A fruitless attempt to storm it–the attackers wading up to their shoulders through the icy river–caused the army to swing to its right. Four miles on, a crossing was effected by the unbroken bridge of Cerisy.[1]

The army was now heading for Amiens, and within a dozen miles of it. Great was the consternation in that city. But it was saved from attack: for next day, November 1, a message was received from King Edward to the effect that he had landed at Calais on October 28, and that the duke of Lancaster was to return at once. It was clever of the messenger, who had a near-hundred-miles journey, to find the duke in only three days.

[1] Almost in the German front line during the summer of 1918.

The army returned to Calais without incident, and thither we also will now direct our attention.

*   *   *

Before leaving England, the king, foreseeing that if he denuded the country of troops the French might be tempted to raid or even invade it in force, issued thorough-going regulations for such a contingency, the details of which we need not enter upon. It may have been these matters, in addition to shipping troubles, that caused the delay in opening the campaign. Walsingham's statement that no fewer than 1,100 vessels were collected must be an exaggeration; such a fleet could transport an army of over 30,000. But the king made use of a procedure adopted in the 1944 invasion of Normandy: he transported his army to Calais in several "lifts", having command of the sea in the Dover Straits. Thereby we see yet another advantage enjoyed by the possession of the Calais beach-head: the troops could be transported piecemeal, and in an unlimited number if there were unlimited time. The duke of Lancaster had taken part of his divisions with him, and possibly some of the Black Prince's crossed at the same time. The enormous train of wagons—necessary because of the denuded state of the country to be traversed—also required much time and tonnage to transport.

THE RHEIMS CAMPAIGN

On October 28, 1359, very early in the morning, King Edward III set out upon his sixth and last campaign. The wind was favourable and strong, and he was enabled to land at Calais that same day. Seven days of strenuous staff-work followed, organizing and arraying the army, and on November 4, Lancaster's raiders having just returned, the army was ready to set out.[1]

[1] The view generally held (and adopted here) that Lancaster's army returned before the army set out is contradicted by le Bel, who may be right, as Lancaster must have made an extremely speedy return if he was back by November 4, but speed was natural to the duke. No doubt his wagon-train was left far in the rear.

The army that set out from Calais in a "do or die" attempt
to end the war in a single winter campaign was in all probability the largest army that had ever left these shores, or was
ever to do so again till the first campaign of Henry VIII in
1513. It can scarcely have been less than 15,000 combatants,
with several thousand non-combatants. The names of the chief
officers should be noted, for they were all names by now
familiar to the reader. The Black Prince, accompanied by his
brothers–the earl of Richmond (John of Gaunt)[1] and Lionel
of Clarence–the duke of Lancaster, the earls of Warwick,
Northampton, March, Salisbury and Stafford, Lord Burghersh,
Sir Reginald Cobham, Sir John Chandos, Sir James Audley
and, of course, Sir Walter Manny. A galaxy! One of the
common soldiers also deserves naming, though his military
career was inglorious–he was taken prisoner. His name was
Geoffrey Chaucer.

The destination was, as we have seen, Rheims. Apart
from the obvious reason for this objective–namely the hallowing of Edward Plantagenet as king of France–there were other
considerations that favoured it, should the anointing project
fail. The expedition, of which there was no attempt at secrecy,
was of so menacing a nature that it might be assumed that the
regent of France would oppose it by force of arms, if he had
the power. Nothing would suit Edward's purpose better than
to cross swords with his French opponent. Now, more than
ever, he was confident of the result. If, on the other hand, the
regent made no attempt to defend the sacred city, or to come
to its assistance, the whole of France would draw the moral:
namely, that the regent was impotent in his own dominion. His
subjects would see and take note of the fact that not only
was the country plunged into chaos and ruin, but that the
English claimant to the crown was free to go wherever he
pleased and do what damage he liked throughout the territories
of a boy regent (dubbed by Ramsay "a sickly, timid lad of

[1] Who had just married the daughter of the duke of Lancaster, thus founding
the "Lancastrian line".

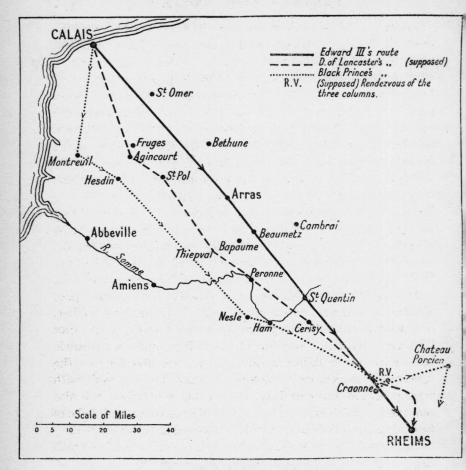

CALAIS

St. Omer

————— Edward Ⅲ's route
— — — D. of Lancaster's ,, (supposed)
.... Black Prince's ,,
R.V. (Supposed) Rendezvous of the
         three columns.

Fruges
Agincourt
Bethune

Montreuil

Hesdin
St Pol
Arras

Cambrai
Beaumetz
Bapaume
Thiepval
R. Somme
Peronne
Amiens
St Quentin

Abbeville

Nesle
Ham
Cerisy

Chateau
Porcien
R.V.
Craonne

Scale of Miles
0   5   10   20   30   40

RHEIMS

17. THE RHEIMS CAMPAIGN

nineteen"), and of an impotent government. For 20 years the iron-willed demi-Frenchman, Edward Plantagenet, had laid claim through his French mother to the throne, and during all those years France had steadily diminished in prosperity and increased in misery. Might it not be as well, for the sake of peace, to yield to the hard logic of events, and acknowledge the ever-victorious Edward as their king? Such might very well become the attitude of the country, thought Edward, as he evolved his plan for a descent on Rheims.

Edward III's strategy in this campaign will repay study. As in his Brittany and Normandy campaigns he decided to advance on a broad front, by parallel columns, each marching on a carefully planned route within supporting distance of its neighbours, yet covering as wide a belt of country as possible. There were to be three columns or divisions, one under the Prince of Wales, one under the duke of Lancaster, and one under the king himself. We know enough about these three itineraries to draw certain conclusions. Fortunately a soldier, who took part in the campaign, afterward wrote about it (not Chaucer). His name was Sir Thomas Gray, and his chronicle was called the *Scalacronica*. From it we are able to plot the itinerary of the Prince's column (in which Gray served) with some precision and certainty. From other sources we can also plot the king's itinerary. The centre column, that of the duke of Lancaster, can easily be interpolated. (See sketch map opposite.)

The route of the right-hand column was as follows: Montreuil, Hesdin, Doullens, Albert, Nesle, Ham, just to the left of La Fere and Laon, to Chateau Porcien and Rethel, 25 miles north-east of Rheims.

That of the left-hand column was by St. Omer, Aire, Lillers, Bethune, Arras, Beaumetz (midway between Bapaume and Cambrai), then practically along what became the line of the Hindenburg Line, by Epehy and Bellenglise to St. Quentin: thence through country less familiar to English soldiers (though known to many of Edward's army of 1339) to a general rendezvous near Craonne.

The centre column must have passed near, if not over, the field of Agincourt, St. Pol, Acheux, Thiepval, Peronne (avoiding the river Somme), thence by Vermand and over what is now the St. Crozat canal, over the 1914 battlefield of Cerisy,[1] and so on to the rendezvous. From Agincourt to Peronne, this column, all unknowingly, trod in the footsteps-to-be (in the reverse direction) of Henry V's army en route for the immortal field of Agincourt.

If we plot these itineraries on a map carefully, we shall discover two striking facts, which go far to confirm the assertion that the marches were carefully plotted in advance. The first fact is that, once the flank columns had diverged from the common starting point to a distance of 20 miles, they kept to this distance, maintaining almost exactly parallel routes as far as St. Quentin. The second fact is that if one draws a straight line from Calais to Rheims, it passes exactly through St. Quentin, and also that the route taken by the king's column never diverges from this straight line by as much as five map miles. This can scarcely be a coincidence and we are sharply reminded of that very direct march of the king across Lower Normandy, followed by the almost geometrically straight one between the Seine and the Somme, as also of Lancaster's straight marches in his Normandy campaign. These four instances compel us to recognize that the English king must have been in possession of some primitive form of map, although there is no specific record of one. (My sketch map is designed to bring out these points.)[2]

This carefully charted itinerary of three parallel columns also calls to mind Napoleon's Ulm campaign. Is it too fanciful to picture Edward, like Napoleon, sprawling on the floor over his map with a primitive pair of dividers in his hand, plotting in advance his great *chevauchée*?

*   *   *

[1] Where the 5th Cavalry Brigade smashed up a column of Uhlans (not to be confused with Cerizy on the Somme).

[2] Edward I had a map made of England, on which the Gough map of 1325 (c) is based, so there is no intrinsic improbability in the existence of a map of northern France.

The duke of Lancaster can have had only a few hours in which to re-shoe his horses and reorganize and refit his tired troops, who had just marched nearly 100 miles in three days, and whose transport was still on the move. He also had to sort out and disband those Germans who would not agree to serve in the coming campaign without pay. Indeed it is quite possible that he delayed his start by at least one day in order to carry out this task, and regained his position abreast of the other two columns by rapid marching. That should be an easy matter, for the rate of march was a leisurely one, being only six miles a day, halts included. If we exclude the halt days, it was still under ten miles a day. The unwieldy baggage train, together with the absence of any imperative need for haste, will account for this. Though Froissart waxes lyrical over the pomp and display of the expedition as it marched out of Calais, it soon degenerated into a dull and rather miserable march. For a steady downpour of cold autumn rain accompanied it and local provender was almost non-existent in the early stages, and the king had issued orders against damage and destruction. This was a welcome innovation; the usual course for an invading army at that epoch of warfare was to ravage and destroy, and the English army had certainly hitherto followed this course. But now, late though it might be, Edward realized that if he was to become the sovereign of the inhabitants through whose lands he was marching, it would be as well to keep on good terms with them. In fact this can be described as not so much a military invasion as a political procession with a military escort: the king was proceeding to his crowning—it was a coronation procession on a large scale.

In spite of the miseries of the march the discipline was of a high order. Straggling was sternly forbidden, and we read that they "did not leave a bag behind them". There was little opportunity for loot or destruction. The king's column was marching in the early stages along almost exactly the same route as that followed only a few days previously by Lancaster's hungry Germans. It was as when a unit occupies billets occupied the previous night by another unit that has bought up (or stolen) all the eggs, and drunk all the beer. Nor was any excitement to be obtained from military encounters, for the French troops had, in obedience to instructions, taken refuge in the walled towns along the route, the capture of which did not fall within the programme of the English king. It is perfectly clear that Edward intended his march to be as much a peace march as possible—unless the French regent dared to presume to cross swords with him.

After advancing for about 80 miles through towns and villages made familiar to English troops of 1914–18, the region between Cambrai and Albert was reached. Here provender was more plentiful and a halt of four days was made. But still it rained. . . .

The march was resumed according to plan, and under the walls of St. Quentin, which was not entered, Lord Burghersh had a satisfactory little fight with a few French knights who were rash enough to sally out of that city. The march was resumed, the king's column continuing on its dead straight route and the other two converging on it. The rendezvous or meeting point was a little to the east of Craonne. Here the army concentrated on November 29, and two councils of war were held. Experiences were exchanged, stock was taken of the situation and arrangements made for approaching the sacred city. The Prince's division was to hold the northern sector, the duke's the east, and the king's the south. This necessitated the columns crossing one another, the king's now being on the south.[1] No news had been heard of any move on the part of the regent, although he had had ample time to reinforce the city, or to advance at the head of the national army of France to encounter the invader outside its walls. Still, the possibility that this might yet occur had to be allowed for, and the march was resumed, with the divisions transposed, on December 1. It was a 30-mile march for the Prince and duke who passed

[1] There is no written authority for this, but the inference is as inescapable as the reason for it is obscure.

through Chateau Porcien, but somewhat less for the king. As the columns converged on the city the tall twin towers of the cathedral came in sight.

It must have been an exciting moment for Edward of Windsor when his eyes first beheld what must have been for months "the city of his dreams". After 21 years of effort, were these dreams at last to come true? Did he experience the feelings and excitement of his great ancestor, Richard Coeur de Lion, when he came in sight of the Holy City of Palestine? History does not relate; nor indeed have we a word from his own pen of this culminating point, as it must have seemed, in his life.

THE SIEGE OF RHEIMS

On arriving in the vicinity of the city of Rheims on December 4 after a 170-mile march, King Edward made a reconnaissance of its walls and fixed the various headquarters. His own headquarters he established at the abbey of St. Basle, nearly ten miles to the south, while those of the Prince were half that distance to the north, and the duke's at Brimont to the east. These distances seem surprisingly large, and may be accounted for in two ways: in the first place the king required a commodious residence for his numerous retinue, and a sufficiently large abbey could not be found nearer the city: in the second place, it indicates that Edward did not intend to make the siege an active military operation, where his personal presence every day would be necessary. It was to be a passive affair; the active part in the proceedings was to be played by the citizens who, as soon as they saw that there was no hope of relief, would come out bearing with them the keys of the city. To mark this feature of the siege still more, Edward issued strict injunctions that the inhabitants were to be treated as if they were friends, and this unusual order was implicitly obeyed, such was the grip that the English king exerted over his army. As Knighton puts it, "the troops behaved as if they were on their own soil".

But it was all of no avail. The king did not know that the regent, or his council, being apprised months in advance of the danger to Rheims, had taken steps to strengthen the defences of the city both in material and men, and had issued strict instructions that it was to hold out, with hints of aid in such an event. Under the heroic archbishop and the count of Porcien the inhabitants responded nobly. The gates were kept closed and appeals for help were smuggled out of the city to Paris.[1]

Thus the days dragged on till Christmas. Most of the besiegers were billeted in the neighbouring villages, and it would be nice to know how these English soldiers spent their Christmas under arms in France. Did they, under the new relationship with the inhabitants, show that adaptability that their descendants did when Christmassing in France and Belgium five and a half centuries later?

Christmas came and went, and the conditions became most unpleasant. The weather was still abominable, and the horses, for the most part picketed out in the open, suffered severely. A static siege, opened and carried on in mid-winter, was until this war an almost unknown phenomenon in medieval warfare. The huts and quarters erected during the siege of Calais were lacking, and something had to be done soon, unless the army was to become immobilized in a foreign country, 200 miles from the coast. An attempt to breach and assault the town must have been a strong temptation to Edward, but he steadfastly set his face against it. Even though he might conceivably storm it without undue damage to materiel or inhabitants, he could not control the assaulters from "running amok" once inside—scarcely a propitious overture to his hallowing by the archbishop of Rheims. He could not hallow himself.[2] This was a quandary that seems to have been lost sight of by the historians.

---

[1] The assertion of *Les Quatre Premiers Valois* that an attempt was made to storm the walls must be dismissed.

[2] The hallowing, not the actual crowning, was the essential part of the ceremony —a king could place the crown on his own head—Napoleon did—but he could scarcely pour oil on himself.

During those anxious weeks of weary waiting, one thing became insistent: the troops must be employed. Unemployment in the field breeds indiscipline. There being as yet no sign of hostile activity in the direction of Paris, it seemed safe to send out minor expeditions on distant missions, and each division was instructed or allowed to carry out raids in its own sector. Four such expeditions at least were sent out. To the north-east Eustache d'Auberchicourt captured Attigny on the Aisne; to the east Lancaster, Chandos, and Audley, roaming wide, came to the strong castle of Cernay, near St. Menehould. This castle possessed two moats, one at least of which was wet. Henry, riding up to it, dismounted from his horse to conduct a reconnaissance on foot. The leading troops, on seeing this, also dismounted, and, if we are to believe Knighton,[1] such was their uncontrollable ardour that they incontinently rushed forward with a shout and after crossing both moats, scaled the walls and captured the town. Then they turned on the castle, but the garrison of this, apparently unnerved at the suddenness and vigour of the attack, surrendered at discretion. This was an affair after Henry of Lancaster's heart, but what military object it served it is difficult to descry. Indeed it has the appearance of being just "a lark" on the part of the delectable and, I think, dapper duke. The very next day he captured another walled town, and this was followed by others. It looks as if the prestige of the English troops was bringing down these fortified places just as in the eighteenth century in southern India the prestige of the English troops of Clive and Stringer Lawrence toppled over semi-impregnable fortresses like so many ninepins.

To resume the catalogue of raids: to the north-west Cormicy was stormed by the earl of March,[2] Lord Burghersh, and John of Gaunt, while to the west a raiding party penetrated right under the walls of Paris. Perhaps we should describe this as a reconnoitring rather than a raiding party, sent out for information about the attitude of the regent. But if so, the

[1] I would not trouble to repeat this improbable-sounding story if it came from Froissart.
[2] The earl died shortly afterwards.

party went about its work in a curious way. Walsingham describes rather humorously how they set up such a din in the suburbs that the garrison of the city thought an attack was imminent.

TO BURGUNDY AND PARIS

By January 10, 1360, all the raiders had returned to camp, and King Edward had to come to an important decision. The Paris raiders had convinced him that the regent could not be coaxed out of his impregnable asylum, nor did the garrison of Rheims show any signs of weakening in their decision to hold out.

Rheims had been plentifully stocked with supplies in view of the siege, and to reduce it by starvation would probably take at least as long as had Calais. In this quandary only two possible courses remained: to take the city by storm, or to give up the siege and undertake some fresh project. The first course Edward still declined to take. His attitude commands admiration, though on wholly military grounds it was a surprising one: with his large and efficient army, with captains experienced in the arts of storming fortifications, and with the threat of outside intervention being now out of the question, it should have been possible to take the city by storm, though no doubt at high cost. Did the king shrink from the idea of high casualties, or was he merely remaining faithful to the course that he had laid out for himself—to secure his hallowing by peaceful persuasion? In view of his stern will-power and implacable resolution I think we may safely impute the latter motive to the English sovereign.

Be that as it may, the military policy of the French government, which was the best possible under the circumstances, presented a difficult problem to Edward.[1] It became necessary for him to frame a new policy. Such a policy may well have been

[1] Edouard Perroy gives the credit for this plan to the 19-year-old Dauphin. "Taught by experience, and influenced by his unwarlike nature, he went on war-strike. It was clever strategy, which was later attributed to du Guesclin's contrivance, but it was that of the Dauphin."

gestating in his mind during the past month, if not before (for we cannot forget those Lenten fishing-boats), and Edward now set it into operation. If the threat to Rheims could not goad the regent into intervention or negotiation, the capital itself must be threatened. But before doing so it would be prudent, seeing that the English army was now far from home and surrounded by potential enemies, to take preliminary steps to safeguard the move. Now the greatest potential danger came from Burgundy, whose duke was the most powerful vassal of France, and must be considered an enemy, although he had taken no active part in the war for many years. A descent upon Burgundy was therefore decided upon.

The nearest point in Burgundy to Rheims was 100 miles due south, and Paris was nearly 150 miles north-west of this point. To reach Burgundy it was necessary to pass through the province of Champagne from north to south. On January 11, 1360, Edward III set out on his new venture. Marching in the same formation of three divisions, each with its own vanguard, the army left Chalons on its right hand and crossed the Marne above it at Poigny on about January 26. Pushing south, the king punished the town of Bar-sur-Aube for some iniquity, and then turned west. Leaving unmolested the little town of Troyes –to become world-famous in 60 years' time–he crossed the Seine at Pont and Mery and pushed southward into Burgundy. The young duke had collected his army at Montréal, but here it remained, for he dared not draw upon himself the formidable English army. The latter therefore roamed his country at will. Various towns were captured, notably Tonnerre, where a welcome stock of Burgundy wine was found–and drunk. The injunctions against ravage and pillage seem to have become a dead letter, whether explicitly or not.

It was in all probability of set policy, intended to cow the duke into submission. But for the moment nothing happened, and Edward seemed in no hurry that it should. February and Lent had arrived. It was the close season for warfare. Fishing took the place of fighting and all the pious knights were enabled to keep the season as laid down, though the common soldiers, we are told, had to fend for themselves. Hunting and hawking were, however, allowed, and the king settled down at Guillon, 40 miles west of Dijon, to a pleasant season of sport. Occasionally a walled town was taken or a monastery pillaged, but in the main Lent was placidly and piously observed. During this period there were some changes among the higher officers. The earl of March died, but we are not told the cause. Most of the German knights departed for their not very distant homes in Lorraine, but their place was more than filled by knights of the Free Companies who had been operating in that part of France for the past 12 months, and who now took regular service in the royal army. Sir Robert Knollys must have been one of these, and there were many others. Also some Gascon lords, including the Captal de Buch of Poitiers fame, in their desire to serve under the banner of the Black Prince, made their way right across France by a devious route which took them through Beauvais, and joined him in Burgundy. What with internal dissension in the country, the Free Companies and the depredations and exactions of the army of England, all northern Burgundy was now in a deplorable state, and the duke at length sent emissaries to sue for peace. Edward was, of course, in a position to demand any terms he desired. These were that there should be a three-year truce, that Burgundy should remain neutral in the war between Edward and the regent, and that it should pay a large indemnity. These humiliating terms were signed on March 10, and five days later the English army set out with its face turned toward Paris.

All was now going according to plan: Lent was nearly over, the spring grass, which would provide fodder for the horses, was beginning to sprout, and if the regent desired to fight for his father's crown, he would now be given the opportunity.

In mid-March the army moved away in a westerly direction toward the county of Nivernais, of which Nevers was the capital. This county promptly compounded against invasion as Burgundy had just done. All danger to flank and rear being now at an end, Edward turned north, and descended the valleys of the Cure and the Yonne,[1] heading for Paris.

An event now occurred on the English shore that had repercussions upon the campaign in France. The offensive is the best form of defensive; and some of the regent's advisers were aware of the fact. Seeing what a very large army the English king had brought with him to the Continent, they supposed that England had been denuded of defenders and that a lodgement of some days, at least, would be possible—sufficient to bring the king hurrying home to the defence of his own land. But they had misjudged their man and forgotten history only 14 years old. For when the Scots had invaded England in 1346 Edward had left its defence to those to whom he had entrusted it before setting out. It was the same again. The far-seeing monarch had made what proved to be ample measures for the defence of the realm when on March 15 a French fleet suddenly appeared off Rye. An actual landing could not be prevented, nor the dreadful atrocities committed at Winchelsea by the French troops (possibly in revenge for the ravages of their native land). But within 24 hours reinforcements were speeding to the spot according to plan, and after a sharp fight the French were driven back to their ships, suffering very heavy casualties.

The outcome was satisfactory, but the stories of atrocities that reached the king (no doubt exaggerated) so stung him and his army to anger that he hastened his march towards Paris, and resumed the old policy of devastation.[2]

On the Tuesday in Holy Week, March 31, the army halted in a line 20 miles south of Paris, between Corbeil and Long-jumeau, the royal headquarters being established at Chante-

---

[1] Passing through the little town of Cravant, to be the scene of a remarkable English victory 63 years later.

[2] Delachenal asserts that the news of Winchelsea dictated Edward's strategy, he having up till that time been uncertain what to do. But Delachenal does not seem to have fathomed, or even suspected, the depth of the English king's strategy throughout the campaign. The Winchelsea raid was repulsed on March 16. Four days later, before the news can have reached him, the King resumed his advance on the French capital.

loupe, near Arpajan, where they remained till the Easter feast
was over. The smoke of some burnings carried out at Long-
jumeau was visible from the walls of Paris and created a panic
in all the suburbs of the city, the terrified inhabitants crowding
into the city for refuge in those long melancholy streams that
have become too familiar in recent wars. A short, abortive
truce conference was held at Longjumeau, to which reference
will be made later.

On the Tuesday in Easter week the advance was resumed,
and the army came to a halt on the line of heights a few miles
to the south-west of the city between Issy and Beaugirard, the
king lodging at Montrouge. Walter Manny now led a party
right up to the walls and tried to exasperate the garrison by his
taunts into making a sortie. In addition, the whole English
army deployed into line and advanced within sight of the walls,
challenging battle. Edward had some reason to believe that the
challenge would be accepted. Froissart speaks of heralds being
sent forward and Knighton says that some arrangement to
engage in a fight was made by the regent but not kept. Whatever be the truth, the French made no more. Strict orders to
this effect had been issued, and they were obeyed by the
garrison, whether willingly or not. However, on April 10 a
deputation treating for peace came out of the city. A conference,
at which the Pope's legates were present, took place at the
abbey of Cluny on the Orleans road, but it led to no conclusion.
The sequel to this conference must have surprised the French
manning the city walls, for 48 hours later a long line of English
troops deployed and advanced close up to the walls. Once
again the garrison did not budge. A few hours elapsed and
the English army had vanished. It was in fact well on its
way to Chartres. The demonstration had been merely a
covering force—a skilful rearguard posted to screen the withdrawal. The English king had made another of his surprise
moves.

Edward III did not commit to paper the motives and
reasons that inspired his various actions throughout this

puzzling campaign, and we are reduced to guessing at them
in practically every case. In most cases, and pre-eminently in
this one, we are obliged to form our conclusions largely by the
logic of subsequent events. We will therefore narrate these
events in brief and then come back to the reasons for this
abrupt withdrawal from the second "city of his dreams" before
scarcely a shot had been discharged by either side.

On Sunday April 12, 1360, the withdrawal began, the general
direction being south-west toward Chartres. The French made
no attempt to follow it up. On Monday there was a terrible
storm, hailstones as large as pigeons' eggs raining down on the
long column and killing several men and horses. According to
the London Chronicle the day became known as Black Monday.[1]
The march was continued by easy stages past Chartres into
the region of Bonneval and Chateaudun, 20 miles south of
that city. One might suppose that the French government and
the people of Paris heaved a sigh of relief at the retreat of
their formidable enemy, perhaps even singing a Te Deum in
Notre Dame. What, in fact, they did was surprising. Though
the danger now appeared to be past, the regent sent emissaries
hurrying after the retreating army to treat for peace! They
caught up with the army near Chateaudun and asked for the
negotiations, broken off on April 10, to be resumed. To this
the king of England agreed, and within eight days a treaty of
peace, based on the terms offered by Edward in the first
Treaty of London, had been drawn up and signed.

That is the outline of the extraordinary story. It presents
a double problem, first the reason for the English abrupt
retreat (if it was a retreat) and second, the anxiety of the French
to come to terms with a retreating opponent approximately on
terms dictated by him. A besieged army that wishes for or is
reduced to suing for terms normally does so as the result of
starvation, of threat of being stormed (when no quarter is

---

[1] Froissart asserts that king and army were frightened and that Edward was
induced to make an immediate peace, but according to Walsingham the storm
had little effect on the march, and Delachenal discredits Froissart's story. Edward
was too tough a man to be diverted from his aim by a bad hailstorm.

given), or of an actual assault. I know of no case in the whole medieval period similar to the one we are considering.

THE TREATY OF BRETIGNY

Let us first consider the English case. Henry Knighton gives no reason for the move; Gray, in his *Scalacronica*, asserts that the move was made in order to find fodder for the horses, it being lacking outside Paris. Froissart states that the king intended to pass down the Loire valley into Brittany, where he would rest and recuperate his army till the late summer and then return to besiege Paris. Was this one of Froissart's reckless statements based on guesswork? It certainly was an obvious guess, for the English army was heading in that direction, and as all prudent commanders keep two or more possible plans in mind, in case things go wrong, Edward probably considered such a course. But it is hard to believe that he had such a design, involving a tame retreat when within sight of his goal, or that his troops, who must have been keyed up with hopes of a spectacular and profitable victory, would have acquiesced in this disappointment—which apparently they did. So the mystery deepens the closer we look into it.

Another assertion of Froissart may lead us toward the solution. He states that the duke of Lancaster, ever avid for battle and adventure, now suddenly became an ardent advocate of peace. The last thing we should expect of this fire-eater! Now, Henry of Lancaster had been English leader in the two abortive peace conferences of April 3 (Good Friday) and April 10. No record exists of the discussions on those occasions, but it is reasonable to suppose that they narrowed the ground between the two parties, and enabled each side to see on which subjects the other side was adamant. Now, Henry of Lancaster had always been *persona grata* with the French, who genuinely admired this dashing and chivalrous soldier. Is it too far-fetched to imagine that at these conferences he gained the confidence of the French delegates, and that in the course of the proceedings of the second conference the French leader, the constable Robert de Fiennes, took Henry aside into an alcove and explained "off the record" (as we might now express it) that *amour propre* prohibited the regent from accepting any terms of duress on the part of a threatening army outside his gates, but that if the English army would be so kind as to move off a few days' march, he knew the regent would jump at the opportunity to accede to the English demands, at least as far as the First Treaty of London? In order to "save face" for the French, secrecy would be essential, and Lancaster on his return would prevail upon the king to give the plan at least a trial. No doubt the English leaders would be let into the secret, under a pledge of secrecy, and a confused story would get about to the effect that Lancaster, who had been seen closeted with the king on his return from the peace conference, had prevailed upon the king to make peace. This in time would come to the ears of Froissart, who then put into the mouth of Lancaster the well-known words of the chronicle.

The above solution is, of course, purely conjectural, as must be any solution, in view of the paucity of recorded facts; but it, and it alone, seems to explain the otherwise curious attitude and actions of both sides in the matter. The one stark and arresting fact is that, as soon as the English "retreated" from Paris, a peace favourable to them was brought about.

If the above is the true explanation, it shows King Edward to be what the French chroniclers and historians are always so ready to call him, an astute diplomat whether in council or in the field.

*   *   *

On April 27 the French delegates arrived at Chartres.[1] The king was now established at Sours, five miles east of the city, and he fixed on a hamlet named Bretigny between that village and the city for the peace conference.[2]

On May Day, 1360, this historic conference assembled.

---

[1] The Black Prince may have had his quarters there: it is stated in Chartres that the name of the Prince appears at the head of a subscription list for the construction of one of the towers of the cathedral.

[2] A stone monument now marks the spot.

There were 16 French and 22 English delegates. It is as well to record the names of the leading delegates to this famous meeting. The leader of the English party was the duke of Lancaster, and he was supported by the earls of Northampton, Warwick, Salisbury, Stafford, Sir Reginald Cobham, Sir John Chandos, Sir Frank Halle (of Auberoche fame), the Captal de Buch, and the inevitable Sir Walter Manny. With what curiosity must the French delegates have gazed on these men whose names had been so prominent throughout the land for nearly a generation.

The French leader seems to have been a priest, the bishop of Beauvais, and many of the members were also priests or civilians.

Of the deliberations we unfortunately have no record, but it appears that the main heads were agreed upon with singular speed, two days sufficing for this purpose. This lends weight to my supposition that much unsuspected headway had been made at the two previous conferences, in spite of their short duration. The terms of the Treaty of Bretigny were slightly, but only slightly, more hard for France than those of the First Treaty of London. The English territorial gains were enlarged by the county of Rouergue (about the same size as that of Kent). The ransom for King John was reduced by one quarter, probably because Edward had the sense to recognize that the original sum was beyond the country's capacity to pay—especially now that no money would be forthcoming from Rouergue.

It followed that since Edward had signed the First Treaty, which he must have considered "an honourable peace",[1] the same honour was satisfied by the Bretigny Treaty, and his vow not to leave France till he had obtained such a peace was carried out.

A further five days were devoted to thrashing out and drafting the numerous and complicated details—another example of expeditious work. The exact nature of these details

---

[1] Technically it was not a peace, for it had to be ratified at Calais in the autumn, under a separate Treaty of Calais.

is not relevant to this book, but it must be noted that they were drawn up with the greatest care, every effort being made by both sides to reduce to a minimum the chance of disputes or conflicts arising from differing interpretations.

The main effect of the Treaty was to return to the English crown her old dominion of Aquitaine, but with this all-important difference that this time it was to be held in absolute right of ownership, the French king abandoning his suzerainty. Thus the main stumbling block to good relations between the two countries—the fact that the king of England was also the vassal of the king of France for his French possessions—was abolished. From now onward there could be permanent peace between the two countries. Edward was to abandon his claim to the French throne, and John was to be released on the payment of an enormous ransom. Calais and Ponthieu were ceded to England.

Great importance was attached to swearing to, and signing, the Treaty.[1] Since King John could not sign it, neither did King Edward, and the two chief signatories thus became the regent and the Prince of Wales.

Leaving the earl of Warwick as Guardian in Normandy and the duke of Lancaster to lead the army home *via* Calais, the king, accompanied by his sons, made straight for home. Setting sail from Honfleur on May 28, he made a speedy crossing, arriving at Rye the same day. Then, without losing a moment, he mounted a horse and rode straight to London, scarcely stopping for rest or refreshment en route. Thus he reached Westminster at 9 o'clock next morning after a journey from France of little over 24 hours. Arrived at Westminster, he met and embraced John de Valois, exclaiming: "You and I are now, thank God, of good accord!" For Edward had acquired a real liking for John, and as long as both kings lived, peace between England and France was, humanly speaking, assured.

Both countries now gave themselves up to thanksgivings and rejoicings. Te Deums were sung and church bells were

[1] The Treaty was cited in the dispute regarding some Channel Islands in 1954.

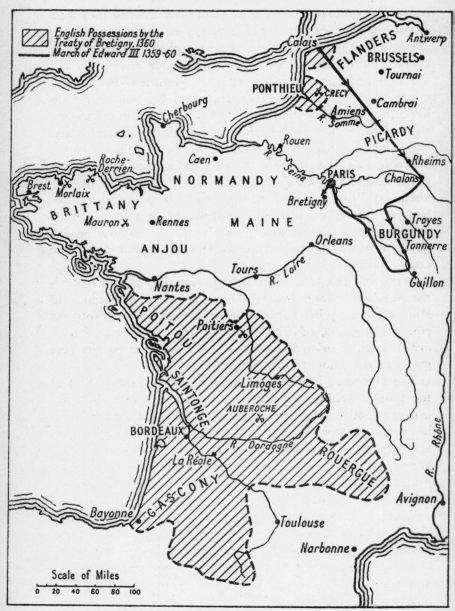

Legend on map:

English Possessions by the Treaty of Bretigny, 1360
March of Edward III 1359-60

Labels on map: Calais, Antwerp, FLANDERS, BRUSSELS, Tournai, PONTHIEU, CRECY, Cambrai, Cherbourg, R. Somme, Amiens, Rouen, Rheims, Caen, R. Seine, PARIS, Chalons, Roche-Derrien, NORMANDY, Bretigny, Brest, Morlaix, BRITTANY, Troyes, Mauron, Rennes, MAINE, BURGUNDY, Tonnerre, ANJOU, Orleans, Tours, R. Loire, Guillon, Nantes, POITOU, Poitiers, Limoges, SAINTONGE, AUBEROCHE, BORDEAUX, R. Dordogne, ROUERGUE, La Réole, GASCONY, R. Rhône, Avignon, Bayonne, Toulouse, Narbonne, PICARDY

Scale of Miles
0 20 40 60 80 100

18. FRANCE AFTER THE TREATY OF BRETIGNY, 1360

350

rung: the roots of antagonism and discord had been rooted up and the seeds of perpetual peace between the two great countries sown. Overhead was the blue sky of heaven—but on the far horizon might be seen a little cloud, no bigger than a man's hand.

APPENDIX

THE NUMBERS OF EDWARD III'S ARMY

All the chroniclers are agreed that the English army was of exceptional size. This was to be expected in view of the king's grim determination this time to leave nothing to chance. Villani gives the figure of 100,000, which is merely another way of saying that it was very large, but that he does not know the figures. Le Bel, writing not long after the event, gives detailed figures for two of the divisions, which bear the impress of being based on some precise information, even though perhaps exaggerated. His total for the king's and Prince's division is 18,500. Froissart adopts le Bel's figures in his first edition, but scales them down in a combination of the Amiens and Abrégées editions by 2,500, bringing the total to 16,000. These figures exclude the division of the duke of Lancaster, so that the grand total cannot well be less than 20,000.

The Dauphin, in a letter dated October 11, stated that at the time of writing, 12,000 troops had landed at Calais. But this does not help us for we do not know what proportion of the army had then landed, nor was the Dauphin likely to have accurate information himself. However, if the divisions of Lancaster and the Black Prince were by then landed, a grand total of 20,000 would not be far from the mark.

The above figures do not take into account the foreign volunteers that eventually marched under the English banner. Knighton states that Walter Manny collected 1,500 of them at Calais, but we do not know how many of them accepted the king's terms, namely that they could not expect any pay, but only booty. The number was probably almost negligible.

The fact that the king did not seem anxious for their presence imparts veracity to his statement that he already had a large enough army for his purpose.

Taking everything into consideration the indications are that the army was at least equal in combatant strength to that of the Crecy campaign, and vastly superior in non-combatants, who must have numbered several thousands. Hence the number of men, armed and unarmed, who set out from Calais in the last expedition of Edward III may have exceeded 20,000.

It is true that Rymer's *Foedera* only records 3,474 infantry as being summoned in England and Wales, but there clearly must be some omissions in this collection of *Foedera*. Ramsay, however, assumes that it is complete and on the strength of it he calculates that the total was under 6,000 combatants. Even so, he fails to take into account any foreign element, or English troops already in Calais or other parts of France.

Moreover, it is probable that Sir Robert Knollys' Grande Compagnie, about 3,000 strong, joined forces in the centre of France where they were operating. Delachenal contents himself with the observation that the figure 20,000 is "probably too high". Ferdinand Lot, another apostle of the low numbers school, follows Ramsay.

SOURCES

The only eye-witness's account we have (for Chaucer wrote nothing) is Sir Thomas Gray, so his *Scalacronica* must take first place. Unfortunately it is all too short. Apart from this, Henry Knighton is our main source. Walsingham, writing later, adds a few facts of his own. Rymer's *Foedera* is essential for the king's measures before setting out to France, and it gives the text of the Treaty of Bretigny, the original of which does not exist in complete form.

Of the neutral writers, le Bel is useful; Froissart copies him, and gives some interesting details of his own about the army; Villani gives a few facts which appear nowhere else.

For the early stages, the French chroniclers are almost valueless, but as the campaign progresses, so they become progressively more useful. The *Grandes Chroniques* is the best, and it prints the Bretigny Treaty. The continuator of de Nangis was in Paris during the siege, so his details are here reliable and to the point. The *Chronique des Quatre Premiers Valois*, though it gives a certain amount of information of its own, is not to be depended upon, and the *Chronique Normande* is no longer of much help.

The only modern works of real assistance, apart from Ramsay's *Genesis of Lancaster*, are of French origin. Two of these, supplemented by some papers in the *Bibliothèque de l'École des Chartes*, Henri Deniflé's *La Désolation des Églises* . . . and Roland Delachenal's *Charles V*, cover the ground between them.

EDWARD III's STRATEGY

There were significant changes in the strategy of the king during the war. He started by amassing allies, but soon learnt to distrust them. He then turned to the strategy of exterior lines, which was rendered possible to an island power in control of the sea.

But absence of communication between his armies caused so many disappointments that in his last campaign he reverted to the strategy of concentration, together with an absence of reliance on allies. This proved to be the correct policy for his times and procured him complete victory.

RETROSPECT

IT was stated in the preface (which may have been skipped by many readers) that the dominant feature of the Crecy War was the person of Edward III–the central figure of the war. Around this remarkable man events pirouetted like dancers round a maypole, or concentrated upon him like filings upon a magnet. That the war was won was due almost entirely to the personality and persistence of a single man, the king of England. Kings, rulers and generals of France came and went during the course of the war, but not the English commander. Throughout a war lasting 22 years– precisely the length of the Napoleonic Wars–Edward pursued relentlessly his main objective: the freeing of the English crown from the vassalage of France, and thereby the termination of a centuries-old conflict.

If the commander changed not, neither did his chief captains. There is a remarkable, perhaps a unique continuity in the high command of the English army. In his first campaign Edward selected as his senior officers Henry of Derby, Warwick, Northampton, Suffolk, Reginald Cobham, and Walter Manny, while Sir John Chandos served as a junior. In his last campaign, 21 years later, he took with him the same six commanders, the only newcomers of note being the Prince of Wales and Lord Burghersh. It is incontestable that the king possessed in a high degree the gift of selecting the right leaders, and it is quite remarkable that, unlike Napoleon's marshals, Edward's generals did not quarrel and fall out among themselves; there is no record of personal feuds or jealousies: all were merged into a veritable "band of brothers", united in devoted service to their king and leader. To this homogeneity in the senior ranks must be attributed much of the English success in the field. Search where I may in the pages of military history, I can find nothing quite to match it.

Now these captains were rugged, masterful soldiers, of differing temperaments, who would not have shown such marked fidelity and devotion to a weakling king: they were the sons of the nobles who had dealt otherwise with his father Edward II. It follows that King Edward must have possessed a dominant yet attractive personality of his own, and that he added to this a natural talent for war and a proficiency in its execution that inspired in them confidence and implicit obedience. This attitude towards their king and commander must have been passed down to the rank and file, for *tel chef, telle troupe*. The confidence thus engendered inspired the whole army with a vibrant morale, without which no army can achieve great things. This in turn reacted upon its discipline, which steadily improved until it attained a high pitch in the final campaign of the war, where privations and frustrations were alike extreme. The army as a whole had also, by dint of much campaigning, reached a high standard of professional ability, and it had been well armed and supplied by a far-seeing commander. There can be no doubt that by the time of the signing of the Treaty of Bretigny the English professional soldier was easily the finest in the world. This is the fundamental reason why a small country like England was able to defeat one several times as large as itself. It follows from this that the English army was then the finest in the world; and this position of pre-eminence it owed to its king—the architect, the *fons et origo* of the whole vast machine.

England was, on military grounds, fortunate in her king. Whether she was equally fortunate on moral grounds it is not within the province of this book to enquire. I will only observe that it must be easy to condemn him on these grounds—to judge by the attitude of most English historians who castigate the king unmercifully. But it is permissible to wonder whether, had the critics lived at that epoch, they would have regarded the matter in the same light. Edward III was a product of his time, a child of his generation, and from all accounts a very likeable child in the period with which we are dealing. Moreover he was genuinely, if narrowly, religious, and it was not a mere formality that he bespoke the prayers of the two archbishops before setting out on his campaigns. Most human actions are the resultant of two or more impulses or motives, and Edward's action in fighting the king of France was no exception to this principle. He was no doubt influenced by the lust for power, and attracted by the glamour and excitement of adventure; but I believe that his dominant motive in so persistently maintaining the struggle was the one given above. He was, according to his lights, doing the right thing, and I will leave it at that.

Whether on material grounds England was fortunate is a fairly easy question to answer, but that also does not strictly appertain to this book. I will therefore confine myself to two observations. During the period covered by this war the internal state of the country was at least as peaceful and undisturbed as in any period of our medieval history: and toward the end, in spite of the ravages of the Black Death, it was rapidly increasing in material prosperity: it really did look as if it paid to go to war. The second observation is that the impact of the series of victories abroad seems to have stoked up the fires of national consciousness and pride in the hearts of this essentially young nation, and it was no mere coincidence that the signing of the Treaty of Bretigny practically coincided with the introduction of the English tongue into Parliamentary proceedings. The Crecy war was responsible for much.

THE AGINCOURT WAR

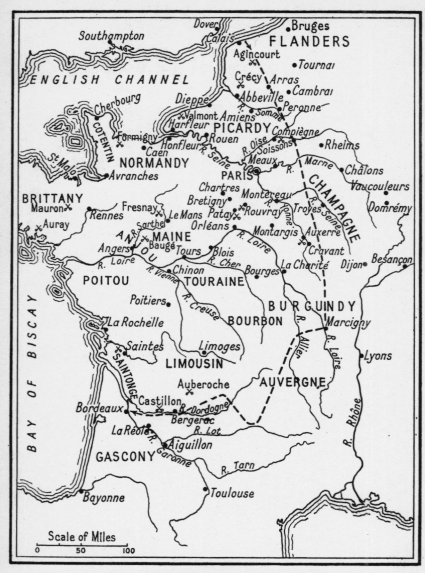

FRANCE DURING THE HUNDRED YEARS WAR
------→ John of Gaunt's Grande Chevauchée

TO JOHN PREST

who took me to Agincourt

CONTENTS

ILLUSTRATIONS AND MAPS

PREFACE

MY previous book on the Hundred Years War, *The Crecy War*, carried the story from its outbreak in 1337 to the Treaty of Bretigny in 1360. The war broke out again in 1369 and lasted, with some intervening truces, till 1453. It is this second war, or portion of war, which, for want of a better title, I call *The Agincourt War*, that is described in the following pages. For all practical purposes it was two, if not three wars, for there was a truce from 1396 to 1415, while by the treaty of Troyes in 1422 the war changed its complexion, the governmental forces of both England and France combining to fight the forces of the Dauphin–"the King of Bourges".

Nevertheless, a central theme runs through the whole 116 years covered by the Hundred Years War–the struggle to maintain an English dominion within the borders of what is now metropolitan France.

The military power and reputation of England was at its height in 1369. We shall see it wane, wax, and wane again. Though the art and conditions of war changed but slightly during the course of this war, we shall see, at its beginning, knights in mail armour, and artillery in its infancy, at its end, knights in full plate armour, *cap-à-pie*, and artillery so powerful that it decided the issue in the last battle of the war.

Much of the campaign was spent in desultory siege operations, lacking in interest; by describing these operations briefly it has been possible to treat the battles in considerable detail.

Agincourt was the dominant battle of the wars, but there were several other battles so little less significant from a military aspect, that I have tried to rescue them from ever-increasing oblivion. In the same way, Henry V was the dominating personality on the stage, but while I have tried to do justice to his prowess and exploits I have tried to penetrate the blinding dazzle that surrounds him and which obscures the abilities

365

and achievements of his chief lieutenants. These men are un-known even by name to most educated persons—except where Shakespeare comes to their help

"Harry the King, Bedford and Exeter, Warwick and Talbot, Salisbury and Gloucester."

These names, and others, such as Huntingdon, Scales, Fastolf and Kyriell, should be in our flowing cups freshly remembered.

For the rest, this volume is framed on the same lines as its predecessor. That is to say, it is designed primarily for the "lay" public rather than for the historian or historical student, and since the average lay reader is repelled by a multitude of footnotes I have reduced these to a minimum. On the other hand I have added an appendix to most chapters which includes a brief note on the sources,[1] and further notes on controversial points. These can of course be skipped by the general reader.

The space devoted to political matters is kept to a minimum, in order to admit greater space for military operations, bear-ing in mind the sub-title, "a military history". The political side cannot however be completely omitted; for instance, the effects of the shortage of money on the operations must be mentioned, but not the causes of that shortage or the measures taken to remedy it; again, the strength of armies must be examined, but not the method of recruitment—except in outline.

The reconstruction of all history is largely conjectural, and this applies more to military than to any other branch of history. It should therefore never be forgotten that there is this element of the conjectural in the reconstruction of all the operations described in this book. It would however be weari-some to the reader were I to qualify almost every other sen-tence with such expressions as "It would seem that", "In all probability", or "The evidence points to the fact that". When in particular doubt or difficulty I have applied the test of what I call "Inherent Military Probability" to the problem and what I.M.P. tells me I usually accept. It is of course easy for

---

[1] In footnote references I have usually inserted the page number only in cases of actual quotation.

the critic to pour ridicule on this method, and many critics
have done so; but I know no other method.

No attempt has been made to keep chapters at a fairly
uniform size. I see no merit in this, and have preferred to em-
body one operation or clear-cut phase of the war in a single
chapter. This should enable the reader to find the section he
wished to consult with a minimum of reference to the index.

The positions of all places mentioned, except very unimportant ones, are either shown on one of the maps or described
in the text.

I am again indebted to Mr. Robin Jeffs of Trinity College
Oxford for reading the MS. and endeavouring to keep me
straight in political matters. If at times I have wandered from
the narrow path of rectitude this must be accounted to me for
waywardness, and not attributed to my mentor. In conclusion
I should like to express my thanks to the officials of the London
Library, who have invariably accorded me courteous attention
and assistance.

ALFRED H. BURNE.

THE AGINCOURT WAR

"Agincourt! Agincourt! Know ye not Agincourt?"

CHAPTER I

THE DUGUESCLIN WAR (1369–96)

"Overhead was the blue sky of heaven – but on the far horizon might be seen a little cloud, no bigger than a man's hand."

WITH the above words ended the book of which this volume is the sequel. The sky was blue, for the kings of England and France, after 22 years of warfare, had sworn eternal friendship: the little cloud indicated the uncertain state of health of the French monarch.

Throughout that period of 22 years, Edward III, king of England, pursued a single aim – the abolition of vassalage to the king of France for his French dominion; and now at last in the year 1360 the Treaty of Bretigny had brought it about.

By this treaty the king of England became the sovereign in his own absolute right of one third of the land of France. This abolition of the homage due by one king to another was calculated to remove the "running sore" that had poisoned the relations of the kings of two neighbouring countries for two centuries. It was all to the good. But it involved the transference by several provinces of France of liege loyalty from one over-lord to another. Although the idea of nationality was not as clear-cut as it was afterwards to become, this transference was bound to set up the sort of condition in a state that a surgical operation sets up in a body. It required a period of complete rest for the new limb to take root and thrive. A period of rest; that was the crux. The best, in fact the only, perceptible condition for this was that king John of France should hold the sceptre in his own country for several years; but his health failed and in 1364 he died, to be succeeded by his son Charles V.

"The death of king John sounded the knell of the Treaty of Bretigny."[1] The new king, Charles V was perhaps the least war-

[1] *The Genesis of Lancaster* by Sir James Ramsay, I, p. 460.

like of French kings, with the possible exception of Charles VII. He had no desire for a new war, but on the other hand he had every desire for revenge. And, being an astute man, he worked patiently for the day when his desire might be fulfilled.

But in the meantime two events of importance occurred. In Brittany "the War of Liberation" had dragged on with alternating fortunes for over 20 years. Of the two claimants to the Duchy, John de Montfort was sponsored by the English, who by this time practically ruled the greater part of Brittany, and Charles de Blois was the French nominee. . . . After a brief truce the war had flared up again, and in 1364 it came to a head. The rival armies met one mile to the north of the little town of Auray, 60 miles south-west of Rennes. In the battle that followed, the Anglo-Breton army, under Sir John Chandos, utterly defeated the French under the count de Blois, who was killed, and a Breton soldier named Bertrand Duguesclin, who was captured. The battle ended the War of Liberation, and ushered in the Golden Age for Brittany.

The second event of importance occurred in the far south. King Pedro the Cruel (who has been maligned by his soubriquet almost as badly as "Butcher Cumberland") had been ousted from the throne of Castile by his bastard half-brother Henry of Trastamare. Pedro appealed for help to the Black Prince, who had been created duke of Aquitaine by Edward III and who held his court at Bordeaux the capital. Prince Edward responded with alacrity to the appeal. Raising an army of Anglo-Gascons—hereinafter called English for short—he crossed the Pyrenees by the pass of Roncesvalles—rendered famous by the epic story of Roland—and advanced through Pamplona to Vittoria, along the same road that Wellington traversed in 1813. Prince Edward came up with the army of Henry of Trastamare on a ridge six miles east of Najera, and gained a signal victory over him. Bertrand Duguesclin, who commanded a French contingent, was again captured. The English pursued the enemy into Najera and rounded up the fugitives in a ravine still called locally "The Ravine of the English".

The Spanish campaign, despite its victorious issue, had calamitous results. Not one penny of the war expenses was received from Pedro (who later was murdered by his half-brother) and it became necessary to impose heavy taxation on Aquitaine in consequence. Early in 1368 the Estates of Aquitaine granted the Black Prince the additional taxation that he asked for, but two of the chief nobles appealed to the king of England against it. Without awaiting his response they then appealed to the king of France. Now, by the Treaty of Bretigny Charles V had of course no jurisdiction in Aquitaine, but his jurists persuaded him, on the grounds that certain terms in the Treaty had not been carried out, that he had. After some hesitation therefore Charles "crossed the Rubicon" and received in audience the two appellants. After this action war became inevitable and on November 30, 1369 the king clinched the matter by confiscating Aquitaine—just as his grandfather had done a generation before.

Before taking this decisive step Charles had prepared for the coming war in various ways: the amassing of war supplies, the enrolling of allies and, most important of all, he cleverly "worked" the lesser landowners of Gascony through the medium of his brother, the duke of Anjou. All this time Edward III, totally unprepared for war, had made conciliatory overtures, but Charles with the bit in his teeth, passed them by unheeded, and even unanswered.

The Prince of Wales's attitude had not been so pacific. When the French king summoned him to Paris he made the famous reply "We shall go to Paris, but with helmets on and sixty thousand troops behind us"—a boast that it was not in his power to make good. To raise an army one tenth that size would have been about as much as was possible at that moment. The war was on!

THE DUGUESCLIN SUB-WAR (1369-96)

The war that ensued, lasting, with short intervals, from 1369 to 1396, has no name. We will call it the Duguesclin Sub-War,[1] after the soldier most closely associated with it. In this war nothing worthy of the name of battle was fought. This was because French armies refused to meet English armies in the field, acting under the strict orders of their king. English armies in consequence were able to roam the country at will, while the French confined themselves to sieges. The war is thus rather lacking in military interest, for there was remarkably little actual fighting.

In spite of the fact that the French had every advantage in war-stores, numbers, allies and surprise, and that they were invading a territory that was already on the verge of revolt, they were strangely hesitant. After over-running, without resistance, the outlying districts of Rouergue they resorted to sporadic assaults on isolated castles. This cautious behaviour may have been inspired by the knowledge that Sir John Chandos had been summoned south from his castle of St. Sauveur-le-Vicomte in Normandy and was soon on the war-path in Poitou.

For the first year of war the results were indeterminate. But a great blow befell the English in the death of the peerless John Chandos, "one of the purest glories of England",[2] before the gate of Lussac, in Poitou.[3] Sir Robert Knowles and Sir Hugh Calverley took up the mantle of Chandos.

LIMOGES

An event took place in the year 1370 which has been so distorted by subsequent writers that it deserves fairly detailed examination. In the course of the French advance the duke of Berry approached Limoges; but there was no reason to assault it for the bishop, who was in control, welcomed the French into the town. When the Black Prince heard of this treachery he was furious; the bishop had been one of his trusted friends, indeed he had stood as godfather to the Prince's son Richard of Bor-

---

[1] It was not a complete war, being terminated merely by a truce.
[2] The tribute of a Frenchman, B. Fillon, in a biography of *Jean Chandos*.
[3] The French still tend his monument at Lussac.

deaux, and there had been no suspicion of his disloyalty. The Prince of Wales vowed vengeance on the bishop, and together with his brother John of Gaunt who had now arrived at Bordeaux with reinforcements from home, he marched on Limoges: that is to say, the army marched; the Prince was too ill and weak, and had to be carried in a litter. The duke of Berry with his army prudently kept out of his way.[1] The English army laid siege to the city, mined it, and in six days carried it by storm.[2] There followed the famous "sack of Limoges".

Many writers—the worst offenders being, I am sorry to say, of English blood—have allowed their too fertile imaginations to run riot in describing the devilries committed by English troops egged on by the Black Prince himself. It may seem curious that a prince of chivalry, such as Edward of Woodstock was, should have descended to such depths of infamy on this one occasion—"the one blot on his escutcheon". But modern research has supplied the answer, and it is a simple one: there was no general massacre of Limoges. The too credulous followers of the recklessly irresponsible chronicler Froissart have seized upon his famous passage; "upwards of 3,000 men, women and children were put to death that day". This passage has been quoted *ad nauseam* by English writers, although Froissart discreetly deleted the number from his subsequent Amiens MS, which, never having been translated into English, was presumably unknown to the above-mentioned writers.

Roland Delachenal quotes Froissart's famous passage where the women and children fling themselves upon their knees before the Black Prince, crying for mercy, and he adds that this passage "is not negligible". Let us see. I once stood on the spot where the Prince's litter is reputed to have rested and tried hard to picture the scene as described by Froissart. I failed. In the first place, the women, in the confusion of the "massacre",

[1] "It is clear that the French feared the Prince of Wales, even though he had to be carried in a litter." *La Désolation des Eglises . . . pendant la Guerre de Cent Ans*, by H. Denifle, Vol. II, p. 559.
[2] Prince Edward seems to have deliberately selected the anniversary of his victory at Poitiers, September 19, for the assault.

would not have been aware of the position of the Prince. Secondly, even if they had known it and had tried to approach him they would have failed. To reach him they would have had to pass up a narrow street, which would be barred by the Prince's escort; indeed, according to Froissart, they would have been struck down had they even attempted it for he states that they were killed wherever the attackers encountered them. Thirdly, the natural instinct of women in a confined town where murder is running riot is to slip out of the town, or to hide in a cellar, not to try to force their way, with their children, up a narrow street into the presence of the Prince. But it is a heart-rending scene, as painted by the shrewd old story-teller who knew well how to work upon the emotions of his readers. "Fut grant pitié"–it was a great pity–is an expression constantly flowing from his pen. In short, the passage *is* negligible: the whole scene was a figment of the chronicler's lurid imagination.

To sum up, the Prince of Wales made an example of the treacherous defenders of Limoges: on that the English chroniclers are insistent and almost gleeful–but he did it by pillage and burning rather than by the taking of life. Even the bishop's life was spared–at the instance of John of Gaunt.[1]

THE GRANDE CHEVAUCHÉE

It would be tedious to recount in detail the many sieges and counter-sieges that took place in the next eight years, while the French slowly closed in on Bordeaux, nor to describe at length the *chevauchées* of the various English armies marching hither and thither through the land of France. There were no less than five of these *chevauchées*. The first, in 1369, was carried out by John of Gaunt, who landed at Calais and marched to Harfleur and back, without a real engagement with the enemy. The second, in 1370, was commanded by a commoner, Sir Robert Knowles. Also landing at Calais, he marched *via* Arras to Troyes, and thence passing Paris made for Brittany. Unfortu-

[1] The sources for the above account are listed in the Appendix to this chapter. For a detailed examination of the affair see an article in *The Fighting Forces* (February 1949), by Lt.-Col. A. H. Burne.

nately he quarrelled with the higher-born nobles, who eventually marched away and never rejoined him. Duguesclin took advantage of this dispersal of forces to pounce on isolated columns and completely break them up. The third campaign, in 1373 was the *Grande Chevauchée* of John of Gaunt, and deserves fuller treatment, for it captured the imagination of the civilized world of his day, and indeed in some respects was an epic resembling that of Christopher Columbus. Gaunt was provided with a huge army, 15,000 strong, and was ordered to take it to the relief of Gascony. Now the French had by this time attained the practical command of the sea and it was almost hopeless to try to go direct by sea. Gaunt accordingly landed at Calais, announcing that he would march right through the middle of France to Bordeaux. This was a map distance of nearly 600 miles through a hostile country. Everywhere he went the French armies evaded him, and hunger became his worst enemy, as, winter approaching, he entered the highlands of central France. Conditions got steadily worse, but Gaunt displayed the iron resolution of his father Edward III. On he marched over the mountains and at last down into the plain of the Dordogne, to reach Bordeaux at Christmas, nearly five months after setting out, having marched about 1,000 miles. He had with him just over half his army, the rest had perished by the wayside.

The result was regarded as rather disastrous by English chroniclers (and by other writers since then), but it was not—and is not—so regarded by the French. The *Grandes Chroniques* wrote that it was "most honourable to the English".

The expedition had in fact achieved considerable results; it had given Brittany a respite, for not only Duguesclin but the duke of Anjou had been hastily recalled from the duchy for the defence of France; it had brought a useful reinforcement to Aquitaine; it had raised the prestige and demonstrated the power of the English army and had brought loss and discouragement and indeed humiliation to its opponents, and had halted their advance into Aquitaine.

*   *   *

The fourth *chevauchée* was undertaken in 1375 by Edmund, earl of Cambridge, who landed in western Brittany and marched right through the duchy from end to end.

The final *chevauchée* was that of the earl of Buckingham, who practically followed in the tracks of Knowles's march into Maine, but continued right on to Rennes, the capital of Brittany, as he had contracted to do.

In the meantime the French were steadily pursuing their campaign of sieges in Gascony, and also operations on the sea, where Admiral de Vienne had considerable successes. Duguesclin was the predominant and most successful of the French generals, and at length Charles V made him Constable of France, probably the first commoner to receive this high honour. It was justified.

The decisive year of the war was 1377, when the French increased their efforts and brought the tide of war within 20 miles of Bordeaux. But it got no further. That same year both Edward III and the Black Prince died, to be followed three years later by Charles V and the Constable Duguesclin.

There was no land fighting of significance after 1380, and after a series of short truces a final truce was signed in 1396, recognizing the *status quo*, and leaving the vital question of the homage unsolved and indeed unmentioned.

*   *   *

What are we to make of this extraordinary war of 27 years in which no real battles were fought and scarcely any out-and-out sieges were carried out, in which however nearly one quarter of the land of France had changed hands? It would almost seem as if nature had asserted herself, and that the transfer of land had taken place by mutual consent, in the natural order of events. In the early stages and on the outer bounds of the newly acquired English territory this was not very far from being the case, for these old possessions of Henry II had long since been in French hands. But even when the fighting approached Bordeaux, in which French soldiers had not been seen for over 200 years, there had been astonishingly little fighting. The fundamental explanation is probably that propounded by Professor Perroy, that the French successes were won "more by diplomacy than by force of arms."[1] Whilst on the purely military side, we may quote with approval the words of that shrewd historian Professor T. F. Tout in *The Political History of England* (1906) –

"When the command of the sea passed to the French and their Spanish allies all hope of retaining Aquitaine was lost."[2]

With so little fighting, it is difficult to assess the military merits of the leadership on either side. One can but admire the spirit of enterprise – and indeed bravado – shown by the three great *chevauchées* of Lancaster, Knowles and Buckingham, whatever their strategical justification. On the French side there were of course a long succession of captures of towns and castles. And this brings us to the Constable of France, Bertrand Duguesclin. This almost incredibly ugly Breton commoner would not have risen to such dizzy heights unless he had possessed exceptional qualities, and yet his bare military record hardly seems to account for it. In both of the only really big battles in which he fought he was defeated and captured, and of his generalship in the field we know scarcely anything. This has probably led the latest French historian of the war to describe him as "a mediocre captain, incapable of winning a battle or being successful in a siege of any scope".[3] Yet this judgement seems altogether too sweeping. If only from the manner in which he swept down on one of Knowles's isolated columns, it is clear that he had the instincts of generalship; and there was more to it than that. Nevertheless, it is probably true to say that he was born at a lucky time; the pendulum was bound to swing against England in far-off Aquitaine once the command of the sea was lost, and whatever soldier happened at that time to be in command would find his cause successful

[1] *The Hundred Years War*, p. 164.   [2] Op. cit., p. 416.
[3] Edouard Perroy, op. cit., p. 148.

whether or not he engaged in any victories in the field or displayed any military genius. Thus the strategy of Duguesclin, whether imposed upon him by his master or not, would have led to ultimate success—as also in all probability would the opposite strategy of offensive action in the field.

Be this as it may, England did not consider herself vanquished in the field. For over ten years the French had evidently not risked a pitched battle. During the last two years England had arrested the French invasion of Gascony, and had herself taken the offensive, one of her armies roaming through France on its way to the succour of Brittany, whilst a second army had marched victoriously to the help of another ally in Spain. If she seemed resigned to writing off her outlying possessions in the south of France, she refused resolutely and obdurately to listen to any proposals to restore the homage that had been abolished at Bretigny or to hand back Calais. It was this obduracy that prevented a permanent peace being concluded; the truce of 1396 merely recognized the *status quo*, and it would require another war to decide the question for good and all.

APPENDIX

A NOTE ON GENERAL SOURCES

On the English side there could scarcely be less material than there is. Aquitaine was far distant, and sea communications were uncertain and infrequent. Rymer's *Foedera* is of course essential for details regarding expeditions and for dates. The standard chroniclers were Adam Murimuth (Continuation), Thomas Walsingham, and for the later part the *Chronicon Angliae* of which Walsingham was also the author. On the French side the *Grandes Chroniques* give by far the most information, though necessarily from the French point of view only. For nearly all the actual details of the fighting we must have recourse to Froissart, who is probably much more accurate here than he was of 1369-96 for the Crecy War.

The war has never been treated as a whole, but of modern

historians Roland Delachenal's *Histoire de Charles V*, Vols. IV
and V (1931), contains the most detailed account and is very
fair and reliable. A few facts not mentioned in Delachenal's
work are contained in *La Désolation des Eglises* . . . *pendant L
Guerre de Cent Ans*, by Henri Deniflé (1899). This French priest
is careful as to his facts but his military appraisals need not be
taken very seriously; he makes a travesty of the various invasions
of France by the English.

The English modern historians for the period are good as
far as they go, T. F. Tout and C. W. Oman in *The Political
History of England* and Sir James Ramsay in *The Genesis of
Lancaster*, Vol. II, are the main authors.

SOURCES FOR THE SACK OF LIMOGES

There are seven contemporary or near contemporary sources
as below, Nos. 1 to 4 are all of French origin and were written
within a very few years of the event.

Source No. 1 is contained in the *Catulaire du Consulat de
Limoges*. It states that the *Cité* (as opposed to the *Ville*[1]) was
taken by Prince Edward and destroyed. Prisoners were taken:
men, women and clergy, bishop and abbot. The city was then
pillaged.

Source No. 2.—An account by one P. Bermondet, notary of
Limoges. He states that Limoges was taken and destroyed by
the lord prince of Aquitaine and his brothers because it had
placed itself in obedience to the king of France.

Source No. 3.—In an *MS of the Abbey of St. Martial* (Limousin).
This states that Limoges was taken and burnt and more than
300 persons were put to death because of the rebellion which
they had made against Prince Edward, duke of Aquitaine.

Source No. 4.—*Written by a monk of the Abbey of Uzerches*
(Limousin), who writes that Limoges was captured by the
lord Prince, the town was burnt and almost destroyed, pillaged

[1] Limoges was in reality two towns: the *Cité* on the banks of the river was
mainly official and ecclesiastical, the cathedral being in the centre of it. Two
hundred yards separated it from the *Ville*, which was twice as large. Both were
fortified: the *Ville* remained always in English hands. Much of the *Cité* wall still
stands, but the gates have gone.

and became almost desolated: monastery and churches were spoiled and polluted (*depredata et polluta*).

*   *   *

Comparing these four sources together, we note several things. First, they are in essential agreement, and in no case contradict one another.

Second, none of them speak of a massacre.

Third, most of the indignation seems to have been caused by the conduct towards the church, its persons and property.

Fourth, such loss of life as occurred seems to have been regarded as military punishment, and no note of condemnation can be found in the account.

Beyond these four primary sources are three others, slightly later and not so reliable.

Source No. 5.—Le Petit Thalamus de Montpellier, merely records that the siege only lasted a few days (important because Froissart states that it lasted a month).

Source No. 6.—La Vie d'Auban V, relates that Limoges was captured and all persons within it. It was totally destroyed except for the cathedral, and the citizens were driven out.

Source No. 7.—Chronique des Quatre Premiers Valois (it was written by a clerk in Normandy several years after the event, and cannot be regarded as very reliable). The English mined the wall, and during the mining operations John of Gaunt [who was the real commander on the spot] met one of the French generals in the mine, and was wounded in a duel with him. [This has also been related of Henry V. It makes a good story.] Many citizens were put to death because they had surrendered to the French.

These last three sources fill in the story of the first four, adding the interesting fact that the citizens were driven out, which implicity denies that they were massacred. These sources were collected by M. Alfred Deroux and published by him in 1906 in his *Le Sac de la Cité de Limoges*.

THE ARMIES

Prior to the reign of Edward III, the English army, like the French, was constituted on a feudal basis, backed by the National Militia or Fyrd. But Edward revolutionized the system, substituting a paid army for foreign service raised by indenture. Certain persons, usually of the nobility, were appointed to recruit a specified number of soldiers, under specified proportions of men-at-arms and archers, with a specified rate of pay, for a specified period. This period seldom exceeded a year in length; at the end of the period the *indentee* (as modern jargon might call him) might be indentured for a further period or he took his discharge. The result of this was that England now possessed a paid, professional, short-service army for foreign service.

France, on the other hand, remained wedded to the feudal system till the closing years of the war. Her internal state had become, in comparison with that of England, primitive and almost anarchical. Thus the army was still a feudal host, of equal lords, with their retainers, over whom the Constable had the slenderest control. The knights and men-at-arms regarded themselves not merely as the backbone of the army: they *were* the army, although, in order to make up numbers, local levies of *les communes* were enrolled, and some foreign mercenaries who wielded the crossbow were recruited chiefly from Italy. But any conception of cooperation between the cavalry and the despised other arms was unheard of. The battle of Crecy had become the stock example of this conception, and France had not yet learnt the lesson, as had her rival many years before. Thus, in spite of her larger population, three or four times as great, France had up to this time never succeeded in putting in the field an army that could stand up to that of Edward III.

In the matter of arms and armament the two armies were not dissimilar. Men-at-arms were armed with a lance (or "spear"), sword, dagger and occasionally battle-mace. Mail armour was now giving place to plate armour, and by the end of the war knights were almost universally armoured *cap-à-pie*. The shield was gradually becoming obsolete, partly owing to the superior defence offered by plate armour and partly to its ineffectiveness against cannon balls. Each man-at-arms was attended by two archers, and often one swordsman, together with one or two pages or *valets aux armes* – an almost synonymous term – who were armed with daggers. The total outfit of four to six constituted a "lance". Herein lies a difficulty. The composition of a lance was always fluid in the English army, and only became standardized in the French army towards the end of the war, when it numbered six (including varlet and page). Moreover it is by no means always clear when the number of lances is given and also the number of archers whether the archers included in the lance are also included in the total number of archers indentured. I have made the rough assumption that in the case of the knighthood their archers are not included in the indentured archers, but that they are so included in the case of the ordinary men-at-arms. In the French army, however, right up to the end of the war, when lances are mentioned we must always multiply this number by four or by six, according to whether we regard pages as "combatants" or not. Ferdinand Lot regards them as non-combatants, but they seem to come under the same category as, for example, the drivers of modern guns, who are certainly combatants.

The English archer was by now usually mounted. Whether mounted or dismounted he carried long-bow, sword and dagger. The bow could be discharged six times a minute, and had an effective range of 250 yards and extreme range of over 350 yards. The French archer, on the other hand, carried a cross-bow. Though more powerful than the long-bow it was four times as slow in its rate of discharge, and had less range. Generally the crossbowmen were Genoese mercenaries.

As for the third arm – the artillery – we hear little of its use in field operations on either side, but in siege operations it was steadily increasing in power and effect and in the last years of the Hundred Years War, as we shall see, it had a predominant effect in securing the surrender of defended towns and castles.

The infantry included in addition to the archers a number of foot spearmen (until their abolition by Henry V), though foreign mercenaries, Flemings, Germans, and also Gascons, etc., were included. Mercenaries also were not favoured by Henry V. As regards armour, archers wore steel helmets and breast-plates or padded hawberks, and spearmen were similarly attired except that they seldom wore breastplates.

DEVELOPMENT DURING THE WAR

In spite of the length of the Hundred Years War, develop-ment or change in arms, armament or method of fighting altered surprisingly little during its course. In two respects only was there a marked progress. The first was in the power and effectiveness of the artillery, of which mention had already been made, and will be again; the other was in the gradual intro-duction of plate armour. It was a very gradual process, and there is little direct evidence as to the rate of its progress. We are for the most part reduced to the evidence of brasses, effigies and stained-glass windows. But the progress was continuous, and at the end of the war body armour for knights was wholly plate. Its effect on the tactics was equally gradual. Its influence here was two-fold: it reduced the mobility of the dismounted men-at-arms, and it reduced the effectiveness of the arrow. As for the first, opinions still differ as to the amount of mobility and agility left to the plate-armoured knight. No doubt suits of armour themselves varied a good deal, there being no "sealed pattern" for them in either army. But generally speaking the tendency was to allow the horse to do the lion's share of the transport work of the knight. The effect of plate armour is easier to descry and define. It clearly rendered the dreaded long-bow less effective. Towards the end of the war we hear less than previously of the casualties caused by it, and instances occurred from time to time when mounted men-at-arms did succeed in breaking through the line of archers. Yet here also, the change was gradual and not well marked.

THE NAVY

Only two major actions took place during the period covered by this book, and there is not much that can be said about the rival fleets, though naval artillery was beginning to make its effect felt. Both countries kept a small number of royal ships-of-war under the direct pay of the king. The bulk of the fleet was collected as occasion warranted, by the simple methods of requisitioning, so many ships being required from each port. In the case of the Cinque Ports there was a sort of standing order or tally for each of them. The French in addition had a number of war-galleys, usually stationed in the Mediterranean, but rowed round to the Channel in the course of the war.

CHAPTER II

THE TRUCE OF 1396-1415

THREE years after the signing of the truce of 1396, Henry IV wrested the throne from his cousin Richard II. The change of sovereign had little effect upon the relations between England and France or on the observance of the truce. France was distracted by internal dissension, and the new English king was at first too preoccupied with consolidating his position at home to make a resumption of the war likely.

An involved political situation now developed, due to two factions, in both England and France, in turn gaining the upper hand and each in turn making commitments which the other faction failed to honour. Thus suspicion between the two countries increased and when in 1413 Henry IV died and was succeeded by his eldest son Henry V, the seeds of open war between France and England had been sown. England still stood by the terms of the Treaty of Bretigny, and would hear of no abatement; on the contrary, the divided state of France seemed to offer a favourable chance of recovering the losses of the previous war. The country rang with the duplicity of France, and war fever began to rise.

This feeling was not discouraged by the young king. Though only 25 years of age it might almost be said that he had been born and brought up in the camp from the age of 12 years.

His attitude, and that of his country, is so well summarized by that careful and profound historian C. L. Kingsford, that I cannot do better than quote it here.

"The idea of war with France was not unpopular. The old traditional and commercial intercourse that bound England to Flanders and Gascony favoured it. The long dispute between the two nations was still unsettled, and the recent action of the French Government had given the English good cause for complaint. To Henry himself, with his high belief in his own rights, the assertion of his claim to the throne of France must have appeared almost in the light of a duty. Possibly he may, even now, have had other motives and dreamed that, when Western Europe was united under his sway, he would restore the unity of the Church and become the leader of Christendom in a new Crusade."[1]

Though it is impossible to say at what precise moment the king "crossed the Rubicon" and decided definitely on war, it must have been sometime in the early spring of 1415. On March 22 he issued a proclamation ordering all soldiers who owed service by virtue of fiefs or wages to rendezvous at London. And yet more plainly and formally was the same announcement made at a great War Council held on April 16. The king also announced that he had appointed his second brother the duke of Bedford as regent in England during his absence. This was followed up by issuing indentures for his expeditionary force, and a general call-up of the shire levies; "embodiment of the militia" it would be called at a later date. The levies in the northern five counties were to remain there on guard against a possible invasion from Scotland (though as its king, James I, was a prisoner in England such an eventuality was unlikely). The remaining levies were to be grouped around the country, facing possible danger from Wales, where Owen Glendower was still antagonistic, or from landings on the coast.

As for the striking force; in recruiting, composition, equipment, organization and method of employment, it was substantially the same as it had been in the day of the king's great-grandfather.[2]

The only two changes since the earlier wars that need be noted are that mail had largely given place to plate armour on men-at-arms, and that the artillery had increased in weight and power. Henry had recently amassed a large force of cannon—some of large calibre—and of cannon balls.

The king's measures for the provision of the ancillary service

---

[1] *Henry V*, p. 110.
[2] See Appendix to Chapter I. The indenture system and description of the army has already been detailed in part I of the book, 'The Crecy War'.

and stores were of a far-seeing and far-reaching nature. Particulars of these are given principally in Rymer's collection of
Foedera. No doubt the stored-up experience of the Edwardian
wars was available. At any rate nothing seems to have been
overlooked, either in the matter of *personnel* or *material*. For
example, we hear of surgeons for the first time, 20[1] of them
being included in the army. Then there were miners, masons,
corderers, turners and carpenters (no less than 1,200 of these),
farriers, chaplains, butchers, bakers, drovers, dyers, skinners,
fishmongers, even minstrels and fiddlers. In addition to the
large number of horses and draught oxen required, large
herds of cattle were also embarked. Then there were of course
carts, wagons and other vehicles, field-ovens and bakeries,
corn-grinders, shovels, picks and saws. And what is most
significant, large quantities of spares of all kinds.

To convey this vast expedition overseas required no less than
1,500 vessels, each of them nominally with over 20 tons portage.
To collect such a number was a matter of some complexity. A
few were specially constructed, and others were purchased in
Flanders and the Netherlands. But the vast majority were requisitioned from the ports all round the coast.

Orders were issued that the whole force, army and fleet, was
to be concentrated in the Southampton-Portsmouth area by
July 1, 1415.

While the expeditionary force was assembling, the French
sent a mission in a final attempt to avert the impending war.
Henry received it in Wolvesey Palace at Winchester, and its
proceedings have a curiously modern ring. It started with toasts
and honeyed words, and ended some days later in anger and
confusion.

*   *   *

On July 2, 1415, the king joined his army and fleet, and he
busily engaged himself in the intricate problem of collecting,
marshalling and supplying the great armada. All the creeks

[1] So Oman: but 13 according to Church.

and inlets along the coast facing the Isle of Wight were filled with shipping, while the interior was steadily filling up with soldiers and camp-followers. Anyone who witnessed the assembly in precisely the same area of the troops destined for a very similar venture 530 years later can perhaps envisage the scene. The task confronting Henry V and his staff was naturally less complicated than that of modern times, but, if less complex it was more difficult owing to the primitive nature of transport and of communications, especially between land and sea.

There is unusually little dispute as to the combatant strength of the army, thanks to what is known as the Agincourt Roll, but which might more accurately be called the Harfleur Roll. What it amounts to is that slightly over 2,000 men-at-arms, 8,000 archers, and 65 gunners, sailed with the expeditionary force. But as regards the numbers of the ancillary or non-combatant services we can but guess. They cannot even be roughly computed from the number of transport vessels, for these varied in size from 20 tons portage to 300 tons portage. But, by comparing the number of vessels required to transport this army with that for the Crecy campaign we realise how enormous and comprehensive these ancillary services must have been. Here are the approximate figures in parallel columns:

Campaign	Combatants	Ships
Crecy	15,000	700
Agincourt	10,000	1,500

On August 16 all was ready and the king took boat from Portchester Castle, where he had been residing, down Portsmouth Harbour, to his flagship the *Trinity Royal*, which was anchored at Spithead. This ship was the pride of the nation, being of the exceptional size of 500 tons portage, with the enormous crew of 300 sailors. Arrived on board, the king hoisted the sail to half-mast, signal for the fleet to concentrate on the flagship.

To carry out this apparently simple operation required four days. When collected they were so tightly packed together that

when one ship caught fire the flames spread to its two neighbours. This was taken as an ill-omen, but when a flock of swans
began to accompany the fleet as it set off, it was realized that
Heaven smiled upon the venture after all.

The summer sun caught the sails, bunting and banners of the
huge concourse and presented such a spectacle as might have
brought Froissart from his grave to depict it.

At 3 p.m. on Sunday, August 11, 1415, the king gave the
signal and, led by his uncle the earl of Dorset with two lanterns
at his masthead, the great fleet slipped slowly down the Channel
past the Isle of Wight and out to sea, sailing in a southerly
direction.

CHAPTER III

THE INVASION OF FRANCE

THE French Government had long been aware that an
invasion of their country was in preparation. But Henry
made great efforts to preserve the secrecy of its destination.
The only recorded statement made by him that I can discover
stated that it might be Aquitaine or "the King of France", a
sufficiently vague term. But the French Government was not
to be hoodwinked into believing that it would be Aquitaine.
Edward III, they recollected, had put out the same suggestion.
Moreover, his wars had shown the hazards attaching to such an
amphibious operation. No, the north coast of France was clearly
indicated. It might be Brittany; Brest and St. Malo had in the
past been favourite landing places for English armies. Or the
king of England might emulate his ancestor and land near
Cherbourg. Harfleur, on the estuary of the Seine, felt itself
threatened and hastily strengthened its defences. Even Flanders
was favoured by some. But the French Government believed
that Boulogne was the actual point of invasion.[1]

The measures taken for defence were, however, singularly
half-hearted. Of the two rival political parties, the Orleanists
were lethargic, and the Burgundians on one pretext or another,
refused to respond to the call for help. The Dauphin, Louis, a
weak youth of 19, was made nominal commander-in-chief, and
the Constable of France, Charles d'Albret, was made his
lieutenant. D'Albret started to collect an army at Rouen, and
stationed a force of 1,500 men under the joint command of himself and Marshal Boucicaut at Honfleur, on the south side of
the Seine estuary opposite Harfleur. But the country as a whole
was listless, being concerned more with the heavy taxation than
with the threatened invasion.

[1] The parallel with 1944 when the Germans believed that the Boulogne area,
not Normandy, was the destination, is inescapable.

Thus the prospects for the invasion were propitious when the English armada disappeared from view to the south of Bembridge, Isle of Wight. What was the destination of the king of England? If we study his recorded words and writings it becomes evident that he was more concerned to recover Normandy than to succour Aquitaine. Normandy was the older patrimony of the two. During a period of over a century it had been in Anglo-Norman hands but for some reason it had not been included in the Treaty of Bretigny. Henry resolved to rectify the omission, and therefore to make that province his first objective.

As for his ultimate aims and his plans for implementing them, not a word escaped his lips—still less his pen. We are in the region of conjecture, but we may obtain some insight into them by the method of what I call Inherent Military Probability. It is inherently probable that the young king had studied closely the successful campaigns of his great-grandfather and his generals—especially Henry of Lancaster, earl of Derby—indeed he may have had converse with some of them, and in particular with his great-uncle John of Gaunt.[1] Henry was 12 years of age when "time-honoured Gaunt" died and he would have eagerly sucked in any reminiscences and stories that he could glean from such a source. Henry V, then, imbibed and digested the lessons to be learnt from the previous wars. Four of these lessons were paramount. First, the difficulties inherent in maintaining a successful war in distant Aquitaine. The French were situated in what we call Interior Lines; they could mass a large army on its borders much more quickly and easily than England could send troops to defend it. Secondly, wide-flung operations on exterior lines were almost doomed to failure owing to shortcomings in communications. Thirdly, France was so well besprinkled with castles and fortified towns that, unless the invader was provided with a siege train, it was almost impossible to occupy effectively hostile territory, and so break the will to resistance of the enemy. Almost—but not quite—as Edward's last

[1] Charles VI had the advice of the Duke of Berri, who had fought at Poitiers.

successful campaign had shown. Fourthly, the value of a firmly established base in France from which to operate had been made manifest. Bordeaux provided one in the south and Calais in the north.

The logical corrollary of these lessons, combined with his own desire first and foremost to recover the ancient duchy of Normandy, was that Normandy should be the primary objective, that a base should be established there, that it should be a harbour analogous to Calais, and that to this end a siege train should be taken out.

Where should this base be established? The estuary of the Seine seemed indicated, and of the two fortresses guarding it, Harfleur on the north side was always regarded as "the key to Normandy", and was therefore the obvious objective. Considerations such as these must have disposed Henry V, as soon as his armada was under way, to issue orders that course was to be set for the mouth of the river Seine. And he followed this up by informing his captains that as a first step he intended to capture Harfleur.

*   *   *

After a smooth 50-hour passage, the fleet cast anchor at 5 p.m. on August 14, 1415, in the mouth of the Seine opposite a bare spit about three miles to the west of Harfleur, where now stands Havre. Though no enemy were visible on shore no one was allowed to disembark till next morning. Before dawn next day a reconnaissance party under the earl of Huntingdon and Sir Gilbert Umfraville landed and soon reported the coast clear. The king then ordered a general but methodical disembarkation, and was himself one of the first to land. His first act was to kneel down on the shore and utter a prayer that in the coming war he might do nothing which would not redound to the honour of God and the furtherance of justice.

The town of Harfleur was of ancient origin and the only harbour on the northern side of the estuary. It was defended by a wall and a wet moat with a perimeter of a little under two

miles. Its position was strong by nature. It lay on the little river
Lézarde, near its entry into the Seine. Consequently the
southern face was protected by that river. On the east were salt
marshes, crossed by a single road; to the north was the valley
of the Lézarde. This had been dammed by the garrison, till the
width of water was about 100 yards. All bridges for some miles
to the north of the town had been destroyed. To the north-west
and west the ground rose gently, and the summit was surmounted by trees and orchards. The river Lézarde flowed
through the town from north-west to south and the harbour was
in the centre of the town. Chains were stretched across the
river at its exit from the town. The chief building was the
church of St. Martin (which still stands). There were three
gates, at the north-east, south-east and south-west respectively.
Temporary barbicans of wood and earth had recently been
thrown up outside the three gates, each surrounded by water.[1]
A low earthen wall had been thrown up on the counterscarp of
the moat. Entrenchments had also been dug along the shore to
impede a landing, but the garrison was too small to man them.
A number of guns were mounted on the walls and in emplace-
ments and stores of quicklime and oil were placed on the
ramparts to throw in the faces of stormers. When all is considered one is not surprised to learn that Harfleur was regarded as impregnable.

*   *   *

THE SIEGE OF HARFLEUR

It took three days to land men, guns and stores. A great camp
was pitched on the hill to the north-west of the town, and about
one mile distant. While the disembarkation was proceeding—
always undisturbed—a welcome reinforcement to the garrison
of 300 men-at-arms under lord de Gaucourt, reached the town
by the south-eastern gate.

The first task facing the English army was obviously to complete the investment on the eastern side. But to reach this side

[1] Part of the eastern gate still stands.

a wide detour to the north was necessary owing to the river valley being flooded by the French. On August 17 the king despatched a column under his oldest brother and chief lieutenant, the duke of Clarence, to make this detour and established the blockade on the east of the town. This was successfully accomplished, and Clarence had the luck to fall in with a convoy intended for the garrison, consisting of guns, arms and ammunition. These were all captured although the garrison sallied out of the town to their rescue. After a sharp fight they were driven back into the town. Thus the "first blood" in the Agincourt War fell to the English.

Harfleur was now completely surrounded, and little help could be expected for it for some time to come. The Constable d'Albret was powerless to cross the estuary to its support, and the English fleet guarded the entrance to the river.

Henry V had now to consider by what means he should capture the town. To reduce it by starvation would take time, and time was precious. The other means were by direct assault, or by methodical breaching of the walls. This in turn could be effected in two ways, by mining or by the comparatively novel method of breaching the walls by artillery fire (for the ancient method, by rams, was rendered impracticable owing to the wide moat).

The king decided first to use his miners. But progress was difficult and slow. Moreover the English miners after the long peace appeared to have lost much of their efficiency and in addition the French possessed miners themselves, and enterprising ones too. They countermined and brought to nought this attempt at the breaching of the walls.

Consequently the king now turned to his artillery. We have no precise details as to its number or weight.[1] A letter written to a priest in Paris places the number of heavy guns at 12, but this was possibly an exaggeration. Three at least were abnormally heavy for they were given special names by the admiring troops—"London", "Messenger" and "The King's Daughter". These began a steady bombardment, aimed principally at

---

[1] It included some "engines of war" such as ballistas.

the walls and towers flanking the three gates and barbicans. But they also fired into the town, and "London" paid special attention to the tower of St. Martin's Church. (Church towers have at all ages had a special attraction to gunners.) When later the town was entered it was observed, that great damage had been done to the church steeple. The bombardment went on, according to one account, by night as well as by day. This, if true, is one of the earliest examples of "night firing" by guns, and one would be interested to have particulars regarding the methods of illuminations and laying employed. But the English gunners had another surprise up their sleeve, as will presently be seen.

The garrison replied with spirit to the bombardment, and damage to the walls and towers, of which there were no less than 26, was repaired by night (from which it would appear that the English night-firing was not very effective.) Meanwhile the weather remained unusually hot; so much so that the knights experienced acute discomfort merely standing up in their full armour. But armour, fortunately for them, was not much in demand at this stage of the siege for it was mainly an artillery combat on each side. The remainder of the army had but little to do – except to eat. There was an abundance of un-ripe fruit available, and the soldier, like Tommy Atkins in all ages, partook of it without discretion or moderation. The natural sequel was widespread trouble, accentuated by the un-healthy night atmosphere on the salt marshes, the lack of sanita-tion and possibly the absence of sufficient exercise. Soon dysen-tery was rife and one of its first victims was bishop Courtenay of Norwich, a close personal friend of the king. The earl of Suffolk was another victim as was also the earl of March but the latter two survived. The epidemic may also have been partly due to some food supplies having been damaged by sea water. The French also suffered from sickness, but it must have been due to other causes. At least one messenger escaped from the stricken town by night with an appeal to the Dauphin for help. But when urged by others to march on Harfleur at about this time he made the amazing reply that the town had already fallen into English hands.

For King Henry there was no rest. He attended to every little detail, being assiduous in all military duties, supervising everything and making constant personal reconnaissances by day, and visiting the watch by night. (The night scene in Shakespeare's play will come to mind.) After the siege had been in operation a fortnight he wrote a significant letter to Bordeaux. In it he asked for guns and wine to be sent, while at the same time he gave a confident, even jubilant account of the siege, and the estimate that it would only last another eight days; after that he would advance on Paris, and finally would march on to Bordeaux. It was soon after the despatch of this letter that the dysentery became serious, but it did not materially affect the course of the siege.

The English artillery concentrated mainly—and rightly—on the south-west gate and barbican (called "The Bulwark" by the attackers.)[1] The main effort of the miners had also been directed against this point, which was evidently regarded by the king as the decisive point of the defences. By September 16, 13 days after Henry's Bordeaux letter, the barbican was in ruins, and the gate behind it was hopelessly damaged. The moat flanking it had been partially filled up with fascines, in readiness for an assault.

In the afternoon of September 16, the day on which bishop Courtenay died, the French made a desperate sortie from the south-west gate. Taking the besiegers unawares they managed to reach the English trenches and to set the wooden palisade on fire. But the defenders rallied rapidly, drove out the French and extinguished the fire. Next day the garrison tried again, but this time the English were on their guard and made short work of the attempt. Then the young earl of Huntingdon, who was in command of that sector of the line, took the offensive himself. He directed his attack on the bulwark, first preparing the ground

---

[1] The Bulwark was circular in shape, about 50 yards in diameter and completely surrounded by a ditch or moat.

by a concentrated bombardment. Moreover he employed a new weapon, probably the invention of the king's chief engineer, "Master Giles". It took the form of what we should now call an incendiary shell; some form of combustible was attached to the stone cannon-balls and ignited and then discharged from the guns against the woodwork of the Bulwark. This was set alight and, the weather being dry, was soon burning furiously. Then the men-at-arms advanced to the attack; crossing the moat dry-shod over the fascines that had been thrown into it, and clambering over the ruined palisade. The defenders could offer no effective opposition and the English entered the blazing Bulwark in triumph. The French fell back across the town moat into the interior and closed the gate behind them before the attackers could pass through it.

The Bulwark was now firmly in English hands and the victorious troops turned their attention to extinguishing the flames. But so fierce was the blaze that it was nearly two days before it was got fully under control and for several days more it was smouldering.

This success was decisive; it put heart into the attackers and corresponding depression into the defenders. The state of these gallant men was now pitiable and hopeless. Of succour from without there was still no sign; they were weakened by disease; food and ammunition were running short, their strongest work had not sufficed to keep out the English, and they were indeed at their last gasp.

This was evident to King Henry, and he resolved to shorten the agony by a general assault unless the garrison immediately surrendered.

After some vague and ineffectual approaches by de Gaucourt next day, Henry issued orders for a general assault on the following morning. The bombardment was to be maintained all night, so that the defenders should get no rest, instructions were issued to each member of the storming party, and the French were left in no misapprehension as to the fate that awaited them next day.

But the threat was sufficient; in the course of the night emissaries slipped out of the town on the comparatively quiet side – the east – and requested the duke of Clarence to prevail on the king to grant them terms. Messages passed throughout the night, and the result was that the town promised to surrender if they were not relieved by the following Sunday, September 22, that is, in three days time.

The final negotiations had been conducted by the bishop of Bangor who assured the garrison "Fear not! The king of England has not come to waste your lands, we are good Christians and Harfleur is not Soissons." This was no empty promise.

The two armies then sat down, silently watching one another, all fighting being suspended. But no succour came to the beleaguered garrison, although the Dauphin had been informed of their plight, and when the stipulated period expired the king sent 500 troops to the gate to demand surrender.

The king's chaplain Thomas Elmham describes the scene that ensued.

"Our King, clothed in royal gold immediately ascended his royal throne, placed under a pavilion on the top of the hill; where his nobles and the principal persons were assembled in their best equipment, his crowned triumphal helmet being held on his right hand unpon a halberd by Sir Gilbert Umfreville. The Lord de Gaucourt came from the [waiting] tent into his presence accompanied by those persons who had sworn to keep the articles, and surrendering to him the keys of the town submitted themselves to his grace."

The chaplain discreetly omits to say that the unfortunate de Gaucourt and his 76 associates were obliged to appear with ropes round their necks; also that the king kept them waiting a good while in the waiting tent before deigning to receive them. All this was, without a doubt, copied from the procedure of his great-grandfather at the surrender of Calais, when the twelve burgesses had to approach him with halters round their necks. It was in both cases an elaborate piece of play-acting, designed to impress them with the might of the English king, and subsequently of his royal magnanimity.

In fact he eventually gave them all a sumptuous supper and

promised them fair and kindly treatment, the details of which he proceeded to enunciate.

His terms, again, were based on those taken by Edward III. That is to say, certain of the knights who seemed good for ransoms were either packed off to England or released on parole in order to allow them to raise the stipulated ransom. Of the remainder, those who were prepared to accept the lordship of the English king were allowed to remain in the town, together with their belongings, while those who were not so prepared were, a few days later, marched out of the town taking with them whatever they could carry, and duly handed over to the French authorities at Lillebonne. Advertisements were then circulated through England inviting merchants and others to come and settle in Harfleur, which Henry was resolved to make like Calais—an English town.

CHAPTER IV
THE MARCH TO AGINCOURT

HARFLEUR was now in English hands: the first stage of Henry V's grandiose plan was accomplished. The question now arose, should he continue with the second stage—an advance on Paris?

There were cogent reasons against it. The reduction of Harfleur had taken longer than had been expected (though five weeks was a reasonable time under the circumstances), and the season was getting late for campaigning. The king of France, it was known, was trying to assemble an army in the Paris-Rouen area, which though poor in quality (as hastily collected armies always are) would be formidable in numbers. But worst of all, the dysentry had made such ravages in the English army that little more than 7,500 fairly healthy troops were now available, the remainder having either died or been shipped back to England. Of the healthy troops 900 men-at-arms and 1,200 archers were allotted for the garrison of Harfleur, under the earl of Dorset. Thus only 900 men-at-arms and 5,000 archers, say 6,000 in all, were available for field operations. It followed that, should the French army challenge a battle, the disparity in numbers would be very great. Was it worth the risk? To march on Paris would mean striking at the enemy where he was strongest; it might have been just feasible with 12,000 men but with only half that number it was clearly inadvisable. When Edward III had invaded France he had taken steps to ensure that the French armed forces were scattered, a large proportion of them being in Gascony. Such was not the case now, and Henry reluctantly abandoned his design on Paris. There remained three possible courses: he might establish with his army a Harfleur Pale, on the lines of the Calais Pale; he could march on Calais, a *chevauchée* typical of his great-grandfather's strategy, or he could leave a garrison in Harfleur and ship the remainder of the army home for the winter.

The king held a war council which examined the matter. The first course does not seem to have had advocates, but on the second there was considerable discussion. As is the nature of war councils the various risks appertaining to a strategy of offence were pointed out by certain members, till a general atmosphere of what we should call "defeatism" was engendered, and in the outcome the council recommended the course which involved the least risk–in this case the return of the army to England.

Henry V stoutly opposed the recommendation of the war council. To do this required some moral courage, despite the prestige attaching to his rank. He was still a young man, and in going against the advice of his council he was taking a great risk; he might conceivably lose his whole army and himself be killed or captured, like the French king 60 years before. The immensity of the risk has impressed the historians of all ages. Their verdict may be summed up as follows: "The risk was unjustifiable; it was a rash, even a madcap, plan." Professor Wyllie himself seems overwhelmed by this impressive flood of opinion and is content to swim with the stream, describing the decision as "the most foolhardy and reckless adventure that ever an unreasoning pietist devised".[1] Only Professor Jacob has ventured to question Wyllie's verdict, and he somewhat mildly suggests that it is "perhaps an exaggeration".[2]

The risk was probably much less than appeared on the surface, for France was in a distracted and divided state: the embers of civil war were still smouldering; the chastening and unifying effect of a common danger–the invasion of their country–had had but little effect. The truth is, France did not possess that feeling of national unity and patriotism that was later engendered in her, largely by Joan of Arc. The duke of Burgundy was the stormy petrel, the incomputable factor. Whilst professing loyalty he made various excuses for not responding to his

[1] *Wyllie*, II, p. 76.   [2] *Henry V and the Invasion of England*, p. 93.

sovereign's summons to service; nor did he permit his son
Philip, count of Flanders (later to be duke Philip the Good of
Burgundy), to serve. All was confusion and disorder, and the
national summons was obeyed only slowly and partially.

*   *   *

The concentration area for the French army was along the
Seine, between Mantes, Vernon and Rouen. The Dauphin had
reached Vernon on September 3, and on the 10th Charles VI,
with befitting ceremony, took the Oriflamme–the national
symbol for the repelling of invasion–from its receptuary in the
cathedral at St. Denys and marched to Mantes, where he
remained.

Meanwhile Boucicaut and D'Albret had moved from Honfleur to Rouen, where they were busy marshalling the advanced-
guard of the national army. By the beginning of October this
force was said to be 14,000 strong. No doubt this is an exaggeration, but it must have exceeded greatly the numbers the
English could put into the field.

Let us presume that Henry was aware of the above, but was
in total ignorance of the effective strength of the rival army at
any given moment. From information gained during the
previous two wars, if from no other source, he would have a fair
idea of the relative positions of the localities in the area Har-
fleur-Paris-Calais. Now his objective was Calais, and to get
there involved a march of a little over 160 miles. By marching
light–that is, with all baggage and supplies carried on pack
animals, he might just accomplish it in eight or nine days. The
distance from Vernon to Calais is the same, but a French army
of newly-formed troops, whose march-discipline would be weak,
and whose army would be encumbered with carts and wagons,
could scarcely do it in under 12 days. Thus, even if both armies
started level, the French army would have little chance of
catching up, still less of intercepting, the English army. But the
two armies were not likely to start level; until the English
actually set off, the French leaders at Vernon would have no
knowledge of what was proceeding, nor would they get this

news till at least 36 hours after the march had begun, for it is nearly 100 miles by road for a scout outside Harfleur to reach Vernon. Thus the French army would start off at least two days behind the English. Hence the danger of Henry being caught by the main French army, if his direct course to Calais was unimpeded, was negligible.

But there is an "if". Could he count on making good the direct route along the sea coast? There were two minor rivers to be crossed, the Béthune and the Bresle, but these would not constitute an obstacle to troops unencumbered with wheels. (The king purposed leaving all his guns behind). There was however the river Somme. Again following the example of his great-grandfather, Henry intended to make use of the Blanche Taque ford a few miles below Abbeville, which he hoped would be undefended. As a step to this end he had sent out a contingent to Calais at the outset of the campaign, with orders to operate in a southerly direction, thereby attracting to itself all local French forces, thus drawing them away from the vital ford.

There was however an unpleasant possibility. What of the troops in Rouen? Might they not intercept the march? On paper it looks as if they might. Rouen is 30 miles nearer Calais than Harfleur. But the chances of such an interception would seem to be small, unless previous knowledge of the direction of the march and its date leaked out. Moreover a sudden departure of the Rouen troops could hardly be undertaken without the permission of the Constable of France, who was then supposed to be in Honfleur, 30 miles away. As we have seen, both Boucicaut and D'Albret had in reality moved to Rouen, but the fact would not have been known to the English scouts, for the wide Seine estuary separated them from the road the Constable would take. Furthermore, Henry might well calculate that the Rouen troops would not dare attack his army in the field unsupported by the French main body. In this calculation, as we shall see, Henry was justified. There was a further contingency, namely that these Rouen troops might march to the Somme, cross it and take up positions on the far bank.

In short there were risks in the English plan, but no military operation is entirely devoid of risk, being dependent for its success on the human element, and frequently on natural elements too—the weather. In war if you risk nothing you gain nothing; and in this case there was a good deal to be gained. The alternative was a return to England. This would be construed as failure in both countries, the king's prestige would fall, there might even be a revolution and he might be supplanted by the legitimate heir to the throne, the earl of March; in any case conditions for a future invasion of France would be bad. On the other hand if Henry succeeded in his march, he would be reviving the memories of similar *chevauchées* which had done much to raise English prestige in the days of Edward III; he would show that an English army could apparently go where it liked in the lands he claimed as his own, and with two bases firmly established on the north coast of France the omens for a further invasion of the Promised Land would be propitious. All this might be accomplished by taking risks. As General Wolfe so truly said:

"In war something must be allowed to chance and fortune, seeing that it is in its nature hazardous and an option of difficulties."

To sum up, it seems to me that, with the information presumably at his disposal, Henry V took a justifiable and commendable risk.

*   *   *

The die was cast: the English army was to attempt to reach Calais overland. King Henry gave out his desire to meet the French army in battle during the operation; but the steps that he had taken to march "light" and as speedily as possible to Calais bear the impression of a directly contrary desire. How are we to account for this seeming contradiction? Up to a point his words seem supported by his deeds. That is to say, he had challenged the Dauphin to personal combat and had waited eight days at Harfleur in order to give time for the reply to arrive. This certainly does not look like the action of a man who wishes to slip away unperceived, yet his later actions do. I suggest that the explanation is that he made a slight change of plan, as a result of the opposition that he encountered from his war council. They had stressed the hazards of the proposed march to Calais, and in order to meet their arguments the king felt constrained to take all possible steps to minimize the chance of an actual encounter with the main French army in the field. This alone, in my opinion, explains the apparent anomaly.

The challenge referred to requires a word of exposition. In it King Henry challenged the Dauphin (his father being half demented) to a personal contest, in order to avoid effusion of blood, the winner to possess the kingdom of France after the death of Charles VI. It is hardly to be supposed that Henry expected the callow youth known as the Dauphin to accept this challenge. Indeed such a challenge strikes our modern minds as similar to the action of a school bully who challenges a smaller boy to a fight. But contemporaries did not take it like that; to them it was "ordeal by battle", and God would give the victory to the rightful claimant—perhaps to David rather than to Goliath—"God defend the right". King Henry was intensely religious, or perhaps we might now say, superstitious; he really believed in the justice of his claim to the crown of France, in a fanatical way and, whether by single combat or by the engagement of his whole army, he was convinced that the Almighty would give him the victory. Moreover he was only following the example of his revered ancestor, who more than once challenged the king of France to single combat, "to avoid useless effusion of blood"—and with the same negative result. The significance of the challenge is, as Ramsay observes, that it discloses the ultimate aim of Henry to be king of all France, a claim that he had never officially put forward.

THE MARCH BEGINS

The eight days having expired without reply being received from the Dauphin, the king gave his final orders for the march. Each man was to carry eight days rations with him, in order to be independent of the hazards of country supply during what was hoped would be only an eight-day march. All possible impedimenta (an apt word in this connection) was to be left behind, the army travelling "light".[1] Strict orders as to behaviour in the country had been issued on landing, and they were now emphasized and given more precision. No one was to fire buildings without orders; to maltreat priests, nuns, women or children; nothing was to be taken from churches or religious houses; no swearing was to be allowed. The king held his army in what for medieval times was an iron discipline. This does not mean that no excesses were committed; indeed the French chroniclers repeat the almost mechanical accusation of fire, robbery and pillage. One chronicler however, has the frankness to record that the English troops did not rob or rape, whereas the French troops in the area did both. Indeed, Joan of Arc, had she but known it, followed much the same line as Henry of Monmouth in her dealings with the troops.

Our sources differ as to the date of the march. Most historians give October 8 or 9, but Wyllie prefers October 6. This early date I doubt, on grounds of inherent military probability. If the army really set out on the 6th it marched only 10 miles on each of the first four days and 20 miles on the two ensuing days. Usually troops march furthest when they are freshest. True, there was slight delay before Montivilliers, and again to the south of Fécamp, but not enough to account for that great disparity. I prefer October 8 as the date.

The army marched in the usual three divisions: vanguard, main body and rearguard. Commanders of the vanguard were Sir Gilbert Umfraville and Sir John Cornwall, two highly trusted leaders. The king himself commanded the main body, being accompanied by his brother the duke of Gloucester and John Holland, later the earl of Huntingdon. The rearguard was under the king's uncle the duke of York with the earl of Oxford. (Shakespeare's earl of Westmorland was not present.) Arques was reached on the fourth day, an average of 15 miles per day (assuming the date of departure was October 8).

[1] But transport was provided for a portion (6 inches long) of the True Cross.

A curious thing happened at Arques. The famous Chateau commanded the bridge over the little river Béthune. It was blocked by the commander of the Chateau, who offered resistance.[1] But when Henry threatened to burn the town unless he gave passage, he not only did so but supplied the army with bread and wine. This stratagem Henry copied, as always, from his great-grandfather, who had adopted it with success in his campaign of 1359. Indeed, Henry continued to apply it with invariable success throughout his march.

Next day, October 12, the army marched a good 20 miles to Eu on the Bresle, where a smart skirmish took place with a strong body of troops. They were however repulsed and bread and wine were dutifully produced as on the previous day. Crossing the Bresle from Inchville to Beauchamps,[2] four miles south-east of the town, the army now set its course for the ford of Blanche Taque, five miles west of Abbeville, marching through Viriville.

But when within a few miles of the ford a prisoner taken at Eu reported that it was defended with stakes and that a strong force under marshal Boucicaut was stationed on the far side. After satisfying himself that the prisoner spoke true,[3] the king came to the reluctant conclusion that he must abandon the attempt to cross the Somme there and instead turned east and marched up the valley, hoping to find an unguarded crossing-place higher up-stream.

It was a nasty shock, and I expect the king was almost as surprised to discover the presence of Boucicaut as we are to read it. How had the French marshal, last heard of in Honfleur, got to the far side of the Somme? This we would all much like to know, but the sources do not give much help. One indeed asserts that he and the Constable d'Albret marched from Rouen via Amiens as soon as they heard that the English army had

[1] The extreme strength of the Chateau may account for the Castellan's contumacy.
[2] According to La Bataille d'Azincourt by René de Belleval, Vol. I (1865) but I cannot find the source.
[3] Waurin, who relates this story, asserts that the statement was not true and that the ford was unguarded, but modern writers discredit this. It is unthinkable that the English king should abandon his plan on the unchecked statement of a prisoner.

set out on its march. This seems impossible. The route *via* Amiens to Abbeville would be almost 100 miles and we must allow seven days for this. If they started the day after getting the news of the English march (which would be very quick action) they could not reach Abbeville *via* Amiens till October 15, two days *after* the English army had passed. But D'Albret evidently was there at least a full day before the English approach, for he seems to have made extensive and successful arrangements for the defence of all the passages over the Somme both above and below Abbeville, destroying the bridges wherever necessary.[1] Moreover, we now know that on the way to Abbeville he had detached Boucicaut to Eu, evidently to act as a delaying force. It was in fact Boucicaut who had opposed the English at Eu, subsequently falling back to Blanche Taque ford.

In the absence of reliable sources, there seem only two possible explanations of Boucicaut's operation. If he did not set out from Rouen till hearing of the departure of the English army, he must have marched light, probably with mounted troops only, followed later by dismounted troops and baggage. In this case, not wishing to become involved in a battle with the whole English army he would give them a wide berth, probably crossing the Somme at St. Remy (four miles east of Abbeville). The other alternative is that the news of the English king's plan leaked out and Boucicaut took the instant decision to forestall him by marching at once. In this case he probably took the direct road to Abbeville. Whether he had the permission of the Dauphin to split the French army in this way or not, his action was a brilliant one and stamps him as a fine commander. He has not been given sufficient credit for it either in England or his own country. His action might well have led to the undoing of the English army.[2]

---

[1] In this matter he seems to have been more prompt and effective than the Germans in their attempt to prevent the British army crossing in their advance from the Seine to the Somme in September 1944.

[2] We know that D'Albret was across the Somme a few days later, and it is probable that the two were acting in concert, so it may well be that D'Albret dispatched the Marshal to act as a rear-guard whilst he himself attended to the Somme crossings.

The English army, altering its course with a heavy heart and much foreboding, soon encountered its first rebuff. The bridge at Abbeville was guarded and Boucicaut's troops were in force on the far side. A few miles further up-stream the bridge at Pont Remy was also defended, and the army went into billets in Bailleul[1] and nearby villages. A 10-mile march.

Next day, the 14th, the search for a crossing was resumed, with the same result, and the army billeted at Hangest, midway between Abbeville and Amiens, a 14-mile march. On the 15th Amiens was given a wide berth and the night was spent at Pont de Metz, two miles south-west of the city. On the 16th they marched to Boves on the Aure.[2] The custodian of the château, after the usual persuasion, gave them bread and wine, the latter in profusion. The troops were tired and thirsty, and partook of the wine so freely that the king gave orders that no more should be served. When someone explained that the soldiers were only filling their water-bottles, the king replied sourly, "Their bottles indeed! They are making big bottles of their bellies and getting very drunk". Which was no doubt the truth.

The little English army was now very dispirited. It was also hungry; the rations carried had almost given out and local produce was hard to come by. For some days they had been living mainly on dried meat and walnuts. And there seemed no end to the march; it was the general opinion that they would have to march to the head-waters of the river, still 50 miles away, in order to get the other side.

On October 17 the army resumed its weary march, this time taking a north-east direction in order to regain the river and make a further attempt at a crossing. A six-mile march brought them opposite the walled town of Corbie, which lies on the northern bank of the river. The bridge was intact and a mounted party of the enemy made a spirited sortie, which for the moment took the English by surprise. But recovering, they

---

[1] The old home of the Balliols. Traces of their motte and bailey castle still exist.
[2] Another motte and bailey castle.

struck back with vigour, driving the French back into the town and taking several prisoners.[1]

Some of these prisoners stated that the French army intended to contest the passage of the invaders, and to make a dead set at the hated longbowmen by mounted attack. On hearing this, the king ordered that henceforth each archer should provide himself with a stake 6 ft. in length and pointed at each end. In case of mounted attack the stake was to be thrust into the ground, the upper end sloping towards the enemy. And so it was done.

It may be that these prisoners also gave the king some information of a valuable kind, namely some topographical particulars as to the course of the Somme up-stream. Whether this be so or not, Henry here made a sudden change in his direction of march, turning nearly 80 degrees to the right instead of continuing to follow the course of the river towards Peronne. It was a decision of great significance, as an examination of the map will show.

From Amiens, the river takes an easterly direction (facing up-stream) for 30 miles to Peronne. It then bends through a right angle to the right, and after going south for 15 miles about Ham it turns gradually to the north-east, as far as St. Quentin. Now the new course followed by the army cut across this great bend in the river, and formed a tangent to the Ham bend. Three advantages might be expected to be gained from this change of course. First, the river would be rejoined at a point considerably higher up where, even if no bridges were available, it might be possible to ford it. Second, if the French army which had been marching abreast of the English army on the northern bank continued to do so, it would, by taking the outside of the bend, have to march 12 to 14 miles further, and so would get one day's march behind. Third, any troops detailed to guard the crossing places in the Ham bend would not be expecting the early arrival of the enemy thus made possible, and might be taken off their

[1] The French would get good warning of the approach from the top of the lofty twin church-towers.

guard. It was in fact a brilliant step on the part of the English king, though it seems to have gone almost unrecognized and unappreciated.

So at Fouilly (south of Corbie) the army turned to its right and mounted the downlands, passing a little to the left of Villers Bretonneux. It is not known where they spent that night, though the implication usually is that it was opposite Corbie. I think this most unlikely and that Harbonnières for the main body and Caix for the advance-guard were the nights' billets.[1] In any case the English army was now entering upon the battlefield of the Somme of 1916 and of the 1918 retreat. For the next 60 miles of their march there will not be a village they passed through that did not see fighting by allied troops (in almost all cases British) during the 1914–18 war.

In either Harbonnières or Caix a soldier entered the church, seized the copper pyx, thinking it was gold, and hid it in his sleeve. When the loss was reported, the king ordered a hue and cry, the culprit was discovered, and by the king's orders hanged from a tree out of hand. There was no further trouble of this nature.

The following day's march brought them to Nesle. The inhabitants showed fight, but the simple threat to burn the fields brought about a change of attitude, and it is said that they informed the king that the fords over the river just ahead were unguarded. Whether or not they gave this information the fact would soon have been discovered, for the army was purposely heading that way with the object of crossing if feasible. At any rate scouts reported that the fords at Voyennes and Bethencourt, three miles north-west of the town, were unguarded, and the army marched off before dawn next day, the 19th, to cross by both simultaneously, the fighting troops making use of the one and the baggage the other.

But there were difficulties. The river valley was wide and marshy all along its course; and the causeways by which alone the army could cross had been destroyed by the defending

---

[1] The Fifth Army held up the German advance in 1918 for two days on this line.

troops. A small vanguard of 200 archers however managed to flounder across and drive off the few half-scared defenders in the vicinity. Thus a small bridge-head was formed whilst the causeways were repaired.

All day long the work of repair went on, the soldiers demolishing houses for timbers and toiling feverishly, for their lives might depend on the results. It was an anxious moment, for the enemy might appear in force before the passage was accomplished.[1]

At about noon on October 19, it became possible to start passing the army over, but it was a tricky business and required careful "traffic control". The king realised the importance of this and he himself supervised the crossing at the ford used by the fighting troops, and two trusted subordinates did the same at the other ford. At about 8 p.m, the last man was across, and the army marched on a few miles in the dark to billets at Athies and Monchy Lagache. "We spent a joyous night" wrote the king's chaplain, and one can well believe it.

Meanwhile, what was the French army doing? We have seen how its advanced-guard under marshal Boucicaut and the Constable d'Albret had set out from Rouen for Abbeville either before or just after the English army started on its march on October 8, also how King Charles VI and the Dauphin had taken up their quarters at Vernon whilst the main body of the French army was assembling at Rouen.

On October 12, while the king of England was approaching Eu the king of France entered Rouen in company with the Dauphin. They had the evident intention of placing themselves at the head of the army and advancing against the English. But no one in the French army relished the idea of being led by a madman or by a nincompoop, and the veteran duke of Berry was deputed to argue his sovereign out of the project. Berry had fought at Poitiers and retained vivid but bitter recollections of that battle and of the fate of the present king's grandfather

[1] The writer may be pardoned if he remarks that he himself experienced just such anxiety at a crossing a few miles down-stream during the Retreat of 1918.

John II. He therefore expostulated firmly with the king, summing up his argument in the words "Better to lose a battle and save the king than lose a battle and lose the king too". The logic of this was unanswerable and both the king and Dauphin consented to remain behind, and that the command should devolve on the dukes of Orleans and Bourbon, until the whole army could be re-united under the command of the Constable d'Albret.

The French army set out for Amiens on, I reckon, the 13th or 14th of October[1] while the English army was pushing its way up the Somme valley between Abbeville and Amiens. The French army must have reached Amiens on the 17th while its rival was passing Corbie. But cutting straight across the great bend traversed by the English army, the French had now almost caught it up. Indeed the fact that Corbie was so strongly garrisoned may indicate that the most advanced troops of the French army were already there. The prisoners taken there seemed to be in communication, at least, with the French main army. D'Albret with the vanguard may be pictured as only a few miles ahead, his face set for Peronne.

So we have this situation; whilst the English were marching across the curve of the Somme, the French, being north of the river, now had the longer route of the two—unless they decided to cross to the south bank, but this was not to be expected of them, for their obvious role was to defend the line of the river, keeping it between the enemy and themselves. Thus on October 18th and 19th, while the English were approaching and crossing the river to the east of Nesle, the French were marching along the north bank of the river to Peronne. There they arrived on the evening of the 19th while the English were in the act of making their hazardous crossing of the river. That night the two armies went to sleep a bare seven miles apart, and with no river dividing them. Decisive events might be expected to happen on the morrow.

---

[1] For a discussion of the march of the French army see the Appendix to this chapter.

But the English troops went to bed that night in high spirits and happy ignorance of the proximity of the enemy, and of the danger that now hung over their heads. For it must be recognized that the French, considering the size, hasty formation and heterogeneous composition of this army, had made remarkable progress and moreover had marched in exactly the right direction. How far this may have been due to accurate information of the English movements, how far to happy intuition and how far to pure luck it is impossible to say, for we do not know what information of their enemy the French possessed. Indeed their movements throughout this crucial campaign have been most inadequately recorded. Possibly this may be due to the unpleasant memories afterwards conjured up by the name Agincourt. (The French later changed the name to Azincourt.)

ACROSS THE SOMME

We now return to the English side. On Sunday, October 20, Henry V seems to have given his tired troops a rest after the exceptional exertions of the previous day. This was natural enough. Before deciding what route to take towards Calais it would be desirable to ascertain the situation of the hostile army; and while scouts were sent northward the king himself seems to have ridden forward. Meanwhile his soldiers fell to speculating as to how many marches it would take them to reach Calais. The "know-alls" declared that they would be there in eight days. Tommy Atkins, in his ignorance has ever been a born optimist.

The question of where lay the French army was soon solved— by the French themselves. For a deputation of three heralds arrived from the French headquarters at Peronne bearing a challenge from the dukes of Orleans and Bourbon. Titus Livius gives a graphic account of the scene. The heralds first approached the duke of York by whom they were led to the king's presence. They promptly fell on their knees, remaining silent until he gave permission for them to speak. They then gave out their message, opening humbly enough—

"Right puissant Prince, great and noble is thy Kingly power; as is reported among our lords. They have heard that thou labourest by thy forces to conquer towns, castles and cities of the realm of Franche, and of the Frenchmen whom thou hast destroyed."

But soon the tone changed, and they came to the point in these words—

"They inform thee by us that before thou comest to Calais they will meet thee to fight with thee."

King Henry, who evidently was now informed of the location of the French army, took this challenge to mean that he would be attacked next day somewhere between his present position and Peronne. He professed to be glad of the opportunity of crossing swords with his opponents. If Titus Livius's account is to be accepted, and I see no reason to doubt it, Henry's reply was a notable one, couched in terms of dignity and quiet pride and confidence.

"To which Henry, with a courageous spirit, a firm look, without anger or displeasure, and without his face changing colour, mildly replied that 'all would be done according to the will of God'. When the Heralds enquired what road he would take, he answered: 'Straight to Calais; and if our adversaries seek to disturb us on our journey, it shall be at their utmost peril, and not without harm to them. We seek them not, neither will the fear of them induce us to move out of our way, or the sight of them cause us to make the greater haste. We advise them, however, not to interrupt our journey nor to seek such an effusion of Christian blood.' "

The author of the *Vita* adds the interesting detail that the king was seated on horseback in the open country, surrounded by his staff when the heralds approached. Maybe he was making a personal reconnaissance to the front when the heralds approached.

Evidently expecting that the French army would advance to the attack when they received his uncompromising reply, King Henry issued a warning order to his army, and selected and started to occupy a position in which to accept battle. It would be interesting to know where this position lay. To anyone acquainted with the ground, it is not difficult to suggest the site of the position selected. The road from Athies to Peronne runs due north for one and a half miles, gradually ascending; it then crosses the great Roman road that runs straight as a die and due east-west right across the Somme battlefields of 1916 and 1918, linking Amiens to St. Quentin. Immediately to the north of the Roman road is a ridge, also running east-west. The Athies-Peronne road crosses this ridge and then sinks gently into the valley of the little river Cologne, and so on into Peronne. This ridge, I make no doubt, was the position selected by the English king.[1]

Throughout the day anxious eyes were strained in the direction of Peronne, four miles ahead; but not a sign of the enemy could be seen, either advancing or taking up a position to the east of the town, barring their own advance. With a sigh of relief the army went to sleep that night: evidently there would be no battle on the morrow.

Meanwhile what had happened to the French army after the sending forth of its challenge? Not one word has come down to us in explanation of the curious course adopted by the French leaders. If as they said, they really intended to bar the Calais road to the English they could not have found a better position in which to do so than that in which they now lay. Peronne itself, combined with the ridge on its eastern side, formed a cork to the bottle in which the English army now found itself. To their left lay the broad marshy valley of the Somme, which they had just, with so great labour, traversed. To their front lay the defended town of Peronne, and to their right front was a ridge, just to the north of, and covered by the river Cologne. There was little chance of circumventing it, for if they attempted a turning movement to the east, the French men-at-arms, who were of course all mounted and who formed the greater part of the army, could sidestep to their left quicker than the English army could move, for the pace of an army is its slowest unit, and the slowest English units were on foot.

[1] Five hundred years later it was occupied by the artillery (in which the writer was serving) of the rear-guard of the Fifth Army during its retreat towards Amiens. It is as unlikely that anyone was aware of the significance of that ridge as that anyone fighting in the Battle of Vittoria was aware that the Black Prince's troops had fought there 450 years before.

The reason why the French, instead of this, marched 13 miles due north, as they did, to Bapaume, is baffling. It may be that the Constable D'Albret, the nominal commander, had contacted the main army in person, after the issue of the challenge, and that he was opposed to risking battle with the English.

Another possibility is that the main body of the army fell back to Bapaume in order to join up with d'Albret's column. If this were so, it would go far to explain the inactivity of the combined French army next day, for a halt would be required in which to amalgamate the two forces which had never seen each other before. This seems the most likely of the two explanations. On October 21 the English army was far from motionless. Pursuant to his stated intention, King Henry gave the order to resume the march on the direct road to Calais.[1] This took the army close past the walls of Peronne. A few French horsemen emerged from its gates and a skirmish took place, but it was devoid of significance. The direct road to Calais lay through Albert, nearly 20 miles to the north-west of Peronne. One mile to the north of Peronne the road crossed the Peronne-Bapaume road up which the French army had marched 24 hours before, leaving unmistakable tracks behind them, a sure indication of the direction of their destination. The English king cannot have failed to be surprised by this, for Bapaume lay a good 10 miles to the right of his own line of march. Did the enemy really intend to bar his road? Or did they intend to attack him on the march from a flank? It was obviously desirable to guard against such an eventuality, and he therefore sent out a right flank-guard, along the high ground to the south-west of Bapaume, from whence any hostile approach would be visible. This ridge-road runs through Combles, Ginchy and Martinpuich, names that became familiar during the 1916 battle of the Somme. The flank-guard observed no motion on the part of

[1] The Duke of York now commanded the vanguard. *The Brut* (*Continuation H*) explains this by stating that for some time the king had lost confidence in York, and that the duke, being aware of the fact, requested to be given the vanguard in order to prove his worth.

the enemy and may be presumed to have spent the night in the Grandcourt-Miraumont area in the valley of the Ancre.[1]

Meanwhile the main body was plodding its way along the direct road to Albert buffeted by rain and wind, and halting for the night probably in the Mametz-Fricourt area, after a march of about 16 miles.

Next day, May 22, it resumed its march (the flank-guard rejoining it on the march), passed through Albert and Bouzincourt, and halted for the night at Forceville, Acheux, and Beauquesne. The last-named place was rather far to the left, and I suspect the advance-guard had missed their way. Such mistakes are easy, even today, when accurate maps are available. The same day the French army, which had been resting at Bapaume the previous day, set off. It had good reason for rest, having marched rapidly and without respite all the way from Rouen, paying little heed to the common foot-soldiers of its company who must have been well-nigh worn out. At Bapaume it had been abreast of the English army, and 10 miles to its flank, but this day it marched, as I reckon it, 16 miles to its opponent's 14 miles and ended up in the Coullemont area about three miles ahead and eight miles on the right flank of the English. In short, the routes were gently approaching one another, the French being always slightly in the lead.

On October 23, the English made a long march of 18 miles, passing three miles to the right of Doullens, through Lucheux, to Bonnières, with advanced-guard, now led by the duke of York, at Frévent. Bonnières was a good two miles to the left of the direct road, and it again looks as if the column had mistaken its way. But as several villages were utilised as billets it may be that the others were on the more direct road.

On the same day the French made a slightly shorter march, to St. Pol or its environs, where it was still nearly three miles ahead, but the distance to the flank had narrowed to three miles. All this time the two armies were said to be out of touch with

---

[1] The area reached by the Ulster Division on the first day of the battle of the Somme.

one another as no music was being played. At this distance
music would have no effect either way, but it is unlikely that
mounted patrols from the two armies were not fully apprised of
the motions of the other army.

Whether or not the main body lost its way, the king certainly
did, and found himself at nightfall two miles in advance of

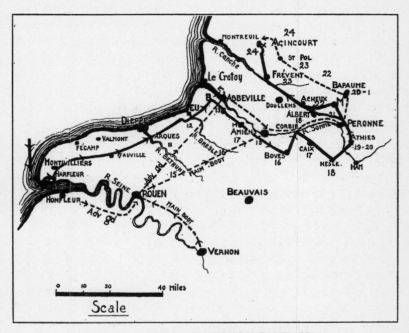

Sketch Map 1; THE AGINCOURT CAMPAIGN

12, 13, etc.	Dates in October	Adv. gd.	Advance-guard
——→	Route of English army	M.	Miraumont
->---→	Routes of French army	B.	Blanche Taque Ford

the village allotted to him for a billet by the harbingers. But
Henry would not withdraw; the billet must advance to him.
He gave the curious reason that, "God would not have me now
go back and forage, for I have my coat-armour on".

From Frévent on October 24 the advanced-guard after a
12-mile march entered the little village of Blangy, in the valley

of the Fernoise. French patrols had recently been seen in the village; evidently the enemy was closing on them at last. Indeed scouts had already reported sighting them three miles to the right. But the king held on his way, refusing to diverge to the left. The river valley at Blangy was crossed by a narrow causeway and the operation was a lengthy one. Meanwhile the advanced-guard had mounted the ridge to the north of the village. Arrived there they saw little more than a mile away to their right a sight to bring their hearts into their mouths. For there, spread out all down the little valley between them and Ambricourt they saw the whole French army strung out, thousands upon thousands of men! "A terrific multitude" wrote the king's terrified chaplain. The king hastened up to the ridge-top to see for himself.[1]

It looked as if the enemy intended to attack from the flank that day, and the king made hasty dispositions to deploy his army in line along the ridge-top.

The English soldiers were put considerably out of countenance when the enormous size of the hostile army became evident and few of them expected to see England again. The French also had apparently been deploying for battle, but after a time they quietly resumed their march. As so often before, we are left guessing as to their intentions. The simplest explanation here seems to be that when their advanced-guard almost blundered into the English advanced-guard on the ridge they halted and sent back for instructions, at the same time forming line to face the enemy. This no doubt resulted in prolonged and excited discussions among the French leaders, ere they decided to resume the march, and take up position a couple of miles further on, barring the road to the English. Thus the march was resumed and at nightfall the French host bivouacked on the open ground astride the road to Calais, just short of the little village of Agincourt. The English army also resumed its march, halting in and around the village of Maisoncelles, one mile short of the enemy, who now completely barred their line

[1] The approximate spot is still easy to identify.

of retreat. A battle on the morrow, the Feast of St. Crispin, seemed inevitable.

APPENDIX

THE ENGLISH MARCH

The course of the march of the English army is not hard to establish within fairly narrow limits. Nor is the speed of the march difficult to compute, if we are agreed on the date of departure. I have accepted the date given by the contemporary *Chronicle of London*–October 8.

I agree with the map in Ramsay's *Lancaster and York* except that it shows the route going through Tréport after passing Eu, and places Tréport on the coast between the estuary of the Bresle and that of the Somme, whereas it is actually on the Bresle estuary. But Ramsay's script does not always agree with his map; he writes that the English army passed to the *left* of Peronne, whereas his map (correctly) shows it as passing to the *right*. His map makes the English pass through Albert, whereas he writes that they passed through "Encre", the medieval name for Albert, but states that it is "on the Miraumont". There is no such river as Miraumont, but there *is* a village Miraumont (famous in the 1914-18 war), which lies on the river Ancre. Ramsay must have misread the map. The fact is that he has jumbled two conflicting accounts: one states that the road passed through Albert, the other through Miraumont, both on the river Ancre. As they are a good seven miles apart, and it is desirable to establish which of the two routes is the correct one, I have conjecturally solved the problem by the test of inherent military probability, and have sent a flank-guard *via* Miraumont, and the main body through Albert. I have not seen this problem discussed by any of the historians, some of whom select one and some the other, without giving their reasons. Wyllie favours Miraumont, but to travel through both Miraumont and Forceville would involve an almost right-angle turn at the former place and would add a good four miles to the march. Professor Jacob also gives Miraumont, but his map seems to indicate Albert. Moreover St. Remy (who gives Miraumont) who might be supposed to have his geographical facts correct, seeing he was with the English army, makes a big geographical error in the very sentence in which he mentions Miraumont. He writes "King Henry passed the river Somme at Esclusier", six miles below Peronne, and 15 miles from the actual crossing place. Waurin and Momstrelet on the other hand make Henry march "straight" to Forceville from near Peronne, which would take him through Albert. I accept this. For the remainder of the march there is no dispute as to the route.

We can now construct a march-table for the English army, with tolerable certainty. It is of course impossible to measure distances with precision, but in the following table I have made ample allowance for twists and turns in the road, but not of course for counter-marches when the wrong turning was taken —a thing that must have often occurred.

THE ENGLISH MARCH

Date	Approx. billets	Miles	Total	Average m.p.d.
Oct.				
8	Depart Harfleur			
11	Arques	60		
12	Eu	21		
13	Bailleul	23	104	17
14	Hangest	15		
15	Pont de Metz	17		
16	Boves	9		
17	Harbonnières	18		
18	Nesle	18		
19	Athies	9	190	14
20	Rest			
21	Mametz	18		
22	Acheux	16		
23	Frévent	20		
24	Agincourt	16	260	17½

From the above table we note that, taking the march in three stages, the march to the Somme was done at 17 miles per day, the march along the Somme at 14 miles per day and the march thence to Agincourt at 17½ miles per day. Including the rest day the whole march of 260 miles was accomplished in 17 days at an average speed of just over 15 miles per day. This was not bad going for hungry men, though of course for the mounted men it was child's play.

The route of the English army was remarkably direct. If a straight line be drawn from Peronne to Calais, a distance of just 100 miles, it will be found that Agincourt lies a bare 10 miles to the left of this line, and that nowhere does the lateral error exceed 12 miles. It is true that the first two days march was 15 degrees to the left of the direct line. But on reaching Acheux this error was largely corrected and from there to Calais the route followed the direct line very closely, the biggest lateral divergence being at Agincourt itself where it was about four miles. This raised the question, did the army possess maps? And if not, how did it estimate the direction of a place 100 miles away? This directness of route had been still more striking in the campaigns of Edward III, and it has led me to the tentative conclusion that some sort of map must have been in the possession of the army. If Edward III had a map of this region of France it is not impossible that Henry V also had one—possibly the identical one used by his great-grandfather.

THE FRENCH MARCH

The route and timing of the French army presents much greater difficulties than does the English, as has been hinted at in the text. Also there is the complication that there are two forces, not one, to consider—the advanced-guard under the Constable Charles D'Albret, and the main body under the dukes of Orleans and Bourbon—at least as far as Peronne. We will take the advanced-guard first. Waurin is our chief source for this. He records that d'Albret, Arthur of Richemont, the duke of Alençon and others were present on the Somme in the Abbeville region when the English army advanced. From the *Chronique de Percival de Cagny* we learn that the Duke of Alençon, "by his diligence managed to reach Abbeville before Henry could reach Blanche Taque", which seems to imply that he marched straight into Abbeville, and not *via* Rouen, as Oman asserts. Now Alençon was Cagny's master and was in the company of D'Albret, which would explain why Alençon rather than the Constable is mentioned; but it is clear that the advanced-guard is indicated. Waurin takes up the tale, telling us that D'Albret "went to Corbie and thence to Peronne, keeping their men always pretty near them on the road". After Peronne, according to him, they moved on to Bapaume. Unfortunately he does not say whether this was before or after joining forces with the main body of the French army. I will revert to this point in due course.

Now let us try to trace the march of the French main body. The date it departed from Rouen where it had been assembling is unknown, but we get an indication from the date of the arrival of the king at Rouen. Various dates are given. The monk of St. Denys, a reliable source, states that Charles VI arrived in Rouen early in October at the head of some of his troops. The exact date was the 12th, and the army would require at least one day to amalgamate the new arrivals with those already collected at Rouen before marching out. Thus the march could hardly have started earlier than October 14 or 15; if it had started earlier it would probably have bumped into the English army in the act of passing Amiens; on the other hand it could hardly have started later as it was in or near Peronne on the 19th. The distance from Rouen to Amiens is just over 50 miles; thus by starting on the 14th or 15th the army might be in Amiens on the 17th. Thence to Peronne is 25 miles: a full day's march on the 18th and a short march on the 19th would take the army there. If the above is what happened the French army must have crossed the tracks of the English army near Pont de Metz about 48 hours later, and reached Amiens on the day that the rival army was passing Corbie 10 miles away. The French were catching up, and the long detour then made by the English army allowed the

French to get right across their path at Peronne as we have seen. And thus it came about that on the 21st the English in their turn crossed the tracks of the French, as we have also seen. All the known facts now seem to fall into a clear pattern.

I do not think there can be much doubt that the above is approximately what happened, but commentators give us little assistance in the elucidation of a real problem. Wyllie is silent on the subject, contenting himself with remarking (in a footnote) that Ramsay shows the French army on his map as marching, "by Beauvais and Montdidier to Amiens and thence round to Ham and Bapaume without touching Peronne", without indicating whether he himself agrees with this astonishing route. As a matter of fact Ramsay's map does not show the French as marching through Amiens at all; from Montdidier it goes to Ham and thence north to Bapaume.

Ramsay gives no authority or reasons for the route he shows; nor does he even refer to his map in the text. His route is of course preposterous, the act of a madman—and the mad king was not present. Beauvais is due east of Rouen; what should induce a French army to take that direction, when its object was to prevent the English army reaching Calais? Its own advanced-guard was busily engaged in this task when the French army left Rouen; the last information it could have had from the front before setting off was that D'Albret was somewhere in the neighbourhood of Abbeville, that is, to the north-east of Rouen, 45 degrees to the left of a line to Beauvais. Moreover in order to prevent the English army reaching Calais the French would try to get to the north of them—not the south. Beauvais is 30 miles south of the Somme, and to wander into that region when the English were trying to cross the Somme would be, as I say, the act of a mad general. The surprising thing is that the French army did not march direct to Abbeville, instead of to Amiens. Presumably the reason was that, knowing or believing D'Albret to be guarding the Somme in the Abbeville area, Orleans and Bourbon rightly judged that the English would be obliged to march up the southern bank of the river

Somme, and might be encountered at Amiens. If this be so, it was a pretty shrewd appreciation and a good mark should be accorded to the French dukes. Reverting to Ramsay's map, if the French had taken the route shown on it their journey to Peronne would have been over 30 miles longer than *via* Amiens, and they could hardly have overtaken the English. Indeed the route from Ham to Bapaume would have taken them through Monchy Lagache, where they might well have bumped into Henry in his billet! A clear indication that the main body marched *via* Amiens is the fact that the duke of Brittany halted in that city, leaving the army to go on without him.

Let us get back to the French army marching along the northern bank of the Somme on October 19, through Corbie, Bray, Clery and under Mont St. Quentin—all localities that figured prominently in the final British advance in 1918. The question to resolve is where did the French army join forces with its advanced-guard? I can find no direct evidence on the point and doubt if there is any. I am reduced to deducing it from a single indication. When the three heralds approached King Henry they were hardly likely to have come from a place so distant as Bapaume, for the English army had only reached its billets in the middle of the preceding night and their billeting area could not have been located till next morning. Bapaume is over 20 miles from Monchy, and to get the news there, prepare the challenge and send off the heralds, and for them to cover the 20 miles, and return with the answer the same day seems unlikely, to say the least. No, I think the challenge must have come from Peronne. Now it was issued by the dukes of Orleans and Bourbon, not by the official commander-in-chief, the Constable D'Albret. Though the dukes are said to have had little regard for him they would hardly have gone to this length, and yet consented to fight under him at Agincourt a few days later. The explanation, I suggest, is that while the main body under the dukes was at Peronne, the advanced-guard had already moved on to Bapaume, as reported by Waurin. If this be so, it is easy to see how the dukes, having issued their challenge continued their march in order to concentrate the whole army at Bapaume before risking an engagement with their opponents.

From Bapaume to Agincourt, there seems no debatable point; in the absence of precise information I have indicated a purely conjectural route, compiled after study of the map.

N.B.–For the sources for the march, see the appendix to the next chapter.

CHAPTER V

AGINCOURT

THE rival armies went to rest, but few to sleep, on the eve of that fateful day of St. Crispin, in very different physical and mental states. The English had marched for 17 days with only one day's rest and had covered 260 miles, an average of 15 miles per day. The greater part of the army, it is true, was mounted, but there remained an appreciable portion of archers on foot. The French had not experienced such a trying and exhausting time. They had certainly marched with speed, covering about 180 miles in ten days, but all save a tiny portion of the combatants were mounted.

The mental state of the two armies was even more dissimilar. The English as a whole believed that they would most of them lose their lives in the inevitable battle next day. The idea of surrender does not seem to have entered the heads of any of them. It was to be literally a case of "do or die". They prepared solemnly for the contest, saw to their weapons, confessed and were shriven, and laid themselves down to rest on the rain-soaked open field. Well might they despair of victory. They had seen the enormous French army, over four times as numerous as their own,[1] which was under 6,000 strong, of whom less than 1,000 were men-at-arms, the rest being archers (for they had no artillery.) It was a small army, but it was homogeneous and it possessed a degree of discipline that was quite unique for that epoch. Let a French contemporary, whose sympathies were French, testify on this score. The monk of St. Denys declared:

"They considered it a crime to have bad women in their camp. They paid more regard than the French themselves for the welfare of the inhabitants, who (consequently) declared themselves in their favour. They closely observed the rules of military discipline and obeyed scrupulously the orders of their King. His words were

[1] See Appendix to this chapter for the numbers.

received with enthusiasm, and not only by the leading men; for the common soldiers also promised to fight to the death."

The king had strictly enjoined complete silence in the lines that night, and his orders were obeyed. Such was the silence that the French outposts suspected that the English were preparing to slip away. St. Remy adds picturesquely, "Not a horse neighed". Henry V worked up his troops to a pitch of fervour and camaraderie akin to that produced by Joan of Arc in the French army marching to the relief of Orleans.

"We few, we happy few, we band of brothers." Shakespeare hit it off perfectly.

In the opposite camp things were vastly different. On the one hand the French lords, at least, were "cock-a-hoop", wagering as to which of them should capture the English king, and so on. It is even stated by Polydore Vergil that they had a cart specially painted in which to promenade their royal captive through the streets of Paris. The other contrast was that in the French camp all was clamour and confusion, attaining almost to chaos. The noise of shouting lords, grooms and servants, reached even to the English lines over half a mile away; the rain was falling steadily most of the night, and the lords were shouting for their varlets, and sending them in all directions in search of straw to lay on the sodden churned-up ground (recently sown with autumn wheat) on which they had to lie. On the one hand was the ordered discipline of a regular trained army of selected soldiers; on the other, a vast rabble-like horde of hastily-raised troops, of a heterogeneous nature, brought together from all parts of France, and even from further afield, and lacking one single undisputed head to whom they could look with reverence and confidence in the ordering of the battle. Indeed there could scarcely have been a greater contrast, except in the arms and armour carried, between two medieval armies.

The English king had billets in the village of Maisoncelles but there could be little sleep for him that night. He must have been in a state of mental excitement. What his inmost feelings were it is difficult to say. Until quite recently he had affected to welcome a battle, and it is generally held that he spoke the truth. But the sight that had greeted him that afternoon, of the vast French army, surely removed any desire that he still retained for a battle. Yet if he felt any misgivings he kept them strictly to himself. The story is well attested, and is not a figment of Shakespeare's imagination, that when the impossibility of avoiding a battle became manifest and Sir Walter Hungerford exclaimed:

"I would that we had 10,000 more good English archers, who would gladly be here with us to-day,"

the king replied:

"Thou speakest as a fool! By the God of Heaven on whose grace I lean, I would not have one more even if I could. This people is God's people, he has entrusted them to me to-day and he can bring down the pride of these Frenchmen who so boast of their numbers and their strength."

But whatever his secret feelings, he had others thing to occupy his mind and attention during the hours of darkness. He was prepared, whatever he might say, to strike a bargain for the possibility of reaching Calais without a battle, and negotiations to that end passed to and fro between the two headquarters, just as they had done in the night before Poitiers. The price he was prepared to pay was the return of Harfleur to its old owners; but the French, confident in their own strength, would not agree to this and the price they proposed was beyond what Henry's pride allowed him to concede. The negotiations thus fell through and a battle next day became inevitable.

At dawn on October 25, 1415, the feast day of St. Crispin and St. Crispianus, the two martyr-cobblers of Soissons, the rain had stopped and the two weary armies roused themselves and were deployed by their respective marshalls in order of battle. The English king, having attended Mass, donned his armour and surcoat, resplendent with leopards of England and the fleur-de-lys of France, his helmet encircled by a golden crown, studded with pearls, sapphires and rubies. He then mounted his grey palfrey, having for some reason removed his spurs; and thus he rode down the line, stopping frequently to harangue the troops and to receive their acclamations.

He then placed himself at the head of the centre division, the duke of York being in command of the right division and the Lord Camoys in command of the left division. The French however appeared not to be ready for battle, and a long and doubtless painful pause ensued, during which we may describe the ground about to be fought over.

It is easily described for it is beautifully symmetrical. If the two contestants really desired a field that would give no advantage to either side as they declared, they certainly found it at Agincourt. As my sketch-map shows, the arena formed a rectangle, the two sides being formed by the woods surrounding the villages of Agincourt[1] and Tramecourt, the open space being 940 yards wide at the narrowest point, and the two ends being formed by the two armies in line, just over 1,000 yards apart. There was a barely perceptible dip between the two armies, but the two flanks fell away appreciably, a surprising discovery to the visitor, for no account mentions the fact. Owing to the slight dip between them the two armies were in full view of one another. Each army filled the open space, a newly-sown wheat-field, and as the arena was slightly wider on the French side it follows that their line was slightly longer than the English, about 1,200 yards to 950. But the French being many times more numerous their line had a similar proportion of extra depth. The English men-at-arms in fact were only four deep, and the archers about seven to the yard. The numbers were so small that the king could not afford a reserve, bar a minute baggage-guard. In this he took a profound risk, but a desperate malady requires a desperate remedy.

There is wide divergence of opinion as to the exact formation of the English army, but I believe it to have been as follows. It consisted in the main of three divisions, each division having

---

[1] The French called it Agincourt at the time; it was at a subsequent date that they changed it to Azincourt.

its men-at-arms in the centre and its archers on the wings. In addition there was a strong force of what we should now call "army archers" attached to no division but formed in two bodies one on each wing. The archers of the centre division would thus be in contact with the archers of the inner wings of the flank divisions; likewise the outside archers of the flank divisions would be in contact with the "army" archers. Thus, looked at from the front at a distance as the French would see them (and this is important for my argument) the English army would appear to have men-at-arms in the centre, divided by two small clumps of archers, while the main archer force would be on the wings. I suggest that the army archers were about 3,100 strong and the divisional archers 1,850. Thus the biggest clumps, viewed from the front, would be on the wings, each nearly 1,900 strong. A simple calculation shows that such a formation should just fill the space of 940 yards between the woods.

The French army, unlike the English, was mainly composed of men-at-arms. These were formed in three lines, all being dismounted except the rear one and two bodies of cavalry, each 600 strong stationed on the two wings. The latter were detailed to open the battle by a mounted attack on the English archers who could be seen grouped on the wings. The French army being practically an undisciplined rabble, when I speak of three lines, I mean in theory only. In practice there was a deal of jostling, squeezing and intermingling of men-at-arms and archers, while the guns seem to have been pushed out of line altogether; it is doubtful if they fired more than a few rounds at the most. For simplicity the sketch map shows only two lines.

*   *   *

Thus the two armies formed up at dawn on October 25, 1415, and for the next four hours they stood motionless, eyeing each other closely, each waiting upon the other to advance. But a battle cannot take place if neither side will advance, and at

11 o'clock the king of England decided to take the offensive himself. "Advance banner," rang out the famous order, on which everyone "knelt down and made a cross on the ground and kissed it".[1] The whole army then began to advance in line.

The French front was, I reckon, 470 yards north of the Agincourt-Tramecourt road and the English army moved steadily forward till it was 170 yards north of the cross-road, 50 yards south of the present coppice wherein lies the main French grave pit. It moved slowly, frequently halting for the heavily-armoured knights to take breath. At extreme bowshot range the army came to a halt, the archers planted their stakes in front of their front rank thus making a sort of fence,[2] and opened fire.

This fire was probably calculated to provoke the French into advancing, for they had few archers with whom to return the fire. It had the desired effect. The mounted cavalry essayed to charge the flank archers according to plan, and as they started to advance, the front line of dismounted men-at-arms also moved forwards, probably without explicit orders from the Constable d'Albret, their nominal commander-in-chief.

The mounted attack of the two flanks was to be made by parties each about 600 strong, (there is much contradiction about the numbers) but owing to the confusion and lack of discipline in the French ranks only a mere 150 or so on each wing actually took part in the attack. That on the Agincourt side was led by Sir William de Savense, whose party in the words of St. Remy:

"threw themselves on the English archers, who had their sharp stakes fixed before them; but the ground was so soft that the said stakes fell. And the French all retreated excepting three men, of whom Sir William was one; to whom it unluckily happened that by their horses falling on the stakes they were thrown to the ground, among the archers and were immediately killed. The remainder, or the greater part of them, with all their horses, from fear of the arrows retreated into the French advanced-guard in which they caused great confusion, breaking and exposing it in many places,

[1] *The Brut (Continuation H)*, (ed. Brie), p. 554.
[2] Monstrelet says, "Each archer placed before himself a stake", which makes nonsense of it.

and caused them to retire to some new-sown ground for their horses were so wounded by the arrows that they were unmanageable. And thus the advanced-guard being thrown into disorder, the men-at-arms fell in great numbers and their horses took to flight behind the lines, following which example numbers of the French fled."

Up to this point I think the story is quite clear and straightforward. But now comes the crucial point. Before quoting it, however, we must glance at the French main body which was now advancing in the centre.

All the authorities agree that when they came into contact with the English they were in such close formation that they could scarcely raise their arms to make use of their weapons. How came this about? Surely they would not form up in such ridiculously close order? I believe two causes conspired to produce this unfortunate and fatal result. Look at the map and you will notice that the width of open space in the French position was about 150 yards wider than in that of the English, and that as the French advanced their frontage would diminish owing to the funnel-shape of the open ground made by the two woods. This was bound to have the effect of compressing the French lines somewhat as they advanced.

But I think there was another and more decisive cause than this. I have described the English men-at-arms as being in three groups, separated by clumps of archers. These archers were formed in wedges (cuneos) which I take to mean the same formation that proved so effective at Crecy, namely bastion-like projections in front of the line of men-at-arms. As the French army advanced they would instinctively, if not by order, concentrate against the English men-at-arms, whom they considered their rightful opponents—not the despised common breed of archers. Indeed one account specifically states that they did so. Moreover the nearer they approached and the more they were goaded by the arrows of the English archers, the more they would tend to flinch away from these archers as they pushed forward into the three ominous re-entrants that the English line in effect comprised.

It should be noted that there is no mention in the above

English account of the horses or men being made immobile by the mud. After all, the English experienced the same mud,

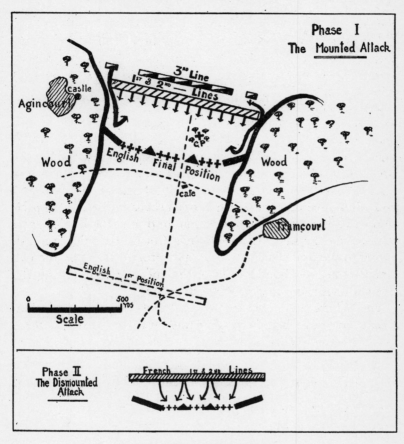

Sketch Map 2; AGINCOURT

++   English men-at-arms   - - - Modern roads

▲   English archers   G.P. Grave pits

▨   French dismounted men

◪   French mounted men

for the rain raineth on the just and the unjust alike, and though the English had had plenty of rain in the night they advanced further through the mud than did their opponents. No, it was arrows not mud, that turned back the French horsemen and started the rot. Nor did the mud prevent the French horsemen from galloping through their own infantry in the course of their flight.

We can now return to St. Remy's account, with the picture of the great mass of the French plodding forward into the centre of the field, goaded by arrows from the front and flanks whilst great breaches were torn in their own ranks by the panicking horsemen.

"The English archers, perceiving this disorder of the advanced-guard, quitted their stakes, threw their bows and arrows on the ground and seizing their swords, axes and other weapons, sallied out upon them, and hastening to the places where the fugitives had made breaches, killed and disabled the French, . . . and met with little or no resistance. And the English, cutting right and left, pushed on to the second line, and then pushed within it, with the King of England in person."

It would seem that only isolated clumps of archers penetrated beyond the wall of dead and dying, that was soon all that was left of the first French line, for their second line was now surging forward, and a great part of it had mingled with the first in an unwieldy conglomeration of armoured men, utterly crowding out the crossbowmen who were originally between the two lines.

The incursion of this second line merely added to the carnage and to the height and thickness of the wall of prostrate forms, on to the top of which the agile and lightly-armed English archers climbed.

Scarcely more than thirty minutes had sufficed to produce this astonishing result, and the battle gradually petered out as fewer and fewer Frenchmen remained on their feet. The contest had been for them a kind of nightmare: the more they pressed forward into the fight the more impossible it became for any of them to fight at all. They could not wield their arms and one man falling would bring down those next to him—and there was no getting up; the pages, one of whose duties it was to help their lords to their feet, were not at hand. It was said that the weight of two men in armour falling on top of a third would take away the breath of the man underneath. Some Englishmen indeed fell victims to this disaster. The duke of York at one period pushed forward into the front line. He over-balanced or was pushed over, and others fell on top of him. When, after the battle was over, his body was pulled out from the shambles he was found to be unwounded but stone dead. He had been suffocated to death. Thus perished the last re-maining grandson of Edward III.

Large numbers of the French men-at-arms met the same fate. Indeed John Hardyng, who was present, declares in his rhymed Chronicle, "More were dead through press than our men might have slain."[1]

Thus in a remarkably short space of time the first two French lines, outnumbering their opponents by at least three to one, had been vanquished. There remained the third line who, it will be remembered, were mounted. They did not advance; to do so would have been quite fruitless; neither did they retire as a body, but there was considerable confusion, and many fainter-hearted men quietly slipped away to the rear. Those who stood fast became visible to King Henry, over the wall of dead. One glance showed him that for the moment at least, no danger need be expected from them, and he allowed the victors to take up the congenial task of taking prisoners and arranging for ransoms. But it was a slow task, and a rather gruesome one, disentangling the living from the dead, prising open helmets, unriveting plate-armour and collecting and marshalling those of the living who could walk. The work had gone on for over two hours when suddenly two disturbing events occurred, one in front, the other in the rear.

Only a small baggage-guard had been provided, and it was quite inadequate to ward off a serious attack. Such an attack was now delivered by an armed marauding body, who broke

---

[1] This is confirmed by *The Brut* (*Continuation H*): "Great people of them were slain without any stroke". (*The Brut*, ed. Brie, p. 555.)

into the camp, and made havoc therein. Not only were the royal beds carried off but the king's chief crown and his seals. At the same time danger suddenly appeared in front. Strenuous efforts had been made by the leaders of the French third line, who were now joined by the duke of Brabant (youngest brother of the duke of Burgundy), with a small body of men. The force thus collecting in his front by itself outnumbered the English army; the English troops were completely off their guard, absorbed in prisoner-taking. Moreover the prisoners had not yet, for the most part, been divested of their armour. The archers thus had their hands full; if they let go of their captives and moved off to repel the impending attack their captives would have been free to pick up weapons that sprinkled the ground and attack them in the rear, possibly in conjunction with their comrades who were still running amok in the English camp. It was an ugly situation; anything might happen. Something had to be done at once, and there seemed only one thing to do: it must be a case of "No quarter" after all: the prisoners must be killed. Sternly the king gave the order, and reluctantly and hesitantly his soldiers obeyed, for it meant to them the loss of ransom. How many were killed is not known, but presently the threat of attack died away and the throat-cutting was stopped.

Some modern English writers have condemned this measure in unmeasured terms: "a cruel butchery" it is dubbed by Ramsay. But needless to say, such things should be judged by the context and customs of the time, and no contemporary chronicler seems to have condemned it, not even the French ones. Indeed one contemporary Frenchman blames his own countrymen for it, on the grounds that their useless rally made this slaughter inevitable. It is also tolerably certain that the French would have done the same under similar circumstances. Indeed 20 years previously on the eve of the Battle of Nicopolis the French commander had cut the throats of 1,000 prisoners, so as not to be encumbered with them next day.[1]

[1] Yet the latest French biographer of Joan of Arc seldom mentions the name of Henry V without the elegant soubriquet "The Cut-throat".

A feature of the battle was the enormous number of Frenchmen killed. The total cannot have been far short of 10,000 and it included three dukes—Alençon, Brabant and Bar—the Constable of France and commander-in-chief Charles D'Albret, together with no less than 90 other lords and 1,560 knights. Indeed it was said that more than half the nobility of France were casualties. The prisoners included both the leading dukes, Orleans and Bourbon, the count Arthur of Richmont and marshal Boucicaut, in fact a "clean sweep" was made of the higher commanders in the French host, which thus became a scattered flock without a shepherd.

The English casualties were at the most a few hundred, mainly wounded; it is impossible to give closer figures than this. The chief victim was of course the duke of York, to whom the credit must go for the provision of double-pointed stakes for the archers. The young earl of Suffolk, whose father had died at Harfleur, also perished.

Of the actions of the French leaders in the battle there is no reliable information, but two stories about King Henry are well attested. At one period of the battle he entered the fray, and at that moment his young brother Humphrey of Gloucester was slightly wounded and fell at his feet. The king stood over his prostrate body till the duke could be dragged away. The other story is that 18 French knights swore that they would hack their way to the king of England and strike down his crown, or perish in the attempt. They perished in the attempt, but not before one of them had got within reach of the king of England and struck him on the helmet, lopping off one of the fleurons of the crown and denting the helmet. The dented helmet now hangs high up on the wall above the tomb of the king in the chapel of Edward the Confessor in Westminster Abbey—surely the most dramatic piece of medieval armour in existence!

In contrast to Crecy and Poitiers, the issue of the Battle of Agincourt was decided in the first half hour. This is the more striking when we remember that the odds were even greater against the victor at Agincourt than at the former two battles, and historians have spilt much ink in trying to find the explanation for the overwhelming success. But I think the answer is not far to seek. Battles can be likened to a tug-of-war. On each side there are a number of factors, all pulling the same way—towards victory. The resultant force of all these factors is the measure of the "pull to victory", and the side which produces the biggest resultant is the winner. It is as simple as that.

In the case of Agincourt, there is no need to label and examine each of these factors in detail, for all the factors except one—relative numbers—were, as far as can be seen, in favour of the English army. Hence the English victory. The result can however be summarized in a single sentence: a regular, trained and disciplined army defeated one that possessed none of these military virtues.

THE RETURN MARCH

On the morrow of the battle of Agincourt the English army resumed its march to Calais. It seems always to be taken for granted that such was the right course; but it is interesting to speculate as to the upshot if King Henry had suddenly reversed his plan, and marched in the opposite direction—on Paris. It is interesting to note that in very similar circumstances Edward III had declined to change his plan after his victory at Crecy, and that both monarchs—though for different reasons—continued their march on Calais. The matter deserves a brief examination.

Consider first the sad plight that France found herself in on the morrow of Agincourt. Her sole army had dissolved overnight. For the time being she was practically defenceless. All her leading men except the old duke of Berry and the duke of Burgundy (and his loyalty was suspect), were out of action. The court seated at Rouen, or what was left of it, was distraught at the news. The king wept and cried, "We be all dead and over-thrown!" According to Juvenal des Ursins, he had but few troops with him at Rouen, which is very likely. It is true that the distance from Rouen to Paris was a four-day march whereas

from Agincourt it was about eight. But the English army would
have had a big start, and might well have reached the French
capital first. Of course the citizens might have shut the gates in
his face as they had done to Edward III 55 years before. On the
other hand, it is at least possible that, faced with the prospect of
further chaos, with a demented king, and a dying Dauphin (he
died a few weeks later) they might have preferred to embrace
the chance of getting some firm and ordered government after
the miseries of the present reign. And the Treaty of Troyes
might have been anticipated by five years. However that may
be, the English army resumed its march on Calais next day,
early in the morning, according to one chronicler; which seems
hard to credit, for there must have been much to do. Prisoners
had to be sorted out, escorts provided and also food, for the
captives could not forage for themselves and would have no
money. The English dead had to be seen to; eventually they
were cremated by placing them in a nearby barn and setting
fire to it. A tally had to be taken, so far as possible, of the high-
born dead on the French side; the body of the Duke of York,
and also that of the earl of Suffolk had to be parboiled, in order
to reduce the weight (the duke had grown corpulent, and heavy)
in order that their bones might be taken home. The captured
armour that was not required had to be disposed of, and so on.

Eventually the army set out, taking the most direct route to
Calais. The 45 miles was covered in four days, without incident.
It must have looked a curious sight as the prisoners (there were
about 2,000 of them) trudged alongside their captors, who
themselves were laden with booty, each with as much as the
man could carry, strung all over his horse. They must have
looked like an army of "White Knights" as described in "Alice
in Wonderland".

On arrival in the Calais Pale the army was met by the earl
of Warwick, the captain of Calais, and conducted into the
town in state. Here a rude awakening met the tired soldiers.
The food which had been sent for their use from England had
not arrived and for some days, owing to bad staff work, they

were in a sorry state. Food and lodgings were hard to come by and there were not enough ships to take them home. In fact it was some time before all got back to England.

The king rode with his two captive dukes beside him, discussing the battle with them. To their enquiry whether he was not now ready for peace he replied that nothing was nearer to his heart. On that Orleans sent a herald to Rouen with the news—but nothing came of it.

After a short stay in Calais King Henry took ship for Dover, and from thence by easy stages he made his way to London, stopping two days in the abbey of St. Augustine at Canterbury. He arrived at Eltham Palace exactly four weeks after the battle. Hither next day came the mayor of London, with 24 aldermen in his train, and followed by no less than 15,000 to 20,000 craftsmen of the City, all mounted on horseback and carrying their trade devices.

The reception in London was worthy of the capital, and was on a scale and magnificence never before witnessed. The culminating scene was in St. Paul's where the king was welcomed by 18 bishops and a solemn Te Deum was sung. It was England's greatest hour of triumph.

APPENDIX

THE NUMBERS

The English army. There is no problem here. Everyone is agreed that the English army numbered about 6,000 – Elmham's figure. It had set out with 900 men-at-arms and 5,000 archers. To this must be added the archers in the lanes of those high-born knights who were not included in the regular ranks of the archers – say 100. This would bring the total to exactly 6,000. From this must be deducted the wastage during the march – sick, wounded, prisoners and possible deserters. Of these numbers we have absolutely no information. That there were some walking sick is evident because they were included in the baggage-guard during the battle. As for wounded and prisoners, casualties were incurred in the skirmishes at Eu and

Corbie, especially the latter, and possibly at other places too. If we allow 5 per cent. for wastage we shall probably not be far wrong. This would bring the effective total at Agincourt to 5,700, and we may feel pretty sure that the correct figure is within 200 of this total.

The French army. To estimate the strength of the French army is a very different proposition. Throughout the Hundred Years War chroniclers show that they have no exact figures and this is not surprising for, as it appears, no exact tallies of dismounted levies, or "Communes", were ever made, and no-one, not even their own commanders, knew what the figures were. The chroniclers were thus reduced to guessing, and the wildness of their guesses may be realized when we note that they varied between 10,000 and 200,000. Clearly it is a waste of time to try to establish the true or even the approximate total from an examination of these figures. We must have recourse to the known factors that may have a bearing on the subject. Of these there are four. The first is that the French largely outnumbered the English. On this point practically all the chroniclers, English, Burgundian and French, are in agreement. Two modern professors have attempted to dispute this fact. Fifty years ago the German Delbrück, flying in the face of all the evidence, asserted that the English outnumbered the French, and in our own day Ferdinand Lot has done the same.[1] Their arguments, if they can be called arguments, are derisory, but since the French professor is widely and rightly revered as a historian, and as his thesis has received no notice or reply on this side of the Channel, his argument must be examined. It occurs on p. 14, vol. II of his *L'art Militaire et les Armées au Moyen Age* (Paris, 1946). His salient point is comprised in a single sentence which must be quoted:

"Sur 800 mètres de front – au maximum – étant donné que la cavalerie se deploie alors sur trois rangs, separés par un espace de 50 mètres environ on ne peut engager plus de 1800 cavalerie au mamimum."

[1] This need occasion no great surprise when we hear that he made the same assertion for Crecy.

He assesses the archers at 3,600, making a total of 5,400. His assessment of men-at-arms is 600 men in each line, on a frontage of two men to three yards. He assumes that each division of men-at-arms was in a single rank, whereas the English were in four ranks (and would no doubt have been in still deeper formation had they had the men). On what grounds does he assume that the French men-at-arms advanced in single rank? It would be a singular and almost unheard-of formation. Moreover, only two French divisions were engaged, so the total of men-at-arms that came to grips with the English was only 1,200, *i.e.*, one-and-a-third men per yard of frontage. Whence then came the corpses that we know built up a formidable wall of dead? Even if every single man-at-arms was killed that would be insufficient to make a wall of any dimension; but we know that by no means every man-at-arms was killed in the engagement. Apart from the unknown number who were despatched after the fighting was over, about 2,000 prisoners were marched away? Whence came these prisoners, if less than that number of men-at-arms were engaged in the fighting? No doubt a few would be crossbowmen, but only a few, for they were scarcely engaged in the battle, being shouldered out by their men-at-arms.

In short it is impossible to reconcile Lot's figures with the general agreed course of the battle.

As opposed to the French professor I may cite the most recent English professor to describe the battle – Professor E. F. Jacob. He contents himself by stating that the French army was "notably superior in size".[1] (Dr. Wyllie estimated that the French army outnumbered the English ten times, but does not give his reasoning in the text; this he reserved for an appendix which most unfortunately he never lived to write.)

Coming now to the second known factor, the battle formation of the two armies. It is known that the English army was formed up in one line, while the French was in three lines or divisions, the rear one being mounted. But there was also an

---

[1] *Henry V and the Invasion of France*, p. 102.

intermediate line between the first and second lines, composed of crossbowmen, archers and guns. If we assume that the depth of each line in both armies was the same, that would make the French nearly four times the number of the English. But the French divisions were probably in deeper formation.

The third known factor is the ground. The width between the two woods is believed not to have altered appreciably. At the place where the French army drew up it is about 1,200 yards wide. As to how many ranks there were in each line, Ferdinand Lot could not know, for no-one knew. If the truth be told, I doubt if there was so regular a formation that anyone could have counted the ranks: I envisage the formation as three conglomerations rather than three neatly formed ranks and lines in dressing so many metres apart, and such evidence as there is tends to show that the lines were densely packed from the start: the wretched archers and cannons were "shouldered" out of the line: there was no space for them to ply their weapons. On the whole an average depth at the outset of five to six per line, would seem reasonable and bring the total (including archers, etc.) to at least 24,000, over four times the English army. Incidentally this figure agrees with the best and most reliable French chronicler, the monk of St. Denys, who states that the French outnumbered the English by four times. Why does professor Lot ignore his own chronicler?

The fourth known factor is the number of casualties, if one may accept it as "known", in view of the usual disagreement among the sources. Dr. Wyllie estimates the number as 10,000. Much the most reliable source for this, I consider, is the MS. of Chateau Ruisseauville. This document was composed locally, and where it gives local topographical information should be worthy of credence. It states that after the battle the bishop of Terouannem accompanied by the abbot of Blangy visited the stricken field of battle, blessed the ground on which the dead still lay and gave orders for grave-pits to be dug for their bodies. It adds that five grave-pits were dug all close together, and upwards of 1,200 bodies buried in each. That would mean upwards of 6,000 burials in that place. Allowing for bodies of knights removed for burial, etc., and remembering that most of the casualties were incurred by the first line, and none by the rear line, it would put the total number engaged in the region of say 20,000 to 30,000.

From several points of view, therefore, the total would appear to lie about 25,000, and I purposely select this round figure in order to show that my estimate is a "round" conjecture.

*   *   *

SOURCES

The sources for the history of Henry V's reign are at first rather confusing, for two reasons. First, their titles are very much alike, and second, the authorship of one of them was in error attributed by Thomas Hearne 200 years ago to Thomas Elmham, whereas he was the author of another of these histories. Consequently when one reads the name Elmham one must know the date of the work in question. The three chief histories are as follows:—

1. *Henrici Quinti Angliae regis gesta.*
2. *Vita et gesta Henrici quinti.*
3. *Vita Henrici Quinti.*

No. 1 is now known to have been written by Thomas Elmham, the king's chaplain, and is sometimes called "The Chaplain's" Account, and sometimes *Gesta*, for short, in order to distinguish it from No. 2 which is sometimes called *Vita* for short, and is by an unknown author, and in Hearne's edition, Thomas Elmham, nowadays described as "Pseudo-Elmham". No. 3 is by an Italian, Titus Livius, and is mainly compiled from Nos. 1 and 2. Of the three the *Gesta* is much the best for our purpose as the chaplain took part in the Agincourt campaign, and wrote his account only two years later; indeed, it is our chief source for the march to Agincourt.

The most important English chronicle of the reign is that of Thomas Walsingham, *Historia Anglicana*, written only a few years after Agincourt.

Three Burgundians also wrote contemporary accounts of the Agincourt campaign, Enguerrand Monstrelet, Le Fèvre, Lord of St. Remy, and Jean de Waurin. Waurin fought in the battle on the French side, St. Remy on the English side; Monstrelet fought on neither but he lived close to the battlefield, and his *Chronique* was published before that of either of the other two. From internal evidence one would say that all three copied from the others in various passages, which at first sight seems absurd. It is indeed an interesting puzzle to unravel, reminding one of the "Synoptic Problem", but whereas we know that Matthew and Luke copied from Mark copiously and Mark copied from neither, Dr. Wyllie asserts that Monstrelet wrote first and that the other two made use of his account. But by comparing carefully the three accounts it would seem that Monstrelet must have written after the other two, although his account was published first and therefore that he copied from them. The other puzzle is to decide whether St. Remy or Waurin copied the other, and strange though it may appear they seem to have copied each other simultaneously. The only possible explanation is that before writing they exchanged experiences and also showed each other their own rough drafts or notes before writing their complete works. It further seems that St. Remy imparted rather more than he borrowed from Waurin. Hence St. Remy's account of the battle must be accounted as the most reliable and informative. The chaplain is undoubtedly reliable as far as he goes (except for his estimate of the French numbers, but this worthy priest witnessed the battle from afar, namely from the baggage lines at Maisoncelles). Still we are much more fortunate in our sources than for Crecy or Poitiers, where no combatant wrote about it,[1] whereas at Agincourt we have three combatants (including John Hardyng, whose rhymed account is however disappointingly short). Thus the battle is exceptionally well documented.

Of the French chroniclers, by far the most reliable is the

---

[1] The two priests who recorded it were out of sight of the battle in the baggage park.

monk of St. Denys who was scrupulously careful with his facts, and even dared to criticize the French high command although he was in essence the Court official historian.

There are several other French chroniclers who add items here and there but who scarcely come within the limits of this short note on sources. The most complete bibliography is contained in Wyllie's *Henry V*, volume III, which cites nearly 3,000 printed books, but it covers the whole reign, not merely the military operations.

Modern accounts of the Agincourt campaign (as opposed to the battle), are disappointingly meagre, especially concerning the French army, which in most books pops up on the eve of the battle out of the blue, so to speak, without any explanation of how it got there. *The Reign of Henry V*, by Dr. J. H. Wyllie, is the most detailed. Next comes *Lancaster and York* by Sir James Ramsay. The account by Sir Charles Oman in his *Art of War in the Middle Ages*, volume II, is good, but shorter still. Ferdinand Lot in his *L'Art Militaire des Armées au Moyen Age* is chiefly concerned to prove that the English outnumbered the French in the battle, and the most recent of all (1951), *La Guerre de Cent Ans* by Edouard Perroy, dismisses the battle in a couple of sentences. Probably the best French account is *La Bataille d'Azincourt* by René de Belleval, published in 1865.

CHAPTER VI

VALMONT AND HARFLEUR

AT the news of how a tiny English army had vanquished a great French army at Agincourt all the world wondered – not least the Emperor Sigismund of Luxemburg (younger brother of "Good King Wenceslas" and more correctly called king of the Romans). This monarch had been foremost in trying to heal the Great Schism of 1378, whereby, to the scandal of the church, two rival popes reigned, one at Rome the other at Avignon. Now the French recognized the Avignon pope and the English the Roman pope. Sigismund realized that England was now such an important power in Europe that no settlement of the problem could be reached without her cooperation. He therefore took upon himself the office of peacemaker. To this end he visited France in 1416, arriving in Paris in mid-March. After a fruitless stay of six weeks he passed on to England.

The duke of Gloucester went down to Dover to meet him. With his retinue he rode into the water, all with drawn swords, as the emperor's boat approached the beach and declared that he could not be allowed to land unless he disclaimed all pretentions to exercise any jurisdiction in England. This the emperor duly disclaimed and he was then permitted to land. On Sigismund's arrival in London the king made amends for any lack of warmth in his welcome at Dover by entertaining him magnificently, and by bestowing upon him the Order of the Garter. Sigismund was thus the first foreign potentate to receive this honour. Possibly the fact that he brought with him what purported to be the heart of St. George had something to do with it.

Under the stimulus of Sigismund, peace negotiations were carried on, though in a desultory fashion, throughout the summer. But King Henry took his stand firmly on the Treaty of Bretigny (which gave back to England all her Aquitaine

451

empire, whilst the English king gave up his claim to the French throne). The French might have agreed to these terms but they would not agree to Henry retaining Harfleur. This was the rock upon which the negotiations broke.

Eventually on August 15 Sigismund and Henry signed at Canterbury the Treaty of Canterbury whereby they swore "eternal friendship" between their countries, and undertook to support one another in any war, whether offensive or defensive.

When the news leaked out the French government were naturally indignant, and declared that Sigismund was a weak creature who had been seduced by the stronger English king. There may be some truth in this.

But the emperor had no military means of rendering effective military support to England, even if he really wished to do so. For one thing, there was what may be loosely described as a buffer state between the two, namely the Flemish territories of the duke of Burgundy. If Burgundy could be drawn into the alliance, thus forming what Professor Jacob calls "The Big Three", the situation would be entirely altered. Henry decided to try to bring this about. He seems to have again been following the example of his great-grandfather in building up a great anti-French alliance in Europe, for he was also making overtures to the Flemish provinces.

Early in October the Big Three met in Calais. John the Fearless, duke of Burgundy, son of Philip the Good, had been enticed to Calais with great difficulty. He was a suspicious man and had demanded that if he came to Calais one of the king's brothers should be handed over as a hostage for his personal safety the while. An elaborate ceremony was therefore enacted on the frontier near Gravelines, which vividly illustrates the degree of insecurity and suspicion that reigned between contiguous states in that era. The duke of Gloucester had been selected as hostage. The meeting was fixed near the mouth of the river Aa, which was tidal. At low water the retinues of the two dukes crossed the stream simultaneously. That done, the two dukes entered the water mounted, met in midstream, shook hands and then passed on–Burgundy to Calais, Gloucester to St. Omer.

Arrived at Calais, Burgundy went into most secret talks with the English king, the details of which were never committed to paper. Henry tried to persuade his guest to sign a paper recognizing him as king of France, and promising him all support. Burgundy would not sign but gave Henry orally to understand that he agreed with it and would give all possible aid when the time came.

*   *   *

The interest now shifts to Harfleur. It will be remembered that King Henry had left there a small garrison under the earl of Dorset to repair the defences and hold it for the king. Artisans and merchants were also enticed thither, the king's aim being to make it a second Calais. In order to secure food and fodder, constant raids into the surrounding country were necessary, and in this connection we meet for the first time one captain John Fastolf, whom we find leading such a raid, in late November, to within six miles of Rouen.

In January, 1416 the garrison was relieved by a new and enlarged one, consisting of 900 men-at-arms and 1,500 archers. This new garrison soon made its presence felt, carrying out a number of successful raids on both sides of the estuary. At the beginning of March the earl of Dorset returned from leave in England, and he soon took action. On March 9, he set out with a force of 1,000 men, all mounted, on a three-day raid to the north-east. All went well, and it reached and set fire to Cany, a little town seven miles south of St. Valery. He then turned for home. His route took him through the villages of Ouainville and Valmont. At the former, three miles west of Cany, and five miles short of Valmont, French patrols spotted the English army, which however continued on its way, suspecting nothing. When near Valmont it suddenly found its way barred by a superior French force, estimated at about 5,000.[1]

---

[1] This is the chaplain's figure and Wyllie accepts it, but 3–4,000 seems a more probable estimate. See below.

It was trapped! This French army was led by Bernard, count
d'Armagnac, who had recently been recalled to Paris from
the south, and created Constable of France. He had brought
with him to Paris an army of 6,000 Gascons. Hearing of the
increased English activity at Harfleur, he had marched north
with 3,000 of his army to deal with it. In addition he picked
up some local garrisons on his arrival in Normandy including
650 men of Rouen, so the total can have been but little short
of 4,000.

The earl of Dorset, seeing that he was about to be attacked,
dismounted his whole force, and sent the horses to the rear, in
the approved English fashion. Then he hastily formed up his tiny
army, in a single line, stretched to the utmost in order not to be
outflanked by the enemy. But it was dangerously thin, and when
the French cavalry threw in one mounted charge after another,
weak places began to appear in what we might call "the Thin
Red Line". Some gaps were made, and excited and exultant
French knights plunged through. Then instead of wheeling
about and finishing off their dismounted opponents, they charged
straight forward against the horses and baggage. To cut down
the grooms and pages tending the horses was a simple matter,
and then the victorious horsemen fell to looting the baggage, in
a fashion typical of cavalry in all countries and all ages.

This misguided action gave a brief respite to the battered
English line, and the earl of Dorset, though grievously wounded
himself, was quick to make use of it. Abandoning his horses
except the handful that he had with him, he reformed his
troops and led them off to a flank where he saw a large garden
surrounded by a tall hedge and ditch. This he lined with his
men, facing all directions. It formed what we might term a
zariba or small "hedgehog" (considering the big part played
by the hedge the latter is "le mot juste"). But his force was
reduced to some 850 fighting men.

Up to now the English, in spite of their surprise and discomfiture, had acquitted themselves well. The fair-minded
monk of St. Denys pays them a handsome tribute:

"In spite of the surprise which an unexpected attack always causes even the most intrepid hearts, the English resisted stoutly. There was a furious mêlée in which the English infantry wounded the greater part of the horses of our auxiliaries (the Gascons?) and put them out of action."

The count d'Armagnac reconnoitred the new position occupied by the English, and the more he looked at it the less he relished the idea of attacking it. Nor were his enemies in a happy position. Outnumbered and practically surrounded, and with their road to Harfleur firmly blocked, they must have felt like King Henry's troops on the eve of Agincourt. As on that occasion, negotiations were set on foot, but, as at Agincourt, nothing came of them. Dorset was anxious to secure some terms by which he would be allowed to continue his homeward march, but the terms offered by the Constable were too high. "Tell your master", declared the earl to the French emissary "that Englishmen do not surrender!"[1]

By this time darkness had fallen, and the bulk of the French army had withdrawn into Valmont to obtain food and rest. The opportunity that had thus arisen did not escape Dorset, and he set about making plans for escape. The details we do not know, but the result is clear: his whole remaining force managed under cover of darkness to creep silently away to the West, without apparent detection.[2] Marching probably through Fécamp and then turning south-west, the little army plodded on another seven miles (making 14 in all) and took cover at about dawn in the wood at Les Loges, four miles east of Etretat. Here they evidently laid up during the hours of daylight, no doubt sleeping most of the day. The French had completely lost track of their opponents. When daylight appeared and it was discovered that the enemy had vanished, Armagnac sent out a force under Marshal Louis de Loigny, his second-in-command, to discover their whereabouts and to bar their road to Harfleur but not to attack them till he himself could come

[1] The details of the negotiations are obscure, as they were in the case of Poitiers and Agincourt; no doubt they were kept as secret as possible.
[2] Wyllie says it was with the connivance of Armagnac but the general sense of the Chronicles does not support this.

up. He was taking no risks, "for he knew that they still could sting".

Darkness fell on the second day of this remarkable but little-known operation,[1] and still the English were "lost". Hope of seeing Harfleur again rose, as the column left the shelter of the wood and set its face for the sea-shore. At or near Etretat they reached the coast. It was Dorset's intention to march along the beach the whole of the distance to Harfleur, his reasoning being that by hugging the sea he had at least one secure flank, besides having thus the best chance of avoiding detection.

It was an arduous march, and the troops became footsore from the rough going over the shingle, for nearly 30 miles in all had to be covered. But on they marched, mile after mile, urged forward by the spur of desperation. After plodding along for 20 miles in this fashion, they rounded the Cap de la Heve just as dawn was breaking and the estuary of the River Seine hove into view. They had almost reached their goal and still they had not been discovered. Spirits rose accordingly; but, alas! one mile further on, when they had reached the foot of the cliffs of St. Andress, they saw on the summit on their left hand a body of French troops. They had been found after all. It was the mounted column of the Marshal de Loigny who, either by shrewd calculation, or from information received from inhabitants during the night, had posted his men in an almost ideal ambuscade. Gleefully the Frenchmen sprang off their horses, and plunged down the hill, regardless of their orders from Armagnac. The prey was too easy to be missed; it could not escape, it would be annihilated or be driven into the sea. It was veritably a case of "Twixt devil and deep sea". Or so it seemed.

But the English remnant, weary, footsore, taken unawares, and undeployed for battle, had still to be reckoned with. Like Sir Richard Grenville and his company "they still could sting".

The shouting Frenchmen, charging down the steep hill by a number of goat-tracks, necessarily lost all semblance of order.

---

[1] Most accounts make it appear that only one night was involved, but a study of the map shows this to be impossible.

Consequently they arrived at the bottom of the cliff piecemeal. The brief period that had elapsed since they had been spotted from the beach had allowed the English to form up in some sort of line. Probably orders were few; indeed Dorset himself cannot have been present with them, for owing to his wound he was being brought round in a boat. Perhaps young John Fastolf took charge; we do not know. But we know the upshot of a desperate and apparently one-sided fight. The French were utterly routed, the English making great play with their axes. Though the numbers killed and captured are in dispute, the Chroniclers, both French and English, are practically unanimous in declaring that the French were completely cut up. One source avers that they were only saved from practical annihilation by the timely arrival of Armagnac with the main body. But even if we had no other evidence this would be hard to believe, for the English had time and opportunity to strip the bodies of the dead French soldiers and coolly cast them into the sea, a procedure they would hardly have engaged in, instead of hurrying on to Harfleur, if the French main body had been in the neighbourhood. Moreover, if Armagnac did arrive in time why did he not attack, instead of waiting to be attacked.

That Armagnac did eventually arrive on the scene is however clear, and here comes the most remarkable episode of the engagement. For when the English, engaged in stripping the corpses, perceived a new enemy, these astonishing troops picked up their arms again and charged straight up the cliff against their new opponents, attacked them, and put them to rout. Armagnac's column fled from the field, making for Rouen. Now the road to Rouen took the fugitives past Harfleur. The garrison of this town were already on the *qui vive*, for the sound of the fighting at Chef de Caux had been wafted to them by the breeze blowing in from the sea. From the top of the walls and towers, or at least from the Church tower they would witness the fight on the cliff-top and the flight of the French across their front. The opportunity was too good to be lost. Mounting their horses in haste they sallied forth and engaged in a hot pursuit for some distance, taking many prisoners. Then they drew rein, and returned in triumph to Harfleur bringing their prisoners and spoils with them. Indeed the unique spectacle may well have been witnessed of the simultaneous entry into Harfleur of two victorious forces, each laden with the spoils of war; the one on horseback from the east, the other on foot from the west.

The deeper I study it the more am I impressed by the achievment of this devoted little band of English soldiers. For pluck, endurance and sheer doggedness, for coolness, discipline, and hitting power when cornered – in short, for all those military virtues that made the reputation of the English army in the Hundred Years War – and has kept it ever since – this epic of Valmont stands with scarcely a rival in the whole of the Hundred Years War.

*　　　*　　　*

BATTLE OF THE SEINE

Harfleur was saved from danger of attack by land, but its trials were not over – they were scarcely begun.

Henry V was trying to make of his Norman acquisition a base in France as firmly established as that of Calais. But he had overlooked the geographical factors. At Calais the English Channel is at its narrowest: at the Seine estuary it is four times as wide. While it was possible to maintain a constant command of the sea at the former this proved impossible at the latter. The French had been quick to sense the inherent weakness of the English position: if a local command of the sea could be obtained in the Seine estuary and maintained, a blockade could be established and Harfleur starved into submission.

Her own maritime resources were not sufficient for the purpose, so she had recourse to Navarre (as had Charles V) and also to Genoa. The Genoese sailors were then accounted the finest in Europe and their warships the most powerful: neither England or France had anything to compete with the Genoese carracks, which out-classed them in size and power. Moreover

France possessed a number of galleys–also emanating from the Mediterranean, which could of course manoeuvre against the wind, whereas the sailing ships of the English could not.

Thus by the Spring of 1416, while Henry V was concerned mainly with the visit of the Emperor Sigismund, France had accumulated a powerful fleet and had concentrated it in the Seine area. The blockade of Harfleur by sea as well as by land was now complete.

After the Valmont raid few supply ships could get through the blockade and the garrison soon began to feel the pinch. The rejoicings in England over the Valmont victory were rudely interrupted by an alarming letter from Dorset setting out the dangers of the situation and the dire need for supplies of all sorts, especially horses and guns. A convoy of supplies was collected at Southampton under the earl of Hungerford, but it does not appear that it was able to deliver its cargoes. At any rate the shortage and privations in Harfleur continued, and Dorset's pleas for help increased in intensity.

But the difficulty of running the blockade steadily increased, and it became apparent that the French had secured the command of the sea in the central sector of the Channel.

It was thus borne in upon the king that if Harfleur was to be saved a major effort would be required. He therefore gave instructions for a great fleet to be collected on the south coast, and he planned to lead it in person to the relief of his Norman possessions. He even got as far as Southampton with this object but the peace negotiations became so urgent that he was obliged to hand over the command to one of his brothers. He selected John, duke of Bedford, his second brother, no doubt as a "consolation prize" for having missed the glories of Agincourt.

Bedford assembled one portion of his fleet at Southampton, while the other collected at Winchelsea; and he fixed the rendezvous for them off Beachy Head.

It was not till the end of July that the two squadrons were ready for action, and Bedford went down to Southampton to take command. Meanwhile tension and excitement was steadily rising in England as fresh messages–possibly of an unduly alarmist nature–kept arriving from the stricken town. The relief operation was complicated by the fact that a portion of the French fleet was in the act of raiding the south-west between Portland and Portsmouth, and when Bedford was ready to set sail to his rendezvous he found his course blocked by enemy ships at Spithead.

Early in August the coast however became clear and Bedford after a stormy passage united his whole fleet at Beachy Head. The Earl of Hungerford was Admiral of the Winchelsea Squadron, and the grand total of the fleet probably exceeded 100, though a German resident in England at the time puts it as low as 70.

The French fleet may be assessed at 150 all told, but in addition to numbers it had, as we have seen, the superiority in big ships. Its Admiral was one Guillaume de Montenay.

By August 14, the fleet was fully assembled and moored off Beachy Head, and early that morning it weighed anchor, and with a fair wind set sail for France. A beacon announcing the fact was lit on Beachy Head, and by a chain of beacons the good news was conveyed to the king who sat awaiting it at Westminster. Immediately he hastened off to his confessor and besought him to pray for divine aid on the operation.

The wind was fair and the fleet made a remarkably rapid crossing and in the evening of that same day they dropped anchor in the mouth of the Seine estuary, the French fleet being further in-shore.

During the night, which was stormy, Bedford sent out rowing-boats to reconnoitre the French dispositions. They came back with the report that the enemy had anchored in mid-stream, and when morning dawned–the wind having abated–the French ships could be seen, drawn up in close order in the centre of the estuary, between Honfleur and Harfleur.

The duke of Bedford then held a war council in his flag-ship. The plan it decided on was a simple one–as all such plans should be. That plan was to drive straight ahead with sails full-set and engage the enemy at close quarters.

The normal procedure of an attacker of that period was to attempt to ram the enemy, ship for ship, or, failing that, to grapple; then to drive the hostile missile-throwers from the shrouds and bulwarks, and finally to board and engage in a hand-to-hand mêlée. Such had been the procedure in general at the battle of Sluys 65 years previously, and such was the procedure adopted now.

We have no specific information as to the dispositions of the French fleet: it seems to have been a dense formation, and it probably was drawn up in no clearly defined lines, as had been the case at Sluys. For though an attack had been foreseen for some weeks, when the English fleet actually hove in sight on the previous evening it had taken the French by surprise. Many of the personnel were on shore and they had to return in haste to their ships and put out into the Channel. Little time was available for it would be dangerous to attempt to manoeuvre in darkness in those constricted waters, and there was a heavy swell on that evening. We can therefore picture the French fleet as drawn up in a serried mass, with a minimum of water-space between each ship.

As the English fleet bore down on them, evidently running before the wind, there can have been little more order in their array than in the French, for Bedford's signal for the advance was a simultaneous one–the blowing of trumpets throughout the fleet, and the fastest sailors would–whether advertently or not–soon take the lead.

Thus as the leading ships got within range of the hostile fleet they must have drawn upon themselves the concentrated fire of their opponents–arrows and crossbow shafts from the nearest, cannon balls and ballista balls from those further off. Thus ere ever they had succeeded in ramming or grappling their opponents the English ships' crews suffered heavy casualties. This was particularly so among those that found themselves opposed by the huge Genoese carracks (probably eight in number) with their towering castle-like poops and prows, from which the defenders could rain down upon the unprotected decks of their attackers darts, stones and iron bolts as well as arrows.

Despite the losses thus caused, the English persevered in their efforts to grapple their opponents, and having grappled, to hold on grimly until their archers had mastered the missile throwers on the decks, in the shrouds and even in the fighting tops of the French, Spanish and Genoese ships.

In a contest of such a nature the details are necessarily swallowed up in the confusion and carnage, and it would be fruitless to attempt to unravel them. There is indeed a statement that a portion at least of the English fleet made a turning movement and attacked the enemy flank. This is hard to credit, for it is doubtful if a squadron not trained to manoeuvre and work together could in those days—whatever the wind conditions—have operated together in such confined waters with effect.

What however seems certain is that the fight lasted for about seven hours—an astonishingly long period under the circumstances, and we can picture the complement of one ship after another succeeding in boarding their "opposite number", and then, by sheer physical strength—in which the English at that period were pre-eminent—either killing their opponents or pushing them into the water, to be drowned. They even succeeded in boarding a number of the lofty carracks by one means or another, and no less than four of them were captured, while a fifth ran aground and was lost. On their side the English lost heavily, 20 of their smaller ships being sunk and their complements drowned.

The issue hung in the balance for a long time; what seems to have decided it was the capture of the four carracks, and the flight of the remainder. Their example was followed by the smaller ships which still remained afloat and navigable—in short the allied fleet disintegrated, dispersed and fled for the shelter of Honfleur harbour. Thus the English fleet was left master of the sea, and the passage to Harfleur was open. It was a victory almost as notable as that of Sluys. But the cost had, this time, been very high. It is useless to attempt to estimate the respective numbers of casualties. The French chroniclers not unnaturally placed the English losses higher than their own, which seems inherently unlikely, whilst on the other side the preposterously low figure of 100 killed given by the *Gesta* (so reliable in everything except in numbers), can be ignored. Amongst the wounded on the English side was the duke of Bedford himself.

When the last French ship had quit the scene of the action the English fleet did not immediately put into Harfleur. For one thing there would not have been room for the whole fleet in such a small harbour. For another the earl of Hungerford, who presumably assumed control on the wounding of Bedford, would be anxious to get the duke home for treatment as speedily as possible, and it would be dangerous to send a single un-escorted ship with its valuable cargo, across the Channel.[1] The wounded men were therefore collected into a portion of the fleet on the spot, and while they set sail for Southampton, taking their prizes with them (the wind presumably having conveniently veered) the remainder continued on its way, and sailed in triumph up the river Lézarde into the beleaguered town, amid the acclamations of its inhabitants.

The relief and rejoicings in England when the great news arrived, were scarcely less marked than those of Harfleur itself. The king, when he heard it, was near Hythe. He sprang to the saddle and galloped to Canterbury, where a solemn *Te Deum* was sung in the cathedral in the presence of the king and the Emperor Sigismund.

Finally, the Genoese carracks were taken over by the English navy, which thus emerged from the operation rather stronger in power than it had entered it.

[1] Also, if the wind was fair for the French making for Honfleur it was probably foul for the English sailing in the opposite direction.

APPENDIX

STRECCHE'S ACCOUNT OF VALMONT

This was the only pitched battle fought in the reign of Henry V after Agincourt. It therefore claims particular attention. The sources for it contain the usual crop of discrepancies and contradictions which have to be elucidated, and as a result of this elucidation my account of the battle differs in some important respects from that usually given. The reason is that I have based it mainly on the chronicle of John Strecche, which is ignored by most historians (though used by Ramsay and Wyllie). It is possible that very few historians of the battle have read it, for it has only been printed of recent years, and both Ramsay and Wyllie worked from the MS. But it would appear that neither of them placed much credence in it. I must therefore give the reasons why I have followed it as closely as I have.

John Strecche was a canon of Kenilworth in the reign of Henry V. It was the king's favourite abode during his brief visits to England during the war, and Strecche would come into contact with members of the royal household who had fought in the wars; thus he would pick up at first- or second-hand a number of stories of the war. As he wrote his chronicle not very long after the death of the king these stories would be fresh in his memory, though they may have been jumbled and distorted in the telling. The account that he gives of Valmont is so markedly different from the others and is so full of circumstantial detail of a kind that one would not expect him to invent, that it is obviously deserving of closer examination than it appears to have received. It hangs together as a story in a convincing way, and in the most important phase of the operations is implicitly and unexpectedly endorsed by a French participant in the battle, as we shall presently see.

As the chronicle has never been translated and as the original appears in a volume not easily come by (*Bulletin of the John Rylands Library, Manchester, Vol.* 16, 1932), I will give a resumé of my own rough translation of the salient passages (square brackets enclose my own comments).

At the outset Strecche gives the numbers of the English army as "1,080 men-at-arms and archers", which is more specific than the "1,000 horsemen" of the *Gesta*, which is the usually accepted figure. On the other hand he gives Armagnac 50,000 men; such absurd exaggerations of the French numbers disfigure his narrative and may have induced Ramsay and Wyllie to treat Strecche's narrative with excessive caution. Here then is a précis of his narrative.

"Before the battle opens Armagnac offers terms of surrender which Dorset declines with disdain. Armagnac then attacks. [The other sources place these palavers after, not before the opening action. Strecche might easily get the order of events wrong from his informants.] In the action that ensues the English lose 400 and the French 3,000. Then the English march towards Harfleur having lost their baggage and all their horses. They march "the whole day" very fatigued, and are followed to a flank by the French. [This is quite different from all the other accounts which place the march in the night, and represent the French as having lost track of them. Probably Strecche confused this march, which took them to Les Loges Wood, with the following one along the sea-shore.] At about vespers the French again attack and the fight goes on till dark. During the night Dorset holds a war council at which Sir Thomas Carew and a Gascon knight urge that in view of their state of fatigue and shortage of food and drink, having already marched a day and a night, they could, without affront to their honour hasten to their refuge (Harfleur). [This is important as showing that the retreat to Harfleur took two marches, not one—as usually stated. I had been driven to this conclusion from a study of the map before reading Strecche's account. I have however followed the other chroniclers in making the marches entirely by night, as I consider this course more in accordance with inherent military probability.] Dorset follows the advice of the two knights and the march is resumed. This time it takes place along the seashore [as in the other sources]. The French follow along the cliffs on the left flank and at dawn take up position on top of the cliffs at Chef de Caux, the modern St. Adresse. The French charge exultantly and carelessly down the steep slope but with unsteady steps, and thus are precipitated over the rocks into the marsh below. "The English, seeing them falling about in this way, attacked and killed them with their axes, stripped their armour off and cast their bodies into the sea. Directly after this they climbed up from the marsh against the army of the count [Armagnac], and fought with their enemy in such a way that the sound reached the inhabitants of Harfleur; and the count and his army were thus forced to turn bridle and quit the field speedily." [All this is utterly at variance with the usually accepted account of Juvenal des Ursins, "If Armagnac had not come up in time Longwy would have been badly mauled". We shall see presently what value to place on Juvenal's statement.] "Which seeing, they who were in the town of Harfleur, mounting their horses, sallied forth at once. And the said count with his troops fled with all their might, and the English captured and killed with the edge of the sword several thousands of them, and then they returned into the town with much booty, heated with the chase, and all refreshed themselves."

Now all this is so very different from the recognized French chroniclers that we turn to the two Frenchmen who took part in the operation and wrote about it afterwards. The first of them, Guillaume de Meuillon, has practically nothing to say; he evidently finds the whole affair distasteful, and passes on as quickly as possible to more pleasant topics. If Armagnac had indeed come up in the nick of time and saved the situation Meuillon might well be expected to mention the fact. The other, Jean Raoulet, is more explicit. He does not give details of the action, though he states that 22 English were killed and 200 taken in the first action (a likely enough figure, the majority probably being in the horse lines); of the action on the Chef de Caux he says, the English defeated the French, many of whom were killed or captured, and then comes the vital sentence, "But D'Armagnac escaped, and hanged many captains and men at Caudebec for running away". Thus the French soldier corroborates in essentials the story told to the English chronicler at the time: the French Constable of France, so far from saving the situation, fled with his army to Caudebec, when he vented his exasperation on his unfortunate officers.

SOURCES FOR VALMONT

There are three main sources for the whole operation, which it is difficult to differentiate in value. Elmham's *Gesta* is usually quoted (at least by English writers) for the respective numbers at the outset, but he exaggerates later on in his narrative. From the Burgundians comes the *Chronique de Normandie* by Sire Georges Chastelain (bound up with Benjamin Williams's edition of the *Gesta*, 1850, with an English translation). This seems to be unbiassed, but was written a good many years after the battle. The virtues of the chronicle of John Strecche have already been referred to. The fourth most useful source, though short, is the *Chronique de Jean Raoulet* (to be found at the end of J. Chartier's *Chronique de Charles VII* (Ed. Viviville). The monk of St. Denys does not seem as unbiassed as he appears in his account of Agincourt, and is full of excuses for the French (though he gives the all-important fact of the English repairing to Les Loges Wood). The same holds good for Pierre Cagny's *Chronique des ducs d'Alençon*, and Juvenal des Ursin's *History of Charles VI*. Little of material value is to be gleaned from the Burgundians Le Fèvre, Waurin and Monstrelet, and the same applies to the English chronicler Thomas Walsingham.

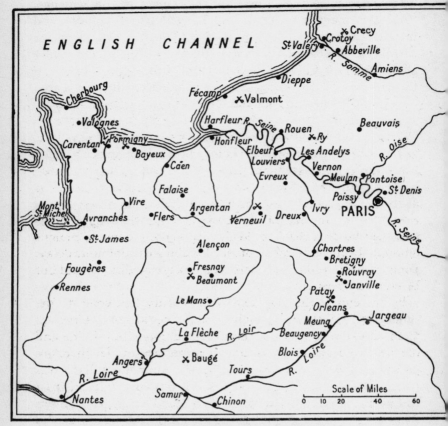

Sketch Map 3; NORTHERN FRANCE

CHAPTER VII

THE CONQUEST OF NORMANDY

WE return to England. Whilst peace negotiations were in train King Henry was steadily building up the military resources of the country with a view to a further campaign in France. This action gave occasion for the French to tax him with duplicity and for the English to praise his foresight. For however sincere he might have been in his desire for a peaceful attainment of his ends, he realized that it was better to negotiate from strength rather than from weakness, and further, that should the negotiations come to naught he would be in a position to pursue his aim without undue delay. For even in those days an overseas military expedition could not be created overnight.

By the end of the year 1416 King Henry had come to the conclusion, rightly or wrongly, that he could not achieve his main aim—the recovery of the old dominion of Aquitaine and the duchy of Normandy—without recourse to arms. He therefore pursued his warlike preparations apace. Every little detail was taken into account. The accumulated experience of past campaigns was made use of; nothing was overlooked that was within the bounds of human perspicacity. In particular, his own painful experiences of the difficulties of river-crossing were not forgotten: for example provision was made for pontoons made of leather stretched on wooden frames. He also built up a royal navy; indeed his reign marks the beginning of the continuous history of the Royal Navy. He realized that the command of the sea was a *sine qua non*.

By April 15, 1417, a number of ships and troops had assembled at Southampton, but there ensued a series of exasperating delays—an almost invariable feature of our medieval amphibious undertakings. One of the pre-essentials for a successful invasion was as we have seen, that the local command of the sea should be assured and maintained. Now, in spite of the great naval victory of Harfleur, Genoese carracks still abounded off the south coast, and in order to sweep a clear channel–to use a modern mine-sweeping term–the earl of Huntingdon was despatched with a fleet in the month of June to do so. On the 29th of the month, near the mouth of the Seine, he came across a strong Genoese fleet, which included nine great carracks and a numerous force of Genoese crossbowmen. There ensued a sea fight that followed the main lines of that of Harfleur. The English ships drove straight ahead into action at close quarters. In so doing they lost heavily at the expert hands of the crossbowmen; but not swerving from their course, they closed with their opponents, grappled and then boarded them. The upshot of a stiff battle lasting three hours was a complete victory for the English. No less than four of the carracks were captured and the rest of the Franco-Genoese fleet dispersed and fled.[1]

The coast was now clear for the invasion. But still there were unforeseen delays and it was not until the end of July that the expeditionary force set sail from Southampton. We know more about the strength and composition of this force than of any other that set out from England in medieval times, thanks to an extant roll sometimes, but wrongly, called the Agincourt Roll. This roll gives the names of 7,839 combatants, but it has two sets of omissions. In the first place, the royal retinues and several others have been omitted. These may amount to as much as 2,800, bringing the total to well over 10,000. Secondly the ancillary services–gunners, sappers, miners and smiths– are omitted, which would bring the grand total to possibly over 11,000.[2] Titus Livius gives a total of 16,400. If this figure is based on exact information it probably includes pages and grooms, all of whom would carry a weapon of personal defence.

[1] The French Chroniclers found it convenient when describing these naval defeats to speak of "the Genoese Fleet" not the Franco-Genoese Fleet.

[2] Professor Waugh deals with the matter in detail in a footnote on p. 52 of Wyllie's third volume, his calculations being based on the unpublished researches of Professor Newhall. He concludes that the total "cannot have reached 11,000". But it seems that he does not include the ancillary services.

By July 30 the whole army was aboard ship and ready to set out for the conquest of Normandy. But few of those on board were aware of their destination. As in the case of Edward III, the king had kept his destination a dead secret. In France the mystification was still greater; the fact that an invasion was imminent had been known for some time, but the wildest guesses were made as to the landing point. Efforts were made to defend most of the harbours along the Channel coast, with the inevitable result that the defence was scattered and weak everywhere. Harfleur was the favourite guess, and after that the Boulogne area.

But King Henry had his eyes fixed on the conquest of Lower Normandy first, *i.e.*, the country to the south of the river Seine, and he had had enough of operating on the wrong side of a river: the landing must thus be to the south of the Seine, not the north of it. Consequently his choice fell upon the mouth of the little river Touques, the site of the modern Trouville.

On July 30 the fleet set sail with great ceremony. The wind being fair, the great expedition made the crossing in two days, and the landing was made on August 1, 1417. Feeble opposition was put up by 500 horsemen, and they were speedily dispersed. The disembarkation was then carried out without incident, and a camp was pitched on the west bank of the river.

The first act of the king, after returning thanks to God, was to appoint his brother the duke of Clarence to be commander-in-chief of the army, and to make no less than 48 new knights. A few miles to the south lay the powerful castle of Bonneville, and the earl of Huntingdon (who seems to have been the king's "maid of all work") was despatched at once to capture it. This proved a simple matter, the garrison offered to surrender unless relieved by August 9. No relief coming, it duly surrendered on that day. So far so good. Two days later the earl of Salisbury began what was to be his long line of conquests by capturing the castle of Auvillers (the modern Deauville). The road was now open to advance east against Honfleur (10 miles), or south against Lisieux (20 miles) or west against Caen (30 miles). The strategical situation of the English army was not dissimilar to that confronting Field-Marshal Montgomery after making his successful landing in 1944. Landings had been made in each case (some 30 miles apart), and against opposition, and modest beach-heads secured. The enemy had in each case expected the landing to be further east, and he was not for the moment capable of holding his ground, still less of driving the invader into the sea. The problem was, should a rapid advance be attempted, or should the ground gained be first consolidated? The decision come to in each case was roughly the same—an attempt to capture Caen before the main weight of the enemy's counter-attack could be mounted.

But here the similarity ends; for whereas the Germans responded rapidly and with vigour to the threatened attack, the French reaction was slow and supine.

The English king, having decided upon making Caen his immediate objective, had to guard against possible interference with his plan. This might come from two quarters—from Honfleur or from Rouen. He had no wish to spend precious time—as he had at Harfleur—besieging Honfleur, which had strong defence. On the other hand the menace from it could not be ignored. He consequently despatched a holding force to prevent any sortie from that town till he should be established at Caen.[1]

But the main danger was to be expected from the direction of Rouen and Paris. A strong force, under the commander-in-chief himself was accordingly thrown out in that direction. Marching swiftly, Clarence captured Lisieux town (but not castle) on August 4, and pushed on to Bernay 10 miles east of it. There being no sign of hostile approach here, Clarence turned west, evidently by pre-arrangement, and, marching rapidly, appeared before the gates of Caen on August 14, just in time to prevent the suburbs being burnt in order to provide the defenders with a good "field of fire". He also managed to take

[1] The only authority for this is a French one, but it seems in accordance with inherent military probability, and I accept it.

the Abbaye aux Dames by surprise. This was a smart piece of work by Clarence and gave the invasion a propitious start.

On the previous day the king had set out with the main army from Touques. Marching *via* Dives and Trearn, he on August 18 joined forces with the duke of Clarence before Caen. The army was reunited and Henry set up his headquarters in the Abbaye aux Hommes which Clarence had also captured. (See Sketch Map 4.)

*   *   *

It may be wondered what the French armed forces were doing, and what steps their government was taking to repel the invader. The short answer is that poor France was still distracted by civil strife, due to the insensate rivalry and hostility between the two leading factions—the followers of Armagnac and of Burgundy. The shifty Burgundy, whom no man could trust, had taken advantage of the impending invasion by the English to conduct a campaign of his own against Paris. Two days before the English expedition sailed, a Burgundian force took Troyes, and directly the duke heard that the English had effected their landing he took the field himself in the north, and advanced towards Paris as far as Corbie.

Faced by this threat, the French government, so far from sending help to Caen which they believed impregnable, recalled the Dauphin to Paris from Rouen where he was in command of a small force. Thus the English had a clear field for their attempt on Caen. In this matter one is constrained to sympathize with the distracted French government in Paris, facing attack from three quarters at once.

*   *   *

The medieval town of Caen cannot be adequately pictured from a verbal description; recourse should be had to the map which appears on p. 477. Soldiers who fought in the town in 1944 might be surprised to hear that the lower town was then an island; this was formed by two branches of the river Orne, for the northern branch has long since dived underground. The castle and hill to the north comprised the old town and the new town is still called the Isle de St. Jean, from the church of that name in the centre of the town. The castle had, and has, a very strong site, two of its sides being precipitous. The castle was the child of William I, strengthened later by his son Henry I. The old town which abutted on to the castle was surrounded by a strong and lofty wall, with numerous towers. A single bridge spanned the river and connected it to the new town, which was also surrounded by a wall. The western wall did not take the course of the river, but cut the island in two, the portion outside the wall being known as La Prairie (as it still is).[1]

The two famous Abbeys, aux Hommes and aux Dames (both built by William I), are a few hundred yards outside the old town, to the west and east of it respectively. They were each easily converted into powerful forts, and from their lofty towers splendid observation of the interior of the town was possible. Great care had been lavished on the defences, and Caen was generally believed to be impregnable—at least until the English had shown that Harfleur had belied that reputation.

The English had brought a large number of great cannons with them, and the slowness of the advance of the main body had probably been in order to keep their artillery with the army. (Some of these cannons were however sent there by boat up the river Orne.)

Arrangements were now made for a methodical siege, on the same lines as that of Harfleur. Gun positions were con-structed, protective trenches dug, other and lighter guns were mounted on the roof and towers of the two abbeys, a collapsible bridge, constructed for the siege of Harfleur—stored there and brought on to Caen in sections—was thrown across the Orne in order to connect the besiegers on both sides of the river; mines were started, and all the paraphernalia of a medieval siege set up. The garrison, for their part, strengthened the walls, mounted light guns on them and prepared for desperate resistance.

[1] It is now a race-course, and unbuilt upon.

Henry decided to attack the new town first, and his plan was to make two breaches, one to the west for the main body, one to the east for the contingent of the duke of Clarence. For the main breach he sited a battery of heavy guns on the Prairie at a distance of 600 yards from the wall to be breached.[1] On the east the breaching guns were sited in the Abbaye aux Dames, at a shorter range. As soon as all the guns were in position the bombardment commenced. It was carried on without intermission until the morning of September 4, by which time practicable breaches had been made. A breach was also started in the south-west angle of the old town wall, but Henry desisted when he perceived that the church of St. Etienne just inside the angle was being damaged by the cannonade. He was ever a punctilious protector of churches.

On the morning of September 4, after hearing three masses, the king gave the signal by trumpet for a simultaneous assault at both breaches. The main assaulting party advanced in three lines, the leading men carrying fascines which they threw into the moat that encircled the wall, and then scrambled across over them. As they set foot on the breach, scaling ladders in hand, the defenders who by this time had manned the wall on each side of the breach, poured down upon the attackers crossbow-shafts, stones, darts, boiling water mixed with fat, lime to blind the eyes and some form of incendiary material, which proved very effective. Against this heroic and determined resistance the English could make no headway. But the king himself came up and with coolheadedness and spirit reorganized his troops and launched a fresh attack.

Meanwhile on the opposite side of the town the assault of Clarence's men was proceeding more favourably; the moat was filled and surmounted, the leading troops climbed the destroyed masonry and rubble of the wall, and one Harry Ingles—his name deserves perpetuation—reached the summit and jumped down into the town. His example was followed and a cheering

[1] Traces of the battery position can still be identified. See Appendix to this chapter.

mass of English soldiers forced their way forward, along-side the north wall, pushing on towards the sound of the fight that their comrades were engaged in at the main breach. It was the story of Badajos, enacted 400 years later. The French defenders of the breach found themselves attacked from front and rear. It was too much for them. They recoiled and scat-tered, and at last the main breach was won. The victorious assailants, bursting through the breach met their comrades inside, headed by the fiery duke of Clarence. King Henry was soon across the breach himself, and the two royal brothers met face to face. It was the greatest moment in the life of Clarence.

The attackers now swept through the whole of the new town, driving the enemy back street by street, and causing heavy casualties. In after years some French chroniclers accused the English of a vile massacre, and a modern English historian has deplored that Henry did not "forbid all massacre and pillage as soon as resistance had ceased".[1] But did Dr. Wyllie pause for a moment, before he wrote those words, to picture the scene, and consider how the king should set about restraining indi-vidual soldiers in the middle of the tumult and confusion that inevitably follows the storming of a town that has refused to surrender? By the custom of war in those days—and for a long time afterwards—when a town refused the call to surrender and it had to be breached no quarter was to be expected once the attackers had got inside it. All adult males were potential soldiers, civilians being indistinguishable from soldiers. The only distinctions that could be made were those of sex and age and the priesthood. Now Henry had strictly charged his troops to respect women, children and priests, also churches and their contents, and it is believed that his orders were very generally complied with. On the evidence, and in view of the circum-stances of the case, I can find nothing for which to condemn the English king. Indeed, when all resistance had clearly ceased he acted with marked leniency, doing all in his power to reconcile the inhabitants to the English rule. One of the first

[1] *Wyllie*, III, 61.

extant documents after the siege records the marriage of an English soldier to a French girl.

The town was now in English hands, but the castle remained to be taken. Henry went about it in an unexpected way. He neither assaulted it nor bombarded it but quietly sat down and

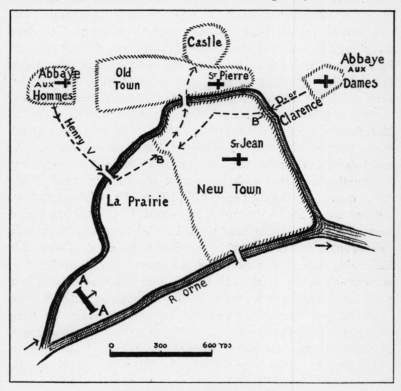

Sketch Map 4; THE SIEGE OF CAEN

A-A Main battery
B, B The breaches

suggested it should surrender. Five days later it agreed to do so, unless relieved by the 19th. No relief coming, it surrendered on the 20th on the most astonishingly easy terms. This surely shows that the English king was anxious to deal as leniently as possible with his opponents whom he hoped shortly to make his loyal subjects. Indeed he here, as always in the Duchy, acted in the most enlightened fashion.

*   *   *

Directly Caen had fallen the king despatched the duke of Gloucester to take Bayeux, which lay 20 miles to the west. The city offered no resistance, and the nearby towns and villages, including such well-known names as Tilly and Villers Bocage, followed suit, such was the power and prestige of the name of Henry V—augmented by exaggerated stories of the size of his army and the terror of his guns. Nor was the lesson of what might happen to a town that refused to surrender lost upon the Normans. The capital of Lower Normandy was in English hands and a firm and conveniently situated base had been secured for further operations. The first phase of the conquest of Normandy was completed according to plan.

*   *   *

What form should future operations take? Before examining this question it will be as well to review the political situation that had suddenly arisen. It was a rather tangled and difficult situation, for there was an unknown factor—the enigmatical duke of Burgundy. On the very day that Caen fell the duke captured Pontoise, only 20 miles north-west of Paris. Crossing the Seine he swept on to Chartres. It looked to Henry as if Paris might fall at any time, and if the English pushed on to Paris themselves it might have the effect of throwing the Armagnacs and Burgundians into each others arms, in common defence of the national capital.

Whether or not Henry had harbourd such an intention, he could not pursue it at the moment; moreover the conquest of Normandy was not yet accomplished. Should he then push east, south or west? Chartres was less than 20 miles from the border of Normandy; if Burgundy were to move in that direction and cross the border it might be awkward and difficult to remove him without open warfare, for he was theoretically an ally. An advance by the English army towards Chartres therefore seemed indicated.

Before putting this plan into effect the king sent out a force to the west of Bayeux to act as a sort of flank-guard in case of any danger developing from the direction of Brittany. This force he placed under the command of Gilbert Talbot, and he placed the trusty Umfraville in command at Caen during his own absence.

By October 1 all was ready for the resumption of the offensive and the army set out. It did not take the road from Caen to Falaise–so much trodden by English troops 500 years later– for Falaise was strongly fortified and would probably delay his army if attacked. Henry therefore by-passed it to the east and marched *via* Trun–the centre of the bottleneck of the "Falaise Pocket" of 1944.

There was no opposition all along the road, and Argentan[1] fell to him after a 40-mile march at the leisurely pace of 12 miles per day. Here the king halted and set up his headquarters, and from it he sent out detachments to make good the country to the east and south practically as far as the frontier of the Duchy. His object was to establish a line of fortified towns guarding this frontier against Burgundy or Armagnac, whichever should feel inclined to attack. Thus a line stretching from Verneuil in the north, southwards to Bellême and thence running west to Alençon was established. Alençon itself offered some slight resistance, but was in English hands well before the end of October.

All had gone well, and only Falaise remained to be taken for the king to be able to claim that he had the whole of southern Normandy in his hands. But Falaise would be a hard nut to crack, and the normal campaigning season was nearly at an end. Political problems had also loomed up in Brittany, Anjou and Maine. All three had become alarmed at the approach of the English army, and had called, though in vain, to Paris for

[1] The scene of Henry II's famous question, "Who will rid me of this turbulent priest?"

help. Receiving no response they took the prudent course of trying to come to terms with the invaders. To this Henry was not averse, and in a short space of time he had made a truce with them all. It was signed on November 16, and the coast was thus clear for the attack on Falaise. The season was, as I have said, late, but Edward III had shown his great-grandson that winter operations were quite feasible, and Henry V was ready to follow the example set him.

The castle and old town of Falaise – the birth-place of William the Conqueror – stands in a picturesque situation on a narrow outcrop of rock. Sharply below it on a little stream lies the lower town with the town washing-place immediately opposite the Castle. The town was surrounded by a wall and, with the castle, formed a strong military fortification. The English army encamped before it on December 1. There was now no need for haste, for the duke of Burgundy had fallen back to Troyes, and the Armagnacs remained quiescent. To storm the town would obviously be a costly operation. Time was no longer a consideration, but English lives were. The king therefore decided merely to blockade and bombard the town, trusting to hunger and cannon-balls to bring about its submission. He went further. Profiting by the experience before the walls of Harfleur, he took active steps to safeguard the health of his troops, and had huts constructed for them as winter quarters.

This plan proved completely successful: the town surrendered on January 2, 1418, and the castle a month later, after the attackers had managed by desperate efforts to make a breach 40 yards wide. This was due partly to the miners and partly to the very powerful artillery that the king brought against it. One cannon at least had the enormous calibre of 20 inches, as is proved by the fact that three cannon-balls of that dimension still lie inside the castle.

*   *   *

It was still winter, but there was to be no let-up in the operations. Three columns at least were sent out to conquer Western

Normandy. The duke of Gloucester commanded the biggest force, 3,000 strong. Its task was to reduce the Cotentin. In rapid succession the duke captured St. Lo, Carentan, Valognes, and the famous castle of St. Sauveur le Vicomte; but Cherbourg itself held him up for some months, being immensely strong.

In the centre, the earl of Huntingdon captured Coutances, Avranche and all the intervening country. Still further south Warwick accounted for the imposing castle of Domfront, but only after a lengthy siege.

In the spring of 1419 the duke of Clarence was sent in the opposite direction to clear up all the country as far as the line of the Seine below Rouen, a task that he accomplished with speed, and without much trouble.

By April practically the whole of Lower Normandy was in English hands and the second stage of the conquest was practically complete. There remained Upper Normandy, north of the Seine, and the capital itself, Rouen.

But before tackling this final task of conquest King Henry applied himself with his usual drive and thoroughness to the formidable task of reconciling his new subjects to English rule. The problem was an intricate one, and is not strictly relevant to this book. Suffice it to say that, pursuing an enlightened policy of appeasement, the king did all in his power by lenient and sympathetic treatment of the inhabitants to win them over, and he met with considerable, even surprising, success.

King Henry decided to lead the great campaign against Rouen in person. All through the month of May preparations went ahead, but when all was in train at the end of the month news came from Paris that altered the whole political situation. On the 29th an uprising against the hated Armagnac placed the city in the hands of the Burgundians. Here they took Armagnac prisoner and a few days later he was murdered by the mob. John the Fearless assumed the supreme power in the state, in close alliance with Queen Isabelle. What followed had been foreseen—and feared in the English camp: he immediately threw off the mask, allied himself with the men of Rouen and sent troops to assist them against the English on the line of the Seine, up to and including Rouen.

Thus when the English army approached Pont de L'Arche, their intended crossing place in the advance on Rouen, they found it strongly held, and the far bank lined with Burgundian troops.

The crossing of the broad and deep river Seine in the presence of the enemy in the month of June 1418 must be regarded as a major military operation. The difficulties were great. The bridge was defended by a walled town on the south side – the side of approach – and the northern end was defended by a square fort. The first endeavour of the English was to capture the town. A fortnight was spent in vain attempts to take it by assault, and a fresh plan had therefore to be devised. At Pont de L'Arche the river contains a string of narrow islands. These, though nearer to the south bank, have the effect of narrowing the 400-yard wide stream to under 200 yards. The army was well provided with boats and pontoons, thanks to the king's foresight. They would now serve a useful purpose. It was a simple task to throw a pontoon bridge from the south bank to the island 400 yards down-stream of the bridge. A large number of small rowing boats were then carried over this bridge by night. The north bank of the island was lined with archers and a forlorn hope of about 60 men under Sir John Cornwall, who had laid a bet with a French knight that he would cross the river that night, crept silently across the bridge on to the island in the early morning. Embarking in the boats and covered by the fire of archers on the island, his little party made the perilous crossing with complete success. The French defenders of the bank were taken by surprise, a landing was effected, the French were routed and a bridgehead was established.[1]

The next step was to capture the square fort guarding the

[1] Wyllie finds the statement "hard to believe" that the archers were able to cover the crossing, but I have satisfied myself from personal inspection that it was perfectly possible. Covering fire by longbowmen at a landing had been practised ever since the Battle of Cadsand in 1338. Though the average width of the river is hereabouts nearly 400 yards, the island is 230 yards wide and the main stream at this point only 170 yards.

northern end of the bridge. Some small guns, mounted on horses, a new development in artillery methods, assisted in the reduction of the fort. Meanwhile two pontoon bridges were thrown across the river one above and one below the town, and a strong force crossed by them to the northern side. Seeing that they were now effectually cut off, and overawed by Henry's vigorous measures, the town surrendered on July 20, 1418.

THE SIEGE OF ROUEN

Rouen, that still enchanting city of towers and spires, was in the fifteenth century one of the largest towns in France, with a population of perhaps 70,000. I measure its defensive wall as almost 6,000 yards.[1] The city had been strengthened and reinforced since the 1415 campaign, and it was easily the most formidably defended place the invaders had yet encountered. The English king had been wise to delay attempting its reduction till the ground was thoroughly prepared by the conquest of Lower Normandy, the amassing of siege stores and bridging material, the concentration of powerful forces and the blocking of the river above and below the city. The capture of Pont de L'Arche was the immediate "curtain raiser'. to the siege. Nine days after the fall of that town the English army approached the capital of Normandy, after it had been reconnoitred by the duke of Exeter who had brought out reinforcements from home.

The plan on p. 485 shows the lay-out of the city. The walls, which had recently been strengthened and provided with more than 60 towers, were pierced by six main gates; one was to the south on the bridge spanning the river, the remainder were sited at equal distances along the perimeter.[2] The walls were well manned with guns and the garrison had been worked up to a high state of morale by its intrepid commander Guy de Bouteille, ably seconded by the commander of the crossbowmen, Alain Blanchard.

[1] Wyllie gives the perimeter as 5 miles.
[2] The line of the walls is now marked by boulevards, with open circular spaces to mark the gateways.

The English army invested the town on all sides at the end of July and the king made his headquarters at the Chartreuse de Notre Dame de la Rose, opposite the Porte St. Hilaire and some 1,200 yards from it. (See Appendix.)

The tasks in front of the besiegers were multiple and difficult. Apart from the immense extent of the defensive line to be blockaded, the waterways above and below the town had to be effectively blocked, and also the way barred to a possible relieving army from Paris.

This brings the duke of Burgundy once more on to the stage. After the murder of Armagnac, duke John and the Queen Isabelle had been in uneasy control of Paris. At the same time they made an uncertain and vague rapprochement with the Armagnacs and they announced that they would go to the help of Rouen. This possibility had to be guarded against.

The final complication was that at the beginning of the siege the army was deficient of a large number of troops, and—still more serious—of siege ordnance. Cherbourg, Domfront and Avranches, though on their last legs, had not actually surrendered at the outset, and most of the siege ordnance was tied up at those places and Gloucester's 3,000 troops were absent. Thus it was out of the question to attempt a breach and a storm, at any rate for some time to come, and Henry decided not to attempt one, but to sit down and starve out the town.

To this end most elaborate measures were adopted, full of interest to the military engineer. Here they can only be summarized. First a line of circumvallation had to be constructed. To judge from a contemporary drawing, it consisted of a wooden palisade and a ditch, which ultimately extended all round the perimeter. Then there was the blocking of the waterways. At the mouth of the Seine an Anglo-Portuguese fleet was in control, but it could not approach the city as Caudebec—midway between the capital and Harfleur—was held by the French. As a first step therefore the earl of Warwick was despatched to deal with this town and to secure the passage for the English fleet. This he did and the Fleet sailed upstream to within sight of Rouen, but could get no further. Nothing daunted, the sailors beached a portion of their ships and dragged them with sails set over-land across the three miles of the great loop in the Seine to the south of the city. Launching them again they drove the French craft back into the city. The waterway was then effectually blocked just out of gun-shot of the town by stretching three great chains across the river, one at water level, one 18 inches below and the other 18 inches above it.

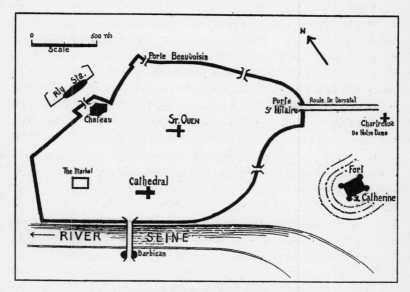

Sketch Map 5; THE SIEGE OF ROUEN

The next necessity was to ensure good communication between the troops situated to the north and to the south of the river. To ensure this an immense wooden bridge was constructed three miles above the town, great piles being driven into the river-bed and the roadway made wide enough to take all traffic.

The chief engineer, who must have been a man of no mean ability, deserves to be named. He was Sir Robert Babthorp, known as the king's controller.

A third preliminary step had to be taken before the city could be considered well and truly besieged. Immediately to the east of the city, and separated from it by some 300 yards of marsh,[1] rose the mountainous-looking hill of St. Catherine, some 400 feet high. On its summit was the fortified monastery of St. Catherine, and nearby the small fort of St. Michel. This hill was held as an outpost by the garrison, and was connected with the town by a subterranean passage.[2]

It was obviously necessary to reduce this outwork, from which the enemy could look right into the English lines, and shoot up the besiegers in the back. The king deputed this task to the earl of Salisbury. It proved a tough one.

Throughout the month of August, Salisbury pursued operations against this formidable obstruction, and at the end of the month he launched an assault. But the ascent was so steep and arduous that the attackers could progress but slowly, and when they reached the summit were repulsed with heavy loss. The garrison were however at the end of their tether and on September 2 the hill was in English possession.

There is no need to recount in detail the story of the dreary three months that followed. The lot of the besiegers was temporarily brightened in November by the receipt of a cargo of wine and beer, the gift of the citizens of London, who thoughtfully included 2,500 mugs. The garrison constantly made gallant but always fruitless sorties. Meanwhile the inhabitants were beginning to feel the pinch of hunger, and resorted to the drastic step of thrusting out of the gates 12,000 unwanted civilians—"bouches inutiles" they had been called when the English did the same thing 200 years before at the famous siege of Château Gaillard. Henry followed the example of the French king on that occasion, and refused to let them pass. He however tempered this severity by allowing his troops to pass to them a portion of their own bread, and at Christmas he provided them with a free meal.

[1] Wyllie states that it was 1 mile wide.
[2] The entrance to this tunnel can still be seen. No-one knows where its exit was, but there seems little reason to doubt that it did reach right into the town.

The inhabitants also made frequent attempts to get messages through to the duke of Burgundy. One such message was carried by an old priest who bluntly told the duke that unless he relieved the city the inhabitants would surrender it and go over to the English side. The duke replied that he would do what he could. What he actually did was to take the sacred Oriflamme from the abbey at St. Denys and march with it as far as Pontoise, under 20 miles, and there he halted. Rouen was not relieved.

On the last day of the year the heroic garrison, urged on by the inhabitants, sent a message that they desired to surrender and, after lengthy negotiations, this was carried out on January 20, 1419. On that morning, perhaps the most auspicious day in the life of the English king, Henry rode out through the convent gateway (it still exists) and entered the city by the Beauvoisin Gate. His mien was modest, and he would have no military triumph. He was entering, not as a conqueror, but as a king "returning to his own", for he and the whole army devoutly believed that it was his by right and that the Valois kings were usurpers. His first steps therefore took him to the cathedral, where he returned thanks to God for his blessings. He was well received by the populace, and immediately set about trying to bring food and amelioration to his new subjects, who were in an appalling state of misery.

*　　　*　　　*

The military effect of the fall of the great city was prodigious. The other towns and castles of northern Normandy almost tumbled over one another in their haste to surrender, even before being summoned. A mere list, with the date of the submission of each is impressive. Lillebourne (January 31); Vernon (February 3); Mantes (February 5); Dieppe (February 8); Gournay (February 9); Eu (February 15); Honfleur (February 25). By the end of the month practically the whole of Normandy was in English hands except five great castles, Mont St. Michel (which was never captured), Château Gaillard, La Roche-Guyon, Gisors and Ivry. These fell after sieges of varying length. Normandy had, after a lapse of 200 years once again become a dependency of the English crown.

APPENDIX

A NOTE ON THE SOURCES

In general the sources remain much as before. Strecche may be said to increase in importance, and Monstrelet to decline. On the French side a new source must from now on be noticed, *Reductio Normanniae*, by Robert Blondel, which may be found in Stevenson's *Expulsion of the English from Normandy*, though it must be treated with caution for Blondel was a virulent Anglophobe. Rymer's *Foedera* remains, as always important and reliable for details on organization and supply and suchlike matters. Interesting items of information also are to be found increasingly in *Collection generale des Documents Français qui se trouve en Angleterre*, by J. Delpit. For the siege of Caen, Walsingham is particularly important and full details of authorities and local items are found in *Siège et Prise de Caen*, by L. Puiseux, a local historian writing in 1858. His story of the siege is the most detailed of any. For the siege of Rouen there are practically no French accounts from the aspect of the garrison, but there is a uniquely valuable account of the siege as a whole from the pen of an English soldier who fought in the retinue of Sir Gilbert Umfraville. His name was John Page, and that is about all we know of him, except that he was the author of a rhymed poem *The Siege of Rouen*, written in English (published in *Historical Collections of a London Citizen*, in the Camden Series (1876)). All modern historians base their account of the siege on this poem; indeed contemporary chroniclers did so too, including even Elmham. The fullest modern history of the siege comes again from the pen of Puiseux, *Siège et Prise de Rouen* (1867), whose map of the town and defences is invaluable. It was whilst writing this history that M. Puiseux discovered the forgotten site of the Chartreuse de Notre Dame de la Rose, which was occupied as the headquarters of Henry V during the siege, and which forms the subject of the appendix (p. 491).

JOHN STRECCHE'S ACCOUNT OF PONT DE L'ARCHE

The account of John Strecche, though no doubt picked up at first- or second-hand from some participant, is of little serious military significance, but it helps to place flesh on the dry bones of the chroniclers' history, besides being entertaining, in the manner of Froissart, for its lively conversations. As, moreover, it has never been done out of Latin into English, it seems worth while giving here my very free translation of the picturesque portions.

To start with, Strecche calls the town Pont Large (Ponte Largo), as no doubt did most English soldiers.[1] The first episode related by Strecche is out of place, but no matter. It concerns the action of Gilbert Umfraville, after effecting the crossing of the river. He surrounded the gateway tower on the northern bank (which we will call the barbican though Strecche calls it the "Bulwark") with an entrenchment, and on it he raised his own standard. When the garrison saw this they sent an English-speaking Scot up the barbican tower, to palaver with the English. (This in itself is of interest as showing the extent to which the French language was becoming extinct in the English army.) The following dialogue then ensued:

The Scot (in a loud voice): "Who is there? Who is the lord of that bulwark? Is he a gentleman?

Umfraville: "Who are you that asks the question?"

The Scot: "If you are a friend of the earl of Kyme (Umfraville) tell him that that standard of his will be in our hands before the hour of vespers."

Umfraville: "So be it, in the name of the Father. And I call God to witness that if my standard is attacked I shall defend it."

Then, as the Scot had foretold, about the hour of vespers 5,000 (!) armed men made a sortie from the barbican gate,

---

[1] In the same manner as Marlborough's soldiers called Bois le Duc "Boiled Duck".

but Umfraville with his handful of men drove them back into the barbican, pursued them and shot at them through the bars of the portcullis which they had lowered just in time, killing and capturing many men.

*   *   *

The other incident took place at the opening of the siege of Pont de L'Arche. A large band of armed rustics had taken up position on the northern bank of the river where they set up a din, shouting and clamouring the whole night long, to such an extent that the repose of the English king and his troops was disturbed. Henry in his wrath sent his favourite "maid of all work" Sir John Cornwall, to parley with the Lord Graville, the governor of the town. Cornwall entered upon his mission with evident relish, and there ensued at the castle gate the following remarkable conversation.

Graville: "Who are you, and what do you want?"

Cornwall: "I am the envoy of the English king, who has sent me to your camp to order you to restrain and punish those rustics yonder who set up a hideous din all night long, thereby disturbing the rest of the king and his army. Moreover you yourselves, if you care for honour, should maintain order and discipline in your camp."

Graville: "We cannot control these louts, so go away and do not vex us."

Cornwall: "Now it is clear that these rustics dominate you, since you dare not punish them. Let *us* into your camp for a short while and we will teach these rustics how to behave."

Graville (mildly): "This, I hope, it shall never be in your power to do."

Cornwall: "You are the lord in the town and you have there a pretty wife, for whom I undertake to give 2,000 crowns for the adornment of her head if I fail in my undertaking that within 15 days[1] our king's army shall cross the river and overpower you

---

[1] Wyllie, for some reason, follows Monstrelet in saying *one* day, which seems militarily improbable.

and those rustics; and you on your side, if I succeed, you shall give me your best charger with best appointments."

Graville: "This I promise, by the oath of a soldier."

The crossing was duly carried out, the French put to flight, while the rustics disappeared into the woods, never to reappear. Graville also fled, and hid himself. But Umfraville found him, and taxed him as follows (speaking in French):

"Graville, Graville, here rides John de Cornwall. You see now how our king has succeeded in crossing the river and in subduing both you and those rustics. Graville, I say, keep your word. Give me your charger, as you have promised."

Then the lord Graville gave Cornwall the charger as he had promised.

THE HEADQUARTERS OF HENRY V AT THE SIEGE OF ROUEN

The headquarters of Henry V were in the Chartreuse, or convent, of Notre Dame de la Rose. A century ago all record and recollection of its site had vanished. In 1867 M. Puiseux, when writing his *Siège et Prise de Rouen* made investigations (which he recorded in a long footnote), and he tracked it down to a site in the Rue de la Petite Chartreuse. This site is now accepted. It is 1,200 yards east of the town walls. Leaving the city by the Porte (now Place) St. Hilaire, proceed along the route de Darnatal (along which encamped the unfortunate *bouches inutiles* during the siege) for 1,200 yards. Then turn to the right down the Rue de la Petite Chartreuse, and on turning the corner to the right, there is a stone wall, on the left of the road, with a gateway through it. The wall is the old convent boundary, and the gateway is apparently the original gateway through which Henry V rode to receive the surrender of Rouen. You are now on historic ground.

Inside the wall is a kitchen garden. Looking half-left you see a detached two-storey building. The upper storey is latticed and modern (used as a granary drying-room); the lower storey is part of the original convent. Its external measurement I make to be 42 feet by 26 feet, and I believe it may be the actual lodgings occupied by the king (though Dr. Wyllie thinks differently). It is now used as a barn or lumber room.

The convent was only 26 years old, having been founded by Archbishop William de l'Estrange in 1392; his only proviso being that the best lodging in the building must always be at his disposal when he wished to stay. After the siege the convent fell on evil days. In 1565 the Huguenots burned the church, and the army of Henri IV did further damage. In 1703 the monks abandoned it altogether for another site. It speedily fell into decay and by 1867 little remained other than the above-mentioned building.

No plaque or inscription marks the place, and it is neglected, ignored and, for all practical purposes, unknown. Yet the words of M. Puiseux are as true today as when they were written nearly 90 years ago: "Il porte l'empreinte des grands souvenirs, et l'archéologue s'arretera avec respect devant cette memorable relique du triomphe d'Angleterre et des dures epreuves que nos pères ont traversés."

CHAPTER VIII

THE TREATY OF TROYES AND THE BATTLE OF FRESNAY

EVEN while the siege of Rouen was in progress, King Henry was in tentative correspondence with count Bernard of Armagnac. This may occasion surprise, so a brief explanation is desirable.

The tangled and tortuous course of events in the diplomatic field at this period of the Hundred Years War is the despair of the historians. Fortunately it is not necessary for our purpose to enter into the matter in detail, but it may be summed up in the following way. Picture a triangular conference-table with one occupant on each side, each of whom is negotiating with his two neighbours simultaneously but separately, these negotiations being directed against the third party. There you have, with but slight exaggeration, the state of affairs at this time. Let us examine each party in turn.

King Henry of England disclosed his policy in a letter to one of his counsellors – a letter full of sound commonsense, for Henry, despite the fanatical side of his character, was a realist where military matters were concerned. The king of England was confident of being able to defeat any army ranged against him in the field, or to take any defended town that he chose. But such operations would entail time, money and casualties, all of which he could ill-afford. He had captured Normandy by force of arms, but if a similar process was to be necessary throughout France, the cost would prove too great. It was therefore essential to resort to diplomatic methods. Translated into plain terms, this meant that he must play off Burgundy against Armagnac, until the country, sighing for settled rule, would turn to him as the only one of the three capable of giving it.

The tergiversations of John, duke of Burgundy are more difficult to follow and explain. He undoubtedly hated the count of Armagnac like poison, and welcomed assistance from Henry in gaining the upper hand over his rival, but whenever he felt that Henry was becoming too powerful in France he drew back, blew cold over an English alliance, and even at times made some pretence of allying himself to Armagnac.

Count Bernard of Armagnac had a more straightforward policy: he hated Burgundy worse than poison, and would stick at nothing to thwart him—short of allowing the English to enter Paris.

Under these conditions, whenever the military situation fluctuated or seemed to, a fresh turn was given to the diplomatic exchanges. What we are here concerned with is, not the course of these fluctuations but their outcome. And the outcome came about in a totally unexpected way.

The chain of events that led up to this was as follows. Directly Rouen fell truces were made with Armagnac and Burgundy and this was followed up by a meeting at Meulan (on the Seine 25 miles below Paris), between the king of England and the queen of France (with Burgundy in attendance). Great precautions were taken against possible treachery, for Burgundy, as we have seen, was suspicious by nature—shifty men always are suspicious. The meeting place was fixed just to the west of the town (near the present railway station), and a ditch with palisaded bank was constructed all round it, to keep unwanted people outside, and to separate the English from the French troops.[1]

The conference lasted from May 29 to June 30, but was abortive. One important event, however, took place. Queen Isabelle brought with her the princess Catherine, to whom the king was to be affianced. Henry kissed her and immediately fell in love with her.

The duke of Burgundy, who had bent the knee to the king of England at Meulan, wasted no time in crossing to the other

---

[1] Part of this bank is still visible.

camp. Eleven days after the end of the conference he did obeissance to the Dauphin of France, in an endeavour to form an alliance against the English. For the moment this conference also was abortive.

The next step in the impending drama came from the English side. Henry, realizing full well the treacherous intent of duke John, broke off the truce the day after the conference was broken off, and struck swiftly and hard. The strongly defended town of Pontoise (which as its name indicates), bridges the river Oise, was distant only 11 miles from Meulan and 20 miles from Mantes, the nearest English garrison. A force was despatched by night to capture this town by a *coup de main*. The storming party, carrying scaling ladders, under the Captal de Buch, approached from the west, while a supporting party under the earl of Huntingdon made a wide circuit to south-east and approached it from the far side. The intention was that the arrival of the two columns should coincide, and that the stormers after effecting an entry should make a dash through the town to the other side and open the gate for Huntingdon's column. The first part worked well; the garrison were taken by surprise and the Captal's party entered, and according to programme made straight for the east gate. But the other column was nowhere to be seen. Meanwhile the whole garrison had been aroused, and it converged on the Captal's slender force. Things began to look serious, when suddenly Huntingdon's column (delayed by losing its way in the dark) arrived just in time to save the situation. Pontoise, for the first time in the Agincourt war (but by no means the last time) fell to an English attack and with it vast stores of every military kind. It was a shrewd, timely, and heavy blow, and it had all and more than all the effect that Henry had looked for. In the first place the duke of Burgundy panicked and hurriedly withdrew the king, Charles, to Troyes. This was just as well, for two days later the duke of Clarence appeared with a column at St. Denys, and on September 9 he was at the gates of Paris. In the second place it produced an effect quite unlooked for and undesired by the English king: it threw Burgundy and Armagnac into each others arms. They resolved to unite against the common enemy, and a meeting for this purpose was arranged to take place at Montereau, a town on the Seine, 20 miles above Paris. Burgundy, suspicious as ever, hesitated for three weeks and only consented to turn up after the most elaborate safeguards against treachery had been made. He had heard rumours of intended treachery, and this time they were not unfounded.

On September 10, 1419, the fateful meeting took place between the Dauphin and the duke of Burgundy. It was on the middle of the bridge over the river Yonne just above its confluence with the Seine. Precise details of what happened are at variance but what is perfectly clear is that Burgundy was brutally struck down and killed while engaged with the Dauphin (who however was not an accomplice). His followers were dispersed, and next day his body was taken to the town church and there buried.[1] The blow on the bridge of Montereau threw the Burgundians into the arms of Henry V: it did for Henry what he could never have done for himself unaided; it secured for his line the crown of France.

The immediate effect of the murder was that the Burgundians and Queen Isabelle both appealed to the English for help against the Armagnacs – the Burgundians in their desire for vengeance and the Queen because she desired to see on the throne of France her daughter Catherine whom she loved, rather than her son Charles, whom she did not love. (In the upshot, the reverse of her desires took place.)

King Henry could demand almost any terms he pleased, and his appellants had a pretty good idea what form they would take. The negotiations, however, were protracted, and it was not till the following spring that a settlement was reached. On April 9, 1420, the "Preliminary Articles" were signed. These

[1] The bridge was destroyed in the war of 1939–45. It spanned the Yonne, not (as Ramsay) the Seine. The church is only 100 yards from the bridge. The duke's body was removed to Dijon two years later, and no visible memorial of him is now in the church.

laid it down that on the death of King Charles VI the crown of England and France should be united in one person, that person being King Henry or his successor. But France was to retain its own laws and government under the king – a situation similar to that which obtained in the United Kingdom between 1603 and the Act of Union. Until the death of Charles VI, Henry Plantagenet should act as regent of France.

Though at the first glance it would appear that Henry had secured all his aims, there were two drawbacks. The first was that, according to the treaty, Normandy would come under the Paris Government (and the same applied to Aquitaine) instead of being under English control. This proviso however seems to have been ignored by both parties, as if by mutual consent. The second drawback was that Henry contracted to continue war against the territories still held by "the so-called Dauphin". But Henry yearned for peace, as we shall presently see.

On May 8, 1420, King Henry set out from Pontoise with a considerable army for Troyes, for the sealing of the treaty,[1] and to obtain a bride. He did not enter the French capital, but passed within sight of its walls, which were crowded with wondering inhabitants. Next day that still remarkable walled town of Provins was reached. On May 20 he entered the city of Troyes, escorted by the young duke of Burgundy, afterwards to be known as Philip the Good.

The meeting of the kings of England and France was ceremonious, but short.

Then, after kneeling dutifully before the Queen, Henry V kissed her daughter; after which they conversed amicably for some time. He then took his departure, recrossed the river to his hostel – and went to bed a happy man. But did he sleep that night? It seems at least doubtful, for the morrow, if all went well, was to see the crown put on his life's labours – in at least a figurative sense.

---

[1] Sometimes called, "the New Peace" to distinguish it from the Treaty of Bretigny which was "the Great Peace".

All *did* go well. The day May 21, 1420, opened with a joint meeting of the councils of the two potentates, at which the treaty was gone through and a few unimportant additions made.

The cathedral was selected as the place for the ceremony of sealing the treaty, in order to give it the greatest possible sanctity. Charles VI was not present, the Queen representing him. Both she and the king of England swore to the treaty, as also did a number of French notables.

Henry was of course delighted at the course events had taken, and he wrote that very day to his brother the regent in England declaring that it inaugurated "perpetual peace" between the two kingdoms.[1] When the news reached Paris "all hands were upraised to Heaven in transports of joy". And on June 14, there was a solemn procession to St. Paul's Cathedral in celebration of the happy event.[2]

But the signing and sealing of the treaty did not close the proceedings of that historic day. Later in the day the Cathedral witnessed the official betrothal of King Henry and the Princess Catherine. Twelve days later the wedding was duly solemnized in the church of St. Jean[3] with magnificent show. The bridal coach was drawn by eight snow-white English horses, the gift of the bridegroom, which must have been brought specially from England for the purpose. The marriage ceremony was performed in the French fashion by the Archbishop of Sens. "The day ended with the wine-cup and the blessing of the bed."

THE BATTLE OF FRESNAY

While the negotiations consummated at Troyes were proceeding, warfare of a rather sporadic nature was proceeding on the confines of Normandy. The last remaining castles in the Duchy were reduced one by one – Gisors, Dreux, Ivry. Last of all – appropriately – the famous Château Gaillard, the "Child of

---

[1] Edward III had expressed a like belief on the signing of the Treaty of Bretigny.
[2] As Professor Jacob points out, the association proposed by Mr. Winston Churchill in 1940 was a closer one than that enacted by the Treaty of Troyes.
[3] Only the nave of the original church survives.

one year" of Cœur de Lion.[1] Nearly all the fighting took the form of reduction or relief of castles and towns. Occasionally there would be a counter-effort by the French, which was in all cases brought to naught. The only real battle in the open field took place during the successful campaign of the earl of Salisbury (king's lieutenant in Lower Normandy) in the spring of 1420. The territory of Maine between Alençon and Le Mans had been temporarily overrun by the English in 1417, but not retained. The earl—"le redoubtable Comte de Salisbury" as a French historian calls him—now undertook the permanent conquest of this region. Advancing south from Alençon with an army of unknown strength he captured in succession, Ballon, Beaumont-le-Vicomte, and Montfort-le-Retrou.[2] He then laid siege to Fresnay-le-Vicomte.

Meanwhile, a large force was being assembled at Le Mans, a large proportion of it being a Scottish contingent that had recently landed in the country. This contingent was 6,000 strong, nearly half the total of English troops in the whole of Normandy at that time. On March 3, 1420, this army, under the command of Rieux, marshal of France, set out from Le Mans to relieve Fresnay, which lay 17 miles to the north. Salisbury evidently got wind of this intention and anticipated it. Without giving up the siege, he detached a force under the earl of Huntingdon and the earl marshal to deal with it. Huntingdon marched south, and the two armies met a short way to the south of Fresnay. Except for the fact that the English laid an ambush for the enemy on the road to Le Mans we have no details of the fight that ensued, nor reliable data as to numbers. The account in the most important source[3] gives the French 15,000, an obviously exaggerated figure, but even if we reduce it five-fold the numbers remaining will still give the contest that ensued the dignity of a battle—the battle of Fresnay. The same

[1] Its shell, mercifully preserved during the war of 1939–45, still stands grim and menacing over the river Seine.

[2] The ruined castles at these places still exist, all on naturally strong sites.

[3] *MS. Bodl. Digby No. 201*, as quoted by Francisque Michel in *Les Ecossais en France*, I. 118 N.

author puts the English at 3,500. Whatever we may make of this, it seems clear that the English were heavily outnumbered by the Franco-Scottish army. The latter seems to have been so confident of victory that the Scots adopted the extraordinary proceeding of taking with them their treasury containing the money for the payment of the troops during the campaign.

Whatever the respective numbers, and whatever the details of the fighting, all sources are in agreement that the result was a complete victory for the English.[1] According to the Bodleian writer, the French lost 3,000 in killed and the captures included their Marshal Rieux, six Scottish knights, the standard of Sir William Douglas (the Scottish commander,) 500 men-at-arms and 12,000 crowns in the Scottish treasury, and, indeed, everything in the allied camp. The Bodleian writer concludes: "And of the English only three were killed and no more, praised be God."

After the battle and the fall of Fresnay,[2] Salisbury rounded off his successful campaign by advancing up to Le Mans, and establishing the boundary there, though he does not appear to have occupied the actual town.

APPENDIX

THE SITE OF THE BATTLE OF FRESNAY

The *Vita* asserts vaguely that the battle took place "near Le Mans". There are difficulties about accepting this statement if we are also to accept the statement of the same authority, (which we may), that the English formed an ambush for the enemy. Le Mans is 20 miles from Fresnay. Salisbury could hardly have despatched Huntingdon's force to meet the enemy until he had certain information of their approach. However slowly they advanced, Huntingdon could therefore hardly have set out till the allies were within 10 miles of Fresnay. How then could he have laid an ambush for them "near Le Mans"?

---

[1] *Gloriosum triumphum* is how the *Vita* describes it.
[2] Situated on a rocky promontory overlooking the river Sarthe. If Salisbury stormed it, it must have been from the town side: the rock is unscalable.

Even if that were possible would an experienced commander such as Salisbury was, have detached a large portion of his small army to such a distance, and still maintained the siege of Fresnay? Moreover, the country near Le Mans does not lend itself to ambushes, which imply concealment on a pass or route by which the enemy is almost bound to come and from which he cannot easily diverge or deploy. Now the valley of the Sarthe to the immediate north of Le Mans is wide and flat, and the only feasible place for an ambush on the road to Fresnay is at the outskirts of Beaumont, 15 miles north of Le Mans. But Beaumont was already in English hands so the allies, whose objective was the relief of Fresnay would have avoided Beaumont. In short, the only place on the direct road from Le Mans to Fresnay at which I can envisage an ambush is at or near St. Christophe, four miles south of Fresnay. This is a likely distance from the main English army at which to make a stand against the enemy, moreover, the village stands upon a steep hill. The road between it and Fresnay runs through various cuttings all of which might form a possible site for an ambush, but I must admit that the present road has a modern appearance, as it winds down the hill. There is however, a direct track through the woods which I have not reconnoitred but which is likely to provide the required defiles for an ambush. These are my reasons for siting the battle about three miles from Fresnay, and naming the battle after that town. The battle deserves a name.

CHAPTER IX

BAUGÉ

FROM the moment the treaty of Troyes was signed, the long war between England and France which had continued intermittently since 1369 was technically over. Henceforth the armies of the two kingdoms were to fight under the banner of the regent of France against the French rebels of King Charles, (now called the Dauphinists). King Henry the regent, was bound by the Treaty to carry on war against these "rebels". That was the theory: in practice the warfare that ensued is treated by historians as a continuation of the Hundred Years War between England and France. As such we must consider it here, for though it was for some years to be waged nominally in the name of the king of France, all men knew that it was in reality a war of Englishmen, with some French allies, against other Frenchmen. Their nominal leader, the Dauphin, now came to be known contemptuously as "the king of Bourges", for it was at Bourges in central France that Charles the Dauphin set up his headquarters, and from Bourges he waged war against his own father. He was the dispossessed son.

King Henry allowed but one day for his honeymoon, and then set out for the siege of Sens, situated on the Seine, 40 miles to the west of Troyes. Thither Henry led his army, accompanied by the French king and the duke of Burgundy and both Courts. But the garrison had no heart for resistance and after a six-day siege it surrendered. The combined armies then turned their attention to Montereau, of notorious fame. The young duke of Burgundy was naturally spoiling for revenge, and he had not long to wait for it. The town was taken by storm on June 23, and the castle surrendered on July 1. Duke Philip entered the parish church, had the coffin containing the body of his murdered father opened, placed the remains in a fresh coffin, and had them sent for burial to the family vault at Dijon.

The next place for reduction was Melun, a powerfully defended town also on the Seine, 30 miles south-east of Paris. This
was a very different proposition. It was well defended, not only
by fortifications but by a resolute and enterprising commander,
the sire of Brabazan. The town was in three portions, the centre
being on an island with suburbs to the east and west. All three
portions were defended by walls and where necessary by a ditch.
The main English camp was on the west side, and the Burgundian camp on the east. Operations were started simultaneously
on both sides, but Henry soon perceived that it would be a
lengthy process and set about making systematic preparations,
such as his great-grandfather had done at the siege of Calais.
Lines of circumvallation were constructed on both sides of the
river, guns were placed in suitable sites and protected against
hostile fire.

The siege opened on July 9, and as it dragged on into the
autumn the zeal of some of the Burgundian leaders, (but not the
duke) began to weaken, and relations between the two camps
to deteriorate. But the king set his face resolutely against resort-
ing to a storm. Time was on his side; he could ill afford heavy
casualties, for the English army, (despite a large reinforcement
brought out by the duke of Bedford) was pitiably weak. Hunger
would do the work cheaper than missiles. As the weeks sped by
an unexpected reinforcement arrived in the allied camp. It
was a great cannon,[1] the gift of the citizens of London, who had
it constructed and sent out at their own expense. They named
it "The London", and it is claimed that it did great execution
and caused great consternation in the garrison.

But when November came round the garrison was in any
case at the end of its tether, and on the 17th of the month an
emissary came out to beg for terms. He approached Sir John
Cornwall, who refused to receive him till he had gone back and
trimmed his beard. This little contretemps did not unduly delay
the negotiations, and on the very next day capitulation terms

---

[1] *Maximum falaricam*, according to *Strecche* (op. cit., p. 183), but evidently a
cannon is indicated.

were agreed. A few days later the two kings with their retinues made a state entry into Paris amid the tumultuous greetings of its hard-tried inhabitants.

English garrisons had already been posted, in agreement with the Burgundians, at the Louvre, (where Henry took up his residence), the Bastille, and the Bois de Vincennes.

The king spent a strenuous month in Paris as regent of France, re-organizing the government. At the end of December Henry departed for Rouen, leaving his brother Clarence as his representative in Paris. On New Year's Eve he and his queen entered the capital of Normandy, and a month later they arrived in England, to receive from the London crowd as enthusiastic a welcome as on their return from the triumph of Agincourt.

When Henry V left France the military situation appeared satisfactory. The Dauphinists were quiescent, and the Anglo-Burgundian sway in northern France appeared to be unquestioned. But it was a deceptive calm. The duke of Burgundy had also left Paris for his duchy, and the simultaneous departure from the centre of the king and duke evidently encouraged the Dauphinists, who were by now recovering from the shock of the treaty of Troyes. They had bargained with the regent of Scotland for help, and ships were collected in France and Spain and sent north to transport the Scottish reinforcements promised by the regent. Moreover the Dauphinist leaders, sitting down and examining their map (if they had one) must have discovered that their strategical position offered great possibilities. This was due to the peculiar disposition of the Burgundian possessions. The old duchy of Burgundy, with the county of Burgundy to the east of it, covered between them all the territory from Savoy in the south-east to Auxerre in the north-west, with Dijon (160 miles south-east of Paris) as its capital. In addition to this, the duke had inherited the county of Artois (capital Arras) and Flanders to the north-east of it. Between these two blocks of Burgundian territory lay Champagne and Picardy. Champagne covered approximately the area between Troyes and the river Marne, while north of it lay Picardy. Between them, these two provinces embraced the lands of the Marne, Aisne and Oise, nearly all of which were in Dauphinist hands. Indeed their influence extended to within 30 miles of Paris, the strongly fortified town of Meaux being held by them. Finally, whilst holding practically all the land south of the Loire, except Gascony, they occupied stretches of the Seine and Yonne, to the south-east of Paris. Thus, not only were the Burgundian territories cut off from one another, but communication between Burgundy and Paris was precarious, while that between Paris and Flanders was in a similar situation.

Early in the New Year matters were worsened by the unexpected defection of Jacques d'Harcourt, sire of Tancarville, to the side of the Dauphin. Harcourt, descendant of the Harcourt who had proved so helpful to Edward III, was a bold and enterprising soldier, and he quickly overran the valley of the lower Somme from about Amiens to the sea. Thus, communications between the English and Flanders were virtually severed.

Meanwhile the duke of Clarence had not been idle. To begin with, he swept south with an army almost to Orleans, a strongly held Dauphinist city. In February, pursuant to instructions imparted to him by King Henry, he set out on a "punitive raid" in Maine and Anjou. What the precise object of this was it is not easy to say. Collecting an army of about 4,000 men at Bernay, midway between Rouen and Caen, and taking the earl of Salisbury as his second-in-command, he advanced south-west to Argentan, thence south to Alençon, and continued along the route taken by Salisbury 12 months before, towards Le Mans. Swerving to his left short of this town (a Dauphinist stronghold), his army crossed the river Huisne 14 miles east of that town, and thence marched 20 miles south-west to Luché, (seven miles east of La Flêche). Here he crossed the river Loir, (not to be mistaken for the Loire, which is 25 miles further south). From Luché he proceeded to Baugé, another 15 miles south-west, whence after a few days halt he marched 22 miles due west to the gates of Angers, the capital of Anjou. Up to this point the

English had encountered scarcely any opposition, but the gates of Angers were shut against them, and the grim and formidable-looking (as it still is) castle of King John did not invite attack. King Henry's orders did not apparently include the storming of defended towns, and to reduce Angers by starvation would have proved a lengthy operation. Clarence therefore fell back to the castle of Beaufort 15 miles east of Angers, and 10 miles south-west of Baugé.[1]

At Beaufort the duke halted his army and gave it a rest. What his next objective was is not clear to the historian and may not have been clear to Clarence. But in any case the matter was solved for him by the Dauphinists. When the news of the English incursion into Maine reached the Dauphin's head-quarters, he decided to employ against them the newly arrived Scottish army, strengthened by such local levies as were available. The army thus produced, slightly over 5,000 in number, assembled at Tours. The Scottish leaders were the Earls of Buchan and Wigtown, and the French were under the Constable de Lafayette. Exact dates of the movements of both sides in this campaign are missing, but it matters not for the understanding of the course of events.

The Allies evidently received information of the halt of the English in Baugé but instead of advancing direct to that place, they marched rather to the north of it, heading for La Flêche. This was presumably in order to place themselves in a position on the invader's line of retreat to Normandy. This shows that they envisaged a battle and considered themselves strong enough to challenge one.

On their arrival at the town of Lude, they may be presumed to have learnt of the new position of the English at Beaufort. Consequently they turned through a right angle to their left, and arrived at Baugé on the evening of Good Friday, March 21. They billeted most of their army in the village of Vieil Baugé, 2,000 yards south-west of the town.

[1] Four square towers of this ancient castle are visible on the left of the road thence to Baugé.

On the following day, Easter Eve, Buchan sent Lafayette to reconnoitre a position suitable for a battle between the two armies. The position was to be, not directly between the rival forces, but astride the road from Beaufort to Tours. This also was a sound move, for it would ensure that the position covered the line of retreat of the allies in case of defeat, whereas if they stood at Baugé they might be driven off this line into Maine and Normandy. Either Buchan or Lafayette was a good strategist.

Lafayette carried out his reconnaissance in the morning, and selected a position at La Lande Chasles, five miles south by east of Baugé.

Meanwhile the duke of Clarence was still halted in Beaufort, with foragers – mainly archers – dispersed over the country-side. One of these parties on approaching Baugé ran into a party of Scots and took some of them prisoners. It is likely that these foragers were under the command of Sir Gilbert Umfraville who sent back the prisoners to headquarters to be interrogated. Clarence was at dinner when they arrived and he carried out the questioning himself, still seated at table. Up till this moment, he had been totally unaware of the propinquity of the enemy. He expressed his annoyance at their appearance on this particular day, for his own troops were dispersed and the next day would be Easter Sunday when he was hardly prepared to fight. Yet he was anxious not to allow two days to elapse before offering battle in case the enemy should elude him. The duke of Clarence was a fiery soldier, imbued with the offensive spirit, a firm believer in its virtues and in his own ability to defeat the French. Moreover he was spoiling for a fight in the open, having missed Agincourt. Not a moment was to be lost; the enemy must not be allowed to give him the slip. Therefore in spite of the fact that his troops were dangerously dispersed and few if any archers (apart from his own body-guard) were immediately available he sprang up from the dinner table leaving his food unfinished, exclaiming, "Let us go against them. They are ours!"

The duke then sent off messengers to his captains to prepare their men-at-arms for battle, without waiting for the archers to come in. He would go on with his men-at-arms, leaving the earl of Salisbury to collect the remainder and bring them on as soon as possible. This course appeared unduly rash to the earl of Huntingdon, but he failed to dissuade Clarence from it.

The duke then set out with a force of men-at-arms numbering something between 1,000 and 1,500 to do battle with the allied army. The little cavalcade moved off at best speed, and in high heart. Sir Gilbert Umfraville and Sir John Grey were apparently out with the foragers when the force set out, and on hearing the news they "chipped in" to the column with only a few personal retainers, while it was on its way. When Umfraville heard what the duke's intentions were he also counselled prudence. But the duke would not hear of it. According to the rhymed chronicle of John Hardyng the following conversation took place. Umfraville reminded the duke that to-morrow was Easter Day, and that it would be better to keep church that day and fight on the Monday. Clarence, possibly misunderstanding Sir Gilbert's motives, replied hotly, "If thou art afraid go home and keep the church," and he reminded the knight that *he* had had the luck to fight at Agincourt, whereas Clarence had not. Umfraville expostulated that he had had no intention of deserting his master: "Nay, my Lord: my cousin Grey and myself have but ten men with us, yet you shall never say that we thus left you." And they rode on together conversing earnestly.[1]

The road approaches Baugé from the south and converges on that from La Lande Chasles. Now it so happened that just as the English were approaching the town, the sire of Layafette was also approaching it with his officers on the conclusion of his reconnaissance. The two parties thus were marching on approximately parallel roads. Presently they came in sight of one another, and Lafayette immediately galloped at full speed into the town shouting a warning to the troops as he entered. To reach it he had to cross the little river Couosnon (only nine feet

---

[1] Since both speakers were dead within an hour of the conversation it is hard to know how its purport could reach Hardyng. The only explanation must be that one of Umfraville's retinue riding close behind his master heard snatches of their converse.

wide at this point), and his warning cries just enabled the few nearby soldiers who were off-duty, to rush to the bridge and man it ere the pursuing English arrived. The English and Scots arrived simultaneously and there followed a hot fight for the possession of the bridge, of sufficiently long duration to enable the earl of Buchan to assemble his main force in or near Vieil Baugé. This village lies on a slight ridge running parallel to the river–and about 300 yards from it.

Though the river itself was but a poor obstacle to mounted men the valley was boggy, which made a crossing other than by the bridge difficult. It was however attempted by Clarence and some of his troops whilst the struggle for the bridge was proceeding. It seems that for the most part his men had to dismount and lead their horses across, and we may picture Clarence himself floundering across in full armour, closely followed by page leading his charger. On gaining the far bank the Scots on the bridge, finding their flank turned, retreated, and the mounted English burst across and pursued them in a northerly direction into the town. Some of the Scots shut themselves up in the parish church, where they were besieged by the exultant English, and confused fighting took place in the streets.

But this was not to the liking of Clarence. His tiny force was rapidly becoming disseminated and the main body of the enemy had yet to be encountered. He therefore halted the troops that still remained under his own hand, and tried to reorganize them on the gentle slope leading up to the Vieil Baugé ridge. He can by now have had with him only a few hundred men, and we can picture them halted, dismounted, resting their panting horses after the nine mile *chevauchée* followed by the exhausting passage across the marsh. Most of the leaders of the tiny band were with him–the earls of Huntingdon and Somerset, the Lord Roos, Sir Gilbert Umfraville, Sir John Grey and others.

Meanwhile events of moment were taking place "the other side the hill". Buchan, by great exertions had managed to collect a considerable proportion of his army, hidden by the village of Vieil Baugé, and he now led them forward over the ridge to join issue with the English. In number they were, to quote a French chronicler Fénin, "incomparably more numerous than the English,"[1] Dr. Waugh computes them as at least 5,000 strong. Moreover they had the advantage of the higher ground. Undeterred by these disadvantages the English duke instantly decided to take the offensive himself. Mounting his horse and ordering his men to follow, he charged straight up the hill into a sea of enemies. Resplendent with his banner flowing and wearing a helmet encircled with a ducal coronet of gold and jewels, he must have been a conspicuous figure, an obvious target for the hostile missiles. Indeed his onset was almost tantamount to suicide.

Be that as it may, the Franco-Scottish army also advanced and the clash must have taken place just below the ridge top, and along the road joining Baugé to Vieil Baugé.[2] The English were almost at once engulfed in the midst of the enemy and a confused and indescribable mêlée took place. One of the first to fall was the gallant Thomas, duke of Clarence. After quoting various circumstantial and detailed accounts by French and Scottish chroniclers, each claiming the honour of striking the mortal blow for their own countrymen, Dr. Waugh coldly concludes, "In short, Clarence died by an unknown hand".[3] It is not surprising that there should be competition in lying to substantiate the claim to have slain in battle the heir presumptive to the English Crown. Such a catastrophe had never previously been known, and it was only to occur once again in English history.

As the mêlée continued, fresh troops were continually being drawn into it as the tail of the strung-out English column came up, while fresh troops were also joining Buchan's forces.

Yet the issue was never in doubt; many of the English were borne down into the marsh by sheer weight of numbers, and either captured there or dispersed. Besides Clarence, Umfraville

[1] *Memoirs de Pierre de Fénin*, p. 154.
[2] A stone monument at this spot commemorates the battle.
[3] Wyllie and Waugh, III, p. 305, n.

and Lord Roos lost their lives, while the earls of Huntingdon and Somerset were both captured. The engagement—it is hardly correct to call it a battle[1]—cannot have lasted long. According to the most reliable account, that of Buchan and Wigtown to the Dauphin, written at midnight that night, it started at one hour before sunset and it was over by dusk.

While these exciting events were being enacted what was the earl of Salisbury doing? It will be remembered that he had received orders to collect the scattered archers and bring them on in the tracks of the duke as soon as he possibly could. This the experienced and faithful Salisbury proceeded to do. But there is an annoying absence of specific information about his movements. It is true that all the English and Burgundian sources are in substantial agreement, but there is not only complete absence of corroboration on the French and Scottish side but certain difficulties about accepting the English account. In fact, Waugh, who has delved more deeply into the whole affair of Baugé than anyone, and to whom I am greatly indebted for his thorough researches and marshalling of evidence, practically discards the accepted Anglo-Burgundian story. For the reasons why I part company with him in this matter see the Appendix to this chapter.

The English account states that the earl of Salisbury, bringing up the remainder of the army, reached the battlefield at dusk, attacked and drove back the allies who were in position on the field and retrieved the bodies of Clarence and other leaders, which were then being carried off in a cart. The body of Clarence was taken away and sent back to England for burial. The last part at least of this story is certainly correct; Clarence's body *was* sent to England.

I will now give my own reconstruction of the story, but it is necessarily conjectural. As soon as he had collected sufficient archers, the earl of Salisbury set out along the road taken by the duke. Whether he left orders for the dismounted archers, the varlets and the baggage train to follow on must remain an open

---

[1] Dr. Waugh calls it "a disorderly scuffle". Op. cit., III, p. 309.

question; fortunately it is immaterial. Marching at top speed the relieving force reached the scene of the fight before it was completely dark. All was quiet, but figures could be seen groping about on the battlefield. They were quickly ridden down and a cart that was hurrying from the field was overtaken and captured. Its grim contents were the dead bodies of the duke and some of his leading captains. In this dramatic form was the dismal intelligence conveyed to Salisbury that the little English force that had set out so joyously only a few hours before had been practically wiped out. It was clear that the allied army must have been of considerable size to effect this, and equally clear that nothing was to be gained now by seeking another encounter with it. It must have been with unspeakably heavy hearts that Salisbury and his archers retraced their steps to Beaufort, bearing with them the body of their beloved leader; for we are told that even many Dauphinists mourned his death. He was (according to St. Remy) esteemed for "his goodness and humility". His military reputation was high and the king seems to have placed more confidence in him than in any of his brothers.

Early next morning, being Easter Day, what remained of the English army begun its sad and hazardous retreat. The prospects of its ever seeing Normandy again cannot have appeared bright, for a superior and victorious army stood in the way. But Salisbury showed his metal, and skilfully evaded the enemy, taking the road to La Flêche instead of the one they had advanced by through Luché. The army managed to reach and to cross the Loir by an improvised bridge of carts and timber which the far-sighted earl had had collected during the march. They entered Le Mans by a *ruse de guerre*, broke down the bridge over the Sarthe behind them, and regained Normandy without ever seeing their opponents.

Indeed, the battle had ended rather tamely for the Franco-Scots. In the last few minutes of daylight the bulk of their army had set off in pursuit of the few fugitives towards the north, leaving the battlefield almost abandoned. Returning from the pursuit late that night the Scottish leaders took up their residence in Baugé town whence at midnight they indited a letter to the Dauphin reporting their victory and appealing to him to advance with them into Normandy. Some troops were next day posted at Ludé in the expectation that the English might try to cross the Loir at that point, but no other steps appear to have been taken to cut off the retreat of the enemy. If any steps were taken they were ineffectual. Dr. Waugh sums up this final phrase of the affair:

"In the sequel English generalship and morale appeared at their best, and the French saw many of the fruits of victory slip from their grasp."[1]

COMMENTS ON BAUGÉ

Baugé holds a place of its own in the military history of the Hundred Years War. It is a mistake to call it–as some English historians have–a skirmish. It was the direct opposite of a skirmish; rather it was a mêlée. The main clash can scarcely have lasted more than twenty minutes at most, and only a few hundred Englishmen were engaged. It was a formless, almost chaotic scrimmage, hardly worthy of the name of battle and there is nothing to be learnt from it either for that or for any other generation. But its results were out of all proportion to its size and nature. And this for two reasons. Easily first was the fact that the heir presumptive to the thrones of England and France had been killed. Such a disaster had never happened previously in recorded English history. Thomas, duke of Clarence, though he had missed Agincourt, had a high military reputation.[2] Forceful, ardent and quite fearless, he was an attractive and appealing character, a knight *sans peur et sans reproche*. Indeed his ardour and fearlessness had been his undoing.

The second reason for the importance of the battle was that it was the first time in the Hundred Years War that an English army had suffered such a defeat–and the fact that its victors were mainly Scots did not diminish the sensation, for French

[1] Op. cit., III, p. 298. [2] Gained originally in Gascony.

propaganda successfully belittled the part played by their allies.

As for the English side, no truer or more exact verdict could be passed than "defeated but not disgraced". When King Henry heard the dire news of the disaster at Baugé and the death of his favourite brother his countenance remained unmoved—and he set about preparing a new army. In the meantime the Dauphin had been stirred into action. The appeal from Buchan found him in Poitiers, and he announced his intention of invading Normandy. But his movements were dilatory, if not hesitant. Arrived in Tours, he remained there several days. During his visit he gave a dinner to the Scottish lords, and to it he invited the captured earls of Huntingdon and Somerset—a pleasing touch of chivalry on the part of a prince about whom little that is flattering has been written. He then made Buchan Constable of France—a tactful, but astonishing honour to a foreigner—and in his company advanced to Le Mans, which was recaptured without difficulty. Here for some unknown reason he halted and made it his headquarters.

Meanwhile the earl of Salisbury had been "scraping the barrel" (of the garrisons in Normandy), to reinforce his depleted army, adding to it a number of Norman knights and their retainers. Early in May, when the French laid siege to Alençon, he marched to its relief. The two armies drew up just outside the town facing one another, but neither would attack. The English were inferior in numbers, but the Dauphin did not relish the idea of a battle with the English in the open. He shortly afterwards raised the siege and marched off in an easterly direction, to besiege Chartres, which was garrisoned in the main by Burgundians.

As a riposte to this, Salisbury undertook the bold project of a raid into Anjou. There was a touch of studied defiance and challenge about this raid, for it set out to do exactly the same thing, and in the same way, as the ill-fated raid of Clarence less than two months before. Moreover it succeeded in its aim: the walls of Angers were again reached without much let or hindrance,and on the return journey large quantities of booty were captured. The earl wrote a jubilant letter about it to the king, and claimed that the English troops were never in better heart. Dr. Waugh rounds off this spring campaign in the following terms:

"In the whole Hundred Years War there was nothing more resolute, prudent and skilful than Salisbury's conduct of the affairs under his direction."[1]

It may be so, but there seems to me to be an absence of firm facts to warrant so unqualified a claim – especially as on the very next page he writes that, had the Dauphin invaded Normandy boldly, Salibury might have been destroyed and the war ended. On this showing, some at least of Salisbury's success was due to the mistakes of his opponent.

Whatever be the truth of this estimate, we can at least agree that, by putting a bold face upon it, Salisbury was able to "keep his end up" in Normandy till the arrival of his king with a fresh army, and to retrieve in a remarkable fashion a situation that looked almost desperate on the morrow of Baugé.

APPENDIX

THE SOURCES

There seems to be more discrepancies and more sheer hard lying on the part of the chroniclers regarding Baugé, than about almost any medieval battle that I know. There may be two reasons for this. In the first place, the chroniclers of four different nationalities or parties are concerned – English, French and Scottish, and Burgundian. Each of the first three would be biased in favour of his own country, and the Burgundians might be fairly neutral, thus making a fourth point of view.

In the second place, there was a natural emulation on the part of the Scots and French to claim the credit for the death of Clarence, and both parties compiled most circumstantial and positive, but mutually incompatible stories of this episode. As

[1] Op. cit., III, p. 315.

for the English, they were equally naturally at pains to emphasize the part played in the final stage of the battle by the arrival of Salisbury's troops. Dr. Waugh cites a long list of sources, but there are only three principal ones, the remainder contributing comparatively little of value. These three are *Vita et Gesta Henrici Quinti*, (cited as *Vita*) by the "Pseudo" Elmham, for the English side, *Liber Pluscardine* for the Scottish side and *Histoire Chronologique du Roy Charles VI*, by Gilles le Bouvier, (sometimes known as le Heraut Berry), on the French side. This valuable work is inaccessible to most people for it is hidden away in Godefroy's *Histoire de Charles VI*, a ghastly folio volume lacking a table of contents and with an almost useless index, published in 1658. To make matters still more confusing, it would appear from Dr. Waugh's method of citation that the references are to *L'Histoire de Charles VII* not *L'Histoire de Charles VI*. To these may be added *Chroniques d'Anjou et de Maine*, though it is not strictly a contemporary source, being written 100 years later, contains much useful material.

THE PART PLAYED BY THE EARL OF SALISBURY

In the body of this chapter I indicated that I could not accept the reconstruction of Dr. Waugh in this matter. In brief, the only statement that he utilizes in the English accounts is that the body of Clarence was recovered on the battlefield. This fact can hardly be disputed, for the army did bring the body back to Normandy with them, whence it was sent to England. But this explanation of the matter is that the episode of the recovery took place next morning. This thesis seems to me to raise more difficulties than are provided by the English account. In order to make it possible for an English force to perambulate the battlefield next day, he suggests that most of the Dauphinist troops were on the east side of Baugé looking for the English there. But could there be a more unlikely quarter for the English to be in? In the first moments of confusion and semi-darkness immediately after the battle was over – a period of relaxation after all battles – the episode described above was quite conceivable, but on the grounds of inherent military probability I cannot conceive it happening in broad daylight next day. Nor on the same grounds can I believe that Salisbury would have sent a flank-guard right up to Baugé, whilst trying to slip away unobserved. Such a flank-guard would necessarily approach the battlefield from the west, and thus would have to pass through Vieil Baugé, a place that would then be occupied by some of the enemy. The only possible direction from which they could have approached the field would be the south. Moreover, assuming that they did succeed in recovering the bodies, they would have to make a detour to the south in order to avoid being intercepted by the enemy. This would give the main army a long start, and how could they be expected to catch up a quickly marching army, encumbered as they would be with dead bodies? In short, this thesis sounds to me wildly improbable.

CHAPTER X

HENRY V'S LAST CAMPAIGN

DURING the months of April and May, 1421, King
Henry was busy raising a new army to take to France. It
was not a large army—900 men-at-arms, 3,300 archers,
but it was unusually well found in ancillary troops, sappers,
miners, pioneers, siege train, etc. The troops were indentured
for six months. The above facts show that the king did not anticipate a winter campaign, but was ready to undertake sieges.

By the beginning of June all was ready; leaving his pregnant
queen in England, Henry, at the stern call of duty, set sail for
France on 10th of the month. He and his army made a speedy
passage from Dover, arriving at Calais the same day. Since his
ultimate destination was Paris, some people have speculated as
to why he did not select the Southampton-Harfleur route, evidently overlooking the slow and uncertain nature of sea voyages
before the days of fore-and-aft rigging. By the Southampton
route more than half the journey would be by water; moreover
the distance from Southampton to Paris is 70 miles more than
by Dover. Furthermore, by clever use of the tides the sea crossing to Calais could usually be assured, while the chance of
interception by a hostile fleet was almost negligible. A landing
in France at the firmly established well-found base of Calais
would provide a firmer start for the campaign than would the
newly acquired base of Harfleur.

There was also a strategical reason for the Calais route, as
well as the logistical one set out above. It is unusual for medieval
commanders to give to posterity the reasons for their courses of
action, and we are usually reduced to deducing them from their
actions. In this case however the king himself gave the main
strategical reason for his selection of the Calais route. The situa-

tion in Picardy was bad: duke Philip had done little to suppress the Dauphinist leader Harcourt, and he probably appealed to the English king for help. At any rate he was very pleased at the prospect of receiving it. Henry had confidence in the power and ability of the earl of Salisbury to hold the enemy for the time being on the borders of Normandy, and he considered it the soundest strategy to start by making good the disturbed and disputed country that separated Paris from Calais. This he could best do by landing at Calais and joining forces with what ever army the Burgundians might provide.

*   *   *

At Calais, then, the English army landed. An advanced guard was sent forward to Paris at once, and the remainder marched straight to Montreuil, 25 miles south. In this pleasant town of historic memories the English king and Burgundian duke met and conferred together. There was ample need for a conference, for on the road Henry had learnt of the advance of the Dauphin to Chartres, which city was then being besieged by him. The earl of Salisbury was by that time far away on his Anjou raid. Should Chartres fall and the Dauphin advance on Paris in the absence of a field army ready to oppose him, there might well be a rising in Paris which the earl of Exeter might find impossible to quell. Anything might then happen. Clearly the presence of the English king with his steadying influence was required in the Isle de France, if only to raise the morale of the defenders. Henry and Philip rode south together from Montreuil discussing the new situation that had arisen. The Burgundian was amenable to the arguments of the Englishman, and agreed to take the field single-handed against Harcourt, thus allowing the English army to push on to the relief of Chartres. The two princes passed over or by the field of Crecy in the course of their ride, and Henry spent a pleasant day's boar-hunting in Crecy forest. At Abbeville the duke turned back to take command of his own army assembled at Arras, while the English army pushed on for the valley of the Seine. Between Vernon and

Pontoise they were quartered, whilst the king rode straight to Paris, to confer with Exeter and the French government and court.

Henry did not stay long in Paris, for the military situation had been transformed, almost overnight. The very sound of the name of the redoubtable English captain had achieved this. On the news of his landing and approach, the Dauphin, who had boasted loudly of his intention to do battle with the English king if he should get the chance, incontinently broke up the siege of Chartres and retreated in a southerly direction. The moment for an English counter-offensive had clearly come. Confidence in the army and the Paris government was restored, while the Dauphinists were correspondingly depressed. The question was, what form should this offensive take? On the eastern border of Normandy, 25 miles north of Chartres and 50 miles west of Paris, lay the town of Dreux, very strongly defended. It was the only considerable Dauphinist stronghold remaining west of the capital. Should the Dauphin be immediately pursued or should this stronghold first be reduced? Without more information as to relative strengths and dispositions it is hard to say, though on general strategical principles one would favour an immediate pursuit and engagement of the chief enemy in the field. The fact is, details of this last campaign of Henry V are distressingly and distractingly meagre, and without them, criticism is, or should be, stifled.[1]

Whether sound or not, Henry decided that his first objective should be the reduction of Dreux. This town, in any case, lay on the route to Chartres and the Loire, and if the siege was not prolonged the delay in the pursuit of the Dauphin might not be material. On July 8, Henry rejoined his army at Mantes, and next day, somewhat surprisingly, he was joined by the duke of Burgundy, with a considerable number of reinforcements at his back. He had come, very faithfully, to the help of his ally in the relief of Chartres. This being no longer necessary, Henry sent

[1] Wyllie, Ramsay, Kingsford and Newall have between them pretty well "scraped the barrel", thereby showing up the more the scantiness of its contents.

him back to deal with Harcourt, but he was much touched at the fidelity of young Philip.

On July 18 he laid siege to Dreux. This was a strongly situated town, but the strength of all defence lies ultimately in the will and spirit of the defenders. The garrison of Dreux, though nearly a thousand strong, were weak in spirit, and after three weeks of siege they asked for terms. On the 20th the English entered the town, and the advance was at once resumed.

Chartres was entered amid great rejoicings. The garrison, both English and Burgundians, had behaved admirably and received Henry's thanks.

On the approach of the English army, the Dauphin, who had temporarily set his headquarters at Vendôme, 12 miles north of Blois, fell back south of the river Loire and was now reported to be concentrating in the Beaugency area, ten miles upstream from Blois. Thither King Henry marched, his army having been reinforced by some Norman levies as well as by detachments from the English garrisons. We can but guess however, at its size, though it seems pretty safe to assume that it was well inferior to the Dauphinist army.

The little town of Beaugency does not belie its name. It is picturesquely poised on an eminence on the north bank of the Loire, with its rather grim castle donjon looking down on the many-arched bridge, which remains today much as it was five centuries ago. The English army arrived opposite the town on September 8, and immediately attacked it. The actual town was taken by assault, but the castle held out. The bridge, which was commanded by the castle, could with difficulty be used while the castle remained intact and as the Dauphinist army was not in sight on the far bank it was necessary to send a reconnoitring force by some other passage.

The river Loire, though wide, is shallow, and a ford was found downstream at St. Dye. By this ford, a force under the command of the earl of Suffolk crossed, and scoured the country-side for the enemy. Working their way downstream they reached the outskirts of Blois without obtaining news of the enemy. No one in the English camp knew where they had gone to – and no one knows today. They disappeared for the time being from the Loire, and from the pages of history.

And now an event that always haunted a medieval army occurred – the outbreak of an epidemic. What its exact nature was we do not know, but it is certain that it carried off a large number of the troops, and at the same time food began to run out. A move to a more salubrious and more fertile area was imperative. Should the army move upstream towards Orleans or downstream towards Tours? Whichever direction they took, it was unlikely that they would now bring the Dauphin to battle; he had shown his colours: evidently he had no intention of crossing swords with his formidable opponent. The probability is that he was well on the way to Chinon, 35 miles south-west of Tours. Henry decided that he must change his objective. He was now confronted with the same problem that had confronted Edward III 60 years before – how to bring to heel an opponent who declined to fight – for it takes two to make a battle. Here, for almost the first time, Henry parted company from his great-grandfather, who had broken the enemy's will by widespread devastation of his country. Henry was regent, and hoped shortly to be king of the land in which he was fighting; he had pledged himself to reduce the places held by the Dauphin, and he now returned to that objective. The obvious area in which to operate was that debatable region to the east and south-east of Paris in Brie and Champagne which, if held by the enemy, threatened to cut off the province of Burgundy from Paris and from Flanders. He therefore turned his face towards the north-east, seeking the lands watered by the rivers Yonne, Seine and Marne. On the way the army passed Orleans. Though some of the suburbs of this great city were captured, there could be no question of sitting down and besieging it with his small army, now racked with disease. The march was resumed, he himself marching north-east to Nemours, near Montereau, and no doubt he lodged in the still-existing castle there. Other troops marched east via Montargis to Villeneuve, an important town on the Yonne, which was immediately attacked. The Burgundians had tried in vain to take it in the previous February, but this time there was but little spirit in the garrison. Perhaps they recollected that the English king had never yet attacked a town that he had not captured, and they decided to anticipate the inevitable and come to terms at once. In a few days the whole valley of the Yonne as far south as Auxerre was cleared of the enemy, and all eyes were now turned upon the one remaining Dauphinist stronghold in those parts, the city of Meaux. Thither the army by diverse routes now directed its steps, the pestilence having apparently abated to a large extent. Descending the valley of the Yonne as far as Sens, the army split up into three divisions, moving on a broad front. One continued to hug the Yonne, treading in the footsteps of that other English army that had followed Edward III in his last campaign. The second struck further to the east, and crossed the Seine at Nogent. The third, still further east, crossed at Pont-sur-Seine, where Edward III's army had crossed in the opposite direction on its way to Burgundy. Thus both these English monarchs traversed much the same ground in their last campaigns. The three columns concentrated on Meaux, which was reached on October 6.

THE SIEGE OF MEAUX

The city of Meaux lies on the river Marne, 25 miles east of Paris. Ten miles on the Paris side, also situated on the Marne, is the town of Lagny. The importance of Meaux lay in the fact that it was the strongest defended post held by the Dauphinists in the region of Paris; from it the communications between the capital and both Burgundy and Flanders could be cut, and from its propinquity, it was a potential menace to the capital itself. It was also the centre for a pillaging band which terrorized the countryside, and led to urgent appeals being made to the English army for its destruction. Until it had fallen, Henry could not claim that he had in any sense carried out his contract to rid the land of Dauphinist dominance in the towns of northern France. There are indeed indications that after the capture of this last stronghold in the north Henry would regard his task as morally accomplished, and that he might then make peace with the Dauphin faction in the south. For in the course of the siege when matters were not going well he complained that he found himself short of men "in the point and conclusion of his labours".

The king had no misconceptions as to the immensity of the task that faced him. No quick and easy reduction of Meaux was to be looked for. In it as we have said, had collected the "scally-wags" of divers nations, English deserters, Scots, wild Irishmen, and the riff-raff of the French population that had ranged themselves under the banner of the Bastard of Vaurus, " a byeword for ferocious cruelty" as Ramsay calls him.[1] All these men had, metaphorically speaking, halters round their necks and they would sell their lives dearly.

Henry therefore made careful and methodical preparations before approaching the town. He made the rendezvous for his army at Lagny, where he had constructed "many wooden engines" according to Monstrelet. This is interesting as showing that nearly a century after the introduction of gunpowder artillery the old mechanical "engines of war" were still employed to supplement the cannons. These "wooden engines" were no doubt ballista, trebuchets and mangonels, throwing great stones, or even carcases of horses into the besieged town, together with "sows" or movable overhead cover for the attackers and possibly rams working at the foot of the walls of the town.

When all was ready, and not till then, he sent the earl of Exeter to make a sudden dash and thus capture the suburbs before the enemy could get wind of it and burn down their buildings. This was successful; Exeter having established himself in the suburbs on October 6, the remainder of the army followed in a few days.

The city of Meaux lay upon the northern apex of a hairpin bend of the river Marne, here about 70 yards wide, a deep, and

[1] Ramsay, op. cit., I, p. 297.

normally slow-flowing stream. A wall and moat surrounded the town, and it was well supplied with artillery. To the south of the river, and inside the bend, which thus protected it on three sides, lay the market, which also was surrounded with a wall while its southern side was protected by a canal, which converted it into an island. Thus, with the river as additional protection, the market was more strongly defended than the town itself.

The king divided his army (which was about 2,500 strong) into four divisions. His own was stationed to the north, his headquarters being St. Faro Abbey. To the east was the earl of March, and to the west the earl of Exeter. South of the river, facing the market, was the earl of Warwick.

It is interesting to note that the Bretons were at this time very divided in their loyalties, and that Arthur of Brittany and his troops assisted in the siege of Meaux, whilst his brother Richard supported the Dauphin.

As a preliminary to the siege, lines of circumvallation and contravallation (that is, facing inwards and outwards) were constructed. King Henry then turned his attention to the reduction of the town. When all his engines and cannons had been placed in position he commenced the systematic bombardment of the gates and walls. The amount of damage done was at first not considerable, or the garrison must have been particularly vigorous in their repair work, because when the month of December came round little impression appears to have been made on the defences. In that month there was prolonged rain and the Marne overflowed its banks, sweeping away the bridge of boats that Henry had constructed to maintain communication with Warwick's division on the south side of the river and forcing the English to evacuate their front trenches. Nearly all the boats were in the possession of the garrison, and Warwick's division was for some days dangerously isolated. The garrison took advantage of this to make sorties by boat. The meadows also were flooded and the king was obliged to send his horses away in order to obtain forage. For food he was largely dependent on a supply line to Paris (much of it being brought from

England), and this was constantly cut or threatened by raiding parties. He was thus forced to picquet the road with troops all the way between his camp and the capital. Thus the see-saw contest proceeded; for every step on the one side a counter was devised on the other.

To add to the difficulties and hardships of the attackers, a sickness epidemic—a feature of most medieval sieges—made its appearance, and the fighting strength was thus reduced at a time when appeals for help were received from Normandy.[1] But whatever the disappointments and difficulties might have been, the king pursued his purpose relentlessly. He had never yet abandoned a siege once he had undertaken it and the very possibility of such a course probably never occurred to him, and he showed his contempt for the faint hearts that began to appear around him. Even the gallant Sir John Cornwall departed for England on sick leave.

Christmas came and went, and still the king remained with his army before the walls of Meaux—like Edward III before Calais. But all was not well with the garrison. The nominal commander was something of a nonentity, and messages were smuggled out of the town to the famous Guy de Nesle, the sire of Offémont, to come and assume command. Offémont responded to this somewhat unattractive offer early in March, (1422). On the 9th of the month, he, with 40 companions, managed to steal through the English lines under cover of darkness and reach a point where the garrison, by pre-arrangement, had let down some scaling ladders (wrapped in cloth to muffle the noise). His leading men had successfully passed over the moat by a plank and were climbing the ladders when they heard a splash behind them. The sire was in the act of following them over the moat when the plank—an old one—broke with his weight and deposited him in the water. Now Offémont was wearing his full armour and its weight bore him down and he was in danger of drowning. Frantic efforts were made to rescue

[1] Salisbury had twice to ask for help, first in the recapture of Avranches, and later in that of Meulan.

him in the darkness. Two lances were handed to him, which he grasped; but, we are told, they were "left in his hands". One can picture the scene, the excitement, the confusion and the resulting clamour. The noise roused the soporific English sentries; the guard was called out and it rushed to the spot. Presumably they were confronted with the rather comic spectacle of a knight in armour up to his neck in the water of the moat, and brandishing two lances – an aquatic Don Quixote. At any rate Guy and all his men were captured.[1]

This failure so disheartened the garrison that the very next day they abandoned the town and took refuge in the market. Before doing this they transferred as much food and stores as possible into the market. These were seen crossing the bridge that connected the town with the market and a vigorous attack was launched in the effort to prevent the move. It came too late to be really effective, but it prevented the desperadoes in control in the city from setting the whole place on fire and slaying all the inhabitants who preferred surrender. The inhabitants as a matter of fact were only too glad to admit the English and to aid them in driving out the Dauphinists.

The bulk of the garrison made good their escape across the river to the market, and King Henry entered the town and transferred his headquarters thither.

The first phase of this great siege was over, but the second – the reduction of the market – was to prove even more arduous. The leaders of the garrison were desperate, knowing that little mercy was to be expected if the place fell, while the patience of the English was becoming strained, and their tempers steeled by the fierce, implacable spirit of their king. Thus the siege of Meaux became an epic, famous throughout the century.

Henry's first attack was directed against the northern face of the market. The garrison had broken down the bridge behind them, and the king set about restoring it. This he did by means of a *beffroi* or movable tower which was manhandled through

---

[1] This episode has been described by some writers as an attempt to relieve the town. It was not. It was an attempt to smuggle in a new Commander.

the streets and on to the English end of the bridge. Halting short of the gap in the bridge, a kind of drawbridge was let down from the *beffroi* and the gap thus bridged. This operation was covered by a "barrage" of missiles from a large number of "engines" stationed at the end of the bridge.

The next step was to obtain possession of the flour mills which lined the southern bank of the river by the bridge (as they still do). To accomplish this the king occupied a small island in mid-stream not far from the bridge. Here he posted a strong force of cannons which directed a heavy bombardment on to the mills, thus enabling the infantry to cross the bridge and capture them in a gallant attack in which the earl of Worcester lost his life. This success not only gave a covered line of approach to the north face of the market but also a foothold on the bank under its walls.

The next step was taken by the earl of Warwick against the southern face of the market. Here he managed to establish his troops across the canal and, covered by a "sow" or movable pent-house, his troops got close up to the wall of an outwork which they took by assault. From here it was possible to direct a very damaging fire on to the interior of the market.

It was now the turn of the western division. The earl of Exeter had handed over the actual command to Sir Walter Hunger-ford, who was a more experienced commander in siege work. The new commander soon made his presence felt. On this side there was an appreciable space between the river bank and the curtain wall. He was able to throw small wooden foot-bridges across, and thus to establish a lodging at the foot of a wall. Pro-tected by a "sow", his miners now sunk a mine, despite a number of desperate and well-led sorties by the garrison.

Last of all, it was the turn of the eastern face. Here the earl of March had a problem all his own, for the river on this side was unusually wide and swift—so swift that boats and bridging could with difficulty be employed. King Henry proved equal to the occasion. He had two large barges lashed together, and on them he constructed a species of *beffroi*, topped with a drawbridge which could be pushed out and lowered on to the top of the wall on that side.[1] It would be impossible to conceal this lofty erection from the eyes of the garrison, who must have watched its progress with trepidation. Appeals to the Dauphin had met with no better response than the appeals of the garrison of Harfleur to his brother Louis had been. Charles was at that moment living a life of luxury in far-off Bourges. Easter had come and gone (Henry granted the enemy a few days truce for the sacred feast), the siege had now lasted over six months; time after time the garrison had countered every attempt of their enemy to effect an entry, but time after time that inexorable foe, like a ferret that has its teeth into a rabbit, returned with some fresh attack. And now yet another attack was plainly brewing. Though food was still plentiful this was the last straw: King Henry had broken their spirit, the voice of their leaders was silenced and the garrison sued for terms.

Henry V was now in one of his grimmest and most unpleasant moods. He and his army had been kept under arms right through the winter, suffering loss and privations, and even insults from the Bastard of Vaurus and his ruffians. He consented to grant terms but they should be "just" terms, which meant that they would not be tempered with mercy. Most of the garrison were to get away with their lives, but there was a long list of exceptions— persons whose lives would be at the disposal of the king, Charles, and his regent, King Henry. The capitulation was written in English only, although it was ostensibly in the names of both kings. This was probably intended as a purposed form of humiliation. Among the names exempted from mercy we find the mysterious phrase, "One that blewe and sounded an Horne during the siege".[2] Thereby must hang some tale but it is lost to history. Some people have connected it with another story,

---

[1] Some writers have regarded this and the other *beffrois* as unique of their kind, the invention of the king's fertile brain. But *beffrois* were a recognized weapon of siege warfare, and the floating one was a counterpart of that constructed by that "leveller of castles" Philip Augustus in his famous siege of Château Gaillard. A huge *beffroi* known as Pompey's Bridge was used as late as A.D. 1601 at the Siege of Ostend.

[2] Rymer's *Foedera*, X, p. 212.

namely that an ass was dragged up to the top of the wall and belaboured till it brayed, when the garrison shouted to the English outside to come to the help of their king who was calling for them. Henry V seems to have had no sense of humour, this being the least attractive side to his complex character and he was much offended by this puerile prank. The condition in the terms of surrender that gave most satisfaction to friend and even foe was the fate accorded to the villainous Bastard of Vaurus. He was ordered to be hanged on the very elm tree outside the town which he had used as a gallows for his many victims in the past.

It was on May 2, 1422, that the capitulation was signed, the siege having lasted longer than any other of King Henry's sieges. Dr. Waugh describes this siege as, "Perhaps Henry's master-piece",[1] a well-deserved tribute. At the first blush, it might be regarded as rather disappointing that such a place should hold out against the might of England at her strongest for over six months, but such events must be judged in the context of their time. The physical strengths of medieval armies was compara-tively small; what swayed the course of history was the moral effect of the operations of those armies, and even more, of their leaders. Here was seen a prince who had never known defeat; disappointments he had had, but he had always managed to overcome them and to come out on top. His iron will had invariably triumphed, and a superstitious generation was pre-pared to regard it as in some way the verdict of God. Much the same had been the case with a previous soldier-king of England, Edward III. In his last campaign he fought no battle; he cap-tured no great town, yet by his persistence in the maintenance of his aim he eventually broke the spirit of his enemies. In like manner his great-grandson in this protracted siege broke the spirit of his enemies; and not only those within the walls of Meaux. The siege had been closely watched from the outside by the neighbouring towns and castles held by the Dauphinists. On its fall they fell too, with scarcely a blow struck. As a result, by

[1] Op. cit., III, p. 338.

the end of June, all Northern France except Guise, St. Valery and Le Crotoy, were in the hands of the Anglo-Burgundians.

      *   *   *

After the capture of Meaux, King Henry returned to Paris, where he met his queen, who had borne him a son, Henry by name, during the siege. In Paris he devoted himself for a time to diplomacy, striving to build up a great alliance against the Dauphin's party. His next campaign, he decided, should be waged in conjunction with the young duke of Burgundy against the elusive Jacques d'Harcourt. The latter had made his base of operations Le Crotoy on the estuary of the Somme. The earl of Warwick was already operating in that direction, and was laying siege to St. Valery, on the opposite side of the estuary. But before plans for this campaign had been fully concerted, the strategical situation was suddenly and unexpectedly altered by a fomidable-looking offensive on the part of the Dauphin, directed at the Burgundian province of Nevers, which lay between the Orleanais and Burgundy. La Charité on the Loire was taken and Cosne on the same river, 50 miles south-east of Orleans, was besieged. The garrison agreed to surrender if not relieved by August 12. Instantly the duke of Burgundy abandoned all thought of proceeding against Harcourt and turned to the south. He had a curious correspondence with the Dauphin in which the two princes agreed to meet in battle on a field to be selected outside the town of Cosne. Thither duke Philip marched with his main army. Being short of archers, he begged Henry to lend him some. The king jumped at this opportunity to show his staunchness to his ally. Not only would he lend archers, but his whole available army, and more still, he would lead it in person.

Late in July the English army, with some adherents from Picardy, concentrated for the campaign near Paris, and began its long march to the south. The route lay through Corbeil, 15 miles south of Paris. Up to this point the king accompanied his army, but found himself unable to ride as he was suffering from some malady, probably dysentry. He was therefore constrained to ride in a horse litter, suffering great pain all the time. Beyond

Corbeil he found it impossible to go, reluctantly handing over the command to the duke of Bedford (who had escorted Queen Catherine from England, bringing some much-needed reinforcements with him). Marching south-east the English army joined forces with that of Burgundy at Vezelay on the Yonne on August 4. The Burgundian army was at full strength and the combined force must have been a formidable one. Continuing on their way (English and Burgundians being mixed in the same formations in order to prevent jealousy) they reached the outskirts of Cosne on the 11th. On the next day the town was due to surrender, the day fixed for the battle.

Of the Dauphin or his army there was no sign. Evidently he had fought shy of the contest. Possibly he had heard a report that the regent was present in person. Whatever the reason, the Dauphinist army had retreated towards Bourges, leaving a mere fringe of patrols on the opposite (west) side of the river.

Duke Philip now took an extraordinary decision. Instead of pursuing the retreating enemy, seizing the opportunity presented by the English troops or at least of retaking La Charité, he immediately fell back to Troyes and disbanded his army. Was his heart in the struggle? It seems doubtful. The English army perforce fell back too, sick at heart. Had their king been still with them, they must have reflected, things might have gone otherwise. But there was worse to come. The king was dying. Bedford was summoned in haste to his bedside at Vincennes, whither the stricken king had been removed.

Bedford, Warwick and other leaders assembled round his bed, while Henry, with two hours of life left him, gave his instructions and advice for the future regulation of affairs. His body might be wracked with pain, but his brain worked as coolly and lucidly as ever. To his eldest brother John of Bedford he bequeathed the regency, with the earnest injunction that he should never give up the contest till all France recognized the treaty of Troyes. Shortly afterwards he died peacefully. The sun of England had set.

*　　　　　*　　　　　*

This book is not a biography of a great king, but we must pause for a while to assess the military talents of Henry of Monmouth.[1] We cannot be sure that he was a great strategist like Edward III, for there is not enough to go upon. Apart from the Agincourt campaign, his warfare consisted for the most part of a series of sieges. Whereas Edward III thought in terms of the movements of armies, Henry's thoughts seemed more concerned with steps of diplomacy. Nor in the field of tactics is there much to be learnt from his actions. How then, it may be asked, did he make such a tremendous impression as a soldier not only upon his own people but upon allies and enemies alike! I think the explanation is that his military greatness lay in the moral sphere. He built up his army on the double foundation of discipline and fervour. The discipline he imparted was astonishingly strict for the age in which he lived, and it stood him in good stead. When things were going badly the fervour, or belief in a cause, was also most marked. He imbued his army with the same firm faith in the righteousness of his cause as he himself held. And all this was stoked up by the fires of religion. In these matters he was perhaps the prototype of Oliver Cromwell, who achieved nothing spectacular as a strategist or tactician, but yet produced an army ready, at long last, to "go anywhere and do anything". Another quality contributing to his military success was his resolution—his refusal to be downcast or to "let up" on anything to which he had put his hand. This, in conjunction with careful forethought and preparation, resulted in success invariably crowning his efforts. His careful forethought was shown strikingly when preparing for his last (and unfought) campaign in the north. Before undertaking it he made arrangements with the people of Amiens to provide food for his army, and even fixed with them the prices that should be paid.

[1] Various French writers of later days have had savage things to say of Henry V. A recent writer delights to call him "The Cut-throat King". But it was not always so. Contemporary French writers, Dauphinist as well as Burgundian, wrote little that was bad and they were practically unanimous in praising his strict sense of justice and his implacable—moderns would say harsh—execution of it. The story goes that on one occasion when one of his brothers was pleading for a malefactor the king answered him, "If it had been even you, my brother, I would have hanged you for it".

None of the above qualities is spectacular, but when combined in one person they represent a formidable combination. But that is not all. Overriding and informing them all was the innate greatness of the man, a greatness that is born witness to by friend and foe alike, a greatness of spirit and character that made all his brothers his dutiful slaves, even after his death. We hear of no petty quarrels among his captains. This was the true greatness that had shone in the character of his great-grandfather, and, in a lesser degree, in his great-uncle the Black Prince, as also in his grandfather, John of Gaunt, whose resoluteness and remorseless determination carried him through difficulties that would have submerged a lesser man. Truly those Plantagenet princes were a "mighty breed of men".

CHAPTER XI

CRAVANT

HENRY V was dead. The linch-pin had fallen out of the coach. John, duke of Bedford, did his best to replace it. It was no easy task, as he must have realized when reviewing the situation that confronted him. We have seen how English fortunes ebbed during the absence in England of the king—not so much from any failings on the part of his subordinates as in the encouragement and improved morale that was thereby engendered in the Dauphinist camp. This swing in military fortune was again to be expected. Bedford was quite a good general, as was shortly to be demonstrated, but he lacked the position and prestige of the late king, and also the military reputation of his dead brother, Thomas of Clarence.

Let us give this military situation a brief glance. The English troops were spread out over an enormous area, nearly as large as England south of a line from the Wash to the Severn estuary. They were pitifully few in numbers for this purpose, probably less than 15,000 combatant troops in all. Bedford saw, as clearly as his brother (who indeed had impressed the point upon him), that his task could only be accomplished if the Burgundian connection was maintained. Ominous cracks were already appearing in it. Duke Philip's conduct during the illness of Henry had been peculiar, not to say suspicious. It would require all the tact and patience at the command of the new regent to cement the uneasy alliance. Fortunately, he was not lacking in experienced and in trusty generals—the chief among them being Salisbury and Warwick—and the morale of the English troops was, so far as we can estimate, still unimpaired; the capture of Meaux and the hasty retreat of the Dauphin from Cosne had evidently raised it. Even so, the prospects of success were not bright, for only a month after the death of the English king, that of the French king followed. This added to the difficulties confronting Bedford, for no longer could orders be issued to the French in the name of their own king, Charles VI, but in that of an absentee infant king, whom Bedford had had proclaimed in Paris as Henry VI of England and France.

Two factors, however, improved the prospects. One was the inertness of the Dauphin who, apart from proclaiming himself king of France as Charles VII, took no active steps to make good his claim. He was reported to be living in luxury in Bourges. The other factor was the sterling character of the duke of Bedford. Now that Henry V was dead there was no better or fitter person in the land to carry on his work than his brother John. Lacking Henry's harshness, he possessed to the full his flair for diplomacy and his strong sense of justice. To these qualities he added a sincere desire to establish enlightened government in France, and strict fidelity to the terms of the Treaty of Troyes. The details of his civil government lie outside the scope of this book, but it may be recorded here that he was outstandingly successful in winning over the leading Burgundians in Paris, to whom he entrusted practically all the reins of government, even appointing his old opponent at the siege of Rouen, Guy de Bouteille, as captain of Paris. The populace tended to follow their leaders, with the result that in future military operations there was usually a strong contingent of French (Burgundian) volunteers, who formed a useful reinforcement to the depleted ranks of the army.

To describe the course of the war during the first year or two of the reign of Henry VI must be the despair of the historian. It is as difficult to discern any clear-cut pattern in it as in much of the Great Civil War.

Military operations were sporadic, spasmodic and of varying fortunes. They consisted, for the most part, of sudden raids by one side or the other, followed by sieges of castles, their capture and recapture almost *ad nauseam*. It is, however, possible to generalize, and to sum up the strategy of the duke of Bedford as an attempt to "tidy up" the military situation before proceeding to further advances. In this he was only following the recent strategy of Henry V. For twelve months, then, after the accession of Henry VI the situation in France may be said to be static.

By a bold stroke the French gained possession of Meulan; the ever-victorious earl of Salisbury, who had become "the hand-maid" of the government just as Henry of Lancaster had been in the Crecy War, was sent to retake it, which he very speedily did. A more serious affair occurred in Anjou. Sir John de la Pole had been ordered to take a force to reduce the formidable fortress of Mont St. Michel. Disregarding his orders, de la Pole carried out a raid into Anjou, up to the gates of Angers, with a small force about 1,600 strong. History continued to repeat itself, for the sire Aumâle with a superior Dauphinist army based on Tours cut in behind him, and waylaid him near Laval on the homeward way. The English force was cut up and its commander deservedly made a prisoner.

As a counter to this setback in the west the English were enjoying marked successes in the north-east, where "the thorn in the flesh" of the Burgundians, Jacques d'Harcourt, was at last being seriously tackled by the earl of Warwick. First of all, Noyelles on the estuary of the Somme was captured. As a result, Harcourt fell back, withdrawing his forces into Le Crotoy. This town was then besieged vigorously and methodically by Sir Ralph Boutellier, and after some months it fell. The detested depredations of Harcourt in Picardy were thus brought to an end, to the great relief of the populace.

On the diplomatic plane, John of Bedford was proving himself a worthy brother to Henry V. His efforts culminated in April 1423 in the tri-partite Treaty of Amiens, a defensive alliance between England, Burgundy and Brittany. It was a great achievement to bring in Brittany, for her duke had been acting in as shifty a manner as the late duke of Burgundy, first leaning towards one side and then to the other. King Henry had laid the foundations of this *rapprochement*, but full credit must be accorded to his brother for bringing it to fruition. This he accomplished

largely by means of two notable marriages. He himself espoused
Duke Philip's fifth sister, Anne, while Arthur of Brittany,
brother of the duke (who fought in the English ranks), married
Philip's eldest sister. The duke of Brittany signed this treaty
despite the treaty contracted in the previous year at Sablé with
the Dauphin. But both Burgundy and Brittany had their
tongues in their cheeks when they signed the Amiens treaty.

To revert to the military aspect. The "tidying up" process was
not yet complete. The duke of Bedford himself did something
towards it in an indirect way. In May he journeyed to Troyes
to receive the hand of his fiancée, Anne of Burgundy, and on
the way back to Paris he fell upon the garrison of Pont-sur-
Seine, which had recently fallen into Dauphinist hands, and
captured the place. He followed this up by clearing up other
bad spots. But Champagne was not yet clear of the enemy, and
Bedford deputed to his most efficient general, the earl of Salisbury, the task of completing the operation. Salisbury commenced by laying siege to Montaiguillon, a small stronghold
near Provins, 50 miles south-east of Paris. Though small, Montaiguillon proved unexpectedly strong and tough, and the siege
was a long one. Whilst thus engaged Salisbury received yet
another task. After the fiasco of Cosne in the summer of 1422
the Dauphin had remained quiescent. But the death of Henry
V, and the resistance of such places as Le Crotoy and Montaiguillon, seem to have spurred him into action. In the summer
of 1423 he formed a new army at Bourges. It must have been of
considerable size, for he collected it from over a wide area. A
large proportion of it was the Scottish contingent under their
marshal, Sir John Stewart of Darnley. There were also contingents from Aragon and even from Lombardy. Stewart was
given the chief command, with the count of Vendôme as his
second. This army the Dauphin despatched into Burgundy,
with orders to take the town of Cravant as a first step. Various
motives have been suggested for this step. For one thing, it was
the region most remote from any English garrisons, and the
Dauphin had already clearly shown that he preferred being

ranged against Burgundians than against English troops. Further, a blow directed against the duchy of Burgundy, while it might relieve the pressure on Montaiguillon, would prepare the way to re-establishing a channel of communications with the remnants of his forces in Picardy and Champagne. To strike at the hostile strategic flank whilst at the same time covering his own communications and threatening the enemy's sensitive spot—his capital—was sound strategy. The degree of success that might be expected from it would depend largely on the reactions of the duke of Bedford.

Bedford's reaction was prompt and vigorous. Reinforcing Salisbury's army with the troops recently brought from England by the earl marshal and Lord Willoughby—about 1,000 in number—he ordered Salisbury to march at once to the relief of Cravant. At the same time the dowager duchess of Burgundy also collected and sent a contingent, which was to form part of Salisbury's army. Auxerre, situated nine miles north-west of Cravant, both towns being on the Yonne, was selected as the rendezvous for the two corps. Thither Salisbury set out in the latter part of July, leaving a small force to continue the siege. The distance was 40 miles and his route would take him through Sens, where he would strike the route of Bedford's army in its march to Cosne the previous year. Thence the two armies marched by the same road, passing through Joigny and Ville-neuve, ascending the wide and rather dull valley of the Yonne.

The size of the English army is given by Waurin as 4,000, a likely enough figure under the circumstances; and as Waurin was himself present and is a reliable chronicler we may safely accept it. Of the Burgundian army we have no information, but it was collected hastily and it is likely to have been neither large nor of good quality. As for the Franco-Scottish army, Waurin is silent, and St. Remy merely states that it was large. Considering the wide area from which it was recruited, and the very large number of casualties incurred in the battle, it must have out-numbered the Anglo-Burgundians by two or three times.

The Burgundians were the first to arrive at Auxerre and, on

July 29, they were joined by the English. It was high time, for the garrison of Cravant were so short of food that they were reduced to eating horses, cats, and even mice. The leaders of the Burgundians, delighted that the English should help, and that their leader should be the great earl of Salisbury, came out of the town on the English approach and escorted them with ceremony into the cathedral city where they received a hearty welcome. Though the two parties had been allies for four years no pitched battle had yet taken place in which both were present. Relations were most cordial and the Burgundians gladly placed themselves under the orders of Salisbury.

The first act was to summon a council of war for that evening, to be held in the nave of the cathedral, which then bore much the same appearance as it does today (though the chancel is newer. On the spot one can easily picture this war council in session. While the council is debating, we will pass on to a description of the beleaguered town of Cravant.

The valley of the Yonne between Auxerre and Cravant is bordered on its eastern side by a line of hills, rising at their highest point, two miles short of Cravant, to some 500 feet above the valley. The town is situated on the southern end of this line, where it descends into the valley. Thus, its northern portion is 100 feet higher than the southern, which is at river level. Three of the medieval gates still stand, and at the highest point of the wall there is a watch-tower, of which more anon. The peculiar thing to note about the situation is that the town does not embrace or even touch the river, which flows past it at a distance at the nearest point of only 160 yards. (It may be conjectured that the river has changed its bed since the original walls of the town were laid out.) The bridge opposite the middle of the town was intact. The river is 40 to 60 yards wide, shallow but not swift, as it flows through the broad valley to Auxerre.

We will return to Auxerre cathedral, where the war council was being held. Whether Waurin was actually present is not known, but it seems likely, for he reported its decisions in great detail. The master-hand of Salisbury is clearly visible throughout, his main object being to weld into one fighting machine two different nationalities. This would not be easy, for the English of those days had a sublime contempt for all foreigners, and were hasty of temper. A quite trivial incident might wreck the whole partnership.

The decisions reported by Waurin may be re-arranged and tabulated as follows:

1. The two national contingents were to form one indivisible army.

2. To ensure this, every man in each contingent was to live in harmony with the others.

3. Two marshals were appointed to control the movements and discipline of the troops, one English and one Burgundian.

4. Each soldier was to carry on his person two days food.

5. Supplementary food for future days was to be provided by the townsmen of Auxerre and sent forward to the army.

6. Each archer was to provide himself with a wooden stake pointed at each end, to plant in the ground to his front.

7. Each soldier was to keep his exact station in the ranks; penalty for falling out being corporal punishment.

8. One hundred and twenty men-at-arms, 60 English and 60 Burgundian, were next morning to go forward as scouts in front of the army.

9. On getting near the enemy, everyone was to dismount, and the horses were to be led a good half-mile to the rear.

10. No prisoners were to be taken until the issue of the battle had been decided. (A wise provision, for the procedure of taking prisoners, including the arrangement of ransom terms, might be a lengthy matter.)

The allied army retired to rest in a happy and confident frame of mind, feeling that its leaders knew their business. Early next morning, July 30, divine service was held, and at 10 a.m. the whole army marched out, "with much brotherly affection" declares Waurin.

Following the right or eastern bank of the river the army marched slowly, the heat being extreme. At about four miles short of Cravant the enemy was sighted "a short league" away, at a place that I will discuss presently. There the army halted for the day. It was a short march, but no doubt Salisbury desired another 24 hours in which his newly-formed army might shake down together.

On Saturday the 31st the march was continued; but not in the same direction. For the French were seen to be drawn up in an extremely strong position.[1] This is given vaguely as "one mile from Cravant", and no one seems to have tried to identify the exact position. But I think it can be easily done. When passing up the valley by road or train on the other bank, the line of hills appears to be continuous, unbroken by any gap in the line of heights. But if one takes the valley road from Cravant along the right bank, at about one-and-a-half miles downstream from Cravant, a sudden cleft in the heights appears at a point where the ridge is at its highest and steepest. This cleft cuts right through it at right angles. If the French held the crest of the gorge with their left resting on the marshy river valley, which there can be little doubt they did, the position would be well-nigh impregnable to a medieval army, and Salisbury was well advised not to attempt it. Instead, he fell back slightly and then crossed to the west of the river at Vincelles, some four miles short of Cravant.[2] Having crossed the river the army advanced south until it came opposite Cravant. But the river separated it from the town to be relieved and the enemy was found to be lining the right bank. What had happened was that the French army, drawn up on its lofty position, had had a good view of the allied army during its turning movement and had consequently moved parallel to it, "descending the hill" as we are explicitly told, prepared to contest the river crossing.

Stated in this way, the manoeuvre of the English commander

---

[1] They had been waiting in that position for three days, so they evidently had early information of the Allies' approach.

[2] Ramsay, who seems to have misread Waurin, makes them cross at Champs, nearly three miles further downstream.

does not look impressive, especially if one works on a small-scale map. For such a map does not show the cleft through the ridge, nor the relationship of the river to the town. In actual fact Salisbury's experienced eye told him that the hill position was not to be tackled, while his scouts had no doubt by this time reported to him that the river ran only 160 yards from the western wall of the town. Thus, if the French tried to oppose the crossing there they would be within missile range of the garrison on the town wall: they would find themselves between two fires.

Nevertheless, the fact remains that when the allies reached the river opposite Cravant they found the French lining the far bank, in spite of any hostile action from the garrison of the town. I fancy they must have provided themselves with some form of parados to their position on the river bank, foreseeing such an eventuality.

THE BATTLE OF CRAVANT (See Sketch Map 6, p. 545)

Salisbury ranged his army along the western bank; the English, who must have formed the major portion of the army, being in the front line. Lord Willoughby had the command of the right, and Salisbury the left.

A long pause – a common feature of medieval battles – now ensued. But after some three hours of waiting for the French to move, Salisbury decided to attack. According to Waurin, no doubt an eye-witness, the earl suddenly shouted, "St. George! Banner advance!" and himself dashed into the water, closely followed by his men-at-arms, while the archers, according to their wont, provided "covering fire". Waurin's account is most circumstantial and rings true. The men crossed "each as best he could", the water reaching in some cases to the knees and in others to the waist.[1] The English men-at-arms must have divested themselves of a great part of their armour (though it is curious that Waurin omits all reference to this) and most of

[1] From local intelligence (for I could not obtain a boat to make my own soundings when visiting the scene) I learnt that it is about 3 ft. deep, at the present time, with some deep pockets. At this point it is 60 yards wide.

them managed to reach the far bank. Seeing this, the Burgundians followed them into the water. A bitter fight then ensued in the narrow strip of ground between river and town.

Meanwhile, on the right, Lord Willoughby had attacked the bridge. It was held by a Scottish contingent who resisted stoutly, and the contest was fierce.[1]

Eventually the day went in favour of the English on the bridge, and the French began to give way. Perceiving this, the garrison commander, who could see every movement from his watch-tower less than 500 yards away, gave the signal to the troops manning the wall, and a sortie was made from the western gate right into the backs of the French engaged in the bridge struggle. The gallant garrison were so weak with hunger that they could scarcely stagger out, but it was the last straw, and the French army took to flight. But escape was difficult: flight direct to the rear was, of course, intercepted by the town; while to the north the ridge had an almost cliff-like steepness, and for men in armour it would be unscalable. Only to the south was there a practicable line of retreat, and to reach it the fugitives had to pass through the gauntlet constituted by the line of English troops on the one side and the garrison on the other. It seems probable that very few men-at-arms can have made good their escape. Certainly that must have been the case with the Scottish Corps, for they were in the front line, and we are told that the Lombards and Spaniards were the first to fly. The Scots, on the other hand, suffered very heavy casualties—one account gives 4,000 killed, another 3,000. For the French contingent Waurin gives 1,200 killed, including no less than 300 to 400 of noble birth. Even French chroniclers admit to a loss of 2,000 to 3,000 Frenchmen. Many prisoners were taken, one account making the number as high as 2,000. Most important of them all were the two commanders of the army, the Constable of Scotland and the count of Ventadour. The unfortunate Sir John Stewart of Darnley was not only captured but lost an

[1] When at a later date the bridge was widened, many skeletons were dredged out of the river under the bridge, a silent testimony to the fight that had waged above it.

eye. (Next time he crossed swords with the English he was again taken prisoner.) The Dauphinist army scattered like sheep with-

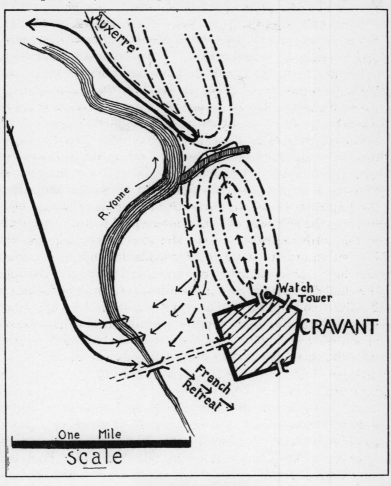

Auxerre

R. Yonne

Watch Tower

CRAVANT

French Retreat

One Mile

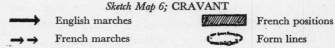
scale

Sketch Map 6; CRAVANT

→	English marches	▨	French positions
⇢ →	French marches	⬭	Form lines

out a shepherd. A contingent was sent in pursuit of them, while the remainder of the allied army entered the gates of Cravant to receive a tumultuous welcome. The following day, Sunday, was spent in the town, the pursuers had returned. On the following Monday the two armies took their leave of one another and marched away, the Burgundians to Dijon and the bulk of the English army back to the siege of Montaiguillon. The French army had literally ceased to exist. The victory was 100 per cent. complete. Thus, by a sudden blow of unlimited dash and daring, the Dauphinist offensive plan for the year 1423 was broken beyond repair. When news of the victory reached Paris, bonfires were lit in the streets by the delighted citizens.

But the results of the battle went even further than this. Salisbury was able to send a corps under the earl marshal to assist the Burgundian, John of Luxemburg, in Eastern Champagne, in driving the French right across the river Meuse into Lorraine. More striking still, another corps under the earl of Suffolk, who had been present at Cravant, plunged into the heart of Burgundy as far as Macon, 100 miles south of Cravant and on the borders of Bourbon, a Dauphinist territory. Thereabouts he captured several strong places, the details of which Waurin unfortunately does not provide. Suffolk then detached Captain Glasdale (afterwards to be prominent at Orleans) still further south to the strong castle of La Roche which he "brought to the obedience of King Henry of England and France". With this series of successes the campaign of 1423 practically came to an end.

COMMENTS ON THE BATTLE

No two medieval battles were alike, and none that I know of even approached Cravant in similarity. It was a crisp, clearcut affair without vicissitudes; and it bore the clear impress of that great soldier Thomas Montagu, earl of Salisbury. From the bare record of his almost unbroken successes and from the confidence that Henry V placed in him, we knew that this could hardly fail to be so, but the details of his work and methods were lacking. One cannot, therefore, be too grateful to John Waurin for his very full and convincing account of the battle, and particularly of the events leading up to it. Waurin tells us

just what we wished to know, the things about which most medieval chroniclers are so aggravatingly silent, either because they
were clerics and did not know, or because they were soldiers and
assumed everyone knew.

Thus we learn six things at least to explain Salisbury's
military success. Notice first his successful efforts to weld
together the heterogeneous elements in his army on the very
eve of battle; the tact with which he employed exactly the same
number of Burgundians as English; the sharing of the duties of
marshal; the strict injuctions as to mutual behaviour.[1] Notice
next his careful foresight and planning—he thought out eventualities and was ready for them. Next, his care for strict discipline, doubtless inherited from his late master. Next, his experienced eye, which told him that the French position was impregnable but that it could be successfully circumvented. Next,
his dash and drive in hazarding a wide river crossing under the
eyes and missiles of the enemy; and, finally, the fighting spirit
that he must have communicated to his troops that induced them
to undertake what seemed such a hazardous operation.

I have referred to the sort of details that Waurin, almost alone
among ancient chroniclers, provides. These details throw valuable light on what we call logistics and the fighting methods of
his age.[2] When Professor Newall in his *The English Conquest of
Normandy* wishes to treat of such matters he goes to Cravant
for his authority (though quoting Monstrelet instead of the
source which the latter copied). As regards weapons and
armour, Waurin tells us how the weight of the armour on that
hot July day—the very height of the summer—bore down on and
wearied the men-at-arms, and he mentions specifically that
these men-at-arms were provided with lances, hatchets and
swords. Shields had by this time practically disappeared from
the battlefield, owing to the increased protection given by plate
armour.

[1] The British army has for centuries had to fight with allies, and it is tempting
to trace the success of Marlborough and Wellington in their relations with their
allies to the example set them by such men as the earl of Salisbury.

[2] The injunction against taking prisoners is an interesting one, doubtless a
hark-back to Agincourt.

APPENDIX

Considering the importance of the battle of Cravant the chroniclers paid remarkably little attention to it, with one noteable exception. This is, perhaps, not to be wondered at on the part of the French writers, but the Scots had nothing to be ashamed about, still less the English; yet both nations have dealt with it perfunctorily. Walsingham had finished writing and Edward Hall, nearly a century later, only provides a list of names. Nor have the Scots much to say about their defeat. It is left to a single Burgundian writer, serving in the English ranks, to provide us with over nine-tenths of the details of the battle. John de Waurin had, it will be recalled, also fought on the English side eight years before on the field of Agincourt, of which battle he provided the most valuable account. It is the same for Cravant. Indeed, it is a case of, "Eclipse first; the rest nowhere". Of the Burgundians, Le Fèvre (sire of St. Remy) condensed his compatriot's account, merely adding a few facts concerning numbers. Monstrelet also condensed, but added nothing whatever. Chastellaine ignored the battle.

The chief French chronicler to notice the battle was Gilles le Bouvier, or Berry the Herald, whose chronicle for the battle is in Godefroy's *Histoire de Charles VII* (1661) (just as his account of Baugé was hidden in the same author's *Charles VI*). His account, though short, adds some particulars as regards personnel on the Dauphinist side, and does not attempt to conceal the extent of the disaster; indeed, he says that the French lost 2,000 to 3,000 in killed and captured. The chronicle of Guillaume Cousinot is also difficult to track down, for it is embodied in a volume edited by Vallet de Viriville in 1850 entitled *Chronique de la Pucelle*, and is generally cited as *Gestes des Nobles Français*, though there is nothing on the title page to indicate its presence in the volume. Cousinot seems to have drawn his account mainly from le Bouvier, but he is even more emphatic about the catastrophic nature of the French defeat. More than once he uses the phrase that it was "grand dommage au roy Charles".

No modern English writer has attempted an adequate description of the battle.

VISITING THE BATTLEFIELD

Cravant is one of the easiest battlefields to find and to follow, although it is one of the least known. Motorists rush past it, within a few yards of its western gate, without so much as seeing it; for the modern road, instead of entering the walled town, bends sharply to the right,[1] and the motorist's eyes are glued to the road. Yet they have just passed over the very bridge on which Lord Willoughby had such a tussle with the Scottish defenders – the same bridge that had echoed to the feet of English soldiers only 12 months before, en route to the relief of Cosne. The town wall is almost intact and the three gateways plainly visible, whilst the watch-tower is in an excellent state of repair. This remarkable tower contains a girdle of circular apertures high up in its wall, too small for the discharge of any missile and quite obviously intended solely as look-outs. I know of no similar tower in England, though some may exist on the Continent. The tower obviously played an important part, not only in the actual battle but in the defence of the town during the siege. Approach to the town from every direction is clearly visible from it.

There is no good hotel in Cravant, but accommodation is easy in the interesting old town of Auxerre, only nine miles to the north, and there is a good train service between the two towns.

Thanks to Waurin's careful description it is easy to follow the course of the battle and to picture the scene, standing on the river bank within sight of the bridge. The watch-tower can also be ascended and from it every detail of the ground can be seen. There can, indeed, be comparatively few other medieval battles where one is so sure of the topographical features as Cravant.

[1] On the bend of the road there is a conveniently situated cafe, also ignored by the motorists.

CHAPTER XII

VERNEUIL:
"A SECOND AGINCOURT"

AFTER the victory of Cravant, affairs, both military and political, continued to go well for the English. On the political side this was almost entirely due to the regent, John, duke of Bedford, who is assessed by Oman as "almost the equal of Henry V as soldier, administrator and diplomatist".[1] By his good sense, fair dealing and tact he managed to endear himself to the Burgundian party, whom he placed in charge of the government in all regions except Normandy. The *Bourgeois de Paris*, a reliable witness, writes of him:

"This Duke was a strenuous man, humane and just, who loved greatly those of the French *noblesse* who adhered to him, virtuously striving to raise them to honour. Wherefore as long as he lived he was greatly admired and cherished by Normans and French of his party."

The details of his administration do not concern us here, but they had a direct bearing upon the military operations, inasmuch as a close and cordial cooperation in the field was maintained between the English and Burgundian armies.

This was well illustrated during the autumn and winter of 1423 in the eastern region where the Burgundian leader, John of Luxemburg, worked hand-in-hand with the earl of Salisbury and his lieutenant, Sir Thomas Rempston. The "tidying up" process continued steadily in the Laon-St. Quentin area, against the garrisons that were still holding out under the Dauphinist leaders La Hire and Poton de Xantrailles, whom we now meet for the first time. Occasional setbacks there were; notably the loss of Compiègne by the Burgundians and their failure to retake it. Bedford had to do the work for them himself early in the following year.

The year 1423 had been a good one for the allies. That of

[1] *Political History of England*, IV, p. 289.

550

1424 was to bring even more striking successes, and this despite the fact that the English, with their allies, were contending against not only the Dauphinists but also the Scots. A constant trickle of Scottish troops had been landing in the country for some years, and in April 1424 a complete army of 6,500 troops under the "war-battered" earl of Douglas landed and joined forces with the Dauphinists in the south. Alexander Douglas, in superseding his son-in-law the earl of Buchan, broke the promise he had made that he would join Henry V if King James were restored to Scotland. James was released and he re-entered Scotland in March, but, despite this, a month later Douglas landed in France, where the Dauphin created him duke of Touraine.

Meanwhile, the English successes were continuing. The ubiquitous and indefatigable earl of Salisbury, with Burgundian aid, subdued nearly all the towns and castles that still held out in the eastern theatre while in the north Le Crotoy fell in March.

Hitherto, the duke of Bedford had confined himself strictly to the instructions bequeathed to him by his brother; and he had carried them out with considerable success. He had established sound and settled government in Paris; he had safeguarded the English conquests in Normandy; he had "tidied up" nearly the whole of the region of northern France; and, above all, he had maintained friendly relations and close co-operation with Burgundy. The time had now come when he felt he could strike out on a line of policy of his own, of a more ambitious nature. In other words, he decided to carry the war into the enemy's country, starting with the conquest of Anjou and Maine. He was encouraged thereto by the numerous contingents of reinforcements that had of recent months joined him from England (notably among them being that of John, Lord Talbot) and amounting in all to about 5,000 men.

The first step was to collect a field army, for at the moment most of the troops were swallowed up in the ever-increasing number of garrisons, and in the scattered columns laying siege to towns and castles, or repelling local raids.

The basis of this army of invasion was the English reinforcement. Next came the contingents from garrison towns. The Normandy garrisons were squeezed dry: out of 4,000 troops so employed Bedford laid hands on 2,000. Finally, he called off the mobile columns, including one now operating far to the south, in Burgundy, under the earl of Salisbury. (Its progress had been so marked that towns as far distant as Lyons began to tremble for their safety.)

By these means the regent managed to assemble at Rouen by mid-July an army at least 10,000 strong. Thither he himself went on the 20th of the month, for he had determined to mark the importance of the operation by taking the command himself. It is probable that it was while at Rouen that the news reached him that the Dauphinists were also collecting a large army, with evident aggressive intentions.

The French command had indeed thrown off the semi-stupor which had afflicted them ever since the day of Agincourt. A resolute attempt was to be made to drive the invader out of Normandy. To this end a levy was declared throughout southern France. Fresh Scottish contingents were enticed over, and mercenaries were raised in Lombardy and elswhere. By these means an army something over 15,000 strong was raised. It assembled along the lower Loire, with advanced headquarters at Le Mans, 40 miles north of that river. By a coincidence both armies were ready to set out practically simultaneously. Furthermore, they both directed their steps towards the same objective.

Some months previously the town of Ivry, 30 miles west of Paris, had been captured by a sudden raid. Bedford despatched the earl of Suffolk to retake it in June. The town fell to him at once, but the garrison shut themselves up in the castle. Mining operations were then resorted to. On July 5, however, the garrison agreed to surrender on August 14, unless previously relieved.[1] It was natural, therefore, that both armies should set their faces in that direction, the one to relieve it, the other to

[1] Most authorities give the date as August 15, the Feast of the Assumption, but Martin Simpson has shown in the *English Historical Review* that the eve of the Feast, not the Feast-day itself is correct. (E.H.R., January 1934.)

effect its speedy fall and, if possible, to cross swords with its opponents. Since the French also announced this intention, a battle appeared imminent.

On August 11, the duke of Bedford marched south from Rouen, arriving the same day at Evreux, 20 miles north-west of Ivry. A contingent of Burgundians under L'Isle Adam had joined the army and, at the last moment, the earl of Salisbury. Meanwhile, the French army was approaching Ivry from Le Mans, 75 miles to the south-west, and had reached Noancourt, 15 miles short of the town. On the 13th, Bedford resumed his march, and that evening joined forces with the earl of Suffolk before the castle of Ivry.

The rival hosts were now within a day's march of each other, and the English fully expected a battle on the morrow—the day fixed for the surrender. The regent drew up his army, ready for attack; but nothing happened; or rather, all that happened was that the garrison marched out and surrendered. It turned out that the advanced scouts of the relieving army had come into contact with the English patrols; it had then been reported to the Franco-Scottish leaders that the main English army had anticipated them. A council of war was thereupon held to decide what action to take. It was of a stormy nature. On the one hand were the Scots and the younger French leaders; on the other, the senior French commanders. The Scots had been "kicking up their heels" at Tours for four months, and were spoiling for a fight with their detested opponents; but the French leaders, the duke of Alençon and the viscounts of Narbonne and Aumâle, had not forgotten the lesson of Agincourt, and were anxious to avoid battle and fall back. Eventually a compromise was reached. The army was to avoid a battle in the open with the English, but was to try and capture as many English towns on the Norman border as could be done without drawing on a battle. A start would be made with the little walled town of Verneuil, which they had passed on their left hand during the previous advance (see Sketch Map 5). Thither they directed their march, and next day effected an entry by the simple expedient of declaring that the English army had been defeated and was in full retreat.[1]

Meanwhile the duke of Bedford, after receiving the keys of Ivry castle and leaving a substantial garrison, had taken what appears on the face of it an astonishing step. Sending off Suffolk with 1,600 men to shadow the French army, he himself returned with his main army that day, August 14, to Evreux. This step has baffled most students, and, indeed, the whole campaign has been baffling owing to the mistake in the date of the surrender. Bedford regained Evreux that night and spent the next day, the Feast of the Assumption, in pious devotions in the cathedral. The only possible explanation is that he had taken the measure of the French generals, realized that there was no danger of immediate attack, and depended on Suffolk to keep him informed of their movements. Meanwhile, being of an intensely religious nature, he was desirous of celebrating the feast in Evreux cathedral. However we look upon it, we cannot palliate such a transgression of an elementary principle of strategy, one which makes it impossible to rate John of Bedford in the very highest rank of military commanders.

Thus, August 15 was spent by the two armies quietly in the respective towns of Evreux and Verneuil, while Suffolk camped in the open between the two, near Breteuil and Damville, some 12 miles north-east of Verneuil (Sketch Map 1). That evening Suffolk sent word to the regent that the French were in possession of Verneuil and Bedford resolved to march next day to meet them in the field. But before doing so he took another step that requires some explanation. He sent away L'Isle Adam with his Burgundian contingent (stated by *The Brut, Continuation* as 3,000 men) to resume their siege operations in Picardy, stating that he had no need of so large an army. One can but suppose that he had in mind his brother's famous remark on the eve of Agincourt, and reckoned to stimulate the pride and confidence of his troops thereby. If this be so, it was

---

[1] As corroboration of this story, they marched some unfortunate Scots troops in sight of the garrison, tied to their horses tails, to represent English prisoners.

certainly a magnificent gesture, and one is loath to condemn it.

On August 16, then, the English army set out to meet its opponents once more, and halted that night at Damville, a 12-mile march.[1] Here, again, a query arises. Why halt so far from the enemy? His troops had had a whole day's rest, and it should have been possible at least to join forces with Suffolk, and to marshall the whole army for battle within reach of Verneuil. Of course it is possible that Bedford possessed more precise and accurate information as to the situation and intentions of the enemy than we are aware of; but it is not likely, for that enemy was himself at the time in two minds as to what to do. Controversy was again raging: to fight or not to fight! And again Douglas and his men were emphatically for fighting. The northerners were not proving very congenial comrades to their allies, one of whom commented on the fanatical hatred displayed by them for their English opponents. However, the Scots got their way this time, and next morning, August 17, the whole allied army was deployed for battle on the open plain one mile to the north of the walls of Verneuil. From its ramparts, and especially from the grim and gaunt Tour Gris of Henry I, spectators of the oncoming battle were to have an excellent view.

*   *   *

A description of the *terrain* will not take long. The ground has changed but little since the battle, in spite of its contiguity to the town. The old town-ditch and traces of the ramparts still remain. To the north the ground is almost flat for one mile. Just to the left of the Damville road lies the farm of St. Denis, the site of a chapel built on the battlefield over the graves of the French dead. It thus pin-points the battlefield as precisely as the abbey at Hastings or the church on Shrewsbury battlefield. The Damville road then slopes very gently downwards for 600 yards into a slight dip at the edge of the forest, through a gap

[1] Some Norman contingents, seeing that a battle appeared inevitable next day, deserted and went home. This must have caused the Regent to regret his action in parting with his Burgundians.

in which the road passes. The ground then rises gently through the forest. The country is cultivated, open and hedgeless, as it probably was at the time of the battle.

THE BATTLE (Sketch Map 7, see p. 559)

On the morning of August 17, 1424, the Franco-Scottish army was early astir, for even if messages had not passed on the previous evening between Bedford and Douglas, as some aver, they were fully aware of the approach of the English army. There are not lacking symptoms of confusion and muddle in the marshalling of this heterogenous array, with at least three tongues – French, English and Italian – and contingents drawn from a wide area, including Brittany. Things were not made easier by the acrimonious conduct of the Scottish leaders who quarrelled among themselves for precedence. There was, doubtless, some intermixture of nationalities, but in the main it may be said that the French occupied the left and the Scots the right of the position. Each division was nominally in three lines, but the three soon became merged in one. On the two flanks were posted smallish bodies of mounted men, as at Agincourt, the remainder of the army being dismounted. The crossbowmen, of whom we hear but little, were interspersed among the men-at-arms. Of artillery in either army we hear nothing. One may picture each division as occupying a frontage of about 500 yards, i.e. 1,000 yards in all; the Damville road dividing the two divisions, and the front line passing through the modern 2-kilometre stone (measured from Verneuil).

The supreme commander was the count d'Aumâle, but it is safe to say that during the battle he exercised no practical influence on its course and particularly on the Scottish division.

While the allied army was debouching on to the plain of Verneuil the English were marching through the forest of Piseux, collecting the scattered forces of the earl of Suffolk *en route*. The combined strength of the army was now reduced to between 8,000 and 9,000, or rather more than half their opponents. The regent's chief lieutenant was the earl of Salisbury.

Nearly all the leaders who afterwards distinguished themselves in the war were present, including the earl of Suffolk, Lord Scales, Sir John Fastolf and Captain Gladstone, the only notable absentee being Lord John Talbot.

*   *   *

As the English descended the hill through the opening in the forest, the allied host could be seen drawn up for battle about one mile away. A glance was sufficient to show Bedford that their flanks were "in the air" but that they were supported by mounted troops. The march continued, down into the dip and up the very gentle slope towards the allied position. At a convenient distance outside missile range Bedford halted and deployed his army, drawing it up parallel to and on the same frontage as his opponents. For Bedford was a conventional soldier of the age of chivalry. Not for him was the surprise action, or the flank attack. He conformed to the practice of his great-grandfather, his grandfather and his brother. After all, he had good precedents. Moreover, he followed his brother's formation at Agincourt pretty closely: everyone was dismounted, the front was in two divisions (of which he himself commanded the right, and Salisbury the left), the men-at-arms occupying the centre of each division, and the archers both flanks (see appendix), and the front consisted of a single line. The sole departure from Agincourt practice was that the regent provided a mobile reserve (described by Waurin as a baggage-guard) of 2,000 archers, whom he stationed to the west of the road, whilst the baggage was slightly further in rear and to the east of the road. Mindful of the fate of the English baggage at Agincourt, Bedford took novel steps to safeguard it: the vehicles were drawn up in close order along the perimeter, while the horses, tethered head to tail in pairs, were placed immediately outside it, in order to supply additional protection to the camp or leaguer other than that supplied by the pages and varlets. Moreover the latter, having no horses to hold, would be free to ply their weapons in active defence.

*   *   *

When both the armies had completed their deployment a pause ensued, a normal precursor of a medieval battle as we have seen. This was to be no chance clash such as the affair of Baugé, but a rare and ordered ordeal by battle on the part of the main armies of England and France—the first for nearly nine years—the only abnormality being the absence of the head of the French state, the 22-year-old Dauphin. It was even more than that: it was, in a sense, an ordeal by battle of three nations, for the Scots regarded themselves as fighting for Scotland and against England rather than for France. And they had Cravant to revenge.

During this pre-battle pause, the duke of Bedford sent forward a herald to Alexander, earl of Douglas, enquiring blandly as to what rules he proposed to observe in the coming fight. If the record is correct he received the grim reply that the Scots would neither give nor receive any quarter.

At about four o'clock, according to Bedford, the two hosts, as if by mutual compact, advanced simultaneously—again as at Agincourt; indeed, that name must have been in the forefront of every man's mind on the field. The duke of Bedford gave the traditional signal, "Avaunt, banners!" and the troops, after kneeling down and reverently kissing the ground, responded with, "St. George, Bedford". The allies countered with "St. Denis, Monjoie!" The English line then stepped forward, slowly and deliberately, uttering what Fortescue describes as

"a mighty cry, the forerunner of that stern and appalling shout which, four centuries later was to strike hesitation into so fine a soldier as Soult."

The allies, on the other hand, advanced impetuously and raggedly—for which the youthful Scottish troops were afterwards blamed.

Each archer carried a double-pointed stake, and when within missile range, say 250 yards, they halted and the stakes were planted in front of the front line. Up to this moment the

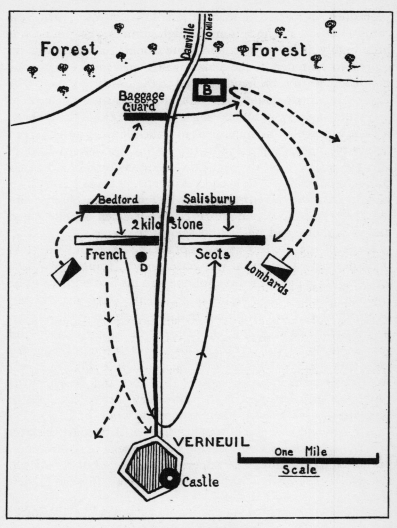

Sketch Map 7; VERNEUIL

D Ferme St. Denis

B English baggage

} English

} French

559

procedure had been a close imitation of that at Agincourt. Now came a variation. The season was high summer, the ground was presumably at its hardest, and some trouble and time was required to hammer in the stakes which, moreover, had to be handed forward from hand to hand to the front-rank men. The French mounted bodies who had orders, as at Agincourt, to open the battle by an attack on the flanks or rear of the archers, took advantage of the time spent in stake-planting and charged before the hedge of stakes was complete. The western body of French cavalry took the archers at a disadvantage and broke through their ranks. The archers instinctively herded into closer clumps (like the Saxons at Mount Badon, and the English infantry at Waterloo) and the French horsemen surged round and past them, and pushed on against the reserve.

Many of the archers were swept to the rear, and the right flank of Bedford's division was left exposed. It must have been an anxious moment for duke John in this his first battle. But he was supported by the admirable behaviour of the men-at-arms of his division. They exhibited that steadfastness that had now become characteristic of English troops in a tight corner—and which was never to desert them in the ages to come. Disregarding the peril on their right, these wonderful soldiers strode straight on right into the ranks of their foes and, bereft of the support of their bowmen on the right, they laid into the French men-at-arms stationed in their immediate front.

The struggle was tough, tougher than at Agincourt declares Waurin, who should know having been present in both battles. But after 45 minutes the superior prowess of the English, though fighting against odds of over two to one (for the French army consisted mainly of men-at-arms), gradually forced their way forward pushing their opponents back. Bedford is said to have wielded a two-handed axe (reminiscent of Harold at Hastings). He had dismounted from the bay charger that had carried him into the battle; he was "large of body, strong of limbs, wise and bold in arms" writes Waurin, and John Hardyng declares that "the regent was there that day as a lion".

Aumâle's own division which was engaged with Bedford's division gradually crumbled up under the intolerable pressure; and then arrived the moment of breaking-strain when a complete formation turns and flees to a man. The French men-at-arms scattered and made for the sheltering walls of Verneuil. Indeed, it is likely that the knowledge of the friendly shelter so close in the rear increased the temptation to retreat. But, alas for them, the pursuit was so close and hotly carried out that many of the fugitives could not reach the gates but plunged into the town ditch, where large numbers of them were drowned,[1] and Aumâle himself was killed.

The presence of this town ditch proved an additional godsend to Bedford for it enabled him to call off the pursuit, collect his scattered troops and return to the battlefield, where fighting was still going on.

This brings us to the earl of Salisbury's division on the English left, where his troops were ranged against the Scots. An even stiffer resistance was put up by these young and untried but doughty troops, who were, of course, picked men of splendid fighting material. They gave as good as they received, or nearly so, for some time, and the sight of their allies on their right quitting the field did not dismay them. Here for the moment we must leave them, fighting lustily in a foreign land for a foreign king.

The mounted body on the allied right flank consisted of 600 Lombard mercenaries. Fine horsemen they were, and under good leadership. Their commander could see that the hostile waggon-leaguer was in their immediate front, apparently unguarded by the English archers in the rear, who were by now engaged with the oncoming French cavalry. The Lombards seized their opportunity, and swinging round the English left flank attacked the baggage. It is, of course, impossible to say how far this encircling movement was influenced by the fire of the archers on Salisbury's left flank. Horses in a mounted action have a way of "taking charge" and swerving away from the missiles, carrying their riders with them willy-nilly. Be this as

---

[1] One report states that the inhabitants closed the gates in their faces.

it may, the result was a complete success for the bold Italian horsemen. They cut down the pages and varlets who offered resistance, broke into and pillaged the baggage-leaguer and loosed and made away with a number of the tethered horses. This was pretty smart work, especially as it was carried out almost under the eyes of the English reserve. The attention of the latter, however, was taken up by the tussle with the cavalry on the other flank, though their commander is open to criticism for not detaching some of his numerous formation to the help of the hard-pressed pages.

The triumph of the Lombards, however, was short lived. As soon as the French cavalry had been disposed of, the reserve turned on the Italians and drove them pell-mell in utter flight right off the field. The success of the French cavalry had been considerable, if only temporary. There is good evidence of fugitives fleeing far to the rear, declaring, in the manner of such people, that all was lost. One of them, a captain Young, was afterwards charged with taking no less than 500 men off the field for which he was afterwards hanged, drawn and quartered – a fate which, complacently observes *The Brut*, was quite right.

Meanwhile, the fight between Salisbury's division and the Scots was proceeding. The reserve, having now successfully disposed of both parties of enemy cavalry was available for further action. But Bedford, far away in pursuit of Aumâle's division, was in no position to give them orders. It mattered not. English archers had shown at Agincourt and elsewhere that they possessed in a high degree, in addition to their other virtues, that of initiative. Looking round for a fresh foe, they could see, and hear, the battle still waging on the left front. This presented a grand opportunity to repeat the example of the captal de Buch in a similar situation at Poitiers. Forming up again and wheeling round to their right they charged into the exposed right flank of the Scottish division, uttering what the good Waurin calls "un merveilleu cry" (sic).[1] The unfortunate Scots, assailed from

[1] Ferdinand Lot goes perhaps too far when he calls this action "une initiative inattendue, inouïe à l'époque." (Op. cit., II, p. 23.)

two sides at once, were now almost at their last gasp. But yet worse was to come.

We left Bedford with his division on the bank of the town ditch, reassembling his victorious troops. Breathless and fatigued as they must have been after nearly an hour's violent physical exertion followed by a pursuit, or, more likely, a painful waddle in full armour in the heat of a summer day, fain would they rest, and scout for drinking-water to relieve their parched lips. But there was more work to be done. Salisbury, outnumbered as he was by his opponents, must be supported. Back into the fight the weary men-at-arms therefore plodded. They arrived in time to strike into the rear of the Scots. This action sealed the fate of the northerners. Now completely surrounded there was nothing left to them but to sell their lives dearly. Escape was impossible, surrender was out of the question, for had not they declared that there was to be no quarter on either side? And it is pretty evident that they were slaughtered where they stood, almost to a man. The exultant English hacked them down with triumphant cries of, "A Clarence! A Clarence!" an obvious allusion to the Battle of Baugé (though it had already been avenged at Cravant).

When the last Scot lay prone the battle came to an end. A great part of the French rank and file had escaped but their leaders had stayed to fight it out, and they were one and all accounted for: Aumâle, the commander, Narbonne, Ventadour, Tonnerre, all were dead, and the duke of Alençon and the marshal Lafayette were prisoners.[1] The Scottish losses were catastrophic, as was only to be expected under the circumstances. Douglas, his son James, and his son-in-law the earl of Buchan, his second-in-command, were also dead. No less than fifty Scottish Gentlemen of rank died that day. Thereafter till the end of the war no considerable Scottish force took the field.

Two days later Bedford wrote a letter to Sir Thomas Rempston, at Guise, stating by count of the heralds no less than 7,262

---

[1] *Harl*, MS. 788, gives the names of 35 French Lords and Knights taken prisoner. Only about 200 prisoners in all were made.

enemies were killed. In a victory bulletin to London the regent might have purposely exaggerated the number of dead, but it seems unlikely that he should do so to one of his junior officers in France. Moreover, the number seems inherently probable; of 6,000 Scots only a handful can have escaped, and this would leave about 1,500 Frenchmen killed out of perhaps 10,000 – ten per cent. No wonder this battle has been likened to that of Agincourt and dubbed by French writers "Un autre Azincourt".

The English losses were about 1,000, a by no means negligible figure. But it was worth the sacrifice. The French army was leaderless, dispirited and dispersed. The Scottish army had ceased to exist. That evening English troops entered Verneuil, and next day a solemn service of thanksgiving was held in the great church. They had much to be thankful for. It was, indeed, a second Agincourt.

* * *

I have only one comment on the battle. Search my memory how I will, I cannot call to mind any medieval battle that involved so happy a co-operation of different formations at a critical juncture as that of Salisbury's division, Bedford's men-at-arms and the English reserve at the battle of Verneuil.

APPENDIX

SOURCES

Owing to the scarcity of modern literature on the battle I will devote more space than usual to the subject of sources. They are fairly numerous, at least 19 contemporary or near-contemporary writers dealing with it, though most of them very briefly. They can be grouped under four headings, English, Burgundian, Dauphinist and Scottish, and they differ but little from the chroniclers of Baugé. The main differences are as follows. On the English side we get an invaluable contribution in *Harleian* MS. 53, included in Brie's edition of *The Brut* as *Continuation H*.

This was first printed by Brie in 1906, and it had not been used by any historian previous to that date nor, so far as I can ascertain, by any historian since. But it is essential to the understanding of the battle, the author being the sole authority for the pursuit of Aumâle by Bedford's division to the town walls, and the subsequent return of the English to the field. We have reached an arid period in our English chroniclers (which possibly accounts for the neglect of the reign of Henry VI by historians). But it is, perhaps, legitimate to include the sixteenth-century chronicler Edward Hall, who adds some useful details about the battle, including the statement that the English had archers in the centre as well as on the wings. Of the Burgundians, though Monstrelet's account is the best known, that of Waurin is *facile princeps*, which is not surprising seeing that he fought in the English ranks, though in what capacity and in what part of the field we unfortunately do not know.

Both Monstrelet and Le Fèvre copy Waurin slavishly. A newcomer among the Burgundians, however, deserves mention, the Bourgeois de Paris, whose *Journal*, though more concerned with the political and social events in Paris, is the work of a contemporary, and fairly reliable one. Of the Dauphinists, perhaps the most original is Raoulet (whom we have cited earlier), and the most copious Thomas Basin, in his *Histoire de Charles VII* (translated from the original Latin into French by E. Samarin). The only really useful Scottish source is again the *Liber Pluscardine*.

No modern writer shows evidence of having visited the battlefield except H. R. Clinton, in his *From Crécy to Assaye* (1881) but he was, of course, handicapped by not having the use of *The Brut*, so his account is incomplete. Other modern writers seem to treat the battle perfunctorily and uncritically: for example, the most recent, Professor Ferdinand Lot, solemnly repeats without comment the (inevitable) story that Bedford struck down Douglas with his own hand. Lot seems, as ever, more interested in the numbers engaged than in the actual fighting. Though usually a careful student of English sources, he does not seem to have been aware of *The Brut Continuation*. And, of course, the English historians Fortescue, Ramsay and Oman laboured under the same disadvantage. (It is a pity Dr. Waugh did not turn his attention to this period.)

It is, perhaps, not surprising that Scottish and French historians have paid little attention to the battle. For example, Michelet in his *History of France* devotes exactly two lines to it. Of the most recent French writer, Ferdinand Lot I have already spoken, and there is really no one else worthy of mention but Vallet de Viriville, who incorporates the most detailed account in his *Histoire de Charles VII* (1861). Du Fresnes de Beaucourt is almost valueless for our purpose.

Finally, for the most documented and best informed, though brief, account of the battle we are indebted to an American, Professor R. A. Newall, whose *The English Conquest of Normandy* was published in 1924. Since that date the only reference to the battle or campaign I can find in the English tongue is an article in the *English Historical Review* for January 1934 by Martin A. Simpson, who, however, stops short of the actual battle.

*   *   *

THE NUMBERS

English. The most careful and most reliable computation of the English numbers has been made by Professor Newall in his *The English Conquest of Normandy*. He computes that Bedford set out from Rouen with 10,000 troops. To these must be added the contingent under Suffolk at Ivry; but we must deduct the garrison left at Ivry, the Burgundian contingent sent away, and the deserters from the Norman contingent on the eve of the battle. We shall probably not be far wrong in assessing the number that actually took part in the battle at between 8,000 and 9,000. This practically tallies with the figure of 9,000 given in *The Brut Continuation*.

French. Here we are confronted by an unusual phenomenon. Almost invariably we find in medieval times that the pro-

tagonists on each side exaggerate the numbers of their enemies
and diminish that of their own side, but here we get the exact
opposite. The average figure given by the Dauphinists (and
Burgundians) is 18,000 to 20,000 Franco-Scots; whilst the duke
of Bedford puts it as low as 14,000 in his letter to Sir Thomas
Rempston. It is true that, writing only two days after the battle,
he could make no more than a guess from the evidence of his
own eyes, and his knowledge of the numbers slain and taken.
Apart from these assessments, the only firm figures we have to
work on is the number of Scots. We may asume that every
available man was put into the field, and, allowing for four
months' wastage, the total must have been at least 6,000. Now
all the accounts seem to imply that the main constituent of the
allied army was French, to whom must be added the Lombards.
If we put this figure at about 9,000 we get a total of about 15,000.
Splitting the difference between the assessments of Bedford and
the French we get 17,000. If we split the difference between
15,000 and 17,000 we get a total of about 16,000, and that is as
far as we can go. The fact that the allied casualities in killed and
captured, and excluding wounded, amounted to nearly 8,000,
shows that the grand total cannot have been far short of 16,000.

Few modern writers attempt an assessment of the numbers.
Ramsay states briefly that the English "may have been 2,000
to 3,000 men" and leaves it at that. One would be glad to know
the reasoning that led to this conclusion. Oman gives no figures
at all, and Lot, after citing fairly fully the medieval figures,
which are unanimous in giving a clear superiority to the French,
refers inconsequentially to this superiority as "réelle ou pré-
tendue" (p. 24). But this lame conclusion–or inconclusion–
does not surprise us.

*   *   *

THE RECONSTRUCTION OF THE BATTLE

Until *The Brut Continuation H* was published the heavy losses
of the French compared with the Scots was something of a

puzzle. But this invaluable document ties up the battle into a comprehensive whole. It also establishes an unusual action in medieval warfare – the concentration on to the vital point of two widely separated units at the critical moment.

This document also enables us to locate the French division on the left of the line. Previous chroniclers were hopelessly at variance on the point, French sources placing Frenchmen in the front line and Scots in the third; whereas the Scottish source, the *Liber Pluscardine*, reverses this position. The fact is, both nations were anxious to appear to have borne the brunt of the fighting. In reality both accounts can be reconciled if we predicate, as I have done, that the Scots, as a formation, were on the right, and the French on the left. On this assumption, and on this alone, the battle seems to make sense, though I am not aware that anyone has suggested this formation before.

I have also disregarded the statement of Waurin (followed by nearly all writers) that the formation in rear was a baggage-guard. Doubtless the guarding of the baggage formed part of its duties, but there must have been more to it than that. Otherwise how are we to explain the original situation of this body, not with nor directly in front of the baggage-leaguer, but on the other flank? The commander of the reserve cannot have believed that his primary duty was to guard the baggage. Moreover, Bedford would hardly have allotted upwards of 20 per cent. of his force for this sole duty.

The last point concerns the formation of the archers. Practically all writers have taken Waurin's statement that the archers were "on the wings" to mean that they were formed in two bodies only, on the two flanks of the army. But this would constitute a striking departure from the formation of Agincourt and Crecy, and we have seen that in all other respects except the reserve (for which there was an obvious explanation) Bedford copied the Agincourt formation almost slavishly. It seemed evident to me that Waurin carelessly omitted the words "of divisions" after "on the flanks", and that his intention was to say that they took up the normal formation, that is, on both flanks of each division (though there may in addition have been, as at Agincourt, bodies of "army archers", as we might call them, on the extreme flanks of the line). Partial confirmation of this view is given by *Hall's Chronicle* which avers that archers were posted both in the front of the battle and on the wings.

CHAPTER XIII

FROM VERNEUIL TO ORLEANS

ON the morrow of the battle of Verneuil the prospects for the English cause were bright. A French field army no longer existed and the Dauphin would find it impossible to create a new one at short notice, for he had spent all available money in raising the one that had just foundered. Humanly speaking, there was nothing to prevent Bedford from advancing straight on Bourges and capturing it. Such action might have resulted in the ending of the war, for the Dauphinists, seeing the utter impotence of the French government, might have lost heart and given up the contest—even as did the inhabitants of Paris in 1360. Of course the Dauphin might have fallen back and set up another capital still further south, such as Toulouse,[1] and the war might have dragged on. Even so, an advance on Bourges would seem to have held out the best chances of a decision and the end of hostilities.

But the duke of Bedford did not take it. Instead he clung to his original plan, the conquest of Maine and Anjou, though he extended his objective to include the reduction of all the territory to the north of the Loire, and an attempt in the west to capture that almost impregnable fortress, Mont St. Michel.

To effect this he divided and scattered his army, entrusting the campaign in Maine to Sir John Fastolf and Lord Scales, the advance to the Loire to the earls of Salisbury and Suffolk, while Sir Nicholas Burdet was directed against Mont St. Michel. He himself departed to Rouen, ostensibly to punish the Norman deserters from Verneuil.

This conduct may appear supine to modern students of war, but before condemning Bedford too severely we should remember two things. First, in those days a war of sieges, such as was now being resumed, was the normal method of fighting;

---

[1] And his domains might then have become the prototype of "Vichy France".

second, both Edward III after Crecy and Henry V after Agincourt had not seized somewhat similar opportunities. There may therefore have been some adverse factors against such a course of which we, at this distance of time, are not aware. But, not knowing of any such, it is difficult for us to place John of Bedford in the highest rank of generals.

But whatever criticism may be passed on the regent, the military situation remained favourable and indeed continued to improve. In all but one theatre progress was registered. It was perhaps slow, but it was sure, and in the months immediately following the battle of Verneuil, the greater part of Maine and Anjou was over-run, the campaign towards the Loire was put in motion, and the few strongholds still holding out in Picardy and Champagne surrendered, and with them the formidable captain La Hire. Best of all perhaps was the loyal and successful co-operation of the duke of Burgundy. He conducted a campaign far to the south and almost reached the town of Macon. Only opposite Mont St. Michel was the general advance stayed.

*   *   *

It seemed to be a case of "all over but the shouting", when suddenly one of those totally unexpected turns of fortune occurred which are at once so upsetting to calculations yet so intriguing to the military historian. To explain what was about to happen we must hark back to the previous year, and dabble in purely political history.

It all started in a simple and apparently harmless way. The young Jacqueline, countess of Hainault and Holland in her own right, had married the boorish duke of Brabant. In 1421 she quarrelled with her husband and fled to the court of England, where she fell in love with the very presentable duke of Gloucester. After some difficulty, she obtained a dubious divorce and married Duke Humphrey. Now the duke of Brabant had assumed the government of Hainault and Holland, and Jacqueline was naturally eager to regain her own dominions. Equally naturally, as it seems to me, her new husband was eager to help her regain her just rights. To this end, he started raising contingents in England to help in the work of ejecting the Brabanters. For this he has been unmercifully condemned by practically all historians, for complications were bound to arise. The trouble was that the duke of Brabant came of the younger branch of the family of Burgundy, and duke Philip hotly espoused the cause of his cousin.

Matters came to a head in October, 1424, when Duke Humphrey and countess Jacqueline landed in Flanders with a contingent of mercenaries. Very soon the countess was in possession of her old domains, and Humphrey sent a force into Brabant which ravaged the country up to the gates of Brussels. The fat was in the fire. Duke Philip threatened even to go to war with England, and a heated correspondence passed between him and Gloucester. Humphrey wrote that Philip ought to espouse the cause of Jacqueline rather than that of duke John of Brabant, and technically there is much to be said for this view. But the sentence that really roused Burgundy was to the effect that he had stated something "contrary to the truth". Philip declared this to be a reflection on his honour and he challenged the Englishman to a duel, the Emperor to be the judge. Humphrey accepted the challenge, and as the Emperor was not forthcoming, Burgundy agreed to accept Philip's suggestion of Bedford as judge – a nice compliment to Duke John. It required all Bedford's tact, diplomacy and patience extending over several months to soothe the feelings of the irate Burgundian.[1]

The threatened breach between the two countries was eventually healed in an unexpected way. The tide of war turned against the Hainault cause, Humphrey went back to England in a somewhat equivocal manner, and never returned to the Continent.

Though Humphrey no doubt deserved the opprobrius epithets cast at him, one cannot overlook the romantic side that was bound to appeal to a high-metalled youth at the side of a

---

[1] His efforts even extended to taking part himself in a joust, a thing he had never done before; he probably lacked something of the martial ardour of his three brothers.

beautiful countess in distress. His conduct was human and understandable; but the consequences were almost disastrous, and with anyone but Bedford in the saddle they would have ended in an open breach with Burgundy, and the end of all English rule in France. And although the breach had been patched up it had unfortunate after-effects: it slowed up the tempo of the war in France at a time when it was looking so promising, and it was the beginning of the "rift in the lute" between England and Burgundy.

For the above reasons, we can pass rapidly over such military operations as there were during this period. The advance in Maine and Beauce (between Chartres and the Loire) came to a standstill, and it was not resumed till the arrival on the scene in the summer of 1425 of the earl of Salisbury with reinforcements.[1] He then carried out yet another of his successful campaigns. After a final "tidying up" of Champagne, he pushed westwards into Beauce, captured Etampes and Rambouillet, and drove forward into Maine. The town of Le Mans, its capital, fell to him on August 10, and Mayenne soon afterwards, and this completed the conquest of Maine. Owing to the absence of any English chroniclers of the period, details are lacking, as they are for most of Salisbury's operations in the war. After this the war languished, the duke of Gloucester again being the indirect cause. This time it was owing to his disturbing influence in home politics – in particular his quarrel with his uncle, Cardinal Beaufort – which entailed the presence of Bedford in England from December, 1425, to April, 1427. Gloucester was the protector in England, but Beaufort was the practical head of the government. Consequently there was a struggle for power between the two men which lasted for nearly 20 years.

While Bedford was in England the only operations that need be noticed were in Brittany, where that arrant turncoat, Jean V, duke of Brittany had now thrown in his lot with the Dauphin. In January, 1426, therefore, a small English force under Sir

[1] Salisbury paid frequent visits to England, and no doubt these visits had the double object – not only of raising reinforcements, but of providing some "Notes from the Front" for their training.

Thomas Rempston invaded the Duchy, and at one time penetrated as far as the capital. Rempston then established his base
in the little town of St. James-de-Beuvron, on the border of
Normandy, midway between Avranches (held by Suffolk) and
Fougères.

The brother of the duke of Brittany, Arthur of Richemont,
who had recently been made Constable of France, raised an
army to take to the help of his brother and in February, 1426, he
advanced to besiege St. James. His army was about 16,000
strong, while that of Rempston's garrison was a mere 600.[1]

The constable had brought with him a powerful force of
artillery, and with it he soon made two breaches in the walls.
On March 6 he assaulted, and a long fierce struggle took place,
lasting till the evening. The hard-pressed garrison then held a
council of war and decided on a desperate expedient. Leaving
a portion of his tiny force to hold the enemy in the breaches,
Rempston with the remainder crept out through a sally port, got
right round the enemy and attacked them in the rear uttering the
war cry: "Salisbury! St. George!". Thus assailed on two sides
at once the French gave way, despite the huge disparity in
numbers; many of them were driven into a nearby lake and
drowned, the remainder fell back to their camp suffering
heavily. But that was not the end. During the night a panic set
in, and burning their tents and abandoning artillery and stores,
the whole army dribbled away and did not stop till they had
reached their original point of departure near Fougères. Their
casualties are given as 600 killed, 50 captured and 18 standards.[2]
De Beaucourt's summing up is:

"Thus fled his army—routed by an enemy 20 times its inferior in
numbers. Thus terminated in a most lamentable reverse an expedition in which he had placed all his hopes."

This extraordinary "Rout of St. James"—one of the most

---

[1] These figures come from French sources and are accepted by both Dr. Cosneau,
in his admirable *Le Connétable de Richemont* and by Du Fresne de Beaucourt in his
Histoire de Charles VI.

[2] Edward Hall claims that the English captured 14 "great guns", 14 barrels
of powder, 300 pipes of wine, 200 pipes of biscuit and flour, 200 "frailes" [*sic*] of
figs and raisins, and 500 barrels of herrings—no doubt in preparation for Lent.

astonishing episodes in the Hundred Years War–puzzled the French chroniclers at the time and French historians since (it has escaped comment by English historians). A contemporary English source for the battle might throw light on it, but there is not one. Various excuses were put forward, but they sound mere palliatives. Whatever the true explanation, the consequences were clear: Arthur de Richemont retreated into Anjou and remained there inactive throughout the ensuing summer. The English remained unmolested at St. James. Two days after the battle the earl of Suffolk, who had evidently learnt of the victory, arrived at St. James with 1,500 troops, rightly resolved to take advantage of this unexpected success. He is, however, open to criticism for not having arrived even earlier. Possibly he had "written off" the town in view of the immense superiority of the French.

The earl of Suffolk now united his force to the garrison and advanced towards Rennes. This town lies 45 miles to the west of St. James; midway between the two is the walled town of Dol (where Harold Godwinson had so distinguished himself when fighting under the banner of Duke William of Normandy). Suffolk occupied Dol without any let or hindrance from the constable de Richemont or Jean V. Further advance proved unnecessary, for the vacillating duke of Brittany now decided that it was time to change his coat again. He sent to apply for a three months' truce, which Suffolk granted. After a little more fighting in the following year this truce ripened into a treaty which was signed in the summer of 1427. By it Jean V recognized Henry VI as king of France. His *volte face* had been complete.

Meanwhile the regent had returned to France, and the arrival of reinforcements enabled him to put fresh vigour into the war. He sent an army 2,000 strong under Warwick and Suffolk into the eastern theatre of the war. On July 1 they laid siege to Montargis, 60 miles south-east of Paris and 40 miles east of Orleans. The siege lasted two months, and was of interest for two reasons. It brought into prominence, in an effort to relieve it, not only La Hire (now released) but a new figure in the person of a bastard son of the late duke of Orleans, known as the Count de Dunois. These two enterprising leaders fell upon a portion of the besieging force, cut it to pieces, captured Suffolk's brother and relieved the town. The English retreated, leaving most of their guns. This was the first "ray of sunshine" (as de Beaucourt called it) that the French had enjoyed; Charles VII described it, at a time when Joan of Arc was still alive, as "le commencement et cause de nostre bonheur". This was an undoubted set-back for the English cause, but exactly how far it set back their progress in the campaign of conquest it is hard to say. The "ray of sunshine" warmed the hearts of the Dauphinists and there were some slight reactions in the west; but the English were apparently not discouraged, nor put off from their resolution to pursue the war vigorously. The trouble was a shortage of troops. It should be noted that for over two years the English had been operating single-handed, for the duke of Burgundy, though he had not openly broken with his allies, had withdrawn his field troops into the Low Countries for the war against Jacqueline. The only Burgundian leader who still kept the field was John de Luxembourg, who–ever faithful to the House of Lancaster–was operating in the Argonne in eastern France. The earl of Salisbury was sent home once more to raise fresh troops, and spent the latter part of 1427 and the spring of 1428 engaged in that duty. His task was not rendered easier by the persistent efforts of Humphrey of Gloucester to revive the war in the Low Countries on behalf of the Countess Jacqueline. Any troops that he could collect for this purpose necessarily reduced the number available for France. Eventually Bedford succeeded in putting a stop to the whole project and Salisbury was able to produce a small army 2,700 strong. With this force he sailed from Sandwich on July 19 and landed at Calais on July 24, 1428, whence he pushed straight on via Amiens to Paris.

While Salisbury was collecting reinforcements in England two isolated actions took place in Maine that deserve notice, for they introduce a new figure to the war with whom we shall have a good deal to do before we finish–John, Lord Talbot.

When Bedford returned from England in the spring of 1427 he had brought in his train Lord Talbot. His first engagement was at the capture of Pontorson by the earl of Warwick. Later he took part in the siege of Montargis, and when the spring of 1428 came round he collected a force at Alençon for some project of which our French informant does not tell us the nature. Whilst thus employed, a message reached him from the garrison of Le Mans, some 30 miles to the south, that the French under the ubiquitous La Hire had seized the town and that they were cooped up in the Tour Ribendèle. Talbot's response was immediate. Marching with only 300 men, "this valiant English chevalier" as the Frenchman Cousinot called him,[1] arrived outside the walls between dawn and sunrise, in other words at the most favourable moment for attack. His troops over-ran the somnolent guards, and rushed into the town shouting "St. George!" The surprise and success was complete; aided by the friendly inhabitants, the French were ejected and the imprisoned garrison rescued.

The second action occurred shortly afterwards when, by another swoop, Talbot captured the town of Laval (midway between Angers and Avranches) which had till then always held out against the English.

These two actions, which were to become typical of Talbot's methods, made a great impression on contemporary French opinion, though they seem to have been allowed to go unrecorded in England.

APPENDIX

THE SOURCES

The four years that intervene between the battle of Verneuil and the siege of Orleans is a bad period for sources. There is an almost complete blank in English chronicle history, while for military operations France is only slightly better provided for. Waurin is almost silent and we must rely more than one would wish on Monstrelet for the Burgundian side. It is true the *Bour-*

[1] *Chronique de la Pucelle* by G. Cousinot, p. 252.

geois de Paris is becoming important, but more for the political than for the military aspect, for he was a civilian resident in Paris. Thus, for the battle of St. James the nearest English chronicler that we can make use of is Edward Hall who wrote a good 100 years later, albeit that his military information is often quite good. Monstrelet's account of St. James is also useful (though ignored by Ramsay for some reason), but, though Ramsay cites *le Bourgeois* for the battle, this author gives no account of it. On the Dauphinist side there are only two real accounts. Easily the best is that of G. Gruel in his *Chronique d'Arthur de Richemont*. The other is *Chronique de la Pucelle*, by G. Cousinot. Of modern histories for the battle we have none in England. In France we have Dr. E. Cosneau's *Le Connétable de Richemont*–the best account–and the *Histories of Charles VII*, by M. Vallet de Viriville (1863) and du Fresne de Beaucourt (1881). In the rather disjointed account of the period by the former I can find no description of the battle, but the latter contains a fair account.

But it is a bleak period for sources on both sides.

CHAPTER XIV

THE SIEGE OF ORLEANS

LATE in July, 1428, Thomas Montague, earl of Salisbury, entered Paris at the head of his army of 2,700 men. The question now arose: how should this army be employed? By collecting contingents from all over occupied France, it was found possible to raise the numbers to about 5,000. Long and careful war councils were held in order to decide on the plan, for it was agreed that a vigorous effort must now be made to bring the war to a conclusion.

Two schools of thought soon arose; the first school advocated the completion of the conquest of Anjou, which meant in practice the capture of Angers its capital; the other school favoured the capture of Orleans. There can be little doubt as to which of these plans represented the soundest strategy. Orleans lies midway between Paris and Bourges, the Dauphin's capital, about 60 miles from each; whilst Angers was more than twice as far from it. Anjou was an old domain of the Plantagenet kings, and its complete domination would not have any direct effect on the Dauphin's cause. It was a very indirect approach to the main objective – the Dauphin's capital. Orleans, as we have seen, constituted the direct approach which is generally the soundest form of strategy. Moreover, its capture would breach the river Loire, which had become the *de facto* boundary of the Dauphinist domains. To rupture this line had long been the aim of the English leaders, but nothing permanent had been accomplished. Orleans was not only midway between the two capitals, but the nearest point to Paris on the vital river Loire. An English army operating in that sector would thus be more easily supplied and reinforced than any other point on the river. But the duke of Bedford favoured the Anjou plan. It is surprising that he should do so, for his previous attempt to conquer Maine and Anjou, though it had made some progress, had not weakened the will of the Dauphinists to fight on, and four more years of warfare had not brought the end appreciably nearer.

For all these reasons the earl of Salisbury, now the most experienced and uniformly successful general on the English side, favoured the direct approach–the maintenance of the objective–which was to hit the enemy where it would hurt him most.

After some weeks of argument the Orleans school prevailed. The regent regretfully acquiesced in it and in mid-August the invading army set out.[1]

THE ORLEANS CAMPAIGN

The earl of Salisbury, decided to make Chartres his first objective. Retaking on the way four towns that had fallen back into Dauphinist hands, he entered the city in the latter half of August and then turned sharply south-east towards Janville 26 miles distant. On the way he captured a number of places with the minimum of resistance except at Puiset, ten miles north of Janville, which had to be stormed.

Janville was a walled town (much of its moat still exists) and had a resolute garrison. Something curious happened here. According to Hall, Bedford intended to reduce the garrison by siege, but his troops, angered by some action on the part of the garrison, "took the bit in their teeth" after only a few days siege, and assaulted the town and took it by storm, "after the most formidable assault that we have ever seen" as Salisbury himself wrote to the mayor and aldermen of the city of London. Sismondi, however, avers that the garrison offered to surrender but that Salisbury, with implacable harshness, would not listen to them but preferred to take it by storm.[2] This seems improbable, to say the least. The English army was already over-small

[1] It is sometimes asserted that Bedford was not aware of Salisbury's intention, on the grounds that Salisbury set off in the direction of Anjou and that Bedford in a famous letter to Henry VI wrote, "Alle things prospered for you till the time of the seage of Orleans, taken God knows by what advice". But Salisbury set out towards Anjou, in order to deceive the enemy, not his own side. As for Bedford's letter, it lays the duke open to the suspicion of prevarication or at least of a *suggestio falsi*, for though he disliked the Orleans project there is no evidence that he did anything to prevent it or to reprimand Salisbury for undertaking it.
[2] *Histoire des Français*, XIII, p. 87.

for the task before it: why then should its commander go out of his way to endanger the lives of his men in a preliminary operation if he could secure his end without striking a single blow?

Janville lies 15 miles north of Orleans, and Salisbury decided (probably in advance) to make of it a sort of forward base, or supply depot, for his army during what he foresaw might be a long and arduous siege of Orleans. The town was well situated for its purpose, being on the direct road from Paris to Orleans and only a day's march from the latter.

The establishment of this base being completed, the next stage of a carefully thought out strategical plan was taken in hand. This was to isolate the city by water, by capturing the Dauphinist defended towns immediately above and below it: that is to say, Jargeau above and Beaugency and Meung below the city. First he turned his attention to the downstream towns. Meung and Beaugency lie 12 and 20 miles respectively below Orleans, both on the northern bank of the Loire. Obviously Meung was the first town to be secured. Now the road from Janville to Meung passes within a few kilometres of Orleans, and it was necessary to use this road for the artillery that might be required in the siege. On September 8, therefore, Salisbury posted a left flank-guard on the outskirts of the city to safeguard the passage of his artillery to the siege. As things happened, the guns were not required, for Meung surrendered tamely, and Salisbury was enabled to pass on to the siege of Beaugency. This proved to be not quite so simple a task, for the château and the abbey, which had been fortified, were just within range of the near end of the many-arched bridge. The garrison confined their defence to the château and bridge. But the English, being now in possession of the bridge at Meung, were able to approach it from the southern bank. The siege opened on September 20, and on the 25th a simultaneous attack was made upon the château from the north and on the bridge from the south after an artillery bombardment. There seems to have been a tussle on the bridge, and one can picture knights in armour being hurled over its parapet into the river, for mail armour has been dredged from the river bed beneath the bridge.[1] The attack was successful and on the 26th the garrison surrendered, and the inhabitants swore fidelity to King Henry VI.

The first stage in the great operation had thus been accomplished and Salisbury, in a letter to the mayor of London, showed justifiable pride in it. He stated that 40 towns, châteaux and fortified churches had fallen into his hands, and this was no empty claim for all 40 have been identified by M. Lognon, and repeated by A. de Villaret.[2]

Salisbury wasted no time, but switched his troops at once to the eastern side of Orleans, and on October 2, Sir William de la Pole laid siege to Jargeau, 12 miles up-stream. Though defended by formidable ramparts and ditch this town only held out for three days, and shortly afterwards Chateauneuf, ten miles further upstream, also fell. Orleans was thus doubly blocked by water on each side and the English army could now settle down to the siege of this redoubtable city. In the words of M. de Villaret:

"Salisbury, with the audacity that proclaims assurance of success, attacked the ancient city, the final hope of the poor King of Bourges and the last rampart of his power."[3]

Jargeau lies on the southern bank of the Loire, and thus enabled de la Pole to march thence to Orleans along this bank and approach the city from the south. This he did on October 7, and appeared in front of the bridge leading across the river into the city the same day. Five days later he was joined by the earl of Salisbury at the head of the main army, who presumably crossed the Loire by the Meung bridge. The whole army now encamped in Olivet, the southern suburb of the city. The earl's chief lieutenants were the earl of Suffolk, his brother de la Pole, Lords Ros and Scales, and Sir William Glasdale. Owing to the necessity of leaving detachments and garrisons on the road his

---

[1] It can now be seen in the town museum. The lower part of the Abbey is now a restaurant and from its terrace the bridge is in full view and the whole scene can be easily envisaged.

[2] *Campagnes des Anglais dans L'Orleanais, La Beauce, Chartraine, et le Gatinais* (Orleans 1893).

[3] Op. cit., p. 70.

army probably did not exceed 4,000 men at this juncture.[1] It was later to be joined by about 1,500 Burgundians, whom Duke John had allowed to take the pay of England. The English artillery was fewer in numbers and less powerful than that of the garrison, but some of the guns could reach the centre of the city at a range of over 1,000 yards.

As for the city of Orleans, an attack had been feared for some years past, and the defences had been greatly strengthened until it was probably the best-defended town in the whole of the Dauphin's dominions. It was also well provided with artillery and ammunition. In the city was at least one great ballista. Side by side with it were some surprisingly big guns. Some of the stone cannon-balls weighed as much as 192 lb., and one of them is recorded as engaging an English ferry—a moving target—at a range that I compute as about 1,400 yards. There were no fewer than 71 guns, many of them made of leather, mounted on the walls. The regular garrison was around 2,400[2] and another 3,000 *milice* were found from the civil population, which numbered over 30,000.

The river was nearly 400 yards broad, shallow, rapid, but navigable, with numerous sand-banks and islands. Over one of these a bridge, 350 metres long, joined the town to the south bank. (See Sketch Map 8, p. 585.) As this bridge comes prominently into the story it must be described. It consisted of nineteen arches, and was built A.D. 1100-1133. (It was demolished in 1760, but the old piles can still be seen when the water is low.) On the southernmost of these arches, and separated from the bank by a drawbridge, a fort with two towers, called Les Tourelles, had been built. An earthwork had also been thrown up on the southern bank as a sort of barbican or horn-work. The city wall was massive, with towers and bastions, and there were five powerfully defended gates.

---

[1] Boucher de Molandon, in *L'Armée Anglaise vaincue par Jeanne d'Arc*, in an exhaustive research makes the number 3,467 "plus 898 pages". Louis Jarry, in an equally careful account, makes it 3,189.

[2] This is de Molandon's figure. Ferdinand Lot reduces it to 1,570, and appears to ignore the *milice*.

Altogether, it was the most formidable obstacle that had confronted the English since the siege of Rouen. It is not surprising if the regent viewed with apprehension the attempt to reduce it with Salisbury's tiny army.

The earl of Salisbury opened operations in the normal style—that is, he directed a cannonade against the Tourelles and the town. After a few days he reckoned that the work was ripe for assault and launched his troops to the attack of the horn-work. The French resisted so strenuously that Salisbury promptly changed his plan. He had brought a large force of miners with him and, having presumably reduced the guns of the horn-work to silence, he set his miners to work against the foundations of the fort. After two days of this the garrison lost heart, abandoned the horn-work and, surprisingly as it seems to us, the Tourelles too, breaking down two arches of the bridge behind them. (The French assert, most improbably, that the English also broke an arch.)

Thus, the first step in the reduction of the town had been achieved, and Salisbury at once set about the second. Having hastily repaired the Tourelles, the next step was reconnaissance, on the result of which he would base his plan of attack. The earl therefore established what we should call his observation post high up in the tower of the Tourelles. At a quiet moment during the dinner hour, when the French gunners had gone to their meal, leaving their cannons loaded and laid, the English commander took a party of his chief officers with him and ascended to this observation post. From it they had a good look at the city and discussed plans for the assault. Now it happened that a lad, the son of one of the gunners, was playing about among the French cannon and, whether for a lark or because he spotted the English party looking out from the Tourelles, he touched off one of the cannons. The earl of Salisbury heard the shot coming and ducked. The cannon-ball hit the lintel of the window, dislodging an iron bar which struck the earl on the side of the face, removing half of it. Since the details of this story are almost the only items that come from English sources, it may be

of interest to reproduce the passage in our earliest printed source,
The Brut, which was almost contemporaneous with the event:

"And tho at the laste, as he was busi to seke and loke upon his
ordynaunce, for to gete it [the town] if he might, a fals thef, a
traitour withynne the towne, shotte a gonne, and the stone smot
this good Earle of Salusbury, and he was dede through the stroke;
wherefore was made grete doole and sorrowe for hys dethe, long
tyme afterward, for the greate doughtynesse and manhood that
was found in hym, and in hys governaunce at all tymes."

The stricken earl was removed to Meung where he died
eight days later, after adjuring his officers gathered round his

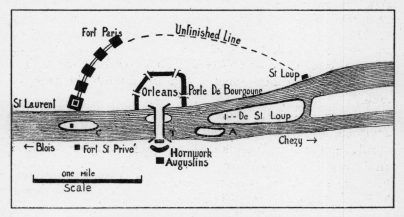

Sketch Map 8: THE SIEGE OF ORLEANS

◼━◼	Line of forts	A	Isle de St. Aignan
T	Tourelles	C	Isle de Charlemagne

bed to persevere with the war till they had obtained complete
victory. His death was a calamity indeed. The French were
fully aware of the extent of it, and the poem *Le Mistère d'Orleans*
puts into the mouth of William Glasdale this lamentation:

> Luy qui a fait et soustenu
> Du tout nostre ost par sa vaillance,
> Et qui très bien entretenu,
> Qu'il avoit conquis toute la France.

There can be no doubt that Salisbury, who had brought
almost as many miners as artillerymen to the siege, had every

intention of taking the town by assault; and had he been spared he would probably have succeeded, for the garrison was then thoroughly demoralized, as we shall see. He was succeeded in the command by the earl of Suffolk, who was opposed to any action of a hazardous nature, and instead of persevering with an operation so well begun, tamely withdrew the field army to winter quarters in the neighbouring towns. He left an isolated garrison under the captain, Sir William Glasdale, in the Tourelles and in a fortification which they threw up round the church of the Augustins immediately to the south of it. Yet though the French in the vicinity were now in overwhelming strength, and had indeed been reinforced by the Count de Dunois, the bastard of Orleans,[1] they left it completely unmolested for three weeks.[2] Thus the action of the English was not so fatuous as it appears to our eyes; it was a "calculated risk", and judging by the result, a justifiable one. This is a point of significance, for it shows what a tremendous power morale was in those days, and will explain much that is otherwise inexplicable in the further course of the siege.

Probably the chief reason for the withdrawal was to preserve the health of the troops whilst billets were being constructed for them outside the walls. The inhabitants had razed to the ground the suburbs outside the walls, including many churches, in order that the besieging army might not find ready-made billets. Again it may be that the breathing space was required in order to bring up heavy ordnance to breach the town walls.

Whatever be the truth of this, and we shall never know the full reasons, the army began to flow back to the siege in December. John Lord Talbot also arrived on December 1,[3] and he and Lord Scales were now associated in the chief command with the earl of Suffolk. This seems an odd and unsatisfactory arrange-

---

[1] Half-brother of the Duke of Orleans, who had been captured at Agincourt and was still a prisoner in England.

[2] Miss Sackville-West well writes: "The English held the French in a snake-like fascination."

[3] Most accounts assert that Talbot shared the command with Suffolk and Scales on the death of Salisbury—which is impossible.

ment. The explanation probably is that Bedford had lost confidence in Suffolk as an independent commander. It may, indeed, be significant that three years previously he had been replaced whilst in command at Pontorson for some reason unknown to us.

John Talbot was a remarkable man. He spent no fewer than 50 years under arms, and was at this time about 46 years old. He soon became known to the French as "The English Achilles", and it is significant that at first his was the only English name known to Joan of Arc.

We can probably deduce the English plan of operations from what followed. The attempt to take the town by a *coup de main* had failed, so recourse was now had to a normal siege procedure of mining and bombardment. But there were abnormal difficulties. The perimeter of the town was 2,000 yards. To construct a besieging line 700 yards outside the wall would require nearly 4,000 yards of fortifications, excluding works on the south bank. These would require a long time to construct, nor were there sufficient troops adequately to man them when constructed. What was to be done? Common-sense would suggest that the work should be commenced on the critical side, *i.e.*, the western, whence reinforcements might arrive from the Dauphin's headquarters at Chinon, and that as time went on and the besieging army was increased, the line might, if necessary, be drawn right round the town, if it had not before then surrendered. This is precisely the procedure followed by the English army.

Here a reference should be made to the map. First of all, a great base camp, as it may be called, was constructed round the church of St. Laurent, on the northern bank, connected with the Tourelles by a fort on the Isle of Charlemagne. Thence in succession to the north a line of four forts (called bastilles), connected by communication trenches, were constructed. An isolated fort was also constructed at St. Loup, one-and-a-half miles east of the town. This work took until about the beginning of April to complete; and meanwhile the eastern side of the town was perforce left open; through this gap reinforcements and supplies could enter the town without much danger, being screened on their way by a forest belt, though occasionally they were cut off. To anticipate, work was put in hand on entrenching this gap, and constructing a bastille, when early in April the Burgundian mercenaries incontinently departed and there were insufficient troops left to complete the work.[1]

The siege operations were mainly of an artillery nature though there were occasional sorties and sallies, and reinforcements in driblets got through. And thus things went on till the beginning of February. The Dauphin now at last bestirred himself and he assembled a relieving force. It was based on Blois, 40 miles downstream from Orleans, and was put under the command of Charles of Bourbon, count of Clermont.

* * *

THE BATTLE OF THE HERRINGS (February 12, 1429)

Meanwhile Lent was approaching, the season when fish must be the staple diet. A convoy was therefore fitted out at Paris and despatched to Orleans early in February. Its commander was Sir John Fastolf, and it consisted of 300 wagon-loads of herrings and other commodities. The escort, all mounted, consisted of about 1,000 archers and some Paris militia. On the 11th of the month it reached the little village of Rouvray, five miles north of Janville, where it spent the night. Next morning it was just setting out when mounted patrols, evidently forming the vanguard of a French army, appeared on the sky-line to the southwest. It was indeed the army of Count Clermont, which was approaching. News of the march of the convoy had reached Blois, and Clermont had instantly decided to march north-east in the endeavour to cut it off from its destination.

Fastolf was a general of great experience. Quick to realize the extent of the danger, he took a step most unusual, if not unprecedented, at that period: he halted his whole convoy and escort in an open space on the road to Janville one mile south of Rouvray.

[1] The ground is now a built-up area and all signs of any entrenchments or works have vanished.

He had recognized that his slow-moving convoy had but little chance of reaching the protection that Janville might provide; and that if caught on the march the line of wagons, which must have been about three miles long, could not be adequately protected by his small force against a mounted adversary who was in fact thrice as numerous as his own escort. He promptly halted and constructed with his wagons a leaguer. It had two openings: these openings he defended with archers; the remainder of the army taking cover inside. Thus when the French came up they found in their path what we might now call a "hedgehog".

This was something novel in medieval warfare, but the count of Clermont, the French commander, fitted his tactics to the novel situation. He was provided with a large number of cannons (of small calibre), whereas the English had none. Instead, therefore, of making a direct attack on them he ordered an artillery bombardment. To this, of course, the English had no reply and they had to "sit and suffer" while casualties steadily mounted. Many of the wagons were holed by the cannon-balls and the herrings spilled on to the ground. If this bombardment had been persisted in there could have been but one outcome— the ignominious surrender of the English army. And it would have constituted the first occasion in military history when guns had brought victory in the field.

But the unpredictable happened. In the French army was a Scottish contingent, small in size. Its commander was Sir John Stewart of Darnley, the Constable of the Scots in France.[1] Clermont's orders were that the whole army (less the gunners and crossbowmen) should remain mounted, but Stewart disregarded this order; he not only dismounted his men but, not waiting for the artillery bombardment to take effect, advanced impulsively to the attack. It encountered the deadly fire of the English archers, and suffered a bloody repulse.

The French men-at-arms then essayed a mounted attack, but this also was disastrous. A Burgundian writer describes how

[1] He had been wounded in the eye and captured by the English at the battle of Cravant six years before, and subsequently released.

the French cavalry spurred their horses on to the stakes that the English archers had stuck into the ground in their front, how the horses were impaled on them and how their riders were pitched forward over their ears. Just what one might have expected to happen! The same writer says that when the Scots saw the outcome of this affray they fled. I doubt this: I think it occurred a little later in the battle.

For the time had come for the counter-attack. Sir John Fastolf now ordered his men-at-arms to get mounted, the archers at the openings made way for them, and two torrents of English cavalry poured out of the leaguer and put the crowning touch to the victory. The Franco-Scottish army was scattered to the winds. The battle of the Herrings, or of Rouvray, was won. Sir John Fastolf delivered his precious supplies to the army in triumph, and returned to Paris for more. The spirits of the English were raised; the hearts of the French drooped to their very nadir.[1] The relieving army had quite unexpectedly been broken into smithereens, and all hope of relief must now be abandoned. Negotiations for surrender were, therefore, put in hand.

But the course of history is inscrutable; even unpredictable. Suddenly there appeared a portent in the west, a comet in the sky: another relieving army was approaching, and at its head, incredible though it sounds, marched a Maid.

JOAN OF ARC AT ORLEANS

Joan of Arc was a peasant girl, about 17 years of age.[2] In her early girlhood she heard what she called her "Voices". The exact nature of these voices is, fortunately, outside the province of this book to examine or pronounce upon. All we are concerned with is the practical effect they had upon her and the practical effect she in turn had upon the military operations.

First the effect upon herself. The Voices convinced her, to the very depth of her being, that it was the will of the King of Heaven

[1] Professor Lot writes (op. cit., p. 37): "This stupid defeat had a disastrous influence on the morale of the French captains. They were firmly convinced of the impossibility of further resistance at Orleans."

[2] There is doubt about her exact age, but Eugène Deprez lends the weight of his great name to the statement that she was born on January 4, 1412.

that the English should be thrown out of France and that she was in some way to be instrumental in their eviction. This developed into the belief that, as a first step, the Dauphin must be anointed with the holy oil at Rheims, after which the English would not be able to stand against the powers of the King of Heaven, wielded terrestrially by the new king, Charles VII. Joan's own first step was therefore obvious: she must impart to the Dauphin the message given her by her Voices. On February 23, 1429, just a fortnight after the battle of the Herrings, she set off from her home on the eastern border of France to seek out the Dauphin in his castle at Chinon, 25 miles south-west of Tours. The ultimate upshot of the interview that she obtained with Charles, in spite of the opposition of la Trémoïlle his chancellor, was that he fitted out a fresh army for the relief of Orleans, placed the duke of Alençon in command of it and allowed Joan, resplendent with banner and a full suit of armour, to accompany it.

On April 27, 1429, the army, about 4,000 strong, set out from Blois, along the south bank of the river. The march was uneventful materially; spiritually it was one of the most important and exciting marches ever made by an army. For that army was spiritually transformed, and it was all the work of the Maid.

Whether they regarded her as a saint or a mascot, the simple credulous French soldiers took heart of grace from her presence among them, and unquestioningly, as far as we can gather, obeyed her behests as to behaviour. And they were exacting and unpopular behests: swearing was to be abolished, loose women were not to be tolerated, and everyone must attend Mass and make his confession. A large body of priests marched at the head of the army chanting psalms. The atmosphere was one of elation, almost of ecstasy, as the troops set out on the gay adventure on which, they knew, Heaven was smiling. In military parlance, their morale was high, and it had been raised by precisely the same means as those employed by Archbishop Thurstan before the battle of the Standard, by Henry V before Agincourt, and by Oliver Cromwell before Dunbar.

Before setting out, Joan dictated a letter to the English, opening with a sentence so astonishing as almost to take the breath away:

"King of England, and you Duke of Bedford . . . render up to the Maid who is sent by God, the King of Heaven, the keys of all the good towns that you have taken and violated in France."

Well might Bedford raise his eyebrows and rub his chin when he received such a missive. It has been averred that terror was struck into the hearts of the English army, but there is no satisfactory evidence that the troops in the English camp, except the leaders, were even aware of the Maid's existence on her arrival outside the city on April 28.

With the army came a convoy of supplies for the city. There were two possible means of getting them into the town without having to risk a battle, to which the French were naturally averse. One was to make a wide circuit to the north through the forest, and approach through the gap between forts Paris and St. Loup; the other was by barge from Chezy five miles upstream, landing them at the Porte de Bourgoyne on the eastern face of the city. This was rendered possible owing to the neglect of the earl of Suffolk to stretch a chain across the river—a laxity that would have horrified Henry V. The count of Dunois[1] who was in command in the town, but in communication with Alençon without, no doubt reported this absence of river barrier and suggested the possibility of this route for the convoy. Thus it was that Alençon led his army by the southern bank of the Loire, contrary to the wish of the Maid that they should follow the northern bank. Why she, being ignorant of the topography, should have any views on the point is not clear. Alençon, for some reason, kept his plan secret from Joan.

To carry out the plan numerous barges were required, but Chezy could not supply them. There were, however, a sufficient number lying idle and empty under the walls of the city. The plan concocted between Alençon and Dunois was therefore as follows. When the wind should be favourable the empty barges

---

[1] Generally known thus, though he was not created count till 1441.

were to sail upstream to Chezy, and meanwhile the army would halt opposite the city, while the convoy marched on to Chezy. There the supplies for the city would be transferred to the barges which could then slip downstream, whatever the direction of the wind.[1] In order to distract attention during the downstream journey Dunois arranged a demonstration against Fort St. Loup. It was no doubt this demonstration, coupled with the fact that St. Loup possessed few cannons, that ensured the success of the project.

The wind changed in the nick of time, and all went according to plan. Joan with a small escort also crossed over the river at Chezy and entered the city overland, next morning, April 30, amid the rejoicings of the populace.

The action of the escorting army was puzzling. It did not cross over the river and enter the town by the unguarded Porte de Bourgoyne, as one might have expected, but immediately returned to Blois, and a few days later set out again for Orleans with further supplies, but this time on the northern bank. The usual surmise is that only a portion of the convoy could be escorted on the first trip, and consequently the army had to return for the other half. It is not easy to see why it should not all have travelled with the first expedition; nor, even if unavoidable, why the previous route which had proved so successful was not again followed. There is, as a matter of fact, evidence contained in the town accounts that some wheat did reach the garrison by water on May 4, so it is just possible (though I have never heard the suggestion advanced) that the army marched by the north bank with the specific object of distracting attention from the convoy which marched in on the south bank.

The relieving army entered Orleans on the morning of May 3. Up to date it would seem that the English had practically ignored the Maid – assuming that they were even aware of her presence. But that was their mistake, and they were soon to

[1] The belief, sponsored by Bernard Shaw's play *St. Joan*, that the problem was merely to cross the river into the town but that this could not be done unless the wind was favourable is of course absurd.

realize it; for later that day, while another attack was being made on Fort St. Loup (probably intended only as a diversion to cover the entry of the wheat), Joan galloped out of the town, joined the attackers and inspired them with such enthusiasm and military zeal that they actually captured and burnt the fort.[1] Probably both sides were equally surprised at this unprecedented occurrence. The fact that Fort St. Loup was so dangerously isolated was evidence of the supreme disdain that the besiegers had for their enemies at this time. However, Talbot, finding that the attack was actually being pressed home, moved round from his headquarters in Fort St. Laurent, picking up a few troops from each fort as he passed, with the intention of going to its relief. But the French, spotting his intention from the walls, sent out a covering force to engage him. The two bodies clashed outside Fort Paris, and at the same time Talbot saw the smoke rising from St. Loup. He realized that he was too late, and had no option but to fall back inside his own lines.

The capture of St. Loup was the turning point of the siege, and in a sense the whole war. What followed in the next few days is highly dramatic, but is already well known and does not raise many problems, so it may be passed over briefly. The next day was Ascension Day, and to show how chroniclers contradicted one another, some assert that Joan refused to fight that day, while others assert the exact opposite, that she wished to attack but was restrained by Dunois. So the attack took place on May 6, and it was directed with sound judgement on the part of Dunois against the Tourelles. The striking force for this task crossed the river by boat to the Isle of St. Aignan, and thence by a short bridge of two boats to the south bank. Why the garrison of the Tourelles allowed this bridge to be constructed does not appear. There is an obvious gap in the narrative at this point, and one man's guess is as good as another's. Mine is that the advanced party crossed by boat and kept the garrison engaged while the bridge was being

---

[1] The so-called fort appears to have been little more than the church of St. Loup put into a state of defence.

built (the small observation post of St. John le Blanc had been evacuated).

The fight for the Augustins fort was a homeric affair. The English were hopelessly outnumbered. Anatole France calculates that no fewer than 4,000 French were concentrated against the work, with 500 English in it and the Tourelles. After an all-day struggle, and several repulses, the fort was at last captured, thanks to the resolution and stimulating influence of Joan. The next morning the attack was resumed, this time against the barbican. The previous day's history was repeated and even intensified. Guns, scaling ladders and mines were brought up; even a fire-ship was rigged out and floated down beneath the drawbridge, which was thus set alight. The retreat of the garrison of the horn-work was thus threatened, and as they fell back into the Tourelles across the drawbridge it collapsed and the gallant Glasdale, waving aloft the banner of the Black Prince's great captain Chandos, was cast into the river and drowned. Last of all, the powder for the cannons failed, until the charge was so small that the cannon-balls merely dribbled out of the muzzles and fell harmlessly into the water. At the same time, the garrison of the town had extemporized the equivalent of what is now known as a Bailey bridge, with which they spanned the broken arches and attacked from the north simultaneously with the attack from the south. This was the last straw; the small remnant of the garrison, that had fought as gallant a fight as is recorded in our annals, surrendered, and the Maid of Orleans three hours later proudly rode her charger across the bridge into the acclaiming city. And well did she deserve her triumph. For there had been no sign of crumbling morale on the part of the English garrison, some of whose names should be rescued from oblivion. Here they are: John Reid, William Arnold, Walter Parker, Matthew Thornton, William Vaughan, John Burford, Pat Hall, Tom Sand, John Langham, Tom Jolly, George Ludlow, Black Harry, Bill Martin, Davy Johnson and Dick Hawke. (Tom Cobley's name does not appear.)

The English leaders had now to make a cruel decision. Their

great advantage over the enemy—the superiority of their morale
—had vanished in a couple of nights, and they were left with an
impossible military position. Heavily outnumbered and out-
gunned, one half of their position—patiently built up in the
course of the previous six months—had crumpled up, the town
walls were as intact as ever, the garrison was indeed increased,
and supplies could be admitted at will; finally, the morale had
passed to the enemy's side. Look where they would, the English
commanders could see no single redeeming feature, and I thnik
they showed their good judgement by bowing to the logic of events
and abandoning what was now shown to be a quite impossible
enterprise. But one action still was open to them, one proud
gesture to show that the English leopard had not got its tail
between its legs. On the morning of May 8, the whole army was
marshalled in battle array and advanced into No Man's Land
opposite the ramparts, where it silently stood, challenging the
French to come out and engage it in open battle. After waiting
for some time, and the French making no indication of desire
to engage, the army quietly filed away to the north "en bon
ordre", as the French chroniclers are forced to admit. There was
no attempt at pursuit. As in the case of Sir Richard Grenville:

> "They dared not touch us again
> For they knew that we still could sting."

Thus did the Maid and the Bastard of Orleans triumph over
the English Achilles.

OBSERVATIONS ON THE SIEGE

To those readers who have obtained their knowledge of the
siege from biographies of Joan of Arc, the above account may
be scarcely recognizable. The Maid herself hardly seems to
come into the story, yet surely she was the central figure in it?
An explanation is obviously required. In the first place, it is
natural that biographies of the Maid should concentrate on her
rather than on the general history and military aspect of the
siege. This tends to give a distorted impression of the course and
importance of events. In the second place, statements made by

contemporary fellow-countrymen may be, consciously or unconsciously, biased. The most reliable statements are those given by eye-witnesses at the *Procès de Rehabilitation*. But even these must be treated with reserve. As M. Edouard Perroy has observed:

"The testimony (of the Procès) relates memories already distant and, so to speak, hazy with legend. It comes from those same countrymen of hers legitimately and sincerely anxious to clear her memory. . . ."[1]

In the third place, testimony from the English side is almost completely lacking, and few writers seem to have made allowance for this. I except M. Boucher de Molandon, whose *L'Armée Anglaise vaincue par Jeanne d'Arc* (1892) is the most thorough investigation into this aspect of the subject that I know. M. de Molandon, after pointing out that a great deal has been written about the raising of the siege, adds:

"But it is evident that, in the absence of any English chronicle giving in detail the general idea and the methods of attack, much remains to be said."[2]

But it is not easy to say it. For we are in the realm of conjecture. A contemporary poem was given the title *Le Mystère d'Orléans*, for the raising of the siege did appear to Frenchmen at the time as a divine mystery. To Englishmen it appears a mystery of another nature. How, they may well ask, came it about that at a time when English military prowess and prestige were at their height could their commanders make so many apparently egregious errors and act in so supine a way as they apparently did? So far as this is true I think it can legitimately be laid at the door of the earl of Suffolk (though Bedford is to be blamed for not troubling to visit the scene of action throughout the siege). Much of the supposed mystery has, it is to be hoped, been cleared up in the preceding narrative. The more complex case of the failure of the besiegers to reinforce the Tourelles in the final attack will be dealt with in an Appendix.

The general conclusion that is forced upon us is that the English commanders, though faced with a tough proposition,

---

[1] *The Hundred Years War*, p. 280.   [2] Op. cit., p. 69.

were making headway with it till the apparition of the Maid, and that this was mainly due to the moral ascendancy they had obtained after 14 years of almost continuous victory. Only four days before the capture of St. Loup a French attack upon Fort Paris was frustrated by what Andrew Lang calls "the dread Hurrah of the English", and years afterwards Dunois testified that prior to the coming of the Maid "two hundred Englishmen would put to flight eight hundred or a thousand Frenchmen". But once the French morale had attained to, or even approached that of the English, the result was almost a foregone conclusion and can be accounted for on purely military grounds without having to invoke the direct intervention of the King of Heaven. There was thus no reason to retail the many stories that attached themselves to the Maid, the "miraculous change of wind", or the rather rude conversations she is said to have had with the English across a No Man's Land 700 yards wide (where sharp eyes on the one hand and strong lungs on the other must have been required). Joan's contribution to the victory was that she roused the fighting spirits of the French, which had lain dormant for so long. This contribution was decisive, and we may say that the main credit for the raising of the siege rests upon that glorious creature, the Maid of Orleans.

APPENDIX

THE SITE OF THE BATTLE OF THE HERRINGS

The situation of the battle of the Herrings is as inaccessible as that of Cravant is accessible. The little village of Rouvray, to give the battle its alternative name, lies away from main roads and railway. To a visitor staying at Orleans and not possessing a car it is practically essential to hire a taxi. And, arrived in Rouvray, it is hard to pick up local knowledge and tradition. It is however available, as will be seen presently. Co-ordinating the various sources it can be stated that the battle took place somewhere between Rouvray and Janville. As these places are nearly six miles apart something more is required. Here

I must have recourse to what I call I.M.P. Let us put ourselves in the shoes of Sir John Fastolf on the morning of the battle. The evidence implies that his army had either just set out or was on the point of setting out when his patrols rode in with the news of the approach of the French. We can picture him riding out along the Janville road in search of a position. He would not have far to go, for the ground was open (as it still is) and the *glacis* smooth. It would take some time to construct a leaguer with as many as 300 wagons, so no time was to be lost. At the first suitable spot outside the village, therefore, the leaguer would be made. At just under a mile outside the village the ground seems eminently suitable, for there is a good unimpeded view in all directions. The road runs along the top of a very slight ridge and at 1,600 yards from the village there is now a small copse – a mere wind screen. On my visit I took some photographs of this spot considering it the most likely locality, and returned to the village – to learn from a *cultivateur* that the locality I had just fixed on was called *le camp ennemi*. I know of no other *ennemi* than the English who have fought in those parts, and if we may assume that the *ennemi* was in fact the English it seems to go far to put the coping-stone on the investigation and to allow us to claim that the copse marks the site of the battle.

A further indication that the battlefield was near the village is the fact that after the battle the villagers issued from their shelters and regaled themselves with the herrings that had been spilt on to the ground from the wagons damaged by the French cannon-balls. Indeed, it was a red-letter day for them, and no wonder they speak, not of the battle, but of the DAY of the Herrings.

THE FAILURE TO REINFORCE THE TOURELLES

The most puzzling problem to some is why Talbot (assuming that he was responsible) failed to reinforce the garrison in the Tourelles. Here we are of course in the realm of conjecture. In the first place, though we know that Dunois planned a holding attack on Talbot's main force at St. Laurent to cover the attack on the Tourelles (just as he had twice previously done against St. Loup), no mention is made of this attack being actually carried out. Historians have concluded that it was not carried out. But this assumption is unwarranted. All eyes were centred on the dramatic events unfolding at the Tourelles, and it is quite natural that the local diarist on whom we largely rely should have omitted reference to such an apparently unimportant affair as the holding attack. But as no mention is made of a change of plan, and as it is inherently probable that Dunois should have stuck to such a sound and indeed obvious plan, I cannot accept silence as an indication of cancellation. Now, if this attack took place as planned it would go far to explain why Talbot could not sally forth to the relief of the Tourelles.

In the second place, how could Talbot expect to render effective aid to the Tourelles? Consider the situation. A glance at the map will show that to approach it he would have to cross over the Isle of Charlemagne, and land opposite the Fort St. Privé. Now the garrison of this fort had evacuated it after the fall of the Augustins. This was, I hold, the first sign of the demoralization caused in the English ranks by the magic of Joan's name. (The idea that Talbot may have *ordered* the evacuation before ever the Tourelles was attacked seems preposterous. Oh, for that English account of the siege!)

The landing on the south bank would thus be opposed, for Dunois was bound to take the elementary precaution of watching the crossing with some of his unemployed troops (only a handful at a time could be employed in the actual assault). Such an opposed landing, improvised as it must be, would present even greater difficulties than those of our troops in Normandy on D Day. Talbot can thus, I think, be absolved of bad leadership on that fatal May 7, 1429.

THE ENGLISH LINES

The most casual glance at the sketch-map of Orleans will bring out the extraordinary lay-out of the English *bastilles* or forts on the north side of the river. The point had been lightly touched on in the narrative, but it deserves some further treatment for those interested in the subject.

On the west side we have a line of five forts, about 400 yards apart, with a double line of circumvallation and contravallation connecting them, whereas on the east side there is a single isolated bastille, on the river bank with a gap of over one and a half miles between it and its neighbour the Fort Paris. Through this gap the enemy could and did often penetrate. There are two explanations. The first one becomes obvious directly one approaches Fort St. Loup. The terrain between the city and this fort is flat, but the fort itself is on a hill, 100 feet high, overlooking the river. Clearly its *raison d'être* was not to complete the girdle of forts but to command the river approaches to the city from the east, and also to form a look-out post in that direction. Owing to the intervening flat ground some species of signals, probably smoke, could be employed to give warning of an attack from that direction. There were, however, two weak points about it: a large island lay under the near bank of the river, thus deflecting the main channel some 700 yards to the south. Even with a numerous force of cannons it would be difficult to hit an enemy moving fast downstream with the current—a fact that Dunois duly appreciated. The second weakness was that the extensive forest of Orleans reached within a short distance of the fort on the north side, thus providing an attacker with a covered line of approach.

The second explanation of this large gap is a simple one: there were insufficient troops to man the other forts adequately and at the same time to construct such a long defensive line, complete with forts (without which it would be valueless at night time). The weakness was not lost upon the English leaders and, after the more vital works on the west side were completed, work was started on the east side too, with a single fort midway between St. Loup and Fort Paris. But the defection of the Burgundians seems to have slowed up the work, if it did not put a a complete stop to it before it had got far enough to be effective. The authority for this is a single sentence in Jean Chartier's

Histoire de Charles VII, and it was overlooked by M. Jollois when he wrote his standard history of the siege and consequently continues to be overlooked in most accounts. Unfortunately, the ground is now a built-up area and all traces of the earthworks or connecting fort have vanished.

Fort Fleury. Nearly two miles to the north of the city there is an old earthwork which Victorian writers ascribed to the English. By any tenets of I.M.P. this claim must be suspect, quite apart from the lack of documentary evidence in support of it; but in any case it has since been established that the earthwork belongs to a quite different period.

A NOTE ON SOURCES ETC.

The primary source for the siege is the *Journal du siège d'Orleans*. As a result of an exhaustive examination made in 1913 by Felix Guillon entitled *Etude Historique sur "Le Journal du siège d'Orleans"*, it is now possible to state that the author of the *Journal* was G. Cousinot, Chancellor of Orleans, who was present throughout the siege and kept the journal from day to day. It was afterwards borrowed largely from by both Berry the Herald, and Jean Chartier (whose books have already been cited), and by Cousinot himself in his *Chronique de la Pucelle*. It is not therefore necessary to cite any other sources.

On the English side there is practically nothing. The period is an arid one as anyone will realize who studies Kingsford's *English Historical Literature in the 15th Century*. We are now well in the 100 years gap between the death of Walsingham, about 1422, and the appearance of the Chronicles of Polidore Vergil and Edward Hall.

The standard history of the siege was written by J. Jollois in 1827, but much more useful for our purpose are the two books by Boucher de Molandon, *L'Armée Anglaise vaincue par Jeanne d'Arc* (1892), and *Première Campagne de Jeanne d'Arc* (1874). Also valuable is *Le Compte de l'armée Anglaise au siège d'Orleans* (1892) by L. Jarry. These two authors have studied the composition of the English army at the siege much more thoroughly than any Englishman. For the early part of the campaign the best account is "*Campagnes des Anglais dans l'Orleanais . . .* " by A. de Villaret (1893). No Englishman has published a detailed study of the campaign or siege.

The battle of the Herrings. The most useful sources are: *Chronique de la Pucelle, Waurin, Le Bourgeois de Paris, Jean Chartier,* and for the Scottish contingent, *Liber Pluscardine.*

N.B.—Sources for Joan of Arc are dealt with in an Appendix to the following chapter.

CHAPTER XV

JOAN OF ARC'S CAMPAIGNS

THE siege of Orleans was over—a siege which the Abbé Dubois described as one of those events on which depend the fate of empires. The news came as a great shock to the duke of Bedford, but he set about scraping together a new army. As for the besieging army, Suffolk stupidly dispersed it, taking about 700 men to Jargeau, while Talbot took the remainder to Meung and Beaugency. On the French side, the count of Dunois followed Suffolk to Jargeau but was repulsed and fell back to Orleans, while the Maid rode off to Tours to announce the glorious news of Orleans to her king.

Charles held some earnest war councils debating the next step. Joan was for raising another army and proceeding with it to the capture of the Loire towns still in English hands, preparatory to marching to Rheims for the sacring and crowning. But Charles and La Trémoïlle were hesitant. The news had reached them that Fastolf was approaching with a new army, and Fastolf was now a name to inspire legitimate fear. Ultimately the persuasive Maid had her way, the duke of Alençon was despatched with an army to Orleans, with Joan in company. Arrived at Orleans, Dunois's garrison was added to it and the whole marched along the south bank of the river to the capture of Jargeau. It was a well-found army, well equipped for a siege and it is said to have been nearly 8,000 in number.

On approaching the town a war council was held to decide whether to proceed with the enterprise. There are two notable points about this council. In the first place it seems extraordinary that, with a powerful army at their back, the resolution of the leaders should have weakened to the extent of contemplating the abandonment of the enterprise before ever it had started.

This can only be put down to the fear of the English military prowess, which could not be dissipated in a night or in a single siege; the captains were looking over their left shoulders wondering what the formidable Fastolf was up to. (There were indeed rumours of his approach.) The second point of significance is that, unlike the procedure at Orleans where the leaders did not usually trouble to call Joan to their councils, on this occasion she attended them all, as if by right. This is good evidence as to the prestige that already attached to the name of the Maid of Orleans.

At this council Joan's voice was raised clamorously in favour of proceeding with the project, and her voice prevailed. The army resumed its march up to the walls of the town, and after a skirmish in which Joan distinguished herself, they drove an English sortie back into the town. Joan that evening approached the walls and uttered the following unforgettable challenge: "Surrender the town to the King of Heaven, and to King Charles, and depart, or it will be the worse for you". Suffolk took no notice of the ravings of this witch, but he did enter into negotiations with Dunois, which, however, came to nothing. Next morning, Sunday, June 12, the besieging artillery were placed in position and the bombardment commenced. With only three shots the great mortar *La Bercère* demolished one of the chief towers, and great damage was done.

After some hours of bombardment another war council was held, and the question was debated whether to go straight to the assault or to await events. Again the voice of the Maid was raised uncompromisingly in favour of immediate assault, and again it was listened to. Scaling ladders were brought forward, and Joan herself mounted one of them. The town was entered and captured, and the escape of the English over the bridge was blocked. The earl of Suffolk, with his brother John, was captured on the bridge. Of his captor he enquired anxiously whether he was a knight. On the Frenchman confessing that he was only a squire, Suffolk knighted him on the spot and, honour being thus satisfied, formally surrendered to his captor.

The whole English garrison, except the nobles who were ransomed, were put to the sword, and the church which had been used by the English troops was looted.

Two towns on the Loire, Meung and Beaugency, remained to be captured before the way would be sufficiently safe to conduct the reluctant Charles to Rheims. This time the French generals acted promptly, for was not Fastolf on the war-path? Jargeau fell on the Sunday (June 12) of a week destined to become memorable. On the Monday the army returned to Orleans, and on the Wednesday resumed its march along the south bank to Meung and Beaugency. The bridge at Meung was reached at nightfall. It was defended by the English, who had made a small bridgehead on its southern end.[1] That night the bridge was won and a small guard was left on it. No attempt was made to take the town, which was separated from the bridge by a meadow.

The army continued along the south bank to Beaugency, where it was found that the English were holding the bridge and château, just as the French had held them in the previous year. The train of siege artillery that had been so effective against Jargeau was soon brought into action and opened on the bridge and château; some of the guns, in order to shorten the range, being floated by barges to a spot opposite the château. But their cannon-balls cannot have had much effect upon the gaunt, grim 12th-century keep of the château (which today looks as if it would never fall). However, the bombardment was kept up all next day (Friday) and that night the defenders, led by Matthew Gough and Richard Gethin, feeling themselves hopelessly out-powered and despairing of relief, compounded with Alençon to quit the town next morning, taking their arms and belongings with them.

On Saturday morning at dawn, therefore, they filed out of the town as agreed, little dreaming that Fastolf's relieving army had been halted within two miles of them on the previous day, and was now preparing to come to their relief along the south

---

[1] No signs remain of this earthwork.

bank. To explain how this astonishing situation arose we must go back to the English side.[1]

On June 5, the army commanded by Sir John Fastolf had marched out for the relief or reinforcement of Jargeau, and any other threatened towns. Its strength is usually given as 5,000, a suspiciously round figure. It is impossible to accept this figure. Less than twelve months previously Bedford had the greatest difficulty in finding about 2,000 men to complete Salisbury's army. In the following February he had been able to find only 1,000 English troops for Fastolf's relief army, and in the intervening four months no reinforcements had arrived from England. It is unlikely that at the second scraping the barrel would produce more men than had the first. As on that occasion, there must have been a considerable addition of *milice* or "Faux Français" who had taken service under the Anglo-Burgundian banners.[2] Even so, it seems improbable that the total can have attained to 3,000.[3] All the best and most active soldiers from the Normandy garrisons had already been taken, and the quality of Fastolf's new army must have been poor. The fact cannot have been hidden from the experienced eye of Sir John–which may explain much of what is to follow.

Marching after depositing a convoy of supplies, for some reason, at Etampes (25 miles south of Paris), Fastolf reached Janville about June 13, only to learn that Jargeau was besieged by a powerful French army. Considering it hopeless to attempt relief, Fastolf turned his eyes towards the twin towns, Meung and Beaugency. On the 16th he was joined by Lord John Talbot with a tiny force of 40 lances and 200 archers, say 300 men in all. He had come from Beaugency, which had been his headquarters since the siege of Orleans, in order to strengthen the relief army that he heard was approaching.

Talbot arrived in the morning, and Fastolf visited him at his

---

[1] Here I have followed Waurin's account. Gruel makes the date of the surrender the Thursday night, which is impossible, for in that case Fastolf would have heard of it in Meung. Moreover Count Charles of Clermont supports Waurin's dating.
[2] Two French sources mention the presence of these "Faux Français".
[3] The earliest French source only makes it 3,500.

lodging for *déjeuner*. Over the meal they discussed plans, and it soon became apparent that they were hopelessly at variance. Talbot, the less experienced soldier of the two, but a man possessed of ardent fighting spirit, argued hotly in favour of an immediate advance, as the Loire towns were obviously threatened, but Fastolf demurred. He knew, better than Talbot, that a poor spirit pervaded his own ranks, and that the efficiency and even loyalty of the French contingent was questionable. He had, moreover, learnt that Bedford was again planning to send reinforcements – probably more were expected from England – and Sir John was in favour of falling back and maintaining a defensive attitude till they arrived. To this Talbot raised violent objection, declaring that he at any rate would go to the relief of Beaugency (which he had just quit!) even if no-one else followed him. This forced Fastolf's hand, and he consented to march next day with his whole force. Early next morning, Saturday, June 17, while the French siege guns were hammering at the château of Beaugency, the English army paraded. But once again Fastolf made an effort to avert what he believed would result in disaster. A war council was held, while the troops, standing fast, must have suspected what was happening, and when at last the word to advance was given it was an army infected by the disharmony of its leaders, that moved off.

The march was, however, carried out fairly speedily, Meung being the first halting place. From here the army necessarily marched along the northern bank of the river, Meung bridge being still held by the French. About two miles short of Beaugency the road mounts a slight ridge, and from its summit another ridge can be seen crossing the road about 800 yards away. On this second ridge a French army was being drawn up in battle order, evidently intending to offer fight. On seeing this, Fastolf took the traditional English action: he halted his army, deployed it for battle in the usual formation; the archers planted their pointed stakes in their front, and all awaited the oncoming French. But nothing happened. The French having completed their dispositions sat firm. Something must be done to stir them to action, and Fastolf sent forward heralds with the proposal that three knights from each should fight out the issue in the space between the two armies. This was a slight variant of the usual challenge, so much favoured by Edward III, of a single combat between the two leaders. But now, as in practically all cases, the French ignored the challenge – and still they did not stir. Fastolf had no intention of taking the offensive himself, the French position appeared too strong for his weak army. He therefore bethought him, in all probability, of the tactics of the earl of Salisbury in a somewhat similar situation on the eve of Cravant: and he took the same course. That is to say, he fell back to Meung, intending to cross the river there, and approach Beaugency from the south side where the bridge was still in English hands. The army accordingly withdrew that evening to Meung, and immediately made preparations to capture the bridge. Cannons were put into position, and during the night they maintained a fire against the defenders on the bridge – one of the earliest recorded cases of "night firing" by artillery.[1]

Saturday, June 18, dawned with the bridge still in French hands. At about 8 a.m. the English assault party were providing themselves with improvised shields from doors, etc., when a galloper arrived with the disturbing news that Beaugency was in the hands of the French and that they were now advancing towards Meung. This settled the matter; the little English army now found itself between two fires north and south of the river; retreat was the only possible course, and with a heavy heart it set out on the return march to Janville. This was the first step, had the troops but known it, in a retreat which was to last with fluctuations for 24 years.

We now return to the French camp. On Friday morning Alençon had received an unexpected and indeed unwelcome

---

[1] The most recent French life of Joan, *Jeanne d'Arc* by Lucien Fabre, states that the bridge was attacked in order to capture the town. This is to put the story upside-down. The bridge could not be attacked until the town was occupied. The real reason why the English attacked the bridge was because they wanted to get to the other side. In war the simplest explanation is usually the correct one.

accession to his strength. Arthur of Richemont, Constable of France, marched into the camp at the head of 1,000 Bretons. Since we last met him fighting in Brittany he had been at the Dauphin's court engaged in a bitter and prolonged struggle for power with La Trémoïlle. In the upshot he was worsted and driven from the court in disgrace. Moreover, Charles forbade Alençon to receive him. The meeting therefore was an embarrassing one. And Count Arthur did not make it less so. He had an awkward manner and unprepossessing appearance – like that other distinguished Breton, Bertrand Duguesclin – being short of stature, dark and thick-lipped.

As soon as he had dismounted from his horse, Joan embraced him around the knees, to receive the gruff response: "Whether you are sent by God I know not; if you are I do not fear you, for God knows that my heart is pure. If you come from the Devil I fear you still less." This undoubtedly authentic utterance throws a useful light on the puzzled attitude of Frenchmen towards the Maid at this period of her career.

Joan acted as peacemaker between the two soldiers, and her task may have been eased and hastened by the abrupt news that Fastolf was approaching at the head of a powerful army. Danger makes good bed-fellows of enemies. Thus it came about that when Alençon started off in pursuit of the English the Constable and his contingent were included in his ranks. The army that set off may have been as high as 6,000 in number.

THE BATTLE OF PATAY (June 18, 1429)

Joan's campaign had started on Sunday at Jargeau. It was now Saturday, the last day of an unforgettable week. The English had suspended the attack on the Meung bridge and had retreated towards Patay, 18 miles away due north. On hearing this news the French leaders exhibited their usual indecision. "You have spurs," exploded Joan, her eyes ablaze, "use them!" They did. Selecting the best mounted men for the vanguard, Alençon ordered a vigorous pursuit. Rapidly the French vanguard gained on their opponents whose pace was necessarily

regulated by the speed of the baggage-train. Thus, when the
English army had reached the vicinity of Patay, the French vanguard was at St. Sigismund, four miles to the south. Here

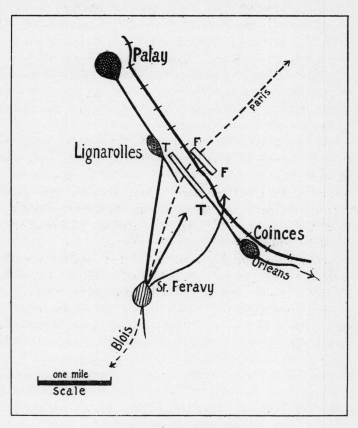

Sketch Map 9: PATAY

T-T Talbot's position   ⟶   French attack
F-F Fastolf's position   - - - - -   Ancient trackway

the French army halted at noon for their mid-day meal, and
resumed the journey two hours later. Hitherto they had not
obtained touch with the English army. Patrols were now sent
out in all directions. Presently word was received that by a

happy chance the English had been located halted just to the south of Patay. It had happened in this way. Advancing north-wards along the Patay road leading patrols had set on foot a stag just north of St. Feravy (see Sketch Map 9). The stag had galloped to the right, and presently the raucous shout of an English "Halloo" had told the French of the presence of the enemy in the vicinity.

The road to Janville diverges from the Patay road two miles to the south of the latter town. On reaching this spot Fastolf received the news from patrols that the French advanced-guard was close on their heels. A hasty council was held, at which there was evidently some difference of opinion. The upshot was that Fastolf agreed, probably with reluctance, to stand his ground, while Talbot with his own 300, reinforced by about 200 "archiers d'élite" from the ranks of Fastolf's host, undertook to occupy and hold a covering position to the south of Patay while Fastolf deployed the main body on the ridge, now marked by the railway two miles south-east of the village.

This was the situation when the startled stag burst through the line of Talbot's archers. Suspecting nothing, they continued the preparation of their position, bringing their stakes to the front and hammering them into the ground in the prescribed fashion. The pick of the troops and the best commanders, Scales, Rempston and Sir Walter Hungerford, were with Talbot, and but slow progress was made with the deployment of the main body of ill-trained soldiers and inexperienced officers on the ridge in rear. Fastolf had not his heart in the business. His was the only English army in France, and he realized (like Admiral Jellicoe on the eve of the battle of Jutland) that he might lose the war in an afternoon.

The position selected by Talbot seems to have run along the road from Lignarolles to Coinces, at the point where it crosses the old Roman road from St. Sigismund to Janville. This point is near the bottom of a slight dip in the ground, which however was calculated to form a suitable locality for its purpose, being a few hundred yards in front of the ridge that Fastolf would hold.

The ground was much enclosed with small copses and hedges, and there was probably a hedge along the road that the archers were to line.

The French army was advancing in the following order. The advanced-guard was composed of specially selected men all well mounted, under the command of La Hire and Poton de Xantrailles, comrades in arms in many an operation. The main body was led by Alençon and Dunois, and with the rear-guard were the Constable de Richemont and Joan of Arc, who was much peeved at being kept back in this way.

Contact with the English rear-guard was obtained shortly after two o'clock in the afternoon. The battle that ensued reached its decision in a matter of minutes and can be described in a few sentences. The French advanced-guard, on topping the slight rise from St. Feravy to Lignarolles, saw the English drawn up in the dip in front of them. Inspired by the *élan* imparted to them by the Maid, and led by the best cavalry commanders in their army, the French horsemen swept impetuously down the slope in a wild avalanche on top of the 400 English archers, who were not ready for them and were taken by surprise. Moreover, the line was turned on each flank and almost before they had realized what was happening they found themselves surrounded. Archers, like gunners, can defend their own front, but are helpless against attack from the flank. They were helpless. Most of them fell. A few managed to get away to the rear, and running back over the ridge added to the confusion that was already affecting Fastolf's heterogeneous collection of soldiers. For the French attack was made in such large numbers and was so closely followed up by the main body, that Fastolf found himself overwhelmed before he could take any effective steps to oppose this surprise attack. It was all outside the experience of any Englishmen in the field. Previously a French antagonist had approached a position held by them with circumspection, even trepidation. But this attack had the unhesitating thrust of a Thomas Dagworth, a Robert Knollys, or indeed of a John Talbot. The Joan of Arc yeast had worked; the loaf was leavened and transformed. The Maid of Orleans, who, with the rear-guard did not see a blow struck—except on an English prisoner[1]—had won the battle of Patay.

Lord Talbot was captured, taken near a prominent bush in his front line, mounted but spurless: evidently a horse had just been brought up for him and he was about to make a dash for it. His was already a name to conjure with in the French army, and his capture was a great morale-raiser in the French ranks. That night he spent in a lodging in Patay, situated in a road which still goes by the name of the Rue Talbot. Next morning the Duke of Alençon who had himself been captured at Verneuil (and had only recently been released) could not resist the temptation of gloating over his prisoner—to receive the dignified response that "it was the fortune of war", a sentiment that seems to have so much impressed the hearers that it was deemed worthy of permanent record by the French Chroniclers.

Lord Scales and other leaders had also been captured, but Fastolf managed to get away and also to save something out of the wreck, though he lost his baggage and guns. He retreated to Janville, 18 miles away. Arrived there he found the gates shut in his face. There was nothing to be done but to continue the weary march to Etampes, another 24 miles, making no less than 60 miles covered that day and night. A terrible journey it must have been for the old warrior, his only consolation being that he could say "I told you so!" But he still had a stout body of English archers around him. They made a firm face to every attack by their pursuers, and when they had exhausted their arrows they attacked their opponents with drawn swords.

*   *   *

When the news of the disaster reached the English and French capitals the reaction was significant. In London a fund was at once raised for the ransom of Lord Talbot. In Paris the wretched Sir John Fastolf was, it is said, deprived of his Garter.[2] He had, it would seem "lost the war in an afternoon".

[1] There is a window depicting this incident in Patay church.
[2] It was later restored to him, and he served again in command in Maine.

The dazzling campaign of a week had ended for Joan in triumph. General Lemoine, after pointing out that this was the only campaign made entirely under the inspiration of Joan, adds admiringly:

"She knew but one method—force, and one argument—battle. . . . Therefore the humble Maid of Domrémy takes her place among the very great generals."[1]

* * *

It might have been supposed that Joan's Voices would have now councilled an immediate advance on Paris, on the well established principle of "striking while the iron is hot". And the prospects of such an advance were rosy. But Joan's eyes were set on Rheims, and the sacred anointing of Charles as the legitimate king of France. As a matter of fact the reverse of Patay had the unexpected effect of a rapprochement between the Burgundians and the English; the duke himself visited Paris and steps were taken to strengthen the defences of the city. He contracted to raise more troops.

Meanwhile Charles was at last on his way to Rheims. By dint of continually pumping courage and confidence into her Prince, Joan ensured that the march should be speedy and almost unopposed. Charles de Valois entered the city of Rheims on July 16, 1429.[2] Next day the anointing and coronation took place, and Charles the Dauphin must now be described as Charles VII. The mission of Joan of Arc was accomplished. It would indeed have been well for France and for England if she had contrived to get killed in the very next engagement. But it was not to be.

* * *

There followed the most bloodless and almost farcical campaign (if it can be called a campaign) of the war. Joan, set upon attacking Paris, dragged a reluctant monarch in that direction. But he kept edging off towards home, till on August 5, the army

[1] *Jeanne d'Arc, Chef de Guerre*, p. 53.
[2] The writer had the luck to be present at the celebrations in Rheims on the 500th anniversary of the historic entry into Rheims.

approached Bray, intending to cross the south bank of the Seine there, and thence back to Bourges. But the duke of Bedford who had not only been reinforced, but had received an undertaking from the unpredictable duke of Burgundy to enter upon active operations in support of his ally, now approached the newly crowned French king, intent upon crossing swords with him. His first step was to post a strong force at Bray to head Charles off that crossing place, whilst he himself advanced with his army to Montereau, 25 miles to the west. Charles, seeing that his project was baulked, turned in his tracks and marched north to Crépy, 40 miles north-east of Paris. To this place Bedford sent a message of studied insolence, that might well be calculated to sting the most phlegmatic coward into aggressive action. It looked for a moment as if this challenge was having its effect, for Charles advanced some 12 miles to Dammartin (20 miles north east of Paris), and there found the English army drawn up to oppose him. A day of skirmishing ensued, and in the evening the French army fell back again. Bedford then advanced to Senlis (12 miles further north) and on August 16 the two armies were again face to face. Bedford drew up his army, blocking the road to Paris, but again the French declined to attack, and their king fell back once more to Crépy.

Seeing that the French had no intention of risking a battle, Bedford took his own army back to Paris, disturbing news having reached him from Normandy. The Constable de Richemont had advanced from Maine and was threatening Evreux, only 25 miles from Rouen. Bedford accordingly took the major part of his army to that region, leaving the Burgundians with a sprinkling of English troops to hold the capital. He had taken stock of the French king and of the danger to be expected from that quarter.

Meanwhile King Charles was finding it more pleasant and profitable to receive the surrender of Burgundian towns such as Compiègne without a blow being struck, than to undertake the hazards of war against the English – a policy in which his evil genius, La Trémoïlle, concurred. All this time he was negotiating with Duke Philip who however proved altogether too dexterous for him. For the time being the lot of this cold and calculating Prince lay with the English party.

Joan was naturally dispirited, but she did not cease to hope. At last her king was induced to quit Compiègne and move forward to St. Denys, (only four miles north of Paris) which had been evacuated by the Burgundians. He arrived there on September 7, Joan and the advanced guard having preceded him by several days. An attack on the capital was planned for the next day. While Alençon watched the Porte St. Denys (from a distance) Joan with her party assaulted the Porte St. Honoré. The Maid exhibited her usual bravery and intrepidity under fire, and the outer ditch was successfully crossed. But it was too late; the defences had recently been strengthened and the attack on the inner ditch failed. Joan was wounded in the leg by a crossbow shaft, and left lying in the open till dark. Alençon held his hand all day and the king did not quit St. Denys. The Maid of Orleans had been deliberately left in the lurch. The evidence is clear enough, although it might appear almost incredible. La Trémoïlle was probably "the villain in the piece".

King Charles now showed his hand; he marched off to the south, ordering Joan to follow. Crossing the Seine at Bray—now undefended—he was on September 21 safely ensconced at Gien, the point of departure for his march to Rheims.

The Maid had failed. It was her first failure; still she had failed, and it was bound to react upon her prestige. But worse was to follow. For nearly two months she was kept inactive at court, and when eventually allowed to take the field again, after a preliminary success in capturing St. Pierre on the upper Loire, she failed for the second time at La Charité. After besieging this town (also on the upper Loire), for a month in bitterly cold weather, and after failing to receive further supplies from the court, she was obliged to abandon the siege. Winter then put an end to operations.

*　　　　　*　　　　　*

We have reached the year 1430. During the early spring, operations languished; indeed Burgundy had arranged a local truce with Charles. But in April he took up arms once more, possibly influenced by the knowledge that a new English army, led by Cardinal Beaufort, with the boy king Henry VI included, was about to land at Calais. Duke Philip now assembled his army at Montdidier (30 miles north-west of Compiègne) and advanced to the recapture of that town. Hearing this, Joan slipped away from the court, then at Sully, with a handful of followers and made her way by stages to Compiègne, which she entered on May 13, three weeks after Henry VI landed at Calais.

The duke of Burgundy was nominally besieging the town, but it was not even as complete an investment as that of Orleans had been. Compiègne lies on the south bank of the river Oise, and the attackers were confined to the north bank. Included in Duke Philip's army was an English detachment under Sir John Montgomery. During the next ten days the Maid took part in some rather petty and abortive manoeuvres on the south bank, but on May 24 she made a sudden sortie with about 500 troops, to the north of the town. Crossing a long causeway her troops surprised and scattered the nearest Burgundian post. But it happened that John of Luxemburg was at the time reconnoitring on a hill in rear. He witnessed the attack, and sent for reinforcements. When they came up a hot fight took place, in which the Maid particularly distinguished herself. While thus engaged, Montgomery's troops attacked her party in the rear. Most of them fled into the city while Joan herself with a tiny band was driven off the causeway and her retreat to the bridge was cut off. She was in fact driven by the English into the arms of the Burgundians and by them she was captured.

Assessed in cold military terms, it seems to have been a happy piece of co-operation between the two allies and there is no need to impute treachery on the part of the French garrison or of members of Joan's party.[1] It was a spirited end to a dazzling and

---

[1] Most history-books state tersely that Joan was captured by the Burgundians. As the above account shows, there is a *suppressio veri* in this statement. It was essentially a combined operation.

utterly unique military career, and one can but regret that the Maid had not the fortune (which she had prayed for) to be killed in an engagement. It would have been better for France and for England, for no person, English, Burgundian or French comes out of the sorry sequel with credit – except that nameless English soldier who dashed into the flames to hand the Maid a rude wooden cross. . . .

At this point, therefore, we take leave of the glorious Maid, for there is no need here to relate the story – more widely known than any other story of medieval times – of how she was sold by the Burgundians to the English, condemned by the French Church and executed by the English army. In passing, one may wonder why the English leaders should have been anxious to take the life of a prisoner whom they deemed no longer an adverse influence to their cause. It may indeed be that they were not particularly anxious, and that there is basis for the story that the earl of Warwick had offered Joan her liberty provided she would promise not to take up arms again.[1]

*   *   *

Be that as it may, we come back to the two questions with which we approached the appearance on the scene of the Maid. What military influence did her Voices have upon Joan, and what practical influence did she have upon the course of the war?

The first question has perhaps been answered inferentially in the preceding pages. No-one pretends that Saint Margaret and Saint Catherine were well-versed in military strategy or that they always guided her aright – for example in her advocacy of an attack on Paris or the relief of Compiègne. Indeed, Joan herself never made such a claim, once her king had been anointed. But what the Voices did do was to inspire her with a burning faith in her mission to rid France of the invaders and in the equally firm belief that this must be accomplished by aggressive action – by the sword. Further, that in order to temper and sharpen that sword the morale of the troops must be raised by a

---

[1] Scurrilous writers have suggested a different proviso.

living faith in victory akin to her own. This achieved, everything else followed the well established war principles of offensive action, the maintenance of the objective – whatever the set-backs and disappointments that had to be encountered – the taking of risks, and the application of speed and surprise. These simple but fundamental military virtues had long lain dormant in the French ranks; it was the Maid, and the Maid alone, who roused them into action.

This leads us on to, and indeed overlaps, our second question and suggests the answer to it: what practical influence did the Maid have upon the course of the war? This question could be answered with greater assurance had the war ended with the death of Joan. But it continued for another generation, indeed the tide turned and for a time seemed to flow quite perceptibly in the opposite direction – as will shortly appear. A further difficulty is that we require to know, not only what practical effects she had upon the fighting capacity and spirit of the French troops but also upon the English troops, and we have very little data to go upon. There is an almost complete silence on the subject of the Maid in contemporary English records, and when all the evidence comes from the enemy's side it has to be treated with caution. Indeed, there is really only one single contemporary English document that bears on the subject. But that is an important document and must therefore be examined closely. I refer to the famous letter written by the Duke of Bedford to the English Council in 1433.

"At the whiche tyme [The Siege of Orleans] there felle by the hand of God, as it seemeth, a greet strook upon your peuple that was assembled there in grete nombre, caused in grete partie as I trowe of lakke of sadde [sound] beleve, and of unlevethefulle [unbelieving] doubte that thei hadde of a disciple and lyme [limb] of the Feende, called the Pucelle, that used false enchauntments and sorcerie; the whiche strook and disconfiture nought only lessed in grete partie the nombre of youre peuple, there, but as welle withdrowe the courage of the remenant in merveilleus wyse; and couragiged youre adverse partie and enemies to assemble them forthwith in grete nombre."[1]

[1] Rymer, IV, p. 408.

This seems pretty clear, though two things must be remembered. First, the letter, though written three years after the capture of the Maid, refers to the effect she had upon the English soldiers during her campaign which was not necessarily a permanent effect. Second, Bedford was naturally looking for a scapegoat, attributing all the evils of the period to the Pucelle, and none to himself or the English leaders. But it is as good evidence as we could wish for that the Maid "started the rot", and in so doing changed the course of military events. Nor is it relevant to remark that she appeared at a fortunate moment, when the Burgundians were tiring of the struggle and when it would seem that the pendulum of fortune was bound to swing back, if not at once then on the death of Bedford, after which the Burgundian alliance could not be expected to endure. All this is of course true, and there were in fact to be (as I have said) some oscillations of the pendulum in the course of the 23 years that supervened after the capture of Joan before the English were finally driven out of France. But all the credit for starting the pendulum in its backward swing, and for starting it in no uncertain manner, must go to that marvellous soul, the pure and peerless Maid of Orleans.

APPENDIX

RECONSTRUCTION OF THE BATTLE OF PATAY

It has been particularly difficult to reconstruct the battle with any degree of confidence, for the sources are obscure and in places conflicting, so that considerable recourse has had to be made to I.M.P. Yet there were two eyewitnesses present who afterwards wrote about the battle: on the English side that ubiquitous Burgundian Jean Waurin, on the French side Guillaume Gruel, a Breton who followed the banner of the Constable de Richemont and afterwards wrote his *Chronicle*. Yet Waurin's account is so confused that one suspects the author had himself a confused notion of what really happened. In at least one passage he wrote *avant-garde* when he must have meant *arrière-garde*. One cannot therefore place as much credence in his story as one

would wish, though most writers appear to accept every statement of his. He marched in the main-body under Fastolf and he
seems more concerned to defend the flight of himself and his
unnamed "capitaine" than to give an explicit account of the
sequence of events.

*   *   *

The first thing is to establish the site of the battle.[1] The
sources are in general agreement that it was:

(*a*) Near Patay. (*b*) To the south of the village.

Other villages mentioned in this connection are St. Sigismund,
St. Feravy, Lignarolles and Coinces. Taking the mean of all
these indications, the site should lie fairly close to Lignarolles.

The English were retreating from Meung towards Janville.
What road would they take? Here local knowledge comes in,
and there is little doubt that it must have been along the old
Roman road that runs between St. Sigismund and St. Feravy
and leaves Lignarolles 1,000 yards on its left. The road Lignarolles–Coinces is also an old track. Next, we may assume that
Talbot's position was astride the road by which the army was
marching *i.e.* the Roman road. This further narrows the search
for his position.

When selecting a position in a hurry, such as in a rear-guard
action, the simplest and easiest position to take up is the one
usually adopted, such as the line of a road. Talbot may thus
have selected the line of the Lignarolles–Coinces road where
it crosses the Roman road. How does this position stand up to
the requirements of the situation? It stands up fairly well. It is
not an ideal position for it crosses the dip; the ridge linking
Lignarolles to St. Feravy would be a stronger position, but not
so easy to take up in a hurry.[2] Moreover the earliest French

---

[1] There is no general agreement as to the site and local information is hard to
come by. Indeed Owen Rutter in his delightful *Land of St. Joan* writes, "The
memory of that field of battle seems to have passed from the memory of man.
At least we could find no-one who could direct us to it, and we returned to Orleans."

[2] Talbot may have purposely left this ridge for Fastolf's force.

JOAN OF ARC'S CAMPAIGNS

source states that the position was not well selected. Finally, a region of hedges would probably have a hedge alongside a road, and according to one account the line was along a hedge. I believe this was the position occupied by Talbot. It is said that the earl was captured close to a prominent bush. His command-post would naturally be in the centre of his line, *i.e.* where it crosses the Roman road. Now it happens that at this spot there is a solitary prominent bush and it will assist the imagination of the visitor to the field to picture Talbot being taken when sitting his horse alongside the bush. We may even go one further and dub it "Talbot's bush". *Le Buisson de Talbot*. There is no monument or memorial on the battlefield. This would be a suitable spot on which to erect one.[1]

SOURCES FOR THE BATTLE OF PATAY

The three earliest sources are the three best. The first takes the form of a letter written in Latin only five weeks after the battle, by Jacques de Bourbon, Comte de la Marche, to the Bishop of Laon. It was not published till 1891 (too late for use by Ramsay). It is included in Charpentier's edition of the *Journal du Siège*. Though it contains some obvious errors, there is a solid core of information in it, and many of its details ring true. Thus it contains the description of La Hire's no doubt rather disorderly charge as "un pêu pêle-mêle". Waurin's account, which should be the best, is confused and probably misleading: Monstrelet copies and improves upon it slightly. The third source is Guillaume Gruel's *Chronicle d'Arthur de Richemont*. Though Gruel was present, his master took no active part in the battle; consequently Gruel did not either, but his account is good as far as it goes. The other French sources add but little to the above three. On the English side there is, as is usual for this period of the war, no chronicle whatever.

I know of no modern work, French or English, that takes into account the topography of the battle.

---

[1] In 1950 the then Curé indicated to the author this dip in the road as the site of the battle; but he gave no reasons for his belief.

Fortunately a bibliography of Joan of Arc would not be appropriate for the purposes of this book. Fortunately, for the number of works on the subject is well-nigh legion: there is in Orleans
a library of several thousand volumes devoted exclusively to the
subject of the Maid. We are merely concerned with works of
assistance to military students. And here we are at once struck
by the dearth of books by English military writers. General
Fuller, it is true, has some arresting things to say about the
Maid in his *Decisive Battles of the Western World* but they are
necessarily strictly condensed, whilst Fortescue cannot find
any space for Joan. French soldiers are of course better
represented, but they tend to be rather uncritically pane-
gyrical. General C. Lemoine however has some useful observations in his *Jeanne d'Arc, Chef de Guerre*. Professor Edouard Perroy
in his admirable *La Guerre de Cent Ans* is balanced but rather non-
committal. In spite of the fact that many lives of the Maid have
appeared since it was published in 1908, Andrew Lang's *The
Maid of France* increases rather than diminishes in stature.
It is understanding, sufficiently detailed and quite useful from
the purely military aspects. The same applies to Owen Rutter's
sympathetic *The Land of St. Joan*.

The two latest books at the time of writing (1955) are M.
Lucien Fabre's *Jeanne d'Arc* and Regine Pernoud's *The Re-
trial of Joan of Arc*. The former is too violently nationalist
and Anglophobe to inspire confidence in a military historian.
For example the author delights in dubbing Henry V "The
Cut-throat King" and he is at pains to discount the tributes paid
to the Duke of Bedford by contemporary Burgundian chroniclers. Madame Pernoud's book on the other hand may be truly
described as "filling a long-felt want", for she translates into
French (here re-translated into English) the Latin of portion
of the *Procès de Condamnation et de Rehabilitation de Jeanne d'Arc*,
which was published by Jules Quicherat in 1841 and partially

translated into French in 1868. I agree with the author that it is strange that this document has been so neglected. Many years ago I enquired of it in a high-class bookshop in Rouen—*in Rouen!* The shopkeeper's face was a complete blank; he had never heard of the book. Though the military detail contained in it is only incidental, it is worth study, if only for the full transcript of Dunois' testimony.

CHAPTER XVI

THE TREATY OF ARRAS

ON May 30, 1430, the sentence on Joan of Arc pronounced by the French ecclesiastics was carried out by the English soldiers. But long before this event the tide of war had begun to turn back in favour of England. Once the Maid was in captivity her influence over the English army evaporated. It was now clear that she was not infallible, and in the eyes of the soldiers she must be a witch—a view that was to be confirmed next year when the church condemned her to be burned. Thus within a month of her capture the strong castle of Château Gaillard had been retaken, to be followed in the succeeding months by the recapture of several towns to the north, east and south of Paris. In fact the situation improved to such an extent that it was deemed safe to convey the young King Henry from Calais to Rouen.

The Burgundians however were not so successful in their campaign; the siege of Compiègne dragged on, the earl of Huntingdon replacing Sir John Montgomery and John of Luxemburg replacing Duke Philip. The latter had gone to take over the province of Brabant which had fallen to him on the death of his cousin. In January 1431 Bedford returned to Paris from Rouen.

Best of all, the redoubtable Poton de Xantrailles had been captured by the earl of Warwick in a brilliant enterprise. With a force of 800 men Xantrailles had set out from Beauvais on a raid towards Rouen. The earl of Warwick got wind of it and hastily collected about 600 men, and advanced rapidly to intercept him. The two forces met in the open at Savignies near Gournay, 20 miles west of Beauvais. It was a one-sided battle, the French putting up very slight opposition; they were utterly defeated and pursued all the way back to Beauvais, while Xantrailles himself and several other knights were captured.

Among these prisoners was a young shepherd whom the Archbishop of Rheims had designed as a successor to the Maid. The Archbishop, who knew Joan well but had received the news of her capture with some complacency, declared that the youth "talks just as well as Joan ever did".

A further notable success was the recovery in the autumn, after three months siege, of Louviers. All was now in order for Bedford's long planned design—the coronation at St. Denys of Henry VI as king of France. This coronation took place on December 16, with due ceremony though without the presence of many notable Frenchmen. But the Paris populace gave the young king a warm welcome, evidently expecting some favours from him—which they did not receive.

The year 1432 followed the general pattern of 1431 except that there were no spectacular English successes, and indeed there were two distinct setbacks. The first was that Chartres fell to the French in March; the second was the siege of Lagny. The duke of Bedford had made this the most important item in the summer campaign. But the French put up a spirited defence, the weather became unbearably hot, and Bedford himself overexerted himself in the heat and suffered some permanent ill-effects. Eventually Dunois brought up a relieving army, and Bedford regretfully abandoned the siege. He also suffered the loss of his wife, Anne of Burgundy, sister of the Duke Philip; thus a link and an important one, in the entente between England and Burgundy was snapped, for there were no offspring of the marriage.

The year 1433 was chiefly marked by successful campaigns in the eastern theatre of the war, mainly undertaken by the Burgundians under Duke Philip. The Duke had become addicted to making short local truces with the Valois, whilst allowing his troops to continue fighting under the English banner for English pay—an economical method of waging warfare. French incursions while the truce was still in operation had however stung him into action. Over the rest of the war-theatre there were alternate gains by each side, which it would merely con-

fuse the reader to recount in detail. A political event of importance however cannot be passed over in silence. The worthless
but all-powerful La Trémoïlle fell at last—assassinated in his bed
at Chinon as the result of a "Court plot", in which his rival the
Constable de Richemont had a hand. His place was taken by
the Queen's brother, Charles of Anjou. It is however difficult to
trace any immediate change in the direction or course of the
war.

The year 1434 opened propitiously. The earl of Arundel conducted a very successful campaign in Maine and Anjou, eventually extending his conquests to the banks of the river Loire.
Unfortunately he was mortally wounded and captured by La
Hire and Xantrailles on the estuary of the Somme next year. A
still more notable commander was however to step into his
shoes. Tremendous efforts had been made in England to raise
the enormous ransom demanded for Lord Talbot. The capture
of Xantrailles therefore came at an opportune moment, for an
exchange between the two warriors was quickly arranged. Talbot landed in France in the Spring, bringing with him 800 men.
He soon made his presence felt. He carried out extensive operations in the area to the north of Paris. He recaptured a large
number of towns, some of which surrendered incontinently on
the mere news that the great Talbot was approaching. Gisors on
the eastern border of Normandy soon fell, and Creil, Clermont
and Crepy in the Oise watershed quickly followed. St. Valery
also was recovered among other places.

The duke of Burgundy was again having successes within his
own borders to the south, and all this time the French reaction
was distinctly and increasingly weak. Charles VII has been
blamed for failing to raise a field army with which to attack the
allies. But the simple truth is that he had not the financial means
to support an army that could do anything effective in face of an
English army in the field. His cause seemed to be in a poor way.
Moreover, throughout the area of the war all semblance of law
and order was vanishing, and brigandage, reminiscent of the
Free Companies of the previous century, was springing up. It

became increasingly difficult to get food into Paris, and the inhabitants sent a despairing appeal to London for reinforcements with which to drive the enemy further from their gates. In Normandy also there were peasant risings, caused more by economic than national or Francophil motives. These were however easily repressed.

But in the late autumn a surprising development and change came over the scene. Duke Philip had recently concluded one of his local truces with the Valois king and negotiations for a possible peace began to appear likely. In January 1435 Philip met at Nevers the heads of the Valois government, and next month preliminaries of peace were signed. But Philip still felt he could not ratify any peace terms without the consent of his ally, so England was invited to be present at a second meeting to be held at Arras in July. The English consented, though without enthusiasm for they had their misgivings. It seemed to them that this was the worst possible time to treat for peace. The king of Bourges seemed to be nearing the end of his tether.[1] A little perseverence, a few more pulls on the rope, and the tug of war would be over. The unknown quantity was the duke of Burgundy; he must at all costs be retained in the alliance, and as much to humour him as for any other reason English plenipotentiaries appeared at the conference chamber at Arras at the appointed time.

The story of the protracted negotiations and bargainings that took place cannot fail to be of interest to the present generation, brought up as it has been on a series of international negotiations of a somewhat similar nature. But we can only summarize them here. The Pope appointed Cardinal Alvergati as his legate and he presided throughout at the conference. The chief English delegate was Cardinal Beaufort.

Scarcely had the proceedings commenced than they were interrupted by an event calculated to wreck the whole conference. La Hire and Xantrailles—the Castor and Pollux of the

[1] "The Valois kingdom was not merely out of breath; it was at the end of its strength." *The Hundred Years War* by Edouard Perroy, p. 290.

Valois army—selected this critical moment to make a raid into
Burgundian territory from Beauvais. They crossed the Somme
at Bray, and worked west towards Corbie. This disturbing news
reached Arras, only 30 miles to the north, while the duke of Burgundy was dining the French envoys. He instantly turned out
a force, to which English and even Valois knights attached themselves, to repel the invader and disturber of the peace. The
"Heavenly Gemini" were encountered near Corbie, but thanks
to the Valois knights, blows were avoided and the raiders were
allowed to return to their own territory, minus their booty and
prisoners. The conference then proceeded.

Each side received secret 'maximum' terms that it was authorized to offer if need be, but each side opened up with proposals
very far apart. Gradually the differences were whittled down,
concessions of territory being made, chiefly on the part of
Charles's party. It soon however became evident that the negotiations would split on the rock of Henry's title to the throne of
France. On this point the English envoys were adamant. Duke
Philip exhausted his utmost powers of persuasion on this issue
with Cardinal Beaufort who, for his part, became so worked up
that the perspiration streamed down his face. It was all of no
use, the negotiations broke down and on September 6 the
English took their departure.

The French delegates, evidently upset and alarmed by the
peremptory departure of the English envoys, sent after them a
fresh proposal that the question of Henry VI's renunciation of
his title as king of France should hang over till he became of age,
on condition that they should at once evacuate all ceded territory. But this last-minute concession was of no avail. Feeling in
London ran high, the mob attacked French domiciles and the
unfortunate messenger, none other than the famous chronicler
Le Fèvre (who relates the story) received the following remarkable reply from the Lord Chancellor:

"The King of England and France, my master, has seen the letters
and offers that you have brought him, which have much displeased
him, and not without reason, for which things he has assembled

those of his blood and Lineage for advice on the subject; and you can now return across the sea."

And that was all.

Seeing that the duke of Burgundy had now shown his hand and was obviously resolved upon an accord with his old enemy, whether the English were agreeable or not, it may be considered that the unbending attitude of the English Government was unreasonable and mistaken. Without the Burgundian alliance the "dual monarchy" could hardly persist indefinitely, and the sensible course was to relinquish the claim to sovereignty, as Edward III had done, and be content with the minor sovereignty of Normandy and Gascony. But in the eyes of the proud and obstinate English people Henry VI was the lawful king of France, Charles having been disinherited by his own father.[1] Mistaken or not, one cannot withold a certain admiration for the pertinacity thus exhibited by the English people – a pertinacity that was to become a part of the national character – the pertinacity that refuses to abandon a struggle or relinquish an aim that it has once embarked upon – as exemplified by the long struggle with Philip II of Spain, Louis XIV of France, Napoleon Bonaparte, Kaiser William and Adolf Hitler of Germany. . . .

* * *

The duke of Burgundy made his peace with Charles. By what processes of casuistry he salved his conscience in breaking unilaterally his alliance with England, sworn to at Troyes, we are not here concerned. The all-important fact is that the alliance which both Henry V and the duke of Bedford so clearly realised to be essential to the endurance of the "dual monarchy" had snapped. John, duke of Bedford, a sick man, saw his life's work crumbling in ruins. His heart was broken; he turned his face to the wall and died.[2]

Of this splendid English prince, a man in advance of his time, who had nursed farseeing projects for the unification and better-

[1] This point is conceded by Professor Perroy, op. cit., p. 292.
[2] He was buried in the chancel of Rouen Cathedral—a pilgrimage to the grave of this great Englishman is therefore easy.

ment of two great nations, it will be sufficient to quote only the tribute of a Frenchman. The Bourgeois of Paris described him as:

"Noble in birth and worth; wise, liberal, feared and loved."

While the peace talks had been going on, military operations had not ceased. In the summer Lord Talbot and the Burgundian leader L'Isle Adam, had carried out successful operations in the Isle de France, retaking many strong places that had fallen into French hands. And early in September he had taken the field with Bedford himself in an attempt to recover St. Denys, which also had been for some time in Valois hands. He had amassed an army 6,000 strong, and the attack was conducted with vigour. After a heavy bombardment an assault with scaling ladders, through the waters of the moat neck-high, was attempted. It failed. But shortly afterwards the garrison despairing of relief, surrendered at discretion.

Some Burgundian troops had assisted in this siege. It was their last cooperation with their allies. A few weeks later they were to be found fighting on the side of the Valois. Duke Philip had offered to remain neutral after the signing of the Treaty of Arras, but the English, infuriated with the "false, forsworn Duke" rejected his offer with contumely, and proudly set about the formidable task of opposing Burgundians and Valois combined. But the defection of Burgundy was fatal to the English cause. The Burgundians in Paris, hitherto faithful to the alliance and to Henry VI, fell away, and when a French army under the Constable de Richemont appeared before the gates on April 13, 1436, they were opened to him. The English garrison was allowed to depart unmolested, but "it was amid the hoots of the burgesses who had once hailed it with delight".

The English cause in France seemed lost.

CHAPTER XVII

THE ENGLISH RECOVERY

THE English cause in France was lost. Or so it must have seemed to most Frenchmen. But they had overlooked two things: the stubborn pride of the English nation, and the presence at the virtual head of their army in France of John, Lord Talbot. But at the outset of this new phase of the war there came a surprising turn of events. Instead of a combined Valois-Burgundian army invading Normandy, such as might have been expected, the fighting was done, not by Armagnacs or Burgundians but by the old allies of England, the Flemings.

It came about in this way. Duke Philip had been piqued by the contemptuous spurning by England of his offer of neutrality, and he conceived a violent hatred of his old ally—a hatred that was reciprocated, for there is no wrath like that of ancient friends who have quarrelled. The English had always regarded Charles with quiet contempt; now they regarded Philip with loathing. The Burgundian resolved to strike back. How could he hurt his old ally with least expense and effort to himself? Calais was the obvious answer. Whatever other possession in France England might be obliged to relinquish, the loss of Calais—a veritable "pistol pointed at Paris"—would hurt her pride the most. Now the Flemish border ran adjacent to the Calais "pale", and the Flemings were his subjects. If he could only persuade them that it was their own (trade) interest to turn the English out of Calais he might utilize them to do the turning out. It was a bright idea, with logic and sound reasoning behind it. Duke Philip tackled the task deftly and successfully. If the Flemings would attack the town on the land side he would blockade it from the sea; relief would be impossible; its fate would be

sealed and the English wool duties would be abolished. The
Flemings were won over by these cajoleries; they collected a
large army, and exuberantly advanced to the attack. But the
English had had warning and counter-measures were taken; a
nation-wide appeal was made for recruits, reinforcements and
supplies were poured into the town, and the duke of Gloucester
was named as the commander of the garrison.

The Flemings duly opened the investment, but things did not
go well for them. The defenders were resolute and even aggressive. As casualties mounted up, the enthusiasm of the Flemings
for the fight diminished–especially as there was no sign of the
promised Burgundian fleet. They complained loudly to their
duke, who responded with excuses, and more promises and
blandishments. With difficulty he prevailed upon the Flemings
to continue the siege. Eventually the fleet did appear, and four
block-ships were fitted out to block the channel leading into the
harbour. One of them however was sunk by gun-fire before it
could be got into position,[1] and the remaining three were run
ashore in the wrong place. At low tide they were high and dry,
and the exultant garrison rushed out, broke them up, and used
the wood for fuel. The Burgundian fleet then sailed ingloriously
home. This was altogether too much for the Flemings; they
were on the point of open revolt, and despite desperate efforts at
pacification on the part of Duke Philip, they broke up their camp
and retreated hastily on Bruges. The garrison pursued them as
far as Gravelines, and made large captures. The duke of Gloucester landed in Calais in time to see his victorious troops re-
enter the town.

Duke Humphrey then conducted a nine days almost bloodless campaign, pushing rapidly into Flanders, burning Bailleul
and Poperinghe, and threatening St. Omer. He then paid off
his army and returned to England. For this critics have blamed
him, suggesting that he might have advanced into Picardy and
captured Arras, the duke of Burgundy's headquarters. But his
army was not fitted out for a field or siege campaign, but solely

[1] One of the earliest instances of ships being sunk by artillery.

for the defence of Calais, and an attack on Arras without a siege train would have been futile.

* * *

Whilst the fate of Calais, that "precious jewel", as English chroniclers lovingly called it, lay in the balance all eyes in England were turned in that direction, little interest being taken in the war with Valois. Indeed the duke of York, who was now sent out as regent was authorized to enter into negotiations with Charles VII, (though nothing came of this). But with the victory over Burgundy at Calais the original war could be resumed with increased vigour. Matters had begun to improve. The panic created by the apparition in the field of the "Limb of the Fiend" had long passed away and the same old resolute spirit of England was reasserting itself. This spirit was incarnated in John Talbot, who soon began to make his presence felt.

THE ENGAGEMENT OF RY

In January 1436 the twin gadflies, La Hire and Poton de Xantrailles had penetrated right up to the gates of Rouen with 1,000 men, hoping to be admitted by French sympathizers. Baffled in this they fell back ten miles in an easterly direction and halted in the village of Ry awaiting reinforcements. Talbot got news of this; hastily collecting a force of 400 men, including Lord Scales and Sir Thomas Kyriell, he galloped out of Rouen in a whirlwind swoop. The little town of Ry lies in a hollow beset on every side by woods. Half a mile to the west, in the direction of Rouen, there is a well defined ridge, over which the Rouen road runs. The top of the ridge is hidden from the village by a screen of trees. The French outposts on this hill were thus invisible to the troops in the town. When Talbot swept down on the outposts, therefore, the surprise was complete. As the outposts came running down the hill panic overtook the troops in billets in the town. La Hire did his best to rally his men in the market square, in the main street, but in vain. He himself was wounded and swept out of the town in the general stampede. Talbot's troopers galloped through the main street in hot pursuit of the fugitives, who fled to the east, leaving a number of high-born knights as prisoners in Talbot's hands, and all their baggage was captured. The victory was complete. Though the numbers engaged were small, the significance of the engagement was great; for the old dash and supremacy in the field of an English force against one over twice its size was once more demonstrated; and the two most famous and skilful French generals had been ignominiously defeated.

*   *   *

John Talbot now looked round for a fresh quarry to attack, and an obvious one came to mind. Pontoise had returned to its French allegiance along with the other towns of the neighbourhood, and its commander was none other than L'Isle Adam, Talbot's comrade-in-arms in the capture of St. Denys two years previously. This acceptance of a key post by his old friend was not appreciated by Talbot and he decided to teach the renegade, as he regarded the Burgundian, a lesson.

We shall have a good deal to do with Pontoise, so it will be well to visualize its aspect and situation. As its name implies, it is the site of a bridge over the Oise, here nearly 100 yards wide. It is on the direct road from Rouen to Paris, and being the lowest bridge on the river was of particular strategic importance, for the Oise in its lower reaches is wide and unfordable. It was the gateway to Paris from the north, and it is not surprising that it had become a military fortress of the first order. Anyone crossing the railway bridge on his way by train to Paris from Dieppe, will realize the significance of the lay-out at a glance, for, towering over and dominating the bridge stand the ruins of the castle, on a rocky cliff—the end of a narrow ridge running north from the river, on which the town lies. A lofty wall, much of which can still be traced, girt the town. Altogether Pontoise was a formidable obstacle, well stocked with military stores and supplies and adequately garrisoned.

Such was the town that John Talbot elected to attack,

although he had only 400 men available for the task and it was
the depth of winter–and a very hard one too. Perhaps this very
fact encouraged the English general to select that season, for it
would favour the element of surprise.

On February 12, 1437, hard on his success at Ry, Lord Talbot
set out from Rouen. Making a dash worthy of Sir Thomas Dagworth, he reached the vicinity of Pontoise utterly unexpected.
The weather was so hard that the river Oise was frozen over and
we are told that Talbot crossed over the ice. This is at first sight
puzzling, for the river is on the far (that is the Paris side) side of
the town, so he should have had no occasion to cross it at all.
The clue seems to lie in the poem of Martial d'Auvergne. He
describes how a party of English troops disguised as villagers and
carrying hampers and baskets of food, as if on their way to the
market, entered the town without exciting suspicion. This they
could hardly expect to do unless they approached from the French
side, *i.e.*, from across the river. Thus it seems that Talbot utilized the ice to get this party across. It is true that Martial says
they were dressed in white, but I fancy he must be mixing it up
with the other party in the operation, namely the scaling party.
Now snow lay deep on the ground, and Talbot clothed his
storming party in white in order to conceal them in their
approach to the walls at daylight next morning. This stratagem
was also completely successful; and the stormers were able to
place their ladders against the walls without attracting attention.
All was quiet and peaceful in the sleeping town, and L'Isle
Adam was in bed, when suddenly a great shout rang out inside
the city: "The town is ours! St. George! Talbot!" This was the
prearranged signal made by the "market men". The stormers
mounted the ladders, entered the now awakening town and
rushed to the gates to open them for the remainders of Talbot's
force. The surprise and the success were equally complete.
L'Isle Adam and his men fled from the town without striking a
blow, leaving all their belongings and an immense quantity of
stores behind them. Thus the gateway to Paris was captured
with the loss of scarcely a man.

But that was not the end of the exploit. Talbot, like the true soldier he was, appreciated the advantage of "striking while the iron is hot". He decided to make practical and instant use of the "gateway". Despite the minute proportions of his force he resolved on attacking Paris itself. Whether this was a mere act of bravado, or whether it was a "calculated risk" on his part we do not know. John Talbot, like all generals of the period, was more proficient with sword than with pen, and his motives and thoughts throughout his campaigns have to be divined from his acts. Whatever the motive, this splendidly audacious action had some initial success. His handful of men penetrated right up to the walls of the capital, crossed the moat over the ice, and made preparations to climb the walls. But the task was beyond them. Assailed by powerful artillery and by crossbow shafts and lances, they were forced to abandon the enterprise and to fall back in good order and good heart to Pontoise.

*   *   *

The English recovery was almost at full flood. Though the duke of York himself had some successes in winning back a few towns in Caux, such as Dieppe, the main credit must go to the triple blow delivered in the winter of 1437 by John, Lord Talbot. Six months later Talbot was again on the warpath. The English still held the two bastions, as it were, on each side of the Somme estuary–St. Valery and Le Crotoy. The Burgundians were besieging the latter in a half-hearted way, and, making no progress, they appealed to the duke of Burgundy for reinforcements. The duke called on John of Luxemburg to supply them, but one Burgundian chief at least remained loyal to his old comrades-in-arms. John stoutly declined to cross swords with the English, and Philip was reduced to conducting the operation himself. Le Crotoy was the nearest coastal town to Calais still in English hands and it would not do to let it fall. The earl of Warwick, now 58 years of age, had just reluctantly succeeded the duke of York as king's lieutenant in France. Recognizing the importance of Le Crotoy he despatched Talbot with an army estimated at 5,000 men, to its relief. The Burgundians are given as 10,000 strong, but both figures can probably be halved.

Talbot, with Kyriell as his chief lieutenant, marched from Rouen to St. Valery. On this occasion he changed his strategy, making no attempt to conceal his march, and indeed issuing a challenge to Burgundy to a fight in the open. Duke Philip did not respond to this but he took alarm, and went in person to Abbeville to strengthen its defences. Whilst he was still there the English resumed their advance. Abbeville being firmly held by the enemy, Talbot resolved to follow the example of Edward III (and the intention of Henry V) and cross the Somme by the famous ford of Blanche Taque. Here history was repeated, for the tide was partly up and the far side was strongly held by Burgundian infantry and artillery. Undeterred by this con- tretemps, Talbot impulsively plunged into the water at the head of his army–up to his chin, it is said (but need not be believed)–struggled across the mile-wide estuary on the narrow causeway, and dispersed the enemy on the far bank with trifling loss to his own army. This was a truly remarkable performance –one that would have been quite impossible against staunch troops. Talbot must have had evidence of the poor quality of these defenders, no doubt local levies, who had no heart for the fight, especially when they learnt the name of the English com- mander. On reaching the far bank Talbot did not turn at once against the besieging army. It had secured itself in a "bastille" or field work similar to those built by the English at Orleans. Talbot's object was to entice them out into the open and in order to do this he started ravaging the surrounding country, penetrating almost to Hesdin, 25 miles to the east, Duke Philip's northern capital. Practically no resistance was offered to the English troops wherever they went or whatever they did. The Burgundian chroniclers are bitter in their contempt for the sorry display exhibited by their men. Talbot then returned towards Le Crotoy. On his approach the garrison of the bastille fled in panic leaving all their artillery and immense quantity of stores. The garrison of Le Crotoy pursued them, according to Monstrelet "shouting after them as they would have done to a ribald mob". The English army returned to Rouen, heavily laden with booty, and well pleased with themselves and with their commander. And well they might be, for Talbot had shown his versatility. His was no one-track mind; his methods had been entirely different to those employed heretofore; he had sized up his opponents correctly—one of the marks of military genius—and had achieved his aim with a minimum of bloodshed.

Eighteen months after Paris had fallen Charles VII deemed it safe to enter his capital. On November 12, 1437, he entered the city amid the plaudits of the populace. But three weeks later he left it again and fell back to his beloved Loire country. The weakness and supineness of the French king at this period has been much criticized by French historians. It is indisputable that Charles had little stomach for the fight—less even than had the preceding Valois kings—but his difficulties at the time, with an uncertain and recently cemented concord with Burgundy, an impoverished treasury, and a state of semi-anarchy due to the French freebooters running riot through the land, were enough to daunt a Churchill. His inactivity immediately after sealing the concord with Burgundy may have also been due in part to the expectation that England would now throw up the sponge.[1]

*   *   *

In 1438 the war languished in the north, partly owing to the famine and plague that affected both France and England. But in the far south it flared up. Ever since 1377 the boundary between English-held Aquitaine and France had been static till 1420. During the next few years the local levies had driven the French back a short distance, recapturing St. Macaire, La Réole and other towns. Thereafter calm descended once more on the scene till this year 1438. There had been no need to call in English troops to defend Gascony, nor even to take part in the 1420 advance, for, as Sir Charles Oman points out:

[1] Adolf Hitler's inactivity in July 1940 was due to a similar miscalculation.

"The English dominion rested, not on the spears and bows of an aline garrison, but on the willing obedience of the whole population."[1]

This is scarcely surprising when we remember that Aquitaine had been an appanage of the English crown for nearly 300 years, and had been governed in an enlightened spirit. However, Charles VII now considered that an opportunity presented itself to drive the English out of Aquitaine, and he collected forces in the south for the purpose. The campaign that ensued was of some military interest strategically, as the French for the first time endeavoured to concert operations by several columns working on exterior lines, in a manner reminiscent of Edward III. But Charles was to learn, as Edward had done, that such operations were beset with difficulties in an age when communications were in a primitive state. The columns were to advance inwards, concentrating for the final assault on Bordeaux, the capital. But co-operation between the columns was bad, indeed almost non-existent, and the successes attained fell far short of what had been planned and expected. Next year the English government sent out an army nearly 3,000 strong, under the earl of Huntingdon, which had little difficulty in driving the French back practically to their starting line.

*   *   *

Both nations were by now growing increasingly weary of the war, but the tragedy was that the English could only obtain peace by renouncing the claim of their king to be the legitimate king of France – an admission that would imply that their 23 years of war had been unjustified – while the French could not be expected to acknowledge the jurisdiction of a second king in their domains whilst they had one who had been anointed with the sacred oil of Rheims in actual possession of the capital. Nevertheless peace was in the air and Cardinal Beaufort, the leader of the peace party in England (the war party being led by the duke of Gloucester) entered into tentative negotiations in the autumn. The upshot of these was that a peace conference was fixed for the following summer. The venue was Calais and the confer-

[1] *Political History*, p. 328.

ence assembled at a spot midway between Calais and Gravelines on July 6, 1439. Memories of the treachery on the bridge
of Montereau were uppermost in the minds of both parties, and
the most elaborate arrangements were made to safeguard
against a repetition of anything of the sort. Cardinal Beaufort
led the English party, and for some reason, the duchess of Burgundy led the French party. The proceedings were protracted,
but we can see in retrospect that they were doomed to failure;
as always, they were shipwrecked on the snag of "the renunciation of the title" of king of France by Henry VI. All that came
out of the conference was a local truce for three years between
England and the duke of Burgundy in the Calais area.

While the peace negotiations were taking place the war was
proceeding. Meaux was now the only town to the east of Paris
in English hands. In July a strong army was fitted out for its
reduction, liberally supplied with siege artillery under one Jean
Bureau. The course of the siege that resulted was singularly
similar to that of Henry V; that is to say, the defence was obstinate, and when the pressure on the town became too great the
garrison crossed the river into the Market. Meanwhile attempts
at relief were being made. Talbot led thither an army of 3,000,
accompanied by the earl of Somerset, and Lord Scales.

Marching straight for Meaux the army arrived in the vicinity
three days after the evacuation of the town. Moreover, the
Constable de Richemont, the French commander, had withdrawn all his troops into the town on hearing of the approach
of the dread Lord Talbot. The latter was intent on a fight
with the Constable, the man to whom he largely owed his
capture at Patay, exactly ten years before. He sent the Frenchman a formal challenge, to which he received no reply. He then
marched his army backwards and forwards in front of the town,
but all to no purpose. His arrival had had an astonishing effect
upon the besiegers, who had now practically themselves become
the besieged garrison. But Richemont did not trust his troops
and would take no risks. His biographer, Dr. Cosneau, frankly
admits the fact.

"The English and their captains, above all Talbot, had a well-established reputation for superiority, Richemont knew them better than anyone."[1]

The supine but correct attitude adopted by Richemont allowed Talbot to pass into the Market fresh stores, and reinforcements. This was accomplished by means of leather boats that had been carried by the army for this purpose. Talbot went further than this. The besiegers had erected a number of bastilles round the town including at least one on an island between the town and Market. Talbot must have felt rather frustrated and disappointed at not being able to inflict much damage on the Constable. To carry the town by assault was out of the question for no siege train had been brought, nor supplies for a long siege. One thing however was possible and that Talbot did. The bastille on the island was too close to the Market to be comfortable. Talbot decided to take it. This he did with speed, killing or capturing the whole of the garrison on the island without let or hindrance from the French troops in the town, only a short distance away, and within easy bow-shot. It was as if the French were hypnotized by the very name of Talbot.

However, in spite of this signal success there was no more that could be done, and, Talbot having "refreshed" the garrison of the Market, took his army back to Rouen. Richemont thereupon resumed the siege and not long afterwards the garrison surrendered on terms. So it would seem that the Constable's rather inglorious procedure was on the short view the correct one.

*　　　*　　　*

AVRANCHES

Lord Talbot led his army back to Normandy and proceeded with the recovery of towns in the Pays de Caux (between Rouen and Dieppe) which had been lost five years before. The Constable de Richemont, as soon as his army was set free by the surrender of Meaux, made no attempt to go to the help of the threatened towns in Caux, but decided to undertake the siege of Avranches, on the borders of Brittany. It has been supposed

[1] *Le Connétable de Richemont*, p. 294, n.

that he expected help from his elder brother the duke of Brittany. But the latter had signed an agreement with England at Calais, and, so far from playing the turn-coat, he promised to support the English cause.[1]

Avranches is picturesquely situated on an isolated hill half a mile to the south of the little river Sée, and four miles from the sea. The tidal waters are fordable in places, and there are occasional fords above the town. In late November Richemont appeared before the town, bringing with him a reinforcement under the command of the duke of Alençon. As soon as Warwick heard of this attack he sent help to the threatened garrison, under the inevitable John Talbot. The French army was about 6,000 strong, and the English decidedly smaller.[2]

In mid-December the English approached from the north and took up position along the north bank of the river Sée facing the town.[3] For some days there was bickering and skirmishing between the sides, whilst Talbot evolved his plan. The main body of the French army was camped between the river and town, and was thus between two fires (much as had been the case at Cravant). Much of the army consisted of ill-disciplined mercenaries, most of whom were in the habit of trickling away when it got dark and sheltering in the nearby villages. Talbot evidently became aware of this and decided to profit by it. He had discovered a ford over the river away to a flank (apparently up-stream) which was either unguarded, being unknown to the French or inadequately guarded at night. On the night of December 22/23 the attack took place. The ford was seized by the English and crossed without difficulty; the attackers then swung inwards parallel to the river and assaulted the French camp. The outposts were all captured or put to flight, and the English penetrated into the sleeping camp. There seems to have been but little resistance, and panic set in. The whole army decamped and dispersed in confusion except a tiny remnant of

[1] Cosneau, citing *Preuves de l'histoire de Bretagne.*
[2] The *Bourgeois de Paris* gives the French as 40,000 and the English 8,000.
[3] Ramsay makes them approach from the south, but Jean Chartier's account (the best) leaves no doubt on the point.

about 100 lances under the Constable. Eventually he also was compelled to retreat, while the English army entered the town in triumph.

The French had retreated in a westerly direction, across the border into Brittany, and the flight was continued without respite as far as Dol, 20 miles to the west. As for the Constable, he made his way as best he could to Paris, minus his army. Here he had an interview with the king, which can scarcely have escaped being stormy; for he told Charles in no uncertain terms that he could do nothing with such an undisciplined rabble as his vanished army. The interview had important results; it strengthened the king in the steps he had already put in hand to reorganize and improve his army. We shall hear more of this later on.

In the early part of the following year, 1440, the English lost a good opportunity for attacking while France was distracted by civil strife. The leaders of the revolt were the dukes of Bourbon and Alençon, the count of Dunois and, of all people, the 16-year-old Dauphin, Louis (later Louis XI), who is described by Ramsay as "a cool astute youth, embued with a profound contempt for his father."[1] It was not till July that the English Government gave orders for the siege of Harfleur, by which time Charles VII had got the revolt under control. It was certainly high time Harfleur was retaken; it had been for five years in French hands, and had become a thorn in the side of the English. The leaders appointed were the earls of Somerset and Dorset (his younger brother), and Lords Talbot and Fauconbridge. Thus the curious and unsound medieval custom of not nominating a supreme commander was followed. In practice Somerset took command of the naval portion of the force and Talbot the land portion. The siege opened in August.[2] The garrison appealed to Charles VII for help and he responded by sending a large army under Richemont and La Hire, (where was Xantrailles?) to its relief. The English army was only 1,000 strong, but they set about their

[1] *Lancaster and York*, II, p. 29.
[2] Ramsay follows Monstrelet in dating it April.

work energetically and thoroughly, constructing double lines of circum- and contra-vallation. Deep continuous ditches and stockaded ramparts were built, instead of the isolated "bastilles" favoured by the French. In addition a defensive line was thrown up along the shore to prevent relief by sea. This was indeed part of the French plan, which comprised a double land attack from two sides together with a simultaneous landing in the estuary.

Some of the French ships must have succeeded in running the gauntlet of Somerset's protective squadron for they were able to approach the town but failed to effect a landing owing to the English shore defences. Both land attacks failed dismally, the English archers causing heavy casualties to the assaulting men-at-arms. This must indicate that they reserved their fire to point-blank range for plate-armour was now fully developed and arrows could only penetrate at the shortest range. The French accepted defeat, and in October fell back to Paris. Shortly afterwards the town surrendered at discretion. A curious incident that ocurred during the French retreat illustrated the fundamentally divided state of the French nation. On the outward march the army had passed through the lands of the duke of Burgundy in the valley of the Somme. They started to retrace their steps along the same route, only to be met by a peremptory demand from the incensed duke that they should keep clear of his domains as they had wrought it so much damage by pillage on the outward march. Count John of Luxemburg also made difficulties about allowing them passage. He was living in retirement, having resolutely declined to take up arms against his old comrades the English in spite of all that Duke Philip could do by threats and cajolery to persuade him. Next January this good friend of the English died, faithful to them to the last.

That same autumn the duke of Orleans, who had been a prisoner in England ever since the Battle of Agincourt, was released; the motive of Henry VI was purely humanitarian; those of his government more calculating; it was hoped that his presence and influence in France would further the English cause, and the duke undertook to do his best in the interests of peace.

THE SEINE ET OISE CAMPAIGN

The chief event of the following year, 1441, was the siege of Pontoise, described by the French historian Du Fresnes de Beaucourt with pardonable exaggeration, as "a veritable siege of Troy". The strategical importance of Pontoise has already been made apparent. While held by the English, only twelve miles from St. Denys, it was a standing menace to the capital. Encouraged by the capture of Creil, thanks largely to Jean Bureau and his artillery, Charles VII decided to attempt the reduction of this key fortress. He was now taking increasing interest in the military operations. He had "witnessed" the siege of Creil from Senlis, some six miles away. This time he led his army in person to the attack on Pontoise, approaching it from the eastern side of the Oise. On June 6, he took up his residence at the Abbey of Maubuisson, two miles short of the river, and opened the siege. The bridge spanning the river was in English hands, with a work forming a barbican (or bridgehead) on the far end of the bridge. It was the lowest bridge on the Oise, which joins the Seine at Conflans six miles to the south. A bridge obviously had to be constructed by the French and this was thrown across the river a short distance down-stream, opposite St. Martin's Abbey. A large bastille was then constructed enclosing the Abbey, and the Dauphin Louis was placed in command of it. There were not sufficient troops however to construct continuous lines of circumvallation round the town, and so (as at Orleans), there was a big undefended gap to the north and east.

The strength of the French investing army may be put, at a very rough guess, at about 5,000. Nearly all the leading French generals, including La Hire and Xantrailles (for the last time together) were present. The Constable was in active command, with Admiral Coëtivi as his second-in-command. The artillery, again under Jean Bureau, was numerous and powerful and it showed its prowess early in the siege. The southern end of the town could not be approached as long as the bridge remained in English hands, and Bureau was set to work on the destruction of the barbican. This he was successful in doing in a few days, together with the destruction of the first three arches of the bridge – a questionable policy, for the attackers would be obliged to repair it themselves before they could make use of it. The first attempt to storm the barbican was defeated with heavy loss, but the second was successful. A powerful battery of guns was also transported across the river and the bombardment of the town commenced in earnest. Several breaches began to appear, but each morning it was seen that the walls appeared as intact as ever; the garrison had been at work on repairs during the night. Sorties were also made from time to time.

While this was going on, Lord Talbot in Rouen had not been idle. He was busy collecting a relief force, complete with food, supplies and ordnance stores for the garrison. Assembling them at Elboeuf, eight miles south of Rouen, he on June 16, marched along the northern bank of the Seine to the relief. Approaching the town from the west, his road took him close past St. Martin's Abbey. The French, as they had done at Meaux, withdrew inside their bastille, and offered no impediment whatever to the entry into the town of the relieving force. This was the direct order of the king: the Constable did not agree with it. Talbot was thus able to replenish the garrison, exchange some worn out soldiers for fresh and strengthen the high command by leaving in it Lords Scales and Fauconbridge. Then he returned the way he had come as far as Mantes, 20 miles distant, where he immediately began collecting a second supply train. With this train Talbot again marched to Pontoise and again he delivered the goods without the French attempting to cross swords with him. It was now becoming obvious that the king had decided on a policy of "non-aggression".

And now a newcomer was to appear on the scene. The earl of Warwick had died in 1439 at the age of 58, and the duke of York, who had held the office for a short time in 1435, was appointed in his stead. After long delays he landed at Harfleur with some reinforcements in June. Arrived at Rouen he set about collecting further supplies for the besieged town, and in the middle of July he set out, Talbot commanding the vanguard. The army was this time on a bigger scale, but there is little indication as to its actual strength. It clearly was much inferior to the French in numbers: the *mot* was shortly to be heard in Paris, "Whenever the French find themselves in a superiority of three to one they immediately retreat." If we assess the English at between 2,000 and 3,000 we shall not be far out.

On the approach of the relieving army, Charles this time withdrew his army across the river, leaving a garrison in the St. Martin's Bastille, under Admiral Coëtivi. Thus York was able to enter the town unmolested, and deliver his supplies.

But this was to be only the beginning of a campaign which possesses an interest—and indeed a humour—seldom surpassed in the war.[1] The leading spirit, if not the architect of the whole operation, was of course John, Lord Talbot. The duke of York opened the proceedings by informing the French king, quite in the style of Edward III, that he intended to cross the Oise with his army whether Charles of Valois liked it or not. The effect of this braggadocio was that Charles extended his troops in a long defensive line along the river from its confluence with the Seine to Creil, a frontage of over 30 miles. York (or shall we say Talbot?) countered this in a way that smacks of the duke of Marlborough of a later era.[2] First he withdrew his army nearly ten miles to the north, well out of sight and touch of the French. From there he marched rapidly to a point on the river near Beaumont, 15 miles upstream from Pontoise. This sector was defended by the Count de la Marche, who had a detachment in Beaumont. The town was attacked, but it was merely a feint; which succeeded in attracting attention and drawing defenders to that point. Meanwhile, the main body was pushing on still further north to opposite the abbey of Royaumont. Here the river (nearly 30 yards wide) was unguarded. A small boat was rowed across, a rope was then stretched across the stream, and the pontoon bridge, made of portable leather boats, specially

[1] Sketch map 10, on page 651, if studied closely, will be found to give an epitome of the campaign, step by step.
[2] In his crossings of the Geet and of the Lines of Non Plus Ultra. But it is unlikely that Marlborough consciously adopted Talbot's method.

brought up for the purpose, was rapidly constructed. The whole army then crossed by this bridge without a blow being struck in its defence. Looked at from any point of view it was a brilliant achievement.

When the startling news reached headquarters at Maubuisson abbey, the Constable de Richemont, a vigorous practical soldier, jumped on to his horse, collected what troops were to hand and galloped to L'Isle Adam, ten miles away upstream, to verify for himself the report. It was all too true. Richemont hastened back and either he or the king decided on a curious step. St. Denys and Paris were obviously threatened, and a portion of the army was at once despatched to St. Denys for its protection. But there was a further danger—the king's own person was in jeopardy. Only a few days before, the army had crossed the Oise from west to east to put the river between themselves and the English. Now the process was reversed, but with the same object: the English were to the east of the river, therefore the French must cross to the west bank, even though it took them away from their base, the capital. Stores were packed up in a hurry and the king and his army made their way across the Oise, while the English army was marching down the left bank of the river, and approaching Maubuisson abbey.

Talbot took possession of the abbey, 24 hours after Charles had quit, with much of the king's belongings and stores still there, for the French had departed in such haste. It seems that they had broken down the Oise bridge after crossing it and York halted for four days whilst repairing the bridge and constructing another at Neuville near Conflans. The English army then crossed and turned south in pursuit of the French king.

Meanwhile Charles, after leaving a strong garrison in the St. Martin's Bastille again under the mis-named Admiral Coëtivi, had retreated still further, in a southerly direction. Not until Charles had placed another river, the Seine, between him and the English did he feel tolerably safe. He took up his residence at the abbey at Poissy, on the south bank of the Seine, some 15 miles south of Pontoise. The inhabitants of Paris

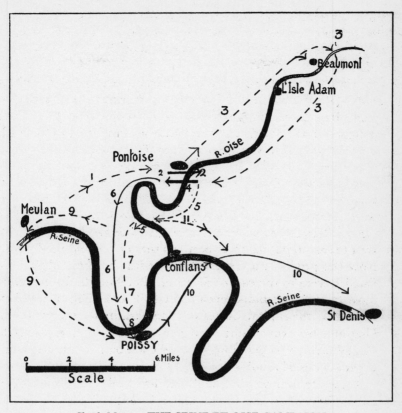

Sketch Map 10: THE SEINE ET OISE CAMPAIGN

- - →   English marches
—→   French marches

1. English enter Pontoise
2. French cross the Oise
3. English cross the Oise
4. French recross the Oise
5. English recross the Oise
6. French retreat to the Seine
7. English pursue to the Seine
8. French cross Seine
9. Talbot crosses Seine
10. French recross Seine
11. York tries to intercept the French

viewed this game of hide-and-seek with disgust and were beginning openly to rate their king as a coward.

After crossing the Seine at Poissy, (doubtless by the very
bridge by which Edward III had crossed during his famous
march to Crecy 95 years before) the French posted a strong
guard at the bridgehead which was soon engaged in hot skirmishing with the English vanguard. The problem now confronting York was how to get at the enemy. Here the fertile brain of
John Talbot came to the rescue. He proposed the following plan
to his chief. He himself would take a small force of 1,000 men
back to Mantes. There he would cross the Seine, and by a
rapid night march would surprise the French in Poissy and set
them off in retreat once more towards St. Denys. To reach it
they would presumably recross the Seine by a bridge slightly to
the east of Conflans. Meanwhile York was to recross the Oise to
the eastern bank at Neuville and lie in wait for the French at
their crossing. Thus they would be driven by Talbot into the
arms of the main English army, and, in the opinion of Bishop
Basin (who alone records the operation in full) nothing could
have saved the king.

The duke of York accepted the plan, and Talbot marched off
to Mantes. Accurate timing between the two disconnected
bodies of the English army was of course essential for the success
of the plan and we may assume that arrangements to this effect
were made. The distance from Mantes to Poissy is 17 miles. As
the success of the operation largely depended upon surprise,
Talbot decided to make the march by night. To do 17 miles in a
single night, whether with or without the aid of the moon is to
ask a lot of the troops. But Talbot asked for it—and received it.
They reached Poissy early in the morning and the surprise was
so complete that when Talbot entered the abbey, where the
king had slept, "his bedclothes were still warm".

King Charles, the reader may not be surprised to hear, was
crossing yet another river, or rather the same river—the Seine—
in the reverse direction, as before. But where was the duke of
York and the main English army? The answer is that they had

been too slow in re-crossing the Oise at Neuville so that the French got across the Seine and back to St. Denys before the duke's army had put in an appearance. They were only in time to see the French marching across their front from a hill, probably just to the north of Herblay (two miles north-east of Conflans).

A curious incident is related by Gruel of this campaign. As soon as the king reached Poissy he had sent off a supply column to Pontoise under the Constable. Xantrailles commanded the vanguard on the outward journey, and the rearguard on the return. On that day the English were throwing their bridge across the river Oise at Neuville, midway between Pontoise and Conflans, so there might be danger from the eastern flank. On the return journey Xantrailles represented this danger to Richemont, strongly urging him to take the roundabout route via Meulan, ten miles down the Seine from Poissy. The Constable agreed and did so. But Xantrailles hung back till the main body was out of sight. He then marched straight for the Poissy bridge, thus arriving well before the main body. He then declared to the king that Richemont had not dared to take the direct route but that he himself had done so. On Richemont's arrival Charles naturally taxed him with this, whereupon the Constable explained the true facts and gave Poton de Xantrailles a good dressing down in the presence of the king. This story illustrates the degree of disharmony and jealousy that reigned in the French army. Indeed the count of St. Pol, a Burgundian, was so disgusted with the turn of events that he marched away with his detachment. And deserters from the army were numerous.

The king of France was now safely back in his capital, at the cost of raising the siege of Pontoise, and at the loss of considerable prestige. Not unnaturally the French were put out of countenance by this unedifying exhibition of the Royal army of France, running away, not once nor twice from a smaller English army. What was to be done about it? Charles held a war council at St. Denys to consider the matter. The problem was partly solved for him by the actions of the duke of York who returned with his army to Rouen. This seems a tame ending to a truly brilliant if short campaign. But logistics are inexorable, and it seems that his army was now practically starving; in fact when they got back to Rouen the haggard appearance of the soldiers was generally remarked on. Moreover, the duke had seen the French army crossing a river four times within 14 days in order to get away from him, and it seemed time to give up such a wild-goose chase.

Charles VII now rose to his full stature as a king, for the first time in his reign. He would listen to no defeatist councils. Perhaps rumours had reached his ears of "cowardice" and he was put upon his metal. *Coûte que coûte* he would persevere with the siege of Pontoise. The English army had disappeared; his own artillery had already made visible marks on the defences of the town; let the good work continue, and success would crown their efforts! Thus reasoned the king, and, turning a deaf ear to the timid councils of some of the staff, thus he ordered. The bridges were once again repaired, the guns were brought out of the shelter of the St. Martin's Bastille, the town was again invested, this time on all sides, and John Bureau again got to work.

So did the other John. The indefatigable Lord Talbot collected yet another train of provisions at Elboeuf, and on August 16 he advanced with it along the direct road to Pontoise. Richemont got news of it, and this time reversed his policy of refusing battle. Instead he collected a field army from the besieging forces and advanced resolutely down the road to meet the English. The two armies met that evening head-on at Vigny, nine miles west of Pontoise. The Constable did not attempt to attack, but neither did he refuse battle. Talbot's object was to conduct his supply column to its destination, his "army" was a mere escort, and it was not his game to attack the French in position. Both forces therefore sat watching each other during the daylight. As soon as it was dark Talbot lit camp-fires and left them burning while he withdrew his troops silently to the rear, then turned sharp to the north, and marched away across the Viosne river, some two miles to the left and then turned straight for Pontoise. The besiegers having been denuded to form Richemont's field force, the English were able to penetrate the French lines in the northern sector, replenish the garrison and return to Rouen, before the Constable could do anything about it. The river Viosne separated the two armies, and though Richemont could see the English approaching the town he could not get across the river to attack them. (Talbot's manoeuvre closely resembled that of Prince Rupert in relieving York in 1644 and was equally sparkling.)

On August 28, Talbot again made a reconnaissance towards the beleaguered town, and took advantage of it on September 6, to make yet another successful relief–the fifth in all–of the town.

But Jean Bureau was now getting his fangs into the defences. On the 16th he took the church of Notre Dame, in a suburb to the west of the town, where he established an observation post, and three days later the general assault was made. The orders for this assault, issued by Admiral Coëtivi, still exist. They show that the walls were assaulted at a large number of points on all sides, in a simultaneous attack. Evidently the necessary breaches had been made. Thanks to the excellent work of the guns, the assault was successful, and after two hours resistance Pontoise at last fell. King Charles himself rode into the town while the fighting was still proceeding, if we are to believe a curious story that Bishop Basin declared he heard from the king's own lips. It was to the effect that an English armed soldier ducked under the belly of the king's charger for protection, and whilst in that constricted position he carried on a fight with his opponents, despite the efforts of Charles to make them desist.[1] As a natural result his unfortunate horse received several sword cuts in the belly.

The capture of Pontoise was a sore blow for the English, after the brilliant campaign that had preceded it. It is also important as marking a distinct step in the evolution of siege artillery. Cannons had recently increased considerably in size and power

---

[1] The author once had a wild boar under his horse's belly and could do nothing about it for the moment, so he can sympathize with King Charles in his predicament.

in the French army, and a man had arisen who understood how to apply their power.[1]

About 500 English soldiers were slaughtered in the garrison, the remainder being put to ransom, including their commander Lord Clinton.

Note. It is pleasant to be able to record that both sides exhanged poems at the opening of the siege, both of which were reproduced by Jean Chartier. The English sent the first, full of braggadocio and challenge. The French poet had rather the best of it in his reply. It is interesting to note that he addressed it to "Vous Anglais et Normans". He is aware of the approach of the duke of York (duc d'Iort): the only other Englishman named is Talbot.

*   *   *

Meanwhile the duke of Orleans had not forgotten his promise to further the cause of peace, and in the spring of 1442 he did his best at a conference at Nevers to produce some accord, but without avail. The real interest of the war now lay in Gascony whither King Charles himself led an army in the summer, and met with a fair amount of success. In taking St. Sever he also captured the Seneschal of Gascony, Sir Thomas Rempston, who thus disappears from our pages. St. Sever was later recaptured, as were many other towns. The whole campaign in fact resolved itself into a series of sieges, and constant changes of ownership, in a rather bewildering fashion. There was however one very notable siege, that of the much-captured La Réole.[2]

The town of La Réole soon surrendered but the very strongly situated castle held out all through the autumn and winter, which was a very hard one. The French in their trenches suffered much from the rigours of the climate and our old friend La Hire literally "met his death of cold". Ramsay describes him as an "utter Free Lance", but we must admit that most of his exploits were achieved under the banner of Charles. He became a national hero and his visage still adorns the Jack in a French pack of cards.

*   *   *

[1] The English also had some powerful cannons, notably the two "Michelets" with which they attempted unsuccessfully to reduce Mont St. Michel. These cannons now lie inside the fortress; they have bores of 15 and 18 inches diameter. But a glance at the strength of that fortress will explain why they failed to breach it.

[2] I calculate that in the course of the Edwardian Wars this town changed hands no fewer than seventeen times.

While the Gascony campaign was dragging on Talbot had returned to England, where he received an enthusiastic welcome – as well he might – and an earldom. Henceforth we should call him the earl of Shrewsbury, but it will be convenient to keep to the name by which he is always remembered. (The French complain, not without reason, of our frequent change of names.) French writers delight to call him "The English Achilles".

Talbot on his return to France in the summer of 1442 captured Conches in Normandy, and in the autumn laid siege to Dieppe, the only port of any size remaining in French hands between St. Valery and Harfleur. Talbot swooped on the place in his usual style, surprising and investing it before the garrison could take effective action. His force, only 1,000 in all, was much too small to invest it completely by land, so he contented himself with constructing a large bastille, in the fashion of the times, on the Pulet Hill to the east of the town, and commanding the harbour. Here he left a garrison on being recalled to Rouen, where he took up the duties of Constable of France. Profiting by his absence the French made several attempts to overrun the bastille, which was in reality more besieged than the town it was nominally besieging. The English however made a gallant and prolonged defence, and it was not till August 1443 that the Dauphin and Dunois, who had been specially sent for the purpose, succeeded in taking it. One of the prisoners was Henry Talbot, a natural son of the earl.

*   *   *

Meanwhile political events at home were obtruding increasingly on the war. The duke of Gloucester was in semi-retirement, his wife having been convicted of intriguing against the king. His loss was Oxford's gain, for it resulted in the formation of the Bodleian Library, built up round good Duke Humphrey's collection of books. The Beaufort party were now supreme and as if to mark their success they arranged for the duke of Somerset, eldest nephew of Cardinal Beaufort, to obtain the command of an army destined for the defence of Gascony, with the title of captain general of Guienne (or Gascony). This appointment was a slight to the duke of York, who was the king's lieutenant for the whole of France. (This was the first rift between the two branches of the House of Lancaster which eventuated in the Wars of the Roses.)

In August 1443 Somerset's army set out. It was about 7,000 strong. But instead of making for Gascony, Somerset for some reason landed at Cherbourg in Normandy. Possibly he shunned the risks of the long sea voyage to Bordeaux. He was ailing in health, and was not pining for unnecessary hardships. From Cherbourg he marched south along the border between Maine and Brittany, and with what appears criminal and almost incredible stupidity, captured La Guerche, a town inside Brittany, 25 miles south-east of Rennes. Stupidity—for Brittany was now in treaty with England. The account of the affair given by the Breton historian Lobinau, writing in 1707, however, puts a different complexion on the matter. He states that the inhabitants were taken by surprise, in view of the treaty made with the late duke, but he adds mildly that circumstances had since changed. He makes no mention of pillage, but says that Somerset set free all who were favourable to the régime, and imprisoned the others. Finally he writes:

"The duke [of Brittany] having given some sum of money to the duke of Somerset, the latter handed back La Guerche and returned into Normandy."[1]

The duke of Somerset then wandered aimlessly through Maine. When his captains asked what his plan was he replied with a frown, "I do not divulge my secret to anyone. If even my own shirt knew my secret I should burn it." Bishop Basin, who tells the story, adds maliciously that it was doubtful whether he knew his own secret. That winter he returned to England without effecting anything—and shortly afterwards he died.

Disappointment at the lack of success of Somerset's expedition was natural, but the government took an over-despondent view

[1] *Histoire de Bretagne*, I, p. 623.

of the matter. After all, the French had had ample forces available to oppose the invasion for operations elsewhere were at a standstill; yet for four months Somerset had been able to roam whither he wished without let or hindrance—as in the days of old. There was no real cause for discouragement; even Edward III had found it difficult to compete with an enemy who refused to fight, and if the government selected a second-rate and ailing commander, as they had done, they had only themselves to blame. The fact is, they were heartily sick of the war and clutched at any straw to get out of it without loss of prestige. The ever-helpful duke of Orleans provided the straw; René, duke of Anjou, was the brother-in-law of Charles VII, and he had an unmarried daughter, Margaret. If Henry VI would take her to wife, the duke argued, a bond of amity and peace between Lancaster and Valois might be knit. The English government embraced the idea, and the earl of Suffolk—that William de la Pole who had been captured on the bridge at Montargis, and afterwards released—was selected to conduct negotiations for peace.

In March 1444 he crossed over to France, and a peace conference took place on the Loire. But difficulties arose; this time the point at issue was no longer the English claim to the throne, for Suffolk was prepared to barter that for the absolute possession of Normandy. It was instead the old question of homage, which had lain dormant for 84 years. Suffolk showed such anxiety to obtain peace that Charles naturally raised his terms, supposing that the English must be negotiating from weakness, always a fatal thing to do. Charles demanded that homage should be done for Gascony and Normandy, and on that the conference broke down. A two years truce was sealed, and Suffolk negotiated the marriage of Margaret of Anjou to Henry VI.

APPENDIX

SOURCES FOR THE SEINE ET OISE CAMPAIGN

Easily the best account is that of Guillaume Gruel, the faithful servant and scribe of the Constable de Richemont. He himself took part in the campaign as a soldier, and his story, though sometimes confused, is first hand, and may be presumed to be reliable. Next come two histories of Charles VII, one by Jean Chartier and the other by Guillaume le Bouvier, the latter being the more detailed of the two; otherwise it is difficult to differentiate between them. Chartier's *Chronique de Charles VII* was published by Vallet de Viriville in 1858, but for Le Bouvier's *Les Chroniques du feu Roy Charles*, one has to go back as far as 1661 when Godefroy incorporated it in his *Histoire de Charles VII*.[1] Incidentally, the name of the author is rather confusing. He is often cited as Berry, or Berry Heraut, or Le Roi Heraut, having served in that capacity to Charles VII. I mention this because he is going to be useful to us.

The fourth source is *Histoire de Charles VII* by Thomas Basin, Bishop of Lisieux. Written in Latin it has fortunately been recently translated into French by Samarin (1933). Basin was not present, but he later became the confidant of the king and much of his account is at least second hand.

Waurin gives what he can pick up from the Burgundian side and borrows from the Armagnac writers, while Monstrelet as usual copies Waurin.

On the English side there is precisely nothing. It is a thousand pities that Talbot did not have his Gruel. We might then have obtained some reliable insight into his mind, while his account might have presented the English achievements in an even more favourable light than do the enemy chroniclers.

Admittedly, it is not easy to piece it all together, in particular the final phase, which is my own construction of a rather obscure and isolated passage in Thomas Basin.

But even as it is, this Seine et Oise campaign can claim to be one of the most remarkable bloodless campaigns of the Middle Ages, and it is astonishing that so little attention has been paid to it by modern writers.

---

[1] Joseph Stevenson in his *Loss of Normandy* published long extracts from it.

CHAPTER XVIII

THE END IN NORMANDY

GLADLY would I pass over in silence the five next years, the two-years truce of Tours–twice extended. For it constitutes one of the most discreditable periods of our history where relations with other countries are concerned. The focus of the whole sorry affair was one matter and one man. The matter was the cession of Maine to France: the man was the earl of Suffolk.

Cardinal Beaufort having retired to his diocese of Winchester, and Somerset having died, the Beaufort power in the government now passed to Suffolk. He started badly; the truce of Tours, in the words of Edouard Perroy "set the seal on the recovery of the Valois and confirmed his conquests".[1]

But worse was to follow. As the price of an extension of the truce Suffolk promised to return Maine to France, and withheld the knowledge as long as he could from the English people. When the news got abroad, a fury of indignation against the earl arose; the people were not as tired of the war as was their government; it had not hit most of them personally and their national pride was touched. There appeared to be no military necessity for the cession. The greater part of Maine had for long years been firmly "in the English obedience". Its capital, Le Mans, was held, and its inhabitants were to all appearances friendly or at least resigned to the English cause. The valley of the Sarthe between the capital and Alençon was studded with English-held castles, and over the rest of the county an English army had recently wandered at will. And all that the nation had received in return was a foreign queen! Suffolk made matters worse for him-

[1] *The Hundred Years War*, p. 311.

661

self in the eyes of history[1] by bowing to the storm and initiating a pitiful policy of prevarication and procrastination in order to get out of his obligations.

In the midst of all this, Suffolk became still more powerful—and therefore still more unpopular—owing to the death in 1447 of the two men who between them had practically ruled England since the death of Henry V. Cardinal Beaufort died in his palace of Wolvesey, the greatest, proudest and richest prince-bishop of England in medieval times, not excepting Cardinal Wolsey. Though for many years the leader of the peace party, he had at the same time conducted the war with sagacity, and during his régime the English cause prospered. His rival, Duke Humphrey of Gloucester, predeceased him by six weeks. As leader of the war party and heir presumptive to the throne, he was naturally the enemy of Suffolk and of Queen Margaret, who as yet was childless. Suffolk and the queen in practice ruled England, for poor Henry VI, though now 23 years of age, was a puppet in their hands. Suffolk hatched a vile conspiracy against his rival and had him arrested on a trumped-up charge. Three days later Gloucester died, under circumstances that looked black for Suffolk. He gave out apoplexy as the cause of death. It matters little whether that be the truth, for one cannot arrest the heir to the throne and ever release him. One is in the position of a snake that has its fangs in the throat of a rival; it dare not leave go. Gloucester would never again have been a free man.

Many opprobrious adjectives can be cast at the good duke with some justification—impulsive, irresponsible, rash, self-centred—but over and above all this he was, in his later years, genuinely concerned for the good of his country. He held a passionate belief in the justice of his country's cause, which he had inherited from his eldest brother, a brother whom he revered and whose wishes he ever regarded as commands.

[1] Recent research is however veering towards less harsh judgement on the earl, especially as regards his initial responsibility for the cession of Maine. But this is no excuse for the shiftiness that he displayed.

[2] See *Humphrey, Duke of Gloucester*, by J. H. Vickers. The author, after thorough examination opines that Gloucester was murdered by a slow poison.

Henry VI was in his eyes the legitimate, duly elected king of France. It was a simple faith; and in that faith he died. And in so doing he had, so far as one can see, the feeling of the nation behind him.

Suffolk had already practically banished his only possible living rival, the duke of York, by appointing him lieutenant of Ireland for ten years. Now there was no enemy left who could harm him—or so Suffolk thought. Being now all-powerful, he made himself duke of Suffolk, and he made Edmund Beauchamp, earl of Dorset, duke of Somerset and king's lieutenant in France.

Meanwhile the shifts and subterfuges by which Suffolk sought to wriggle out of his undertaking to hand over Le Mans to France by a specified date, continued with wearisome evasions, till at last Charles VII lost all patience and decided on a resumption of the war.

The king of France had been steadily increasing the efficiency and strength of his army during the truce whereas Suffolk had been whittling down the English armed forces, fondly supposing that he could obtain a favourable peace by friendly gestures such as the cession of Maine, and the marriage of Margaret. He seemed oblivious to the fact that good peace terms have, throughout history, only been obtained through strength and bargaining power. He had deliberately reduced his bargaining power by the needless cession of Maine. Worse still, though the balance of military power had now swung to France he continued to act and talk in the lordly manner of Henry V. The French king, on the other hand had at long last realized that battles do help in ridding a country of an invader, and he was becoming in a sense almost fond of war—that is, on its strategical and planning side. The study of it was no longer repellent to him, he busied himself in logistics, and found that he rather liked them.

All this changed state of affairs on both sides of the line was hidden from Suffolk, who instigated some semi-freebooter English troops to sack the town of Fougères in Brittany, and declined to give redress, though strongly pressed by both the new Duke Francici and by King Charles VII. A resumption of the war was thus inevitable, and indeed Charles may be praised for his patience and forbearance–unless it be that an earlier declaration of war would not have "suited his book".

The king of France had by this time completed the formation of what may be called his "new model" army. It was constituted somewhat on English lines; that is to say, the feudal element had almost disappeared, and its place had been taken by a paid professional army, at least as far as the mounted portion was concerned. It had a fairly definite organization in which the constitution of the "lance" becomes clearly defined. This consisted of six mounted men, the man-at-arms, one swordman, two archers, one *valet aux armes* and one page. Ferdinand Lot says that the latter two were unarmed, but they carried at least a dagger each, and though useless for offensive action they would be useful for the defence of the wagon lines, etc., as were English pages. The latter were included in the number of the retinues, so for the purposes of comparison we should perhaps reckon a French lance at six men.

Now for the first time in the Hundred Years War we get some reliable figures regarding French strengths. Professor Lot has collected them with great care, but there remain so many *lacunae* that we are still rather in the dark. The following basic figure seems at least established. In the king's pay were 1,500 lances, or 9,000 mounted men. To this must be added 1,500 lances, in Languedoc, making a total of 12,000 mounted men on the king's pay-roll. There were other lances called "petites ordanances" which might bring the total up to 15,000. Of dismounted troops–almost exclusively crossbowmen–there was an unknown number. They constituted a paid militia, somewhat after the English model. Lastly, there were the permanent garrisons of defended towns, principally archers, whose numbers it is quite impossible to compute. From the above we must deduct the troops required in Gascony–again impossible to compute, but we must add the armies provided by the duke of Burgundy for operations in eastern Normandy, and the duke of Brittany who now came out openly on the side of Charles.

Looking at the matter as a whole, it seems impossible to pare down the total numbers available for field operations against Normandy much below 30,000. Against this total, what had the English to show? As the reign of Henry VI advances it becomes increasingly difficult to estimate numbers in France, largely because we have no figures for wastage. Under this heading come deserters, who towards the end of the war became a considerable item. In the palmiest days early in the reign it is doubtful if the army in France ever topped 15,000, and nearly all these were normally employed on garrison duties. When a particular effort was planned in the field the bulk of the army for the operation was usually sent out from home. Moreover, of latter years Suffolk had cut down the numbers, and been backward in providing pay, though parliament must share the blame for this. It therefore seems safe to assert that no field army could be provided without depriving the garrisons and leaving them dangerously weak. This will help to explain why in the operations about to be described we hear little of English armies in the field.

Early in July, Charles had sent to seek the advice of the duke of Burgundy as to whether he should go to war. But before receiving the reply, and indeed before issuing his ultimatum, two of his columns commenced operations. The campaign that ensued is singularly lacking in military interest. The reason is not far to seek. The English having no field army, field operations could not take place; consequently the war devolved into a succession of sieges. Most of these were short, almost "token" sieges leading to speedy surrenders on easy terms. Now one siege – still more one surrender – is much like another, and it would be tedious to relate each in detail – even if we possessed those details. It did however possess a certain strategical interest, though even this was somewhat illusory. Charles was, as we have said, beginning to fancy himself as a strategist, and he determined to apply the strategy followed by him in Gascony (and so loved by Edward III); that of exterior lines. He stationed no less than four columns round the circumference of Lower Normandy, and gave them orders to advance inwards and simultaneously. Now the successful application of exterior lines strategy depends, as we have seen so often, on the possession of good communications between columns, and also on resolute commanders. It would seem that the French possessed neither of these for they advanced with circumspection and with an absence of any detectable co-operation between columns. This however did not much matter in the absence of an opposing field army which might strike at one of the isolated columns.

Somerset employed a method that looks supine but which in reality was the only feasible procedure–that of "sitting and suffering". Each town in turn was summoned to surrender, and the smaller ones usually did so. Isolated, with no prospects of relief, often with a Norman commander, always with a partially Norman garrison, and sometimes with an English commander married to a local Norman lady, there was little inducement to hold out long. Any such inclinations were speedily stifled by Jean Bureau's guns.

It is difficult to be certain as to the real feelings of the population. French chroniclers naturally depicted them as burning to escape from "*le joug Anglais*" and to return to their beloved and native France. But this over-simplifies the matter. Normandy was not yet a fully fledged part of France; it had been in English occupation for a third of a century,[1] and it must have appeared to the average inhabitant that they were now permanently linked to England. His attitude was perhaps akin to that of the townsman in the Great Civil War–anxious to be upon the winning side. As it became more and more evident that France would be the winner, adherence to her cause became ever more popular. The rapid fall of one town effected and led to the still more rapid defection of its neighbours. It was like a river approaching a waterfall; the current becomes ever more rapid, till at last nothing can prevent the water falling into the abyss below.

[1] Not to mention the whole of the twelfth century.

The invasion of Normandy can be likened to a boy nibbling round the edge of a biscuit. Four armies converged on the duchy from east, south and west. King Charles attached himself to the eastern one, commanded by Dunois, and directed on the capital. It arrived before the gates of Rouen on October 16, 1449, and Dunois endeavoured by a stratagem to scale the walls. He nearly succeeded, but Talbot rushed to the rescue in the nick of time and the French were driven out. There followed an unexpected event. At that moment a deputation of inhabitants was in England appealing to the king to send English troops to defend the city against the invaders. But the inhabitants were divided in their loyalties, as I have suggested was the case elsewhere. Next day portions of the mob so worked upon Somerset that he weakly allowed the archbishop to negotiate for a surrender. What John Talbot's feelings were we do not know. King Charles took up his residence at the monastery of St. Catherine overlooking the city whilst the parlies proceeded. But they were protracted, and on October 19 the mob seized the gates and opened them to the French. Somerset fell back to the citadel (where Joan of Arc had been imprisoned) and after further negotiations, a treaty on honourable terms was signed. Eight hostages were selected including Talbot, and Somerset marched out with the remainder of the army to Caen.

In December, Harfleur was besieged and Jean Bureau's artillery made short work of it. Next month, January 1450, Honfleur followed suit. All that was now left of Normandy was the central area including Caen, Bayeux, Falaise and the Cherbourg peninsula.

Meanwhile in England there was a storm of fury; and naturally it was centred on the head of Suffolk. The bare possibility of losing Normandy had never crossed the mind of anyone, least of all the ineffable government, who throughout the twelve months preceding the invasion had sent no reinforcements or supplies to the threatened duchy. An army was hastily raised, fitted out and placed under Sir Thomas Kyriell. Now that Talbot had gone, Kyriell was the most experienced commander left, if we exclude Sir John Fastolf, who had long been restored to favour and to the Garter, and had for some years been acting as military advisor to the great council – a post apparently akin to what we might now call director of military operations.

The army consisted of a mere 2,500 men. It was collected at Portsmouth during the autumn, was land-bound for a long period by adverse winds and did not set sail until March 1450.

Kyriell's orders were to land at Cherbourg (which was still in English hands) and march straight to the relief of Bayeux, which was now threatened. He landed at Cherbourg on the 15th but departed from his orders at the request of the local authorities to retake Valognes (in the middle of the Cherbourg peninsula) before pushing on to Bayeux. Not only did he accede to their wishes, but he requested the duke of Somerset, the governor of Normandy, to send reinforcements to him. This Somerset weakly did, scraping together 1,800 men from Bayeux, Caen and Vire. This brought Kyriell's army up to slightly over 4,000 men and enabled him to capture the town of Valognes, though not without considerable casualties. Valognes fell on April 10, and the army resumed its advance to Bayeux two days later, having already consumed nearly four weeks.

The situation when Kyriell landed in France was that, in addition to Rouen, most of the towns in the eastern and southern parts of the duchy had fallen into French hands, and the king was slowly advancing west on Caen. The four weeks delay had also given time for various French columns in Western Normandy to work towards Cherbourg, hunting for the English army. Chief among these was the army of the count of Clermont, the young son of the duke of Bourbon. His headquarters were at Carentan, 20 miles west of Bayeux and 30 miles south of Cherbourg.

At Coutances, a further 20 miles south-west of Carentan, lay some 2,000 men under the Constable de Richemont. These two columns, if they could join hands, would make an army about

5,000 strong, sufficient to confront Kyriell with. Thus, when on April 12 Kyriell set out from Valognes with some 3,800 men,[1] Clermont was only six miles from the route he must take, while Richemont was about 25 miles from it.

Clermont could, of course, easily intercept Kyriell single-handed – if he dared – but Richemont could not expect to get there in time. Valognes and Coutances were, however equi-distant from Bayeux, and by marching thither on the direct road through St. Lô, Richemont ran a good chance of getting there first. He accordingly set out for St. Lô. This was sound military judgement.

The direct road to Bayeux for the English army crossed the estuary of the river Vire by a causeway four miles long. It was only passable at low water and Kyriell must have had an anxious time waiting for the tide to fall, being aware of the presence of Clermont's army at Carentan, only six miles away. The picture of Edward III's crossing of the Somme before Crecy must have come into his mind.

But Clermont sat as tight as a badger. He refused to be drawn by the clamour of the inhabitants of Carentan, who eventually surged out on their own and engaged the English rearguard as it waded through the water waist-deep. The English army continued on its way unmolested, and camped for the night beside a little stream ten miles further on, being still ten miles short of Bayeux. It was the 14th of April. That night Richemont billeted at St. Lô, 19 miles to the south-west, while Clermont remained motionless in Carentan, 15 miles west of Kyriell. The latter had only to continue his march next morning and by mid-day he should be secure in Bayeux.

THE BATTLE OF FORMIGNY, APRIL 15, 1450 (Sketch Map 11, see p. 675.)

As the sun rose on that fateful mid-April day, the little army of Sir Thomas Kyriell might be seen grouped in the shallow valley in which the tiny village of Formigny nestled. It was a

---

[1] Allowing for the casualties at Valognes.

pleasant spot surrounded by orchards, fruit-trees and gardens, now in full April bloom. A handy brook supplied the necessary water, and a good direct route, the "grand chemin", provided an easy connection and communication with Bayeux.

It was no place to dally in, but Kyriell was an experienced soldier. Why then did he not continue his march, in compliance with his orders, to the safety that Bayeux could provide? History is silent on the point, but I fancy the clue to the problem can be found in the actions of Sir Matthew Gough, the commander of the reinforcements. The troops were not tired; they had only marched 30 miles in three days—an average speed for that period. While the army was sitting motionless round Formigny, Gough was speeding into Bayeux, ten miles in rear. For what purpose? The strong presumption is that Kyriell had a plan of his own, which would not entail continuing the march to Bayeux, and that he had sent Gough in order to obtain approval of it, and possibly reinforcements wherewith to carry it out. What was this project? Again the natural presumption is that Kyriell, who was of course aware by this time of Clermont's column in Carentan, believed he had an opportunity of falling upon it while it was still unsupported by any other column, for it is unlikely that he was aware of Richemont's march to St. Lô the previous day. No contemporary English account of the battle exists, and the French chroniclers cannot have known what the English plan was. My conclusion is thus mere conjecture, but it is in accordance with IMP.

Thus, the morning of April 15 saw the English army stationary, whilst its opponents were hour by hour drawing nearer to it and to each other.

The previous evening the count de Clermont had sent word to the Constable de Richemont at St. Lô of the movements of the English, with the request that he would come to his support in an attack on them the following day. What reply Richemont sent we do not know, but his actions make its purport pretty clear; for he set off up the road to Formigny. Was this a lucky shot, or had definite information of the enemy's position at

Formigny come in during the night? It is impossible to say; which is a pity, for if the Constable was acting merely on an intuition it stamps him as a great general, and confirms my opinion that he was not only the most experienced, but easily the most skilful French general living.

Clermont had the shorter distance to cover and the better road; he was, therefore, the first to gain contact with the enemy. This happened in the early afternoon. Kyriell had, of course, on the previous evening, posted outposts on the low ridge covering his rear, *i.e.* facing west. The slope is gentle and the ridge-top only 50 feet above the valley bottom. The top of the ridge is 800 yards from the little brook that winds down the valley, and astride the road on the ridge-top we may safely locate the line of outposts. Preparations to man it would have been put in hand during the morning, and when the enemy was signalled approaching, every available man was put to work completing it. Kyriell had at his command nearly 4,000 men and Clermont something over 3,000. (See Appendix on numbers.) Kyriell had originally only 425 men-at-arms and if we add 500 from the Gough contingent and allow for casualties at Valognes, sickness etc., we may put the number at about 800. It is important to assess this figure, for thereby we can compute the approximate length of the line. Let me explain.

Kyriell formed up his battle line in a strikingly similar manner to that employed by Henry V at Agincourt. That is to say, it consisted of a thin line of dismounted men-at-arms, interspersed by three clumps of archers, which projected like bastions in front of the spearmen's line. Also as at Agincourt, the number of men-at-arms was so small that no reserve was possible, nor indeed could they form more than a single line and it had to be supplemented by a second line of archers and a third line of billmen. (Billmen had only recently made their appearance in battle.)

The line of men-at-arms was thus about 700 yards in all, and if we allow 80 yards frontage for each archer clump, which I reckon is about right, we get a total length of front of slightly under 1,000 yards, or say 450 yards each side of the road.[1]

Kyriell's headquarters was no doubt on or near the stone bridge, which existed even in those days, alongside which the memorial chapel was afterwards erected. As was usual, the archers planted stakes in their front and, as at Bannockburn and later in Brittany, holes and short trenches were dug all along the front of the line to impede the hostile cavalry. We are often left wondering as to how the troops obtained entrenching tools. In this case we are specifically informed they utilized their swords and daggers. This was doubtless the normal method.

A slightly higher ridge runs eastwards on the south side of the road. This ridge was crowned by a windmill and from it a good view could be obtained southwards over the valley of the river Aure and warning could be obtained of the approach of any enemy from that direction. A small detached force seems to have been posted on this ridge – a sensible step.

It was about 3 o'clock in the afternoon. The French army approached, marching straight up the road. On getting near the position held by the English they deployed in three lines to right and left of the road, in a parallel line to that of their opponents, and distant from it "two bow-shots", *i.e.* about 600 yards.

A pause now ensued, during which the English improved their defences. This pause was to allow Clermont to confer with his officers. He was young and inexperienced and, though he wished to attack, his officers, who had a wholesome respect for an English army in position, and who could not forget Agincourt and Verneuil, tried to dissuade him. The English, they pointed out, were probably superior in numbers and it would require a two to one superiority on the part of the French to defeat them. Better wait till the Constable came up. Such was the advice given, but the headstrong Clermont, probably

[1] Sir James Ramsay, who has a curious propensity for placing the line askew to the natural front and sometimes even perpendicular to it, does so in this case, and his beautifully coloured map – the only one I know of in this country – shows the position running along the Bayeux road, facing south instead of west.

supported by the younger officers who had grown to manhood
since Agincourt and who were sick of hearing the word mentioned as an excuse for inaction, took the bit in his teeth and
ordered his troops to the assault.

The French men-at-arms for the most part dismounted and
advanced "impetuously" on foot. But the English line stood firm
behind their stakes and pot-holes and the attackers made no
impression. The archers exacted a heavy toll, enfilading the line
of pot-holes at short range and from the two flanks. Mounted
attacks on the flanks met with the same reception. The action
went on for two hours, with no result. Then the French remembered their guns. Two "culverins", heavy field guns, were
dragged out in front of their line and galled the English position.
This proved too much for the archers who broke their ranks and
with headstrong initiative charged forwards straight upon the
offending cannon. The French gunners were all dispatched or
dispersed and the triumphant archers, not knowing how to spike
the guns, began to drag them back into their own lines. Here
the accounts are hopelessly conflicting and we cannot be sure
whether they succeeded or whether the French recaptured them.
It matters not; the incident is picturesque and consequently has
been seized upon by all writers, but it is of trifling importance.
What matters is that the French had by this time suffered so
heavily that they began to melt off the field. One of their leaders,
Pierre de Brezé, distinguished himself by rallying many of the
fleeing archers. The French had plainly shot their bolt and it has
been conjectured that, if Kyriell had "plucked the golden
moment" and launched a general counter-attack, the enemy
would have been completely routed. But two things happened,
or rather one thing happened and a second did *not* happen.
Kyriell did *not* attack, but sat motionless in his position, while
from the south, in the very nick of time for the French, the army
of the Constable appeared over the skyline.

Of the details of Richemont's approach march we unfortunately know nothing, but it is probable that the sound of the culverins firing reached him and told him what he wanted to know:

the English must be standing at Formigny. By this time the Constable had reached the village of Trevières, one and a half miles due south of Formigny, on the banks of the river Aure.

Climbing the steep slope to the north of it, Richemont reached the windmill on the summit, and tradition asserts that he climbed it to get a view of the battle. Likely enough, if the ground was as thickly timbered as it is to-day. Otherwise he could have taken in the situation at a glance from ground levels and the spectacle was enough to gladden his heart. For the English were heavily engaged, fighting with their flanks and backs to him. What an opportunity! But the Constable was a cautious man. He could also see signs of the French rout. It would take some time to get up his own army on to the ridge-top and deploy it for the attack. What if by that time Clermont's troops had disappeared completely off the battlefield? He would then be left to face a victorious and greatly superior English army single-handed.

Richemont decided to get in touch with Clermont before committing his own army. He accordingly rode forward, crossed the brook by a ford (probably the one marked on my sketch-map) and managed to find Clermont. A hasty consultation was held and it would seem that Clermont placed himself under the orders of the older man. At any rate an agreement was reached: Clermont would rally his army and return to the attack, engaging the northern half of the hostile line, while Richemont attacked the southern half.

Richemont returned to his own army, which he deployed on top of the ridge by the windmill. He then advanced down the hill towards the English left, being careful to extend his left across the brook, so as to contact Clermont's right flank.

By this time Kyriell had become aware of the approach of the Constable's army. Whether or not he had contemplated turning to the attack of the defeated enemy in his front, (which seems likely) such a thing was now out of the question. He must form front to the new enemy, and that quickly, for the windmill was less than a mile from his nearest flank, and the enemy could approach rapidly down the hill.[1] There being now signs that Clermont's troops were now rallying, Kyriell's course was obvious. While still holding a front against the old enemy he must form a second front to face the new one. This could be done partly by refusing the extreme left of the line, and partly by

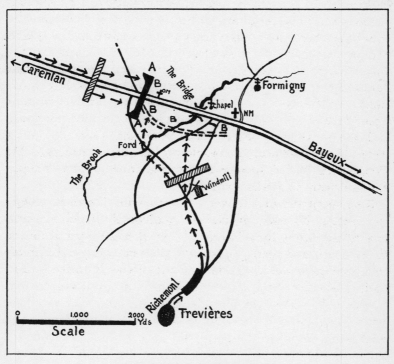

Sketch Map 11: FORMIGNY

A-A English position phase I
B-B English position phase II

O.M. Old monument
N.M. New monument

withdrawing troops from the old line and extending the flank with them. This was a difficult and complicated manoeuvre to carry out without previous warning in the heat of battle, but there was no alternative for he possessed no reserve. It was done,

[1] The situation was strikingly similar to that at Waterloo when the Prussians appeared on the field—as had also been the previous strategy.

after a fashion, but the confusion and disorder must have been fearful. However, a French chronicler pays tribute to the courageous way the English faced up to the new emergency–"They held themselves grandly" he writes. Their line was now bent back into a right angle or rough semi-circle, with the bridge as centre.

As Richemont's attack developed in full view of Clermont's troops, the latter, thus enheartened, returned to the attack. The weakened English line crumbled under the shock and the defenders gave ground everywhere. Step by step they fell back to the bridge, round which the heaviest fighting now developed. (A field by the bridge was until recently known as Le Champ Anglais.) The pressure of the double attack steadily increased, till it became a case of "Sauve qui peut!".

Matthew Gough, who had been hurriedly recalled from Bayeux in time to take part in the battle, managed to cut his way out with a portion of his men and to regain Bayeux. Kyriell was not so fortunate; he was surrounded and captured. The English were now split up into small packets, each of which fought on individually and stubbornly. Little quarter seems to have been asked or offered and one party of about 500 English archers fought it out to the death in a garden by the brook-side, selling their lives dearly to the last man. We know not the names of these men, but we are put in mind of Newcastle's famous regiment of White Coats, on the field of Marston Moor, 200 years later. No memorial marks the spot where these nameless heroes stood and died to a man.

The battle was over; the English army was practically wiped out; Normandy was lost for ever.

*   *   *

COMMENTS

This battle contained a strategical feature almost unique in medieval warfare. That is to say, two armies operating on exterior lines effected a concentration on the battlefield. The concentration of Wellington and Blücher on the field of Waterloo was not more timely and more effective than that of Clermont and Richemont on the field of Formigny. In both cases the operation that Napoleon was never tired of warning against was carried out successfully. The question naturally arises, how much did this happy result owe to luck and how much to good management?

It is impossible to answer this question with any assurance, for the records fail us. The difficulty of bringing about concentration on the battlefield, before the advent of modern inventions had improved communications out of all knowledge, was extreme; this accounts for the rarity of successful undertakings of this nature and for Napoleon's reiterated warning. Unfortunately there is no space here to go into this fascinating subject, but I think that, however great the luck in this case, we must salute Arthur of Brittany for his courage and tactical skill in carrying out what luck may or may not have put in his path.

The powerful influence of one battle on another was perhaps never more strikingly shown than in that of Agincourt on Formigny. Agincourt in its turn was influenced by Crecy and Poitiers, and Crecy in its turn by Halidon Hill and Dupplin Moor.

Of the soldierly qualities of the Englishmen of that day, the battle is an eloquent witness; of the leadership displayed it is more difficult to make an estimate, mainly because no English combatant had the heart to write, or even talk, about the battle and consequently our Chronicles were reduced to copying the French accounts. If we knew more we might condone Kyriell's actions. He was a veteran of the war, with a good record. We must be content to give him the benefit of the doubt. We should however have been better pleased if he had met his death in the field as did the great Talbot three years later at Castillon. Instead he ended on the traitor's scaffold, 21 years later. The sole contemporary English criticism of Kyriell that I have found is contained in a memorandum submitted to the great council by their advisor, Sir John Fastolf, shortly after the battle. He writes of Kyreill as "negligently tarrying in Normandy, and sped him not to go spedly to [Somerset]".[1]

THE FINAL PHASE

The news of the complete destruction of England's last army came as a thunder-clap to the government and people. Fastolf set about raising another army 3,000 strong, but events in Normandy moved too fast for him. Instead of advancing straight on Caen, the French turned south to Vire. Six days sufficed to capture it with its commander Lord Scales, who thus passes out of these pages. There were now but half a dozen defended towns, but all had strong garrisons. Clermont and Richemont here parted company, the former to Bayeux, which soon fell, the latter to assist Duke Francis of Brittany in the siege of Avranches. This outpost of Normandy had acquired a great reputation, having valiantly sustained the siege of 1439, as we have seen. The heroic wife of its captain, John Lampet, donned the trousers to rally the garrison, and when all hope had gone, resumed the skirt in order to conduct negotiations with the duke. Francis fell in love with this amazon, but fell ill and died shortly afterwards. John Lampet, according to the contemporary, "List of Cities . . . taken from the English. . . . "

"come to England and died of grief."[2]

The time was now ripe for the siege of Caen. No less than four columns concentrated against it – the fruition of the strategic plan of Charles VII. In it was the remnants of the main English forces in Normandy, under the duke of Somerset (who had his wife and children with him). The "List of Cities . . . " gives the French as 100,000 strong, and they may well have been up to one fifth of that number. The siege followed somewhat similar lines to that of Henry V. The town was surrounded by troops, the two great abbeys were occupied and a vigorous bombardment opened by Jean Bureau on June 5. But there was no

---

[1] *Collections of William of Worcester*, printed in Stevenson's *Letters and Papers*, II, Part 2, p. 595.

[2] Stevenson, op. cit., II, p. 633.

storm; after standing three weeks bombardment the English came to terms. The "last straw" was a cannon-ball which penetrated the ducal nursery, the duchess being in the room at the time. The duke of Somerset was granted a free passage to England, the prospect of which he did not relish. Instead he got himself conveyed to Calais.

But all was not over yet. Falaise, the appanage of the captive earl of Shrewsbury, was now besieged by Xantrailles, and an early surrender was negotiated in return for the the liberation of its lord. Thus John Talbot once again became a free man, and promised (so it is said) not again to put on armour against Charles VII.

Last of all came Cherbourg. To the Constable and Clermont, who were by now a firm combination, was granted the honour and triumph of the final siege. They were accompanied by Jean Bureau, who now surpassed himself. The most advantageous site for his battering artillery was on the sands, which however were submerged by every flood-tide. But Bureau was equal to this. Just before each tide rose he had the guns plastered in tallow and hides (thus "waterproofing" them in a manner unconsciously copied nearly 500 years later). There they were left till the tide fell again, when the bombardment was resumed. The English garrison under Thomas Gower, as if conscious of the historic nature of the occasion, put up a splendid resistance and stretched the great French besieging force to the full, exacting a heavy toll in killed and wounded, including that gallant sailor, Admiral Coëtivi. But the end was inevitable, and on August 11, 1450, the English rule in northern France came to an end.

Seven days later John Paston's servant wrote to him wistfully:

"This morning was it told that Shirburgh is goon, and we have not now a foote of londe in Normandie."[1]

THE LOSS OF NORMANDY

It was of course inevitable that Normandy should eventually be completely absorbed by France. A tract of the earth's surface

[1] *Paston Letters*, I, p. 139.

of the size and shape of modern France, almost surrounded by water and mountains was bound by the process of inter-marriage and inter-communication to become a single political entity in the long run. The English had had only a short run – a mere 30 years – one tenth of their dominance in Gascony. Never-theless there was no overriding political reason why the inevit-able should happen so suddenly in 1450. It is true that the Maid had stirred and stimulated the sense of patriotism and national-ism in France proper. But it is at least doubtful if she had had much influence in Normandy; all that the Normans knew about her came from the English garrison or the Church; from both sources they heard that Joan was a witch – a limb of the devil – and it would be surprising if they did not believe it. Though England and Normandy had been bad neighbours, being rivals on the sea, there were still some historic and blood links between the two countries and as long as the people were better governed and more secure in their persons than their neighbours in metro-politan France, they had little inducement to try to upset what was beginning to look like a permanent connection with the people *outre la Manche*.

It would seem then, that the sudden overrunning of their country must be assigned to other than political, social or eco-nomic causes. In fact, the whole course of events can be ex-plained on purely military grounds and on no other. It can be expressed in a single sentence: so long as England was able to put and maintain in the field a more effective striking force than her opponents, she was able to maintain her position indefinitely; but when the balance of military power passed to the other side, her dominion in France was doomed. When we enquire WHY the balance of military power veered from one side to the other we at once find ourselves in the domain of politics, economics, and social history – factors which it is outside the scope of this book to examine.[1]

It only remains to record with a satisfaction that I will not

---

[1] They have been well set out by Professor Edouard Perroy in his book *The Hundred Years War*.

attempt to disguise, that the duke of Suffolk was arraigned by
the Commons, banished by the king, captured by some English
ships (including one of the king's), beheaded on a boat gunwale
and his headless body cast on to the sands at Dover. Sir Charles
Oman thrice describes him as "the shuffling Suffolk". If we add
the adjective "shifty' that will suffice for his epitaph. And now
let us try and forget the man.

APPENDIX

THE NUMBERS

Numbers in a medieval battle are usually the most controversial item. This is not surprising; records were few, and sometimes altogether absent; estimates as to numbers were wild and
often biased; our checks on their veracity, where they do exist,
are scanty. The result is that most conflicting estimates as to
numbers are still being made by historians. Formigny is no
exception, although the degree of difference is not nearly so
wide as that of the other great battles of the war.

The French chroniclers and the official bulletin all assert
that the English outnumbered the French. This might be due
to patriotic pride; indeed a French writer suggests that the
French claim to absurdly few casualties was due to an attempt
to make the result appear due to Divine interposition. Modern
French writers accept the old figure unquestioningly. The last
to do so is Professor Ferdinand Lot.

His figure for the English (slightly under 4,000) need not
detain us, for I arrived at the same result (though not for precisely the same reasons). M. Lot, who is the exponent of small
numbers in medieval war, accepts the figure given by the
official bulletin of 3,000 for Clermont's army, though it had
every motive to minimize the French numbers. At the same
time he rejects the statement (again likely not to be exaggerated,
to say the least) made by Jean Chartier that Richemont besides
his lances had 800 archers. (Blondel also confirms the presence
of these archers.) This Ferdinand Lot will not allow, on the

grounds that to take dismounted archers would be "extremely perilous". The professor may think so, but count de Richemont may not have shared this opinion; and in any case, why should Chartier and Blondel expressly state the fact if there were no dismounted archers present? By this arbitrary reasoning M. Lot is able to show that the French had rather fewer men than the English. My own computation is as follows. To the official figure of 3,000 for Clermont I think we must add some hundreds. The number of Richemont's lances is variously given as 200, 220, 250 and 300, the last being the usual figure. Accepting this and counting only four armed men per lance, we get a minimum of 1,200, plus 800 archers, total 2,000. The grand total of the two armies can thus safely be placed at something over 5,000.

It may be objected that the figure 4,000 for the English is too low seeing that the number of dead alone is given as 3,774 in the official bulletin. The exactitude of this figure is at first sight impressive, but on second thoughts it becomes suspicious. We know that the English were buried in 14 grave-pits extending over a fairly wide area. The corpses would be stripped and thrown into these pits simultaneously, since the whole army which did not pursue, would be available for the purpose. Was there a clerk at each pit narrowly counting the corpses? And were no dead French bodies included in the pits? A naked French body would look much like an English one. I think it more likely that the figure 3,774 was deliberately fabricated for propaganda purposes, in order to enhance the measure of victory, and underline its miraculous nature.

CLERMONT'S DEFEAT IN PHASE ONE

The official bulletin spoke of a "skirmish", not a genuine attack, by Clermont, and this word has been accepted by most modern writers, including Sir Charles Oman and Sir James Ramsay, the only two modern English historians to devote attention to the battle. Unfortunately for the official bulletin, Admiral Coëtivi, one of Clermont's senior captains, "spilt the beans" in a letter written only four days after the battle. After relating the English defeat he adds:

"But, to tell the truth, I believe that God brought us M. le Constable, for if he had not come at the time and by the manner that he did, I doubt if, *entre nous*, [*sic*] . . . we should have got through the battle without irreparable damage for they were half as strong again as we were."

THE ENGLISH POSITION IN PHASE TWO

It is here that the chroniclers are most obscure and most at variance. I have had to draw largely on I.M.P. in order to resolve the matter to my own satisfaction. The reader must judge whether the course of events as described above seems a natural one. Both Ramsay and Oman disagree with me and with each other and Lot (as always) is more interested in the relative numbers engaged than in the course of the battle. As for other writers I can find nothing of note in the French language since about 1900 when the 450th anniversary of the battle produced a number of papers on the subject. No two exactly agree, and the one which goes into the matter the most thoroughly, providing a number of maps, is unfortunately guilty of inventing a valley which does not exist (thereby rendering my investigation on the field unduly difficult and prolonged – till I discovered his error).

SOURCES FOR FORMIGNY

The main, in fact practically the only, English source for the battle is the "List of cities . . . " under the heading *William of Worcester's Collection*, edited and translated in J. Stevenson's *Letters and Papers*. . . . Incidentally, these *Letters and Papers*, though they add little to our knowledge of military operations, become increasingly useful for the logistical side of the war; (but they are clumsily edited; to ascertain the provenance of many of the letters and papers in Vol. I and Vol. II, Part 1, it is essential to have by one Vol. II, Part 2).

On the French side the sources are naturally plentiful, though, as mentioned in the text, they copy one another to a large extent. Charles Joret, in his *Bataille de Formigny* (1903) gives no

less than 15 sources and transcribes the relevant passages from
most of them.[1] His book is the best published on the battle. The
chief chroniclers are, Jean Chartier, Berry the Herald, Robert
Blondel,[1] Guillaume Gruel, Thomas Basin, all of whom have
already been cited in these pages. A brief allusion to some
modern works has also been made and need not be repeated
here; but to them should be added Du Fresne de Beaucourt's
Histoire de Charles VII.

[1] J. Stevenson in his *Expulsion of the English from Normandy* prints the original
Latin of Blondel's *De Reductione Normanni* and Berry's *Le Recouvremont de Normandie*
in the original French from his *Histoire de Charles VII,* and also an English translation.

CHAPTER XIX

CASTILLON

NORMANDY having been regained, Charles VII turned
his attention to Gascony. But he made his usual
thorough preparations and it was not till nearly a
year later that he was ready to strike. The Count de Dunois then
led a large French army into Gascony.

Few English troops remained in the duchy, and the Gascons
were much too weak to offer effective resistance. On June 30,
1451, the French entered Bordeaux, and all seemed over. But
the unexpected happened, as it so often does in our history. The
French may have regarded themselves as liberators, but the
inhabitants of Bordeaux looked upon them as conquerors. Not
for 300 years had the streets of Bordeaux seen a French soldier.
In addition, there were economic and commercial reasons – the
wine trade, above all – for their preference for the English, which
we need not go into here. Suffice it that the king of France himself admitted that the Gascons preferred the English as their
masters. "Everyone knows", he wrote six years later to the king
of Scotland, "that it (Gascony) has been English for 300 years
and that the people of the region are at heart completely inclined
towards the English party."

The burgesses of Bordeaux, therefore, did not settle down
quietly under their new masters, and in March, 1452, some of
the leading citizens sailed to London to entreat Henry VI to
send an army of deliverance. In spite of the domestic troubles
that were developing, Henry not only complied but appointed
to the command the foremost captain of the day, John Talbot,
earl of Shrewsbury. He had literally grown grey in the service of
arms, for at his last battle he was reputed eighty years of age.
Though according to my calculations he cannot have passed his
seventieth year, that was a great age for his or any other period.

His fame had become so great, and the French dread of him so deep, that mothers could be heard to quieten their fractious offspring with the threat that "Tal-bote" would have them. (In this respect Talbot must be bracketed with Marlborough and Napoleon.) Later, we shall see an equally striking example of the hold that he acquired over the imagination of the people of France.

The English expeditionary force was about 3,000 strong—rather a small army, one would say, for the reconquest of a dominion. Small or not, however, it appeared sufficient. Talbot landed in Gascony on October 17, 1452, and Bordeaux ejected the French garrison, joyfully opened its gates to him, and hailed their deliverer as "Le Roi Talbot". Most of western Gascony followed suit, and the few towns occupied by a French garrison in the Bordelais which did not capitulate were taken by force.

So the winter passed, while Charles VII did not stir. The English, it seemed, had come back to stay. But the king of France, who did nothing in a hurry, began in the spring of 1453 to collect an army. This time there was to be no mistake about it: an overwhelming force should be assembled, nothing less would suffice against Le Roi Talbot. By mid-summer, 1453, Charles was ready to strike. The strategy he adopted was similar to that which had proved successful in Normandy three years previously: it was that of operations on exterior lines. Three armies were to approach Bordeaux simultaneously, one from the south-east, one from the east and one from the north-east, while the king himself held his reserve well to the rear. The French were in overwhelming superiority, though probably no one army by itself outnumbered the Anglo-Gascon army that the earl of Shrewsbury could put into the field. Reinforcements under his favourite son, Lord de Lisle, had arrived, but the total at Talbot's disposal cannot be exactly estimated owing to scanty Gascon records. It may have been as much as 6,000.

The French advanced slowly and cautiously, and by mid-July the centre army had reached Castillon, a small walled town 30 map miles east of Bordeaux. Meanwhile, Talbot sat tight in the capital, waiting for the French armies to advance closer so as to enable him in a single rapid march to swoop on the nearest of them and defeat it before the other could come to its assistance. This was the best answer to the strategy of Charles.

Unfortunately for Talbot's strategy, the inhabitants of Castillon, which was of course in imminent danger, did not see any attractions in it. They objected to being "thrown to the lions", and clamoured for help. In this they were backed up by the burgesses of Bordeaux. Talbot explained to them as patiently as he could the nature of his strategy, and assured them that he was only biding his time and would strike in due season. The burgesses were inclined to disbelieve him and he lost much of his phenomenal popularity and prestige. The earl was deeply hurt by this disbelief in his good faith, and eventually, against his better judgement, he yielded to the clamour and decided to go at once to the help of the threatened Castillon.

The army that was about to lay siege to the town had been collected from many parts of France, including Brittany, and had at least six commanders who seem to have acted as a committee. This was a very unsatisfactory arrangement, but it was alleviated by the fact that a chief of staff (as we should now call him) had been appointed, and the actual dispositions were left to him. The person in question was that stocky little Frenchman, Jean Bureau. He had graduated in the English service in his youth, but had afterwards transferred his allegiance to the Valois king. When Charles decided on a campaign for the recovery of Gascony he had commissioned Bureau to construct a great park of siege and field guns for the purpose. Of these no less than 300 cannon, great and small, accompanied the centre army if we are to believe the chroniclers, though the number is probably exaggerated. The men-at-arms and archers numbered something between 7,000 and 10,000.

On arrival opposite the walls of Castillon, Bureau who seems to have been the *de facto* commander adopted what may appear curious procedure. Instead of constructing lines of circumvallation round the town, with possibly a line of contravallation

facing the direction whence Talbot's relieving army might be
expected to approach, Bureau set to work to construct an entrenched camp for the bulk of his army. Nor did he site it to
the west of the town, so as to cut it off from reinforcements, but
on the east side, and 2,000 yards distant, well out of range of the
town's guns. Why did he take this curiously defensive step? It is
true that he had done something of the sort on occasion in Normandy, but I fancy his main motive was one of fear–fear of
Talbot. If he sited his camp to the west of the town he might
find himself caught between two fires, the town garrison on the
east, the relieving army on the west. Whatever his motives,
Bureau set 700 pioneers to digging and building. For four days,
July 13th to 16th, they worked night and day, and at the end of
that time a deep continuous ditch backed by a palisaded rampart surrounded his camp on three sides. This camp (Sketch
Map 12, page 693) was 700 yards long and on an average 200
yards wide, situated with its long side parallel to and abutting
the river Lidoire. The main entrance was on the south side, and
a footbridge probably spanned the river on the north. Along the
north side, the camp perimeter followed the river bank which,
being ten feet high and almost perpendicular, acted as a rampart, with the river as ditch. No digging was therefore required
on this side.

The camp was, as the map shows, of a most extraordinary
shape.[1] Its area was nearly 30 acres–and its shape was exactly
as shown on my map, for its lines can still be traced on the ground.
(The grounds for this remarkable assertion are given in the
Appendix.) Roughly, it was designed to afford the artillery a
maximum of oblique and enfilade fire, and the hand of an artilleryman is discernible in its planning.

The guns were placed round the perimeter of the camp and,
if there were as many as 300, they must have been almost wheel
to wheel in an unbroken line–a fact that makes me doubt the
accuracy of this figure. In addition to the troops encamped in

[1] Its shape has, however been plausibly explained by Major J. L. Nicholson,
O.B.E., R.E., in an article in *The Royal Engineers Journal* (1949, p. 290).

the new work, Bureau (or the committee) stationed 1,000 archers in the priory of St. Lorent, 200 yards north of the town (the site is now occupied by the railway station), to act as an outpost against the approach of the English army; and also a force of 1,000 or more Bretons in the woods on the high ground to the north of the camp. All was now ready to commence the siege works, or to resist attack by Talbot, should he accept the challenge.

We must return to Bordeaux. But prior to narrating the movements of the relieving army I must warn the reader that, as was almost always the case in our infrequent defeats of medieval days, no English participant seems to have troubled to tell his story to our chroniclers. Consequently, for every single fact relating to the campaign we have to go to the French sources. These were, not unnaturally, considerable in number and volume, but however fair and truthful they may have tried to be, a certain amount of bias cannot have been avoided. It is, therefore, all the more remarkable that they show a singular unanimity and emphasis, amounting almost to enthusiasm, regarding the prowess and achievements of the "English Achilles", as the earl of Shrewsbury was dubbed by them. Whereas they seldom mention the names of the French commanders, that of Talbot is forever on their lips. This reverence for their great opponent has extended even to modern times. In *La Conquête de Guyenne*, by Henri Ribadien, the French author provides but a single illustration; it is not, as might have been expected, of some French commander, such as Jean Bureau, but of Talbot the Englishman. As I say, the amount of bias is small and, as their accounts contradict one another but little, we can reconstruct the story with some assurance.

*   *   *

THE BATTLE

The earl of Shrewsbury, once having made up his mind acted with lightning speed. No doubt his troops had already been warned to expect a rapid move at short notice. Certainly they got little notice now. Parading his army in the early hours of

July 16, Talbot marched out of the city at the head of his mounted men, the dismounted troops following as fast as they could. After a gruelling march of nearly 20 miles at the height of the Gascon hot weather, the army reached Libourne on the river Dordogne by sun-down. But there was little rest in store for them. Talbot had decided upon a night march, and not only a night march but one by unfrequented tracks through the forest along the high ground to the north of the Dordogne valley, instead of by the direct and easier road which led up the valley. A few hours' rest was therefore allowed, during which the veteran earl himself obtained a little sleep. On again at about midnight they went, the mounted troops still leading, with the foot soldiers plodding miles behind. This mounted force was tiny in size, a mere 500 men-at-arms and 800 archers, according to Aeneas Piccolomini. The route would take them through St. Emilion, that delectable centre of a famous wine district; after which it would follow the crest of the ridge to the north of the valley.

As dawn broke on the 17th the advanced-guard reached the woods to the immediate north of the Priory of St. Lorent, without encountering any hostile patrols. The presence of the French archers in the priory had been reported to Talbot, and his night march was no doubt undertaken with the object of surprising this force, for until it was accounted for the main French army could not be attacked. The garrison of the priory may be supposed to have had sentries out on the main road facing west, but they would hardly suspect the presence of the enemy in the almost trackless woods at daybreak without any previous intimating of their approach. Talbot would be aware of this, and his decision to make a bold and sudden attack from the woods, which at this point reached almost down to the priory, was a natural one and was in accordance with the English tradition built up during the Hundred Years War. It met with rapid and complete success. The luckless French archers, taken unawares, many of them being still in their beds, put up but a feeble resistance, and such as were not cut down fled to the refuge of the

French camp. While the fight lasted, the main French army made no attempt to send aid to the priory. This is not surprising; there was little time, even if they had been aware of the attack, which they probably were not, for they were out of sight of the priory, which was distant from the camp about a mile, and no cannons took part in the engagement.

It was a brilliant little affair, and must have "put up the tails" of the attackers. The driving power of the aged leader in this headlong advance, and his sure grip and skill in arriving at precisely the right place at the right time, despite the difficulties of a night march through 12 miles of unmapped woodland, compel our admiration and must have proved to his troops that age had not dimmed his prowess. The whole operation was similar to, and probably based on, Talbot's own night march and attack on the French at Pontoise 16 years before. It showed a nice judgement on his part, and it is noteworthy that Frenchmen of his time described him as a man of good judgement. But the very success of this affair was to have the most unexpected and sinister results, as we shall shortly see.

Some men-at-arms pursued the fleeing archers right up to the French camp and came back with useful reports as to its position and nature. The question for Talbot was now whether to push straight on to the attack, striking while the iron was hot, or to await the arrival of his infantry who were still some miles in rear. He decided on the latter course: the enemy in the camp had been aroused, surprise was now out of the question; his own men were fatigued with a 30-mile march on empty stomachs, followed by a fight; the French archers had left plenty of food and drink in the priory, and so the earl ordered some of this food to be issued to the troops, after which they were to get what rest they could. He also sent forward Sir Thomas Evringham to make a careful reconnaissance of the camp. It would be hard to criticize this course of action.

Talbot now ordered his chaplain to prepare a celebration of the Mass for himself, while his men were breaking their fast. But just before it was ready, a messenger dashed in from the town

stating breathlessly that the French were in full retreat; their
horsemen could be seen from the town walls hastily quitting
their camp, and leaving a trail of dust behind them. What was to
be done? Cancel the previous orders and put in an improvised
attack? Allow the enemy to retreat if he wished to? Or await
the arrival of the infantry and then, if not too late, attack? The
last course was urged upon him by Sir Thomas and others, but
it was not in the nature of the old warrior to let go a chance of
this sort. The enemy was in retreat, he should be scattered to
the winds! Swearing to his chaplain that he would not hear Mass
until he had beaten the French, he gave orders for an instant
attack and pursuit. Calling for his charger he mounted and led
his army out of the priory. He must have been a striking figure,
on his white cob, his white locks surmounted by a purple velvet
cap—for he wore no armour. (When released after his second
captivity in 1450, he had—so it is said—sworn to the French
king never again to wear armour against him. This vow he was
now keeping to the letter.)

And now was seen the true subtlety of the siting of Bureau's
camp. If attacked from the north the assailant would be confronted by the river and steep bank; if from the west—the direct
line of approach—the frontage presented would be only 200
yards, insufficient for full deployment of the attacking army; if
from the south, the assailants would have to pass across the front
of the camp at a short distance from it, since the Dordogne
flowed only 600 yards south of the camp, and moreover the
English would have to fight with their backs to a broad swift-
flowing river.

Despite these disadvantages, Talbot decided to attack from
the south. To do this his army had to ford the little river Lidoire
600 yards short of the camp. This was successfully done, and the
advance was continued towards the hostile camp. But a dreadful surprise was in store for the Anglo-Gascon army. Instead of
being in full flight, the French were standing their ground,
their guns almost wheel to wheel, their infantry manning the
parapets, motionless and ready. What had gone wrong? Simply

this; when the fleeing archers took refuge in the camp which
was already uncomfortably crowded, in order to make room

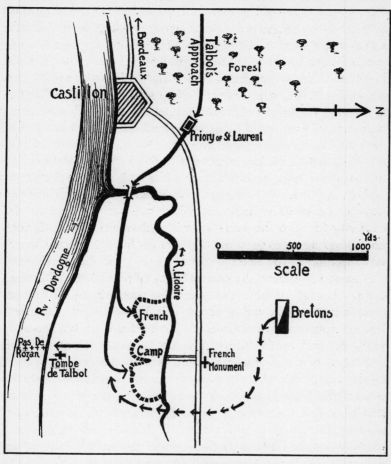

Sketch Map 12: CASTILLON

➡️ English movements

➡️ French movements

for them the horses, or a portion of them, had to be turned
out; it was the sight of the varlets riding these horses away at a
gallop that had misled the Gascon watchers into supposing that

the whole army was in retreat. Thus the surprise and flight of the archers had led to their victors themselves being surprised. The serried ranks of the French army ranged in position must have been an almost unnerving sight; and the decision to be taken by Talbot a fateful one. His mounted troops were outnumbered by over six to one, and there was no knowing when and how many of his main army would join in the fight. But the veteran earl did not hesitate. Quietly confident in the invincibility of his troops he would not deign to give a counter-order. Deploying his slender force opposite the southern face of the camp, he dismounted everyone, he himself alone remaining mounted. A conspicuous sight to the French defenders was this solitary horseman on the white cob and wearing no armour, and they did not fail to remark on it when describing the battle in after-years.

The signal for the assault was given, banners were unfurled[1] and, with the battle-cry of "Talbot! St. George!", the Anglo-Gascons advanced and engaged. A desperate and confused contest then took place along most of the line.[2] The ditch was fortunately dry and those who escaped the first rounds from the formidable French artillery plunged into it and engaged in a desperate struggle to mount the parapet. In places this was done; notably at the gateway to the camp, where Sir Thomas Evringham (who had advised against an immediate attack) planted his banner on the top of the parapet, only to fall dead next moment. All the while the French cannon were pounding the attackers with crossed and enfilade fire at point-blank range, and sometimes as many as six men would fall to a single cannon-ball. Thus the struggle swayed for over an hour, while the leading units of the dismounted force arrived in driblets and rushed straight into the battle. Eventually there must have been close on 4,000 Anglo-Gascons present on the field. Even so, the attackers were badly outnumbered, and were also deprived of the support of their own guns, none of which arrived in time for the battle.

---

[1] Some of these banners—if we are to believe Jean Chartier, were inscribed with rude remarks about the claims of Charles to be the legitimate king of France.
[2] "Un grant et terrible assault" (*Chartier*).

In spite of all these disadvantages encountered by the English army, French chroniclers admit that the issue remained in doubt till the sudden appearance on the field of the Bretons. It will be remembered that they had been stationed in the woods to the north of the camp. Swooping down from the heights and crossing the Lidoire, on the east side of the camp, a party of these men, all picked troops, made an unexpected inroad into the exposed right flank of the already hard-pressed attackers. Talbot drew off some of his men to oppose the new foe. Noticing this partial withdrawal the garrison of the camp, reinforced by the remainder of the Bretons, left their defences and with all forces combined drove their enemy back towards the river Dordogne.

The English army scattered in flight, the majority falling back direct to the rear. Thus the main body of fugitives found themselves on the bank of the river Dordogne. By the natural process of trial and error, and after a number had been drowned,[1] they discovered a practicable ford. This ford is now called the Pas de Rozan and has been used at exceptionally low water within living memory. Here the earl of Shrewsbury, who had been swept along in the retreat, tried no doubt to organize a defensive line covering the ford, actively supported by his son, the Lord de Lisle. But the pressure of the enemy grew ever greater, and eventually a chance cannon-ball struck the famous white palfrey which fell, bringing the old earl with it to the ground and pinning him underneath. In this defenceless posture a Frenchman named Michael Perunin was able to deal him the death blow with a battle-axe on his unprotected skull. His son, Lord de Lisle, died with him. That was the end of the battle, the Anglo-Gascon army dispersed, and Gascony was lost to England for ever.

The body of the earl of Shrewsbury was found next day, with great difficulty, and only recognized by a missing tooth. According to one account he was buried where he fell. Whether this is

---

[1] In 1954 a spear-head was found in the river bed near the ford—no doubt dropped by a drowning English man at arms. An iron cannon ball, 5 inches in diameter, was found near the same spot.

true or not, the body was removed shortly afterwards to Falaise, where it was reburied, the skull being taken to England and buried in the parish church at Whitchurch, Salop. In about 1493 Sir Gilbert Talbot removed the body to the same resting place. The grave was opened in 1860 and "the true cause of death was seen to be a blow from a battle-axe on the skull".

So died the English Achilles, and after the battle a monument was raised to him by the victorious French generals. It was called Notre Dame de Talbot. The spot came to be known as La Tombe de Talbot, and it is still marked on the map as Monument de Talbot. The chapel was destroyed during the revolution, but a modern cross has since been erected on the spot. It originally had no inscription on it, but I was told that Talbot's name did appear on the old one. On the 600th anniversary of the battle a plaque, presented by the local commune was unveiled.[1]

Of the many tributes paid to the dead warrior by contemporary French chroniclers, I will quote but one, that of Matthew d'Escoucy:

"Such was the end of this famous and renowned English leader who for so long had been one of the most formidable thorns in the side of the French, who regarded him with terror and dismay."

One is forcibly reminded of the saying, "A prophet is not without honour, save in his own country".

With the loss of the battle, the English Dominion of Gascony was lost and on October 10, 1453, the reluctant Bordelaise received once more in their midst the French conquerors. The Hundred Years War was at last over.

APPENDIX

SOURCES

There are no English sources for the battle. The main French sources are as follows (the length of time in years after the battle being given in brackets):

---

[1] The author was privileged to be present at this ceremony, and now possesses the unveiling flag.

1. A letter from Angoulême, written two days after the battle, giving a second-hand account of it. (Printed in *Bibliothèque de l'École des Chartes*, 1846.)

2. A short letter from Charles VII, written six days after the battle and based on the above.

3. The official account, written by Berry the Herald, last printed by the *Société de l'Histoire de France* 1863. (One year.)

4. *Histoire de Charles VII* by Jean Chartier, edited by Vallet de Viriville in 1863. (A few years.)

5. *Chronique de Matthieu d'Escoucy* in *Société de l'Histoire de France*, 1863. (About 12 years.)

6. *Les Vigiles*, a poem by Martial d'Aubergne, last printed in 1724. (Not cited by Ramsay.)

7. *Histoire de Gaston IV* by Lesuer, printed in 1826. (Also not cited by Ramsay.) (23 years.)

8. *Histoire de France* by Thomas Basin, last printed in 1944. (24 years.)

Of modern works none exists in the English language. The classical French account is in *La Conquête de la Guyenne* by Henri Ribadieu (1866).

THE FRENCH CAMP

The claim made in the text that the lines of the French camp are still visible (though not in their totality) requires some justification. A sentence in a scarce French book written in 1866 that the lines could then be traced, caught my eye and attention. On investigating the subject I found that in the 17th century, the lines were reported to be still visible. I further found the statement made in 1863 by Leo Drouyn in *La Guyenne Anglaise* that they were still visible but that in 25 years they would have completely disappeared. This statement was repeated three years later by Henri Ribadieu in his *La Conquête de la Guyenne*. I found a copy of Drouyn's book in the British Museum, and to my satisfaction it contained a large-scale plan of the camp. I made a tracing of it and took it out to Castillon in 1948. As there had been no reference in any book that I could find, referring to the existence of the lines during the last 82 years I was not hopeful. However I had no difficulty in finding the lines, exactly as depicted on Drouyn's map. My delight was unbounded. The existing lines take the form of a continuous ditch, on the average now one foot deep and about two yards wide. They are the easier to trace since they for the most part have been utilized by the farmers to form field boundaries (in one case a farm boundary). I did not however succeed in locating the supposed grave-pits possibly because the grass was long in that area, and about to be mown. I think there is little doubt that the very indentated trace (it measures nearly 1,600 yards) was in order to provide enfilade fire for the guns, and also to find room in a single line for the great number of guns present. I reckon that 250 guns could at a pinch have been placed in position along the east, south and west sides.

THE NUMBERS

Anglo-Gascons. The earl of Shrewsbury took out with him 3,000 troops. Reinforcements brought by his son, Lord de Lisle, brought this up to about 5,500. But we do not know, (1) the wastage, (2) the proportion put into the field, (3) the number of Gascons engaged. One thing is clear: Talbot set out at short notice taking with him only troops already concentrated at Bordeaux, and without the possibility of picking up more than a handful en route. I should suppose that the resulting number of English troops available could hardly exceed 4,000; if we add as an outside figure 2,000 Gascons it makes the "ceiling" 6,000. Now Jean Chartier gives the figures 5,000 to 6,000, and Professor Lot accepts this. So do I.

French. M. Lot gives the accepted strength of the French army as 9,000, but he adds that the French camp would not be large enough to hold this number and he concludes:

"The most probable thing is that the forces present were approximately equal in number—6,000 men."

This is rather a lame and inconsequential assessment, and one would like to know the basis on which the professor has come

to this conclusion. In any case his argument leaves out of account
the archers in the priory of St. Lorent and the Bretons in the
woods, each 1,000 strong. This would leave only 4,000 to garrison the camp. The horses should only take up one sixth to one
quarter of the space. The men would have no tents, it being high
summer. To man the perimeter at one man per yard would con-
sume over 2,000 men and the remainder would not require much
sleeping space. In short, I consider the camp large enough for
the numbers stated, and that the French army was approximately 9,000 strong. As to how many of the 6,000 Anglo-
Gascons ever reached the field of battle history is silent.

RETROSPECT

IT is easy to become cynical about the Hundred Years War, and especially about this latter part of it, which for convenience I have called the Agincourt War. For, after 115 years of intermittent strife, England had lost all her traditional possessions in France, and the only asset she could show for all her efforts was a harbour in the extreme north – Calais. Moreover she only relinquished a war on the Continent to become engaged in a fresh one at home. And she had yet to learn that civil strife is the worse evil of the two, for the latter is founded upon envy and and ambition (disguised as "the better government of the realm"), whereas the foreign war can – as this one did – unite a country's inhabitants in a common task.

On the credit side of the account, the Hundred Years War produced a breed of mighty men and illustrious leaders such as can stand comparison with those of any other century in our history. The Crecy War produced a galaxy of great men whose names should in our flowing cups be remembered – Edward III, the Black Prince, Henry of Lancaster, Sir John Chandos, Sir Thomas Dagworth, and many others. The Agincourt War, though not quite so prolific, brought to the fore great leaders such as Henry V, Bedford, Salisbury, and the peerless John Talbot. The country had basked in the sun of their greatness and waxed prosperous in the process, despite taxation for the war. A strong national spirit had been born, one that a generation of civil strife was to prove powerless to eradicate.

France, on the other hand, found herself after the war in a weaker state than that in which she had entered upon it. In the words of Edouard Perroy, "France emerged weakened and worn, and incapable for centuries of resuming her former position." On the other hand, the war had provided her with a band of national heroes, Duguesclin, Dunois, Richemont, La Hire and of course Joan of Arc, and in a specialist sphere Jean Bureau, the greatest artilleryman of his day. The bone of contention – the homage – that had embittered the relations of the two countries for exactly 300 years had been dropped, and for 60 years they were to be at peace with one another.

Yet the long war had ended on an ironical note that was to puzzle the international jurists for another 350 years. (It was not till 1803 that the *fleur de lys* disappeared off the national flag of England.) No treaty of peace was signed, the English claim to the throne of France was not dropped (for England would not consider herself defeated) and the question of the homage lapsed simply because no fief remained in English possession on which it could be claimed. Juridically, I suppose, the war has not yet ended.

INDEX

Aa, river, 452

Abbeville, 155, 157–8, 160, 162, 166, 169, 174–5, 183, 405, 409–11, 414–15, 425–6, 519

Acheux, 334, 420, 424–5

Adam, L'Isle, 553–4, 632, 636–7, 650

Agache, Gobin, 158, 162

Agen, 117–18

Agenais, 110, 122, 127

Agincourt, 11, 173, 184, 188, 238, 242, 301, 321, 334, 390, 416, 422, 424–5, 428–9, 433, 435, 441–3, 445, 448, 449–51, 455, 459, 467, 504, 507–8, 533, 547–8, 552–4, 556–8, 560, 562, 564, 568–9, 571, 586, 646, 671–3, 677, 700

Agincourt Roll, 390, 470

Aiguillon, 113–14, 116–18, 121–3, 137, 220, 222

Aisne, river, 505

Albert, 336, 419–20, 423–4

Albert, Charles d', 392, 396, 404–5, 409–10, 414–15, 419, 425–8, 435, 441

Alençon, 479, 499, 505, 514, 577, 661

Alençon, Count of, 180, 183

Alençon, Duke of, 425–6, 441, 553, 563, 591–2, 604, 606, 609–10, 613–14, 617, 644–5

Alvergate, Cardinal, 629

Amboise, 279, 281, 284

Ambricourt, 422

Amerigo, 225–6

Amiens, 149, 153, 155–7, 166, 183, 187, 212, 247–8, 271, 285, 329, 409–12, 415, 426–8, 505, 533, 576

Amiens, Treaty of, 537–8

Ancre, 423

Angers, 67, 84, 276, 284, 505–6, 514, 537, 577, 579

Anjou, 479, 505, 514, 537, 551, 570–71, 579–80, 628

Anjou, Charles of, 628

Anjou, Henry Plantagenet, Count of, 17, 20

Anjou, Margaret of, afterwards wife to Henry VI, 659, 662–3

Anjou, René, Duke of, 377, 659

Annequin, Godfrey d', 161

Antwerp, 21, 24–5, 49–50, 53

Aquitaine, 100, 122, 258, 277, 326, 349, 373, 377, 379–80, 392–3, 452, 469, 497, 640–41

Aragon, 538

Arc, Joan of, 403, 408, 431, 440, 576, 587, 590–98, 600, 604–5, 609–10, 613–15, 617–21, 624, 626–7, 667, 680, 700

Argentan, 269–70, 479, 505

Argonne, 576

Armagnac, Count Bernard d', 454–7, 465–7, 473, 479, 481, 484, 493–4, 496

Armagnac, Count Jean d', 250–51, 253, 255–8, 276

Arques, 408–9, 424

Arras, 22, 32, 34, 52, 58, 61, 149, 212, 271, 329, 333, 504, 519, 629–30, 634–5

Arras, Treaty of, 632

Array, Commissioners of, 27

Artevelda, Jacques van, 51–2, 60–62, 89

Artois, 22, 136, 504

Artois, Robert of, 21, 48, 56, 70, 74, 80–84

Arundel, Earl of, 181, 227, 628

Athens, Duke of, 48

Athies, 414, 417, 424

Attigny, 339

Auberchicourt, Eustace de, 339

Auberoche, 105–7, 112–13, 120, 128–9, 130, 219–20

Audenarde, 57

703

Richemont, Arthur of, 425, 441, 525,
    538, 574–5, 610, 613, 616–17, 621,
    628, 632, 642–5, 647–8, 650,
    653–5, 659, 668–74, 676–9,
    681–2, 700
Rieux, Marshal of France, 499–500
Roche–Derrien, 87–90, 96, 109, 192,
    220, 323
Romans, Charles, King of the, 175
Romarentin, 277
Roncesvalles, 372
Roos, Lord, 509, 511, 582
Rouen, 140, 148–50, 206, 261, 266,
    271, 392, 402, 404–5, 409–10,
    414, 420, 426–7, 442, 444, 453–4,
    457, 473, 481–5, 487–8, 491,
    493–4, 504–5, 536, 552–3, 566,
    570, 584, 616, 626, 631, 635–7,
    639–40, 643, 648, 653–5, 657,
    667–8
Rouergue, 374
Rouvray, 588, 590, 598
Rozan, Pas de, 695
Ruisseauville, Chateau, *Manuscript*,
    447
Rus, 537
Rutter, Owen, 622, 624
Ry, 635, 637
Rymer, 63, 223, 327, 352, 380, 389,
    488, 529
Rysbank, 213

Sablé, 538
Saintes, 232–4, 241
Saintonge, 122–3, 126–7, 232, 234
Salic law, 20, 67
Salisbury, Earl of, 11, 45, 48, 52, 227,
    252, 292, 294, 298, 301, 319, 331,
    348, 471, 486, 499–501, 505, 508,
    511–12, 514–17, 519, 521, 526, 535,
    537–40, 542–3, 547, 550–53,
    556–7, 561–4, 571, 573, 576,
    579–82, 584–5, 607, 609, 700
Sandwich, 79, 576
Sarthe, river, 500–501, 512, 661
Savense, Sir William de, 435
Savignies, 626
Savoy, 504

Savoy, Duke of, 175, 214
Scales, Lord, 557, 570, 582, 586, 612,
    614, 635, 642, 648, 678
Scheldte, River, 21–2, 57, 60
Scotland, 18–20, 211, 218–19, 224, 247,
    249–50, 388
Scotland, King of, 43, 48, 95, 127, 211,
    218
Sée, river, 644
Seine, River, 149–51, 154, 169, 204,
    322, 334, 341, 392, 394, 395,
    404–5, 410, 456, 458, 459–60,
    470–71, 478, 481–2, 484–5, 494,
    496, 499, 502–3, 505, 519, 522–3,
    615, 617, 647–8, 650, 652–3
Senlis, 616, 647
Sens, 498, 502, 523, 549
Shakespeare, William, 11, 366, 398,
    408, 431–2
Shrewsbury, Earl of *see* Talbot, Lord
Sigismund, Emperor, 451–2, 459, 463
Sicily, King Robert of, 49
Simpson, Martin, 552, 566
Sismondi, 580
Sluys, 28, 52, 54, 228–9, 306–7, 461,
    463
Soissons, 400, 432
Somerset, Earl of, 509, 511, 524, 642,
    645–6, 657–9, 661, 666–8, 678–9
Somme, river, 149, 153, 155–6, 161–2,
    166, 174, 204, 214, 329, 334, 405,
    409–10, 412, 415–16, 418–19,
    423–5, 427–8, 505, 531, 537, 628,
    630, 638–9, 646, 669
Spain, 380
Spithead, 390
St. Andréss, 456
St. Augustine, Abbey of, 444
St. Christophe, 501
St. Crozat Canal, 334
St. Denys, 498, 617, 632, 636, 647,
    650, 652–3
St. Denys, Abbey of, 487
St. Denys, Monk of, 426, 430, 447,
    450, 454, 467
St. Dye, 521
St. Emilion, 690
St. Feravy, 612–13, 622

READ MORE IN PENGUIN

In every corner of the world, on every subject under the sun, Penguin represents quality and variety – the very best in publishing today.

For complete information about books available from Penguin – including Puffins, Penguin Classics and Arkana – and how to order them, write to us at the appropriate address below. Please note that for copyright reasons the selection of books varies from country to country.

In the United Kingdom: Please write to *Dept. EP, Penguin Books Ltd, Bath Road, Harmondsworth, West Drayton, Middlesex UB7 0DA*

In the United States: Please write to *Consumer Sales, Penguin Putnam Inc., P.O. Box 12289 Dept. B, Newark, New Jersey 07101-5289.* VISA and MasterCard holders call 1-800-788-6262 to order Penguin titles

In Canada: Please write to *Penguin Books Canada Ltd, 10 Alcorn Avenue, Suite 300, Toronto, Ontario M4V 3B2*

In Australia: Please write to *Penguin Books Australia Ltd, P.O. Box 257, Ringwood, Victoria 3134*

In New Zealand: Please write to *Penguin Books (NZ) Ltd, Private Bag 102902, North Shore Mail Centre, Auckland 10*

In India: Please write to *Penguin Books India Pvt Ltd, 11 Community Centre, Panchsheel Park, New Delhi 110017*

In the Netherlands: Please write to *Penguin Books Netherlands bv, Postbus 3507, NL-1001 AH Amsterdam*

In Germany: Please write to *Penguin Books Deutschland GmbH, Metzlerstrasse 26, 60594 Frankfurt am Main*

In Spain: Please write to *Penguin Books S. A., Bravo Murillo 19, 1° B, 28015 Madrid*

In Italy: Please write to *Penguin Italia s.r.l., Via Benedetto Croce 2, 20094 Corsico, Milano*

In France: Please write to *Penguin France, Le Carré Wilson, 62 rue Benjamin Baillaud, 31500 Toulouse*

In Japan: Please write to *Penguin Books Japan Ltd, Kaneko Building, 2-3-25 Koraku, Bunkyo-Ku, Tokyo 112*

In South Africa: Please write to *Penguin Books South Africa (Pty) Ltd, Private Bag X14, Parkview, 2122 Johannesburg*

PENGUIN ONLINE

INSPECTION COPY REQUESTS

Lecturers in the United Kingdom and Ireland wishing to apply for inspection copies of Classic Penguin titles for student group adoptions are invited to apply to:

Inspection Copy Department
Penguin Press Marketing
80 Strand
LONDON
WC2R 0RL

Fax: 020 7010 6701

E-mail: academic@penguin.co.uk

Inspection copies may also be requested via our website at:
www.penguinclassics.com

Please include in your request the author, title and the ISBN of the book(s) in which you are interested, the name of the course on which the books will be used and the expected student numbers.

It is essential that you include with your request your title, first name, surname, position, department name, college or university address, telephone and fax numbers and your e-mail address.

Lecturers outside the United Kingdom and Ireland should address their applications to their local Penguin office.

Inspection copies are supplied at the discretion of Penguin Books

READ MORE IN PENGUIN

ARCHAEOLOGY

The Penguin Dictionary of Archaeology
Warwick Bray and David Trump

The range of this dictionary is from the earliest prehistory to the civilizations before the rise of classical Greece and Rome. From the Abbevillian handaxe and the god Baal of the Canaanites to the Wisconsin and Würm glaciations of America and Europe, this dictionary concisely describes, in more than 1,600 entries, the sites, cultures, periods, techniques and terms of archaeology.

The Complete Dead Sea Scrolls in English   Geza Vermes

The discovery of the Dead Sea Scrolls in the Judaean desert between 1947 and 1956 transformed our understanding of the Hebrew Bible, early Judaism and the origins of Christianity. 'No translation of the Scrolls is either more readable or more authoritative than that of Vermes' *The Times Higher Education Supplement*

Ancient Iraq   Georges Roux

Newly revised and now in its third edition, *Ancient Iraq* covers the political, cultural and socio-economic history of Mesopotamia from the days of prehistory to the Christian era and somewhat beyond.

Breaking the Maya Code   Michael D. Coe

Over twenty years ago, no one could read the hieroglyphic texts carved on the magnificent Maya temples and palaces; today we can understand almost all of them. The inscriptions reveal a culture obsessed with warfare, dynastic rivalries and ritual blood-letting. 'An entertaining, enlightening and even humorous history of the great searchers after the meaning that lies in the Maya inscriptions' *Observer*

READ MORE IN PENGUIN

RELIGION

The Origin of Satan Elaine Pagels

'Pagels sets out to expose fault lines in the Christian tradition, beginning with the first identification, in the Old Testament, of dissident Jews as personifications of Satan ... Absorbingly, and with balanced insight, she explores this theme of supernatural conflict in its earliest days' *Sunday Times*

A New Handbook of Living Religions
Edited by John R. Hinnells

Comprehensive and informative, this survey of active twentieth-century religions has now been completely revised to include modern developments and recent scholarship. 'Excellent ... This whole book is a joy to read' *The Times Higher Education Supplement*

Sikhism Hew McLeod

A stimulating introduction to Sikh history, doctrine, customs and society. There are about 16 million Sikhs in the world today, 14 million of them living in or near the Punjab. This book explores how their distinctive beliefs emerged from the Hindu background of the times, and examines their ethics, rituals, festivities and ceremonies.

The Historical Figure of Jesus E. P. Sanders

'This book provides a generally convincing picture of the real Jesus, set within the world of Palestinian Judaism, and a practical demonstration of how to distinguish between historical information and theological elaboration in the Gospels' *The Times Literary Supplement*

Islam in the World Malise Ruthven

This informed and informative book places the contemporary Islamic revival in context, providing a fascinating introduction – the first of its kind – to Islamic origins, beliefs, history, geography, politics and society.

READ MORE IN PENGUIN

HISTORY

A History of Twentieth-Century Russia Robert Service

'A remarkable work of scholarship and synthesis . . . [it] demands to be read' *Spectator*. 'A fine book . . . It is a dizzying tale and Service tells it well; he has none of the ideological baggage that has so often bedevilled Western histories of Russia . . . A balanced, dispassionate and painstaking account' *Sunday Times*

A Monarchy Transformed: Britain 1603–1714 Mark Kishlansky

'Kishlansky's century saw one king executed, another exiled, the House of Lords abolished, and the Church of England reconstructed along Presbyterian lines . . . A masterly narrative, shot through with the shrewdness that comes from profound scholarship' *Spectator*

American Frontiers Gregory H. Nobles

'At last someone has written a narrative of America's frontier experience with sensitivity and insight. This is a book which will appeal to both the specialist and the novice' James M. McPherson, Princeton University

The Pleasures of the Past David Cannadine

'This is almost everything you ever wanted to know about the past but were too scared to ask . . . A fascinating book and one to strike up arguments in the pub' *Daily Mail*. 'He is erudite and rigorous, yet always fun. I can imagine no better introduction to historical study than this collection' *Observer*

Prague in Black and Gold Peter Demetz

'A dramatic and compelling history of a city Demetz admits to loving and hating . . . He embraces myth, economics, sociology, linguistics and cultural history . . . His reflections on visiting Prague after almost a half-century are a moving elegy on a world lost through revolutions, velvet or otherwise' *Literary Review*

READ MORE IN PENGUIN

PENGUIN CLASSIC BIOGRAPHY

 Highly readable and enjoyable biographies and autobiographies from leading biographers and autobiographers. The series provides a vital background to the increasing interest in history, historical subjects and people who mattered. The periods and subjects covered include the Roman Empire, Tudor England, the English Civil Wars, the Victorian Era, and characters as diverse Joan of Arc, Jane Austen, Robert Burns and George Melly. Essential reading for everyone interested in the great figures of the past.

Published or forthcoming:

E. F. Benson	**As We Were**
Ernle Bradford	**Cleopatra**
David Cecil	**A Portrait of Jane Austen**
Roger Fulford	**Royal Dukes**
Christopher Hibbert	**Charles I**
	The Making of Charles Dickens
Christopher Hill	**God's Englishman: Oliver Cromwell**
Marion Johnson	**The Borgias**
James Lees-Milne	**Earls of Creation**
Edward Lucie-Smith	**Joan of Arc**
Philip Magnus	**Gladstone**
John Masters	**Casanova**
Elizabeth Mavor	**The Ladies of Llangollen**
Ian McIntyre	**Robert Burns**
George Melly	**Owning Up: The Trilogy**
Raymond Postgate	**That Devil Wilkes**
Peter Quennell	**Byron: The Years of Fame**
Lytton Strachey	**Queen Victoria**
	Elizabeth and Essex
Gaius Suetonius	**Lives of the Twelve Caesars** translated by Robert Graves
Alan Villiers	**Captain Cook**

READ MORE IN PENGUIN

PENGUIN CLASSIC HISTORY

 Well written narrative history from leading historians such as Paul Kennedy, Alan Moorehead, J. B. Priestley, A. L. Rowse and G. M. Trevelyan. From the Ancient World to the decline of British naval mastery, from twelfth-century France to the Victorian Underworld, the series captures the great turning points in history and chronicles the lives of ordinary people at different times. Penguin Classic History will be enjoyed and valued by everyone who loves the past.

Published or forthcoming:

Leslie Alcock	**Arthur's Britain**
John Belchem/Richard Price	**A Dictionary of 19th-Century History**
Jeremy Black/Roy Porter	**A Dictionary of 18th-Century History**
Ernle Bradford	**The Mediterranean**
Anthony Burton	**Remains of a Revolution**
Robert Darnton	**The Great Cat Massacre**
Jean Froissart	**Froissart's Chronicles**
Johan Huizinga	**The Waning of the Middle Ages**
Aldous Huxley	**The Devils of Loudun**
Paul M. Kennedy	**The Rise and Fall of British Naval Mastery**
Margaret Wade Labarge	**Women in Medieval Life**
Alan Moorehead	**Fatal Impact**
Samuel Pepys	**Illustrated Pepys**
J. H. Plumb	**The First Four Georges**
J. B. Priestley	**The Edwardians**
Philippa Pullar	**Consuming Passions**
A. L. Rowse	**The Elizabethan Renaissance**
John Ruskin	**The Stones of Venice**
G. M. Trevelyan	**English Social History**
Philip Warner	**The Medieval Castle**
T. H. White	**The Age of Scandal**
Lawrence Wright	**Clean and Decent**
Hans Zinsser	**Rats, Lice and History**

READ MORE IN PENGUIN

PENGUIN CLASSIC MILITARY HISTORY

This series acknowledges the profound and enduring interest in military history, and the causes and consequences of human conflict. Penguin Classic Military History covers warfare from the earliest times to the age of electronics and encompasses subjects as diverse as classic examples of grand strategy and the precision tactics of Britain's crack SAS Regiment. The series will be enjoyed and valued by students of military history and all who hope to learn from the often disturbing lessons of the past.

Published or forthcoming:

Correlli Barnett	**Engage the Enemy More Closely**
	The Great War
David G. Chandler	**The Art of Warfare on Land**
	Marlborough as Military Commander
William Craig	**Enemy at the Gates**
Carlo D'Este	**Decision in Normandy**
Michael Glover	**The Peninsular War**
	Wellington as Military Commander
Winston Graham	**The Spanish Armadas**
Heinz Guderian	**Panzer Leader**
Christopher Hibbert	**Redcoats and Rebels**
Heinz Höhne	**The Order of the Death's Head**
Anthony Kemp	**The SAS at War**
Ronald Lewin	**Ultra Goes to War**
Martin Middlebrook	**The Falklands War**
	The First Day on the Somme
	The Kaiser's Battle
Desmond Seward	**Henry V**
John Toland	**Infamy**
Philip Warner	**Sieges of the Middle Ages**
Leon Wolff	**In Flanders Fields**
Cecil Woodham-Smith	**The Reason Why**

BY THE SAME AUTHOR

CLASSIC MILITARY HISTORY

The Battlefields of England

Hastings, Bosworth Field, Stamford Bridge ... the bloody battles of England have dramatically changed the course of our country's history. They were scenes of great heroism and also cowardice, of military genius and fatal errors, and are an essential part of our national heritage.

Here Alfred H. Burne, one of the most distinguished authorities on the history of land warfare, brings the turbulent and terrible struggles that have shaped our violent history to life. His superb guide makes it possible for readers to follow the course of thirty-nine landmark battles, from AD 51 to 1685, as if they were on the battlefields themselves. It includes fifty maps and seventeen drawings, detailed analyses of the conflicts and their aftermath, and informed and intelligent commentary on the contradictory statements found in contemporary records, which were often written by scribes who were not present at events – or doctored for political propaganda.

Containing the famous *The Battlefields of England* and *More Battlefields of England* in one volume, this is the first edition of Burne's magisterial work with all the battles arranged in chronological order.